California Real Estate Principles

NINTH EDITION

Dennis J. McKenzie

Mary Ellen Brady
Cerritos College

Edwin Estes, Jr.
Mt. San Antonio College

CENGAGE
Learning™

Australia • Brazil • Japan • Korea • Mexico • Singapore • Spain • United Kingdom • United States

California Real Estate Principles, Ninth Edition
Dennis J. McKenzie, Mary Ellen Brady, and Edwin Estes

Vice President/Editorial Director: Dave Shaut

Acquisitions Editor: Sara Glassmeyer

Developmental Editor: Arlin Kauffman

Sr. Marketing and Sales Manager: Mark Linton

Sr. Content Project Manager: Holly Henjum

Sr. Frontlist Buyer, Manufacturing: Charlene Taylor

Production Technology Analyst: Starratt Scheetz

Sr. Art Director: Pam Galbreath

Production Service: PreMediaGlobal

Text Designer: Patti Hudepohl

Cover Designer: Jeff Bane, CMB Design Partners

Cover Images: top: © Sklep Spozywczy/shutterstock; middle: © Dwights/Dreamstime.com; bottom: © Chris Rodenberg Photography/shutterstock

For product information and technology assistance, contact us at
Cengage Learning Customer & Sales Support, 1-800-354-9706

For permission to use material from this text or product, submit all requests online at **www.cengage.com/permissions**
Further permissions questions can be emailed to
permissionrequest@cengage.com

Exam*View*® is a registered trademark of eInstruction Corp. Windows is a registered trademark of the Microsoft Corporation used herein under license. Macintosh and Power Macintosh are registered trademarks of Apple Computer, Inc. used herein under license.

© 2011 Cengage Learning. All Rights Reserved.

Cengage Learning WebTutor™ is a trademark of Cengage Learning.

Library of Congress Control Number: 2010930164

ISBN-13: 978-0-538-73965-8

ISBN-10: 0-538-73965-7

Cengage Learning
5191 Natorp Boulevard
Mason, OH 45040
USA

Cengage Learning products are represented in Canada by Nelson Education, Ltd.

For your course and learning solutions, visit www.cengage.com Purchase any of our products at your local college store or at our preferred online store **www.cengagebrain.com**

Printed in the United States of America
1 2 3 4 5 6 7 14 13 12 11 10

Brief Contents

Contents

4 REAL ESTATE AGENCY 94

5 REAL ESTATE CONTRACTS AND MANDATED DISCLOSURES 120

10 THE ROLE OF ESCROW AND TITLE INSURANCE COMPANIES 294

11 LANDLORD AND TENANT RELATIONS 316

Student Learning Outcomes 316

11.1 LEASES 317

Types of Leasehold Estates • Requirements for a Valid Lease • Other Provisions • Security Deposits • Assignment Versus Sublease of the Lease • Lease with Option to Buy • Major Types of Leases • Important Concepts

11.2 DUTIES AND RESPONSIBILITIES OF LANDLORDS AND TENANTS 328

Landlord's Duties and Rights • Tenant's Duties and Rights • Rental Offset • Rental Payments to Neutral Escrow

11.3 EVICTIONS AND OTHER WAYS TO TERMINATE RENTAL AGREEMENTS 331

Unlawful Detainer Action • Three-Day Notice Versus 30 or 60-Day Notice • Serving Notice • Superior Court • Sheriff Evicts the Tenant • Delays and Appeals • Termination of Lease • Mobile (Manufactured) Home Park Tenants

11.4 PROPERTY MANAGEMENT 334

Field of Property Management • Compensation

CHAPTER SUMMARY 336

IMPORTANT TERMS AND CONCEPTS 337

PRACTICAL APPLICATION 337

REVIEWING YOUR UNDERSTANDING 337

12 LAND-USE PLANNING, SUBDIVISIONS, FAIR HOUSING, AND OTHER PUBLIC CONTROLS 342

Student Learning Outcomes 342

12.1 GOVERNMENT LAND-USE PLANNING 343

Private Deed Restrictions • Public Land-Use Controls • Planning • General Plan • Zoning • Controversy: Local Versus State and Federal Planning

12.2 SUBDIVISIONS 348

Subdivision Laws • Out-of-State and Foreign Land • Red Tape • Land Project Right to Rescind Sale • Interstate Land Sales Full-Disclosure Act

12.3 COMMON INTEREST DEVELOPMENTS (CIDs) 353

Condominiums • Planned Unit Development (PUD) • Stock Cooperatives and Community Apartments • Disclosure Requirements • Recreational Developments Selling Undivided Interests • Time-Sharing Ownership

12.4 HOUSING AND CONSTRUCTION LAWS 356

State Laws and Regulations

12.5 FAIR HOUSING 357

State Laws and Regulations • Federal Laws • Senior Citizen Housing • Many Other Laws

Preface

The revision of this California Real Estate Principles text was a collaborative effort. The authors worked in conjunction with real estate agents and attorneys as well as a number of instructors from both community colleges and real estate schools. The most up-to-date information was researched and applied so students will be able to utilize their knowledge from this book for the California Department of Real Estate (DRE) state license examination.

This informative text will assist the student in preparing for the California real estate state examination using the various practice test questions contained within this book. For additional preparation, students are encouraged to purchase the *California Real Estate License Preparation* text by William H. Pivar and Dennis McKenzie, published by Cengage Learning. This exam prep textbook contains thousands of additional practice test questions and follows the same format as this *California Real Estate Principles* textbook.

NEW TO THIS EDITION

This edition is one of the most current and practical textbooks on real estate principles in California. Changes in this ninth edition include the following:

- Chapter 1: Explain the meaning of the California Domestic Partnership Law, including family code and a website that discusses this law.
- Chapter 2: New examples for "Probate" and "Other Characteristics of Joint Tenancy" sections.
- Chapter 3: Define and discuss a party wall.
- Chapter 4: Agency and Disclosures: Updated forms have now been incorporated, including the Agent's Visual Inspection

Disclosure (AVID), an update on dual agency relationships, agency by estoppel, a clarification of the employment relationship between brokers and salespeople, updated amounts available under the DRE Recovery Fund, and an explanation of Buyer Agency.

- Chapter 5: Define and discuss Authorization to Sell. Update numbers in net listing example. Included the CAR form RPA CA, updated in 2010.
- Chapter 7: Explanation of Loan Modifications and typical lender requirements to obtain one.
- Chapter 8: Explanation of the Savings and Loan Crisis of the early 1990s, the Financial Crisis of 2008, FHA updates, the California Home Buyer Tax Credit, the SAFE ACT and what it means to mortgage brokers.
- Chapter 9: Explanation of the new Home Valuation Code of Conduct (HVCC) and how it affects agents.
- Chapter 10: Update closing costs example paid by seller.
- Chapter 11: 30- versus 60-day notices.
- Chapter 12: Explanation of redevelopment agencies and condemnation, a clarification of *Jones v. Mayer* and the Civil Rights Act of 1866, and an explanation of the Senior Citizens Exemption to age discrimination and the requirements of senior communities under the law.
- Chapter 15: Updated license requirements for becoming a salesperson. New section on becoming a part-time real estate salesperson. Added new exam questions and answers.

Global Changes: Vocabulary and terms surrounding real estate principles have grown with the alphabet soup of the new regulations. While the principle language can at first seem complicated, as you progress through the chapters, you will find that the text makes them easier to understand. The glossary will add to your understanding and is a great asset when you need to check the meaning of a word or term. Use of the online flashcards for electronic vocabulary review at www.cengage.com/realestate/mckenzie is recommended.

Each chapter in the book is self-contained, allowing instructors to adapt the book to various course formats. Instructors and students alike will appreciate the practical application and multiple-choice questions—both designed for testing, learning, and review of the material covered in each chapter.

SUPPLEMENTS

Instructors who adopt this textbook receive access to an instructor's manual written by the authors. Each chapter is supported with chapter objectives, a suggested lesson plan, a 10-question review quiz of the previous chapter, and a 30-question chapter quiz and test for checking student understanding of the material. The manual also provides three exams: an exam covering Chapters 1 through 5, Chapters 6 through 10, and Chapters 11 through 15 that consists of 100 four-part multiple-choice questions; the final exam covers the entire book and includes 100 four-part multiple-choice questions, including answers.

Online WebTutor™ support for WebCT™ and BlackBoard® is also provided. Designed to accompany this textbook, WebTutor is an e-learning software solution that turns everyone in your classroom into a front-row learner. Whether you want to Web-enhance your class or offer an entire course online, WebTutor allows you to focus on what you do best—teaching. More than just an interactive study guide, WebTutor is an anytime, anywhere online learning solution providing reinforcement through chapter quizzes, multimedia flashcards, e-mail discussion forums, and other engaging learning tools.

Classroom PowerPoint® presentation slides also support each chapter by outlining learning objectives, emphasizing key concepts, and highlighting real-world applications to help further engage learners and generate classroom discussion. These instructional support materials are available online only to adopters from the text companion site www.cengage.com/realestate/mckenzie.

This text may also be integrated with the *Instructor Guide* and *Student Study Guide* published by the California Community College Real Estate Education Center.

ACKNOWLEDGMENTS

Any book, in its final form, is the result of the time and talents of many individuals. While we cannot acknowledge all of the contributors, we are grateful for their review of information, their insights, and their suggestions—all of which have enhanced this edition. We hope that we have successfully included the information that they so generously provided.

We would also like to express our appreciation to those who served as reviewers and who provided insightful comments and valuable suggestions: Shad Jefferies, *San Diego Mesa College*; Timothy R. Durfield, *Citrus College*; Jill Carter, *West Los Angeles College*; and Ray Solis, *Mira Costa College*.

About the Authors

Mary Ellen Brady has been a successful California real estate broker and real estate salesperson for nearly twenty years. She is the owner of her own real estate company in addition to being the Real Estate Department chair and teaching at Cerritos College.

In 1993, 1996, and 1997, Ms. Brady was named the REALTOR® of the Year by the Downey Association of REALTORS®. She was President of the Women's Council of REALTORS® in 1997 and President of the Downey Association of REALTORS® in 1998. She has functioned as president and chair for many prestigious boards throughout the years. She received the impressive Norm Wurst Award for her contributions to real estate education from the California Real Estate Educator's Association in 2007.

In addition to obtaining her Graduate REALTOR® Institute (GRI) designation, Mary Ellen has also acquired her e-PRO, NAH-REP Certified Professional, and Senior Real Estate Specialist (SRES) designations. She has participated in negotiation and mediation training in association with the Pepperdine University School of Law, Straus Institute for Dispute Resolution.

Edwin Estes received his bachelor of arts degree from the University of Southern California and his juris doctorate degree from the Pepperdine University School of Law. A real estate licensee since 1976, he received his California broker's license in 1984 and has been a member of the California State Bar since 1983. Since that time, he has been active in real estate brokerage management, counseling, development, and investment brokerage. He is a former arbitrator for the American Arbitration Association and has served as a judge pro tem for the California Superior Court.

Professor Estes has been teaching Graduate REALTOR® Institute (GRI) classes as a master instructor for the California Association of REALTORS® since 1991; in addition to obtaining the real estate designations of Certified Commercial Investment Member (CCIM), Certified Real Estate Brokerage Manager (CRB), Graduate REALTORS Institute (GRI), Accredited Buyer Representative (ABR), Accredited Buyer Representative Manager (ABRM), e-PRO, and Senior Real Estate Specialist (SRES), he is also an accomplished community college instructor, and serves as the Real Estate Program coordinator for Mt. San Antonio College.

Mary Ellen Brady
Edwin Estes Jr.

Dedication

The world of real estate lost a legend with the passing of Dennis McKenzie. Authoring many books that changed and shaped real estate education, Dennis was a well-recognized course author and instructor and the recipient of the CARET Teacher of the Year award. Dennis was the director of the College of the Redwoods' real estate curriculum and was a popular real estate course instructor.

We will miss Dennis's infectious enthusiasm, his inquisitive mind, and his inexhaustible energy. His contributions to California real estate education and to the overall real estate community will be long remembered.

Chapter

1

WELCOME

People study real estate for a variety of reasons. Some wish to become real estate agents, and they are reading this book because enrolling in a course in Real Estate Principles is required before they are allowed to sit for the California real estate sales examination. Some people study real estate to be better informed consumers as they work with agents to buy or sell a personal residence. Still others study real estate as a way to acquire investments that can generate rental income for their retirement years.

Whatever the reason, this book provides a strong basic understanding of the principles of California real estate. The format of the book has been designed to logically take a reader step by step through the study of real estate. The book ends with a complete discussion of the requirements necessary to become a licensed real estate salesperson or broker and a 150-question practice examination similar in format to the state test.

Why are the licensing requirements at the end of the book rather than the beginning? Two reasons: (1) Those who think they are interested in a career as a real estate professional should study the information in the book first to see if they are comfortable with the topic, and (2) some readers wish to become informed consumers and real estate investors and are not interested in a career as a real estate agent.

However, if you wish to know the California real estate license requirements before you begin your study of real estate, you are encouraged to begin your reading with Chapter 15; then you can return to Chapter 1. The choice is up to you. You can also refer to the California Department of Real Estate (DRE) website at www.dre.ca.gov.

Introduction to Real Estate

STUDENT LEARNING OUTCOMES

In this first chapter, the historical, legal, civic, and economic importance of real estate is stressed. This chapter also highlights the characteristics of and differences between real and personal property and their effect on today's real estate market. At the conclusion of the chapter, you will be able to do the following:

1. Trace the history of real estate property ownership in California.
2. List the four-part definition of *real property*. Distinguish the difference between real and personal property.
3. Explain the term *bundle of rights* and list each of those rights.
4. List the five legal tests of a fixture and explain their meaning.

1.1 PRESENT AND HISTORICAL IMPORTANCE OF REAL ESTATE

Real estate touches the lives of more people than any other single commodity. Real property represents a significant portion of wealth and contributes to a substantial amount of commerce in the United States.

Impressive Statistics

Of the almost 2.5 billion acres of land in the United States, over 100 million acres are in California. (See the Special Interest Topic on page 4.) According to the U.S. Census Bureau, the population in California is approximately 37 million, with a projected increase of millions more in the next decades. These statistics are important only if they help people to become aware of the significance of real estate in their lives.

Historical Importance of Real Estate

California has perhaps the most interesting history of any state in the Union. The historical story of California can be told in terms of the use and occupancy of its land.

The earliest inhabitants of California were the Native Americans. Although they frequently led a nomadic existence, they were still governed by tribal rights to the land they occupied, including hunting, fishing, and gathering. The Native Americans respected and cherished the land because they recognized that their survival was based on products derived from the land.

Spanish Rule

In 1513, a Spanish explorer by the name of Vasco Núñez de Balboa first sighted the Pacific Ocean and claimed it for the king and queen of Spain. Many other Spanish explorers followed in the ensuing years. The years 1542 to 1822 were known as the period of exploration, discovery, and colonization.

The Spanish colonizers established forts, called *presidios*, in selected areas along the California coast to protect against invaders. Communities and agricultural villages known as *pueblos* appeared throughout the state to supply food for colonizers. During this period, the land was under Spanish domination. All land was held in the name of the king and queen of Spain, and private activities were governed by Spanish law. Spain did not recognize the ownership rights of Native Americans.

During the Spanish occupation of California, missionaries strived to spread Christianity among the natives by establishing a string of twenty-one missions ranging from San Diego to Sonoma, north of San Francisco.

Mexican Rule in California

In April 1822, Mexico, then a territory of Spain, established its independence and, in the process, took over the territory of California. During the Mexican reign, colonization of the territory of California continued to expand. Large Mexican land grants, called *ranchos*, were created and given to private citizens. Much of this rancho land was converted to agricultural use.

Under Mexican rule, colonization was encouraged, and land grants made extensive private ownership a reality for the first time in California's history.

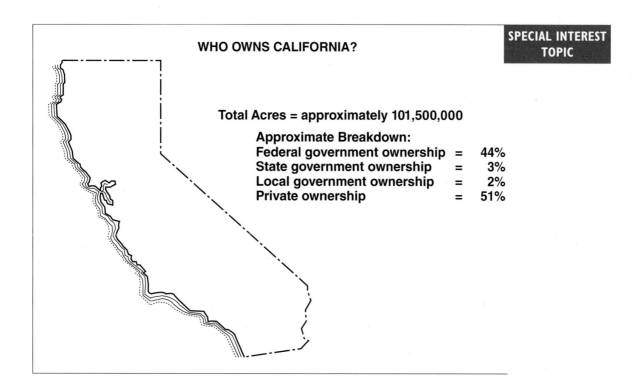

WHO OWNS CALIFORNIA?

SPECIAL INTEREST TOPIC

Total Acres = approximately 101,500,000

Approximate Breakdown:
Federal government ownership	=	44%
State government ownership	=	3%
Local government ownership	=	2%
Private ownership	=	51%

American Rule in California

American settlers coming from the east were confronted by Mexican authorities, and these tensions led to the Mexican-American War in 1846. In 1848, the **Treaty of Guadalupe Hidalgo** ended the war with Mexico, and California became a territory of the United States.

California achieved full statehood on September 9, 1850, and from that time on, the population rapidly increased, aided by the gold rush in the Sacramento Valley. The new California legislature adopted a land ownership recording system, which recognized and protected some, but not all, of the early Mexican land grants.

1.2 PROPERTY RIGHTS

As you launch your study of real estate, it is important to differentiate between real estate in a physical sense, such as land and buildings, and real property in the legal sense, such as property rights. The law defines *property* as "that which is the subject of ownership." The law explains ownership as essentially "the right of one or more persons to possess and to use the thing which is owned, to the exclusion of others." In a legal sense, then, the word *property* does not refer exclusively to the physical thing owned. The law is also concerned with the rights and the interests the owner has in the thing he or she owns.

What kind of rights does an individual have as an owner of real property? The law designates the rights that accompany ownership as the **bundle of rights**.

These rights include the following:

BUNDLE OF RIGHTS

The right to own property

The right to possess property

The right to use property

The right to enjoy property

The right to encumber property or borrow money on property

The right to dispose of property

The right to exclude those who do not share ownership of the property

Although owners of real estate have a bundle of rights, they also have certain responsibilities to other persons regarding the use they can make of their property. Their rights are not absolute or unlimited. Ownership rights are subject to government control to promote public health, safety, and welfare. Zoning, building codes, and antidiscrimination laws are all examples of government control of property rights.

1.3 REAL PROPERTY VERSUS PERSONAL PROPERTY

To better understand laws and regulations relating to the acquisition and transfer of real property, a person needs to distinguish between real and personal property.

The law states that anything that is not real property is personal property. Likewise, any property that is not personal property is real property. To fully understand this concept, you need to understand what is meant by real property.

Real property consists of the following:

1. Land
2. That which is affixed to the land
3. That which is appurtenant or incidental to the land
4. That which is immovable by law

Land

Land is the solid material of the earth, such as soil, rock, or other substances. It can be composed of mountains, valleys, swamps, or any other kind of terrain. The technical definition of *land* includes the following:

1. Surface of the land
2. Airspace above the land
3. Materials and substances beneath the surface to the center of the earth

Surface of the Land

The surface of the land is defined as the space on the surface of the earth upon which people live. This includes *lateral support*, which is support from adjoining land, and *subjacent support*, which is support from underlying strata.

Airspace

Airspace (air rights) is more difficult to define. Modern theories based on air travel generally agree that an owner of real property owns a reasonable amount of airspace above his or her land, with the remainder being a public highway. Moreover, landowners have the right to prevent a use of airspace that would interfere with their use and quiet enjoyment of the land. However, the issue of what

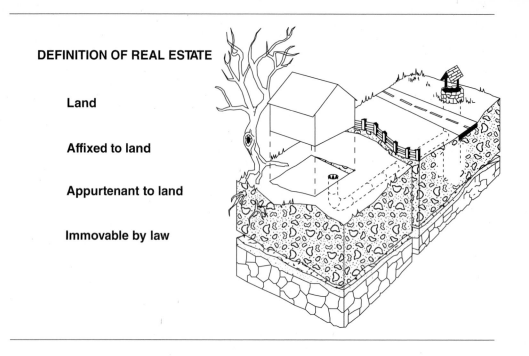

DEFINITION OF REAL ESTATE

Land

Affixed to land

Appurtenant to land

Immovable by law

constitutes a *reasonable amount* is currently determined by the courts on a case-by-case basis whenever a lawsuit arises between disputing parties.

Minerals in the Ground

Solid minerals contained in the land—such as coal, iron ore, gold, or silver—are real property until they are taken from the ground, at which time they become personal property. A landowner who deeds the land to another conveys the minerals contained in the land, unless the mineral rights are reserved or have already been sold to some other party. When mineral rights have been reserved by the former owner or conveyed to another person, the owner of the mineral rights has an implied easement to enter upon the surface of the property to extract the minerals. Oil and gas are special classes of minerals and are governed by the *rule of capture*, also known as the *law of capture*; because of their shifting nature, they are not considered capable of absolute or exclusive ownership until reduced to capture, or possession. However, the right to drill for oil and gas rests with the surface landowner or with the owner of the mineral rights if those rights belong to someone other than the surface landowner. Once oil and minerals are brought to the surface, they are considered personal property.

Water Rights

A working knowledge of the water rights of a property owner should include an understanding of the following issues:

1. Underground water rights
2. Riparian water rights
3. Right of appropriation

Underground Water

Underground or percolating water is water that is not confined to a well, a defined channel, or a water bed. In California, the land-owner has neither ownership of specific underground water nor absolute ownership of waters running across or bordering property, such as a lake or a stream. Under the Concept of Reasonable Use, the landowner may take, in common with other owners, only his or her share of underground (percolating) waters for beneficial use. In a dispute, California regulatory agencies and the courts determine a *reasonable use*.

Riparian Rights

Owners of land that borders on a river or another water course enjoy certain benefits regarding use of the water, under a concept known as **riparian rights**. Although these landowners have no absolute ownership of the waters, each owner has a personal right, along with other landowners, to use such waters in a "reasonable manner." Basically, each owner has a right to an amount of water in proportion to the amount of land owned that borders the water course and in light of the needs of all interested parties.

Right of Appropriation

The **right of appropriation** is that right given to the state to give permission to a nonriparian owner to take water from a river or lake.

Affixed to the Land

The second component of the definition of real property is "that which is affixed to the land," or anything regarded as a permanent part of the land. This includes

1. things permanently resting on the land, such as buildings.
2. things permanently attached to a building, such as fixtures.
3. things attached to the land by roots, such as trees and shrubs.

Natural trees, shrubs, and vines that are rooted in the ground are generally considered to be part of the land. In other words, natural vegetation is real property until severed or gathered, at which time it becomes personal property. On the other hand, farm produce and growing crops that are the result of annual labor are considered to be goods and are governed by laws of personal property. Growing vegetable crops are sometimes referred to as **emblements**.

Appurtenant to the Land

The third component of the definition of real property is "that which is appurtenant or incidental to the land." That which is **appurtenant** to the land is anything that, by right, is used by the land for its benefit and "goes with the land." Examples include the following:

1. Easements, such as the rights of way over adjoining lands, or passages for light, air, or heat from or across the land of another. (Easements are discussed in detail in a subsequent chapter.)
2. Stock in a mutual water company. A mutual water company is a nonprofit organization that is created to provide water to property owners within a specific district. Usually, each share is considered to be appurtenant to a specific piece of real property and cannot be sold separately. In other words, the stock is considered real property and transfers with the property.

Immovable by Law

Real property is also defined as any property that is immovable by law. When the law declares that an item of personal property is required to stay with the land, that item then becomes real property.

Personal Property

As was indicated previously, anything that is not real property is personal property. Personal property is movable, whereas real property is considered to be immovable. Other names for personal property are *chattels* or *choses*. Examples of personal property include bonds, money, contracts, furniture, automobiles, and mortgages.

Other distinctions that might be made between real and personal property include these:

1. Contracts involving the sale of real property must be in writing and signed by the person whose title is being transferred. In the sale of some personal property, the transaction need not be in writing if the price is low enough. However, prudence suggests that all personal property sales contracts should be in writing to avoid

CHANGING CHARACTER OF PROPERTY

real property   personal property

real property   personal property

misunderstandings. The contracts themselves are personal property even though the contracts might refer to the sale of real property.

2. Personal property, when sold, is usually transferred by use of a bill of sale. Real property is transferred by delivery of a written instrument called a *deed*.

The Status of Property Can Change

Real property can become personal property, and personal property can become real property. For example, trees growing in a forest are considered real property. When the trees are cut and transported to the sawmill, where they are made into boards, they become personal property. When the boards are used in the construction of a building, this changes them back to real property. If the building eventually outlives its usefulness and is torn down, the salvaged lumber becomes personal property once again.

1.4 FIXTURES

Fixtures are items that were originally personal property but are now attached to the land in such a manner as to be considered part of the land itself, thus becoming real property. Depending on the specific circumstances, certain items of personal property may become so integrated with the land that they are considered to be part of the real property and, consequently, belong to the current owner of the real estate.

The concept of fixtures can become a touchy question when land is bought or sold or when a tenant makes improvements on the property. If a legal dispute arises, the court must make a decision as to whether the property in question is a fixture and must remain with the real property or whether the item is still personal property and can be removed and taken by the seller or the tenant. If allowed to be taken, the seller and/or tenant must repair all damage caused by the removal.

Memory Tool Five Tests of a Fixture "MARIA"
Method of attachment
Adaptability
Relationship
Intention
Agreement

Tests of a Fixture

To help determine whether an item is a fixture, which makes it real property, or is not a fixture, which makes it personal property, the courts have established the five **tests of a fixture**, which are method of attachment, adaptability, relationship of parties, intention of parties, and agreement between parties.

1. The courts are concerned with the *method* by which the property is incorporated into or attached to the land and its consequent degree of permanence. In other words, is the property nailed, cemented, welded, or bolted down? Or is it simply leaning against the building or hanging on the wall?

2. The courts are concerned with the *adaptability* to ordinary use of the attached personal property. In other words, is the item in question customized, or can it easily be used in some other building? Wall-to-wall carpeting is considered a fixture because it was cut for a room of a particular size and shape and the carpet is attached to a tack strip that is nailed to the floor, whereas a standard 9′ × 12′ rug is personal property because it is readily movable from house to house. Customized draperies or fireplace screens may also become fixtures.

3. The courts are concerned with the *relationship* between the person who adds the article and the party with whom he or she may be transacting business. In other words, is the dispute between a landlord and a tenant, a buyer and a seller, or a borrower and a lender? In a dispute between a landlord and a tenant, the courts tend to favor the tenant; between a buyer and a seller, the courts tend to favor the buyer; and between a borrower and a lender, the courts lean toward the lender.

4. The *intention* of the person attaching the personal property to the land is a very important issue. Intention is indicated by action or agreement of the parties, whether it be expressed or merely implied. If intention can be proved, the courts consider this the most important test.

5. The courts also look to the existence of any *agreements between the parties* regarding the item in question. In other words, has a right to the property in question been established by the signing of an agreement? Is the item mentioned in the real estate listing or purchase contract?

Take Proper Precautions

Many times problems arise between buyers and sellers regarding fixtures. Therefore, it is in the best interest of all parties to spell out clearly in the purchase contract the intentions of the seller and buyer regarding the items of personal property or fixtures and whether or not they will remain with the property. The purchase contract should state whether the washer and dryer, stove, or other questionable items are remaining with the property or if the seller reserves the right to remove these items after the sale.

Exception to the Fixture Rule

For every good rule, there is often an exception. In the case of fixtures, certain items remain personal property after they have been affixed to real property. Articles of personal property that a business tenant has attached to real property because of their need to be used in a trade or business are called **trade fixtures**. Examples are shelving, counters, or cash registers used by a business but not sold as merchandise to customers.

These trade fixtures are viewed as the personal property of the business tenant, and the tenant has the right to remove these items. The tenant must repair any damage caused by the removal. However, a residential tenant in a house or an apartment might install room dividers or different light fixtures. These fixtures may or may not be viewed as the personal property of the tenant. As noted earlier, the courts tend to favor the tenant. In many cases, these fixtures may be removed by the tenant, provided the premises are not damaged in the process of removal. However, the right to remove is not absolute; it depends on the circumstances in each case.

Special Issue: California Domestic Partnership Law

Effective January 1, 2005, a California law, AB 205, created many new rights and responsibilities for registered domestic partners. (FAMILY CODE SECTION 297-297.5 pertains to Registered Domestic Partners [RDP]. See www.leginfo.ca.gov for more information.) Some of these rights and responsibilities have a major impact on real estate principles and will be noted as you proceed through the book.

Many of the California real estate laws and regulations stating the rights of husbands and wives now include the same rights for registered domestic partners. However, AB 205 did not change real estate issues reserved for husbands and wives that are found in the California Constitution. Constitutional changes involve a complicated process that extends beyond the passage of AB 205. In addition, federal laws and regulations do not recognize California's domestic partnership law. For example, California domestic partners are not currently allowed to file federal joint income taxes. Domestic partners are not currently allowed the same Social Security and Medicare benefits as married couples. Also, many other states will not recognize this California law, so domestic partners may not get the same rights if they move to another state. AB 205 is a very complicated law, and where this law impacts major real estate principles we have tried to make mention of same. However, all domestic registered partners are cautioned to seek professional legal advice before making any real estate decisions. **This textbook is designed to provide accurate information. However, neither the authors nor the publisher is engaged in rendering legal, tax, or other professional service. If such assistance is required, the services of a competent professional person should be sought**.

CHAPTER SUMMARY

California's colorful history is closely tied to the concept of land ownership. A study of the early inhabitants of the state gives a better understanding of the foundation upon which real estate laws and regulations have been built.

Ownership of real property includes certain property rights called the *bundle of rights*. The bundle of rights include the right to own, possess, use, enjoy, encumber, dispose of, and exclude.

Real property is defined as (1) land; (2) that which is appurtenant to the land, such as easements or stock in a mutual water company; (3) that which is affixed to the land, known as *fixtures*; and (4) that which is immovable by law.

The status of property can change. Real property can become personal property, and personal property can be changed to real property. In determining the status of real versus personal property, the courts have developed five tests to determine whether an item is a fixture. These tests are method of attachment, adaptability, relationship of the parties, intention of the parties to the transaction, and the existence of an agreement between the parties involved (the MARIA memory tool).

IMPORTANT TERMS AND CONCEPTS

appurtenant

bundle of rights

emblements

fixtures

right of
appropriation

riparian rights

tests of a fixture

trade fixtures

Treaty of Guadalupe
Hidalgo

PRACTICAL APPLICATION

1. After purchasing a home, the new owner applies for a building permit to add another bedroom and bath. The city building department requires a $1,000 application fee and refuses to issue the permit until acceptable plans are submitted showing that the project meets all construction codes. How does this building department requirement conflict with the basic bundle of rights?

2. After the close of the sale, the seller of a home removes a 8′ × 10′ metal prefab storage shed from the property. The buyer states that the shed is real property and should stay on the property as part of the sale. Who is right? How could this problem have been avoided?

3. How do trade fixtures differ from regular fixtures?

REVIEWING YOUR UNDERSTANDING

1. Which group of explorers and colonizers set up presidios and pueblos in the early days of California?
   a. Mexicans
   b. British
   c. Spanish
   d. Native Americans

2. Which of the following is not considered to be one of the bundle of rights? The right to
   a. own property.
   b. pay taxes.
   c. enjoy.
   d. encumber.

3. Which of the following is considered *land* and, therefore, is real estate?
   a. Oil deposits beneath the surface
   b. Harvested crops
   c. Trade fixtures
   d. Reasonable airspace above the land

4. The right of the owner of land bordering on a river to use the river water in a reasonable manner is called
   a. appropriation rights.
   b. take-out rights.
   c. riparian rights.
   d. subjacent privileges.

5. Wall-to-wall carpeting in a single-family dwelling is usually considered to be
   a. a fixture.
   b. a chattel.
   c. removable.
   d. separate property.

6. Which of the following is considered appurtenant to the land and upon sale or other transfer stays with the land and is not taken by the former owner?
   a. Stock in a mutual water company
   b. Trade fixtures
   c. An easement
   d. Both a and c

7. All other things being equal, in a dispute between a buyer and a seller over a fixture, the courts tend to favor
   a. the seller.
   b. the buyer.
   c. the one with the most money.
   d. neither party.

8. In what year was California granted statehood?
   a. 1821
   b. 1846
   c. 1848
   d. 1850

9. The main feature of personal property is
   a. its title is transferred by a deed.
   b. its immobility.
   c. its value is always less than that of real property.
   d. its mobility.

10. Which two terms do not belong together?
    a. Bundle of rights—use and enjoyment
    b. Real estate—land
    c. Reasonable use—water rights
    d. Personal property—easement

11. An orange tree in a suburban backyard is real property. An orange on the ground that has fallen off the tree is
    a. real property.
    b. a fixture.
    c. personal property.
    d. real estate.

12. Unless otherwise noted, mineral rights
    a. transfer with the land.
    b. are the personal property of the owner.
    c. are always reserved by the former owner.
    d. never carry an implied right to enter the land for extraction.

13. Mortgages and deeds of trust are
    a. real property.
    b. personal property.
    c. fixtures.
    d. emblements.

14. The right of the state to give permission to a nonriparian owner to take water from a river or lake is called a
    a. riparian right.
    b. possessor right.
    c. percolating right.
    d. right of appropriation.

15. Which mineral is not considered capable of absolute or exclusive ownership until reduced to possession?
    a. Gold
    b. Oil
    c. Iron
    d. Silver

16. The words *chattel* and *chose* stand for
    a. fixtures.
    b. real estate.
    c. personal property.
    d. real property.

17. Which of the following is not considered a test of a fixture?
    a. Relationship of the parties
    b. Method of financing
    c. Intention of the parties
    d. Method of attachment

18. Personal property that is attached to the land in such a manner that it becomes part of the real property is called a(n)
    a. fixture.
    b. chattel.
    c. chose.
    d. emblement.

19. Arnold and Sally are tenants in an apartment. They add temporary shelves in the kitchen. When they move, the shelves will probably be considered
    a. trade fixtures.
    b. real property.
    c. appurtenances.
    d. personal property.

20. Garcia leases a retail store and operates a jewelry business. When she moves, her business machines and shelves will probably be considered
    a. trade fixtures.
    b. real property.
    c. appurtenances.
    d. personal property.

Chapter

2

In Part I of this chapter, you will study land descriptions, stressing the lot, block, and tract; metes and bounds; and U.S. government survey methods for describing and locating land.

You will also explore five ways of acquiring title to real estate, including an explanation of deeds used in California. At the conclusion of Part I, you will be able to do the following:

1. List the three methods used to legally describe and locate land.
2. Find a parcel of land using each of the three location methods and be able to calculate acreage.
3. Outline five ways of acquiring title to real estate.
4. Discuss the difference between a grant deed, quitclaim deed, and warranty deed.
5. Briefly describe the purpose of the California recording system.

Part I: Legal Descriptions, Methods of Acquiring Title, and Deeds

2.1 LAND DESCRIPTIONS

Three reasons the description of real property is essential are as follows:

1. To specifically identify and locate areas of real property ownership.
2. To satisfy buyers who are interested in the precise dimensions and area of their property.
3. To minimize land description disputes between neighbors by establishing set boundary lines.

In addition to these three reasons, the law requires that every parcel of land sold, mortgaged, or leased must be properly described or identified. Legal descriptions are usually based upon the field notes of a civil engineer or a surveyor. When dealing with real property, recorded descriptions usually can be obtained from title insurance policies, deeds, deeds of trust, or mortgages.

Engineers and surveyors establish exact directions and distances by means of transits and measuring devices. Aerial photography and Global Positioning Systems (GPS) are also used in modern mapping.

Early Methods Used

Today's survey methods are a far cry from the methods used in early California. One early method of land measurement employed two people on horseback. Each rider dragged an end of a cord or rawhide strip, called a *thong*, which was about 100 *varas* in length. (A *vara* is about 33 inches.) One rider remained stationary while the other rode past. When the length of the thong was reached, the process was repeated by the other rider until one of them arrived at the end of the property. The number of thong lengths passed was counted, and the dimensions of the property were determined.

In another early method, the circumference of a wagon wheel was measured. A leather strip was tied to a spoke, and then, by rolling the wheel on the ground, the revolutions of the wheel were counted and the distance recorded.

Present-day Land Descriptions

Three major methods are used today to legally describe and locate land. They are as follows:

1. Lot, block, and tract system.
2. Metes and bounds system.
3. U.S. government survey, commonly called the *U.S. section and township system*.

Lot, Block, and Tract System

Dividing a large parcel of land into smaller parcels is called *subdividing*. The California Subdivision Map Act requires that all new subdivisions be either mapped or platted. A map of each subdivision is recorded in the recorder's office of the county in which the land is located.

At the time a subdivision map is filed in the county recorder's office, it is assigned a tract name and/or number. Once subdivision maps are recorded, legal descriptions are created by making reference to a particular lot in the block in that tract in which the property is located.

> *Example:* "All of lot 4 in Block A of Tract number 2025 in the city of Bellflower, Los Angeles County, California. As per map recorded in Book 76 page 83 of maps in the office of the recorder of said county." This type of identification is commonly found in urban areas of California, where extensive subdividing has taken place. (See Figure 2.1.)

Metes and Bounds System

The **metes and bounds** system of land location is used most often when the property in question is not covered by a recorded subdivision map or when the property is so irregular in shape that it is impractical to describe under the section and township system.

Metes refer to the measurement of length, using items such as inches, feet, yards, rods, meters, and miles. *Bounds* refer to the use

FIGURE 2.1

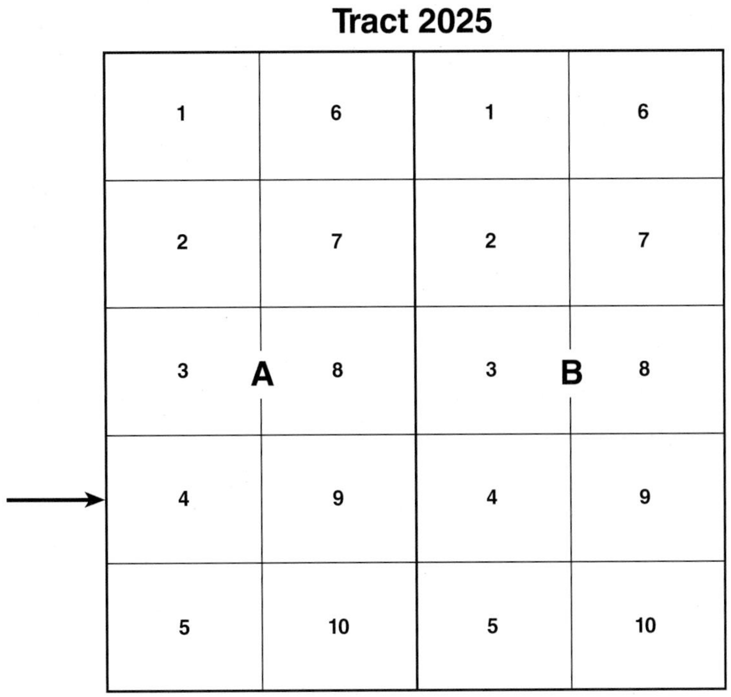

Tract 2025

of boundaries, both natural and artificial, such as rivers, roads, fences, boulders, creeks, and iron pipes. So the term *metes and bounds* means to measure the boundaries. This system is one of the oldest methods used to describe land, and it is used in both rural and urban areas. A common term used in the metes and bounds system is *benchmark*. A benchmark is a mark on a fixed or enduring object, such as a metal stake or rock, and it is often used as an elevation point by a surveyor.

Another term is *angular lines*. Many surveys using metes and bounds descriptions are based on angles and directions from a given north–south line, which is obtained with a compass. Angles are a deflection from this north–south line. Deflections are to the east or west of the north–south line.

There are 360° in a circle and 180° in a half-circle. Each degree is divided into sixty minutes, and each minute is divided into sixty seconds. The bearing of a course is described by measuring easterly or westerly from the north and south lines. (See Figure 2.2.) Although the metes and bounds land description is one of the oldest forms, it is also one of the most complicated. The system ranges from simple distances between given landmarks to surveyor readings based on angles found in the arc of a circle.

FIGURE 2.2

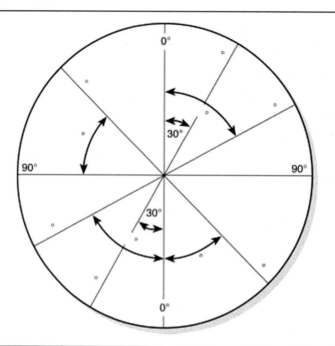

In using the metes and bounds method, three important points must be stressed:

1. You must start at a given point of beginning.
2. You must follow, in detail, the boundaries of the land in courses, distances, and directions from one point to another.
3. You must return to the point of beginning, thus enclosing the boundary lines.

Example: Here is a legal description using the metes and bounds method. "Beginning at a point on the southerly line of Harbor Ave., 200 ft. westerly of the southwest corner of the intersection of Harbor Ave. and 8th St.; running thence due south 300 ft. to the northerly line of Cribbage St.; thence westerly along the northerly line of Cribbage St., 200 ft.; thence northerly and parallel to the first course, 300 ft. to the southerly line of Harbor Ave.; thence easterly along the southerly line of Harbor Ave., 200 ft. to the point of beginning." (See Figure 2.3.)

One major weakness in using a metes and bounds system is that markers or points of beginning often disappear or are moved or replaced. In later years, this makes it difficult to find the exact corners of a parcel.

FIGURE 2.3

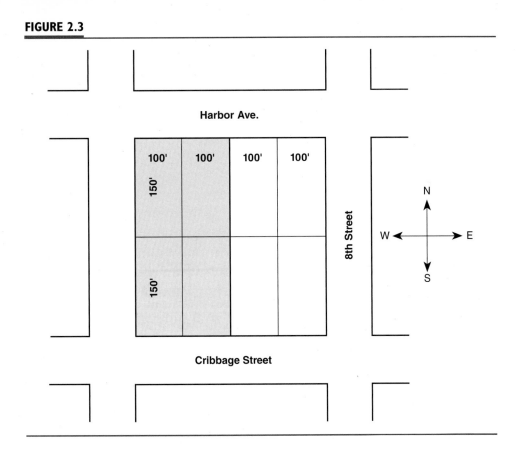

U.S. Government Section and Township System

The U.S. government section and township method of survey is used primarily to describe agricultural or rural land. The system originated in the late 1780s with a survey of public lands made by the U.S. surveyor general. The **U.S. government survey system** establishes monuments as points of beginning. The monuments are intersected by two imaginary lines: one running east and west, called a *base line*, and another running north and south, called a *meridian line*.

Because of its peculiar shape, the state of California requires three of these principal base lines and meridians, as shown in Figure 2.4. They are as follows:

1. *Humboldt Base Line and Meridian*, which is the point of beginning for describing land in the northwestern part of California. The actual point of beginning is on Mt. Pierce, just south of Eureka, California. (See Figure 2.4.)
2. *Mt. Diablo Base Line and Meridian*, which is the point of beginning for describing land in the central and northeastern part of California. The actual point of beginning is on Mt. Diablo, near Walnut Creek, California.

FIGURE 2.4

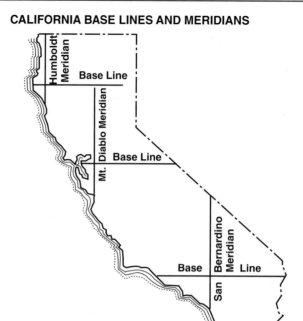

CALIFORNIA BASE LINES AND MERIDIANS

3. *San Bernardino Base Line and Meridian,* which is used to describe land in southern California. The actual point of beginning is the intersection of Base Line Street and Meridian Avenue in the city of San Bernardino, California.

Range lines run parallel to the principal meridians at six-mile intervals. *Township lines* (sometimes referred to as *tier lines*) run parallel to the principle base lines at six-mile intervals. The result is a grid of squares, or townships, each township containing approximately thirty-six square miles.

To identify each of these townships, a numbering system utilizing an assignment of two location numbers was devised. The identity of each township is determined by its position north or south of the base line and east or west of the meridian line. An example of a legal description might be "Township 2 North, Range 3 East, San Bernardino Base Line and Meridian. (T2N, R3E, SBBL & M)." The *X* indicates the township. (See Figure 2.5.)

Sections in a Township

Townships are, in turn, divided into sections. Each township contains thirty-six squares, or sections. Each section is one mile square.

FIGURE 2.5

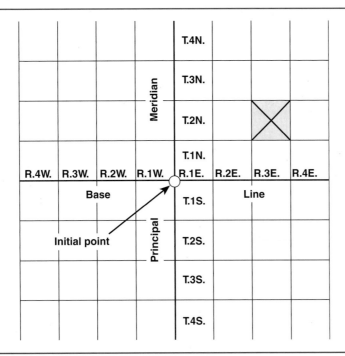

These sections are uniformly numbered from 1 to 36, with Section 1 located in the northeast corner of the township.

Not only is each section one mile square, but also each contains 640 acres. Each section can be divided into smaller parcels of land, as follows:

A quarter of a section = 160 acres

A quarter of a ¼ section = 40 acres

A quarter of a ¼ of a ¼ section = 10 acres

The division can be smaller and smaller until the size of the parcel is identified. The division need not be in quarters; it can also be in halves. (See Figures 2.6 and 2.7)

Pitfall

Because of the earth's curvature, some sections in townships are distorted and may not contain a full 640 acres; thus, computing acreage under the U.S. government system provides approximate figures. An accurate measure of actual acreage is best left to licensed civil engineers and surveyors.

These additional measurements will help in computing land measurements:

FIGURE 2.6

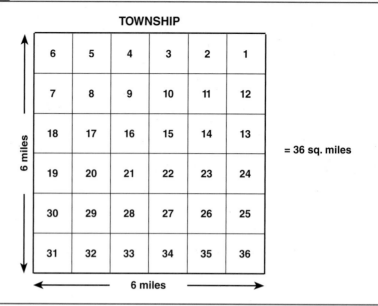

FIGURE 2.7

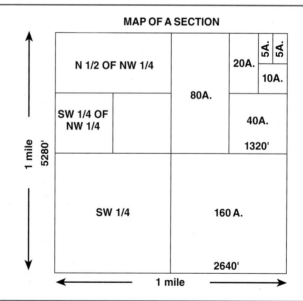

One mile = 5,280 feet or 320 rods

One rod* = 16 ½ feet

One acre = 43,560 square feet

*Rods are used as a measurement in land surveying.

One square acre = 208.71 feet

Commercial acre = standard acre less land needed for streets, sidewalks, and curbs

2.2 METHODS OF ACQUIRING TITLE

Chapter 1 discussed the difference between real and personal property. Section 2.1 of this chapter illustrated the three main ways of legally describing real property. The next logical step is to describe how a person goes about acquiring legal title to real property. According to the California Civil Code, the five legal ways of acquiring property are by will, succession, accession, occupancy, and transfer.

Acquiring Property by Will

A will is a legal instrument by which a person over the age of eighteen and of sound mind disposes of property upon his or her death. California law recognizes three types of wills: (1) a witnessed will, (2) a holographic will, and (3) a statutory will. (See Figure 2.8.)

A **witnessed will** is a formal typewritten document signed by the individual who is making it, wherein he or she declares in the presence of at least two witnesses that it is his or her will. The two witnesses, in turn, sign the will. This document should be prepared by an attorney.

A **holographic will** is a document written, dated, and signed in its entirety in the handwriting of the maker. It requires no witnesses. A **statutory will** is a preprinted form approved by the state in which a person merely fills in the blanks, usually without formal legal assistance. This statutory will requires at least two witnesses. At one time, another will—an oral will in contemplation of death, called a

FIGURE 2.8

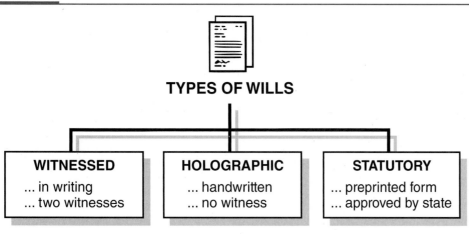

nuncupative will—was occasionally recognized. But today oral dying declarations are, for the most part, ignored by the probate courts.

Special Terms

A will is also called a *testament.* Special terms relating to wills are as follows:

> *Testator:* Male person who makes a will.
>
> *Testatrix:* Female person who makes a will.
>
> *Executor:* Male person named in the will by the maker to handle the estate of the deceased.
>
> *Executrix:* Female person named in the will by the maker to handle the estate of the deceased.
>
> *Administrator:* Male person appointed by the court to handle the estate when no will is left.
>
> *Administratrix:* Female person appointed by the court to handle the estate when no will is left.
>
> *Devise:* A gift of real property by will.
>
> *Devisee:* Person receiving real property by will.
>
> *Bequest, legacy:* A gift of personal property by will.
>
> *Legatee:* Person receiving personal property by will.
>
> *Codicil:* A change in a will.
>
> *Intestate:* A situation in which a person dies without leaving a will; he or she is said to have died intestate.
>
> *Testate*: A situation in which a person dies leaving a will.

Probate

Legal title to property being acquired by will is subject to the control of the probate court. The purpose of a **probate** hearing is to identify the creditors of the deceased and to pay off these creditors. Then if any property remains, the probate court determines the identity of the rightful heirs and distributes the remaining property.

The law requires that upon the death of the owner, all property is subject to the temporary possession of an **executor** (or **executrix**, if female) or an **administrator** (or **administratrix**).

Probate action takes place in superior court, and the estate property may be sold during the probate period for the benefit of the heirs or to cover court costs. If a probate sale takes place, certain guidelines are set by the court. The general guidelines are as follows:

1. The initial offer in a probate real estate sale must be for at least 90 percent of the appraised value of the property.

2. Once the initial offer is made, the court is petitioned to confirm the sale, and at the hearing, the court may accept additional bids.

3. The first additional bid must be an increase of at least 10 percent of the first $10,000 of the original bid and 5 percent of any excess. For example, if the original bid is in the amount of $259,000, the first overbid would be 10% of the first $10,000, which is $1,000, and the remaining excess of $249,000 is then multiplied by 5% which would be $12,450. The first overbid would then be $272,450. Subsequent bids may be for any amount set by the court.

4. The court confirms the final sale and sets the broker's commissions if a broker is involved.

Probate fees paid to executors, administrators, and attorneys are set by the courts and vary depending on the size and complexity of the estate. Certain types of property holdings need not be probated, which is discussed in Part 2 of this chapter.

Independent Administration of Estate Act

Under this act, if all heirs agree in advance, the complicated open-court probate sale rules mentioned above are avoided. Under the Independent Administration of Estate Act, the executor/executrix or administrator/administratrix can sell the property directly to a specific buyer, similar to a regular real estate sale. The sale is still subject to court approval, but no open-court hearing for other potential bidders is required. But if all heirs do not agree, which is occasionally the case, the previously described open-court sale rules apply.

Acquiring Property by Succession

When a deceased person leaves no will, the law provides for the disposition of his or her property. The state of California dictates who will get the property under the law of **intestate** succession. **Succession** means the handing down of property to another person. (See Figure 2.9.)

When a person dies intestate, the property of the deceased is divided into two categories: separate property and community property. The laws of intestate succession are different for each of these categories. When a person dies without a will and leaves separate property, this means that the surviving spouse or **registered domestic partner**, a person, other than a spouse, with whom one cohabits, did not have an interest in said property. If a person

FIGURE 2.9

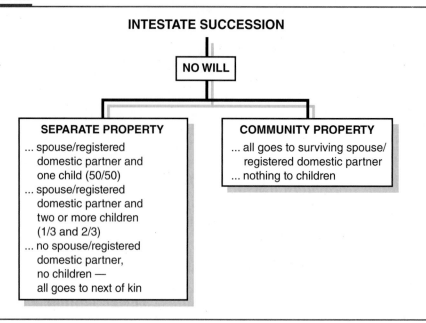

When *separate property* is involved, the following disposition of property is made:

1. When a deceased person leaves a spouse or registered domestic partner and one child, the separate property is divided one-half to the spouse or registered domestic partner and one-half to the child.

2. When a deceased person leaves a spouse and two or more children, the spouse/registered domestic partner receives one-third and the children equally divide the other two-thirds.

3. Other divisions are made by the courts in the event that a person dies leaving no spouse or registered domestic partner and no children. The usual rule is that the property goes to the next of kin, such as parents, brothers, sisters, and so on.

When a person dies intestate and leaves community property, the deceased person's community interest passes to the surviving spouse or registered domestic partner. The children, if any, get nothing.

Keypoint
On matters regarding wills and estates, always consult an experienced attorney! Do-it-yourself estate planning is not recommended!

Acquiring Property by Accession

You may acquire title to property that is added to your existing real estate. This process is called **accession**.

Examples include (1) accretion, (2) avulsion, (3) addition of fixtures, and (4) improvements made in error. (See Figure 2.10.)

Accretion

The gradual accumulation of soil on property bordering a stream, a river, or an ocean shoreline is called **accretion**. The soil thus deposited is referred to as **alluvion** or *alluvion deposits*. The gradual wearing away of land by the action of water and wind is known as *erosion*. Reliction occurs when the waterway, sea, or river recedes permanently below the usual water line. When this takes place, the owner of the property that borders on the waterway, sea, or river may acquire title to the newly exposed land.

Avulsion

Avulsion occurs when a river or stream, during a storm or earthquake, carries away a part of the bank and bears it to the opposite bank or to another part of the same bank. The owner of the part carried away may reclaim it within one year after the avulsion. However, the owner must reclaim the title by applying some act of ownership, such as cultivation of the soil, within one year; if not, the land belongs to the owner of the property to which the land is now attached.

For urban readers, this discussion regarding rivers and water rights may seem out of place. But in rural California, especially

FIGURE 2.10

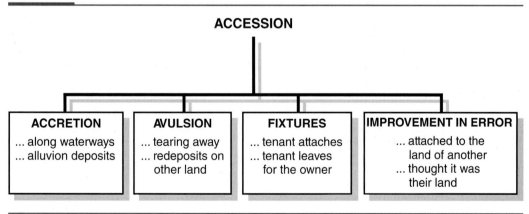

northern California, these topics are an important aspect of real estate principles.

Addition of Fixtures

Addition of fixtures occurs when a person affixes something to the land of another without an agreement permitting removal. The thing so affixed may then become the property of the landowner.

Improvements Made in Error

An *improvement made in error* occurs when a person, in good faith, erroneously affixes improvements to the land of another. In some cases, these erroneous improvements may pass to the land-owner. But in most cases, the person who made the improvements in error is permitted to remove the improvements and pay the cost to restore the property to its original condition.

Acquiring Property by Occupancy

Real property or the use of real property may be gained through

(1) abandonment and (2) adverse possession. (See Figure 2.11.)

Abandonment

A party who holds a leasehold interest (the tenant) in a piece of property may abandon his or her interest or any improvements made thereon. If this should occur, the landlord may reacquire possession and full control of the premises. In other words, when a tenant leaves before the lease expires, the landlord may reacquire the use of the property at that time and in some cases not be

FIGURE 2.11

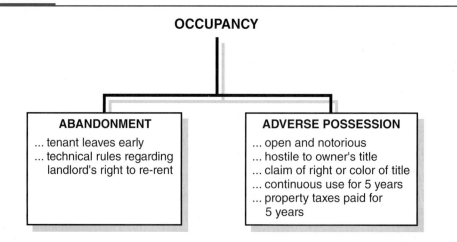

obligated to refund rental payments or return any improvements made on the property. There are technical rules regarding the landlord's right to re-rent the property. If a tenant abandons the premises and leaves personal property, the landlord may, after due notification, dispose of such personal property.

Adverse Possession

Adverse possession is the process by which title to another's property is acquired without compensation. Ownership may develop into legal title if five conditions are met.

Five elements of adverse possession

1. There must be actual occupation, open and notorious. This means the claim of possession must not be kept a secret. In other words, if the present owner inspects the property, the possession or use by another person should be apparent. You do not actually have to reside on the property, but you must show your intentions of holding and possessing the land through some type of improvement to the land. For example, if the property were farmland, the cultivation of crops, the grazing of cattle, or the fencing of the property might constitute possession.

2. There must be occupancy hostile to the true owner's title (wishes). Hostile does not mean physical confrontation. Hostile means a person is using the property without permission and not making rental payment of any kind to the owner. Permission to use the property defeats the hostile use and prevents acquiring title by adverse possession.

3. There must be a *claim of right or color of title*. Under claim of right, the claimant enters as an intruder and remains; under color of title, claimants base their right on some court decree or upon a defective written instrument.

4. There must be *continuous and uninterrupted possession* for a period of five years.

5. There must be the *payment by the possessor of all real property taxes* levied and assessed for a period of five consecutive years. The fact that the true owner is also paying the taxes does not necessarily defeat the rights of the adverse possessor, as long as the possessor pays the taxes first.

Adverse possession is not common in California because of the five requirements listed previously. It is not possible to obtain title by adverse possession to public lands or against an incompetent private landowner. Title insurance and marketable title cannot be obtained until a court, under a quiet title action, rules that the adverse possession vested valid title. In short, if you acquire title by adverse possession, it will be difficult to finance or sell the property without first going to court.

Acquiring Property by Transfer

Without question, the most common method of acquiring property is by transfer. When property is conveyed from one person to another by act of the parties or by act of law, title is acquired by transfer. There are five basic types of property transfers: (1) private grant, (2) public grant, (3) gift, (4) public dedication, and (5) court action (or involuntary transfer). (See Figure 2.12.)

Private Grant

Private grant occurs when an owner voluntarily conveys his or her ownership rights to another. The basic instrument used in this transaction is a deed. (Deeds are discussed in detail in Section 2.3.)

Public Grant

When a governmental agency deeds property to an individual or institution, it is called a **public grant**. In the early years of U.S. history, public grants were made through laws enacted by Congress.

The Preemption Act of 1862 allowed persons living on federal land, who were known as *squatters*, to acquire 160 acres of land at

FIGURE 2.12

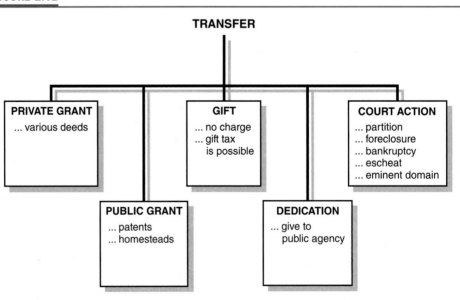

a small fee. The Homestead Act of 1862 allowed vast stretches of public land to be homesteaded. Heads of families or persons over twenty-one years of age could obtain 160 acres. They had to file a declaration of homestead with the county recorder or at a land office and had to agree to occupy and improve the land. After residing on it for five years and paying a small fee, they received a document from the government called a *patent*, which conveyed the title from the government to the homesteader.Other public grants were made by the government for railroads, educational institutions, national parks, cities, and towns.

Gift

A property owner may voluntarily transfer property to a private person or an organization without giving or receiving any consideration or compensation. In the case of real property, the transfer normally is evidenced by a gift deed. Depending on the value of the gift, there may or may not be a gift tax liability. The person who gives the gift is called the *donor;* the person who receives the gift is called the *donee*.

Public Dedication

A property owner may also give land to a public body for a particular use such as a street, a park, bridges, schools, playgrounds, and so on. This act is called *public dedication*. The dedication is valid only if the public body accepts the property.

Court Action (Involuntary Transfer)

A court of law may be called upon to transfer legal title in a variety of situations. The most common of these involuntary transfers are partition action, foreclosure action, bankruptcy, escheat, and eminent domain. (See Figure 2.13.)

Partition action is a court action wherein the co-owners of property may sue other co-owners for severance of their respective interests. If the property cannot be physically divided, the court can order a sale and divide the proceeds among the former owners.

Foreclosure action takes place when a person holding a delinquent lien on a property institutes proceedings requesting the forced sale of property. In California, delinquent real estate loans are foreclosed using a process called a *trustee's sale*, which is discussed in Chapter 7.

FIGURE 2.13

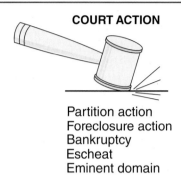

COURT ACTION

Partition action
Foreclosure action
Bankruptcy
Escheat
Eminent domain

Bankruptcy can be either voluntary or involuntary. When an individual cannot meet credit obligations, he or she may voluntarily file bankruptcy or may be adjudged bankrupt by the courts. Title to real property is then vested in a court-appointed trustee, who sells the property to pay the claims of creditors. Under certain circumstances, a family home can be protected against forced sale by the bankruptcy court.

Escheat is the legal process whereby ownership of property reverts to the state due to lack of heirs or want of legal ownership. The probate courts do all in their power to locate possible heirs. After escheat proceedings are instituted, the title is held in trust by the state for a set time. If at the end of that time no heirs have been located, title to the property transfers to the state. Every year, millions of dollars' worth of property escheats to the state of California because of the lack of heirs.

Eminent domain is the power of the state to take land from private ownership by due process of law. Use of eminent domain is often referred to as *condemnation proceedings*. These proceedings may be instituted by all levels of government and by public utilities or railroads.

Two conditions are legally required to use the power of eminent domain:

1. The property must be taken for a public use, * as found to be the case in *Kelo v. New London* (Connecticut), a U.S. Supreme Court ruling.
2. The owner must be paid just compensation. Most courts have ruled that the "fair market value" based on an appraisal is the proper method for determining just compensation.

---

*See *Kelo v. City of New London*, 545 U.S. 469 (2005).

2.3 INSTRUMENTS USED IN THE TRANSFER OF REAL PROPERTY

Under English common law, a written document was not needed to transfer title to real property. Rather, a twig, a stone, or a handful of dirt passing from one owner to the next owner in the presence of witnesses was symbolic of the transfer of property. Other methods of transfer were simply a statement made before witnesses in sight of the land, followed by entry upon the land by the new owner. Today under California law, the transfer of ownership of real property may be done by a single written instrument known as a *deed*.

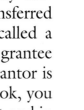

A deed is a written document by which (when properly executed, delivered, and accepted) title to real property is transferred from one person, called a **grantor**, to another person, called a **grantee**. The grantor is the person who gives title, and the grantee is the person who receives title. In a real estate sale, the grantor is the seller and the grantee is the buyer. Throughout this book, you will find words to designate the parties in an agreement that end in the letters *or* and *ee*, such as the following:

Trustor and trustee

Lessor and lessee

Vendor and vendee

Optionor and optionee

To understand these terms, remember this rule:

> *The* or *ending denotes the giver, and the* ee *ending indicates the receiver.*

Example: A lessor (owner or landlord) gives a lease to the lessee (tenant).

Essentials of a Valid Deed

To be valid, a deed must contain certain essential elements:

1. *The deed must be in writing.* Legal instruments required to be in writing come under the Statute of Frauds. According to this statute, when the title to real property is to be voluntarily conveyed, it must be accomplished by an instrument in writing, usually a deed.

2. *Parties must be correctly described and identified.* For a deed to be valid, the parties must be properly described. This means that the grantor (seller) and the grantee (buyer) must be certain and absolute.

For a Deed to be Valid

It must be ...

1 in writing,

2 with the parties correctly described,

3 with a competent grantor and capable grantee,

4 with a clear description,

5 granting clause, and

6 bearing the signature of the grantor.

> *Example:*   A deed from A to B or C is not absolute. The word *or* creates the problem. A deed from A to B and C is absolute. The word *and* makes it certain.

Because so many individuals have like or similar names, the parties to a deed must be identified as clearly as possible to avoid any later confusion as to true identity.

If possible, the full legal name should be used and the legal status of the individual should be shown. Remember, the full name includes middle name or initial, if any, and the legal status refers to the relationship between parties, such as husband and wife.

3. *Grantor must be competent to convey and grantee capable of receiving title.* Everyone is competent to convey except:
   a. *Minors:* persons under the age of eighteen years, unless the minor is classified as emancipated, in which case a minor can legally contract for real estate. An emancipated minor is normally a person under eighteen years who is married or in the armed services.
   b. *Incompetents:* persons of unsound mind, judicially declared incompetent.
   c. *Convicts:* persons imprisoned for life or under a death penalty.

Question: Can an infant take title to real property?
Answer: Yes, an infant can receive title by gift or inheritance but cannot convey title without a guardian or other court approval.
Question: Question: Can a person take title under an assumed name?
Answer: Yes, but upon resale, he or she may have difficulty proving identity for a notary public.

4. *Description of the property must be clear.* The property in the deed must be correctly described; this means any description that clearly identifies the property so it can be located with certainty meets the test of the law. In most cases, the legal description is a lot, block, and tract; a metes and bounds; or a U.S. government survey description.

5. *There must be a granting clause.* A granting clause means the deed must contain words indicating the intention of the owner to convey the property. The exact words are not specified; however, the words *I hereby grant, I hereby convey*, or *I hereby transfer* satisfy the requirements of a granting clause.

6. *Deed must contain the signature of the grantor.* To be valid, a deed must be signed by all grantors named in the deed. If there is more

than one owner, all owners must sign. For instance, both husband and wife must sign a deed to convey community property. Only the grantor(s) sign a deed, not the grantee(s).

Under certain guidelines, state law allows a grantor's name to be signed by an *attorney in fact,* a person acting under a valid power of attorney.

California permits a person who is unable to sign his or her name to sign by mark as long as two witnesses are present. One of the witnesses then signs the deed according to the manner prescribed by law.

Delivery of the Deed is Required

A deed is not effective unless it is delivered to and accepted by the grantee. This does not mean a mere turning over of the physical possession of the document. The grantor must have a clear and honest intention to pass title immediately, before there is a legal delivery.

1. *Evidence of delivery.* The best evidence is actually handing the deed to the grantee. However, manual delivery is not necessary, as a deed may be delivered to a third party for the benefit of the grantee—for example, depositing the deed in escrow. Again, manual delivery does not in itself constitute delivery; the proof lies in the intent of the grantor to pass title. Recording of the deed, if and when it happens, presumes valid delivery.

2. *Time of delivery.* To be effective, a deed must be delivered to the grantee during the grantor's lifetime. It cannot be used to take the place of a will. A deed that is delivered to a grantee with the condition that it is not to take effect until the death of the grantor is not valid because the intent to pass title would not occur during the lifetime of the grantor.

3. *Date of delivery.* A deed is presumed to be delivered as of its date of writing or execution. If no date exists on the deed, the legal date is presumed to be the date of delivery. The lack of a date on the deed does not invalidate the deed.

4. *Conditional delivery.* Delivery of a deed must be absolute. It cannot be delivered to a grantee subject to conditions. For example, in an attempt to avoid the cost of probate, A gives a deed to B, telling B she is not to record the deed until A dies. This is a conditional delivery and is not a valid deed or transfer.

Acceptance

The deed must be accepted by the grantee, and this acceptance must be voluntary and unconditional. Acceptance is usually accomplished by words, acts, or conduct on the grantee's part that lead to the presumption of voluntary acceptance. An example of acceptance is the recording of the deed by the grantee.

Acknowledgment

A deed is a real estate document that need not be recorded to be valid. However, if the grantee wishes to record the deed, it must first be acknowledged.

An **acknowledgment** is a formal declaration before a duly authorized officer (usually a notary public) by the person who signed a document, stating that the signature is voluntarily given and that he or she is the person whose signature appears on the document.

Nonessentials in a Deed

Many of the items listed previously are essential for a deed to be valid. Some items, however, are not legally required but are commonly found in a deed.

Legally, a deed *does not* need to contain but commonly has (1) an acknowledgment, (2) a date, and (3) a recording number issued by the county.

However, it must be remembered that a deed is void or invalid if the

1. grantor is incompetent.
2. deed is signed in blank.
3. deed is not delivered.
4. deed is a forgery.
5. grantee does not exist (fictitious or deceased).
6. deed is altered in escrow.

TYPES OF DEEDS

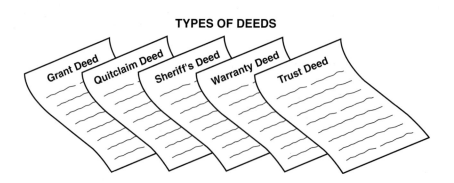

Grant Deed

In California, the **grant deed** is the most commonly used instrument for transferring title to real estate. A grant deed carries two *implied warranties*—meaning that although the warranties are not written in the deed, the law says they apply. An example of a grant deed is shown in Figure 2.14.

The implied warranties in a grant deed are that

1. the grantor has not already conveyed title to any other person.
2. the estate being conveyed is free from encumbrances made by the grantor or any other person claiming under the grantor, other than those disclosed to the grantee.

Notice that these implied warranties do not state that the grantor is the owner or that the property is not encumbered. Rather, they state that the grantor has not deeded to others and that the property is free of encumbrances made by the grantor. This is why a potential buyer should insist that a policy of title insurance be issued as a condition of the purchase.

In addition to transferring legal ownership, a grant deed can be used to create easements and land use restrictions. A grant deed also conveys any after acquired title. *After acquired title* means that after the grantor deeds the property to the grantee, if the grantor should later acquire an additional interest in the property, that interest automatically passes to the grantee.

Quitclaim Deed

A **quitclaim deed** provides the grantee with the least protection of any deed. A quitclaim deed carries no implied warranties and no after acquired title provisions. Under a quitclaim deed, the grantor merely relinquishes any right or claim he or she has in the property. If the grantor has absolute ownership, that is what is conveyed. If the grantor has no claim or ownership right, this type of deed transfers what the grantor has—nothing! In other words, a quitclaim deed merely says, "Whatever interest I have in the property is yours; it may be something, or it may be nothing."

The quitclaim deed is usually used to remove certain items from the public record, such as the removal of an easement or a recorded restriction. It is not normally used in a buy-and-sell transaction.

Sheriff's Deed

The court may order an owner's property sold after a lawsuit and the rendering of a money judgment against the owner. The

FIGURE 2.14

RECORDING REQUESTED BY

AND WHEN RECORDED MAIL DOCUMENT AND
TAX STATEMENT TO:

NAME

STREET
ADDRESS

CITY, STATE &
ZIP CODE

TITLE ORDER NO.   ESCROW NO.   SPACE ABOVE THIS LINE FOR RECORDER'S USE ONLY

GRANT DEED

APN:

The undersigned grantor(s) declare(s)_____
DOCUMENTARY TRANSFER TAX $
☐ computed on full value of property conveyed, or
☐ computed on full value less linens and encumbrances remaining at time of sale.
☐ Unincorporated Area   City of_____

FOR VALUABLE CONSIDERATION, receipt of which is hereby acknowledged, I (we)

hereby remise, release and grant to

the following described real property in the City of _____, County of_____
State of California, with the following legal description:

_____
              Date

_____

_____

STATE OF _____

COUNTY OF _____

On_____ before me,_____ ,
              (Date)   (Name and title of the officer)
personally appeared _____ , who proved to me on the basis of
                              (Name of person signing)
satisfactory evidence to be the person(s) whose name(s) is/are subscribed to the within instrument and acknowledged to me that he/she/
they executed the same in his/her/their authorized capacity(ies), and that by his/her/their signature(s) on the instrument the person(s), or the
entity upon behalf of which the person(s) acted executed the instrument.

I certify under PENALTY OF PERJURY under the laws of the State of California that the foregoing paragraph is true and correct.

WITNESS my hand and official seal.

_____
              Signature of officer

MAIL TAX STATEMENT AS DIRECTED ABOVE

* There are various types of deed forms depending on each person's legal status. Before you use this form you many want to consult an attorney
if you have questions concerning which document form is appropriate for your transaction.

successful bidder at this type of sale receives a sheriff's deed, which contains no warranties. In some courts, this sale is conducted by a commissioner instead of the sheriff, and the deed issued is called a *commissioner's deed*.

Gift Deed

A person who wishes to give real estate to another may convey title by using a gift deed. The legal consideration given in a gift deed is usually "love and affection." A gift deed is valid unless it is being used to defraud creditors, in which case the creditors may institute legal action to void the deed.

Tax Deed

A tax deed is issued by the tax collector after the sale of land that previously reverted to the state because of nonpayment of property taxes. The tax sale procedure is presented in Chapter 13.

Warranty Deed

A warranty deed is seldom used in California. Under a warranty deed, the grantor is legally responsible to the grantee for the condition of the title. Sellers in California are reluctant to assume this liability and rarely sign warranty deeds. Instead, sellers sign grant deeds and leave the legal responsibility for the condition of the title to title insurance companies.

Trust Deed (or Deed of Trust)

A trust deed conveys "bare legal title" (but no right of use or possession) to a third party called a *trustee*. This deed differs from others in that title is held by the trustee merely as security for a loan (lien) until such time as the loan is paid off or until the borrower defaults on his or her payments. Trust deeds are financing instruments, and they are explained in Chapter 7.

Deed of Reconveyance

This deed is executed by the trustee to the borrower (trustor). When a beneficiary (the lender) notifies the trustee that the trustor has repaid a loan, the trustee reconveys the title back to the trustor using a deed of reconveyance. This instrument is also involved with the financing of real estate and is discussed in Chapter 7.

Trustee's Deed

This deed conveys title to a successful bidder at a trustee's sale (foreclosure). A trustee's deed contains no warranties. A trustee's deed and the foreclosure process are discussed in Chapter 7.

2.4 THE RECORDING SYSTEM

The recording of a deed and many other title instruments, although not required by law, protects the new owner's rights. Under the Spanish and Mexican governments, there were no recording laws in California. Shortly after California became a state, the legislature adopted a recording system by which evidence of title or interest in real property could be collected and held for public view at a convenient and safe place. This safe public place is the county recorder's office.

To be accepted for recording by a county recorder, the deed must have the following:

1. An acknowledgment (be notarized)
2. Name and address to which future tax statements can be mailed
3. Basis for computing the transfer tax
4. Names of all parties involved in the transaction
5. An adequate legal description
6. Payment of a recording fee

Once a document is recorded, it is said that the world has constructive notice of the contents of the document.

The recording system also shows sequential transfers of property from the original owner to the present owner. This successive list of owners is called a *chain of title*.

Recorded documents are filed in books called *grantor–grantee indexes*. Most counties have reduced their title records to microfilm or microfiche for easy handling and storage. These title records are frequently transferred by title companies to computers, making it easier for the title company to research a property.

A general rule says, "The first to record is the first in right."

> *Example:*   A deeds to B, who does not record. If A then deeds to C, who does record, under the general rule, C would probably get the property because C recorded first.

However, there are two exceptions to this rule:

1. If a party or grantee is the first to record, but is aware of another party (an earlier grantee for example) who has an interest in the property, the first party to record would be second to the interest of the other earlier party.
2. If the first party failed to record but took possession of the property, the possession by an unrecorded owner can defeat a later recorded deed by another person.

Example: A deeds to B, who does not record, but B takes physical possession of the property. A then deeds to C, who does not make a physical inspection of the property. C then records the deed. Who will probably win? Answer: B, because physical possession gives actual notice to all parties, including C, that B has a prior interest in the property.

Moral: Always physically inspect a property before you purchase. Do not rely on the public records only!

CHAPTER SUMMARY, PART I

There are three major types of land descriptions: lot, block, and tract; metes and bounds; and the U.S. government survey system. Five ways of acquiring title to property are by will, succession, accession, occupancy, and transfer.

To be valid, a deed must contain certain essential elements, and the deed must have proper delivery and acceptance. Major types of deeds are grant deed, quitclaim deed, warranty deed, sheriff's deed, and gift deed. The most common is the grant deed, and it contains two implied warranties.

California has adopted a recording system designed to protect the rights of property owners and lien holders.

IMPORTANT TERMS AND CONCEPTS

accession

accretion

acknowledgment

addition of fixtures

administrator (or administratrix)

adverse possession

alluvion

avulsion

eminent domain

escheat

executor (or executrix)

foreclosure action

grant deed

grantee

grantor

holographic will

intestate

metes and bounds

partition action

private grant

probate

public grant

quitclaim deed

registered domestic partner

statutory will

succession

trust deed

U.S. government survey system

warranty deed

witnessed will

PRACTICAL APPLICATION

1. S ½ of SW ¼ of the SW ¼ of the NW ¼, and the SW ¼ of Section 5. How many acres? Using the grid below, shade in the parcel.

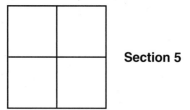

Section 5

2. At a probate sale for a vacant lot, the initial accepted offer to purchase is $200,000. If you wish to place the next additional bid, what is the minimum you must bid?

3. Garcia deeds real property to Williams using a grant deed. Shortly thereafter, the county abandons an alley easement at the rear of the property. Garcia maintains that the alley area is his, whereas Williams says it belongs to her. Based on your knowledge of grant deeds, who is probably right?

REVIEWING YOUR UNDERSTANDING

1. Ms. Jones was killed in an automobile accident. When the courts were called upon to distribute her property, they found she had died intestate. This means that she died
   a. leaving no property.
   b. leaving no heirs.
   c. in debt.
   d. without a will.

2. If a married man with two children died without leaving a will, separate property that was purchased by him before he married and was maintained as separate property during the marriage would be distributed as follows:
   a. One-half to the children
   b. One-half to the widow
   c. All to the widow
   d. One-third to the widow and two-thirds to the children

3. How many acres are there in a parcel of property that includes the following: the NW ¼ of the SW ¼, the E ½ of the NW ¼, and the NE ¼ of the SW ¼ of Section 5?

   a. 320 acres

   b. 160 acres

   c. 40 acres

   d. 80 acres

4. The state urgently needs a piece of property to complete a project for public use. The owner did not wish to sell. Which method could be used to acquire the property?

   a. Dedication

   b. Escheat

   c. Police power

   d. Eminent domain

5. The term *escheat* is a legal term meaning

   a. a fraud has been committed.

   b. an agent's license has been revoked.

   c. property with a mortgage can be conveyed.

   d. title has reverted to the state.

6. The water flowing down a river gradually builds up the land along the bank by leaving deposits of soil; this action is called

   a. accretion.

   b. reliction.

   c. avulsion.

   d. erosion.

7. All of the following statements concerning wills are correct except which?

   a. A statutory will uses a form approved by the state.

   b. A holographic will can be signed by an *X* if it is witnessed.

   c. An administratrix is appointed by a probate court.

   d. A person who receives real property by will is known as a devisee.

8. Deeds are used to transfer property. Which deed contains no implied or expressed warranties?
   a. Warranty deed
   b. Grant deed
   c. Quitclaim deed
   d. Interspousal grant deed

9. The executrix of an estate is
   a. selected by the heirs.
   b. appointed by the superior court.
   c. named in the testator's will.
   d. named by the decedent's attorney.

10. To be valid, a deed must
    a. contain a proper description of the property.
    b. be signed by a competent grantee.
    c. be recorded.
    d. be dated.

11. "Beginning on a point on the North line of Bard Avenue distant 218.00 feet East from the Northeast corner of Bard Avenue and Elm Street." This legal description is
    a. metes and bounds.
    b. lot, block, and tract.
    c. U.S. government survey.
    d. townships and sections.

12. Which of the following is not a base and meridian found in California?
    a. Humboldt
    b. Mt. Diablo
    c. Mt. Shasta
    d. San Bernardino

13. Which measurement is incorrect?
    a. Acre = 43,800 square feet
    b. Mile = 5,280 feet
    c. One square acre = 208.71 feet
    d. Township = 6 miles square

14. Hostile, open, and notorious use of another person's land for five years is required for title by
    a. will.
    b. succession.
    c. accession.
    d. adverse possession.

15. An instrument by which the government grants title to a person is a(n)
    a. homestead.
    b. partition action.
    c. patent.
    d. escheat.

16. Recording of a deed gives
    a. actual notice.
    b. constructive notice.
    c. physical notice.
    d. vested notice.

17. A deeds to B, who does not record the deed or take physical possession of the property. A then deeds to C, who had no notice of the prior deed to B. C records the deed. In a dispute over title between B and C, which rule would be important?
    a. All deeds must be recorded to be valid.
    b. He or she who records first is the first in right.
    c. All deeds must be acknowledged to be valid.
    d. The date of the deed determines who is first.

18. Which statement regarding deeds is false?
    a. A minor who is not emancipated can receive title but cannot convey title without court action.
    b. Incompetent persons cannot convey title without court action.
    c. A person cannot take legal title under an assumed name.
    d. A valid deed need not be recorded.

19. An after acquired title provision occurs in a
    a. grant deed.
    b. quitclaim deed.
    c. sheriff's deed.
    d. tax deed.

20. Who signs a grant deed?
    a. Lessor
    b. Mortgagor
    c. Grantee
    d. Grantor

Part II: Estates and Methods of Holding Title

Part II discusses freehold and less-than-freehold estates. In addition, various methods of holding title (including joint tenancy, tenancy in common, community property, living trust, and tenancy in partnership) are presented, stressing the characteristics, advantages, and disadvantages of each. At the conclusion of Part II, you will be able to do the following:

1. Explain the difference between freehold and less-than-freehold estates.
2. Describe the key differences in taking title to property as joint tenants as opposed to tenants in common.
3. Explain the difference between community property and separate property.
4. Discuss the concepts of cohabitation, equity sharing, and living trusts.

2.5 ESTATES

An **estate** is defined as the degree, quantity, nature, and extent of interest a person has in property. If the estate is in real property, you have a real estate interest. Real property estates fall into two major classifications: freehold estates and less-than-freehold estates.

Freehold Estates

A **freehold estate** refers to one's interest as an owner of real property. Freehold estates can be subdivided into fee estates and life estates. (See Figure 2.15.)

FIGURE 2.15

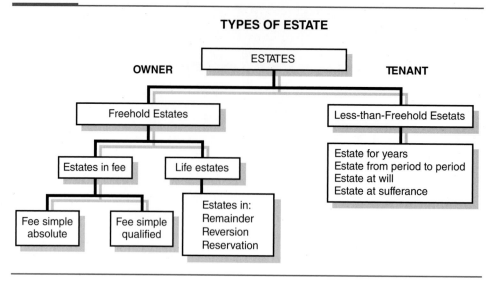

1. Fee estates or fee simple estates can be divided into the following:
   a. **Fee simple absolute**, which the owner holds without any qualifications or limitations, such as private deed restrictions. All government ordinances and limitations still apply. This is the highest form of interest an individual can have in land.
   b. **Fee simple qualified** (*defeasible*), which the owner holds subject to special conditions, limitations, or private deed restrictions that limit the use of the property.

   Example: A parcel of land may carry a restriction that prohibits the sale of alcoholic beverages on the premises. If the owner fails to adhere to the restriction, the owner may be liable in a lawsuit for damages, or in extreme cases the title may revert back to the grantor or creator of the restriction.

2. **Life estates** are created by deed or will for the life of one or more designated human beings. The life tenant has all the rights of possession, or income, during the life of the designated person(s). However, the holder of a life estate cannot deed or lease a property beyond the life of the designated person. If the person granting the life estate designates that the title is to go to some other person upon the death of the life estate holder, the person so designated is said to have an **estate in remainder**.

Example: In Figure 2.16, A deeds a life estate to B for the life of B. When B dies, the property passes to C. B holds the life estate; C holds the estate in remainder.

If the property is to be returned to the person who gave the life estate or to his or her heirs, that person is said to have an **estate in reversion**.

Example: In Figure 2.17, A deeds a life estate to B for B's life, with the provision that when B dies, the title reverts back to A. B holds a life estate; A holds the *estate in reversion*.

Another possibility is a *grant reserving a life estate*. Among life estates, this is probably the most common situation.

Example: In Figure 2.18, A deeds title to B, but A reserves or keeps a life estate for the rest of A's life. Upon the death of A, possession and use pass to B.

FIGURE 2.16

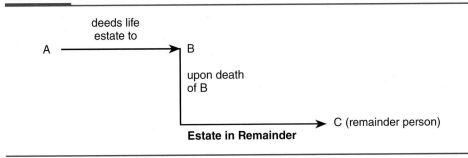

FIGURE 2.17

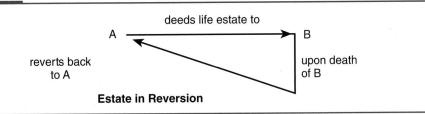

FIGURE 2.18

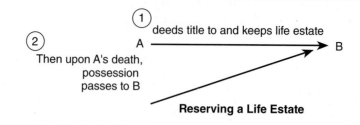

Reserving a Life Estate

As previously mentioned, a holder of a life estate cannot deed or lease property beyond the length of the life of the designated person. For example, assume that A holds title for life and, upon A's death, title is to pass to B, the remainder person. If, during A's life, A leases the property to C, upon A's death the lease is canceled and B, the remainder person, receives title free of the lease. If C wishes to continue to lease the property, C needs to negotiate a new lease with B.

Finally, freehold estates, both fee simple and certain parts of life estates, are considered durable and capable of being transferred by inheritance upon death. Therefore, freehold estates are sometimes called *estates of inheritance*.

Less-than-Freehold Estates

Less-than-freehold estates are interests held by tenants who rent or lease property. Tenants are also called *lessees* or *leaseholders* and are discussed in detail in Chapter 11.

2.6 METHODS OF HOLDING TITLE

When people acquire ownership of real property, they must decide how to hold title. Title may be held separately in one person's name alone or concurrently with other people.

Ownership in Severalty

When a person acquires real property and holds title solely in his or her own name, it is technically known as **ownership in severalty**. In other words, he or she alone enjoys the ownership benefits, including the complete bundle of rights, and "severs" his or her relationship with others.

A person can hold title in severalty in one of the following ways, depending on the owner's legal status:

As single

As unmarried

As married

As a registered domestic partner

As a widow or widower

A person who wishes to indicate **separate property** ownership can add the words *sole* and *separate property* to any of the choices listed. A corporation can hold title in severalty, such as "Acme Company, a California Corporation."

Concurrent Ownership

Concurrent ownership is when two or more people hold title together. There are numerous types of concurrent ownership, but the most important are joint tenancy, tenancy in common, community property, and tenancy in partnership.

Joint Tenancy

Joint tenancy exists when two or more persons are joint and equal owners of the same undivided interest in real property. To create and maintain a valid joint tenancy, four unities must exist:

1. *Unity of time.* This means that the owners must have acquired their interest at the same time.

2. *Unity of title.* This means that all owners must come into title on the same document. Consider this example: A and B are joint tenants. B sells her interest to C. A and C are tenants in common because they each took title on a different document at a different time.

3. *Unity of interest.* This means that all owners must have equal shares or interest in the property. For example, if there are two owners, each must have a one-half interest; with four owners, each must have a one-quarter interest; with eight owners, each must have a one-eighth interest; and so on.

4. *Unity of possession.* This means that all owners must have equal rights of possession. No one owner can be prevented from using the property by the other owner(s).

If any of these unities are missing, the joint tenancy is invalid and the rules of tenancy in common apply.

Important Characteristics

The most important characteristic of joint tenancy is the **right of survivorship**. This means that if one tenant dies, the surviving joint tenant(s) acquire the deceased's interest without a court action such as a probate.

Example:

1. A and B take title to property as joint tenants. B dies; A becomes the sole owner because of the right of survivorship.

2. A, B, and C take title to a property as joint tenants. C dies and her interest automatically passes to the survivors, A and B. A and B are still joint tenants between each other, each owning a one-half interest in the property.

Other Characteristics of Joint Tenancy

In addition to the four unities (time, title, interest, and possession) and the right of survivorship, joint tenancy has these important characteristics:

1. You cannot will your interest in joint tenancy property.

2. Interest in the property is undivided. In other words, each owner can use every square foot, and he or she cannot say, "This is my half and this is yours."

3. No probate procedure is required to distribute the interest upon the death of one of the owners. The interest goes to the surviving co-owners. However, some paperwork is required to shift the remaining interest to the surviving joint tenant. But this paperwork is minor in comparison to a complete probate.

4. A joint tenant may sell or convey his or her interest without approval of the other tenant(s). This action may break the joint tenancy and create a tenancy in common. For example; A , B and C are joint tenants. C sells his interest to X. A and B are still joint tenants with each other but now they are also tenants in common with X.

   Example: A and B are joint tenants. B sells her interest to C. A and C are now tenants in common. Why? Because B's act of selling to C violated the unities of time and title.

5. A corporation is not allowed to hold title as a joint tenant because, in theory, a corporation never "dies."

6. A surviving tenant acquires the interest of the deceased joint tenant and is free from the debts created individually by the deceased joint tenant.

Tenancy in Common

When two or more persons are owners of an undivided interest in property, they can hold title as tenants in common. **Tenancy in common** has these characteristics:

1. There is no right of survivorship, meaning that upon the death of a tenant in common, his or her interest passes to the heirs, not the surviving co-tenants. This requires a probate proceeding.
2. Each owner may hold an unequal interest; that is, he or she may own unequal shares.

> *Example:* A, B, C, and D hold title as tenants in common. These owners might share their interest as follows:

A might own one-quarter interest.
B might own one-eighth interest.
C might own one-eighth interest.
D might own one-half interest.

> Contrast this with joint tenancy, which requires all owners to have equal shares or interest.

3. Each owner has equal rights of possession and must pay his or her share of the expenses, such as property taxes.
4. Each owner may will his or her interest to his or her heirs, and upon death, the heirs take their place along with the other owners as tenants in common.
5. Each co-tenant may sell, convey, or encumber his or her interest without the consent of the co-tenants.

> *Example:* A and B are tenants in common. A dies and his interest passes to his heir, X. X and B become tenants in common.
> *or*
> A, B, and C are tenants in common. If C sells her interest to D, then A, B, and D become tenants in common.

What If?

To test your understanding of the difference between joint tenancy and tenants in common, answer the following questions.

1. A and B are joint tenants. If B dies, who gets what?
2. A and B are joint tenants. If B sells to C, what is the relationship between A and C?

continued

3. A and B are tenants in common. If B dies, who gets what?
4. A and B and C are joint tenants. C sells his interest to D. What is the relationship between A and B and D?

Answers

1. B's interest passes to A, who now holds title in severalty.
2. A and C are tenants in common.
3. A and the heirs of B are tenants in common.
4. A and B are joint tenants to each other and tenants in common with D.

Tenancy in Business Partnership

Tenancy in partnership exists when two or more persons, as partners, pool their interests, assets, and efforts in a business venture, with each to share in the profits or the losses. This type of business organization includes general partnerships and limited partnerships, and many rules and regulations are involved. The following discussion outlines only the real estate aspects of partnerships, not the legal or accounting aspects. Tenancy in partnership has the following real estate characteristics:

1. Each partner has an equal right with other partners to possession of specific partnership property for partnership purposes. This means a partner only has the right to use the property for business, not for personal purposes, unless the other partners agree to the personal use.
2. A partner's right in the partnership property is not assignable except in connection with the assignment of rights of all the partners in the same property.
3. A partner's right in the partnership property is not subject to attachment or execution, except on a claim against the partnership.
4. There is a form of survivorship when one partner dies.

   Example: A and B own property as partners. A dies; B receives title in trust until the disposition of the property. In other words, the title rests in the survivor only long enough to carry on the business for the sole purpose of winding up the partnership affairs.

Limited Partnership

Sometimes title to real estate is held by a limited partnership. Under a limited partnership, one or more general partners have unlimited liability and usually a series of limited partners have limited liability. *Limited liability* means that if all legal requirements have been met, the limited partners can lose only their investment and cannot be held liable for partnership debts. Most real estate syndicates hold title as a limited partnership.

Community Property

Community property ownership is another form of ownership held by more than one person, but in this case, the property can be held only by a husband and wife or by registered domestic partners. Community property is defined as all property acquired during a valid marriage or registered domestic partnership. California is a community property state; therefore, all California property acquired by a husband and wife or by registered domestic partners during marriage is presumed to be community property. However, there are a few exceptions.

1. All property owned by husband or wife before marriage or registered domestic partnership can remain separate property after-marriage or registered domestic partnership as long as the property is not commingled with community property, causing it to lose its separate property identity.
2. All property acquired by gift or inheritance by either spouse during marriage or registered domestic partnership remains separate property as long as it is not commingled with community property.
3. All income and profits from separate property as well as any property acquired from the proceeds of separate property remain separate property as long as said income and profits are not commingled with community property.

In effect, a husband and wife are general partners, as are registered domestic partners, each owning one-half of the community property.

Each spouse or partner has equal management and control of the community property. Neither spouse or partner may convey or encumber real estate held as community property unless the other spouse or partner also signs the contracts or documents involved.

Each spouse or partner has the right to dispose of his or her half of the community property by will to whomever he or she wishes. But if either spouse or partner dies intestate, the surviving spouse or partner receives all the property; the children, if any, get nothing.

Another Choice

Effective for deeds or documents recorded after July 2, 2001, a husband and wife or registered domestic partners may hold title as "community property with right of survivorship." This means upon the death of one spouse or partner, the surviving spouse or partner receives title without a special spousal or partner probate. In short, married couples and registered domestic partners now have a choice. They may (1) hold title as regular community property and keep the right to will their separate interest or (2) hold title with the right of survivorship and automatically guarantee that upon death of one spouse or partner, the property will go to the surviving spouse or partner without any probate. In addition, there are some tax differences between the two choices. If a married couple acquired title as community property prior to July 2, 2001, and wish to switch, they need to discuss with their tax and legal experts the pros and cons of redeeding to take advantage of this more recent choice (see California Civil Code Sec.682.1).

Community property does not need to be probated if the deceased spouse or partner leaves his or her interest to the surviving spouse or partner. But if the deceased spouse's or partner's interest is left to someone other than the surviving spouse or partner, the estate must be probated.

For Married Couples or Registered Domestic Partners, Which is Best: Joint Tenancy or Community Property?

The answer is complicated and should be discussed with a tax attorney. Some of the main issues to compare are income tax basis upon death, estate taxes, and probate procedures (if any). Also, the trend toward deeding title into a **living trust** may need to be discussed with a tax attorney. Real estate licensees and escrow officers are neither qualified nor allowed to give buyers and existing owners advice on how to hold title. (See Table 2.1.)

TABLE 2.1 The Basics of Co-Ownership.

	Tenancy in Common	Joint Tenancy	Community Property
Who Can Hold Title?	Any 2 or more persons	Any 2 or more persons	Husband and wife and registered domestic partners
Ownership Interest	Can be any percentage, equal or not	All shares must be equal	Equal shares
Upon Death	Probate usually required	No probate, right of survivorship, no will allowed	Special probate; right to will; intestate goes to surviving spouse or partner; after July 2001, optional right of survivorship
Disposition of Title	Convey interest without others' permission	Convey interest without others' permission	Need both signatures to convey title

Cohabitation and Property Rights

In 1976, in the famous *Marvin v. Marvin* case involving the late actor Lee Marvin, California courts held that unmarried persons who cohabitate may create property rights and obligations by oral agreement. The bottom line is that unmarried people who cohabitate might need to discuss this situation with an attorney. They may find it advisable to reduce to contract form an agreement on how to handle previously owned property and property accumulated during cohabitation, in the event they separate at a later date.

Equity Sharing

Equity sharing is when an owner-occupant and a nonresident owner-investor pool their money to buy a home. The down payment is split according to an agreed percentage, and both parties are on the deed and mortgage. The owner-occupant pays rent to the nonresident owner-investor for a portion of the home owned by the investor. The nonresident owner-investor then uses the rent money to join with the owner-occupant to pay the monthly mortgage payments. The equity share contract spells out who is responsible for taxes, insurance, and upkeep. Some day in the future, the home is either refinanced or sold, and the parties split the net proceeds according to a prearranged percentage. Equity share arrangements are complicated and should not be undertaken without advice from legal and tax experts.

Living Trust

As the value of estates increases, the tendency is for people to look for ways to minimize the cost of probate. One trend has been to place all real estate and other valuable property into a living trust. The owner transfers the property to the trust and frequently names himself or herself as trustee with the right to change the terms and scope of the trust as he or she sees fit. While in the trust, he or she enjoys all the privileges of ownership. Upon death, title passes to the named beneficiaries without the time and delay of a probate. A living trust does not eliminate estate taxes but rather eliminates the cost of probate. A person should contact an attorney before entering into a living trust to discuss its pros and cons.

CHAPTER SUMMARY, PART II

Freehold estates consist of fee estates and life estates, representing the rights of an owner of real property. Fee estates are either fee simple absolute with no private restrictions or fee simple qualified with some private limitations and restrictions. Life estates are granted for the life of one or more persons and may be a remainder, reversion, or reservation type.

Ownership in severalty is when title is held in sole ownership. Concurrent ownership is when title is held by two or more persons. Common examples of concurrent ownership are joint tenancy, tenancy in common, tenancy in partnership, and community property. In California, property acquired by a husband and wife during marriage and by partners while domestically registered is considered to be community property. Property acquired by a spouse or partner before marriage or registration, or property acquired by inheritance or gift during marriage or registration, is considered separate property unless it is commingled with the community property. An increasing number of people are choosing to hold title in a living trust. Methods of holding title have important estate and income tax consequences that should be discussed with a qualified attorney before a selection is made.

IMPORTANT TERMS AND CONCEPTS

community property	freehold estate	ownership in severalty
estate	joint tenancy	right of survivorship
estate in remainder	less-than-freehold estate	separate property
estate in reversion		tenancy in common
fee simple absolute	life estate	tenancy in partnership
fee simple qualified	living trust	

PRACTICAL APPLICATION

1. Chan owns real property and deeds a life estate to Washington. Upon Washington's death, title is to pass to Adams. While holding a life estate, Washington leases the property for five years to Santos. Two years later, Adams dies; one year later, Chan and Washington both die. Upon Washington's death, who is entitled to possession of the property?

2. Nguyen and Harris purchased twenty acres as joint tenants. Harris then sold one-half of her undivided interest to Battino. Shortly thereafter, Harris died. What is the legal relationship between Nguyen and Battino, and what percentage interest is owned by each?

3. Bill and Sara Belinski, husband and wife, purchased a home in California as community property. Later Sara's parents died and left her a five-unit apartment in Los Angeles. The apartments are professionally managed, and all rental proceeds are placed in a separate account under Sara's name alone. Sara uses the rental proceeds to pay tuition for the children, who are still in college. The Belinskis are now in the process of a divorce. What are the community property issues?

REVIEWING YOUR UNDERSTANDING

1. Which of the following statements is false?
   a. The right of survivorship is present in a tenancy in common.
   b. A life estate tenant is responsible for payment of the property tax.
   c. A leasehold estate is a less-than-freehold estate.
   d. Unity of possession is present in joint tenancy and tenancy in common ownerships.

2. Which of the following terms do not belong together?
   a. Joint tenancy, probate hearing
   b. Tenancy in common, equal interest
   c. Tenancy in common, severalty estate
   d. All of the above

3. Which of the following is considered to be a less-than-freehold estate?
   a. Fee simple absolute
   b. Life estate
   c. Leasehold estate
   d. Fee simple defeasible

4. The single most important characteristic of joint tenancy is
   a. equal rights of use.
   b. equal interest.
   c. right of survivorship.
   d. right to encumber.

5. It is impossible for a corporation to legally hold title as a
   a. trustee.
   b. joint tenant.
   c. tenant in common.
   d. California corporation.

6. Which of the following is not one of the four unities of joint tenancy?
   a. Time
   b. Interest
   c. Security
   d. Title

7. A deeds a life estate to B; upon B's death, title is to pass to C. This is an example of a
   a. perpetual estate.
   b. less-than-freehold estate.
   c. remainder estate.
   d. fee simple estate.

8. The term *fee simple defeasible* is best described in which statement?
   a. Owner holds a title without limitations.
   b. Owner holds a less-than-freehold estate.
   c. Owner holds title subject to deed restrictions.
   d. Owner holds an estate in remainder.

9. Smith and Dang are joint tenants; Dang sells his half of the property to Brown. Brown will take title with Smith as
   a. joint tenants.
   b. tenants in common.
   c. ownership in severalty.
   d. separate property.

10. Community property is defined as property acquired by a husband and wife or registered domestic partners
    a. before marriage or domestic registration.
    b. after marriage or domestic registration.
    c. by either party by gift or inheritance.
    d. before or after marriage or registration.

11. Real estate syndicates usually hold title to property as
    a. general partnership.
    b. limited partnership.
    c. tenants in common.
    d. tenancy in partnership.

12. Freehold estates are sometimes called estates of
    a. inheritance.
    b. will.
    c. accession.
    d. years.

13. Ownership in severalty refers to holding title as
    a. joint tenants.
    b. an individual.
    c. co-ownership.
    d. partners.

14. Garcia owned a life estate in a property. Garcia leased the property to Williams for five years. Two years later, Garcia died. The lease is
    a. valid and in force for the rest of the term.
    b. valid for a two-year period after the death of Garcia.
    c. invalid from the beginning; a life estate owner cannot sign a lease.
    d. canceled and invalid upon Garcia's death.

15. A, B, and C are joint tenants, and they hold title to the NW ¼ of Section 24 in some township. C deeds her interest to D.
    a. D is a joint tenant with A and B.
    b. D acquired approximately 53.33 acres.
    c. D owns a one-third interest in 160 acres.
    d. A, B, and D are all tenants in common with each other.

16. In California, without any evidence to the contrary, a husband and wife or registered domestic partners are presumed to hold title as
    a. tenants in common.
    b. joint tenants.
    c. community property.
    d. tenancy in partnership.

17. To be valid, all owners must have equal shares, except for
    a. community property.
    b. joint tenancy.
    c. tenants in common.
    d. All of the above must have equal shares.

18. For a married person or registered domestic partner, which of the following is most likely to be separate property? Real estate recently acquired by
    a. gift.
    b. severalty.
    c. purchase.
    d. foreclosure.

19. Which real estate owner is usually considered to be liable only for the amount of invested capital, not the owner's personal assets?
    a. Tenant in common
    b. General partner
    c. Joint tenant
    d. Limited partner

20. Regarding the best method for buyers to hold title:
    a. Real estate agents should tell buyers the best way.
    b. Buyers should seek advice from their attorneys.
    c. Joint tenancy is always the best method.
    d. For married couples and registered domestic partners in California, community property is the only method allowed.

Chapter

3

STUDENT LEARNING OUTCOMES

In this chapter, you will study money and nonmoney encumbrances. The discussion of nonmoney encumbrances centers on easements, encroachments, and private and public restrictions.

Money encumbrances are defined as liens. The liens discussed include mechanics' liens, tax liens, special assessment liens, attachments, and judgment liens.

In addition, the California homestead law is presented, illustrating how homeowners can protect their homes against a forced sale by certain types of creditors. At the conclusion of the chapter, you will be able to do the following:

1. Define encumbrance, lien, easement, and encroachment.
2. Explain the difference between private deed restrictions and public restrictions.
3. Describe the key characteristics of mechanics' liens and judgment liens.
4. Discuss the details of the California homestead law.

Encumbrances, Liens, and Homesteads

3.1 ENCUMBRANCES

In real estate, an **encumbrance** is anything that burdens the owner's title with a legal obligation. It is any right or interest in the property possessed by someone other than the owner.

Encumbrances fall into two basic categories: *nonmoney encumbrances* and *money encumbrances*.

Nonmoney (Physical) Encumbrances

Nonmoney encumbrances affect the physical condition or use of the property. Examples include easements, public and private restrictions, and encroachments—as opposed to money encumbrances, such as real estate loans or property taxes, where the property is held as security for repayment of a debt.

Easements

An easement is a right to enter or use another person's property, or a portion thereof, within certain limitations without paying rent or being considered a trespasser. In California, the most common type of easement is a right-of-way, also called an easement for ingress (entering) and egress (exiting) the property.

Two important terms used in connection with a right-of-way are **dominant tenement** and **servient tenement**. The property that benefits from the use of the easement (Property B in Figure 3.1) is described as the dominant tenement. The property subject to the easement or upon which the easement is imposed (Property A in Figure 3.1) is described as the servient tenement.

FIGURE 3.1

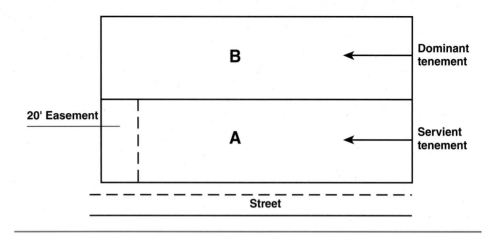

A right-of-way easement is usually designated as nonexclusive, meaning that when it is created, it doesn't prevent the owner from using the land, including that part covered by the easement. The owner's use (servient tenement), however, cannot interfere with the right of use by the dominant tenement.

In addition to a right-of-way, other examples of easements include the right to take water, wood, minerals, and other named items; the right to receive air and light; or the right to use a wall as a **party wall**. A party wall is a dividing partition between two adjoining buildings (or units) that is shared by the tenants of each residence or business.

When an easement is created, it is usually considered to be appurtenant or belonging to the land. This means the easement is considered real property and stays attached to the property in the event of a sale or another title transfer. When an easement "runs with the land," it is called an **easement appurtenant**.

Some easements do not have a dominant tenement. This is known as an **easement in gross**. For example, when a utility company erects poles or strings wire over private lands, the utility company obtains an easement in gross. Easements in gross allow someone to pass over the land for personal use, not to reach an adjoining parcel of land. This means no dominant landowner is being served; hence, no dominant tenement exists.

Creation of Easements

Easements can be created in a number of ways. The most common ways are by (1) deed, (2) necessity, (3) dedication, (4) condemnation, and (5) prescription. (See Figure 3.2.)

FIGURE 3.2

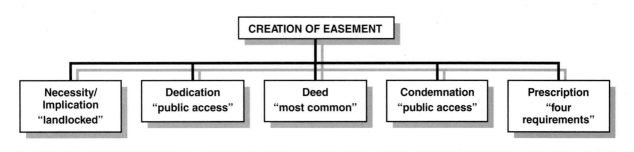

By Deed

Easements are not created orally; instead, they are set forth in the form of a written grant (such as a deed or contract). An easement must comply with all the legal requirements of a deed and be signed by the owner of the property (servient tenement) over which the easement lies.

> *Example:* (1) **A** deeds an easement to **B** to cross A's property, or (2) **A** deeds title to **B** but reserves an easement over **B's** property for **A's** use. Easements created by a written deed or contract are also called *expressed easements.*

By Necessity or by Implication

When a buyer discovers that he or she has no access to the street without passing over the property of another, the buyer's property is considered "landlocked." In this situation, the landlocked buyer can appeal to the courts and ask for an easement by necessity over the portion of land, if any, which the seller of the land-locked parcel may still own. If the seller of the landlocked parcel does not own an adjoining parcel to cross over, the buyer of the landlocked parcel may be permanently landlocked. However, a recent court case, *Kellogg v. Garcia* 102 Cal. App. 4th 796 (2002), may allow under some circumstances an easement over nearby property.

An easement can also be implied. For example, A deeds a portion of his or her land to B, but fails to grant an easement for access. However, an existing road runs over the remaining portion of the land owned by A. In this circumstance, B usually has an implied right to use the road over A's property to get to B's property. To obtain an easement by necessity, previous common ownership is required.

By Dedication

An owner may voluntarily dedicate an easement for public access. An example might be when an owner gives the public the right to cross over his or her land to reach the beach.

By Condemnation

Often an easement is created through condemnation. This means that government, as well as utility companies and railroads, may acquire an easement against the wishes of an owner through a legal process known as *eminent domain*. The law states that the condemned easement must be acquired for public use and the owner reimbursed for the value lost to the property.

By Prescription

An easement by prescription is created when a person acquires an easement in another person's property by reason of use. To obtain an easement by prescription in another person's property, a person must comply with four basic requirements:

1. A person must openly and notoriously use the land of another.
2. The easement use must be continuous and uninterrupted for five years.
3. The easement use must be hostile to the true owner's wishes, meaning without the owner's permission.
4. There must be a claim of right or color of title. This means the easement user must believe he or she has some right to cross the land of another or have a document that falsely purports to give the easement user an easement right.

Termination of an Easement

Easements can be terminated in several ways. (See Figure 3.3.)

1. The most common way to terminate an easement is by express release. The dominant tenement usually issues a quitclaim deed to the servient tenement owner, which extinguishes the easement.
2. Another way easements can be terminated is by a court proceeding called a *quiet title action*. The purpose of a quiet title action is to establish title against adverse claims to real property or any interest in the property. (Code Civ. Proc. §760.020)
3. When the owner of the dominant tenement property becomes the owner of the servient tenement property, the easement is terminated by merger of title. In other words, you cannot have an easement over your own property!

FIGURE 3.3

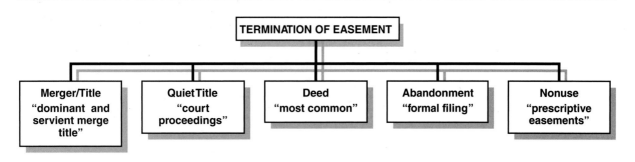

4. The filing of a formal abandonment can terminate an easement.

5. A prescription easement can be terminated automatically by nonuse for a period of five years. However, termination by nonuse applies only to prescriptive easements, not deeded easements.

Other Types of Nonmoney Encumbrances

In addition to easements, other examples of nonmoney encumbrances include private deed restrictions, public restrictions, and encroachments.

Private Deed Restrictions

A seller of property can place in a deed certain legal restrictions or limits on the use of the property being sold. The restrictions can apply not only to the new owner, but also to all subsequent owners. These restrictions are often referred to as *CC&Rs*, which stands for covenants, conditions, and restrictions.

A **covenant** is a promise or an agreement on the part of the individual accepting it to do or not do certain things. If a grantee (buyer) violates a covenant, he or she has broken a promise or agreement, and the grantor (seller) may institute court proceedings. The grantor may sue for dollar damages or get an injunction against the grantee prohibiting continuation of the violation of the promise.

A **condition** is a restriction that places a limitation on the grantee's (buyer's) ownership. The main difference between a covenant and a condition is the degree of punishment if a violation occurs. If a condition is violated, the grantor may have the right to demand the forfeiture of the grantee's title to the property. However, a violation of a covenant normally only allows money damages, or a cease-and-desist order may be issued by a judge or other governmental authority.

Some restrictions are legal and some are not. A classic example of restrictions that are unethical, illegal, and unenforceable are those relating to discrimination. Any discrimination based on race; color; creed; religion; national origin; sex; sexual orientation; marital, registered domestic partnership, and family status; or physical handicap is prohibited by state and/or federal law. A detailed discussion of fair housing laws is presented in Chapter 12.

Public Restrictions

When the government imposes restrictions on property, they are called **public restrictions**. Using a provision called *police power,* government has the right to impose restrictions on the use of private property to protect the health, safety, morals, and welfare of its citizens.

Police power includes such public restrictions as the following:

1. Zoning regulations that dictate what type of land use may exist in a given geographical area
2. Building codes that mandate rules and regulations governing the quality and size of construction
3. Health codes to protect and regulate the quality of domestic water and the effectiveness of sanitation systems

Encroachments

Another type of physical nonmoney encumbrance is an encroachment. An **encroachment** is the wrongful construction of a building or an improvement on or over the land of another. Examples of possible encroachments are shown in Figure 3.4.

FIGURE 3.4

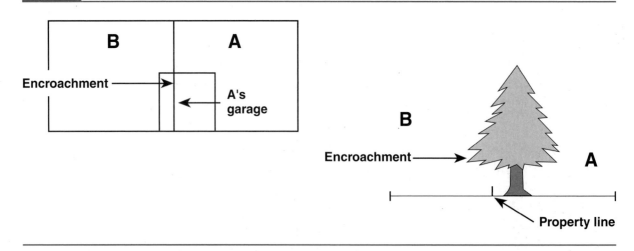

According to the Statute of Limitations, the party whose land is encroached upon has only three years in which to bring action for the removal of any such encroachment. If the owner allows the time limitation to run out, the owner runs the risk that the encroachment on the property becomes permanent. However, some encroachments are above the ground, such as a neighbor's tree limb extending into your airspace. This type of encroachment has no statute of limitation, and an action for removal can be brought at any time.

3.2 LIENS

A **lien** is a money encumbrance. In this type of encumbrance, a specific property is held as security for the payment of a money debt. Liens can be classified as voluntary, involuntary, general, or specific. (See Figure 3.5.)

Voluntary Lien

A **voluntary lien** is freely accepted by the property owner. An example of a voluntary lien is a mortgage or a deed of trust, which an owner signs when obtaining a real estate loan. (Deeds of trust and mortgages are discussed in detail in Chapter 7.)

Involuntary Lien

An **involuntary lien** is one imposed by law that the owner does not freely accept. Examples of involuntary liens include mechanics' liens, tax liens, attachments, and judgment liens.

FIGURE 3.5

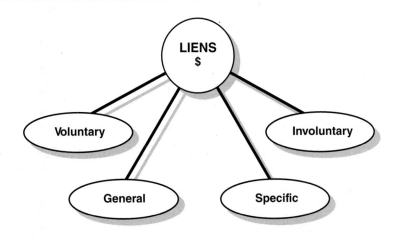

General Lien

A lien that applies to all the property of an owner, unless exempt by law, is a **general lien**. Examples of general liens include income tax and judgment liens.

Specific Lien

A lien against a particular single piece of property is a **specific lien**. Examples of specific liens include mortgages, trust deeds, taxes on real property, and mechanics' liens.

Types of Liens

Mechanics' Liens

Before discussing the details of a mechanics' lien, you need to know what is meant by a *mechanic*. A mechanic is anyone hired to do work that improves real property. In short, a mechanic is anyone who performs labor, bestows services, or furnishes material or equipment on a construction project. This includes contractors, subcontractors, carpenters, plumbers, painters, plasterers, laborers, material and equipment suppliers, architects, and landscape gardeners, as well as those workers involved in the demolition and removal of old buildings and the grading and filling of land.

The California State Constitution allows any qualified mechanic who does not receive payment to file a lien against the specific property upon which work was done. The **mechanics' lien** must be based on a valid contract, written or verbal, between the claimant and the owner or the owner's general contractor. The mechanics' lien law is based on the theory that improvements contribute additional value to the land; therefore, the property owner should be held responsible for wages and materials that led to the improvements.

The key provisions of the mechanics' lien law are illustrated in Figure 3.6.

Preliminary Notice

The law requires that all mechanics and material suppliers must give written notice to the owner, the general contractor, and the construction lender, if there is one, of their right to file a lien against the property if they are not paid. This notice should be

FIGURE 3.6

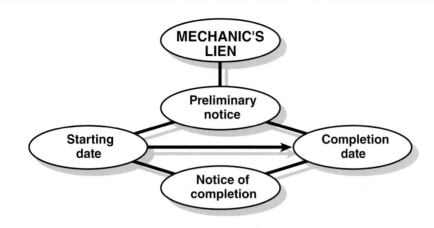

served within twenty days of the first furnishing of labor, services, equipment, or material to the job site.

Failure to give the preliminary notice within twenty days does not preclude the right to give a preliminary notice at a later time, but the mechanic's claim rights may be subordinated to other claims.

Starting Date

For a valid mechanics' lien to be created, the law requires that the lien must be recorded within a specified period of time after completion of the project. The law has determined the following situations to be equivalent to completion:

1. Owner occupies the property, and work stops.
2. Owner accepts the work as being completed and files a document called a *notice of completion.*
3. Work on the project ceases for a continuous sixty-day period.
4. Work ceases for a continuous period of thirty days or more, and the owner files a notice of cessation.

Notice of Completion

A **notice of completion,** if filed by the owner or the general contractor, must show the date of the completion, the name and address of the owner, the nature of the interest or estate of the owner, a description of the property, and the name of the contractor (if any). To be valid, a notice of completion must be recorded within ten days after the completion of the project.

Statutory Time Period

Two situations establish time periods for filing a mechanics' lien.

1. If the owner files a notice of completion, the original contractor has sixty days in which to file a lien; all others have thirty days.
2. If no notice of completion is filed or if the notice is invalid, all parties, including the contractors and subcontractors, have ninety days to file from the day work was finished.

In summary, when an owner correctly files a notice of completion, it shortens the time period a work person has to file a mechanics' lien.

Termination of a Mechanics' Lien

1. A mechanics' lien is terminated when the debt has been paid, either by voluntary action or by forced foreclosure sale.
2. A mechanics' lien is automatically terminated if the mechanic fails to institute a court foreclosure within ninety days after filing the mechanics' lien. In other words, once a mechanics' lien is recorded, a mechanic has only ninety days to bring foreclosure action. If mechanics wait more than ninety days, they lose their right to foreclosure upon the property. They still can personally sue the owner for the amount owed, but they cannot foreclose on the mechanics' lien and force the sale of the property.

Notice of Nonresponsibility

If a tenant orders work on a property without the landlord's approval, can the landlord be held responsible for any unpaid work? The answer is yes. However, a landlord can protect against mechanics' liens resulting from work ordered by a tenant if the landlord files a **notice of nonresponsibility**.

This notice of nonresponsibility must be filed within ten days of the date of discovery that the work is being done. It is filed by recording a copy of a notice of nonresponsibility in the county recorder's office and posting a notice on the property. This gives the workers notice that the owner will not be financially responsible for the work being done, and the workers must look to the tenant for payment.

Priority of Claim

When a mechanics' lien is placed against a given piece of property, its priority over a construction loan is determined by the beginning date of the project. The law states that even though a mechanics' lien is recorded after a construction loan is recorded, the mechanics' lien is given priority if any work has been done or materials furnished prior to recording the construction loan. Ordinarily, a title insurance company first inspects the property to make sure no work has been done or materials delivered prior to the recording of the construction loan.

If there are multiple mechanics' liens against a property, they all share on a parity with each other. This means that the first mechanic to record a lien does not have a superior right over the second mechanics' lien, and so on. If there are multiple mechanics' liens and the property is sold for lien payments, each mechanic receives a share of the proceeds based on his or her *pro rata* (proportionate) share of the work.

Summary of Mechanics' Lien Dates

1. Preliminary notice should be given within twenty days of the beginning of work.
2. If the owner files a notice of completion within ten days of completion of the project:
   a. Original contractors have sixty days to file.
   b. All others have thirty days to file.
3. If the owner does not file a notice of completion or if the notice is invalid, all mechanics have ninety days to file from the day that work was finished.
4. Once a valid mechanics' lien is filed, the mechanic must bring a court foreclosure action within ninety days to enforce the lien.
5. A notice of nonresponsibility must be filed by the landlord within ten days of the discovery of work ordered by a tenant.

Finally, a property owner who hires a contractor might consider having the contractor provide a performance bond in which, for a fee, an insurance company guarantees payment in the event the general contractor fails to complete the project and/or fails to pay the subcontractors.

Tax Liens

The purpose of taxation is to provide money to cover government expenses. A tax lien arises when a person does not pay taxes when they are due and his or her property is encumbered to ensure payment.

Tax liens may include these:

1. Unpaid real property taxes
2. Unpaid income taxes
3. Unpaid estate taxes
4. Unpaid gift taxes

Taxes and their consequences are covered in detail in Chapter 13. The point stressed here is that government has the power to levy taxes. If the taxpayer refuses to pay the levy, government has the right to place a lien against the taxpayer's property and foreclose upon the property for back taxes.

Special Assessments

Special assessments are levied against property owners in a certain assessment district. The basic purpose is to defray the cost of specific local improvements, such as streets, sewers, schools, and so on. Even though assessments are usually paid with property taxes, they differ in that property taxes are a general tax levied to pay general government expenses, whereas assessments are for a single purpose. If a person refuses to pay the assessment, government and/or bondholders can foreclose upon the assessee's property. Special assessments are discussed in Chapter 13.

Attachments and Judgments

An **attachment** is a legal process whereby property, personal or real, is seized pending the outcome of a court action. A **judgment** is a decision of the court as a result of a lawsuit. A judgment is the final determination of the rights of the parties involved in a court proceeding.

The purpose of the attachment is to have the property of the defendant available to satisfy a judgment if it is rendered in favor of the plaintiff. In some cases, it may take several months before the case is tried and a judgment issued. During this time, an unscrupulous defendant might secretly sell or give away his or her property, making it impossible for the plaintiff to satisfy the judgment.

Under an attachment, the seizure and holding of the property is merely symbolic. The defendant may still keep the property, but a notice is posted on the property and the attachment is recorded.

The attachment remains a lien upon all real property attached, three days from the date of levy. However, so much property is exempt from attachment (such as a personal residence, most of the debtor's wages, and so on) that the use of an attachment has declined in recent years. Instead of seeking an attachment, many creditors go directly for a judgment.

A judgment (court decision) does not automatically create a lien on real property. For a judgment to become a lien, an *abstract of the judgment* (summary of the judgment) must be recorded with the county recorder. It then becomes a general lien on all real property located in the county in which the abstract is recorded.

The judgment lien normally runs for ten years. Any real property acquired during the ten-year period in the county where the abstract is filed automatically becomes encumbered by the judgment lien. The abstract of judgment may be recorded in any number of California counties. If a creditor wishes to tie up anything a debtor might own in California, the creditor can record the abstract of judgment in all fifty-eight counties. Abstracts of judgments from California courts cannot normally be recorded in other states. A separate court proceeding is needed in each state.

Writ of Execution

To collect on a judgment, the creditor requests a **writ of execution**. Under a writ of execution, the court orders the sheriff to seize and sell the property to satisfy the judgment. A public auction is then held, and the property is sold to the highest bidder.

In the event that the judgment is paid before the sale, the judgment creditor issues to the judgment debtor a satisfaction of judgment. When this notice is recorded, the judgment is released and the lien is lifted from the property.

3.3 HOMESTEAD LAW

The California homestead law is designed to protect a homeowner's equity in a personal residence from forced sale by certain types of creditors. The term **homestead** means a personal dwelling and should not be confused with the federal homestead laws of early American history, where the government gave away land to encourage settlement.

Declared versus Automatic Homestead

There are two types of homesteads in California: a formal declared homestead and an automatic homestead called a *dwelling house exemption*. The formal declared homestead requires an owner to correctly complete and file a homestead document at the county recorder's office, whereas a dwelling house exemption is available to all valid homeowners who have not previously filed a document at the county recorder's office. The dollar protections are the same, but there are other differences that will be pointed out in the following discussion.

Requirements for a Formal Declared Homestead

Certain essentials must be observed in the filing of a formal homestead exemption. If these rules are not followed, the formal homestead is void and the automatic dwelling exemption usually applies.

1. A formal homestead must be recorded to be valid. A homestead declaration must be recorded in the recorder's office, showing that the claimant is a head of family, if such is the case, or when the declaration is made by the wife, that the husband has not made such a declaration and that she, therefore, makes it for their joint benefit. In addition to a husband or wife, the state liberally interprets a *head of family* to be any person who lives in his or her home and provides for any relative living in the same home. Registered domestic partners are entitled to head-of-household homestead rights.
2. The formal homestead statement must declare that the claimant is residing on the premises and claims this as a homestead.
3. The formal homestead statement must include a description of the premises. The dwelling house may be a single- or multiple-family dwelling, a condominium, a stock cooperative, a community apartment project, a mobile home, or a yacht. Any owner-occupied residential property can be used, but the owner may have only one homestead exemption at a time.

No previous formal filing is required for the automatic dwelling house exemption, but the home must be a principal residence and the debtor-homeowner must appear in court and claim the dwelling house exemption.

Dollar Protection for Formal and Automatic Homestead

Effective January 1, 2010, the head of the household is entitled to exemption protection of $100,000. Heads of households sixty-five years and older and certain low-income homeowners fifty-five to sixty-four years old are allowed a $175,000 exemption. Single persons who are not considered low income and are under the age of sixty-five years are usually allowed a $75,000 exemption. These exemption figures do not reflect the actual value of the property. The homestead exemption is intended to protect the equity the owner has in the property.

When the courts rule that a home has too much equity and, therefore, is to be sold to satisfy the debts of the homeowner, the owner retains the exemption portion and the creditor is awarded the difference.

Example :

Homestead Property A
$500,000 home
−460,000 loan
$40,000 equity

This home cannot be sold by judgment creditors as the equity is within the homestead exemption.

Homestead Property B
$500,000 home
−0 loan
$500,000 equity

This home can be sold by judgment creditors as the equity exceeds the homestead exemption. However, the homeowner (debtor) is allowed to keep the amount of the exemption, and the creditor only gets the excess.

$500,000 equity
−$100,000 exemption for head of family
$400,000 excess to creditor if needed

The proceeds from any forced sale are allocated in the following order:

1. To the discharge of all prior liens and encumbrances exempt from homestead.
2. To the homestead claimant (homeowner), the amount of the exemption.
3. To the satisfaction of the execution.
4. To the homestead claimant if a balance is left over.

The Six-Month Rule

In the event the homeowner wishes to sell to move to another home or if the owner is forced to sell the home to satisfy an execution and the homeowner's equity is converted to cash, a homeowner with a valid formal declaration of homestead applies what is known as the six-month rule.

The owner has six months in which to invest his or her equity money in a new home. The homeowner may then file a homestead on the new home and thereby continue to protect the equity against creditors up to the exemption amount. *The homeowner who relies on the automatic dwelling house exemption does not get to use this six-month rule to protect the equity exemption upon resale.*

> Remember that the law states that a party cannot have more than one homestead at the same time and that a homestead can be placed only on owner-occupied residential property.

Homestead Protection

Homesteads, both formally declared and automatic, protect against forced sale of a family home because of bankruptcy and execution of judgments as long as the equity in the home does not exceed the homestead exemption.

Homesteads do not protect against forced sale of a family home resulting from mortgage or trust deed foreclosures and mechanics' liens. Even if the homestead is recorded before the trust deed and mechanics' lien, *a homestead never defeats a trust deed or mechanics' lien.*

Termination of Homestead

A homestead may be terminated in one of two ways:

1. The owner may sell the home, which automatically terminates a homestead. On the other hand, a formally declared homestead is not terminated if the owner merely moves out and rents the home. The rule is that a property must be owner occupied at the time of filing the formal homestead. An owner can later move and rent the property and still have a valid homestead. *But when a homeowner relies on the automatic dwelling exemption and then moves out, there is a loss of the homestead protection.*

2. A homeowner who has filed a formal declaration of homestead can terminate a homestead by filing a notice of abandonment. If one spouse or registered domestic partner dies, the homestead stays in force for the surviving spouse or partner. A dissolution of marriage or registered domestic partnership does not terminate a homestead if one spouse or partner remains in possession of the property. However, when death or dissolution results in only one occupant, the exemption will be reduced from $100,000 to $75,000, due to the homeowner becoming single again, unless the person is sixty-five years or older or fifty-five to sixty-four years and of low income; then the exemption remains $175,000.

CHAPTER SUMMARY

Encumbrances are burdens on title that can be either physical or money encumbrances. Physical (nonmoney) encumbrances include easements, private and public restrictions, and encroachments. Money encumbrances are called *liens*, and they include mechanics' liens, tax liens, judgment liens, mortgages, and deeds of trust. An easement is a right to use the land of another. The most common easement is a right-of-way for ingress and egress. Easements are created by deed, implication, necessity, dedication, condemnation, and prescription. They may be removed by deed, court action, merger of title, filing of an abandonment, or nonuse for five years in the case of prescriptive easements.

Private restrictions placed in a deed are known as *CC&Rs*, a term that stands for covenants, conditions, and restrictions. Public restrictions such as zoning, building codes, health regulations, and so on are imposed by governments.

An encroachment is the wrongful extension of a building or improvement on or over the land of another. There are statutory time periods in which an owner must sue to force removal.

Liens (money encumbrances) may be voluntary or involuntary and may be general or specific. Mechanics' liens are involuntary liens placed upon a property by anyone who performs labor, provides a service, or furnishes equipment or supplies on a construction project to guarantee that they are paid for their services. Starting dates and completion dates are extremely important, and the law specifies the exact time limits involved in carrying out a mechanics' lien right.

Judgments are considered general liens and may attach all property owned by the debtor in the county in which the abstract of judgment is filed. An abstract of judgment creates a lien for ten years on real estate located within the county where the judgment is recorded.

The homestead law provides a limited amount of protection in the event a judgment is obtained against a homeowner. If a homestead is properly completed and recorded, the head of a household is entitled to a $100,000 exemption; persons sixty-five or over and low-income people fifty-five to sixty-four get $175,000, whereas a single person under sixty-five years receives $75,000. A homestead can be applied only on owner-occupied residential property, and only one homestead can be held at a time. Homesteads can be terminated by selling the property or filing a declaration of abandonment or, in the case of the automatic dwelling house exemption, by moving out of the home.

IMPORTANT TERMS AND CONCEPTS

attachment	general lien	notice of
condition	homestead	nonresponsibility
covenant	involuntary lien	party wall
dominant tenement	judgment	public restrictions
easement	lien	servient tenement
appurtenant	mechanics' lien	six-month rule
easement in gross	notice of	specific lien
encroachment	completion	voluntary lien
encumbrance		writ of execution

PRACTICAL APPLICATION

1. How does an easement by prescription differ from adverse possession?

2. You wish to have a contractor build a home on your lot. You insist that the contractor be licensed, be bonded, and carry adequate workers' compensation insurance and other liability insurance.

You are also concerned about the mechanics' lien rules. Fill in the correct days for each situation.

a. Preliminary notice should be served within _____ days from the first furnishing of labor or materials on your home site.

b. A notice of completion should be filed by you within _____ days after the completion of the home.

c. After filing your notice of completion, the general contractor has _____ days to file a lien, while the subcontractors have _____ days.

d. If your notice of completion is filed incorrectly and hence is invalid, all workers have _____ days to file a lien.

e. If a mechanics' lien is filed, it automatically terminates if court action is not instituted within _____ days.

3. A forty-five-year-old head of household has correctly filed a formal declaration of homestead. The condo is worth $250,000 and has a first loan of $125,000, plus a $35,000 homeowner equity second loan. A judgment creditor petitions the court to force the sale of the condo for the payment of a $25,000 debt. Assuming the court orders the sale of the condo, how will the proceeds be distributed?

REVIEWING YOUR UNDERSTANDING

1. An easement on a parcel of land may be removed from the records by one of the following:
   a. Reconveyance deed
   b. Unlawful detainer action
   c. Recording a quitclaim deed executed by the user of the easement to the servient tenement
   d. Lis pendens action

2. Materials were delivered to a building site for the construction of a commercial building. To be sure the supplier can collect for the cost of the material, he or she should file a
   a. homestead declaration.
   b. preliminary notice.
   c. surety bond.
   d. subordination lien.

3. The terms *ingress* and *egress* refer to
   a. utilities.
   b. streams.
   c. encroachments.
   d. easements.

4. An easement is an example of
   a. general lien on real property.
   b. an encumbrance on real property.
   c. an equitable restriction on real property.
   d. a specific lien on real property.

5. A formally declared homestead can be terminated in all of the following ways, except by
   a. renting the property.
   b. making untrue statements in the homestead declaration.
   c. selling the property.
   d. filing an abandonment of homestead.

6. When a property owner discovers that a neighbor has built a structure on a portion of his or her property, how long does the property owner normally have to bring an action against the neighbor?
   a. Six months
   b. Two years
   c. Three years
   d. Fifteen years

7. A mechanics' lien can be filed and recorded for the benefit of
   a. painters.
   b. subcontractors.
   c. material suppliers.
   d. all of the above.

8. Which document does not need to be recorded to be valid?
   a. Mechanics' lien.
   b. Feed.
   c. Formal homestead declaration.
   d. None of the above need to be recorded to be valid.

9. One way of acquiring an easement is by prescription. All of the following are required for the creation of this type of easement, except
   a. paying the property taxes for five years.
   b. using the property hostile to the true owner's wishes.
   c. using the property openly and notoriously.
   d. having some right of claim or color of title.

10. A plaintiff takes a case to court and obtains a judgment. To create a lien on the defendant's property, the plaintiff must record a(n)
    a. writ of attachment.
    b. abstract of judgment.
    c. writ of execution.
    d. lis pendens action.

11. A telephone company's right to enter your property to maintain power lines is an example of
    a. a servient tenement.
    b. a mechanics' lien.
    c. an easement in gross.
    d. an easement appurtenant.

12. A thirty-five-year-old head of household files a legally declared homestead against a $480,000 home that has a $370,000 loan against the property. A judgment creditor attempts to force the sale of the home. If the home is sold, the judgment creditor is allowed how much from the sale proceeds?
    a. $35,000
    b. $75,000
    c. $100,000
    d. Nothing

13. If zoning laws allow a property to be used in such a manner that is prohibited by a lawful deed restriction, the
    a. owner must file a quiet title action.
    b. zoning allowance should prevail over a deed restriction.
    c. deed restriction should prevail.
    d. owner must file a quitclaim deed.

14. Which of the following is an involuntary lien?
    a. Homestead
    b. Encroachment
    c. Mortgage
    d. Judgment

15. Private deed restrictions are known as *CC&Rs*. The first *C* stands for
    a. condition.
    b. covenant.
    c. convenient.
    d. cooperative.

16. Once properly recorded, an abstract of judgment is good for
    a. ten years.
    b. seven years.
    c. five years.
    d. three years.

17. If an owner files a notice of completion, a general contractor has how many days to file a mechanics' lien?
    a. Ninety days
    b. Sixty days
    c. Thirty days
    d. Ten days

18. If an owner files a notice of completion, a subcontractor has how many days to file a mechanics' lien?
    a. Ninety days
    b. Sixty days
    c. Thirty days
    d. Ten days

19. If a landlord wishes to be protected from a mechanics' lien on work ordered by a tenant, upon discovery of the work, the landlord must file a notice of nonresponsibility within how many days?
    a. Ninety days
    b. Sixty days
    c. Thirty days
    d. Ten days

20. Which of the following is a general lien?
    a. Real Estate Property taxes
    b. Special assessment
    c. Mortgage
    d. Judgment

Chapter

4

In recent years, the laws regarding a real estate agent's duties have changed drastically. This chapter defines the term *agency*, discusses the creation of agencies, and analyzes the duties and responsibilities of real estate agents. At the conclusion of the chapter, you will be able to do the following:

1. Define agency and list the three ways in which agencies are created.
2. Discuss the fiduciary relationship that exists between a principal and a real estate agent.
3. Explain the difference between single agency and dual agency.
4. List and give examples of several real estate agency violations.
5. Describe the agency differences between salespersons and brokers.
6. List and give examples of six ways in which real estate agencies are terminated.

Real Estate Agency

4.1 AGENCY

The California Civil Code defines *agency* as "the representation of another person called a principal, by an agent, in dealings with third persons." An **agent**, therefore, is empowered to represent a **principal** in negotiating with a third party for the principal's benefit. Agencies are not required by law. However, because of the complexity of business and for convenience, principals frequently prefer to have experts represent them in transactions. Common examples of agents include travel agents, insurance agents, and real estate agents. There are two broad categories of agency. The first category is called **general agency**; the second is called **special agency**. A general agent is one who has broad powers to act on behalf of the principal. A special agent has limited or well-defined powers, frequently confined to a single transaction. Most real estate agencies are special in nature, with powers normally limited to the sale of a specific property. (See Figure 4.1.)

FIGURE 4.1

REAL ESTATE AGENCY

Principal		Agent		Third party
Seller	Appoints →	Real Estate Broker	To find →	Buyer

Employer-Employee and Independent Contractor Distinctions

A real estate agency differs from an employer-employee relationship; it also differs from an independent contractor relationship. An employer-employee relationship exists when an individual is hired by another to perform certain services under the strict supervision of the employer. The degree of direct control over the individual hired is important in determining whether that individual is an employee or independent contractor.

For example, assume Santos hired Brown to perform office work. Santos requires that Brown work from 9:00 A.M. to 5:00 P.M. Monday through Friday. Santos carefully supervises the method in which Brown performs work duties. Further, Santos provides fringe benefits and deducts money from Brown's paycheck each week for income taxes and Social Security. Under these circumstances, Brown is clearly an employee and an employer-employee relationship exists. An **independent contractor** relationship exists when an individual is hired to accomplish results and little or no supervision is required. Assume Santos hires West Company to perform janitorial services for an office. Santos pays West Company a fixed amount of money per month and does not supervise West Company. West Company is free to clean the office at a self-determined pace and at the company's own time schedule, provided it is after business hours. Further, Santos does not provide fringe benefits and does not take deductions for Social Security or income taxes out of West Company's pay. West Company, under these circumstances, is probably an independent contractor and not an employee.

A real estate agency differs from an employer-employee relationship and an independent contractor relationship. Whereas an employee works for an employer and is under the control of the employer for all work activities, a real estate agent's activities are not under the complete control of a principal. For example, most sellers do not tell a real estate broker when to open the real estate office, when to take a lunch hour, or when to return home!

A real estate agency is also different from an independent contractor relationship in that the agent is not free to do anything to achieve a sale. An agent must respect the lawful instructions of the principal. For example, a seller engages a real estate agent to find a buyer under certain lawful terms and conditions that the agent must follow to receive a commission.

A further distinction exists within a real estate brokerage. Due to the independent nature of the relationship between real estate salesperson and broker, an independent contractor relationship is usually recognized for income tax–reporting purposes. But because the real estate law requires the broker to supervise the activities of his or her salespeople, the real estate commissioner regards the relationship between a broker and his or her salespeople to be like that of an employer and employee.

Creation of Real Estate Agencies

Agencies are created in three ways: by agreement, by ratification, and by estoppel. (See Figure 4.2.)

By far, the greatest number of real estate agencies are created by agreement. The principal (usually the seller) appoints a real estate agent in writing, or by their mutual actions. The authorization to sell (listing agreement) is the document most frequently used to appoint real estate agents. The authorization to sell specifies the powers delegated to the agent, the terms and conditions of the proposed sale of the property, and the circumstances under which a brokerage commission is earned, as well as the brokerage amount. As will be outlined in Chapter 5, there are different types of listing agreements—each with different powers of agency.

The second method of creating an agency is by *ratification*. Under this concept, no agency is currently in existence; however, a series of events then occurs that creates an agency relationship. In other words, an unauthorized agent performs a service on your behalf of which you were unaware. Upon learning of the service, which turns out to be beneficial, you accept the responsibility for the agent's act. As an example, assume Chang, a real estate broker, approaches Johnson with an offer from a buyer to buy Johnson's store when Johnson had not previously considered selling the

FIGURE 4.2

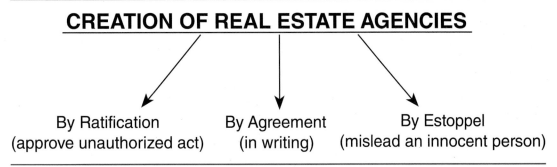

CREATION OF REAL ESTATE AGENCIES

By Ratification
(approve unauthorized act)

By Agreement
(in writing)

By Estoppel
(mislead an innocent person)

store. Johnson likes the price and terms, and decides it would be advantageous to sell the property. By accepting the offer and agreeing to pay a commission, Johnson has created an agency with broker Chang. In essence, Johnson ratified broker Chang's unauthorized actions by accepting the buyer's offer.

The third method of creating an agency is by *estoppel*. In an estoppel situation, an individual knowingly allows another person to perform tasks beneficial to that individual. Later, the individual determines that the person did not act properly and decides to pursue legal recourse but may be prevented from doing so because there was no legal duty to care for that individual. For example, say Dang was selling his own home. Agent Jones offered Dang a price that was clearly below market value, but Dang was not aware of the market value of his property. During the transaction, Jones assisted Dang with the paperwork but never formally became Dang's agent. After the close of escrow, Dang discovers he underpriced his property and wants to sue Jones. Dang would only be able to recover from Jones if he could prove Jones had a duty to care for him. Such a duty exists between an agent and his or her principal, which you will learn as a fiduciary duty. In order to recover from Jones, Dang would have to show that Dang relied on the efforts of Jones and that Jones in fact performed the actions of an agent. This legal theory is called *agency by estoppel*.

Actual Versus Ostensible Agent

Sometimes on the state real estate examination and in agency discussions, this question comes up: What is the difference between an actual agent and an ostensible agent? Answer: An actual agent is directly appointed by a principal using a written contract where the agent is granted certain powers to act on behalf of the principal. An ostensible agent is appointed when a principal knowingly allows innocent third parties to believe that an unauthorized person is the principal's agent. If this occurs, the principal may be held liable for the unauthorized agent's actions.

Fiduciary Relationship

When a real estate agent is appointed by the principal (seller) to represent the seller in negotiations with a buyer, a *fiduciary relationship* is created. This **fiduciary** relationship is one of loyalty, obedience, and confidentiality and obligates the agent to act in the principal's best interest. This relationship is probably the agent's most important duty. An agent cannot act in a manner that is detrimental to this fiduciary relationship. The agent (1) cannot profit from the agency without the consent of the principal, (2) must obey all lawful instructions of the principal, and (3) must keep all information told to the agent by the principal confidential unless instructed to disclose or such disclosure is required by law. An agent may not discriminate in the rental or sale of real property.

Seller's Agency

The majority of real estate agencies are created when a seller (principal) appoints a real estate broker (a **seller's agent**) to find a buyer for the seller's property. The agency relationship is between the seller and the broker, not between the broker and the buyer. Therefore, a real estate broker is legally bound to do the very best for the seller, which includes trying to get the best price and terms for the property.

Although the real estate broker may not be the buyer's agent, the broker owes a degree of good faith to the buyer. The agent must be honest and truthful and disclose any known defects in the property. Above all else, an agent must not misrepresent the property to a prospective buyer.

Buyer's Agency

Although not as common, a buyer may appoint a real estate broker to be the **buyer's agent** to find property for the buyer. Under these circumstances, the buyer's broker is bound to reveal this fact to the seller. With a buyer's broker agency, the fiduciary relationship is between the buyer and the real estate broker, not between the seller and the buyer's broker.

Single Versus Dual Agency

When a real estate broker acts as an agent to only the seller or only the buyer, this is called a **single agency**. A real estate broker may represent both the buyer and seller in the same transaction, but only with the knowledge and consent of both parties. This is called **dual agency**. (*Note:* Two real estate agents working for the same broker will be a dual agency if one agent has the buyer and the other has the seller because it is the broker who determines the agency relationship.) Although common, dual agencies are considered by many attorneys as a conflict of interest with the potential for lawsuits. Real estate agents often carry errors-and-omissions insurance to help protect against this problem.

Agency Disclosure Requirements

California law requires all real estate agents to disclose in writing to the buyer and the seller whether the real estate broker is the agent of the seller, the buyer, or both. The buyer and the seller must sign a consent form approving the real estate agency status. The agency disclosure must be done before the seller signs the listing contract and before the buyer signs the purchase contract. The disclosure is done in three steps: disclosure, election, and confirmation.

Step 1: The real estate agent discloses or presents the choice of being the agent for only the seller, for only the buyer, or for both.
Step 2: The seller and/or buyer make their choices known.
Step 3: The agent, seller, and buyer sign the required form.
(See Figure 4.3.)

How the agency disclosure is made is a bit confusing. Cal. Civil Code 2079.14 requires the listing agent to disclose only to the seller and the selling agent to disclose to *both* the seller and the buyer, unless one agent represents both seller and buyer, in which case a single disclosure is made to the seller and the buyer. It is important to remember that agency relationships are determined by the broker, not the individual salesperson or agent who is working for a brokerage company. When the law speaks of an *agent*, it is referring to all licensees working for a single real estate brokerage company.

Subagents and Cooperating Agents

If the seller gives permission in the listing agreement, a real estate agent can assign some of his or her duties to other licensed agents. These other agents are called *subagents*. The same fiduciary relationship exists between the subagent and the principal as exists between the listing agent and the principal. Subagents are required to try to get the best price and terms for the seller even if the subagent is from another office and has independently found a buyer.

Due to the conflict and possible liability issues raised by subagency, most real estate agents feel uncomfortable acting as subagents, instead preferring to be viewed as *cooperating agents*, who attempt to find a buyer for the other broker's listing and then to act as the agent of the buyer, not the subagent of the seller.

Buyer Agency

From a legal perspective, there is less risk to agents if they remain in single agency. Multiple Listing Service rules have been changed

FIGURE 4.3

CALIFORNIA
ASSOCIATION
OF REALTORS®

DISCLOSURE REGARDING
REAL ESTATE AGENCY RELATIONSHIP
(As required by the Civil Code)
(C.A.R. Form AD, Revised 11/09)

When you enter into a discussion with a real estate agent regarding a real estate transaction, you should from the outset understand what type of agency relationship or representation you wish to have with the agent in the transaction.

SELLER'S AGENT
A Seller's agent under a listing agreement with the Seller acts as the agent for the Seller only. A Seller's agent or a subagent of that agent has the following affirmative obligations:
To the Seller: A Fiduciary duty of utmost care, integrity, honesty and loyalty in dealings with the Seller.
To the Buyer and the Seller:
    (a) Diligent exercise of reasonable skill and care in performance of the agent's duties.
    (b) A duty of honest and fair dealing and good faith.
    (c) A duty to disclose all facts known to the agent materially affecting the value or desirability of the property that are not known to, or within the diligent attention and observation of, the parties. An agent is not obligated to reveal to either party any confidential information obtained from the other party that does not involve the affirmative duties set forth above.

BUYER'S AGENT
A selling agent can, with a Buyer's consent, agree to act as agent for the Buyer only. In these situations, the agent is not the Seller's agent, even if by agreement the agent may receive compensation for services rendered, either in full or in part from the Seller. An agent acting only for a Buyer has the following affirmative obligations:
To the Buyer: A fiduciary duty of utmost care, integrity, honesty and loyalty in dealings with the Buyer.
To the Buyer and the Seller:
    (a) Diligent exercise of reasonable skill and care in performance of the agent's duties.
    (b) A duty of honest and fair dealing and good faith.
    (c) A duty to disclose all facts known to the agent materially affecting the value or desirability of the property that are not known to, or within the diligent attention and observation of, the parties.
An agent is not obligated to reveal to either party any confidential information obtained from the other party that does not involve the affirmative duties set forth above.

AGENT REPRESENTING BOTH SELLER AND BUYER
A real estate agent, either acting directly or through one or more associate licensees, can legally be the agent of both the Seller and the Buyer in a transaction, but only with the knowledge and consent of both the Seller and the Buyer.
In a dual agency situation, the agent has the following affirmative obligations to both the Seller and the Buyer:
    (a) A fiduciary duty of utmost care, integrity, honesty and loyalty in dealings with either the Seller or the Buyer.
    (b) Other duties to the Seller and the Buyer as stated above in their respective sections.
In representing both Seller and Buyer, the agent may not, without the express permission of the respective party, disclose to the other party that the Seller will accept a price less than the listing price or that the Buyer will pay a price greater than the price offered.
The above duties of the agent in a real estate transaction do not relieve a Seller or Buyer from the responsibility to protect his or her own interests. You should carefully read all agreements to assure that they adequately express your understanding of the transaction. A real estate agent is a person qualified to advise about real estate. If legal or tax advice is desired, consult a competent professional.
Throughout your real property transaction you may receive more than one disclosure form, depending upon the number of agents assisting in the transaction. The law requires each agent with whom you have more than a casual relationship to present you with this disclosure form. You should read its contents each time it is presented to you, considering the relationship between you and the real estate agent in your specific transaction.
**This disclosure form includes the provisions of Sections 2079.13 to 2079.24, inclusive, of the Civil Code set forth on page 2. Read it carefully.
I/WE ACKNOWLEDGE RECEIPT OF A COPY OF THIS DISCLOSURE AND THE PORTIONS OF THE CIVIL CODE PRINTED ON THE BACK (OR A SEPARATE PAGE).**

Buyer/Seller/Landlord/Tenant_____ Date _____

Buyer/Seller/Landlord/Tenant_____ Date _____

Agent _____ DRE Lic. # _____
                        Real Estate Broker (Firm)
By _____ DRE Lic. # _____ Date _____
      (Salesperson or Broker-Associate)

AGENCY DISCLOSURE COMPLIANCE (Civil Code §2079.14):
• When the listing brokerage company also represents Buyer/Tenant: The Listing Agent shall have one AD form signed by Seller/Landlord and a different AD form signed by Buyer/Tenant.
• When Seller/Landlord and Buyer/Tenant are represented by different brokerage companies: (i) the Listing Agent shall have one AD form signed by Seller/Landlord and (ii) the Buyer's/Tenant's Agent shall have one AD form signed by Buyer/Tenant and either that same or a different AD form presented to Seller/Landlord for signature prior to presentation of the offer. If the same form is used, Seller may sign here:

_____ _____   _____ _____
  Seller/Landlord   Date   Seller/Landlord   Date

REBS INC®
Published and Distributed by:
REAL ESTATE BUSINESS SERVICES, INC.
a subsidiary of the California Association of REALTORS®
525 South Virgil Avenue, Los Angeles, California 90020

EQUAL HOUSING OPPORTUNITY

Reviewed by _____ Date _____

AD REVISED 11/09 (PAGE 1 OF 2) PRINT DATE

DISCLOSURE REGARDING REAL ESTATE AGENCY RELATIONSHIP (AD PAGE 1 OF 2)

FIGURE 4.3 *(continued)*

CIVIL CODE SECTIONS 2079.13 THROUGH 2079.24 (2079.16 APPEARS ON THE FRONT)

2079.13 As used in Sections 2079.14 to 2079.24, inclusive, the following terms have the following meanings:
(a) "Agent" means a person acting under provisions of title 9 (commencing with Section 2295) in a real property transaction, and includes a person who is licensed as a real estate broker under Chapter 3 (commencing with Section 10130) of Part 1 of Division 4 of the Business and Professions Code, and under whose license a listing is executed or an offer to purchase is obtained. **(b)** "Associate licensee" means a person who is licensed as a real estate broker or salesperson under Chapter 3 (commencing with Section 10130) of Part 1 of Division 4 of the Business and Professions Code and who is either licensed under a broker or has entered into a written contract with a broker to act as the broker's agent in connection with acts requiring a real estate license and to function under the broker's supervision in the capacity of an associate licensee. The agent in the real property transaction bears responsibility for his or her associate licensees who perform as agents of the agent. When an associate licensee owes a duty to any principal, or to any buyer or seller who is not a principal, in a real property transaction, that duty is equivalent to the duty owed to that party by the broker for whom the associate licensee functions. **(c)** "Buyer" means a transferee in a real property transaction, and includes a person who executes an offer to purchase real property from a seller through an agent, or who seeks the services of an agent in more than a casual, transitory, or preliminary manner, with the object of entering into a real property transaction. "Buyer" includes vendee or lessee. **(d)** "Dual agent" means an agent acting, either directly or through an associate licensee, as agent for both the seller and the buyer in a real property transaction. **(e)** "Listing agreement" means a contract between an owner of real property and an agent, by which the agent has been authorized to sell the real property or to find or obtain a buyer. **(f)** "Listing agent" means a person who has obtained a listing of real property to act as an agent for compensation. **(g)** "Listing price" is the amount expressed in dollars specified in the listing for which the seller is willing to sell the real property through the listing agent. **(h)** "Offering price" is the amount expressed in dollars specified in an offer to purchase for which the buyer is willing to buy the real property. **(i)** "Offer to purchase" means a written contract executed by a buyer acting through a selling agent which becomes the contract for the sale of the real property upon acceptance by the seller. **(j)** "Real property" means any estate specified by subdivision (1) or (2) of Section 761 in property which constitutes or is improved with one to four dwelling units, any leasehold in this type of property exceeding one year's duration, and mobile homes, when offered for sale or sold through an agent pursuant to the authority contained in Section 10131.6 of the Business and Professions Code. **(k)** "Real property transaction" means a transaction for the sale of real property in which an agent is employed by one or more of the principals to act in that transaction, and includes a listing or an offer to purchase. **(l)** "Sell," "sale," or "sold" refers to a transaction for the transfer of real property from the seller to the buyer, and includes exchanges of real property between the seller and buyer, transactions for the creation of a real property sales contract within the meaning of Section 2985, and transactions for the creation of a leasehold exceeding one year's duration. **(m)** "Seller" means the transferor in a real property transaction, and includes an owner who lists real property with an agent, whether or not a transfer results, or who receives an offer to purchase real property of which he or she is the owner from an agent on behalf of another. "Seller" includes both a vendor and a lessor. **(n)** "Selling agent" means a listing agent who acts alone, or an agent who acts in cooperation with a listing agent, and who sells or finds and obtains a buyer for the real property, or an agent who locates property for a buyer or who finds a buyer for a property for which no listing exists and presents an offer to purchase to the seller. **(o)** "Subagent" means a person to whom an agent delegates agency powers as provided in Article 5 (commencing with Section 2349) of Chapter 1 of Title 9. However, "subagent" does not include an associate licensee who is acting under the supervision of an agent in a real property transaction.

2079.14 Listing agents and selling agents shall provide the seller and buyer in a real property transaction with a copy of the disclosure form specified in Section 2079.16, and, except as provided in subdivision (c), shall obtain a signed acknowledgement of receipt from that seller or buyer, except as provided in this section or Section 2079.15, as follows: **(a)** The listing agent, if any, shall provide the disclosure form to the seller prior to entering into the listing agreement. **(b)** The selling agent shall provide the disclosure form to the seller as soon as practicable prior to presenting the seller with an offer to purchase, unless the selling agent previously provided the seller with a copy of the disclosure form pursuant to subdivision (a). **(c)** Where the selling agent does not deal on a face-to-face basis with the seller, the disclosure form prepared by the selling agent may be furnished to the seller (and acknowledgement of receipt obtained for the selling agent from the seller) by the listing agent, or the selling agent may deliver the disclosure form by certified mail addressed to the seller at his or her last known address, in which case no signed acknowledgement of receipt is required. **(d)** The selling agent shall provide the disclosure form to the buyer as soon as practicable prior to execution of the buyer's offer to purchase, except that if the offer to purchase is not prepared by the selling agent, the selling agent shall present the disclosure form to the buyer not later than the next business day after the selling agent receives the offer to purchase from the buyer.

2079.15 In any circumstance in which the seller or buyer refuses to sign an acknowledgement of receipt pursuant to Section 2079.14, the agent, or an associate licensee acting for an agent, shall set forth, sign, and date a written declaration of the facts of the refusal.
2079.16 Reproduced on Page 1 of this AD form.
2079.17 (a) As soon as practicable, the selling agent shall disclose to the buyer and seller whether the selling agent is acting in the real property transaction exclusively as the buyer's agent, exclusively as the seller's agent, or as a dual agent representing both the buyer and the seller. This relationship shall be confirmed in the contract to purchase and sell real property or in a separate writing executed or acknowledged by the seller, the buyer, and the selling agent prior to or coincident with execution of that contract by the buyer and the seller, respectively. **(b)** As soon as practicable, the listing agent shall disclose to the seller whether the listing agent is acting in the real property transaction exclusively as the seller's agent, or as a dual agent representing both the buyer and seller. This relationship shall be confirmed in the contract to purchase and sell real property or in a separate writing executed or acknowledged by the seller and the listing agent prior to or coincident with the execution of that contract by the seller.
(c) The confirmation required by subdivisions (a) and (b) shall be in the following form.

(DO NOT COMPLETE. SAMPLE ONLY)	is the agent of (check one): ☐ the seller exclusively; or ☐ both the buyer and seller.
(Name of Listing Agent)	

(DO NOT COMPLETE. SAMPLE ONLY)	is the agent of (check one): ☐ the buyer exclusively; or ☐ the seller exclusively; or ☐ both the buyer and seller.
(Name of Selling Agent if not the same as the Listing Agent)	

(d) The disclosures and confirmation required by this section shall be in addition to the disclosure required by Section 2079.14.

2079.18 No selling agent in a real property transaction may act as an agent for the buyer only, when the selling agent is also acting as the listing agent in the transaction.

2079.19 The payment of compensation or the obligation to pay compensation to an agent by the seller or buyer is not necessarily determinative of a particular agency relationship between an agent and the seller or buyer. A listing agent and a selling agent may agree to share any compensation or commission paid, or any right to any compensation or commission for which an obligation arises as the result of a real estate transaction, and the terms of any such agreement shall not necessarily be determinative of a particular relationship.

2079.20 Nothing in this article prevents an agent from selecting, as a condition of the agent's employment, a specific form of agency relationship not specifically prohibited by this article if the requirements of Section 2079.14 and Section 2079.17 are complied with.

2079.21 A dual agent shall not disclose to the buyer that the seller is willing to sell the property at a price less than the listing price, without the express written consent of the seller. A dual agent shall not disclose to the seller that the buyer is willing to pay a price greater than the offering price, without the express written consent of the buyer. This section does not alter in any way the duty or responsibility of a dual agent to any principal with respect to confidential information other than price.

2079.22 Nothing in this article precludes a listing agent from also being a selling agent, and the combination of these functions in one agent does not, of itself, make that agent a dual agent.

2079.23 A contract between the principal and agent may be modified or altered to change the agency relationship at any time before the performance of the act which is the object of the agency with the written consent of the parties to the agency relationship.

2079.24 Nothing in this article shall be construed to either diminish the duty of disclosure owed buyers and sellers by agents and their associate licensees, subagents, and employees or to relieve agents and their associate licensees, subagents, and employees from liability for their conduct in connection with acts governed by this article or for any breach of a fiduciary duty or a duty of disclosure.

AD REVISED 11/09 (PAGE 2 OF 2)

Buyer's Initials (_____)(_____)
Seller's Initials (_____)(_____)

Reviewed by _____ Date _____

EQUAL HOUSING
OPPORTUNITY

DISCLOSURE REGARDING REAL ESTATE AGENCY RELATIONSHIP (AD PAGE 2 OF 2)

Source: Reprinted with permission of California Association of REALTORS®.

to allow compensation from the seller or the listing agent to the selling or cooperating agent regardless of the agency relationship. Now, agents may represent buyers in single agency while still receiving compensation from the seller or the listing agent. This practice of an agent representing only buyers is known as *buyer agency*, and some companies have developed a business model of only representing buyers and refusing to take listings from sellers.

Buyer's agents, wishing to better serve their clients, may now enter into formal written buyer representation agreements with their buyers. These agreements, similar in concept to a listing agreement between a seller's agent and a seller, require the buyer to pay a commission to his or her agent if the agent is not being compensated from the listing agent or the seller. This allows buyer's agents more freedom to provide better service to their buyers. Buyer's agents, under a buyer representation agreement, may now negotiate with "For Sale By Owner" properties, and owners of unlisted properties without concern about being paid. If the seller is not willing to pay a commission to the agent, the buyer representation agreement provides that the buyer will pay the commission.

4.2 SOME AGENCY VIOLATIONS

There are over 500,000 real estate licensees in California. The percentage of licensees who violate agency laws is very small. Of those who are disciplined, most have committed violations unintentionally or through ignorance. Through education, examination, and on-the-job training, real estate licensees learn their duties and responsibilities and, therefore, reduce the possibility of agency violations. The following, from the Department of Real Estate (DRE) Reference Book (available to download at http://www.dre.ca.gov), are examples of types of agency violations. The appropriate sections of the Real Estate Law are cited as a reference.

> **Trust fund–handling problems.** Section 10145. Number one on the DRE's list of violations are issues dealing with trust funds. **Trust funds** are defined as money or other items of value that an agent receives on behalf of a principal in the course of a real estate transaction that requires a license. General trust fund rules are outlined in the next section, but the point stressed here is that the most common agency violation is the failure to handle trust funds in an appropriate manner, as outlined by law and DRE regulations.

Misrepresentation. Section 10176(a). Many complaints received by the real estate commissioner allege **misrepresentation** on the part of the broker or salesperson. This includes not only what was said but also the failure of a broker or salesperson to disclose a material fact about the property. Can a real estate agent legally withhold information about a defect in the property? No. Failure to disclose is a type of misrepresentation!

False promise. Section 10176(b). A false promise and a misrepresentation are not the same thing. A misrepresentation is a false statement of fact. A **false promise** is a false statement about what the promiser is going to do in the future. To prove false promise, the injured party must show that the promise was impossible of performance and that the person making the promise knew it to be impossible. An example might be "Buy this home and it will double in value in six weeks!"

Commingling and conversion. Section 10176(e). **Commingling** takes place when a broker has mixed the funds of his or her principal with the broker's own money. **Conversion** is not the same thing as commingling. Conversion is misappropriating and using the client's money. This is a crime that carries a jail sentence.

Definite termination date. Section 10176(f). This section of the law requires a specified termination date for all exclusive contracts between a real estate agent and a principal relating to transactions for which a real estate license is required. What a definite termination date is has been the subject of a number of lawsuits. Generally, if a definite date is specified in the contract or if a definite period of time is indicated, the requirement is satisfied. However, if it cannot be determined from the exclusive listing contract when the listing is to expire, then the real estate agent may be in violation of the law.

Secret profit. Section 10176(g). **Secret profit** cases usually arise when the broker, who already has a higher offer from another buyer, makes a low offer, usually through a "dummy" purchaser. The difference is the secret profit. This is sometimes referred to as *divided agency;* agents must always disclose any self-interest they might have in a transaction and obtain their principal's consent. Many attorneys contend that an agent is guilty of secret profit or divided agency if the real estate agent derives any profit other than the agreed commission without disclosing the nature of the profits to the principal.

Other possible violations include dishonest dealing, obtaining a license by fraud, false advertising, conviction of crime, negligence, misuse of a trade name, inducement of panic selling, in addition to many others.

Trust Funds

A broker is required to keep an official record of all deposits that pass through his or her real estate business. This account must be kept using acceptable accounting procedures and is subject to audit by the California real estate commissioner.

Although not required by law, many real estate brokers open a trust fund account at a financial institution where all monies received on behalf of clients and customers can be deposited for safekeeping. Withdrawals can be made only by the broker or other authorized persons. The broker cannot put his or her personal funds in this trust fund account, with the exception of up to $200 to cover bank service fees.

If a broker receives a deposit from a prospective buyer *who does not instruct that the deposit be held uncashed*, the broker must, within three business days, do one of the following:

1. Give the deposit to the principal (the seller).
2. Put the deposit in escrow.
3. Put the deposit in a trust fund account.

If the broker fails to do one of these three things within three business days, the broker could be found guilty of commingling.

If asked by the prospective buyer to hold the deposit pending the seller's acceptance of the offer, then upon acceptance, the broker must, within three business days, do one of the three actions mentioned above.

Basic Rules of Entries

Trust fund records must be kept in chronological sequence in a DRE-approved columnar form or by a method deemed an acceptable accounting practice. If the funds *are not deposited* into a broker's trust fund bank account, the items must be entered in a trust fund logbook outlining what happened to the funds. If the funds are deposited into a broker's trust fund bank account, another entry must be made in another account in the name of the beneficiary of the funds. This is called a *double-entry accounting system*.

The bank account must be reconciled monthly with the bank statement, and the bank account must be reconciled monthly with each separate beneficiary. The broker's trust fund account must be kept in an institution insured by a government agency. If a DRE audit of a broker's trust fund finds a violation, the broker must bear the cost of the audit and, depending on the violation, the broker may lose his or her real estate license.

A more detailed explanation of trust fund requirements can be found in the required three-hour DRE continuing education course, Trust Fund Handling.

Recovery Fund

The state of California has a program whereby the public can recover money when there are certain uncollectable court judgments obtained against a real estate licensee on the basis of fraud, misrepresentation, deceit, or conversion of trust funds in a transaction. Called the **recovery fund**, this program is financed using a portion of real estate licensing fees. Signed into law by President Obama in April 2009, the maximum amount of money a person can receive from the fund is currently limited to $50,000 per individual claim, up to a $250,000 maximum for multiple claims against any one real estate licensee.

Responsibilities of Principals to Agents and Buyers

Agency is a two-way street. Real estate agents owe certain duties and responsibilities to principals; principals, in turn, owe certain responsibilities to agents. A principal must tell the real estate agent of any known defects in the property so the agent can properly disclose the defects to a prospective buyer. If the seller knows of a property defect and fails to tell the real estate agent, the seller can be held legally accountable. In short, a seller should not withhold pertinent information or distort facts about the property. In California, sellers of 1-4 residential units are required to complete and hand to the buyer, prior to the sale, a complete written disclosure regarding the property known as a Transfer Disclosure Statement. (See Chapter 5.)

Sellers usually enter into a contract (listing agreement) to have an agent sell their property. These contracts should be honored, and commissions should be paid when the property is sold. Sellers should not deal directly with prospective purchasers procured by the agent to evade the payment of a commission.

"As Is" Sale

This brings up the concept of an "as is" sale. Although an "as is" sale is legal, laws and regulations require that the buyer be fully informed as to the condition of the property, including any known defects, before the buyer becomes bound by a purchase contract. If the buyer is fully informed and still wishes to proceed with the sale, then an "as is" transaction is permissible. *Caveat emptor*, the Latin phrase meaning "let the buyer beware," is no longer a defense in court in a real estate transaction. If a seller withholds material facts about the property, such as structural defects known to the seller, the seller can be sued by the buyer.

4.3 REGULATION OF BROKERS AND SALESPEOPLE

Real Estate Broker Versus Salesperson

Although brokers and salespersons are licensed by the state of California's DRE, a salesperson's license is valid only when he or she is working for a real estate broker. It is through this association with the real estate broker that a salesperson also becomes an agent. Therefore, only a real estate broker can contract directly with a principal. A real estate salesperson must use the broker's name when signing a listing agreement with a seller. (Requirements to become a licensed real estate agent are discussed in detail in Chapter 15.)

Considered an employee of the broker by the DRE for supervision purposes, a real estate salesperson is usually (as mentioned above) considered an independent contractor with the broker for other purposes such as income tax withholding, Social Security, and so on. The broker must supervise the real estate activities of all salespersons under the broker's jurisdiction. In other matters, however, the broker usually treats the salesperson as an independent contractor and does not require the salesperson to be at work at certain hours. The salesperson is responsible for final results, not the method used to attain the results.

By law, real estate salespersons are required to have a written employment contract with their broker. Commission details between the broker and salesperson should also be in writing. A real estate salesperson can receive compensation only from his or her broker. When escrow is closed, the escrow company usually sends the entire commission to the employing broker, who in turn writes a separate check to the salesperson for his or her share.

Violation of agency law by a real estate salesperson may subject the salesperson to disciplinary action and may also be a cause for disciplinary action against the employing broker who by law is responsible for certain acts of the salesperson. (See Figure 4.4.)

Piece of the Pie

"I want a real estate license so I can get a share of the commission when I buy and sell my own properties." Some people do not wish to become real estate agents to serve the public, but want a license to deal on their own account. Is this a good idea? The answer is not clear-cut—it depends!

When a licensee buys and sells real estate as a principal, regulations require the licensee to disclose to the opposite party that he or she has a real estate license. Sometimes sellers and/or buyers refuse to deal with licensees as principals for fear that the licensee will take advantage of them. In some cases, the seller allows the buyer-licensee a portion of the commission. However, in some instances, the seller absolutely refuses to allow the listing broker to share the commission with a buyer-licensee.

Working Out-of-State Properties

Problem: A California broker wants to list or sell a property in another state where the California agent is not licensed.

Solution: The California broker refers the transaction to a licensed broker in that particular state. Both brokers agree to then share the commission.

Regulation of Real Estate Agents

Real estate agents are regulated by government agencies and professional trade associations. The California real estate commissioner, using the employees of the California DRE, is empowered to enforce the real estate law and to issue regulations that are enforced in the same manner as law. (See Chapter 15 for details regarding the real estate commissioner's regulation of licensees.)

Commissioner's Former Code of Ethics

At one time, the California real estate commissioner established, by regulations, a code of ethics and professional conduct that applied to all real estate licensees. The code of ethics listed examples of unethical behavior by real estate licensees and required that licensees refrain from such behavior. In addition, the code of ethics outlined positive steps real estate licensees could undertake to improve the public's image of a real estate agent. In 1997, a regulation repealed the code in an effort to reduce the number of regulations over the real estate business. However, many topics regarding violations in the former code of ethics are still illegal in other code sections under California law.

FIGURE 4.4

CALIFORNIA
ASSOCIATION
OF REALTORS®

INDEPENDENT CONTRACTOR AGREEMENT
(Between Broker and Associate-Licensee)
(C.A.R. Form ICA, Revised 4/09)

This Agreement, dated _____, is made between _____
_____("Broker") and
_____ ("Associate-Licensee").
In consideration of the covenants and representations contained in this Agreement, Broker and Associate-Licensee agree as follows:

1. BROKER: Broker represents that Broker is duly licensed as a real estate broker by the State of California, ☐ doing business as
_____ (firm name), ☐ a sole proprietorship, ☐ a partnership, or ☐ a corporation.
Broker is a member of the _____
Association(s) of REALTORS®, and a subscriber to the _____
Multiple Listing Service(s). Broker shall keep Broker's license current during the term of this Agreement.

2. ASSOCIATE-LICENSEE: Associate-Licensee represents that: **(i)** he/she is duly licensed by the State of California as a ☐ real estate broker, ☐ real estate salesperson, and **(ii)** he/she has not used any other names within the past five years, except
_____. Associate-Licensee shall keep his/her license current during the term of this Agreement, including satisfying all applicable continuing education and provisional license requirements.

3. INDEPENDENT CONTRACTOR RELATIONSHIP:
A. Broker and Associate-Licensee intend that, to the maximum extent permissible by law: **(i)** This Agreement does not constitute an employment agreement by either party; **(ii)** Broker and Associate-Licensee are independent contracting parties with respect to all services rendered under this Agreement; and **(iii)** This Agreement shall not be construed as a partnership.
B. Broker shall not: **(i)** restrict Associate-Licensee's activities to particular geographical areas, or **(ii)** dictate Associate-Licensee's activities with regard to hours, leads, open houses, opportunity or floor time, production, prospects, sales meetings, schedule, inventory, time off, vacation, or similar activities, except to the extent required by law.
C. Associate-Licensee shall not be required to accept an assignment by Broker to service any particular current or prospective listing or parties.
D. Except as required by law: **(i)** Associate-Licensee retains sole and absolute discretion and judgment in the methods, techniques, and procedures to be used in soliciting and obtaining listings, sales, exchanges, leases, rentals, or other transactions, and in carrying out Associate-Licensee's selling and soliciting activities; **(ii)** Associate-Licensee is under the control of Broker as to the results of Associate-Licensee's work only, and not as to the means by which those results are accomplished; **(iii)** Associate-Licensee has no authority to bind Broker by any promise or representation; and **(iv)** Broker shall not be liable for any obligation or liability incurred by Associate-Licensee.
E. Associate-Licensee's only remuneration shall be the compensation specified in paragraph 8.
F. Associate-Licensee who only performs as a real estate sales agent, shall not be treated as an employee for state and federal tax purposes. However, an Associate-Licencee who performs loan activity shall be treated as an employee for state and federal tax purposes unless the activity satisfies the legal requirements to establish an independent contractor relationship.
G. The fact the Broker may carry workers' compensation insurance for Broker's own benefit and for the mutual benefit of Broker and licensees associated with Broker, including Associate-Licensee, shall not create an inference of employment.
(Workers' Compensation Advisory: Even though Associate-Licensees may be treated as independent contractors for tax and other purposes, the California Labor and Workforce Development Agency considers them to be employees for workers' compensation purposes. According to that Agency: **(i)** Broker must obtain workers' compensation insurance for Associate-Licensees and **(ii)** Broker, not Associate-Licensees, must bear the cost of workers' compensation insurance. Penalties for failure to carry workers' compensation include, among others, the issuance of stop-work orders and fines of up to $1,000 per agent, not to exceed $100,000 per company.)

4. LICENSED ACTIVITY: All listings of property, and all agreements, acts or actions for performance of licensed acts, which are taken or performed in connection with this Agreement, shall be taken and performed in the name of Broker. Associate-Licensee agrees to and does hereby contribute all right and title to such listings to Broker for the benefit and use of Broker, Associate-Licensee, and other licensees associated with Broker. Broker shall make available to Associate-Licensee, equally with other licensees associated with Broker, all current listings in Broker's office, except any listing which Broker may choose to place in the exclusive servicing of Associate-Licensee or one or more other specific licensees associated with Broker. Associate-Licensee shall provide and pay for all professional licenses, supplies, services, and other items required in connection with Associate-Licensee's activities under this Agreement, or any listing or transaction, without reimbursement from Broker except as required by law. Associate-Licensee shall work diligently and with his/her best efforts to: **(i)** sell, exchange, lease, or rent properties listed with Broker or other cooperating Brokers; **(ii)** solicit additional listings, clients, and customers; and **(iii)** otherwise promote the business of serving the public in real estate transactions to the end that Broker and Associate-Licensee may derive the greatest benefit possible, in accordance with law. Associate-Licensee shall not commit any unlawful act under federal, state or local law or regulation while conducting licensed activity. Associate-Licensee shall at all times be familiar, and comply, with all applicable federal, state and local laws, including, but not limited to, anti-discrimination laws and restrictions against the giving or accepting a fee, or other thing of value, for the referral of business to title companies, escrow companies, home inspection companies, pest control companies and other settlement service providers pursuant to the California Business and Professions Code and the Real Estate Settlement Procedures Acts (RESPA). Broker shall make available for Associate-Licensee's use, along with other licensees associated with Broker, the facilities of the real estate office operated by Broker at _____
and the facilities of any other office locations made available by Broker pursuant to this Agreement.

ICA REVISED 4/09 (PAGE 1 OF 3)

Broker's Initials (_____)(_____)
Associate-Licensee's Initials (_____)(_____)

Reviewed by _____ Date _____

EQUAL HOUSING
OPPORTUNITY

FIGURE 4.4   *(continued)*

5. **PROPRIETARY INFORMATION AND FILES:** **(A)** All files and documents pertaining to listings, leads and transactions are the property of Broker and shall be delivered to Broker by Associate-Licensee immediately upon request or termination of this Agreement. **(B)** Associate- Licensee acknowledges that Broker's method of conducting business is a protected trade secret. **(C)** Associate-Licensee shall not use to his/her own advantage, or the advantage of any other person, business, or entity, except as specifically agreed in writing, either during Associate-Licensee's association with Broker, or thereafter, any information gained for or from the business, or files of Broker.

6. **SUPERVISION:** Associate-Licensee, within 24 hours (or ☐ _____) after preparing, signing, or receiving same, shall submit to Broker, or Broker's designated licensee: **(i)** all documents which may have a material effect upon the rights and duties of principals in a transaction, **(ii)** any documents or other items connected with a transaction pursuant to this Agreement in the possession of or available to Associate-Licensee; and **(iii)** all documents associated with any real estate transaction in which Associate-Licensee is a principal.

7. **TRUST FUNDS:** All trust funds shall be handled in compliance with the Business and Professions Code, and other applicable laws.

8. **COMPENSATION:**

   A. TO BROKER: Compensation shall be charged to parties who enter into listing or other agreements for services requiring a real estate license:

   ☐ as shown in "Exhibit A" attached, which is incorporated as a part of this Agreement by reference, or

   ☐ as follows: _____
   _____
   _____

   Any deviation which is not approved in writing in advance by Broker, shall be: **(1)** deducted from Associate-Licensee's compensation, if lower than the amount or rate approved above; and, **(2)** subject to Broker approval, if higher than the amount approved above. Any permanent change in commission schedule shall be disseminated by Broker to Associate-Licensee.

   B. TO ASSOCIATE-LICENSEE: Associate-Licensee shall receive a share of compensation actually collected by Broker, on listings or other agreements for services requiring a real estate license, which are solicited and obtained by Associate-Licensee, and on transactions of which Associate-Licensee's activities are the procuring cause, as follows:

   ☐ as shown in "Exhibit B" attached, which is incorporated as a part of this Agreement by reference, or

   ☐ other: _____
   _____
   _____

   C. PARTNERS, TEAMS, AND AGREEMENTS WITH OTHER ASSOCIATE-LICENSEES IN OFFICE: If Associate-Licensee and one or more other Associate-Licensees affiliated with Broker participate on the same side (either listing or selling) of a transaction, the commission allocated to their combined activities shall be divided by Broker and paid to them according to their written agreement. Broker shall have the right to withhold total compensation if there is a dispute between associate-licensees, or if there is no written agreement, or if no written agreement has been provided to Broker.

   D. EXPENSES AND OFFSETS: If Broker elects to advance funds to pay expenses or liabilities of Associate-Licensee, or for an advance payment of, or draw upon, future compensation, Broker may deduct the full amount advanced from compensation payable to Associate-Licensee on any transaction without notice. If Associate-Licensee's compensation is subject to a lien, garnishment or other restriction on payment, Broker shall charge Associate-Licensee a fee for complying with such restriction.

   E. PAYMENT: (i) All compensation collected by Broker and due to Associate-Licensee shall be paid to Associate-Licensee, after deduction of expenses and offsets, immediately or as soon thereafter as practicable, except as otherwise provided in this Agreement, or a separate written agreement between Broker and Associate-Licensee. **(ii)** Compensation shall not be paid to Associate-Licensee until both the transaction and file are complete. **(iii)** Broker is under no obligation to pursue collection of compensation from any person or entity responsible for payment. Associate-Licensee does not have the independent right to pursue collection of compensation for activities which require a real estate license which were done in the name of Broker. **(iv)** Expenses which are incurred in the attempt to collect compensation shall be paid by Broker and Associate-Licensee in the same proportion as set forth for the division of compensation (paragraph 8(B)). **(v)** If there is a known or pending claim against Broker or Associate-Licensee on transactions for which Associate-Licensee has not yet been paid, Broker may withhold from compensation due Associate-Licensee on that transaction amounts for which Associate-Licensee could be responsible under paragraph 14, until such claim is resolved. **(vi)** Associate-Licensee shall not be entitled to any advance payment from Broker upon future compensation.

   F. UPON OR AFTER TERMINATION: If this Agreement is terminated while Associate-Licensee has listings or pending transactions that require further work normally rendered by Associate-Licensee, Broker shall make arrangements with another associate-licensee to perform the required work, or Broker shall perform the work him/herself. The licensee performing the work shall be reasonably compensated for completing work on those listings or transactions, and such reasonable compensation shall be deducted from Associate-Licensee's share of compensation. Except for such offset, Associate-Licensee shall receive the compensation due as specified above.

9. **TERMINATION OF RELATIONSHIP:** Broker or Associate-Licensee may terminate their relationship under this Agreement at any time, with or without cause. After termination, Associate-Licensee shall not solicit: **(i)** prospective or existing clients or customers based upon company- generated leads obtained during the time Associate-Licensee was affiliated with Broker; **(ii)** any principal with existing contractual obligations to Broker; or **(iii)** any principal with a contractual transactional obligation for which Broker is entitled to be compensated. Even after termination, this Agreement shall govern all disputes and claims between Broker and Associate-Licensee connected with their relationship under this Agreement, including obligations and liabilities arising from existing and completed listings, transactions, and services.

Broker's Initials   (_____)(_____)
Associate-Licensee's Initials (_____)(_____)

| Reviewed by _____ Date _____ |

ICA REVISED 4/09 (PAGE 2 OF 3)

EQUAL HOUSING OPPORTUNITY

FIGURE 4.4   *(continued)*

10. **DISPUTE RESOLUTION:**
    A. Mediation: Mediation is recommended as a method of resolving disputes arising out of this Agreement between Broker and Associate-LIcensee.
    B. Arbitration: All disputes or claims between Associate-Licensee and other licensee(s) associated with Broker, or between Associate-Licensee and Broker, arising from or connected in any way with this Agreement, which cannot be adjusted between the parties involved, shall be submitted to the Association of REALTORS® of which all such disputing parties are members for arbitration pursuant to the provisions of its Bylaws, as may be amended from time to time, which are incorporated as a part of this Agreement by reference. If the Bylaws of the Association do not cover arbitration of the dispute, or if the Association declines jurisdiction over the dispute, then arbitration shall be pursuant to the rules of California law. The Federal Arbitration Act, Title 9, U.S. Code, Section 1, et seq., shall govern this Agreement.

11. **AUTOMOBILE:** Associate-Licensee shall maintain automobile insurance coverage for liability and property damage in the following amounts $_____/$_____. Broker shall be named as an additional insured party on Associate-Licensee's policies. A copy of the endorsement showing Broker as an additional insured shall be provided to Broker.

12. **PERSONAL ASSISTANTS:** Associate-Licensee may make use of a personal assistant, provided the following requirements are satisfied. Associate-Licensee shall have a written agreement with the personal assistant which establishes the terms and responsibilities of the parties to the employment agreement, including, but not limited to, compensation, supervision and compliance with applicable law. The agreement shall be subject to Broker's review and approval. Unless otherwise agreed, if the personal assistant has a real estate license, that license must be provided to the Broker. Both Associate-Licensee and personal assistant must sign any agreement that Broker has established for such purposes.

13. **OFFICE POLICY MANUAL:** If Broker's office policy manual, now or as modified in the future, conflicts with or differs from the terms of this Agreement, the terms of the office policy manual shall govern the relationship between Broker and Associate-Licensee.

14. **INDEMNITY AND HOLD HARMLESS; NOTICE OF CLAIMS: A.** Regarding any action taken or omitted by Associate-Licensee, or others working through, or on behalf of Associate-Licensee in connection with services rendered or to be rendered pursuant to this Agreement: (i) Associate-Licensee agrees to indemnify, defend and hold Broker harmless from all claims, disputes, litigation, judgments, awards, costs and attorney's fees, arising therefrom and (ii) Associate-Licensee shall immediately notify Broker if Associate-Licensee is served with or becomes aware of a lawsuit or claim regarding any such action. **B.** Any such claims or costs payable pursuant to this Agreement, are due as follows:
    ☐ Paid in full by Associate-Licensee, who hereby agrees to indemnify and hold harmless Broker for all such sums, or
    ☐ In the same ratio as the compensation split as it existed at the time the compensation was earned by Associate-Licensee
    ☐ Other: _____
    _____
    Payment from Associate-Licensee is due at the time Broker makes such payment and can be offset from any compensation due Associate-Licensee as above. Broker retains the authority to settle claims or disputes, whether or not Associate-Licensee consents to such settlement.

15. **ADDITIONAL PROVISIONS:** _____
    _____

16. **DEFINITIONS:** As used in this Agreement, the following terms have the meanings indicated:
    (A) "Listing" means an agreement with a property owner or other party to locate a buyer, exchange party, lessee, or other party to a transaction involving real property, a mobile home, or other property or transaction which may be brokered by a real estate licensee, or an agreement with a party to locate or negotiate for any such property or transaction.
    (B) "Compensation" means compensation for acts requiring a real estate license, regardless of whether calculated as a percentage of transaction price, flat fee, hourly rate, or in any other manner.
    (C) "Transaction" means a sale, exchange, lease, or rental of real property, a business opportunity, or a manufactured home, which may lawfully be brokered by a real estate licensee.

17. **ATTORNEY FEES:** In any action, proceeding, or arbitration between Broker and Associate-Licensee arising from or related to this Agreement, the prevailing Broker or Associate-Licensee shall be entitled to reasonable attorney fees and costs.

18. **ENTIRE AGREEMENT:** All prior agreements between the parties concerning their relationship as Broker and Associate-Licensee are incorporated in this Agreement, which constitutes the entire contract. Its terms are intended by the parties as a final and complete expression of their agreement with respect to its subject matter, and may not be contradicted by evidence of any prior agreement or contemporaneous oral agreement. This Agreement may not be amended, modified, altered, or changed except by a further agreement in writing executed by Broker and Associate-Licensee.

Broker: **Associate-Licensee:**

_____   _____
(Brokerage firm name)   (Signature)

By _____   _____
Its Broker/Office manager (circle one)   (Print name)

_____   _____
(Print name)   (Address)

_____   _____
(Address)   (City, State, Zip)

_____   _____
(City, State, Zip)   (Telephone)   (Fax)

_____
(Telephone)   (Fax)

THIS FORM HAS BEEN APPROVED BY THE CALIFORNIA ASSOCIATION OF REALTORS® (C.A.R.). NO REPRESENTATION IS MADE AS TO THE LEGAL VALIDITY OR ADEQUACY OF ANY PROVISION IN ANY SPECIFIC TRANSACTION. A REAL ESTATE BROKER IS THE PERSON QUALIFIED TO ADVISE ON REAL ESTATE TRANSACTIONS. IF YOU DESIRE LEGAL OR TAX ADVICE, CONSULT AN APPROPRIATE PROFESSIONAL.

This form is available for use by the entire real estate industry. It is not intended to identify the user as a REALTOR®. REALTOR® is a registered collective membership mark which may be used only by members of the NATIONAL ASSOCIATION OF REALTORS® who subscribe to its Code of Ethics.

R E B S | **I N C** ®   Published and Distributed by:
REAL ESTATE BUSINESS SERVICES, INC.
a subsidiary of the California Association of REALTORS®
525 South Virgil Avenue, Los Angeles, California 90020

ICA REVISED 4/09 (PAGE 3 OF 3)   Reviewed by _____ Date _____

INDEPENDENT CONTRACTOR AGREEMENT (ICA PAGE 3 OF 3)

Source: Reprinted with permission of California Association of REALTORS®.

Filing Complaints

If a person wishes to file a complaint about a real estate agent, the procedure is to send a written complaint to the real estate commissioner. The commissioner then assigns the complaint to a deputy for investigation. Statements about the incident are taken from witnesses and the licensee. In addition, the real estate agent's records and accounts may be audited. An informal conference may be called to allow the investigating deputy to determine the seriousness of the complaint. If a violation of the law has occurred, a formal hearing is called and the agent's license may be suspended or revoked. Every year the commissioner receives several thousand complaints about real estate licensees, but after an investigation, a majority are dismissed as not being in violation of real estate law or regulations.

Trade Associations

There are several national, state, and local professional real estate trade associations, such as the National Association of REALTORS® and the National Association of Real Estate Brokers. The role of trade associations is presented in detail in Chapter 15. The point stressed here is that real estate trade associations have membership rules and codes of ethics to help monitor the activities of their members. This indirectly works as a form of self-regulation. Members who violate the real estate trade association rules of conduct can be suspended from membership and, in the process, lose many benefits.

4.4 TERMINATION OF A REAL ESTATE AGENCY

There are six basic ways to terminate a real estate agency. (See Figure 4.5.)

1. Termination by *completion of the agency agreement.* The agent fulfills his or her responsibilities by securing a buyer who is ready, willing, and able to buy the property on the exact terms of the listing or on other terms agreeable to the seller. When this occurs, the agent is eligible for the commission and is normally paid at close of escrow.

2. Termination by *expiration of time.* If an agent fails to find a ready, willing, and able buyer by the termination date of the listing, the agency is terminated. Most listings contain a clause, however, that allows the agent to give the seller a list of prospects to whom the agent has shown the property during the term of the listing. If any of these prospects buys the property directly from the seller or through another broker during the designated protection period after the listing expires, the agent

FIGURE 4.5

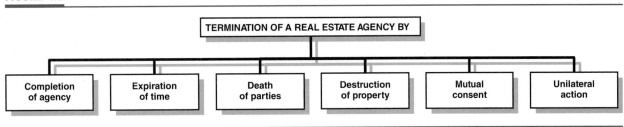

is entitled to a commission. In a buyer's agency the exact same issues apply, except the word *buyer* is substituted for *seller*. Additional details are presented in Chapter 5.

3. Termination by *death of the principal or death of the agent.* An agency is automatically terminated if the principal or the agent dies during the term of the listing. One exception is if the principal dies after a purchase agreement is signed, in which case the agent is entitled to the commission. The sale is usually binding on the heirs of the decedent.

4. Termination by *destruction of the property.* If a major catastrophe such as an earthquake or a fire occurs, causing damage to the property, the agency is terminated.

5. Termination by *mutual consent.* The principals and the agent can mutually agree to terminate the agency.

6. Termination by *unilateral action of the agent or the principal.* Either party can terminate the agency unilaterally. However, the party that cancels the agency may be liable for damages. If a principal cancels the agency, the agent is usually entitled to the full commission or, at a minimum, to reimbursement for expenses and time spent.

CHAPTER SUMMARY

An agency relationship is created when a principal appoints an agent to represent the principal in dealings with third parties. A real estate agency is usually created when a seller appoints a real estate broker to find a buyer for the seller's property. There are two broad categories of agency: general agency and special agency. Real estate agents are usually special agents. When a real estate broker represents only the seller or only the buyer, it is called a single agency. If the broker represents both the buyer and seller, it is called a dual agency. A real estate agency differs from an employer-employee relationship and an independent contractor relationship.

Agencies are created in three ways: by agreement, by ratification, and by estoppel. Most real estate agencies are created by written agreement. A fiduciary relationship is established when a real estate agent is appointed by the principal. This relationship is one of binding trust and loyalty and obligates the real estate agent to act in the principal's best interest. The agent, nonetheless, owes the opposite party a full disclosure of all known defects. A real estate agent must be honest and truthful and must not misrepresent the sale. Agency violations may include trust fund–handling problems, misrepresentation, false promise, commingling, definite termination date, and secret profit. A principal should advise a real estate agent of any known defects to the property. A seller should not withhold information from the real estate agent or buyer. A seller can be held liable for distortion of facts about the property.

A real estate broker can contract directly with a principal, whereas a salesperson cannot. Only through the real estate salesperson's association with a broker does the salesperson become an agent. Salespersons must have a written employment contract with a broker and can receive compensation only from the employing broker.

Real estate agents are regulated by the California DRE and by professional trade associations if they are members of those organizations.

Agencies are terminated by completion of the agency agreement, by expiration of time, by death of the principal or agent, by destruction of the property, by mutual consent, and by unilateral termination by the agent or the principal.

IMPORTANT TERMS AND CONCEPTS

agent	fiduciary	recovery fund
buyer's agent	general agency	secret profit
commingling	independent	seller's agent
conversion	contractor	single agency
dual agency	misrepresentation	special agency
false promise	principal	trust fund

PRACTICAL APPLICATION

1. Real estate salesperson Ames from Vista Realty is the agent for the sale of the Alvarez home at 123 Main Street, Somewhere, CA. Salesperson Jones also works for Vista Realty and brings in an offer on the Alvarez home from Buyer Patel. Explain the agency relationship between Alvarez, Vista Realty, and Patel.

2. A real estate salesperson from Acme Properties shows a potential buyer a home listed with Lake Realty. While showing the home,

the Acme agent mentions that based on the information supplied by Lake Realty, the home is 2,100 square feet and the lot is one-half acre. In fact, the home is 2,000 square feet and the lot is only one-quarter acre. Which real estate company is guilty of misrepresentation? How should the salesperson from Acme Properties have handled the situation?

3. Excellent Realty has a signed contract to act as the exclusive agent for the seller of a condo (priced at $375,000) for a period of ninety days. Within sixty days, a buyer is found who makes an offer of $360,000. Prior to accepting the offer, the seller dies. The heirs then cancel the agreement with Excellent Realty. Excellent Realty contends that it is entitled to a commission based on the $360,000 offer. The heirs deny that they must pay the commission. Who is right and why?

REVIEWING YOUR UNDERSTANDING

1. A real estate agency exists between
   a. the seller and buyer.
   b. the broker and principal.
   c. the borrower and lender.
   d. the landlord and tenant.

2. A fiduciary relationship is best described as
   a. ethics and loyalty.
   b. ethics and trust.
   c. trust and confidence.
   d. loyalty and confidentiality.

3. A real estate salesperson is a(n)
   a. direct agent.
   b. agent by virtue of his or her association with a broker.
   c. employee of the seller.
   d. employee of the buyer.

4. The use of cooperating agents is illegal under California law.
   a. True
   b. False

5. A real estate agency can be created by all of the following, except by
   a. ratification.
   b. agreement.
   c. estoppel.
   d. doctrine of realty determination.

6. All of the following are methods of terminating a real estate agency, except for
   a. estoppel.
   b. mutual consent.
   c. completion of agency.
   d. expiration of time.

7. A home seller must inform his or her real estate agent when the seller is aware of
   a. termite infestation discovered earlier.
   b. a leaky roof.
   c. an inoperative fireplace.
   d. all of the above.

8. All of the following are true, except:
   a. Real estate salespersons and brokers are required to be licensed.
   b. A real estate broker, not the salesperson, is appointed by the principal to be the agent.
   c. A salesperson collects his or her commission directly from the seller.
   d. A dual agency means the real estate broker represents both the buyer and seller.

9. A seller's real estate agent owes the buyer
   a. the duty to see that the property is sold at the lowest possible price.
   b. a disclosure of known defects.
   c. a fiduciary relationship.
   d. the right to know the seller's lowest acceptance price.

10. The real estate commissioner
    a. administers the real estate law.
    b. issues regulations that have the force of law.
    c. heads the Department of Real Estate.
    d. all of the above.

11. If a real estate salesperson decides to work for a new broker, the existing listings obtained by the salesperson belong to whom?
    a. The salesperson
    b. The former broker
    c. The new broker
    d. The seller, who can automatically cancel the listing

12. Unless instructed to hold the check uncashed, a buyer's deposit must be placed with the appropriated party or account within how many business days?
    a. Three
    b. Five
    c. Seven
    d. Nine

13. Ms. Lightdeer showed a property to Mr. and Mrs. Chu without having an agency agreement with the owner. Later the owner accepted the offer to purchase, which was submitted by Ms. Lightdeer on behalf of Mr. and Mrs. Chu. The owner consented to Ms. Lightdeer's unauthorized acts. Under these circumstances, an agency could be created by
    a. fiduciary.
    b. estoppel.
    c. ratification.
    d. assumption.

14. The maximum amount per individual claim against the Department of Real Estate Recovery Fund is
    a. $10,000.
    b. $20,000.
    c. $50,000.
    d. $100,000.

15. A real estate broker who has been appointed in writing to be a property owner's agent to find a buyer under a specified set of terms is best described as
    a. a general, ostensible agent.
    b. a general, actual agent.
    c. a special, actual agent.
    d. a special, ostensible agent.

16. A real estate agent mistakenly states that the portable dishwasher is included in the sales price of the home. This agent is guilty of
    a. false promise.
    b. misrepresentation.
    c. divided agency.
    d. secret profit.

17. When a real estate agent mixes his or her personal funds with that of a principal, the agent is guilty of
    a. commingling.
    b. conversion.
    c. trust funding.
    d. embezzlement.

18. In today's real estate market, when a real estate agent uses agents from other real estate companies to help find a buyer, the other agents are called
    a. principals.
    b. listing agents.
    c. cooperating agents.
    d. finder agents.

19. Homeowner Raymond appoints Broker Cecilia to find a buyer. Later a qualified buyer is found, all papers are signed, and all loans are approved. The home is scheduled to be transferred on June 1. On May 30, Homeowner Raymond dies. Which best describes the situation?
    a. The real estate agency is canceled, and Broker Cecilia has not earned the commission.
    b. The real estate agency is canceled, and Broker Cecilia has earned the commission.
    c. The sale is probably not binding on the heirs of Raymond.
    d. The sale and agency are terminated by expiration of time.

20. All of the following are true, except:
    a. All real estate brokers are required to establish reasonable procedures to supervise the activities of salespersons transacting business under the name of the broker.
    b. "As is" home sales are allowed in California if proper disclosures are given.
    c. By law, real estate salespersons are required to have a written contract with their employing broker.
    d. A majority of real estate complaints against agents are valid enough to warrant disciplinary action by the real estate commissioner.

21. A real estate broker is allowed to keep _____ of his or her money in a trust fund to handle bank service charges.
    a. $200
    b. $300
    c. $400
    d. $500

22. When attempting to become an agent for a home seller, the seller asks the agent if he or she would be willing to reduce the amount of the commission. An acceptable reply would be:
    a. The commission is set by law, and I cannot change it.
    b. The commission is set by our local trade association, and I cannot change it.
    c. The commission is set by our company policy, and I cannot change it.
    d. The commission is set by the Real Estate Commissioner, and I cannot change it.

23. Which of the following might be considered an example of secret profit and a violation of the law?
    a. Seller sells for 50 percent more than he or she paid for the property.
    b. Buyer believes the property is worth more than the asking price.
    c. Broker receives a referral fee from a title company without telling the principals in the sales transaction.
    d. Broker earns a commission after showing the property to only one buyer, who then purchases within one week.

24. Under a buyer's agency, the fiduciary relationship is between the broker and the
    a. seller.
    b. buyer's broker.
    c. buyer.
    d. seller and buyer.

25. When a California real estate broker sells a property in another state where the California agent is not licensed, the use of a licensed broker in the other state does not allow the California broker to share in the commission.
    a. True
    b. False

STUDENT LEARNING OUTCOMES

This chapter presents the legal requirements for an enforceable real estate contract. The chapter includes a definition of a contract, outlines the essential elements of a valid contract, and discusses how contracts are terminated. Two important real estate contracts, the authorization to sell (listing agreement) and the purchase agreement (deposit receipt), are discussed. Copies of these and other contracts used in a typical residential sale are presented in the chapter appendix. At the conclusion of the chapter, you will be able to do the following:

1. Define contracts and list the legal requirements for an enforceable contract.
2. Describe how contracts are terminated or discharged.
3. List seven provisions that should be part of a real estate contract.
4. Explain the purpose of an authorization to sell (listing agreement) and discuss the various types of listing agreements.
5. Discuss the essential elements of a purchase agreement.
6. Discuss the purpose of an option contract.
7. Explain the use of a counteroffer form.
8. Describe the major mandated disclosures that must be given in a residential real estate transaction.

Real Estate Contracts and Mandated Disclosures

5.1 LEGAL REQUIREMENTS FOR ENFORCEABLE CONTRACTS

A **contract** is generally defined as an agreement between two or more persons, consisting of a promise or mutual promises to perform or not to perform certain acts. If the contract is executed under proper conditions, the law enforces the contract and requires the parties to abide by the terms or incur damages. A **unilateral contract** is created by only one party extending a promise without a reciprocal promise by another party. An example is a reward. If you lose your wallet and offer $100 for its return, this is a unilateral contract because you promise to pay $100 in exchange for an act (find and return your wallet).

However, most real estate contracts are **bilateral contracts** in nature, in which a promise from one person is made in exchange for a promise from another person. For example, in a listing agreement a seller promises to compensate the broker to achieve the purpose of the agreement. The broker in turn promises to use due diligence in attempting to find a ready, willing, and able buyer for the property under terms that are acceptable to the seller.

A contract may be created by expression or by implication. An **expressed contract** is one wherein the parties have agreed to perform an act or acts verbally or under a written agreement. An **implied contract** is one wherein the parties have not formally agreed verbally or through a written agreement to perform an act. Instead, they agree to perform by their actions rather than by their words.

For example, say you reach agreement with a contractor to build a fence around your home and you mutually agree to a style, a size, costs, and a starting date. Under these circumstances, you have probably created an expressed contract. On the other hand, assume you had talked to the contractor about the fence but your discussions were inconclusive and no promises were made. The next day the contractor appears on your property with a load of materials and begins building the fence. If you do not stop the contractor and the fence is built, an implied contract may be established.

A contract can also be labeled as an executed contract or an executory contract. In an **executed contract,** all parties have performed and fulfilled their obligations. An **executory contract** means that some act of the contract remains to be completed by one or more of the parties. A real estate listing agreement, discussed later in this chapter, is a good example of an executory contract. Here a seller promises to pay a commission if the broker finds a buyer under terms acceptable to the seller. This is an executory contract that will not be completed until the broker finds an acceptable buyer. Once a buyer is found who is acceptable to the seller, the listing agreement becomes a complete or executed contract. (See Figure 5.1.)

Legal Effects of Contracts

Once a contract is created, what are the prospects that the agreement will stand up in court in the event of a dispute? Here are four important legal terms regarding contracts:

1. *Valid.* A **valid** contract is one that is binding and enforceable. You can sue on it; it is considered the best type of contract you can have.

2. *Void.* A **void** contract is an agreement that the courts will not consider a contract; in other words, the contract has no legal

FIGURE 5.1

TYPES OF CONTRACTS

UNILATERAL	=	PROMISE FOR AN ACT
BILATERAL	=	PROMISE FOR A PROMISE
EXPRESSED	=	VERBAL OR WRITTEN
IMPLIED	=	CREATED BY ACTIONS
EXECUTORY	=	SOME ACTION NEEDED
EXECUTED	=	COMPLETED CONTRACT

Most real estate agreements are expressed bilateral contracts.

effect. An example is a contract by a minor (someone under 18 years of age) to purchase a home. A minor may acquire real property through a will or by a gift. However, a minor may not buy or sell real property except through a court-appointed person acting on the minor's behalf. An exception is a category of minor called an *emancipated minor*. Examples of emancipated minors are those minors who are married or serving in the military or whose parents have been relieved of legal responsibility for their minor's actions. Emancipated minors can legally contract for real property.

3. *Voidable.* A **voidable** contract exists where one of the parties (the injured party) has the option of proceeding with the contract or calling it off. Examples include contracts entered into because of duress (force), menace (threat of force), undue influence (pushed by a person with excess power), or fraud (misrepresentation).

4. *Unenforceable.* An **unenforceable** contract appears to be valid but cannot be sued upon. An example is an oral agreement for the sale of real property by an agent for a commission. A California law called the **Statute of Frauds** requires that certain contracts, including real estate contracts, must be in writing to be enforceable. (See Figure 5.2.)

FIGURE 5.2

LEGAL EFFECTS OF CONTRACTS

✓ **VALID**
binding and enforceable

✓ **VOIDABLE**
one party can cancel due to fraud, duress, or undue influence, but the other side cannot cancel

✓ **UNENFORCEABLE**
appears valid, but cannot be enforced in court

✓ **VOID**
no legal effect, no contract

FIGURE 5.3

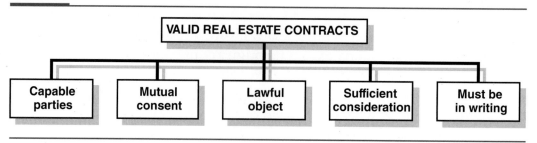

Essential Elements of a Real Estate Contract

The five essential elements for an enforceable real estate contract are (1) parties capable of contracting; (2) mutual consent; (3) lawful object; (4) a sufficient consideration; and (5) according to the Statute of Frauds, it must be in writing. (See Figure 5.3.)

Parties Capable of Contracting

For a contract to be valid, there must be at least two or more parties with the legal capacity to contract. As a general rule, anyone is capable of contracting. However, there are some exceptions. A minor is incapable of contracting for real property unless the minor is emancipated. Persons who are declared incompetent by the courts cannot contract. Like minors, however, incompetents can acquire title to real property by gift or by will. Certain classifications of convicts are considered incapable of contracting. On the other hand, foreigners can buy and sell real property, although there are certain state and federal withholding regulations when selling real property. Partnerships and corporations are regarded as artificial beings and can also hold and dispose of real property.

Mutual Consent

The parties to a contract must mutually agree to be bound by the terms of the contract. This is exemplified by an offer by one party and an acceptance by the other. The offer must be definite and certain in its terms. A typical example is where a buyer makes an offer to purchase real estate under certain terms and conditions. The seller then accepts the offer, and the acceptance is communicated either in person, by mail, by fax, or electronically to the buyer. This offer and acceptance constitute mutual consent.

Lawful Object

A contract must have a lawful object. An object refers to what is required to be done or not to be done. A contract is void if there is a single object and that one object is unlawful or impossible to perform. If there are many lawful objects in the contract and one or more unlawful objects, usually only the lawful objects are valid; the other objects are void. A contract for a gambling debt in California or a contract to commit a crime is not a lawful object. Therefore, the contracts are not valid.

Sufficient Consideration

Consideration is defined as "a benefit conferred or agreed to be conferred on the person making the promise or on any other person or a detriment suffered or agreed to be suffered." Consideration can be as simple as the return of one promise for another promise. The consideration must have some value. In many cases, the consideration is money, but it need not be. It must be something of value in exchange for something of value and is termed a "valuable" consideration. For example, love and affection might be considered "valuable" or "good" consideration on a gift deed. If there is a dispute as to what constitutes "sufficient" consideration, the parties to the contract may need to bring a court action to clarify the issue.

The Statute of Frauds

According to the *Statute of Frauds* in the California Civil Code, a real estate contract must be in writing to be enforceable in court. Similarly, any change from the original contract must also be in writing and dated and initialed by the parties involved. The purpose of the law is to prevent perjury, forgery, and dishonest conduct on the part of unscrupulous people in proving the existence and terms of certain important types of contracts. The so-called parol evidence rule applies. This rule states that oral evidence may not be used to modify a written contract that appears to be complete. Oral evidence is allowed to prove fraud or other illegal aspects of a written contract. Practically speaking, a written contract is simply a good way to help eliminate ambiguities and misunderstandings that might arise at a later date.

The California Civil Code requires that the following contracts must be in writing to be enforceable:

1. An agreement that, by its terms, is not to be performed within a year from the making thereof.
2. A special promise to answer for the debt, default, or miscarriage of another, except in the cases provided for in Civil Code Section 2794.

3. An agreement made on consideration of marriage other than a mutual promise to marry.

4. An agreement to lease real estate for more than one year or for the sale of real property or of an interest therein. A lease for one year or less need not be in writing to be valid.

5. An agreement authorizing or employing an agent, broker, or any other person to purchase or sell real estate or to lease real estate for a period longer than one year or to procure, introduce, or find a purchaser or seller of real estate or a lessee or lessor of real estate where such lease is for a period longer than one year, for compensation or a commission.

6. An agreement that, by its terms, is not to be performed during the lifetime of the promisor or an agreement to devise or to bequeath any property or to make any provision for any reason by will.

7. An agreement by a purchaser of real property to pay an indebtedness secured by a mortgage or deed of trust on the property purchased, unless assumption of said indebtedness by the purchaser is specifically provided for in the conveyance of such property.

Any contract that does not comply with the preceding is not void, but is unenforceable.

Discharge of Contracts

Contracts can be discharged in a number of ways. **Full performance** is the normal situation, wherein the parties accomplish what they set out to do in the contract. At the other extreme is a *breach* of the contract, which means that at least one of the parties did not fulfill its part of the agreement. In the case of a breach, the injured party has a number of legal remedies available.

Two of the more common remedies are to (1) sue for damage or (2) *sue for specific performance*. When you sue for damages, you are attempting to receive monetary compensation for the damage because the other party will not complete the contract. When you sue for specific performance, you are asking the court to compel the other party to perform according to the contract.

Statute of Limitations

To initiate a lawsuit, the **Statute of Limitations** states that you must begin the lawsuit within a legally prescribed time period. If you fail to initiate the lawsuit within the time period outlined in the Statute of Limitations, you may have no remedy in the courts and your rights to sue are said to have "outlawed." Four real estate examples of Statute of Limitation periods are as follows:

1. Three years to bring action for removal of encroachments.
2. Four years to bring action on a written contract.
3. Five years to bring action for recovery of title to property.
4. Ninety days after filing a mechanic's lien, the mechanic must bring a court foreclosure to enforce the lien.

Sometimes, even though the issue is within the Statute of Limitations, certain rights may be set aside using the Doctrine of Laches. This doctrine states that if an unreasonable delay in bringing an action results in an unfair situation for a defendant, the extent of the lawsuit might be limited.

Other ways to discharge a contract include the following:

1. Part performance
2. Substantial performance
3. Impossibility of performance
4. Agreement between the parties
5. Release
6. Operation of law
7. Acceptance of a breach of contract

Provisions in Contracts

The following basic provisions should be part of a real estate contract:

1. The date of the agreement
2. The names and addresses of the parties to the contract
3. A description of the property
4. The consideration
5. Reference to the creation of new mortgages or deeds of trust, if any, and the terms thereof; also, the terms and conditions of existing mortgages, if any
6. Any other provisions that may be required or requested by either of the parties
7. The date and place for closing the contract

In the real world, most real estate contracts are preprinted forms that cover the current legal requirements per California law.

Real Estate Licensees Should not Practice Law

A real estate agent is not licensed to practice law. Therefore, a real estate agent should not create a contract from a blank sheet of paper.

Current practice allows a real estate agent only to fill in blanks on a preprinted real estate form.

On some occasions, a discrepancy occurs between a preprinted clause in a contract and a handwritten clause. The usual rule is that the handwritten clause supersedes the preprinted clause.

5.2 AUTHORIZATION TO SELL

Commonly referred to as the *listing agreement,* the authorization to sell is one of the most common contracts found in a real estate transaction. An authorization to sell is the formal contract wherein the owner of the property (the seller) will act in good faith to accomplish the sale of the property under certain stipulated conditions. The listing agreement creates a contract between a real estate broker and the seller.

As noted in the previous chapter, the authorization to sell also establishes an agency relationship between the broker and the principal. This agency is referred to as a **fiduciary relationship**.

An authorization to sell is a bilateral contract in that there is an exchange of promises. The seller promises to sell at a stipulated price and to pay the broker a commission upon delivery of a ready, willing, and able buyer. The broker promises to use diligence in attempting to procure a purchaser. The seller may make additional promises regarding the terms. Thus, there is a promise for a promise—the required ingredient for a bilateral contract.

Different Types of Authorization to Sell

There are essentially four different types of authorization to sell: (1) open listing, (2) exclusive agency listing, (3) exclusive authorization and right-to-sell listing, and (4) net listing.

All of these should be in writing, and real estate regulations require that all parties must be given copies at the time of signature. (See Figure 5.4.)

Open Listing

The **open listing** is one that can be given simultaneously to more than one agent. Only one commission is payable, and it is paid to the agent who first procures an offer acceptable to the seller. Even the owner can sell the property to his or her own prospective buyer without paying a commission to any agent. For these reasons, most agents are generally reluctant to spend their time on this type of listing arrangement.

FIGURE 5.4

TYPES OF LISTINGS

Open
Exclusive Agency
Exclusive Right to Sell
Net

Exclusive Agency Listing

In an **exclusive agency listing,** one broker is named in the contract. The named broker may cooperate with other brokers and agree to share his or her commission with them if they bring in a buyer. The seller reserves the right to sell the property him- or herself to prospects he or she finds without paying a commission. An exclusive agency listing must have a definite termination date.

Exclusive Authorization and Right-to-Sell Listing

The **Exclusive Authorization and Right-to-Sell listing** is the most common form of listing used in the real estate business. The broker is entitled to a commission no matter who sells the property, including the owner, during a specific time period. Because the broker can expect compensation (assuming the property is reasonably salable), the broker is willing to spend considerable time attempting to find a buyer. The broker is also more likely to spend money to advertise and promote the property.

If authorized by the seller, the listing broker may cooperate with other brokers, who help the listing agent find a buyer and agree to split the commission. An exclusive authorization and right-to-sell listing, like the exclusive agency listing, must contain a definite termination date. If a real estate agent accepts any exclusive listing without a definite termination date, he or she is in violation of the real estate law.

See the appendix of this chapter for an example of an Exclusive Authorization and Right-to-Sell listing form.

Net Listing

Under a **net listing**, the seller stipulates a set sum of money that the seller wants regardless of the final sale price of the property. For example, assume that a seller of a home states that he or she wants to net $62,000 cash from the sale after paying off a $325,000 existing loan and $4,000 in escrow, title, and other seller closing costs. The broker is free to sell the property for any price as long as the price covers the seller's net, loan payoff, and $4,000 in closing costs.

Assume the broker finds a buyer who will pay $425,000 for the property. The broker would then earn a commission of $34,000, computed as follows:

$425,000	Sales price
− 325,000	Seller's existing loan balance
−4,000	Seller's closing
−62,000	Seller's net
$ 34,000	Broker's commission

The commission would then represent 8% of the sales price:

$34,000 commission ÷ $425,000 sales price=8% commission rate

Due to past abuses by some real estate agents, California law requires that the broker must notify the seller of the size of the broker's commission and obtain the seller's approval before the net sale can close. The idea is that if the seller feels the broker misled the seller regarding the size of the seller's potential net, the seller will have a chance to halt the sale. If the real estate broker fails to comply with this presale disclosure, the seller may later institute a lawsuit against the broker and the broker's license may be revoked or suspended by the California real estate commissioner. A net listing may be taken on an open, exclusive agency, or exclusive authorizations and a right-to-sell basis.

Multiple Listing Service

The **multiple listing service (MLS)** is a listing service usually controlled by a group of brokers who are affiliated with a real estate association. Listings are placed on the MLS, and that information is then disseminated to all members of the MLS. Some limited information about the listed property is also released to the public via numerous websites. The seller gets significantly greater market exposure through this type of service, given that most MLS systems have hundreds, even thousands, of members. Through the use of computers, this kind of quick mass exposure gives the seller a better chance of receiving the best possible price and terms.

The exclusive authorization and right-to-sell listing contract is widely used when submitting or inputting a listing on the MLS. Under the terms of MLS, the listing broker controls the listing and agrees to split the commission in some manner with the cooperating agents. A property can be submitted to MLS only if the agent has the prior written permission of the seller.

5.3 PURCHASE AGREEMENT AND DISCLOSURE RULES

The *Real Estate Purchase Agreement,* commonly called the **deposit receipt,** is a contract between the buyer and the seller that outlines the terms for the purchase of real property. It also acts as a receipt for the buyer's deposit toward the purchase of the property. In addition, the purchase agreement spells out the details regarding the payment of the broker's commission and frequently sets up the guidelines for the escrow instructions.

The Offer and Acceptance

The prospective buyer stipulates the price and terms of the offer, and the offer is then put on the purchase contract form. By regulation, all offers received by the broker must be presented to the seller. If the seller accepts the offer, communication of acceptance must be delivered back to the buyer or authorized third party (usually the buyer's agent) either in person, by mail, by fax, or electronically. At that time, there is a binding contract because offer, acceptance, and notification of the acceptance have occurred. At any time prior to receiving communication that the seller has accepted the offer, the buyer can withdraw the offer and not be liable on the contract.

California real estate regulations used to require the broker or the broker's designee to review and initial the purchase agreement within five business days. As of 1997, a regulation removed this five-day requirement. The broker must now show that he or she has reasonably supervised the transaction. Signed copies of the offer and the acceptance must be left with all parties at the time they sign. Then a final completed copy with all signatures must be given to all parties.

Rejection of the Offer

If the terms of the offer are unacceptable, the seller can reject the offer outright. The legal effect of this is that no contract exists because there has been no acceptance. The buyer, however, may make another offer.

COUNTEROFFERS

If the seller believes that the offer is basically a good one but there should be a change in price or terms, the seller can make a counteroffer to the buyer. A **counteroffer** by the seller automatically does away with the buyer's original offer and, in effect, is merely an offer made by the seller to the buyer. As such, the legal requirements for withdrawal or acceptance and communication of acceptance exist in reverse order. If the buyer accepts the changes, that fact must be indicated in writing, and communication of acceptance of the counteroffer must be delivered back to the seller. At any point prior to the communication of acceptance of the counteroffer, the seller may withdraw the counteroffer.

See the appendix of this chapter for an example of a Real Estate Purchase Agreement.

Real Estate Transfer Disclosure Statement

In California, sellers of one to four residential units must furnish buyers with a completed Transfer Disclosure Statement (TDS). This disclosure statement details various facts about the property—needed repairs, the condition of appliances, improvements added with or without building permits, the existence of any known harmful substances, and so on.

The details noted are based upon an inspection conducted by the real estate agents involved in the sale and upon statements made by the seller. This TDS must be provided even if the transaction is an "as is" sale. The responsibility for providing this disclosure rests with the real estate agents. If no agents are involved, the seller must provide the statement. The transfer disclosure statement must be signed by the buyers, the sellers, and all real estate agents involved in the transaction. Ideally, the TDS should be given to the buyers before they sign the purchase contract. If the TDS is given after the purchase contract is signed, the buyer has a three-day right to cancel the sale.

See the appendix of this chapter for an example of a Real Estate Transfer Disclosure Statement.

Summary of Mandated Disclosure Requirements

To protect consumers, many mandated disclosures are required in a real estate transaction. Some of the disclosures are the sole responsibility of the seller, others are the sole responsibility of the real estate agent, and still others are the joint responsibility of the seller and the real estate agent. So in addition to the disclosure of the status of the agency relationship covered in Chapter 4, "Real Estate Agency," and the Real Estate Transfer Disclosure Statement (TDS) mentioned previously, the following summary provides the major mandatory disclosures that must be made in a simple 1- to 4-unit real estate sales transaction.

1. *Disclosure Regarding Real Estate Agency Relationship.* (See discussion and form in Chapter 4.) This requires that a real estate agent and principal agree on the person the licensee represents in the sales transaction. The disclosure must take place during the listing and selling process. Principal(s) and agent(s) must sign the disclosure form.

2. *Real Estate Transfer Disclosure Statement.* (See the discussion above and the form in the appendix of this chapter.) Prior to the closing of the sale, the seller must give the buyer a statement regarding the condition of the property. If a real estate agent is involved in the sale, the agent must also do a physical inspection and report his or her findings. Seller, buyer, and real estate agent, if any, all sign the form. In a few instances, this form may not be required. See qualified experts for details.

3. *Residential Environmental and Earthquake Hazards Disclosures.* The buyer is given a booklet entitled "Environmental Hazard and Earthquake Guide," and the buyer and seller sign a disclosure form addressing various earthquake issues, including a braced water heater, a bolted-down foundation, unreinforced masonry, and other building construction items. The booklet also discusses hazardous wastes, asbestos, formaldehyde, lead paint, mold, and radon gases.

4. *Natural Hazard Disclosure Statement.* Sellers are required to issue a separate disclosure report regarding possible natural hazards. The report must answer the following questions. Is the property in any of the following:

   A. a special flood area?
   B. an area of potential flooding if a dam fails?
   C. a very high fire severity area?
   D. a wildland forest fire risk area?
   E. an earthquake fault zone?
   F. seismic hazard zone?

   In addition, the report also discloses whether the property is located in an area subject to a Mello-Roos Community District and/or a 1915 Bond Act assessment.

All of these topics make reference to various agencies and code sections. Because of the complexity of these disclosures, most sellers pay to have a professional company present this disclosure to the buyer.

5. *Common Interest Development General Information.* If the buyer is making a purchase in a planned unit development (PUD) or other type of common interest development, said buyer(s) must be given information about the covenants, conditions and restrictions (CC&Rs), and the amount of the homeowner dues. In addition, the financial status of the owner's association and any pending lawsuits must be disclosed.

6. *Seller Financing Addendum and Disclosure Statement.* If a sale involves a *seller carry loan,* then a statement clearly outlining all the financing terms and conditions must be signed by the buyer, seller, and real estate agent, if any. This statement must be signed before the buyer signs the promissory note and other critical loan papers.

7. *Other required disclosures are frequently found in the purchase contract.* (See the California Residential Purchase Agreement and Joint Escrow Instructions form in the appendix of this chapter.)

   A. *Megan's Law.* Buyer is given notice that a data bank is available to screen the nearby area for registered sex offenders. See http://caag.state.ca.us/megan/index.htm.

   B. *Military Ordnance Location.* Buyer is given notice if the home has an existing or former military training facility within one mile of the property. The issue is the possibility of hazardous bombs and other explosives near the home.

   C. *Home Inspection Notice.* Buyer must sign an *Importance of a Home Inspection notice.* The purpose is to encourage the buyer to order an independent home inspection prior to purchasing the property.

   D. *Water Heater Bracing and Smoke Detector Notice.* Buyer must be given notice that the water heater is braced according to building codes and that the property meets the legal requirements for properly operating smoke detectors.

The above list includes many major, but not all, material facts and disclosures that should be given to a buyer in a 1- to 4-unit residential real estate transaction. Individual cases and circumstances will vary. For additional information about what other disclosures might be required in a particular sales transaction, readers should get appropriate legal advice or consult other qualified experts.

OPTIONS

An **option** is a contract between the owner of a property (the optionor) and a potential purchaser (an optionee). Under an option, the optionor gives to the optionee the right to purchase real estate under a set of terms and conditions within a designated time period. To be binding, the optionee must pay consideration to the optionor.

Here is the key point: The optionee is not required to exercise the option (purchase the property). The optionee has the choice of buying or not buying. If the optionee decides to buy, the owner must sell under the terms of the option. If the optionee decides not to buy, the optionor (owner) keeps the option fee.

Sometimes a combination of lease and option is used, by which a person leases the property for a certain time and then has the option to purchase the property when the lease expires. The use of lease or option agreements usually increases during "tight" markets when sellers have a difficult time finding buyers. The seller attempts to entice someone to purchase by allowing the person(s) to rent for a while, then buy later—a sort of try-before-you-buy situation.

Broker Supervision and Recordkeeping

A broker is required to exercise reasonable supervision over the activities of his or her salespeople. Reasonable supervision includes the establishment of policies, rules, procedures, and systems to review, oversee, inspect, and manage the activities that require a real estate license.

A real estate broker is required to keep copies of all listings, deposit receipts, canceled checks, trust funds, and any other documents in connection with any sale transaction for at least three years. Forms pertaining to acting as a mortgage broker must be kept for four years. As noted in Chapter 4, a broker must also maintain current trust fund records.

5.4 SAMPLE CONTRACTS

The appendix of this chapter includes samples of contracts and forms typically used in a simple real estate residential sale. The forms are copyrighted by the CALIFORNIA ASSOCIATION OF REALTORS® and are reprinted with permission by the CALIFORNIA ASSOCIATION OF REALTORS®. Endorsement is not implied.

The forms are as follows:

1. Residential Listing Agreement (Exclusive Authorization and Right to Sell)
2. Seller's Advisory
3. California Residential Purchase Agreement and Joint Escrow Instructions
4. Real Estate Transfer Disclosure Statement (This form is being revised and will be available in November, 2010.)
5. Buyer's Inspection Advisory

Real estate contracts and forms are subject to change as new laws and/or regulations are enacted. A situation may occur in a real estate transaction that would require a specialized, as opposed to standard, form. All parties should seek legal and other advice from qualified professionals.

CHAPTER SUMMARY

A contract is an agreement between two or more persons, consisting of a promise or mutual promises to do or not to do certain acts. In a unilateral contract, a promise is made by one party in exchange for an act by another party. In a bilateral contract, one party exchanges promises with another party. Contracts may be created by expression or implication. Contracts can be valid, void, voidable, and unenforceable.

There are five essential elements of a real estate contract: (1) parties capable of contracting; (2) mutual consent; (3) a lawful object; (4) sufficient consideration; and (5) according to the Statute of Frauds, the contract must be in writing. An executed contract is one that has been completed or fulfilled. An executory contract is one that remains to be fulfilled.

Full performance discharges or terminates a contract. Contracts can also be terminated by expiration of time and mutual consent, in addition to other technical means. A breach of contract means that at least one of the parties did not fulfill its part of the agreement. The two most common remedies for a breach are to sue for damages or to sue for specific performance. The Statute of Limitations prescribes the time period within which a lawsuit must be filed. Beyond the prescribed period, a person's rights are said to have outlawed.

A real estate contract should contain the date of the agreement, the names and addresses of the parties, a description of the property, the consideration, the mortgage terms, the date and place of closing the contract, and any other provisions required or requested by the parties. A listing agreement is the contract between the principal, usually the seller, and the real estate broker. Types of listings include the open, exclusive agency, exclusive authorization and right-to-sell, and net listing. The multiple listing service (MLS) is an organization whereby member brokers agree to pool listings and share information and commissions.

The Purchase Agreement is the contract between the buyer and seller. To be binding, certain requirements must be met. Common real estate forms are provided in this chapter. For 1- to 4-unit residential properties, various disclosure statements must be presented to the buyer before the close of the sale.

IMPORTANT TERMS AND CONCEPTS

bilateral contract

contract

counteroffer

deposit receipt

exclusive agency listing

exclusive authorization and right-to-sell listing

executed contract

executory contract

expressed contract

fiduciary relationship

full performance

implied contract

multiple listing service (MLS)

net listing

open listing

option

statute of frauds

statute of limitations

unenforceable

unilateral contract

valid

void

voidable

PRACTICAL APPLICATION

1. Sara Hennings, age 17, joins the Army and then signs a lease agreement and moves into an apartment near the base. Using correct contract language, describe in complete detail Sara's contract, beginning with words such as *unilateral, bilateral, expressed, implied, executed, executory, valid, void, voidable,* and *unenforceable.*

2. Homeowner Vargas signed a 180-day exclusive authorization and right-to-sell listing with Sunrise Realty. After 90 days, Vargas unilaterally canceled the listing and gave it to Ambrosini Properties, who 10 days later brought in a full-price offer. The sale closed and a full commission was paid to Ambrosini Properties. Later Sunrise Realty filed a lawsuit for another full commission. What are the legal issues?

3. An old run-down rental home is listed for sale with a real estate company in "as is condition." The seller knows that the roof leaks and that the electrical system frequently shorts out and blows fuses. The seller does not mention this to the listing real estate agent. A buyer agrees to purchase the home "as is." For the seller and the real estate agent, what are the Real Estate Transfer Disclosure Statement requirements?

REVIEWING YOUR UNDERSTANDING

1. All of the following are covered by the Statute of Frauds, except for
   a. the payment of an agent's commission.
   b. a two-year lease.
   c. an agreement not to be performed within the lifetime of the promisor.
   d. a six-month tenancy.

2. Which of the following is not considered an essential element of a real estate contract?
   a. Consent of the parties
   b. A lawful object
   c. Consideration
   d. Parol evidence

3. Contracts may be discharged by
   a. impossibility of performance.
   b. agreement of the parties.
   c. both (a) and (b).
   d. none of the above.

4. The most common form of listing agreement found in California is
   a. an open listing.
   b. an exclusive authorization and right-to-sell listing.
   c. a net listing.
   d. an exclusive agency listing.

5. By law, which of the following listings must have a definite termination date?
   a. Net listing
   b. Exclusive agency
   c. Exclusive authorization and right-to-sell listing
   d. Both (b) and (c)

6. Of the following listings, which stipulates that the agent may earn anything over the seller's stipulated amount after giving the seller proper disclosure?
   a. Net listing
   b. Exclusive agency
   c. Exclusive authorization and right-to-sell listing
   d. Open listing

7. A listing is
   a. a unilateral contract.
   b. a bilateral contract.
   c. both (a) and (b).
   d. none of the above.

8. A deposit receipt is
   a. a receipt for the buyer's deposit.
   b. a real estate purchase contract when properly executed.
   c. a common term for the purchase contract.
   d. all of the above.

9. Which of the following statements is true if, during the escrow process but prior to closing the sale, a fire destroys the home being sold?
   a. Buyer must complete the purchase.
   b. Buyer need not complete the purchase, but seller retains the deposit.
   c. Buyer need not complete the purchase and is entitled to the deposit back.
   d. Buyer must complete the purchase for the land, not the remains of the building.

10. After signing a deposit receipt, the seller decides not to sell. The buyer can do all of the following, except which?
    a. Cancel the agreement and get a refund of any deposit.
    b. Sue for specific performance.
    c. Sue on criminal grounds.
    d. Sue for money damages.

11. A contract that still needs some action by one or more of the parties is
    a. executory.
    b. executed.
    c. valid.
    d. voidable.

12. Within the prescribed time period, an inexcusable delay might limit a lawsuit according to the
    a. Statute of Frauds.
    b. Statute of Limitations.
    c. Doctrine of Laches.
    d. Stoppel of Contracts.

13. Which best describes a voidable contract?
    a. Valid and enforceable
    b. Valid on its face, but for some reason cannot be sued upon
    c. Valid on its face until the injured party voids the contract
    d. Void on its face until enforceable

14. A 17-year-old divorced man wishes to sell his separate real property. A real estate broker legally:
    a. can accept the listing.
    b. cannot accept the listing until the owner is 18 years old.
    c. can accept the listing only if the owner has a legal guardian.
    d. cannot accept the listing unless the owner's parents consent.

15. The real estate transfer disclosure statement is signed by whom?
    a. Buyer only
    b. Seller only
    c. Seller and agent/broker only
    d. Buyer, seller, and agent/broker

16. Which of the following requires a real estate agent to do a physical inspection of the home and report the results of said inspection?
    a. A disclosure regarding real estate agency relationship
    b. A natural hazard disclosure statement
    c. A common interest development general information
    d. A real estate transfer disclosure statement

17. Megan's Law is concerned with which issue?
    a. The location of registered sex offenders
    b. The possibility of mold and its required disclosure
    c. The issue of AIDS and/or death in the home
    d. The hazards of earthquakes and unbraced water heaters

18. Prior to signing a listing agreement, the seller asks the real estate agent, "What is the commission rate in our area?" According to regulations and the CALIFORNIA ASSOCIA-TION OF REALTORS® Residential Listing Agreement in the appendix of this chapter, the correct answer is which of the following?
    a. "6 percent."
    b. "All commission rates are negotiable."
    c. "The association of REALTORS® says 7 percent."
    d. "The Department of Real Estate says no more than 10 percent."

19. When an offer from a potential buyer is presented to the seller, the seller asks if the buyer is a member of a minority race. The broker presenting the offer should respond as follows:
    a. "Yes, I think so."
    b. "I don't know, but I'll find out and let you know before you are legally required to sell."
    c. "By law and per my business practice, that information is not relevant."
    d. "No, I checked them out per your previous request."

20. The disclosure requirement concerned with special flood areas, dam failure, high fire severity, wildland forest fires, earthquake fault zones, and seismic hazard zones is the
    a. real estate transfer disclosure statement.
    b. residential environmental and earthquake hazards disclosures.
    c. natural hazard disclosure statement.
    d. home inspection notice.

21. When a buyer is purchasing a condominium or a unit in a planned unit development (PUD), said buyer must be given which of the following regarding the CC&Rs, homeowner dues, and financial and legal status of the homeowner's association?

  a. A seller financing addendum and disclosure statement

  b. A real estate transfer disclosure statement

  c. A common interest development general information

  d. A natural hazard disclosure statement

22. According to the residential listing agreement in the appendix of this chapter, a real estate broker is entitled to the commission if the property is sold during the listing period by

  a. the seller.

  b. the listing broker.

  c. the cooperating broker, if any.

  d. any of the above.

23. A buyer and seller sign a valid California Residential Purchase Agreement and Joint Escrow Instructions contract as outlined in the appendix of this chapter. Per the terms of the contract, any statutory and lead disclosures cannot be waived by the mutual agreement of the buyer and the seller.

  a. True

  b. False

24. Per the buyer's inspection advisory form that appears in the appendix of this chapter:

  a. The broker is presumed to be an expert in all areas listed on the form.

  b. The square footage of the home and lot has been verified by the seller.

  c. The seller is required to repair all disclosed defects.

  d. The purchase agreement obligates the seller to make the property available to the buyer for the investigations.

25. The real estate transfer disclosure statement that appears in the appendix of this chapter requires the form to be signed by the listing real estate agent, not by a separate real estate agent who represents the buyer.

  a. True

  b. False

Appendix

Sample Forms

The appendix of this chapter includes samples of contracts and forms typically used in a simple real estate residential sale. The forms are copyrighted by the CALIFORNIA ASSOCIATION OF REALTORS® and are reprinted with permission by the CALIFORNIA ASSOCIATION OF REALTORS®. Endorsement is not implied.

The forms are as follows:

1. Residential Listing Agreement (Exclusive Authorization and Right to Sell) (Figure 5.5)
2. Seller's Advisory (Figure 5.6)
3. California Residential Purchase Agreement and Joint Escrow Instructions (Figure 5.7)
4. Real Estate Transfer Disclosure Statement (Figure 5.8)
5. Buyer's Inspection Advisory (Figure 5.9)
6. Agent Visual Inspection Disclosure (Figure 5.10)

Real estate contracts and forms are subject to change as new laws and/or regulations are enacted. Situations may occur in a real estate transaction that require specialized, as opposed to standard, contract forms. All parties should seek legal and other advice from qualified professionals.

FIGURE 5.5

RESIDENTIAL LISTING AGREEMENT
(Exclusive Authorization and Right to Sell)
(C.A.R. Form RLA, Revised 4/07)

a1. EXCLUSIVE RIGHT TO SELL: _____ ("Seller")
hereby employs and grants _____ ("Broker")
beginning (date) _____ and ending at 11:59 P.M. on (date) _____ ("Listing Period")
the exclusive and irrevocable right to sell or exchange the real property in the City of _____,
County of _____, Assessor's Parcel No. _____,
California, described as:_____ ("Property").

2. ITEMS EXCLUDED AND INCLUDED: Unless otherwise specified in a real estate purchase agreement, all fixtures and fittings that are attached to the Property are included, and personal property items are excluded, from the purchase price.
ADDITIONAL ITEMS EXCLUDED: _____.
ADDITIONAL ITEMS INCLUDED: _____
Seller intends that the above items be excluded or included in offering the Property for sale, but understands that: **(i)** the purchase agreement supersedes any intention expressed above and will ultimately determine which items are excluded and included in the sale; and **(ii)** Broker is not responsible for and does not guarantee that the above exclusions and/or inclusions will be in the purchase agreement.

3. LISTING PRICE AND TERMS:
    A. The listing price shall be: _____
    _____ Dollars ($ _____).
    B. Additional Terms: _____
    _____.

4. COMPENSATION TO BROKER:
Notice: The amount or rate of real estate commissions is not fixed by law. They are set by each Broker individually and may be negotiable between Seller and Broker (real estate commissions include all compensation and fees to Broker).
    A. Seller agrees to pay to Broker as compensation for services irrespective of agency relationship(s), either ☐ _____ percent of the listing price (or if a purchase agreement is entered into, of the purchase price), or ☐ $ _____, AND _____, as follows:
        (1) If during the Listing Period, or any extension, Broker, Seller, cooperating broker, or any other person procures a buyer(s) who offers to purchase the Property on the above price and terms, or on any price and terms acceptable to Seller. (Broker is entitled to compensation whether any escrow resulting from such offer closes during or after the expiration of the Listing Period.)
    OR (2) If within _____ calendar days **(a)** after the end of the Listing Period or any extension; or **(b)** after any cancellation of this Agreement, unless otherwise agreed, Seller enters into a contract to sell, convey, lease or otherwise transfer the Property to anyone ("Prospective Buyer") or that person's related entity: **(i)** who physically entered and was shown the Property during the Listing Period or any extension by Broker or a cooperating broker; or **(ii)** for whom Broker or any cooperating broker submitted to Seller a signed, written offer to acquire, lease, exchange or obtain an option on the Property. Seller, however, shall have no obligation to Broker under paragraph 4A(2) unless, not later than **3 calendar days** after the end of the Listing Period or any extension or cancellation, Broker has given Seller a written notice of the names of such Prospective Buyers.
    OR (3) If, without Broker's prior written consent, the Property is withdrawn from sale, conveyed, leased, rented, otherwise transferred, or made unmarketable by a voluntary act of Seller during the Listing Period, or any extension.
    B. If completion of the sale is prevented by a party to the transaction other than Seller, then compensation due under paragraph 4A shall be payable only if and when Seller collects damages by suit, arbitration, settlement or otherwise, and then in an amount equal to the lesser of one-half of the damages recovered or the above compensation, after first deducting title and escrow expenses and the expenses of collection, if any.
    C. In addition, Seller agrees to pay Broker: _____.
    D. Seller has been advised of Broker's policy regarding cooperation with, and the amount of compensation offered to, other brokers.
        (1) Broker is authorized to cooperate with and compensate brokers participating through the multiple listing service(s) ("MLS") by offering MLS brokers either ☐ _____ percent of the purchase price, or ☐ $ _____.
        (2) Broker is authorized to cooperate with and compensate brokers operating outside the MLS as per Broker's policy.
    E. Seller hereby irrevocably assigns to Broker the above compensation from Seller's funds and proceeds in escrow. Broker may submit this Agreement, as instructions to compensate Broker pursuant to paragraph 4A, to any escrow regarding the Property involving Seller and a buyer, Prospective Buyer or other transferee.
    F. **(1)** Seller represents that Seller has not previously entered into a listing agreement with another broker regarding the Property, unless specified as follows: _____.
        (2) Seller warrants that Seller has no obligation to pay compensation to any other broker regarding the Property unless the Property is transferred to any of the following individuals or entities: _____
        _____.
        (3) If the Property is sold to anyone listed above during the time Seller is obligated to compensate another broker: **(i)** Broker is not entitled to compensation under this Agreement; and **(ii)** Broker is not obligated to represent Seller in such transaction.

Seller acknowledges receipt of a copy of this page.
Seller's Initials (_____)(_____)

RLA REVISED 4/07 (PAGE 1 OF 3) Print Date

Reviewed by _____ Date _____

EQUAL HOUSING OPPORTUNITY

RESIDENTIAL LISTING AGREEMENT - EXCLUSIVE (RLA PAGE 1 OF 3)

FIGURE 5.5 *(continued)*

Property Address: _____ Date: _____

5. **OWNERSHIP, TITLE AND AUTHORITY:** Seller warrants that: **(i)** Seller is the owner of the Property; **(ii)** no other persons or entities have title to the Property; and **(iii)** Seller has the authority to both execute this Agreement and sell the Property. Exceptions to ownership, title and authority are as follows: _____.

6. **MULTIPLE LISTING SERVICE:** All terms of the transaction, including financing, if applicable, will be provided to the selected MLS for publication, dissemination and use by persons and entities on terms approved by the MLS. Seller authorizes Broker to comply with all applicable MLS rules. MLS rules allow MLS data to be made available by the MLS to additional Internet sites unless Broker gives the MLS instructions to the contrary. MLS rules generally provide that residential real property and vacant lot listings be submitted to the MLS within 48 hours or some other period of time after all necessary signatures have been obtained on the listing agreement. However, Broker will not have to submit this listing to the MLS if, within that time, Broker submits to the MLS a form signed by Seller (C.A.R. Form SEL or the locally required form) instructing Broker to withhold the listing from the MLS. Information about this listing will be provided to the MLS of Broker's selection unless a form instructing Broker to withhold the listing from the MLS is attached to this listing Agreement.

7. **SELLER REPRESENTATIONS:** Seller represents that, unless otherwise specified in writing, Seller is unaware of: **(i)** any Notice of Default recorded against the Property; **(ii)** any delinquent amounts due under any loan secured by, or other obligation affecting, the Property; **(iii)** any bankruptcy, insolvency or similar proceeding affecting the Property; **(iv)** any litigation, arbitration, administrative action, government investigation or other pending or threatened action that affects or may affect the Property or Seller's ability to transfer it; and **(v)** any current, pending or proposed special assessments affecting the Property. Seller shall promptly notify Broker in writing if Seller becomes aware of any of these items during the Listing Period or any extension thereof.

8. **BROKER'S AND SELLER'S DUTIES:** Broker agrees to exercise reasonable effort and due diligence to achieve the purposes of this Agreement. Unless Seller gives Broker written instructions to the contrary, Broker is authorized to order reports and disclosures as appropriate or necessary and advertise and market the Property by any method and in any medium selected by Broker, including MLS and the Internet, and, to the extent permitted by these media, control the dissemination of the information submitted to any medium. Seller agrees to consider offers presented by Broker, and to act in good faith to accomplish the sale of the Property by, among other things, making the Property available for showing at reasonable times and referring to Broker all inquiries of any party interested in the Property. Seller is responsible for determining at what price to list and sell the Property. **Seller further agrees to indemnify, defend and hold Broker harmless from all claims, disputes, litigation, judgments and attorney fees arising from any incorrect information supplied by Seller, or from any material facts that Seller knows but fails to disclose.**

9. **DEPOSIT:** Broker is authorized to accept and hold on Seller's behalf any deposits to be applied toward the purchase price.

10. **AGENCY RELATIONSHIPS:**
    A. **Disclosure:** If the Property includes residential property with one-to-four dwelling units, Seller shall receive a "Disclosure Regarding Agency Relationships" form prior to entering into this Agreement.
    B. **Seller Representation:** Broker shall represent Seller in any resulting transaction, except as specified in paragraph 4F.
    C. **Possible Dual Agency With Buyer:** Depending upon the circumstances, it may be necessary or appropriate for Broker to act as an agent for both Seller and buyer, exchange party, or one or more additional parties ("Buyer"). Broker shall, as soon as practicable, disclose to Seller any election to act as a dual agent representing both Seller and Buyer. If a Buyer is procured directly by Broker or an associate-licensee in Broker's firm, Seller hereby consents to Broker acting as a dual agent for Seller and such Buyer. In the event of an exchange, Seller hereby consents to Broker collecting compensation from additional parties for services rendered, provided there is disclosure to all parties of such agency and compensation. Seller understands and agrees that: **(i)** Broker, without the prior written consent of Seller, will not disclose to Buyer that Seller is willing to sell the Property at a price less than the listing price; **(ii)** Broker, without the prior written consent of Buyer, will not disclose to Seller that Buyer is willing to pay a price greater than the offered price; and **(iii)** except for (i) and (ii) above, a dual agent is obligated to disclose known facts materially affecting the value or desirability of the Property to both parties.
    D. **Other Sellers:** Seller understands that Broker may have or obtain listings on other properties, and that potential buyers may consider, make offers on, or purchase through Broker, property the same as or similar to Seller's Property. Seller consents to Broker's representation of sellers and buyers of other properties before, during and after the end of this Agreement.
    E. **Confirmation:** If the Property includes residential property with one-to-four dwelling units, Broker shall confirm the agency relationship described above, or as modified, in writing, prior to or concurrent with Seller's execution of a purchase agreement.

11. **SECURITY AND INSURANCE:** Broker is not responsible for loss of or damage to personal or real property, or person, whether attributable to use of a keysafe/lockbox, a showing of the Property, or otherwise. Third parties, including, but not limited to, appraisers, inspectors, brokers and prospective buyers, may have access to, and take videos and photographs of, the interior of the Property. Seller agrees: **(i)** to take reasonable precautions to safeguard and protect valuables that might be accessible during showings of the Property; and **(ii)** to obtain insurance to protect against these risks. Broker does not maintain insurance to protect Seller.

12. **KEYSAFE/LOCKBOX:** A keysafe/lockbox is designed to hold a key to the Property to permit access to the Property by Broker, cooperating brokers, MLS participants, their authorized licensees and representatives, authorized inspectors, and accompanied prospective buyers. Broker, cooperating brokers, MLS and Associations/Boards of REALTORS® are **not** insurers against injury, theft, loss, vandalism or damage attributed to the use of a keysafe/lockbox. Seller does (or if checked ☐ does not) authorize Broker to install a keysafe/lockbox. If Seller does not occupy the Property, Seller shall be responsible for obtaining occupant(s)' written permission for use of a keysafe/lockbox.

13. **SIGN:** Seller does (or if checked ☐ does not) authorize Broker to install a FOR SALE/SOLD sign on the Property.

14. **EQUAL HOUSING OPPORTUNITY:** The Property is offered in compliance with federal, state and local anti-discrimination laws.

15. **ATTORNEY FEES:** In any action, proceeding or arbitration between Seller and Broker regarding the obligation to pay compensation under this Agreement, the prevailing Seller or Broker shall be entitled to reasonable attorney fees and costs from the non-prevailing Seller or Broker, except as provided in paragraph 19A.

16. **ADDITIONAL TERMS:** _____
_____
_____

Seller acknowledges receipt of a copy of this page.
Seller's Initials (_____)(_____)

RLA REVISED 4/07 (PAGE 2 OF 3)

Reviewed by _____ Date _____

EQUAL HOUSING
OPPORTUNITY

RESIDENTIAL LISTING AGREEMENT - EXCLUSIVE (RLA PAGE 2 OF 3)

FIGURE 5.5 (continued)

Property Address: _____ Date: _____

17. **MANAGEMENT APPROVAL:** If an associate-licensee in Broker's office (salesperson or broker-associate) enters into this Agreement on Broker's behalf, and Broker or Manager does not approve of its terms, Broker or Manager has the right to cancel this Agreement, in writing, within **5 Days** After its execution.

18. **SUCCESSORS AND ASSIGNS:** This Agreement shall be binding upon Seller and Seller's successors and assigns.

19. **DISPUTE RESOLUTION:**

   A. **MEDIATION:** Seller and Broker agree to mediate any dispute or claim arising between them out of this Agreement, or any resulting transaction, before resorting to arbitration or court action, subject to paragraph 19B(2) below. Paragraph 19B(2) below applies whether or not the arbitration provision is initialed. Mediation fees, if any, shall be divided equally among the parties involved. If, for any dispute or claim to which this paragraph applies, any party commences an action without first attempting to resolve the matter through mediation, or refuses to mediate after a request has been made, then that party shall not be entitled to recover attorney fees, even if they would otherwise be available to that party in any such action. THIS MEDIATION PROVISION APPLIES WHETHER OR NOT THE ARBITRATION PROVISION IS INITIALED.

   B. **ARBITRATION OF DISPUTES: (1)** Seller and Broker agree that any dispute or claim in law or equity arising between them regarding the obligation to pay compensation under this Agreement, which is not settled through mediation, shall be decided by neutral, binding arbitration, including and subject to paragraph 19B(2) below. The arbitrator shall be a retired judge or justice, or an attorney with at least 5 years of residential real estate law experience, unless the parties mutually agree to a different arbitrator, who shall render an award in accordance with substantive California law. The parties shall have the right to discovery in accordance with California Code of Civil Procedure §1283.05. In all other respects, the arbitration shall be conducted in accordance with Title 9 of Part III of the California Code of Civil Procedure. Judgment upon the award of the arbitrator(s) may be entered in any court having jurisdiction. Interpretation of this agreement to arbitrate shall be governed by the Federal Arbitration Act.
   (2) EXCLUSIONS FROM MEDIATION AND ARBITRATION: The following matters are excluded from mediation and arbitration: (i) a judicial or non-judicial foreclosure or other action or proceeding to enforce a deed of trust, mortgage, or installment land sale contract as defined in California Civil Code §2985; (ii) an unlawful detainer action; (iii) the filing or enforcement of a mechanic's lien; and (iv) any matter that is within the jurisdiction of a probate, small claims, or bankruptcy court. The filing of a court action to enable the recording of a notice of pending action, for order of attachment, receivership, injunction, or other provisional remedies, shall not constitute a waiver of the mediation and arbitration provisions.
   "NOTICE: BY INITIALING IN THE SPACE BELOW YOU ARE AGREEING TO HAVE ANY DISPUTE ARISING OUT OF THE MATTERS INCLUDED IN THE 'ARBITRATION OF DISPUTES' PROVISION DECIDED BY NEUTRAL ARBITRATION AS PROVIDED BY CALIFORNIA LAW AND YOU ARE GIVING UP ANY RIGHTS YOU MIGHT POSSESS TO HAVE THE DISPUTE LITIGATED IN A COURT OR JURY TRIAL. BY INITIALING IN THE SPACE BELOW YOU ARE GIVING UP YOUR JUDICIAL RIGHTS TO DISCOVERY AND APPEAL, UNLESS THOSE RIGHTS ARE SPECIFICALLY INCLUDED IN THE 'ARBITRATION OF DISPUTES' PROVISION. IF YOU REFUSE TO SUBMIT TO ARBITRATION AFTER AGREEING TO THIS PROVISION, YOU MAY BE COMPELLED TO ARBITRATE UNDER THE AUTHORITY OF THE CALIFORNIA CODE OF CIVIL PROCEDURE. YOUR AGREEMENT TO THIS ARBITRATION PROVISION IS VOLUNTARY."
   "WE HAVE READ AND UNDERSTAND THE FOREGOING AND AGREE TO SUBMIT DISPUTES ARISING OUT OF THE MATTERS INCLUDED IN THE 'ARBITRATION OF DISPUTES' PROVISION TO NEUTRAL ARBITRATION."

   Seller's Initials _____/_____   Broker's Initials _____/_____

20. **ENTIRE AGREEMENT:** All prior discussions, negotiations and agreements between the parties concerning the subject matter of this Agreement are superseded by this Agreement, which constitutes the entire contract and a complete and exclusive expression of their agreement, and may not be contradicted by evidence of any prior agreement or contemporaneous oral agreement. If any provision of this Agreement is held to be ineffective or invalid, the remaining provisions will nevertheless be given full force and effect. This Agreement and any supplement, addendum or modification, including any photocopy or facsimile, may be executed in counterparts.

By signing below, Seller acknowledges that Seller has read, understands, received a copy of and agrees to the terms of this Agreement.

Seller _____ Date _____
Address _____ City _____ State _____ Zip _____
Telephone _____ Fax _____ E-mail _____

Seller _____ Date _____
Address _____ City _____ State _____ Zip _____
Telephone _____ Fax _____ E-mail _____

Real Estate Broker (Firm) _____ DRE Lic. # _____
By (Agent) _____ DRE Lic. # _____ Date _____
Address _____ City _____ State _____ Zip _____
Telephone _____ Fax _____ E-mail _____

THIS FORM HAS BEEN APPROVED BY THE CALIFORNIA ASSOCIATION OF REALTORS® (C.A.R.). NO REPRESENTATION IS MADE AS TO THE LEGAL VALIDITY OR ADEQUACY OF ANY PROVISION IN ANY SPECIFIC TRANSACTION. A REAL ESTATE BROKER IS THE PERSON QUALIFIED TO ADVISE ON REAL ESTATE TRANSACTIONS. IF YOU DESIRE LEGAL OR TAX ADVICE, CONSULT AN APPROPRIATE PROFESSIONAL.
This form is available for use by the entire real estate industry. It is not intended to identify the user as a REALTOR®. REALTOR® is a registered collective membership mark which may be used only by members of the NATIONAL ASSOCIATION OF REALTORS® who subscribe to its Code of Ethics.

Published and Distributed by:
REAL ESTATE BUSINESS SERVICES, INC.
a subsidiary of the California Association of REALTORS®
525 South Virgil Avenue, Los Angeles, California 90020

Reviewed by _____ Date _____

RLA REVISED 4/07 (PAGE 3 OF 3)

RESIDENTIAL LISTING AGREEMENT - EXCLUSIVE (RLA PAGE 3 OF 3)

Source: Reprinted with permission of California Association of REALTORS®

FIGURE 5.6

CALIFORNIA
ASSOCIATION
OF REALTORS®

SELLER'S ADVISORY
(C.A.R. Form SA, Revised 10/01)

Property Address: _____ ("Property")

1. **INTRODUCTION:** Selling property in California is a process that involves many steps. From start to finish, it could take anywhere from a few weeks to many months, depending upon the condition of your Property, local market conditions and other factors. You have already taken an important first step by listing your Property for sale with a licensed real estate broker. Your broker will help guide you through the process and may refer you to other professionals as needed. This advisory addresses many things you may need to think about and do as you market your Property. Some of these things are requirements imposed upon you, either by law or the listing or sale contract. Others are simply practical matters that may arise during the process. Please read this document carefully and, if you have any questions, ask your broker for help.

2. **DISCLOSURES:**

    A. **General Disclosure Duties:** You must affirmatively disclose to the buyer, in writing, any and all known facts that materially affect the value or desirability of your Property. You must disclose these facts whether or not asked about such matters by the buyer, any broker, or anyone else. This duty to disclose applies even if the buyer agrees to purchase your Property in its present condition without requiring you to make any repairs. If the Property you are selling is a residence with one to four units, your broker also has a duty to conduct a reasonably competent and diligent visual inspection of the accessible areas and to disclose to a buyer all adverse material facts that the inspection reveals. If your broker discovers something that could indicate a problem, your broker must advise the buyer.

    B. **Statutory Duties** (For one-to-four Residential Units):

    (1) You must timely prepare and deliver to the buyer, among other things, a Real Estate Transfer Disclosure Statement ("TDS"), and a Natural Hazard Disclosure Statement ("NHD"). You have a legal obligation to honestly and completely fill out the TDS form in its entirety. (Many local entities or organizations have their own supplement to the TDS that you may also be asked to complete.) The NHD is a statement indicating whether your Property is in certain designated flood, fire or earthquake/seismic hazard zones. Third-party professional companies can help you with this task.

    (2) Depending upon the age and type of construction of your Property, you may also be required to provide and, in certain cases you can receive limited legal protection by providing, the buyer with booklets titled "The Homeowner's Guide to Earthquake Safety," "The Commercial Property Owner's Guide to Earthquake Safety," "Protect Your Family From Lead in Your Home" and "Environmental Hazards: A Guide For Homeowners and Buyers." Some of these booklets may be packaged together for your convenience. The earthquake guides ask you to answer specific questions about your Property's structure and preparedness for an earthquake. If you are required to supply the booklet about lead, you will also be required to disclose to the buyer any known lead-based paint and lead-based paint hazards on a separate form. The environmental hazards guide informs the buyer of common environmental hazards that may be found in properties.

    (3) If you know that your property is: **(i)** located within one mile of a former military ordnance location; or **(ii)** in or affected by a zone or district allowing manufacturing, commercial or airport use, you must disclose this to the buyer. You are also required to make a good faith effort to obtain and deliver to the buyer a disclosure notice from the appropriate local agency(ies) about any special tax levied on your Property pursuant to the Mello-Roos Community Facilities Act.

    (4) If the TDS, NHD, or lead, military ordnance, commercial zone or Mello-Roos disclosures are provided to a buyer after you accept that buyer's offer, the buyer will have 3 days after delivery (or 5 days if mailed) to terminate the offer, which is why it is extremely important to complete these disclosures as soon as possible. There are certain exemptions from these statutory requirements. However, if you have actual knowledge of any of these items, you may still be required to make a disclosure as the items can be considered material facts.

    C. **Death and Other Disclosures:** Many buyers consider death on real property to be a material fact in the purchase of property. In some situations, it is advisable to disclose that a death occurred or the manner of death. However, California Civil Code Section 1710.2 provides that <u>you have no disclosure duty</u> "where the death has occurred more than three years prior to the date the transferee offers to purchase, lease, or rent the real property, or [regardless of the date of occurrence] that an occupant of that property was afflicted with, or died from, Human T-Lymphotropic Virus Type III/Lymphadenopathy-Associated Virus." This law does not "immunize an owner or his or her agent from making an intentional misrepresentation in response to a direct inquiry from a transferee or a prospective transferee of real property, concerning deaths on the real property."

    D. **Condominiums and Other Common Interest Subdivisions:** If the Property is a condominium, townhouse, or other property in a common interest subdivision, you must provide to the buyer copies of the governing documents, the most recent financial statements distributed, and other documents required by law or contract. If you do not have a current version of these documents, you can request them from the management of your homeowners' association. To avoid delays, you are encouraged to obtain these documents as soon as possible, even if you have not yet entered into a purchase agreement to sell your Property.

SA REVISED 10/01 (PAGE 1 OF 2) Print Date

Seller's Initials (_____)(_____)

| Reviewed by _____ Date _____ |

EQUAL HOUSING
OPPORTUNITY

SELLER'S ADVISORY (SA PAGE 1 OF 2)

FIGURE 5.6   *(continued)*

Property Address: _____ Date: _____

3. **CONTRACT TERMS AND LEGAL REQUIREMENTS:**
    A. **Contract Terms and Conditions:** A buyer may request, as part of the contract for the sale of your Property, that you pay for repairs to the Property and other items. Your decision on whether or not to comply with a buyer's requests may affect your ability to sell your Property at a specified price.
    B. **Withholding Taxes:** Under federal and California tax laws, a buyer is required to withhold a portion of the purchase price from your sale proceeds for tax purposes unless you sign an affidavit of non-foreign status and California residency, or some other exemption applies and is documented.
    C. **Prohibition Against Discrimination:** Discriminatory conduct in the sale of real property against individuals belonging to legally protected classes is a violation of the law.
    D. **Government Retrofit Standards:** Unless exempt, you must comply with government retrofit standards, including, but not limited to, installing operable smoke detectors, bracing water heaters, and providing the buyer with corresponding written statements of compliance. Some city and county governments may impose additional retrofit standards, including, but not limited to, installing low-flow toilets and showerheads, gas shut-off valves, tempered glass, and barriers around swimming pools and spas. You should consult with the appropriate governmental agencies, inspectors, and other professionals to determine the retrofit standards for your Property, the extent to which your Property complies with such standards, and the costs, if any, of compliance.
    E. **Legal, Tax and Other Implications:** Selling your Property may have legal, tax, insurance, title or other implications. You should consult an appropriate professional for advice on these matters.
4. **MARKETING CONSIDERATIONS:**
    A. **Pre-Sale Considerations:** You should consider doing what you can to prepare your Property for sale, such as correcting any defects or other problems. Many people are not aware of defects in or problems with their own Property. One way to make yourself aware is to obtain professional home inspections prior to sale, both generally, and for wood destroying pests and organisms, such as termites. By doing this, you then have an opportunity to make repairs before your Property is offered for sale, which may enhance its marketability. Keep in mind, however, that any problems revealed by such inspection reports should be disclosed to the buyer (see "Disclosures" in paragraph 2 above). This is true even if the buyer gets his/her own inspections covering the same area. Obtaining inspection reports may also assist you during contract negotiations with the buyer. For example, if a pest control report has both a primary and secondary recommendation for clearance, you may want to specify in the purchase agreement those recommendations, if any, for which you are going to pay.
    B. **Post-Sale Protections:** It is often helpful to provide the buyer with, among other things, a home protection/warranty plan for the Property. These plans will generally cover problems, not deemed to be pre-existing, that occur after your sale is completed. In the event something does go wrong after the sale, and it is covered by the plan, the buyer may be able to resolve the concern by contacting the home protection company.
    C. **Safety Precautions:** Advertising and marketing your Property for sale, including, but not limited to, holding open houses, placing a keysafe/lockbox, erecting FOR SALE signs, and disseminating photographs, video tapes, and virtual tours of the premises, may jeopardize your personal safety and that of your Property. You are strongly encouraged to maintain insurance, and to take any and all possible precautions and safeguards to protect yourself, other occupants, visitors, your Property, and your belongings, including cash, jewelry, drugs, firearms and other valuables located on the Property against injury, theft, loss, vandalism, damage, and other harm.
    D. **Expenses:** You are advised that you, not the Broker, are responsible for the fees and costs, if any, to comply with your duties and obligations to the buyer of your Property.
5. **OTHER ITEMS:**_____
    _____
    _____
    _____
    _____

Seller has read and understands this Advisory. By signing below, Seller acknowledges receipt of a copy of this document.

Seller _____ Date _____

Print Name _____

Seller _____ Date _____

Print Name _____

Real Estate Broker _____ By _____
                                                      (Agent)

Address _____ City _____ State _____ Zip _____

Telephone _____ Fax _____ E-mail _____

Published and Distributed by:
REAL ESTATE BUSINESS SERVICES, INC.
a subsidiary of the California Association of REALTORS®
525 South Virgil Avenue, Los Angeles, California 90020

SA REVISED 10/01 (PAGE 2 of 2)

Reviewed by _____ Date _____

SELLER'S ADVISORY (SA PAGE 2 OF 2)

Source: Reprinted with permission of California Association of REALTORS®

FIGURE 5.7

CALIFORNIA
RESIDENTIAL PURCHASE AGREEMENT
AND JOINT ESCROW INSTRUCTIONS
For Use With Single Family Residential Property — Attached or Detached
(C.A.R. Form RPA-CA, Revised 4/10)

Date _____

1. **OFFER:**
   A. **THIS IS AN OFFER FROM** _____ ("Buyer").
   B. **THE REAL PROPERTY TO BE ACQUIRED** is described as _____
      _____, Assessor's Parcel No. _____, situated in
      _____, County of _____, California ("Property").
   C. **THE PURCHASE PRICE** offered is _____
      _____ (Dollars $ _____).
   D. **CLOSE OF ESCROW** shall occur on _____ (date) (or ☐ _____ **Days** After Acceptance).

2. **AGENCY:**
   A. **DISCLOSURE:** Buyer and Seller each acknowledge prior receipt of a "Disclosure Regarding Real Estate Agency Relationships" (C.A.R. Form AD).
   B. **POTENTIALLY COMPETING BUYERS AND SELLERS:** Buyer and Seller each acknowledge receipt of a disclosure of the possibility of multiple representation by the Broker representing that principal. This disclosure may be part of a listing agreement, buyer representation agreement or separate document (C.A.R. Form DA). Buyer understands that Broker representing Buyer may also represent other potential buyers, who may consider, make offers on or ultimately acquire the Property. Seller understands that Broker representing Seller may also represent other sellers with competing properties of interest to this Buyer.
   C. **CONFIRMATION:** The following agency relationships are hereby confirmed for this transaction:
      Listing Agent _____ (Print Firm Name) is the agent of (check one):
      ☐ the Seller exclusively; or ☐ both the Buyer and Seller.
      Selling Agent _____ (Print Firm Name) (if not the same as the Listing Agent) is the agent of (check one): ☐ the Buyer exclusively; or ☐ the Seller exclusively; or ☐ both the Buyer and Seller. Real Estate Brokers are not parties to the Agreement between Buyer and Seller.

3. **FINANCE TERMS:** Buyer represents that funds will be good when deposited with Escrow Holder.
   A. **INITIAL DEPOSIT:** Deposit shall be in the amount of ....$ _____
      (1) Buyer shall deliver deposit directly to Escrow Holder by personal check, ☐ electronic funds transfer,
      ☐ Other _____ within 3 business days after acceptance
      (or ☐ Other_____);
      OR (2) (If checked) ☐ Buyer has given the deposit by personal check (or ☐ _____)
      to the agent submitting the offer (or to ☐ _____), made payable to
      _____. The deposit shall be held uncashed until Acceptance and
      then deposited with Escrow Holder (or ☐ into Broker's trust account) within **3** business days after
      Acceptance (or ☐ Other_____).
   B. **INCREASED DEPOSIT:** Buyer shall deposit with Escrow Holder an increased deposit in the amount of ....$ _____
      within _____ **Days** After Acceptance, or ☐ _____.
      If a liquidated damages clause is incorporated into this Agreement, Buyer and Seller shall sign a
      separate liquidated damages clause (C.A.R. Form RID) for any increased deposit at the time it is
      deposited.
   C. **LOAN(S):**
      (1) FIRST LOAN: in the amount of ....$ _____
      This loan will be conventional financing or, if checked, ☐ FHA, ☐ VA, ☐ Seller (C.A.R. Form SFA),
      ☐ assumed financing (C.A.R. Form PAA), ☐ Other _____. This loan shall be at a fixed
      rate not to exceed _____% or, ☐ an adjustable rate loan with initial rate not to exceed ____%.
      Regardless of the type of loan, Buyer shall pay points not to exceed ____% of the loan amount.
      (2) ☐ **SECOND LOAN** in the amount of ....$ _____
      This loan will be conventional financing or, if checked, ☐ Seller (C.A.R. Form SFA), ☐ assumed
      financing (C.A.R. Form PAA), ☐ Other _____. This loan shall be at a fixed rate not to
      exceed _____% or, ☐ an adjustable rate loan with initial rate not to exceed ____%. Regardless
      of the type of loan, Buyer shall pay points not to exceed ____% of the loan amount.
      (3) FHA/VA: For any FHA or VA loan specified above, Buyer has **17 (or** ☐ _____**) Days** After
      Acceptance to Deliver to Seller written notice (C.A.R. Form FVA) of any lender-required repairs or
      costs that Buyer requests Seller to pay for or repair. Seller has no obligation to pay for repairs or
      satisfy lender requirements unless otherwise agreed in writing.
   D. **ADDITIONAL FINANCING TERMS:** _____
      _____
   E. **BALANCE OF PURCHASE PRICE OR DOWN PAYMENT** in the amount of ....$ _____
      to be deposited with Escrow Holder within sufficient time to close escrow.
   F. **PURCHASE PRICE (TOTAL):** ....$ _____

Buyer's Initials (_____)(_____)   Seller's Initials (_____)(_____)

RPA-CA REVISED 4/10 (PAGE 1 OF 8) Print Date BD Apr 10

Reviewed by _____ Date _____

CALIFORNIA RESIDENTIAL PURCHASE AGREEMENT (RPA-CA PAGE 1 OF 8)

FIGURE 5.7 *(continued)*

Property Address: _____   Date: _____

    G. **VERIFICATION OF DOWN PAYMENT AND CLOSING COSTS:** Buyer (or Buyer's lender or loan broker pursuant to 3H(1)) shall, within **7 (or** ☐ _____**) Days** After Acceptance, Deliver to Seller written verification of Buyer's down payment and closing costs. (If checked, ☐ verification attached.)

    H. **LOAN TERMS:**

        (1) LOAN APPLICATIONS: Within **7 (or** ☐ _____**) Days** After Acceptance, Buyer shall Deliver to Seller a letter from lender or loan broker stating that, based on a review of Buyer's written application and credit report, Buyer is prequalified or preapproved for any NEW loan specified in 3C above. (If checked, ☐ letter attached.)

        (2) LOAN CONTINGENCY: Buyer shall act diligently and in good faith to obtain the designated loan(s). Obtaining the loan(s) specified above **is a contingency** of this Agreement unless otherwise agreed in writing. Buyer's contractual obligations to obtain and provide deposit, balance of down payment and closing costs **are not contingencies** of this Agreement.

        (3) LOAN CONTINGENCY REMOVAL:

           (i) Within **17 (or** ☐ _____**) Days** After Acceptance, Buyer shall, as specified in paragraph 14, in writing remove the loan contingency or cancel this Agreement;

      OR (ii) (If checked) ☐ the loan contingency shall remain in effect until the designated loans are funded.

        (4) ☐ **NO LOAN CONTINGENCY** (If checked): Obtaining any loan specified above is NOT a contingency of this Agreement. If Buyer does not obtain the loan and as a result Buyer does not purchase the Property, Seller may be entitled to Buyer's deposit or other legal remedies.

    I. **APPRAISAL CONTINGENCY AND REMOVAL:** This Agreement is (**or, if checked,** ☐ is NOT) contingent upon a written appraisal of the Property by a licensed or certified appraiser at no less than the specified purchase price. If there is a loan contingency, Buyer's removal of the loan contingency shall be deemed removal of this appraisal contingency (**or,** ☐ if checked, Buyer shall, as specified in paragraph 14B(3), in writing remove the appraisal contingency or cancel this Agreement within **17 (or ____) Days** After Acceptance). If there is no loan contingency, Buyer shall, as specified in paragraph 14B(3), in writing remove the appraisal contingency or cancel this Agreement within **17 (or** ☐ ____**) Days** After Acceptance.

    J. ☐ **ALL CASH OFFER** (If checked): Buyer shall, within **7 (or** ☐ _____**) Days** After Acceptance, Deliver to Seller written verification of sufficient funds to close this transaction. (If checked, ☐ verification attached.)

    K. **BUYER STATED FINANCING:** Seller has relied on Buyer's representation of the type of financing specified (including but not limited to, as applicable, amount of down payment, contingent or non contingent loan, or all cash). If Buyer seeks alternate financing, (i) Seller has no obligation to cooperate with Buyer's efforts to obtain such financing, and (ii) Buyer shall also pursue the financing method specified in this Agreement. Buyer's failure to secure alternate financing does not excuse Buyer from the obligation to purchase the Property and close escrow as specified in this Agreement.

4. ALLOCATION OF COSTS (If checked): Unless otherwise specified in writing, **this paragraph** only determines who is to pay for the inspection, test or service ("Report") mentioned; it **does not determine who is to pay for any work recommended or identified in the Report.**

    A. **INSPECTIONS AND REPORTS:**

        (1) ☐ Buyer ☐ Seller shall pay for an inspection and report for wood destroying pests and organisms ("Wood Pest Report") prepared by _____ a registered structural pest control company.

        (2) ☐ Buyer ☐ Seller shall pay to have septic or private sewage disposal systems inspected _____.

        (3) ☐ Buyer ☐ Seller shall pay to have domestic wells tested for water potability and productivity _____.

        (4) ☐ Buyer ☐ Seller shall pay for a natural hazard zone disclosure report prepared by _____.

        (5) ☐ Buyer ☐ Seller shall pay for the following inspection or report _____.

        (6) ☐ Buyer ☐ Seller shall pay for the following inspection or report _____.

    B. **GOVERNMENT REQUIREMENTS AND RETROFIT:**

        (1) ☐ Buyer ☐ Seller shall pay for smoke detector installation and/or water heater bracing, if required by Law. Prior to Close Of Escrow, Seller shall provide Buyer written statement(s) of compliance in accordance with state and local Law, unless exempt.

        (2) ☐ Buyer ☐ Seller shall pay the cost of compliance with any other minimum mandatory government retrofit standards, inspections and reports if required as a condition of closing escrow under any Law. _____.

    C. **ESCROW AND TITLE:**

        (1) ☐ Buyer ☐ Seller shall pay escrow fee _____.
        Escrow Holder shall be _____.

        (2) ☐ Buyer ☐ Seller shall pay for **owner's** title insurance policy specified in paragraph 12E _____.
        Owner's title policy to be issued by _____.
        (Buyer shall pay for any title insurance policy insuring Buyer's **lender,** unless otherwise agreed in writing.)

    D. **OTHER COSTS:**

        (1) ☐ Buyer ☐ Seller shall pay County transfer tax or fee _____.

        (2) ☐ Buyer ☐ Seller shall pay City transfer tax or fee _____.

        (3) ☐ Buyer ☐ Seller shall pay Homeowners' Association ("HOA") transfer fee _____.

        (4) ☐ Buyer ☐ Seller shall pay HOA document preparation fees _____.

        (5) ☐ Buyer ☐ Seller shall pay for any private transfer fee _____.

        (6) ☐ Buyer ☐ Seller shall pay for the cost, not to exceed $ _____, of a one-year home warranty plan, issued by _____, with the following optional coverages:
        ☐ Air Conditioner ☐ Pool/Spa ☐ Code and Permit upgrade ☐ Other: _____.
        Buyer is informed that home warranty plans have many optional coverages in addition to those listed above. Buyer is advised to investigate these coverages to determine those that may be suitable for Buyer.

        (7) ☐ Buyer ☐ Seller shall pay for _____.

        (8) ☐ Buyer ☐ Seller shall pay for _____.

Buyer's Initials (_____)(_____)   Seller's Initials (_____)(_____)

RPA-CA REVISED 4/10 (PAGE 2 OF 8)

| Reviewed by _____ Date _____ |

EQUAL HOUSING OPPORTUNITY

CALIFORNIA RESIDENTIAL PURCHASE AGREEMENT (RPA-CA PAGE 2 OF 8)

FIGURE 5.7 *(continued)*

Property Address: _____   Date: _____

5. **CLOSING AND POSSESSION:**
   - **A.** Buyer intends (or ☐ does not intend) to occupy the Property as Buyer's primary residence.
   - **B.** **Seller-occupied or vacant property:** Possession shall be delivered to Buyer at 5 PM or (☐ _____ ☐ AM/☐ PM), on the date of Close Of Escrow; ☐ on _____; or ☐ no later than _____ **Days** After Close Of Escrow. If transfer of title and possession do not occur at the same time, Buyer and Seller are advised to: **(i)** enter into a written occupancy agreement (C.A.R. Form PAA, paragraph 2); and **(ii)** consult with their insurance and legal advisors.
   - **C.** **Tenant-occupied property:**
     - **(i)** **Property shall be vacant** at least 5 (or ☐ _____) **Days** Prior to Close Of Escrow, unless otherwise agreed in writing. **Note to Seller: If you are unable to deliver Property vacant in accordance with rent control and other applicable Law, you may be in breach of this Agreement.**
     - **OR (ii)** (if checked) ☐ **Tenant to remain in possession.** (C.A.R. Form PAA, paragraph 3)
   - **D.** At Close Of Escrow, **(i)** Seller assigns to Buyer any assignable warranty rights for items included in the sale, and **(ii)** Seller shall Deliver to Buyer available Copies of warranties. Brokers cannot and will not determine the assignability of any warranties.
   - **E.** At Close Of Escrow, unless otherwise agreed in writing, Seller shall provide keys and/or means to operate all locks, mailboxes, security systems, alarms and garage door openers. If Property is a condominium or located in a common interest subdivision, Buyer may be required to pay a deposit to the Homeowners' Association ("HOA") to obtain keys to accessible HOA facilities.

6. **STATUTORY DISCLOSURES (INCLUDING LEAD-BASED PAINT HAZARD DISCLOSURES) AND CANCELLATION RIGHTS:**
   - **A.** **(1)** Seller shall, within the time specified in paragraph 14A, Deliver to Buyer, if required by Law: **(i)** Federal Lead-Based Paint Disclosures (C.A.R. Form FLD) and pamphlet ("Lead Disclosures"); and **(ii)** disclosures or notices required by sections 1102 et. seq. and 1103 et. seq. of the Civil Code ("Statutory Disclosures"). Statutory Disclosures include, but are not limited to, a Real Estate Transfer Disclosure Statement ("TDS"), Natural Hazard Disclosure Statement ("NHD"), notice or actual knowledge of release of illegal controlled substance, notice of special tax and/or assessments (or, if allowed, substantially equivalent notice regarding the Mello-Roos Community Facilities Act and Improvement Bond Act of 1915) and, if Seller has actual knowledge, of industrial use and military ordnance location (C.A.R. Form SPQ or SSD).
     - **(2)** Buyer shall, within the time specified in paragraph 14B(1), return Signed Copies of the Statutory and Lead Disclosures to Seller.
     - **(3)** In the event Seller, prior to Close Of Escrow, becomes aware of adverse conditions materially affecting the Property, or any material inaccuracy in disclosures, information or representations previously provided to Buyer, Seller shall promptly provide a subsequent or amended disclosure or notice, in writing, covering those items. **However, a subsequent or amended disclosure shall not be required for conditions and material inaccuracies** of which Buyer is otherwise aware, or which are **disclosed in reports provided to or obtained by Buyer or ordered and paid for by Buyer.**
     - **(4)** If any disclosure or notice specified in 6A(1), or subsequent or amended disclosure or notice is Delivered to Buyer after the offer is Signed, Buyer shall have the right to cancel this Agreement within **3 Days** After Delivery in person, or **5 Days** After Delivery by deposit in the mail, by giving written notice of cancellation to Seller or Seller's agent.
     - **(5) Note to Buyer and Seller: Waiver of Statutory and Lead Disclosures is prohibited by Law.**
   - **B.** **NATURAL AND ENVIRONMENTAL HAZARDS:** Within the time specified in paragraph 14A, Seller shall, if required by Law: **(i)** Deliver to Buyer earthquake guides (and questionnaire) and environmental hazards booklet; **(ii)** even if exempt from the obligation to provide a NHD, disclose if the Property is located in a Special Flood Hazard Area; Potential Flooding (Inundation) Area; Very High Fire Hazard Zone; State Fire Responsibility Area; Earthquake Fault Zone; Seismic Hazard Zone; and **(iii)** disclose any other zone as required by Law and provide any other information required for those zones.
   - **C.** **WITHHOLDING TAXES:** Within the time specified in paragraph 14A, to avoid required withholding, Seller shall Deliver to Buyer or qualified substitute, an affidavit sufficient to comply with federal (FIRPTA) and California withholding Law (C.A.R. Form AS or QS).
   - **D.** **MEGAN'S LAW DATABASE DISCLOSURE:** Notice: Pursuant to Section 290.46 of the Penal Code, information about specified registered sex offenders is made available to the public via an Internet Web site maintained by the Department of Justice at www.meganslaw.ca.gov. Depending on an offender's criminal history, this information will include either the address at which the offender resides or the community of residence and ZIP Code in which he or she resides. (Neither Seller nor Brokers are required to check this website. If Buyer wants further information, Broker recommends that Buyer obtain information from this website during Buyer's inspection contingency period. Brokers do not have expertise in this area.)

7. **CONDOMINIUM/PLANNED DEVELOPMENT DISCLOSURES:**
   - **A.** **SELLER HAS: 7 (or ☐ _____) Days** After Acceptance to disclose to Buyer whether the Property is a condominium, or is located in a planned development or other common interest subdivision (C.A.R. Form SPQ or SSD).
   - **B.** If the Property is a condominium or is located in a planned development or other common interest subdivision, Seller has **3 (or ☐ _____) Days** After Acceptance to request from the HOA (C.A.R. Form HOA): **(i)** Copies of any documents required by Law; **(ii)** disclosure of any pending or anticipated claim or litigation by or against the HOA; **(iii)** a statement containing the location and number of designated parking and storage spaces; **(iv)** Copies of the most recent 12 months of HOA minutes for regular and special meetings; and **(v)** the names and contact information of all HOAs governing the Property (collectively, "CI Disclosures"). Seller shall itemize and Deliver to Buyer all CI Disclosures received from the HOA and any CI Disclosures in Seller's possession. Buyer's approval of CI Disclosures is a contingency of this Agreement as specified in paragraph 14B(3).

8. **ITEMS INCLUDED IN AND EXCLUDED FROM PURCHASE PRICE:**
   - **A.** **NOTE TO BUYER AND SELLER:** Items listed as included or excluded in the MLS, flyers or marketing materials are **not** included in the purchase price or excluded from the sale unless specified in 8B or C.
   - **B.** **ITEMS INCLUDED IN SALE:**
     - **(1)** All EXISTING fixtures and fittings that are attached to the Property;
     - **(2)** EXISTING electrical, mechanical, lighting, plumbing and heating fixtures, ceiling fans, fireplace inserts, gas logs and grates, solar systems, built-in appliances, window and door screens, awnings, shutters, window coverings, attached floor coverings, television antennas, satellite dishes, private integrated telephone systems, air coolers/conditioners, pool/spa equipment, garage door openers/remote controls, mailbox, in-ground landscaping, trees/shrubs, water softeners, water purifiers, security systems/alarms; (If checked) ☐ stove(s), ☐ refrigerator(s); and _____.
     - **(3)** The following additional items:_____
     - **(4)** Seller represents that all items included in the purchase price, unless otherwise specified, are owned by Seller.
     - **(5)** All items included shall be transferred free of liens and without Seller warranty.
   - **C.** **ITEMS EXCLUDED FROM SALE:** Unless otherwise specified, audio and video components (such as flat screen TVs and speakers) are excluded if any such item is not itself attached to the Property, even if a bracket or other mechanism attached to the component is attached to the Property; and _____.

Buyer's Initials (_____)(_____)

RPA-CA REVISED 4/10 (PAGE 3 OF 8)

Seller's Initials (_____)(_____)

| Reviewed by _____ Date _____ |

EQUAL HOUSING OPPORTUNITY

FIGURE 5.7 *(continued)*

Property Address: _____ Date: _____

9. **CONDITION OF PROPERTY:** Unless otherwise agreed: **(i) the Property is sold (a) in its PRESENT physical ("as-is") condition as of the date of Acceptance and (b) subject to Buyer's Investigation rights; (ii)** the Property, including pool, spa, landscaping and grounds, is to be maintained in substantially the same condition as of the date of Acceptance; and **(iii)** all debris and personal property not included in the sale shall be removed by Seller by Close Of Escrow.
   - **A.** Seller shall, within the time specified in paragraph 14A, DISCLOSE KNOWN MATERIAL FACTS AND DEFECTS affecting the Property, including known insurance claims within the past five years, and make any and all other disclosures required by law.
   - **B.** Buyer has the right to inspect the Property and, as specified in paragraph 14B, based upon information discovered in those inspections: (i) cancel this Agreement; or (ii) request that Seller make Repairs or take other action.
   - **C. Buyer is strongly advised to conduct investigations of the entire Property in order to determine its present condition. Seller may not be aware of all defects affecting the Property or other factors that Buyer considers important. Property improvements may not be built according to code, in compliance with current Law, or have had permits issued.**

10. **BUYER'S INVESTIGATION OF PROPERTY AND MATTERS AFFECTING PROPERTY:**
   - **A.** Buyer's acceptance of the condition of, and any other matter affecting the Property, is a contingency of this Agreement as specified in this paragraph and paragraph 14B. Within the time specified in paragraph 14B(1), Buyer shall have the right, at Buyer's expense unless otherwise agreed, to conduct inspections, investigations, tests, surveys and other studies ("Buyer Investigations"), including, but not limited to, the right to: **(i)** inspect for lead-based paint and other lead-based paint hazards; **(ii)** inspect for wood destroying pests and organisms; **(iii)** review the registered sex offender database; **(iv)** confirm the insurability of Buyer and the Property; and **(v)** satisfy Buyer as to any matter specified in the attached Buyer's Inspection Advisory (C.A.R. Form BIA). Without Seller's prior written consent, Buyer shall neither make nor cause to be made: **(i)** invasive or destructive Buyer Investigations; or **(ii)** inspections by any governmental building or zoning inspector or government employee, unless required by Law.
   - **B.** Seller shall make the Property available for all Buyer Investigations. Buyer shall **(i)** as specified in paragraph 14B, complete Buyer Investigations and, either remove the contingency or cancel this Agreement, and **(ii)** give Seller, at no cost, complete Copies of all Investigation reports obtained by Buyer, which obligation shall survive the termination of this Agreement.
   - **C.** Seller shall have water, gas, electricity and all operable pilot lights on for Buyer's Investigations and through the date possession is made available to Buyer.
   - **D. Buyer indemnity and Seller protection for entry upon property:** Buyer shall: **(i)** keep the Property free and clear of liens; **(ii)** repair all damage arising from Buyer Investigations; and **(iii)** indemnify and hold Seller harmless from all resulting liability, claims, demands, damages and costs of Buyer's Investigations. Buyer shall carry, or Buyer shall require anyone acting on Buyer's behalf to carry, policies of liability, workers' compensation and other applicable insurance, defending and protecting Seller from liability for any injuries to persons or property occurring during any Buyer Investigations or work done on the Property at Buyer's direction prior to Close Of Escrow. Seller is advised that certain protections may be afforded Seller by recording a "Notice of Non-responsibility" (C.A.R. Form NNR) for Buyer Investigations and work done on the Property at Buyer's direction. Buyer's obligations under this paragraph shall survive the termination or cancellation of this Agreement and Close Of Escrow.

11. **SELLER DISCLOSURES; ADDENDA; ADVISORIES; OTHER TERMS:**
   - **A. Seller Disclosures (if checked):** Seller shall, within the time specified in paragraph 14A, complete and provide Buyer with a:
      ☐ Seller Property Questionnaire (C.A.R. Form SPQ)   **OR**   ☐ Supplemental Contractual and Statutory Disclosure (C.A.R. Form SSD)
   - **B. Addenda (if checked):**   ☐ Addendum #_____ (C.A.R. Form ADM)
      ☐ Wood Destroying Pest Inspection and Allocation of Cost Addendum (C.A.R. Form WPA)
      ☐ Purchase Agreement Addendum (C.A.R. Form PAA)   ☐ Septic, Well and Property Monument Addendum (C.A.R. Form SWPI)
      ☐ Short Sale Addendum (C.A.R. Form SSA)   ☐ Other
   - **C. Advisories (If checked):**   ☑ Buyer's Inspection Advisory (C.A.R. Form BIA)
      ☐ Probate Advisory (C.A.R. Form PAK)   ☐ Statewide Buyer and Seller Advisory (C.A.R. Form SBSA)
      ☐ Trust Advisory (C.A.R. Form TA)   ☐ REO Advisory (C.A.R. Form REO)
   - **D. Other Terms:** _____

12. **TITLE AND VESTING:**
   - **A.** Within the time specified in paragraph 14, Buyer shall be provided a current preliminary title report, which shall include a search of the General Index. Seller shall within 7 Days After Acceptance give Escrow Holder a completed Statement of Information. The preliminary report is only an offer by the title insurer to issue a policy of title insurance and may not contain every item affecting title. Buyer's review of the preliminary report and any other matters which may affect title are a contingency of this Agreement as specified in paragraph 14B.
   - **B.** Title is taken in its present condition subject to all encumbrances, easements, covenants, conditions, restrictions, rights and other matters, whether of record or not, as of the date of Acceptance except: **(i)** monetary liens of record unless Buyer is assuming those obligations or taking the Property subject to those obligations; and **(ii)** those matters which Seller has agreed to remove in writing.
   - **C.** Within the time specified in paragraph 14A, Seller has a duty to disclose to Buyer all matters known to Seller affecting title, whether of record or not.
   - **D.** At Close Of Escrow, Buyer shall receive a grant deed conveying title (or, for stock cooperative or long-term lease, an assignment of stock certificate or of Seller's leasehold interest), including oil, mineral and water rights if currently owned by Seller. Title shall vest as designated in Buyer's supplemental escrow instructions. THE MANNER OF TAKING TITLE MAY HAVE SIGNIFICANT LEGAL AND TAX CONSEQUENCES. CONSULT AN APPROPRIATE PROFESSIONAL.
   - **E.** Buyer shall receive a CLTA/ALTA Homeowner's Policy of Title Insurance. A title company, at Buyer's request, can provide information about the availability, desirability, coverage, survey requirements, and cost of various title insurance coverages and endorsements. If Buyer desires title coverage other than that required by this paragraph, Buyer shall instruct Escrow Holder in writing and pay any increase in cost.

13. **SALE OF BUYER'S PROPERTY:**
   - **A.** This Agreement is NOT contingent upon the sale of any property owned by Buyer.
   - **OR B.** ☐ (If checked): The attached addendum (C.A.R. Form COP) regarding the contingency for the sale of property owned by Buyer is incorporated into this Agreement.

Seller's Initials (_____)(_____)

RPA-CA REVISED 4/10 (PAGE 4 OF 8)

Reviewed by _____ Date _____

CALIFORNIA RESIDENTIAL PURCHASE AGREEMENT (RPA-CA PAGE 4 OF 8)

FIGURE 5.7 *(continued)*

Property Address: _____ Date: _____

14. **TIME PERIODS; REMOVAL OF CONTINGENCIES; CANCELLATION RIGHTS:** The following time periods may only be extended, altered, modified or changed by mutual written agreement. Any removal of contingencies or cancellation under this paragraph by either Buyer or Seller must be exercised in good faith and in writing (C.A.R. Form CR or CC).

   A. **SELLER HAS: 7 (or ☐ _____) Days** After Acceptance to Deliver to Buyer all Reports, disclosures and information for which Seller is responsible under paragraphs 4, 6A, B and C, 7A, 9A, 11A and B, and 12. Buyer may give Seller a Notice to Seller to Perform (C.A.R. Form NSP) if Seller has not Delivered the items within the time specified.

   B. **(1) BUYER HAS: 17 (or ☐ _____) Days** After Acceptance, unless otherwise agreed in writing, to:
       (i) complete all Buyer Investigations; approve all disclosures, reports and other applicable information, which Buyer receives from Seller; and approve all other matters affecting the Property; and
       (ii) Deliver to Seller Signed Copies of Statutory and Lead Disclosures Delivered by Seller in accordance with paragraph 6A.
     (2) Within the time specified in 14B(1), Buyer may request that Seller make repairs or take any other action regarding the Property (C.A.R. Form RR). Seller has no obligation to agree to or respond to Buyer's requests.
     (3) Within the time specified in 14B(1) (or as otherwise specified in this Agreement), Buyer shall Deliver to Seller either (i) a removal of the applicable contingency (C.A.R. Form CR), or (ii) a cancellation (C.A.R. Form CC) of this Agreement based upon a remaining contingency or Seller's failure to Deliver the specified items. However, if any report, disclosure or information for which Seller is responsible is not Delivered within the time specified in 14A, then Buyer has **5 (or ☐ _____) Days** After Delivery of any such items, or the time specified in 14B(1), whichever is later, to Deliver to Seller a removal of the applicable contingency or cancellation of this Agreement.
     (4) Continuation of Contingency: Even after the end of the time specified in 14B(1) and before Seller cancels this Agreement, if at all, pursuant to 14C, Buyer retains the right to either (i) in writing remove remaining contingencies, or (ii) cancel this Agreement based upon a remaining contingency or Seller's failure to Deliver the specified items. Once Buyer's written removal of all contingencies is Delivered to Seller, Seller may not cancel this Agreement pursuant to 14C(1).

   C. **SELLER RIGHT TO CANCEL:**
     (1) Seller right to Cancel; Buyer Contingencies: If, within time specified in this Agreement, Buyer does not, in writing, Deliver to Seller a removal of the applicable contingency or cancellation of this Agreement then Seller, after first Delivering to Buyer a Notice to Buyer to Perform (C.A.R. Form NBP) may cancel this Agreement. In such event, Seller shall authorize return of Buyer's deposit.
     (2) Seller right to Cancel; Buyer Contract Obligations: Seller, after first Delivering to Buyer a NBP may cancel this Agreement for any of the following reasons: **(i)** if Buyer fails to deposit funds as required by 3A or 3B; **(ii)** if the funds deposited pursuant to 3A or 3B are not good when deposited; **(iii)** if Buyer fails to Deliver a notice of FHA or VA costs or terms as required by 3C(3) (C.A.R. Form FVA); **(iv)** if Buyer fails to Deliver a letter as required by 3H; **(v)** if Buyer fails to Deliver verification as required by 3G or 3J; **(vi)** if Seller reasonably disapproves of the verification provided by 3G or 3J; **(vii)** if Buyer fails to return Statutory and Lead Disclosures as required by paragraph 6A(2); or **(viii)** if Buyer fails to sign or initial a separate liquidated damages form for an increased deposit as required by paragraphs 3B and 25. In such event, Seller shall authorize return of Buyer's deposit.
     (3) Notice To Buyer To Perform: The NBP shall: **(i)** be in writing; **(ii)** be signed by Seller; and **(iii)** give Buyer at least **2 (or ☐ _____) Days** After Delivery (or until the time specified in the applicable paragraph, whichever occurs last) to take the applicable action. A NBP may not be Delivered any earlier than **2 Days** Prior to the expiration of the applicable time for Buyer to remove a contingency or cancel this Agreement or meet an obligation specified in 14C(2).

   D. **EFFECT OF BUYER'S REMOVAL OF CONTINGENCIES:** If Buyer removes, in writing, any contingency or cancellation rights, unless otherwise specified in a separate written agreement between Buyer and Seller, Buyer shall with regard to that contingency or cancellation right conclusively be deemed to have: **(i)** completed all Buyer Investigations, and review of reports and other applicable information and disclosures; **(ii)** elected to proceed with the transaction; and **(iii)** assumed all liability, responsibility and expense for Repairs or corrections or for inability to obtain financing.

   E. **CLOSE OF ESCROW:** Before Seller or Buyer may cancel this Agreement for failure of the other party to close escrow pursuant to this Agreement, Seller or Buyer must first Deliver to the other a demand to close escrow (C.A.R. Form DCE).

   F. **EFFECT OF CANCELLATION ON DEPOSITS:** If Buyer or Seller gives written notice of cancellation pursuant to rights duly exercised under the terms of this Agreement, Buyer and Seller agree to Sign mutual instructions to cancel the sale and escrow and release deposits, if any, to the party entitled to the funds, less fees and costs incurred by that party. Fees and costs may be payable to service providers and vendors for services and products provided during escrow. **Release of funds will require mutual Signed release instructions from Buyer and Seller, judicial decision or arbitration award. A Buyer or Seller may be subject to a civil penalty of up to $1,000 for refusal to sign such instructions if no good faith dispute exists as to who is entitled to the deposited funds (Civil Code §1057.3).**

15. **REPAIRS:** Repairs shall be completed prior to final verification of condition unless otherwise agreed in writing. Repairs to be performed at Seller's expense may be performed by Seller or through others, provided that the work complies with applicable Law, including governmental permit, inspection and approval requirements. Repairs shall be performed in a good, skillful manner with materials of quality and appearance comparable to existing materials. It is understood that exact restoration of appearance or cosmetic items following all Repairs may not be possible. Seller shall: **(i)** obtain receipts for Repairs performed by others; **(ii)** prepare a written statement indicating the Repairs performed by Seller and the date of such Repairs; and **(iii)** provide Copies of receipts and statements to Buyer prior to final verification of condition.

16. **FINAL VERIFICATION OF CONDITION:** Buyer shall have the right to make a final inspection of the Property within **5 (or _____) Days** Prior to Close Of Escrow, NOT AS A CONTINGENCY OF THE SALE, but solely to confirm: **(i)** the Property is maintained pursuant to paragraph 9; **(ii)** Repairs have been completed as agreed; and **(iii)** Seller has complied with Seller's other obligations under this Agreement (C.A.R. Form VP).

17. **PRORATIONS OF PROPERTY TAXES AND OTHER ITEMS:** Unless otherwise agreed in writing, the following items shall be PAID CURRENT and prorated between Buyer and Seller as of Close Of Escrow: real property taxes and assessments, interest, rents, HOA regular, special, and emergency dues and assessments imposed prior to Close Of Escrow, premiums on insurance assumed by Buyer, payments on bonds and assessments assumed by Buyer, and payments on Mello-Roos and other Special Assessment District bonds and assessments that are a current lien. The following items shall be assumed by Buyer WITHOUT CREDIT toward the purchase price: prorated payments on Mello-Roos and other Special Assessment District bonds and assessments and HOA special assessments that are a current lien but not yet due. Property will be reassessed upon change of ownership. Any supplemental tax bills shall be paid as follows: **(i)** for periods after Close Of Escrow, by Buyer; and **(ii)** for periods prior to Close Of Escrow, by Seller (see C.A.R. Form SPT or SBSA for further information). TAX BILLS ISSUED AFTER CLOSE OF ESCROW SHALL BE HANDLED DIRECTLY BETWEEN BUYER AND SELLER. Prorations shall be made based on a 30-day month.

Buyer's Initials (_____)(_____)   Seller's Initials (_____)(_____)

RPA-CA REVISED 4/10 (PAGE 5 OF 8)

Reviewed by _____ Date _____   EQUAL HOUSING OPPORTUNITY

CALIFORNIA RESIDENTIAL PURCHASE AGREEMENT (RPA-CA PAGE 5 OF 8)

FIGURE 5.7 *(continued)*

Property Address: _____ Date: _____

18. **SELECTION OF SERVICE PROVIDERS:** Brokers do not guarantee the performance of any vendors, service or product providers ("Providers"), whether referred by Broker or selected by Buyer, Seller or other person. Buyer and Seller may select ANY Providers of their own choosing.

19. **MULTIPLE LISTING SERVICE ("MLS"):** Brokers are authorized to report to the MLS a pending sale and, upon Close Of Escrow, the sales price and other terms of this transaction shall be provided to the MLS to be published and disseminated to persons and entities authorized to use the information on terms approved by the MLS.

20. **EQUAL HOUSING OPPORTUNITY:** The Property is sold in compliance with federal, state and local anti-discrimination Laws.

21. **ATTORNEY FEES:** In any action, proceeding, or arbitration between Buyer and Seller arising out of this Agreement, the prevailing Buyer or Seller shall be entitled to reasonable attorney fees and costs from the non-prevailing Buyer or Seller, except as provided in paragraph 26A.

22. **DEFINITIONS:** As used in this Agreement:
   A. **"Acceptance"** means the time the offer or final counter offer is accepted in writing by a party and is delivered to and personally received by the other party or that party's authorized agent in accordance with the terms of this offer or a final counter offer.
   B. **"C.A.R. Form"** means the specific form referenced or another comparable form agreed to by the parties.
   C. **"Close Of Escrow"** means the date the grant deed, or other evidence of transfer of title, is recorded.
   D. **"Copy"** means copy by any means including photocopy, NCR, facsimile and electronic.
   E. **"Days"** means calendar days. However, after Acceptance, the last **Day** for performance of any act required by this Agreement (including Close Of Escrow) shall not include any Saturday, Sunday, or legal holiday and shall instead be the next Day.
   F. **"Days After"** means the specified number of calendar days after the occurrence of the event specified, not counting the calendar date on which the specified event occurs, and ending at 11:59 PM on the final day.
   G. **"Days Prior"** means the specified number of calendar days before the occurrence of the event specified, not counting the calendar date on which the specified event is scheduled to occur.
   H. **"Deliver", "Delivered"** or **"Delivery"**, regardless of the method used (i.e. messenger, mail, email, fax, other), means and shall be effective upon (i) personal receipt by Buyer or Seller or the individual Real Estate Licensee for that principal as specified in paragraph D of the section titled Real Estate Brokers on page 8; OR (ii) if checked, ☐ per the attached addendum (C.A.R. Form RDN).
   I. **"Electronic Copy"** or **"Electronic Signature"** means, as applicable, an electronic copy or signature complying with California Law. Buyer and Seller agree that electronic means will not be used by either party to modify or alter the content or integrity of this Agreement without the knowledge and consent of the other party.
   J. **"Law"** means any law, code, statute, ordinance, regulation, rule or order, which is adopted by a controlling city, county, state or federal legislative, judicial or executive body or agency.
   K. **"Repairs"** means any repairs (including pest control), alterations, replacements, modifications or retrofitting of the Property provided for under this Agreement.
   L. **"Signed"** means either a handwritten or electronic signature on an original document, Copy or any counterpart.

23. **BROKER COMPENSATION:** Seller or Buyer, or both, as applicable, agree(s) to pay compensation to Broker as specified in a separate written agreement between Broker and that Seller or Buyer. Compensation is payable upon Close Of Escrow, or if escrow does not close, as otherwise specified in the agreement between Broker and that Seller or Buyer.

24. **JOINT ESCROW INSTRUCTIONS TO ESCROW HOLDER:**
   A. **The following paragraphs, or applicable portions thereof, of this Agreement constitute the joint escrow instructions of Buyer and Seller to Escrow Holder,** which Escrow Holder is to use along with any related counter offers and addenda, and any additional mutual instructions to close the escrow: 1, 3, 4, 6C, 11B and D, 12, 13B, 14F, 17, 22, 23, 24, 28, 30, and paragraph D of the section titled Real Estate Brokers on page 8. If a Copy of the separate compensation agreement(s) provided for in paragraph 23, or paragraph D of the section titled Real Estate Brokers on page 8 is deposited with Escrow Holder by Broker, Escrow Holder shall accept such agreement(s) and pay out of Buyer's or Seller's funds, or both, as applicable, the respective Broker's compensation provided for in such agreement(s). The terms and conditions of this Agreement not specifically referenced above, in the specified paragraphs are additional matters for the information of Escrow Holder, but about which Escrow Holder need not be concerned. Buyer and Seller will receive Escrow Holder's general provisions directly from Escrow Holder and will execute such provisions upon Escrow Holder's request. To the extent the general provisions are inconsistent or conflict with this Agreement, the general provisions will control as to the duties and obligations of Escrow Holder only. Buyer and Seller will execute additional instructions, documents and forms provided by Escrow Holder that are reasonably necessary to close the escrow.
   B. A Copy of this Agreement shall be delivered to Escrow Holder within **3** business days after Acceptance (or ☐ _____). Escrow Holder shall provide Seller's Statement of Information to Title company when received from Seller. Buyer and Seller authorize Escrow Holder to accept and rely on Copies and Signatures as defined in this Agreement as originals, to open escrow and for other purposes of escrow. The validity of this Agreement as between Buyer and Seller is not affected by whether or when Escrow Holder Signs this Agreement.
   C. Brokers are a party to the escrow for the sole purpose of compensation pursuant to paragraph 23 and paragraph D of the section titled Real Estate Brokers on page 8. Buyer and Seller irrevocably assign to Brokers compensation specified in paragraph 23, respectively, and irrevocably instruct Escrow Holder to disburse those funds to Brokers at Close Of Escrow or pursuant to any other mutually executed cancellation agreement. Compensation instructions can be amended or revoked only with the written consent of Brokers. Buyer and Seller shall release and hold harmless Escrow Holder from any liability resulting from Escrow Holder's payment to Broker(s) of compensation pursuant to this Agreement. Escrow Holder shall immediately notify Brokers: **(i)** if Buyer's initial or any additional deposit is not made pursuant to this Agreement, or is not good at time of deposit with Escrow Holder; or **(ii)** if either Buyer or Seller instruct Escrow Holder to cancel escrow.
   D. A Copy of any amendment that affects any paragraph of this Agreement for which Escrow Holder is responsible shall be delivered to Escrow Holder within **2** business days after mutual execution of the amendment.

Buyer's Initials (_____)(_____)

Seller's Initials (_____)(_____)

| Reviewed by _____ Date _____ |

RPA-CA REVISED 4/10 (PAGE 6 OF 8)

CALIFORNIA RESIDENTIAL PURCHASE AGREEMENT (RPA-CA PAGE 6 OF 8)

FIGURE 5.7 *(continued)*

Property Address: _____   Date: _____

25. **LIQUIDATED DAMAGES: If Buyer fails to complete this purchase because of Buyer's default, Seller shall retain, as liquidated damages, the deposit actually paid. If the Property is a dwelling with no more than four units, one of which Buyer intends to occupy, then the amount retained shall be no more than 3% of the purchase price. Any excess shall be returned to Buyer. Release of funds will require mutual, Signed release instructions from both Buyer and Seller, judicial decision or arbitration award. AT TIME OF THE INCREASED DEPOSIT BUYER AND SELLER SHALL SIGN A SEPARATE LIQUIDATED DAMAGES PROVISION FOR ANY INCREASED DEPOSIT (C.A.R. FORM RID).**

Buyer's Initials _____/_____	Seller's Initials _____/_____

26. **DISPUTE RESOLUTION:**
   A. **MEDIATION:** Buyer and Seller agree to mediate any dispute or claim arising between them out of this Agreement, or any resulting transaction, before resorting to arbitration or court action. **Buyer and Seller also agree to mediate any disputes or claims with Broker(s) who, in writing, agree to such mediation prior to, or within a reasonable time after, the dispute or claim is presented to the Broker.** Mediation fees, if any, shall be divided equally among the parties involved. If, for any dispute or claim to which this paragraph applies, any party (i) commences an action without first attempting to resolve the matter through mediation, or (ii) before commencement of an action, refuses to mediate after a request has been made, then that party shall not be entitled to recover attorney fees, even if they would otherwise be available to that party in any such action. THIS MEDIATION PROVISION APPLIES WHETHER OR NOT THE ARBITRATION PROVISION IS INITIALED. Exclusions from this mediation agreement are specified in paragraph 26C.
   B. **ARBITRATION OF DISPUTES:**
   Buyer and Seller agree that any dispute or claim in Law or equity arising between them out of this Agreement or any resulting transaction, which is not settled through mediation, shall be decided by neutral, binding arbitration. Buyer and Seller also agree to arbitrate any disputes or claims with Broker(s) who, in writing, agree to such arbitration prior to, or within a reasonable time after, the dispute or claim is presented to the Broker. The arbitrator shall be a retired judge or justice, or an attorney with at least 5 years of residential real estate Law experience, unless the parties mutually agree to a different arbitrator. The parties shall have the right to discovery in accordance with Code of Civil Procedure §1283.05. In all other respects, the arbitration shall be conducted in accordance with Title 9 of Part 3 of the Code of Civil Procedure. Judgment upon the award of the arbitrator(s) may be entered into any court having jurisdiction. Enforcement of this agreement to arbitrate shall be governed by the Federal Arbitration Act. Exclusions from this arbitration agreement are specified in paragraph 26C.
   "**NOTICE: BY INITIALING IN THE SPACE BELOW YOU ARE AGREEING TO HAVE ANY DISPUTE ARISING OUT OF THE MATTERS INCLUDED IN THE 'ARBITRATION OF DISPUTES' PROVISION DECIDED BY NEUTRAL ARBITRATION AS PROVIDED BY CALIFORNIA LAW AND YOU ARE GIVING UP ANY RIGHTS YOU MIGHT POSSESS TO HAVE THE DISPUTE LITIGATED IN A COURT OR JURY TRIAL. BY INITIALING IN THE SPACE BELOW YOU ARE GIVING UP YOUR JUDICIAL RIGHTS TO DISCOVERY AND APPEAL, UNLESS THOSE RIGHTS ARE SPECIFICALLY INCLUDED IN THE 'ARBITRATION OF DISPUTES' PROVISION. IF YOU REFUSE TO SUBMIT TO ARBITRATION AFTER AGREEING TO THIS PROVISION, YOU MAY BE COMPELLED TO ARBITRATE UNDER THE AUTHORITY OF THE CALIFORNIA CODE OF CIVIL PROCEDURE. YOUR AGREEMENT TO THIS ARBITRATION PROVISION IS VOLUNTARY.**"
   "**WE HAVE READ AND UNDERSTAND THE FOREGOING AND AGREE TO SUBMIT DISPUTES ARISING OUT OF THE MATTERS INCLUDED IN THE 'ARBITRATION OF DISPUTES' PROVISION TO NEUTRAL ARBITRATION.**"

Buyer's Initials _____/_____	Seller's Initials _____/_____

   C. **ADDITIONAL MEDIATION AND ARBITRATION TERMS:**
   (1) **EXCLUSIONS:** The following matters shall be excluded from mediation and arbitration: (i) a judicial or non-judicial foreclosure or other action or proceeding to enforce a deed of trust, mortgage or installment land sale contract as defined in Civil Code §2985; (ii) an unlawful detainer action; (iii) the filing or enforcement of a mechanic's lien; and (iv) any matter that is within the jurisdiction of a probate, small claims or bankruptcy court. The filing of a court action to enable the recording of a notice of pending action, for order of attachment, receivership, injunction, or other provisional remedies, shall not constitute a waiver or violation of the mediation and arbitration provisions.
   (2) **BROKERS:** Brokers shall not be obligated or compelled to mediate or arbitrate unless they agree to do so in writing. Any Broker(s) participating in mediation or arbitration shall not be deemed a party to the Agreement.

27. **TERMS AND CONDITIONS OF OFFER:**
   This is an offer to purchase the Property on the above terms and conditions. The liquidated damages paragraph or the arbitration of disputes paragraph is incorporated in this Agreement if initialed by all parties or if incorporated by mutual agreement in a counter offer or addendum. If at least one but not all parties initial such paragraph(s), a counter offer is required until agreement is reached. Seller has the right to continue to offer the Property for sale and to accept any other offer at any time prior to notification of Acceptance. If this offer is accepted and Buyer subsequently defaults, Buyer may be responsible for payment of Brokers' compensation. This Agreement and any supplement, addendum or modification, including any Copy, may be Signed in two or more counterparts, all of which shall constitute one and the same writing.

28. **TIME OF ESSENCE; ENTIRE CONTRACT; CHANGES:** Time is of the essence. All understandings between the parties are incorporated in this Agreement. Its terms are intended by the parties as a final, complete and exclusive expression of their Agreement with respect to its subject matter, and may not be contradicted by evidence of any prior agreement or contemporaneous oral agreement. If any provision of this Agreement is held to be ineffective or invalid, the remaining provisions will nevertheless be given full force and effect. Except as otherwise specified, this Agreement shall be interpreted and disputes shall be resolved in accordance with the laws of the State of California. **Neither this Agreement nor any provision in it may be extended, amended, modified, altered or changed, except in writing Signed by Buyer and Seller.**

Buyer's Initials (_____)(_____)   Seller's Initials (_____)(_____)

RPA-CA REVISED 4/10 (PAGE 7 OF 8)

Reviewed by _____ Date _____

EQUAL HOUSING OPPORTUNITY

CALIFORNIA RESIDENTIAL PURCHASE AGREEMENT (RPA-CA PAGE 7 OF 8)

FIGURE 5.7 (continued)

Property Address: _____ Date: _____

29. EXPIRATION OF OFFER: This offer shall be deemed revoked and the deposit shall be returned unless the offer is Signed by Seller and a Copy of the Signed offer is personally received by Buyer, or by _____ who is authorized to receive it, by 5:00 PM on the third Day after this offer is signed by Buyer (or, if checked, ☐ by _____ ☐AM/☐PM, on _____(date)). Buyer has read and acknowledges receipt of a Copy of the offer and agrees to the above confirmation of agency relationships.

Date _____   Date _____
BUYER _____   BUYER _____

(Print name) _____   **(Print name)** _____

(Address) _____
☐ Additional Signature Addendum attached (C.A.R. Form ASA).

30. ACCEPTANCE OF OFFER: Seller warrants that Seller is the owner of the Property, or has the authority to execute this Agreement. Seller accepts the above offer, agrees to sell the Property on the above terms and conditions, and agrees to the above confirmation of agency relationships. Seller has read and acknowledges receipt of a Copy of this Agreement, and authorizes Broker to Deliver a Signed Copy to Buyer.
☐ (If checked) **SUBJECT TO ATTACHED COUNTER OFFER (C.A.R. Form CO) DATED:** _____.

Date _____   Date _____
SELLER _____   SELLER _____

(Print name) _____   **(Print name)** _____

(Address) _____
☐ Additional Signature Addendum attached (C.A.R. Form ASA).

(_____/_____) **CONFIRMATION OF ACCEPTANCE:** A Copy of Signed Acceptance was personally received by Buyer or Buyer's
(Initials) authorized agent on (date) _____ at _____ ☐AM/☐PM. **A binding Agreement is created when a Copy of Signed Acceptance is personally received by Buyer or Buyer's authorized agent whether or not confirmed in this document. Completion of this confirmation is not legally required in order to create a binding Agreement. It is solely intended to evidence the date that Confirmation of Acceptance has occurred.**

REAL ESTATE BROKERS:
A. Real Estate Brokers are not parties to the Agreement between Buyer and Seller.
B. Agency relationships are confirmed as stated in paragraph 2.
C. If specified in paragraph 3A(2), Agent who submitted the offer for Buyer acknowledges receipt of deposit.
D. **COOPERATING BROKER COMPENSATION:** Listing Broker agrees to pay Cooperating Broker **(Selling Firm)** and Cooperating Broker agrees to accept, out of Listing Broker's proceeds in escrow: (i) the amount specified in the MLS, provided Cooperating Broker is a Participant of the MLS in which the Property is offered for sale or a reciprocal MLS; or (ii) ☐ (if checked) the amount specified in a separate written agreement (C.A.R. Form CBC) between Listing Broker and Cooperating Broker. Declaration of License and Tax (C.A.R. Form DLT) may be used to document that tax reporting will be required or that an exemption exists.

Real Estate Broker (Selling Firm) _____ DRE Lic. # _____
By _____ DRE Lic. # _____ Date _____
Address _____ City _____ State _____ Zip _____
Telephone _____ Fax _____ E-mail _____

Real Estate Broker (Listing Firm) _____ DRE Lic. # _____
By _____ DRE Lic. # _____ Date _____
Address _____ City _____ State _____ Zip _____
Telephone _____ Fax _____ E-mail _____

ESCROW HOLDER ACKNOWLEDGMENT:
Escrow Holder acknowledges receipt of a Copy of this Agreement, (if checked, ☐ a deposit in the amount of $ _____), counter offer numbered _____, ☐ Seller's Statement of Information and ☐ Other _____ _____, and agrees to act as Escrow Holder subject to paragraph 24 of this Agreement, any supplemental escrow instructions and the terms of Escrow Holder's general provisions if any.

Escrow Holder is advised that the date of Confirmation of Acceptance of the Agreement as between Buyer and Seller is _____.

Escrow Holder _____ Escrow # _____
By _____ Date _____
Address _____
Phone/Fax/E-mail _____
Escrow Holder is licensed by the California Department of ☐ Corporations, ☐ Insurance, ☐ Real Estate. License # _____

PRESENTATION OF OFFER: (_____) Listing Broker presented this offer to Seller on _____ (date).
  Broker or Designee Initials

REJECTION OF OFFER: (_____)(_____) No counter offer is being made. This offer was rejected by Seller on _____ (date).
  Seller's Initials

THIS FORM HAS BEEN APPROVED BY THE CALIFORNIA ASSOCIATION OF REALTORS® (C.A.R.). NO REPRESENTATION IS MADE AS TO THE LEGAL VALIDITY OR ADEQUACY OF ANY PROVISION IN ANY SPECIFIC TRANSACTION. A REAL ESTATE BROKER IS THE PERSON QUALIFIED TO ADVISE ON REAL ESTATE TRANSACTIONS. IF YOU DESIRE LEGAL OR TAX ADVICE, CONSULT AN APPROPRIATE PROFESSIONAL.

This form is available for use by the entire real estate industry. It is not intended to identify the user as a REALTOR®. REALTOR® is a registered collective membership mark which may be used only by members of the NATIONAL ASSOCIATION OF REALTORS® who subscribe to its Code of Ethics.

Published and Distributed by:
REAL ESTATE BUSINESS SERVICES, INC.
a subsidiary of the CALIFORNIA ASSOCIATION OF REALTORS®
525 South Virgil Avenue, Los Angeles, California 90020

Reviewed by
Broker or Designee _____ Date _____

EQUAL HOUSING OPPORTUNITY

REVISION DATE 4/10

CALIFORNIA RESIDENTIAL PURCHASE AGREEMENT (RPA-CA PAGE 8 OF 8)

Source: Reprinted with permission of California Association of REALTORS®

FIGURE 5.8

CALIFORNIA
ASSOCIATION
OF REALTORS®

REAL ESTATE TRANSFER DISCLOSURE STATEMENT
(CALIFORNIA CIVIL CODE §1102, ET SEQ.)
(C.A.R. Form TDS, Revised 10/03)

THIS DISCLOSURE STATEMENT CONCERNS THE REAL PROPERTY SITUATED IN THE CITY OF _____
_____, COUNTY OF _____, STATE OF CALIFORNIA,
DESCRIBED AS _____.
THIS STATEMENT IS A DISCLOSURE OF THE CONDITION OF THE ABOVE DESCRIBED PROPERTY IN COMPLIANCE
WITH SECTION 1102 OF THE CIVIL CODE AS OF (date) _____. IT IS NOT A WARRANTY OF ANY
KIND BY THE SELLER(S) OR ANY AGENT(S) REPRESENTING ANY PRINCIPAL(S) IN THIS TRANSACTION, AND IS
NOT A SUBSTITUTE FOR ANY INSPECTIONS OR WARRANTIES THE PRINCIPAL(S) MAY WISH TO OBTAIN.

I. COORDINATION WITH OTHER DISCLOSURE FORMS

This Real Estate Transfer Disclosure Statement is made pursuant to Section 1102 of the Civil Code. Other statutes require disclosures, depending upon the details of the particular real estate transaction (for example: special study zone and purchase-money liens on residential property).

Substituted Disclosures: The following disclosures and other disclosures required by law, including the Natural Hazard Disclosure Report/Statement that may include airport annoyances, earthquake, fire, flood, or special assessment information, have or will be made in connection with this real estate transfer, and are intended to satisfy the disclosure obligations on this form, where the subject matter is the same:

☐   Inspection reports completed pursuant to the contract of sale or receipt for deposit.
☐   Additional inspection reports or disclosures: _____
_____

II. SELLER'S INFORMATION

The Seller discloses the following information with the knowledge that even though this is not a warranty, prospective Buyers may rely on this information in deciding whether and on what terms to purchase the subject property. Seller hereby authorizes any agent(s) representing any principal(s) in this transaction to provide a copy of this statement to any person or entity in connection with any actual or anticipated sale of the property.

THE FOLLOWING ARE REPRESENTATIONS MADE BY THE SELLER(S) AND ARE NOT THE
REPRESENTATIONS OF THE AGENT(S), IF ANY. THIS INFORMATION IS A DISCLOSURE AND IS NOT
INTENDED TO BE PART OF ANY CONTRACT BETWEEN THE BUYER AND SELLER.

Seller ☐ is ☐ is not occupying the property.

A. The subject property has the items checked below (read across):

☐ Range	☐ Oven	☐ Microwave
☐ Dishwasher	☐ Trash Compactor	☐ Garbage Disposal
☐ Washer/Dryer Hookups		☐ Rain Gutters
☐ Burglar Alarms	☐ Smoke Detector(s)	☐ Fire Alarm
☐ TV Antenna	☐ Satellite Dish	☐ Intercom
☐ Central Heating	☐ Central Air Conditioning	☐ Evaporator Cooler(s)
☐ Wall/Window Air Conditioning	☐ Sprinklers	☐ Public Sewer System
☐ Septic Tank	☐ Sump Pump	☐ Water Softener
☐ Patio/Decking	☐ Built-in Barbecue	☐ Gazebo
☐ Sauna		
☐ Hot Tub	☐ Pool	☐ Spa
☐ Locking Safety Cover*	☐ Child Resistant Barrier*	☐ Locking Safety Cover*
☐ Security Gate(s)	☐ Automatic Garage Door Opener(s)*	☐ Number Remote Controls ____
Garage: ☐ Attached	☐ Not Attached	☐ Carport
Pool/Spa Heater: ☐ Gas	☐ Solar	☐ Electric
Water Heater: ☐ Gas	☐ Water Heater Anchored, Braced, or Strapped*	
Water Supply: ☐ City	☐ Well	☐ Private Utility or
Gas Supply: ☐ Utility	☐ Bottled	Other ____
☐ Window Screens	☐ Window Security Bars ☐ Quick Release Mechanism on Bedroom Windows*	

Exhaust Fan(s) in _____ 220 Volt Wiring in _____ Fireplace(s) in _____
☐ Gas Starter _____ ☐ Roof(s): Type: _____ Age: _____ (approx.)
☐ Other: _____
Are there, to the best of your (Seller's) knowledge, any of the above that are not in operating condition? ☐ Yes   ☐ No. If yes, then
describe. (Attach additional sheets if necessary): _____

(*see footnote on page 2)

TDS REVISED 10/03 (PAGE 1 OF 3) Print Date

Buyer's Initials (_____)(_____)
Seller's Initials (_____)(_____)

Reviewed by _____ Date _____

EQUAL HOUSING
OPPORTUNITY

REAL ESTATE TRANSFER DISCLOSURE STATEMENT (TDS PAGE 1 OF 3)

FIGURE 5.8 *(continued)*

Property Address: _____ Date: _____

B. Are you (Seller) aware of any significant defects/malfunctions in any of the following? ☐ Yes ☐ No. If yes, check appropriate space(s) below.

☐ Interior Walls ☐ Ceilings ☐ Floors ☐ Exterior Walls ☐ Insulation ☐ Roof(s) ☐ Windows ☐ Doors ☐ Foundation ☐ Slab(s) ☐ Driveways ☐ Sidewalks ☐ Walls/Fences ☐ Electrical Systems ☐ Plumbing/Sewers/Septics ☐ Other Structural Components

(Describe: _____

_____

_____)

If any of the above is checked, explain. (Attach additional sheets if necessary.): _____

_____

_____

_____

_____

*This garage door opener or child resistant pool barrier may not be in compliance with the safety standards relating to automatic reversing devices as set forth in Chapter 12.5 (commencing with Section 19890) of Part 3 of Division 13 of, or with the pool safety standards of Article 2.5 (commencing with Section 115920) of Chapter 5 of Part 10 of Division 104 of, the Health and Safety Code. The water heater may not be anchored, braced, or strapped in accordance with Section 19211 of the Health and Safety Code. Window security bars may not have quick release mechanisms in compliance with the 1995 edition of the California Building Standards Code.

C. Are you (Seller) aware of any of the following:

1. Substances, materials, or products which may be an environmental hazard such as, but not limited to, asbestos, formaldehyde, radon gas, lead-based paint, mold, fuel or chemical storage tanks, and contaminated soil or water on the subject property . . . . ☐ Yes ☐ No
2. Features of the property shared in common with adjoining landowners, such as walls, fences, and driveways, whose use or responsibility for maintenance may have an effect on the subject property . . . . ☐ Yes ☐ No
3. Any encroachments, easements or similar matters that may affect your interest in the subject property . . . . ☐ Yes ☐ No
4. Room additions, structural modifications, or other alterations or repairs made without necessary permits . . . . ☐ Yes ☐ No
5. Room additions, structural modifications, or other alterations or repairs not in compliance with building codes . . . . ☐ Yes ☐ No
6. Fill (compacted or otherwise) on the property or any portion thereof . . . . ☐ Yes ☐ No
7. Any settling from any cause, or slippage, sliding, or other soil problems . . . . ☐ Yes ☐ No
8. Flooding, drainage or grading problems . . . . ☐ Yes ☐ No
9. Major damage to the property or any of the structures from fire, earthquake, floods, or landslides . . . . ☐ Yes ☐ No
10. Any zoning violations, nonconforming uses, violations of "setback" requirements . . . . ☐ Yes ☐ No
11. Neighborhood noise problems or other nuisances . . . . ☐ Yes ☐ No
12. CC&R's or other deed restrictions or obligations . . . . ☐ Yes ☐ No
13. Homeowners' Association which has any authority over the subject property . . . . ☐ Yes ☐ No
14. Any "common area" (facilities such as pools, tennis courts, walkways, or other areas co-owned in undivided interest with others) . . . . ☐ Yes ☐ No
15. Any notices of abatement or citations against the property . . . . ☐ Yes ☐ No
16. Any lawsuits by or against the Seller threatening to or affecting this real property, including any lawsuits alleging a defect or deficiency in this real property or "common areas" (facilities such as pools, tennis courts, walkways, or other areas co-owned in undivided interest with others) . . . . ☐ Yes ☐ No

If the answer to any of these is yes, explain. (Attach additional sheets if necessary.): _____

_____

_____

_____

_____

Seller certifies that the information herein is true and correct to the best of the Seller's knowledge as of the date signed by the Seller.

Seller_____ Date _____

Seller_____ Date _____

Buyer's Initials (_____)(_____)
Seller's Initials (_____)(_____)

TDS REVISED 10/03 (PAGE 2 OF 3)

Reviewed by _____ Date _____

🏠 EQUAL HOUSING OPPORTUNITY

REAL ESTATE TRANSFER DISCLOSURE STATEMENT (TDS PAGE 2 OF 3)

FIGURE 5.8 *(continued)*

Property Address: _____   Date: _____

III. AGENT'S INSPECTION DISCLOSURE
(To be completed only if the Seller is represented by an agent in this transaction.)

THE UNDERSIGNED, BASED ON THE ABOVE INQUIRY OF THE SELLER(S) AS TO THE CONDITION OF THE PROPERTY AND BASED ON A REASONABLY COMPETENT AND DILIGENT VISUAL INSPECTION OF THE ACCESSIBLE AREAS OF THE PROPERTY IN CONJUNCTION WITH THAT INQUIRY, STATES THE FOLLOWING:

☐ Agent notes no items for disclosure.

☐ Agent notes the following items: _____

_____

_____

_____

_____

Agent (Broker Representing Seller) _____ By _____ Date _____
                                  (Please Print)   (Associate Licensee or Broker Signature)

IV. AGENT'S INSPECTION DISCLOSURE
(To be completed only if the agent who has obtained the offer is other than the agent above.)

THE UNDERSIGNED, BASED ON A REASONABLY COMPETENT AND DILIGENT VISUAL INSPECTION OF THE ACCESSIBLE AREAS OF THE PROPERTY, STATES THE FOLLOWING:

☐ Agent notes no items for disclosure.

☐ Agent notes the following items: _____

_____

_____

_____

_____

Agent (Broker Obtaining the Offer) _____ By _____ Date _____
                                  (Please Print)   (Associate Licensee or Broker Signature)

V. BUYER(S) AND SELLER(S) MAY WISH TO OBTAIN PROFESSIONAL ADVICE AND/OR INSPECTIONS OF THE PROPERTY AND TO PROVIDE FOR APPROPRIATE PROVISIONS IN A CONTRACT BETWEEN BUYER AND SELLER(S) WITH RESPECT TO ANY ADVICE/INSPECTIONS/DEFECTS.

I/WE ACKNOWLEDGE RECEIPT OF A COPY OF THIS STATEMENT.

Seller _____ Date _____   Buyer _____ Date _____

Seller _____ Date _____   Buyer _____ Date _____

Agent (Broker Representing Seller) _____ By _____ Date _____
                                  (Please Print)   (Associate Licensee or Broker Signature)

Agent (Broker Obtaining the Offer) _____ By _____ Date _____
                                  (Please Print)   (Associate Licensee or Broker Signature)

SECTION 1102.3 OF THE CIVIL CODE PROVIDES A BUYER WITH THE RIGHT TO RESCIND A PURCHASE CONTRACT FOR AT LEAST THREE DAYS AFTER THE DELIVERY OF THIS DISCLOSURE IF DELIVERY OCCURS AFTER THE SIGNING OF AN OFFER TO PURCHASE. IF YOU WISH TO RESCIND THE CONTRACT, YOU MUST ACT WITHIN THE PRESCRIBED PERIOD.

A REAL ESTATE BROKER IS QUALIFIED TO ADVISE ON REAL ESTATE. IF YOU DESIRE LEGAL ADVICE, CONSULT YOUR ATTORNEY.

SURE TRAC
The System for Success®

Published and Distributed by:
REAL ESTATE BUSINESS SERVICES, INC.
a subsidiary of the California Association of REALTORS®
525 South Virgil Avenue, Los Angeles, California 90020

Reviewed by _____ Date _____

EQUAL HOUSING OPPORTUNITY

TDS REVISED 10/03 (PAGE 3 OF 3)

REAL ESTATE TRANSFER DISCLOSURE STATEMENT (TDS PAGE 3 OF 3)

Source: Reprinted with permission of California Association of REALTORS®

FIGURE 5.9

CALIFORNIA
ASSOCIATION
OF REALTORS®

BUYER'S INSPECTION ADVISORY
(C.A.R. Form BIA, Revised 10/02)

Property Address: _____ ("Property").

A. IMPORTANCE OF PROPERTY INVESTIGATION: The physical condition of the land and improvements being purchased is not guaranteed by either Seller or Brokers. For this reason, you should conduct thorough investigations of the Property personally and with professionals who should provide written reports of their investigations. A general physical inspection typically does not cover all aspects of the Property nor items affecting the Property that are not physically located on the Property. If the professionals recommend further investigations, including a recommendation by a pest control operator to inspect inaccessible areas of the Property, you should contact qualified experts to conduct such additional investigations.

B. BUYER RIGHTS AND DUTIES: You have an affirmative duty to exercise reasonable care to protect yourself, including discovery of the legal, practical and technical implications of disclosed facts, and the investigation and verification of information and facts that you know or that are within your diligent attention and observation. The purchase agreement gives you the right to investigate the Property. If you exercise this right, and you should, you must do so in accordance with the terms of that agreement. This is the best way for you to protect yourself. It is extremely important for you to read all written reports provided by professionals and to discuss the results of inspections with the professional who conducted the inspection. You have the right to request that Seller make repairs, corrections or take other action based upon items discovered in your investigations or disclosed by Seller. If Seller is unwilling or unable to satisfy your requests, or you do not want to purchase the Property in its disclosed and discovered condition, you have the right to cancel the agreement if you act within specific time periods. If you do not cancel the agreement in a timely and proper manner, you may be in breach of contract.

C. SELLER RIGHTS AND DUTIES: Seller is required to disclose to you material facts known to him/her that affect the value or desirability of the Property. However, Seller may not be aware of some Property defects or conditions. Seller does not have an obligation to inspect the Property for your benefit nor is Seller obligated to repair, correct or otherwise cure known defects that are disclosed to you or previously unknown defects that are discovered by you or your inspectors during escrow. The purchase agreement obligates Seller to make the Property available to you for investigations.

D. BROKER OBLIGATIONS: Brokers do not have expertise in all areas and therefore cannot advise you on many items, such as soil stability, geologic or environmental conditions, hazardous or illegal controlled substances, structural conditions of the foundation or other improvements, or the condition of the roof, plumbing, heating, air conditioning, electrical, sewer, septic, waste disposal, or other system. The only way to accurately determine the condition of the Property is through an inspection by an appropriate professional selected by you. If Broker gives you referrals to such professionals, Broker does not guarantee their performance. You may select any professional of your choosing. In sales involving residential dwellings with no more than four units, Brokers have a duty to make a diligent visual inspection of the accessible areas of the Property and to disclose the results of that inspection. However, as some Property defects or conditions may not be discoverable from a visual inspection, it is possible Brokers are not aware of them. If you have entered into a written agreement with a Broker, the specific terms of that agreement will determine the nature and extent of that Broker's duty to you. **YOU ARE STRONGLY ADVISED TO INVESTIGATE THE CONDITION AND SUITABILITY OF ALL ASPECTS OF THE PROPERTY. IF YOU DO NOT DO SO, YOU ARE ACTING AGAINST THE ADVICE OF BROKERS.**

E. YOU ARE ADVISED TO CONDUCT INVESTIGATIONS OF THE ENTIRE PROPERTY, INCLUDING, BUT NOT LIMITED TO THE FOLLOWING:
1. **GENERAL CONDITION OF THE PROPERTY, ITS SYSTEMS AND COMPONENTS:** Foundation, roof, plumbing, heating, air conditioning, electrical, mechanical, security, pool/spa, other structural and non-structural systems and components, fixtures, built-in appliances, any personal property included in the sale, and energy efficiency of the Property. (Structural engineers are best suited to determine possible design or construction defects, and whether improvements are structurally sound.)
2. **SQUARE FOOTAGE, AGE, BOUNDARIES:** Square footage, room dimensions, lot size, age of improvements and boundaries. Any numerical statements regarding these items are APPROXIMATIONS ONLY and have not been verified by Seller and cannot be verified by Brokers. Fences, hedges, walls, retaining walls and other natural or constructed barriers or markers do not necessarily identify true Property boundaries. (Professionals such as appraisers, architects, surveyors and civil engineers are best suited to determine square footage, dimensions and boundaries of the Property.)
3. **WOOD DESTROYING PESTS:** Presence of, or conditions likely to lead to the presence of wood destroying pests and organisms and other infestation or infection. Inspection reports covering these items can be separated into two sections: Section 1 identifies areas where infestation or infection is evident. Section 2 identifies areas where there are conditions likely to lead to infestation or infection. A registered structural pest control company is best suited to perform these inspections.
4. **SOIL STABILITY:** Existence of fill or compacted soil, expansive or contracting soil, susceptibility to slippage, settling or movement, and the adequacy of drainage. (Geotechnical engineers are best suited to determine such conditions, causes and remedies.)

BIA REVISED 10/02 (PAGE 1 OF 2) Print Date

Buyer's Initials (_____)(_____)
Seller's Initials (_____)(_____)

| Reviewed by _____ Date _____ |

EQUAL HOUSING
OPPORTUNITY

BUYER'S INSPECTION ADVISORY (BIA PAGE 1 OF 2)

FIGURE 5.9 *(continued)*

Property Address: _____   Date: _____

5. **ROOF:** Present condition, age, leaks, and remaining useful life. (Roofing contractors are best suited to determine these conditions.)

6. **POOL/SPA:** Cracks, leaks or operational problems. (Pool contractors are best suited to determine these conditions.)

7. **WASTE DISPOSAL:** Type, size, adequacy, capacity and condition of sewer and septic systems and components, connection to sewer, and applicable fees.

8. **WATER AND UTILITIES; WELL SYSTEMS AND COMPONENTS:** Water and utility availability, use restrictions and costs. Water quality, adequacy, condition, and performance of well systems and components.

9. **ENVIRONMENTAL HAZARDS:** Potential environmental hazards, including, but not limited to, asbestos, lead-based paint and other lead contamination, radon, methane, other gases, fuel oil or chemical storage tanks, contaminated soil or water, hazardous waste, waste disposal sites, electromagnetic fields, nuclear sources, and other substances, materials, products, or conditions (including mold (airborne, toxic or otherwise), fungus or similar contaminants). (For more in formation on these items, you may consult an appropriate professional or read the booklets "Environmental Hazards: A Guide for Homeowners, Buyers, Landlords and Tenants," "Protect Your Family From Lead in Your Home" or both.)

10. **EARTHQUAKES AND FLOODING:** Susceptibility of the Property to earthquake/seismic hazards and propensity of the Property to flood. (A Geologist or Geotechnical Engineer is best suited to provide information on these conditions.)

11. **FIRE, HAZARD AND OTHER INSURANCE:** The availability and cost of necessary or desired insurance may vary. The location of the Property in a seismic, flood or fire hazard zone, and other conditions, such as the age of the Property and the claims history of the Property and Buyer, may affect the availability and need for certain types of insurance. Buyer should explore insurance options early as this information may affect other decisions, including the removal of loan and inspection contingencies. (An insurance agent is best suited to provide information on these conditions.)

12. **BUILDING PERMITS, ZONING AND GOVERNMENTAL REQUIREMENTS:** Permits, inspections, certificates, zoning, other governmental limitations, restrictions, and requirements affecting the current or future use of the Property, its development or size. (Such information is available from appropriate governmental agencies and private information providers. Brokers are not qualified to review or interpret any such information.)

13. **RENTAL PROPERTY RESTRICTIONS:** Some cities and counties impose restrictions that limit the amount of rent that can be charged, the maximum number of occupants; and the right of a landlord to terminate a tenancy. Deadbolt or other locks and security systems for doors and windows, including window bars, should be examined to determine whether they satisfy legal requirements. (Government agencies can provide information about these restrictions and other requirements.)

14. **SECURITY AND SAFETY:** State and local Law may require the installation of barriers, access alarms, self-latching mechanisms and/or other measures to decrease the risk to children and other persons of existing swimming pools and hot tubs, as well as various fire safety and other measures concerning other features of the Property. Compliance requirements differ from city to city and county to county. Unless specifically agreed, the Property may not be in compliance with these requirements. (Local government agencies can provide information about these restrictions and other requirements.)

15. **NEIGHBORHOOD, AREA, SUBDIVISION CONDITIONS; PERSONAL FACTORS:** Neighborhood or area conditions, including schools, proximity and adequacy of law enforcement, crime statistics, the proximity of registered felons or offenders, fire protection, other government services, availability, adequacy and cost of any speed-wired, wireless internet connections or other telecommunications or other technology services and installations, proximity to commercial, industrial or agricultural activities, existing and proposed transportation, construction and development that may affect noise, view, or traffic, airport noise, noise or odor from any source, wild and domestic animals, other nuisances, hazards, or circumstances, protected species, wetland properties, botanical diseases, historic or other governmentally protected sites or improvements, cemeteries, facilities and condition of common areas of common interest subdivisions, and possible lack of compliance with any governing documents or Homeowners' Association requirements, conditions and influences of significance to certain cultures and/or religions, and personal needs, requirements and preferences of Buyer.

Buyer and Seller acknowledge and agree that Broker: **(i)** Does not decide what price Buyer should pay or Seller should accept; **(ii)** Does not guarantee the condition of the Property; **(iii)** Does not guarantee the performance, adequacy or completeness of inspections, services, products or repairs provided or made by Seller or others; **(iv)** Does not have an obligation to conduct an inspection of common areas or areas off the site of the Property; **(v)** Shall not be responsible for identifying defects on the Property, in common areas, or offsite unless such defects are visually observable by an inspection of reasonably accessible areas of the Property or are known to Broker; **(vi)** Shall not be responsible for inspecting public records or permits concerning the title or use of Property; **(vii)** Shall not be responsible for identifying the location of boundary lines or other items affecting title; **(viii)** Shall not be responsible for verifying square footage, representations of others or information contained in Investigation reports, Multiple Listing Service, advertisements, flyers or other promotional material; **(ix)** Shall not be responsible for providing legal or tax advice regarding any aspect of a transaction entered into by Buyer or Seller; and **(x)** Shall not be responsible for providing other advice or information that exceeds the knowledge, education and experience required to perform real estate licensed activity. Buyer and Seller agree to seek legal, tax, insurance, title and other desired assistance from appropriate professionals.

By signing below, Buyer and Seller each acknowledge that they have read, understand, accept and have received a Copy of this Advisory. Buyer is encouraged to read it carefully.

_____   Date _____   _____   Date _____
Buyer Signature   Buyer Signature

_____   Date _____   _____   Date _____
Seller Signature   Seller Signature

Published and Distributed by:
REAL ESTATE BUSINESS SERVICES, INC.
a subsidiary of the California Association of REALTORS®
525 South Virgil Avenue, Los Angeles, California 90020

Reviewed by _____ Date _____

EQUAL HOUSING OPPORTUNITY

BIA REVISED 10/02 (PAGE 2 OF 2)

BUYER'S INSPECTION ADVISORY (BIA PAGE 2 OF 2)

Source: Reprinted with permission of California Association of REALTORS®

FIGURE 5.10

CALIFORNIA ASSOCIATION OF REALTORS ®

AGENT VISUAL INSPECTION DISCLOSURE
(CALIFORNIA CIVIL CODE § 2079 ET SEQ.)
For use by an agent when a transfer disclosure statement is required or when a seller is exempt from completing a TDS
(C.A.R. Form AVID, Revised 11/07)

This inspection disclosure concerns the residential property situated in the City of _____,
County of _____, State of California, described as _____
_____ ("Property").

California law requires, with limited exceptions, that a real estate broker or salesperson (collectively, "Agent") conduct a reasonably competent and diligent **visual** inspection of reasonably and normally accessible areas of certain properties offered for sale and then disclose to the prospective purchaser material facts affecting the value or desirability of that property that the inspection reveals. The duty applies regardless of whom that Agent represents. The duty applies to residential real properties containing one-to-four dwelling units, and manufactured homes (mobilehomes). The duty applies to a stand-alone detached dwelling (whether or not located in a subdivision or a planned development) or to an attached dwelling such as a condominium. The duty also applies to a lease with an option to purchase, a ground lease or a real property sales contract of one of those properties.

California law does not require the Agent to inspect the following:
• Areas that are not reasonably and normally accessible
• Areas off site of the property
• Public records or permits
• Common areas of planned developments, condominiums, stock cooperatives and the like.

Agent Inspection Limitations: Because the Agent's duty is limited to conducting a reasonably competent and diligent visual inspection of reasonably and normally accessible areas of only the Property being offered for sale, there are several things that the Agent will not do. What follows is a non-exclusive list of examples of limitations on the scope of the Agent's duty.

<u>Roof and Attic:</u>   Agent will not climb onto a roof or into an attic.

<u>Interior:</u>   Agent will not move or look under or behind furniture, pictures, wall hangings or floor coverings. Agent will not look up chimneys or into cabinets, or open locked doors.

<u>Exterior:</u>   Agent will not inspect beneath a house or other structure on the Property, climb up or down a hillside, move or look behind plants, bushes, shrubbery and other vegetation or fences, walls or other barriers.

<u>Appliances and Systems:</u>   Agent will not operate appliances or systems (such as, but not limited to, electrical, plumbing, pool or spa, heating, cooling, septic, sprinkler, communication, entertainment, well or water) to determine their functionality.

<u>Size of Property or Improvements:</u>   Agent will not measure square footage of lot or improvements, or identify or locate boundary lines, easements or encroachments.

<u>Environmental Hazards:</u>   Agent will not determine if the Property has mold, asbestos, lead or lead-based paint, radon, formaldehyde or any other hazardous substance or analyze soil or geologic condition.

<u>Off-Property Conditions:</u>   By statute, Agent is not obligated to pull permits or inspect public records. Agent will not guarantee views or zoning, identify proposed construction or development or changes or proximity to transportation, schools, or law enforcement.

<u>Analysis of Agent Disclosures:</u>   For any items disclosed as a result of Agent's visual inspection, or by others, Agent will not provide an analysis of or determine the cause or source of the disclosed matter, nor determine the cost of any possible repair.

What this means to you: An Agent's inspection is not intended to take the place of any other type of inspection, nor is it a substitute for a full and complete disclosure by a seller. Regardless of what the Agent's inspection reveals, or what disclosures are made by sellers, California Law specifies that a buyer has a duty to exercise reasonable care to protect himself or herself. This duty encompasses facts which are known to or within the diligent attention and observation of the buyer. Therefore, in order to determine for themselves whether or not the Property meets their needs and intended uses, as well as the cost to remedy any disclosed or discovered defect, **BUYER SHOULD: (1) REVIEW ANY DISCLOSURES OBTAINED FROM SELLER; (2) OBTAIN ADVICE ABOUT, AND INSPECTIONS OF, THE PROPERTY FROM OTHER APPROPRIATE PROFESSIONALS; AND (3) REVIEW ANY FINDINGS OF THOSE PROFESSIONALS WITH THE PERSONS WHO PREPARED THEM. IF BUYER FAILS TO DO SO, BUYER IS ACTING AGAINST THE ADVICE OF BROKER.**

Buyer's Initials (_____)(_____)
Seller's Initials (_____)(_____)

EQUAL HOUSING OPPORTUNITY

AVID REVISED 11/07 (PAGE 1 OF 3)   Print Date

Reviewed by _____ Date _____

AGENT VISUAL INSPECTION DISCLOSURE (AVID PAGE 1 OF 3)

FIGURE 5.10 *(continued)*

Property Address: _____   Date: _____

Inspection Date/Time: _____   Weather conditions: _____
Other persons present: _____

THE UNDERSIGNED, BASED ON A REASONABLY COMPETENT AND DILIGENT VISUAL INSPECTION OF THE REASONABLY AND NORMALLY ACCESSIBLE AREAS OF THE PROPERTY, STATES THE FOLLOWING:

Entry (excluding common areas): _____
_____
_____

Living Room: _____
_____
_____

Dining Room: _____
_____

Kitchen: _____
_____

Other Room: _____
_____
_____

Hall/Stairs (excluding common areas): _____
_____
_____

Bedroom # __: _____
_____
_____

Bedroom # __: _____
_____

Bedroom # __: _____
_____
_____

Bath # ____: _____
_____

Bath # ____: _____
_____

Bath # ____: _____
_____

Other Room: _____
_____
_____

Buyer's Initials (_____)(_____)
Seller's Initials (_____)(_____)

AVID REVISED 11/07 (PAGE 2 OF 3)

Reviewed by _____ Date _____

EQUAL HOUSING OPPORTUNITY

AGENT VISUAL INSPECTION DISCLOSURE (AVID PAGE 2 OF 3)

FIGURE 5.10 *(continued)*

Property Address: _____ Date: _____

Other Room: _____

_____

_____

Other: _____

_____

_____

Other: _____

_____

_____

Other: _____

_____

_____

Garage/Parking (excluding common areas): _____

_____

Exterior Building and Yard - Front/Sides/Back: _____

_____

_____

Other Observed or Known Conditions Not Specified Above: _____

_____

_____

This disclosure is based on a reasonably competent and diligent visual inspection of reasonably and normally accessible areas of the Property on the date specified above.

Real Estate Broker (Firm who performed the Inspection) _____

By _____ Date _____
            (Signature of Associate Licensee or Broker)

Reminder: Not all defects are observable by a real estate licensee conducting an inspection. The inspection does not include testing of any system or component. Real Estate Licensees are not home inspectors or contractors. BUYER SHOULD OBTAIN ADVICE ABOUT AND INSPECTIONS OF THE PROPERTY FROM OTHER APPROPRIATE PROFESSIONALS. IF BUYER FAILS TO DO SO, BUYER IS ACTING AGAINST THE ADVICE OF BROKER.

I/we acknowledge that I/we have read, understand and received a copy of this disclosure.

Date _____   Date _____

SELLER _____   SELLER _____

Date _____   Date _____

BUYER _____   BUYER _____

Real Estate Broker (Firm Representing Seller) _____ Date _____

By _____
            (Associate Licensee or Broker Signature)

Real Estate Broker (Firm Representing Buyer) _____ Date _____

By _____
            (Associate Licensee or Broker Signature)

Published and Distributed by:
REAL ESTATE BUSINESS SERVICES, INC.
a subsidiary of the California Association of REALTORS®
525 South Virgil Avenue, Los Angeles, California 90020

AVID REVISED 11/07 (PAGE 3 OF 3)

| Reviewed by _____ Date _____ |

AGENT VISUAL INSPECTION DISCLOSURE (AVID PAGE 3 OF 3)

Source: Reprinted with permission of California Association of REALTORS®

Chapter

6

This chapter will help you to understand the fundamentals of mathematics as they apply to real estate. Basic concepts of addition, subtraction, multiplication, division, fractions, and decimals are briefly reviewed to set a solid foundation for more complicated real estate computations. At the conclusion of the chapter, you will be able to do the following:

1. Solve problems related to investments, discounting notes, appraisals, commissions, interest and loans, cost and selling price, square footage and area calculations, prorations, and documentary transfer taxes.

2. Use amortization and other tables to simplify real estate mathematical computations.

Practical Real Estate Mathematics

6.1 REVIEW OF FUNDAMENTALS

The practical application of real estate mathematics creates apprehension in some people. The use of calculators and the development of tables can help alleviate the fear of math. An understanding of the simple formulas presented in this lesson can help you gain confidence in your ability to solve everyday real estate mathematical problems.

The difficulty some people have with mathematics comes from a lack of knowledge or a forgetfulness of some of the basic rules of mathematics, particularly with regard to percentages, decimals, and fractions.

Decimals

Before solving various real estate mathematical problems, it is helpful to review the concept of decimals. A **decimal** is the period that sets apart the whole number from the fractional part of a number. The position of the decimal in a number determines the value of the number.

All numbers to the right of the decimal are less than one. The first position to the right of the decimal is the "tenth" position, the second is the "hundredth," the third is the "thousandth," the fourth is the "ten thousandth," the fifth is the "hundred thousandth," and so on.

To the left of the decimal are the whole numbers. The first position is known as the "units" position, the second is the "tens," the third is the "hundreds," the fourth is the "thousands," the fifth is the "ten thousands," the sixth is the "hundred thousands," and so on. Table 6.1 may help you clarify the relationships among percentages, decimals, and fractions.

Converting Percentages to Decimals

To remove the percent sign, simply move the decimal two places to the left to form a usable decimal number. (See Table 6.2.)

Many times an answer will appear as a decimal. If you wish to convert the answer to an answer with a percent sign (%), simply reverse the procedure. (See Table 6.3.)

Addition of Decimal Numbers

When adding numbers with decimals, place figures in a vertical column, making sure each decimal is in a direct vertical line.

TABLE 6.1

Percentage (%)	Decimal	Fraction
4.5	0.045	45/1000
6.67	0.0667	1/15
10	0.10	1/10
12.5	0.125	1/8
16.67	0.1667	1/6
25	0.25	1/4
33.33	0.333	1/3
50	0.50	1/2
66.67	0.6667	2/3
75	0.75	3/4
100	1.00	1/1

TABLE 6.2

8%	converts	.08
25%	converts	.25
9.5%	converts	.095
105%	converts	1.05

TABLE 6.3

.08	converts to	8%
.25	converts to	25%
.095	converts to	9.5%
1.05	converts to	105%

Example:

$$126.06$$
$$5.715$$
$$\underline{400.8}$$
$$532.575$$

Subtraction of Decimal Numbers

The same procedure is used to subtract one decimal number from another.

Example:

$$\$18,450.60$$
$$\underline{-425.20}$$
$$\$18,025.40$$

Multiplication of Decimal Numbers

Multiply the two numbers in the normal fashion and then mark off as many decimal places in the answer as there are in the two numbers being multiplied.

Example:

$$7.064 \quad \text{(multiplicand)}$$
$$\underline{\times 37.6} \quad \text{(multiplier)}$$
$$265.6064 \quad \text{(product)}$$

Division of Decimal Numbers

In a division problem that contains a decimal in the divisor, you must remove that decimal before proceeding with the problem. Mentally move the decimal in the dividend the same number of places shown in the divisor. Add zeros to the dividend if the dividend has fewer digits than are needed to carry out the division process. The decimal point in the quotient (answer) will appear directly above the imaginary decimal in the dividend.

Example:

$$\qquad\qquad 6000 \quad \text{(quotient)}$$
$$\text{(divisor)}.045\overline{)270.000} \quad \text{(dividend)}$$

When no decimal appears in the divisor, the decimal in the quotient will appear directly above the decimal in the dividend.

Example:

$$\qquad 3.02$$
$$24\overline{)72.48}$$

6.2 VARIABLES

Most real estate problems involve three variables—two known and one unknown. You must find the unknown variable. The three variables are termed *paid*, *made*, and *rate* (%). These basic formulas evolve from the illustration:

$$\text{Made} = \text{Paid} \times \text{Rate}$$
$$\text{Paid} = \text{Made} \div \text{Rate}$$
$$\text{Rate} = \text{Made} \div \text{Paid}$$

In any problem involving these formulas, one quantity is unknown. You must determine from the given information whether to multiply or divide the other variables to compute the third variable.

To assist in this process, Table 6.4 equates various real estate terms with the terms *made*, *paid*, and *rate*.

Investment Problems

To find the amount of money to be invested when the income and rate of return are known:

$$\text{Amount invested (paid)} = \frac{\text{Income (made)}}{\text{Rate (\% of return)}}$$

To find the rate (%) of return when the income and the amount invested are known:

$$\text{Rate (\%)} = \frac{\text{Income (made)}}{\text{Amount invested (paid)}}$$

TABLE 6.4

Amount Made	Amount Paid	Rate (%)
1. Income (earned per year)	Amount of investment	Percentage return
2. Sales commission	Selling price	Rate of commission
3. Documentary transfer tax	Taxable equity	Transfer tax rate
4. Monthly rent	Investment amount	Rate of return
5. Annual net income	Property value	Capitalization rate
6. Interest	Principal	Rate × Time
7. Discount amount	Loan balance	Rate of discount
8. Area of property	Length	Width

To find the income when the amount invested and the rate (%) are known:

Income (made) = Amount invested (paid) × Rate (%)

Sample investment problems using the preceding formulas follow.

> **Caution**
> When you are given monthly figures, convert them to annual figures (for example, $80 per month × 12 months = $960 per year).

Problem 1

If an investor wants to earn $50 per month from a savings account and the account pays 5 percent simple interest, how much must be put in the account?

The given variables are

Income = $600 per year ($50 × 12 months)
Rate of return = 5%

The unknown variable is the amount of investment. By substituting in the formula, you obtain

$$\text{Amount} = \frac{\$600}{5\% \text{ or } .05} \qquad .05\overline{)\begin{array}{c} 12{,}000 \\ 600.00 \end{array}}$$

Amount of investment = $12,000

Problem 2

An investor bought a small lot for $85,000 cash. Assume the lot was later listed for sale and sold for $125,000. What is the rate (%) of profit the investor made on this sale?

The given variables are

Paid = $85,000
Made = $40,000 ($125,000 − $85,000)

The unknown variable is the rate of profit. By substituting in the formula, you obtain

$$85{,}000\overline{)\begin{array}{c} .4706 \\ 40{,}000 \end{array}} \quad \text{or} \quad 47.06\%$$

Discounting Notes

Problem 3

A \$5,000 note for a loan from a private lender is to be paid off in 12 months. The borrower is to pay the \$5,000 plus 8 percent interest on the due date. An investor purchases the note today at a discount rate of 10 percent. What is the investor's rate of return on the amount invested?

The first step is to determine the amount made.

$$\text{Paid} \times \text{Rate} = \text{Made}$$

By substituting in the formula, you obtain

\$5,000 × .08 = \$400 (interest to the lender on due date)
\$5,000 × .10 = \$500 (discount allowed investor)
Made = \$900 (\$400 + \$500)
Paid = \$5,000 less 10%, or \$4,500

The given variables are

Made = \$900
Paid = \$4,500

The unknown variable is the rate (%).

$$\text{Made} \div \text{Paid} = \text{Rate}$$

Substitution results in

$$4500 \overline{\smash{)}900.00}^{\,.20 \text{ or } 20\%}$$

Rate or percentage of profit = .20, or 20%

Appraisal Problems

In appraisal problems, use the formula:

$$\text{Paid} \times \text{Rate (\%)} = \text{Made}$$

Reconstructed, the choices become:

1. Value of property × Capitalization rate = Net income or net loss
2. Value = Made ÷ Rate (capitalization rate)
3. Capitalization rate = Made ÷ Paid (value of property)
4. Income or loss = Paid × Capitalization rate

Problem 4

After all operating expenses have been deducted, an older triplex nets an income of $500 per month per apartment unit. A prospective investor is interested in purchasing the property, and he or she demands an investment rate (**capitalization rate**) of 6 percent. What is the maximum the investor should pay for the triplex?

$500 per unit × 3 units = $1,500 net income per month
$1,500 × 12 months = $18,000 annual net income

The given variables are

Made = $18,000
Rate = 6%

The unknown variable is the paid. Substitution in the formula results in

$$\frac{300,000}{.06 \,)\overline{18,000.00}}$$

The investor should pay no more than $300,000.

Problem 5

An investor pays $600,000 for an older six-unit apartment house that has a gross income of $700 rent per month per unit with total expenses of $14,400 per year. What capitalization rate (%) will the investor make on the purchase price?

Gross income = 12 months × 700 = $8,400 × 6 units
                                 = $50,400
Less expenses   −14,400
Net income (made) $36,000

By substituting in the formula

$$\frac{.06}{600,000 \,)\overline{36,000.00}}$$

The capitalization rate = 6%.

Commission Problems

In commission problems:

Paid figure refers to the selling price.

Rate is the commission rate.

Made is the amount of commission.

Problem 6

A real estate salesperson found a buyer for a $300,000 condo. The seller agreed to pay the broker a 6 percent commission on the sale. The broker pays the salesperson 40 percent of the commission. What is the salesperson's commission?

The unknown variable is the made. Substitution in the formula results in

Paid = $300,000 (selling price)
Rate = 40% of 6%
Made (commission) = Paid (selling price) × Rate

$300,000 $18,000
 × .06   × .40
$ 18,000 Total commission $ 7,200 Salesperson's commission

The amount of the salesperson's share of the $18,000 total commission is $7,200.

Problem 7

A real estate office lists a parcel of land for $800,000 with an agreed commission of 10 percent. The broker presents an offer for 10 percent less than the listed price, which the seller agrees to accept if the broker reduces the amount of commission by 25 percent. If the broker agrees to the reduction, what is the amount of the commission?

The missing variable is the made.

Paid = $800,000 less 10% ($80,000) = $720,000
Rate = 10% less 25% = 7.5% or (.075)

Thus, the formula becomes Selling Price × Commission Rate = Commission Amount.

Therefore: $800,000 listing price − 10% = $720,000 selling price
            10% − 25% = 7.5% commission rate (.10 − .025 = .075)
Then: $720,000 × 7.5% = $54,000 commission

There are a variety of **commission splits** in actual practice.

A broker may take a listing, make the sale, and receive the entire commission. One or more salespersons in a broker's office may be involved; if so, they divide the commission with the broker.

A listing may be taken by Broker A and placed in multiple listing. If the sale is made by Broker B, he or she splits the commission with Broker A's office. One of Broker B's salespersons may make the sale. If so, the salesperson splits the office's share of the commission with Broker B.

Commission splits between multiple listing brokers vary, with 50/50 being the most common. In some cases, this split is 40 percent to the listing broker's office and 60 percent to the selling broker's office.

When the listing and the sale are in-house, the splits may be as follows:

- 20 percent to the listing salesperson
- 40 percent to the salesperson making the sale
- 40 percent to the broker

  OR

- 35 percent to the listing salesperson
- 35 percent to the salesperson making the sale
- 30 percent to the broker

The amount of the commission split depends on the individual broker's commission schedule. An example of a possible commission split between real estate brokers and salespersons may be as follows: Assume that $400,000 is the sales price for a home and the seller agrees to pay a 6 percent commission. Then 6% × $400,000 = $24,000 commission. The $24,000 commission may be divided up between brokers and salespeople as shown in Figure 6.1.

Interest and Loan Problems

Interest is the charge for the use of money. The dollar amount of interest is determined by the rate of interest charged and the amount of money borrowed. When borrowing money, the

FIGURE 6.1

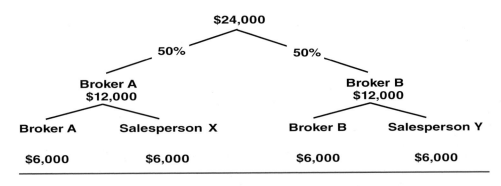

borrower is obligated to pay back the amount borrowed as well as interest per agreed terms between the borrower and the lender.

> **Note**
> When working with interest problems, be sure to convert monthly figures to annual figures.

To solve interest problems, you will use these terms and formulas. **Interest** is the charge for the use of money expressed as dollars. **Principal** is the amount of money borrowed.

Rate is the percentage of interest charged on the principal.

Time represents the interval between payments on principal and/or interest. In the formula, time is expressed as years or a fraction of a year. Interest = Principal × Rate × Time (I = P × R × T).

By applying this formula to the standard "made, paid, rate" formula, the paid figure refers to the amount of the loan or the principal, rate (%) is the rate of interest multiplied by the years or fraction of a year, and made is the amount of interest expressed in money. As a result, the following formulas are derived:

$$\text{Amount of loan} = \frac{\text{Amount of interest}}{\text{Rate of interest} \times \text{time}} \quad \text{or } P = \frac{I}{R \times T}$$

$$\text{Rate of interest} = \frac{\text{Amount of interest}}{\text{Amount of loan} \times \text{time}} \quad \text{or } R = \frac{I}{P \times T}$$

Amount of interest = Amount of loan × Rate of interest × Time or
I = P × R × T

Problem 8

If you borrowed $8,000 for one year and paid $640 interest, what rate of interest did you pay?

The known variables are

Paid = $8,000
Made = $640 × 1 year = $640 per year

Substitution results in

$$\text{Rate} = \text{Made} \div \text{Paid or } \frac{I}{P \times T}$$

$$\frac{.08}{\$8000/640.00} \quad \text{or} \quad \frac{640}{8000 \times 1}$$

Problem 9

If one month's interest is $1,000 on a seven-year straight note (interest-only note) and the note calls for interest at 6 percent per year, what is the amount of the loan?

The known variables are

Rate = 6%
Made = $1,000 × 12 months = $12,000 interest per year

Substitution in the formula results in

$$\text{Paid} = \text{Made} \div \text{Rate}$$

$$.06\overline{)12,000.00} \quad \begin{array}{c} 200,000 \end{array}$$

Proof:
$$\begin{array}{rl}
\$200,000 & \text{Principal} \\
\times\ .06 & \text{Rate} \\
\hline
\$12,000 & \text{Interest paid for year}
\end{array}$$

Cost and Selling Price Problems

When dealing with cost problems, you are given a selling price and are asked to calculate the profit or the cost before a fixed profit. The first step is to consider the cost figure as 100 percent. Next, add the profit percent to the 100 percent and divide the total percentage into the selling price.

Problem 10

A person sold a rural property for $60,000, which allowed her to make a 20 percent profit. What did she pay for the property?

Substitution in the formula results in

$$\text{Cost} = \text{Selling price} \div (\text{Profit \%} + 100\%)$$

$$\text{Cost} = 1.20\overline{)60,000.00}^{\ 50,000}$$

She paid $50,000 for the property.

Problem 11

Another problem arises when the seller receives a given net amount and you are asked to establish the selling price or amount of the loan.

For instance, you offer your lot for sale, asking for a certain net amount. A broker who found a buyer delivered a check to you for $85,500. The broker had already deducted 10 percent for commission and seller closing cost. What did the lot sell for?

The formula used to solve this problem is

$$\text{Selling price} = \frac{\text{Net amount received}}{100\% - \text{Commission rate}}$$

Substitution in this formula results in

$$\text{Selling price} = \$85,000 \div (100\% - 10\%) \text{ or } 90\%$$

$$\text{Selling price} = .90\overline{)85,500.00}^{\,95,000}$$

6.3 SQUARE FOOTAGE AND AREA CALCULATION

Problems related to square footage are simple. This technique is used when you want to know the number of square feet in a property. Once you determine the square footage, you can refer to an index on residential property to determine the cost per square foot or to obtain estimates per square foot from local contractors. The cost per square foot multiplied by the square footage gives an estimated new construction cost of a building.

The basic formula for determining the area of a piece of property is

$$\text{Area} = \text{Length} \times \text{Width}$$

The following formulas can be used:

Area = Length × Width
Length = Area ÷ Width
Width = Area ÷ Length

Problem 12

What is the depth, or length, of a piece of vacant land containing six acres with a width, or front footage, of 400 feet on a county road? (Remember, there are 43,560 square feet in an acre.)

Convert the piece of property into square feet by multiplying 43,560 by 6 = 261,360 square feet.

Substitution in the formula results in

Length = Area ÷ Width
Length = 261,360 ÷ 400 = 653.4 feet
Proof: 400 feet × 653.4 feet = 261,360 square feet

If the piece of property you are measuring is irregular in shape, try to make rectangles and triangles of the area given (Area of a triangle = Altitude × Base ÷ 2). An example of this type of computation is given in Problem 13.

Problem 13

Use Figures 6.2 and 6.3 to compute the square footage of the lot and then find the total construction cost of the garage and house. Assume contractors are quoting $50 per square foot for garages and $100 per square foot for homes.

Insert dotted lines in the diagram to form a rectangle A and a triangle B.

Improvements

1. Compute the area in rectangle A as follows: 110 × 100 = 11,000 square feet.
2. Compute the area of triangle B as follows: 40 × 100 ÷ 2 = 2,000 square feet.

Thus, the size of the lot is 11,000 + 2,000 = 13,000 square feet. To figure the area in the house:

1. Place dotted lines as indicated in the diagram, thus forming three rectangles (C, D, E) in the house.
2. Compute the area of each rectangle as follows:

   Rectangle C = 25 × 20 = 500 square feet
   Rectangle D = 60 × 20 = 1,200 square feet
   Rectangle E = 20 × 35 = 700 square feet
   Total = 2,400 square feet in house

3. Compute the area of the garage as follows: 20 × 25 = 500 square feet.

FIGURE 6.2

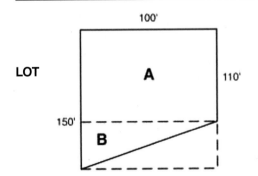

FIGURE 6.3

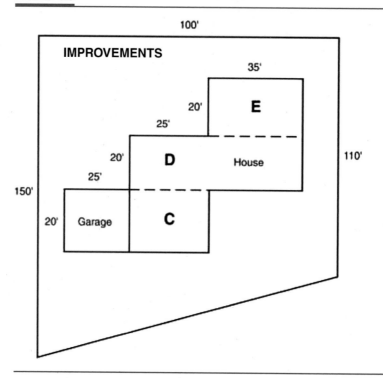

4. Compute the costs as follows:

2,400 square feet × $100 per square foot	=	$240,000
500 square feet × $50 per square foot	=	$ 25,000
Total	=	$265,000

Answers

13,000 square feet in the lot; $265,000 cost of construction for the total improvements

6.4 PRORATIONS

Ownership of real property entails certain expenses. Some of these expenses are paid in advance; others, in arrears. They may be paid for by the seller prior to the sale of the property, or the buyer may assume costs owed by the seller at the close of escrow.

It is only fair that expenses paid in advance should be credited (allocated) to the seller and debited (charged) to the buyer; by the same token, expenses owed by the seller and not paid by the seller prior to the close of escrow, but to be paid later by the buyer, should be debited to the seller and credited to the buyer.

Proration is the act of making an equitable distribution of these expenses in escrow at the close of the sale.

There are four basic steps in proration:

1. Determine whether the amount should be a credit or a debit to the seller or the buyer.
2. Determine the number of days to be prorated.
3. Tabulate the cost per day.
4. Multiply the number of days by the cost per day.

> **Remember**
> For simplicity in determining prorations, assume there are 30 days in a month and 360 days in a year.

Expenses that are normally subject to proration are real property taxes and assessments, interest on loans assumed, hazard insurance, and prepaid rents if the property is income producing.

Problem 14

Ms. A sells her rural cabin on September 1, 2007. She has an existing loan of $100,000 on the cabin. The interest on the loan is 9 percent. Buyer B assumes Ms. A's loan with interest paid to August 15, 2007. The seller has paid for an existing three-year hazard insurance policy for $360 per year, paid by Ms. A until October 15, 2008. Ms. A also neglected to pay her property taxes of $1,800 for the year. The tax year runs July 1, 2007, through June 30, 2008. What is the interest proration, and who is credited or debited? What is the insurance proration, and who is credited or debited? What is the tax proration, and who is credited or debited?

To figure the proration on the interest:

Step 1: August 15 to September 1, 2007 = 15 days
Step 2: $100,000 × 9% ÷ 360 = $25 per day
Step 3: 15 days × $25 per day = $375 interest
Step 4: Credit the buyer and debit the seller.

To figure the proration on the insurance policy:

Step 1: September 1, 2007, through October 15, 2008 = 405 days
Step 2: $360 ÷ 360 = $1 per day
Step 3: 405 days × $1 = $405
Step 4: Credit the seller and debit the buyer.

To figure the tax proration:

Step 1: July 1 to September 1, 2007 = 60 days
Step 2: $1,800 ÷ 360 = $5 per day
Step 3: 60 days × $5 = $300
Step 4: Debit the seller and credit the buyer.

> **Note**
> A general rule to use in proration is: When the expenses are paid beyond escrow, credit the seller and debit the buyer. When the expenses are paid short of escrow, debit the seller and credit the buyer.

6.5 DOCUMENTARY TRANSFER TAX

When real property is transferred, state law allows the county recorder to apply a **documentary transfer tax**. The amount of the tax is placed on the deed and is computed based on the following schedule:

1. $1.10 for $1,000 of value transferred, or $0.55 for every $500 or fraction thereof.
2. When the terms of the sale are all cash, the documentary transfer tax is paid on the entire sales price. A new loan by the buyer is treated the same as an all-cash sale.
3. When the buyer assumes the seller's existing loan, the amount of the loan on property is exempt and is subtracted from the total selling price. The tax is computed only on the equity amount. The transfer tax can be paid by the buyer or the seller, but custom usually has the seller pay the tax.

In some areas, cities are allowed to levy a real estate transfer tax on top of this statewide documentary tax. These transfer taxes are not standardized and vary from city to city. They are not presented in this book.

Problem 15

A home is sold for $510,000. The buyer puts some cash down and obtains new financing for the balance of the sales price. What is the documentary transfer tax?

$$\frac{\$510,000}{1,000} = 510 \times \$1.10 = \$561 \text{ Documentary transfer tax}$$

Problem 16

A one-bedroom condo is sold for $237,500. But in this case, the buyer assumes the seller's existing $200,000 loan. What is the documentary transfer tax?

$237,500 Sales price
− 200,000 Existing loan assumed
$37,500 Equity transferred

$$\frac{\$37,500}{1,000} = 37.5 \times \$1.10 = \$41.25 \text{ Documentary transfer tax}$$

6.6 USE OF FINANCIAL TABLES

To facilitate mathematical computations, financial calculators, computers, and/or tables are used.

Interest Computation

This chapter previously discussed how to compute the amount of interest to be paid using the formula $I = P \times R \times T$. Remember that computations are usually based on a 30-day month and 360-day year.

Take a look at an example using the conventional method and an interest table. (See Table 6.5.)

Problem 17

What is the interest on a $6,500 loan for one year, three months, and twenty days at 9 percent interest?

Conventional Method

$P \times R \times T = I$

Principal is $6,500

Rate is 9%

Time is 470 days (1 year + 3 months + 20 days)

Thus

$$\$6,500 \times .09 \times 1.3056^* = \$763.78 \text{ (actual)}$$

$$^*\frac{470 \text{ days}}{360 \text{ days}} = 1.3056$$

TABLE 6.5 Interest Table Figured on $1,000 360 Days to the Year.

Days	5%	6%	7%	8%	9%	10%
1	0.1389	0.1667	0.1944	0.2222	0.2500	0.2778
2	0.2778	0.3333	0.3889	0.4444	0.5000	0.5556
3	0.4167	0.5000	0.5833	0.6666	0.7500	0.8334
4	0.5556	0.6667	0.7778	0.8888	1.0000	1.1112
5	0.6944	0.8333	0.9722	1.1111	1.2500	1.3890
6	0.8333	1.0000	0.1667	1.3333	1.5000	1.6668
7	0.9722	1.1667	1.3611	1.5555	1.7500	1.9446
8	1.1111	1.3333	1.5556	1.7777	2.0000	2.2224
9	1.2500	1.5000	1.7500	2.0000	2.2500	2.5002
10	1.3889	1.6667	1.9444	2.2222	2.5000	2.7780
11	1.5278	1.8333	2.1389	2.4444	2.7500	3.0558
12	1.6667	2.0000	2.3333	2.6666	3.0000	3.3336
13	1.8056	2.1667	2.5278	2.8888	3.2500	3.6114
14	1.9444	2.3333	2.7222	3.1111	3.5000	3.8892
15	2.0833	2.5000	2.9167	3.3333	3.7500	4.1670
16	2.2222	2.6667	3.1111	3.5555	4.0000	4.4448
17	2.3611	2.8333	3.3055	3.7777	4.2500	4.7226
18	2.5000	3.0000	3.5000	4.0000	4.5000	5.0004
19	2.6389	3.1667	3.6944	4.2222	4.7500	5.2782
20	2.7778	3.3333	3.8889	4.4444	5.0000	5.5560
21	2.9167	3.5000	4.0833	4.6666	5.2500	5.8338
22	3.0556	3.6667	4.2778	4.8888	5.5000	6.1116
23	3.1944	3.8333	4.4722	5.1111	5.7500	6.3894
24	3.2222	4.0000	4.6667	5.3333	6.0000	6.6672
25	3.4722	4.1667	4.8611	5.5555	6.2500	6.9450
26	3.6111	4.3333	5.0555	5.7777	6.5000	7.2228
27	3.7500	4.5000	5.2500	6.0000	6.7500	7.5006
28	3.8889	4.6667	5.4444	6.2222	7.0000	7.7784
29	4.0278	4.8333	5.6389	6.4444	7.2500	8.0562
30	4.1667	5.0000	5.8333	6.6666	7.5000	8.3340

31st day

Use of Interest Table

1 year and 3 months = 15 months

Under the 9% column in Table 6.5, the 30-day factor = 7.5000.

15 months × 7.5000 = 112.50 + the 20-day factor of 5.00 = 117.50

$117.50 × 6.5 (number of thousands in $6,500) = $763.75

Amortization Tables

Amortization tables can be used to compute monthly payments for various loan amounts at various interest rates and terms. A typical table showing various rates of interest and length of loans (called *terms*) is shown in Table 6.6.

TABLE 6.6   Table of Monthly Payments to Amortize $1,000 Loan.

Term of Years	6%	7%	8%	9%	10%	11%	12%
10	11.11	11.62	12.14	12.67	13.22	13.78	14.35
15	8.44	8.99	9.56	10.15	10.75	11.37	12.00
20	7.17	7.76	8.37	9.00	9.66	10.32	11.01
25	6.45	7.07	7.72	8.40	9.09	9.80	10.53
30	6.00	6.66	7.34	8.05	8.78	9.52	10.29
40	5.51	6.22	6.96	7.71	8.49	9.28	10.09

A typical table shows along one axis a list of various loan terms expressed in years and along the other axis various amounts of interest. At the intersection of any two axes in the table is found the monthly payment to pay off $1,000 at various interest rates.

Problem 18

A $100,000 loan for thirty years at 7 percent interest will have what monthly payment? To solve this problem using an amortization table, use the following procedure:

Go to the 7 percent interest column in Table 6.6, and follow it down to the thirty-year line. There you will find the factor 6.66. This means $6.66 per month will pay off $1,000 in thirty years. The loan amount is $100,000; therefore,

$$\frac{\$100,000}{\$1,000} = 100$$

Thus, $100 \times \$6.66 = \$660$ per month (rounded), which will pay off a $100,000 loan at 7 percent in thirty years.

Problem 19

If an individual made payments of $1,234.60 per month, including 9 percent on a fully amortized thirty-year loan, what was the original amount of the loan?

In Table 6.6, the point where the thirty-year line intersects with the 9 percent interest line is $8.05 for a $1,000 loan.

$1,234.60 ÷ 8.05 = 153.37 × 1,000 = $153,366 loan (approximate)

Problem 20

If you borrowed $48,000 from a personal finance company using a fully amortized home equity loan and were to make payments of

$495.45, including 11 percent interest, how many years would it take to pay off the loan?

Solution:

Reduce $48,000 to the amount of each payment per $1,000 as follows:

$$\$495.45 \div 48 = \$10.32$$

Using the 11 percent interest column in Table 6.6, locate the amount $10.32. This amount falls on the twenty-year loan term line. It will take approximately twenty years to pay off the $48,000 loan.

Problem 21

If an individual borrowed $250,000 for a home loan, payable $1,834.41 per month, including interest, for a period of thirty years, what would be the rate of interest?

Solution:

Divide $1,834.41 by 250 to determine the amount of each payment per $1,000:

$$\$1,834.41 \div 250 = \$7.34$$

Using Table 6.6, the intersection of the thirty-year line and the $7.34 = 8 percent interest rate.

Real World of Real Estate

Today's real estate professionals use financial calculators and computers to do real estate math problems. Due to the large variety of models and software, it is impossible to illustrate the keystrokes and software used to arrive at the answers presented in this chapter. The California Department of Real Estate (DRE) allows some models of calculators to be used during the state real estate examination as long as the calculator is silent, is not programmable, and does not have a printout tape. Check with the DRE for allowable models.

CHAPTER SUMMARY

This chapter laid the foundation for real estate mathematics by discussing the basic computations using decimals and fractions when adding, subtracting, multiplying, and dividing.

In most real estate transactions, there are three variables—two of them are given, and you must solve for the third. Three formulas can be used to solve many real estate problems:

$$\text{Made} = \text{Paid} \times \text{Rate (\%)}$$
$$\text{Rate (\%)} = \text{Made} \div \text{Paid}$$
$$\text{Paid} = \text{Made} \div \text{Rate (\%)}$$

Problems related to investments, discounting notes, appraisals, commissions, interest and loans, cost and selling price, and square footage and area were presented. Prorations and the documentary transfer taxes were computed.

As an aid to rapid calculation, interest tables, amortization tables, and financial pocket calculators can reduce the time needed to determine a correct answer.

IMPORTANT TERMS AND CONCEPTS

amortization
   tables

capitalization rate

commission split

decimals

documentary
   transfer tax

interest

principal

proration

rate

PRACTICAL APPLICATION

1. You are thinking about buying a property that is listed for $300,000. The seller has owned the property for five years, and you are curious as to what the seller originally paid for the property. The seller's deed in the county recorder's office shows a Documentary Transfer Tax of $244.75 based on an all-cash sale price. How much did the seller pay for the property? If you buy the property for $400,000, not counting closing cost, what gross percentage profit will the seller make?

2. The N ½ and the NW ¼ of the SW ¼ of Section 9 are sold for $5,000 per acre. The commission rate is 10 percent with Broker A getting 50 percent and Broker B getting 50 percent. You work as a salesperson for Broker B, who agrees to give you 60 percent for your sales effort. How much commission do you earn?

3. A 2,000-square-foot tract home with a 500-square-foot garage can be built for $125 per square foot for the home and $30 per square foot for the garage. Other improvements, including the land, will cost $60,000. If the developer wishes to resell the home for a 20 percent profit, what should the resale price be?

REVIEWING YOUR UNDERSTANDING

Note: Some of the problems require using the tables presented in Chapter 6.

1. An investor is thinking about purchasing an older four-unit apartment. Each one-bedroom unit rents for $600 per month, with a vacancy factor of 5 percent and operating expenses of $8,000 annually. To realize a capitalization rate of 6 percent, how much should the investor pay for the property? (Round answer to nearest dollar.)
   a. $317,670
   b. $318,421
   c. $320,974
   d. $322,667

2. Ms. B sold her vacant lot for $63,000. This was 20 percent more than she paid. The commission to the broker and other selling costs amounted to 6 percent of the selling price. How much was her net profit?
   a. $12,600
   b. $6,720
   c. $15,250
   d. $5,250

3. Mr. A wishes to place a lump sum into a savings account that will pay 6 percent interest. He hopes to earn $150 in monthly interest. To realize this monthly interest income, how much must he deposit?
   a. $15,000
   b. $9,000
   c. $25,000
   d. $30,000

4. Ms. Jones purchased a small studio condo for $170,000; she assumed an existing loan for $140,000. The seller agrees to pay the documentary transfer tax. What is the tax?

   a. $187

   b. $33

   c. $45

   d. $154

5. Mr. and Mrs. Chu prepaid their annual property taxes of $720 to July 1, 2008. They sold their condo on April 1, 2008. On the settlement sheet, what entry would be made?

   a. Debit the seller $180

   b. Credit the seller $240

   c. Credit the buyer $180

   d. Credit the seller $180

6. Seller sold a home for $600,000. It was purchased one year ago for $400,000. What percentage gross profit was realized on the sale?

   a. 66.5%

   b. 50%

   c. 33.33%

   d. 48%

7. Broker Santos listed vacant land, and the seller agreed to pay a 6 percent commission. If the commission amounted to $18,000, what was the listing price?

   a. $108,000

   b. $195,000

   c. $300,000

   d. $405,000

8. If you were to borrow $42,000 using your home's equity line of credit and make fully amortized payments for 15 years, including 9 percent interest, using the amortization table, what would be your monthly payments?
   a. $426.30
   b. $10.15
   c. $375.20
   d. $315.00

9. If you owned a rectangled four-acre parcel of land and wished to divide it into eight equal lots each 400 feet deep, what would be the width of each lot?
   a. 55.40 feet
   b. 54.45 feet
   c. 435.6 feet
   d. 45.54 feet

10. A payment of $840 per month principal and interest is made on a $66,000 home equity loan, which includes interest at 10 percent. How much of the payment is principal the first month?
    a. $550
    b. $100
    c. $95
    d. $290

11. A 1,920-square-foot home can be built for $100 per square foot. The 425-square-foot garage can be built for $30 per square foot. The 8,000-square-foot lot sells for $15 per square foot. What will the entire property cost?
    a. $324,750
    b. $320,250
    c. $318,500
    d. $204,750

12. A $425,000 amortized loan at 10 percent interest, payable at $3,861.98 per month, will take approximately how long to pay off?

 a. 15 years

 b. 20 years

 c. 25 years

 d. 30 years

13. A commercial property generates $60,000 annual net income, and prevailing capitalization rates in the market are 8 percent. What is the maximum price a buyer should pay for this property?

 a. $700,000

 b. $725,000

 c. $730,000

 d. $750,000

14. Broker A employs Salesperson B under the following terms: In-house sales shall be split 20/40/40. Salesperson B, who did not list the property, finds a buyer for Broker A's vacant land listing at a price of $179,500. The seller agrees to pay a 7 percent commission. What will be Salesperson B's share?

 a. $12,250

 b. $7,350

 c. $5,026

 d. $2,450

15. A buyer offers to purchase a manufactured home for $225,000 and applies for a 90 percent loan at 7 percent interest-only payments, all due in five years. If granted, what will be the monthly loan payments?

 a. $1,312.50

 b. $1,875.00

 c. $1,777.95

 d. $1,181.25

16. You are trying to figure out what a person paid for a property. The deed in the courthouse shows a county documentary transfer tax of $206.25 based on the full cash price. What is the estimated purchase price of the property?
    a. $187,500
    b. $206,250
    c. $226,875
    d. $319,680

17. A one-fifth-acre parcel sold for $13 per square foot. The commission was 9 percent. The salesperson received a 50 percent split. How much did the salesperson receive? (Round answer to nearest dollar.)
    a. $6,371
    b. $5,097
    c. $4,113
    d. $3,987

18. A condo escrow closed 9/10/XX. The buyer's first payment on the $150,000 purchase money loan at 9 percent amortized for thirty years is due 10/1/XX. The lender wants twenty days' worth of interest paid by the buyer in escrow as a closing cost. The interest on the buyer's closing statement is
    a. $750 and will show as a credit.
    b. $750 and will show as a debit.
    c. $805 and will show as a credit.
    d. $805 and will show as a debit.

19. A buyer purchases a used mobile home and lot for $127,000, putting 10 percent down and obtaining a new first loan for 80 percent at 9 percent amortized for thirty years but due in five years. The seller carries a 10 percent second loan at 10 percent amortized for twenty years but due in three years. The buyer's total monthly loan payments will be how much? (Round answer to nearest dollar.)
    a. $1,217
    b. $1,146
    c. $941
    d. $893

20. A large apartment building loan of $2,500,000 at 9 percent amortized for thirty years will have how much interest allocated in the first payment?
    a. $225,000
    b. $20,125
    c. $19,375
    d. $18,750

Chapter 7

This chapter stresses the legal aspects of real estate finance. At the conclusion of the chapter, you will be able to do the following:

1. Describe the types of promissory notes and explain adjustable rate loans.
2. Explain deeds of trust (trust deeds) and installment sales contracts and describe the foreclosure process (trustee's sale).
3. Define acceleration, alienation, subordination, and prepayment penalty clauses.
4. Outline the principles of the Real Property Loan Law and truth-in-lending regulations.

Introduction to Real Estate Finance

7.1 REAL ESTATE FINANCING INSTRUMENTS

Access to money and credit is the key factor in most real estate transactions. Real estate is expensive, and few people ever accumulate enough savings to pay all cash for property. Therefore, the completion of a real estate sale hinges on the buyer's ability to obtain financing. Even people who have sufficient funds rarely pay cash for real estate. Income tax deductions and an investment concept called **leverage** (see this chapter's appendix) in some cases favor purchasing real estate with borrowed funds. Thus, whether by necessity or by choice, financing is essential for most real estate transactions.

Real Estate Financing Process

Real estate financing usually involves five phases: (1) application, (2) analysis, (3) processing, (4) closing, and (5) servicing. (See Figure 7.1.)

The lending process begins by having the prospective borrower complete a lender's loan application. A loan application form requests information about the borrower's financial status, such as level and

FIGURE 7.1

REAL ESTATE FINANCING PROCESS

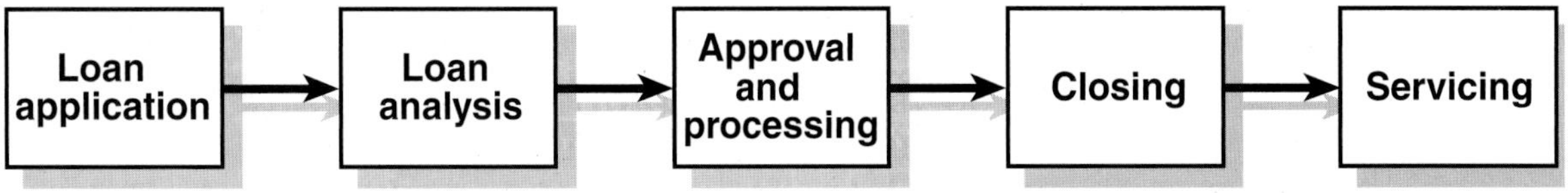

consistency of income, personal assets, existing debts, and current expenses. The loan application form also asks for data concerning the property, including its location, its age, the size of the lot, and any existing improvements.

Once the application is completed, the lender reviews the form and uses it as a screening device to determine whether the prospective borrower and the subject property appear to meet the lender's requirements. If it becomes obvious that the borrower or the property is unacceptable for a loan, the lender informs the applicant. If it appears that the borrower and the property might be acceptable, the analysis phase begins.

Analysis involves an in-depth appraisal of the property and a professionally compiled credit report on the prospective borrower. After the appraisal and credit report are completed (and assuming both are favorable), the lender presents the terms and cost of financing to the borrower. The borrower may accept, reject, or attempt to negotiate the financing terms with the lender. Assuming an agreement is reached, the processing phase begins.

Processing involves drawing up loan papers, preparing disclosure forms regarding loan costs, and issuing instructions for the escrow and title insurance company. Each lender establishes its own processing pattern in view of its special in-house needs.

Once the loan package has been processed, the closing phase begins. Closing the loan involves signing all loan papers and then, in conjunction with the other terms of the sale, transferring the property. In southern California, an independent escrow company, the escrow department of a title company, or (in some cases) the broker handles the entire escrow. In much of northern California, once the loan papers are signed, they are forwarded to the escrow department of a title insurance company, which closes the sale.

After the title has been transferred and the escrow is closed, the loan-servicing phase begins. *Loan servicing* refers to the record-keeping process once the loan has been placed. Many lenders do their own servicing, while others pay independent mortgage companies to handle the paperwork. The goal of loan servicing is to see that the lender makes the expected yield on the loan by promptly collecting and processing the loan payments with minimum cost.

Promissory Notes

When money is borrowed to purchase real estate, the borrower agrees to repay the loan by signing a *promissory note*, which outlines the terms of repayment and sets the due date. The promissory note is legal evidence that a debt is owed. The types of promissory notes in general use are the *straight note, installment note,* and *negative amortized note.*

Straight Note

The straight note is frequently referred to as an interest-only note. Under a **straight note**, the borrower agrees to pay the interest, usually monthly, and to pay the entire principal in a lump sum on the due date. For example, if you borrow $100,000 for 30 years at 10 percent interest rate using a straight note, the monthly payments would be $833.33 per month. The $833.33 payments cover just the monthly interest. Thus, 30 years hence, on the due date, you must pay back the entire $100,000 principal. In other words, the payments were only large enough to cover the monthly interest and did not reduce the $100,000 principal. (Proof: $100,000 × 10%=$10,000 ÷ 12 months=$833.33 per month.) (Ten percent is used for illustration purposes only. Actual interest rates will vary.)

Installment Note

The second and by far the most common type of real estate promissory note is the installment note. An **installment note** requires payments that include both principal and interest. If you borrow $100,000 for 30 years at 10 percent interest payable at $877.57 per month, including both principal and interest, you will find that at the end of 30 years, the entire debt is liquidated. Each monthly payment of $877.57 includes the monthly interest due and reduces a portion of the $100,000 principal. By the time the due date arrives 30 years hence, the entire principal has been paid back. *An installment loan that includes principal and interest of equal installment payments that liquidate the debt is called a fully amortized loan.* Under a fully amortized loan, no large balloon payment must be paid on the due date of the loan, as the loan is completely paid off.

One variation of the installment note is to have monthly payments that are large enough to pay the monthly interest and reduce some of the principal, but the monthly principal portion is not sufficient to entirely liquidate the debt by the due date. Thus, on the due date, the remaining unpaid principal must be paid in a lump sum, often referred to as a **balloon payment**. (Any payment more than twice the lowest payment amount is called a *balloon payment.*) One hundred thousand dollars for 30 years at 10 percent interest payable at $850 per month would require a balloon payment of $62,325.20 on the due date. Why? Because the $850 per month was enough to cover the monthly interest ($833.33), but it was not enough to cover the monthly interest and all of the monthly principal, which would have taken $877.57 per month. Thus, the difference over the 30-year life of the loan comes to $62,325.20, which must be paid on the due date in the form of a balloon payment. Loan payments and balloon payments can be calculated using financial tables or financial calculators.

Finally, some borrowers sign negative amortized promissory notes. **Negative amortized** means that the loan payment does not cover even the monthly interest. Each month this shortage is added to the principal owed, resulting in an increased loan balance, which, in turn, incurs additional interest. As mentioned above, a $100,000 loan at 10 percent payable interest would be a monthly payment of only $833.33 ($100,000 × 10% ÷ 12 mo.). If a borrower paid only $750 per month, the difference between the interest-only payment of $833.33 and the $750 payment would be $83.33. Each month this additional $83.33 amount would be added to the $100,000 loan and begin to accrue interest.

If this continued for 30 years, the borrower would still owe a balloon payment of $288,373.99 on top of paying $750 per month for 30 years! The total paid would be $750 × 360 payments (30 years × 12) = $270,000 + $288,373.99 balloon payment, for a grand total of $558,373.99 to pay off a $100,000 negative amortized loan payable for $750 per month at 10 percent over 30 years! Of course, in the real world, most people do not stay in a home and pay for 30 years. They usually sell or refinance long before 30 years, and the balance owed on a negative amortized loan is far less than that illustrated above. But the lesson learned is that a negative amortized loan is one where a loan balance grows each and every year prior to payoff.

Adjustable Rate Loans

Most real estate lenders qualify a borrower for either a fixed interest rate or an adjustable rate loan. The fixed interest rate is the traditional real estate loan where the interest rate does not change over the life of the loan. Under the **adjustable rate** plan, the rate may move up or down. Therefore, the monthly payment may decrease or increase over the life of the loan.

How Does It Work?

Adjustable rate loans, usually called *adjustable rate mortgages* (ARMs), have the following characteristics:

1. They are usually offered at a lower initial interest rate than traditional fixed interest rate loans.

2. Once the initial interest rate is established, the rate is tied to some neutral index, which is beyond the control of the lender or the borrower.

3. The index is usually a government index. Examples are the One Year Treasury Spot Index, the Treasury 12-Month Average Index, or the 11th District Cost-of-Funds Index. Other indexes used are tied to certificate of deposit (CD) rates, prime rates, or even a European rate known as the London Interbank Offered Rate (LIBOR). The distance between the actual rate paid by the borrower and the index is called the *margin*. A typical margin is 2 percent to 3 percent.

4. Although not required, most lenders place a cap on how high the rate can climb. A typical cap is 5 percent or 6 percent; therefore, if the initial interest rate is 6 percent, the maximum it can rise to is 11 percent or 12 percent.

5. The adjustment period can vary, with some lenders adjusting the rate at six-month, one-year, or three-year intervals.

6. The maximum increase or decrease per period is established in the lender's contract, with a maximum change of 1 percent per six-month adjustment period being typical.

7. If the interest rate increases because of a change in the index, in some cases, the borrower may have the option of (a) increasing the monthly payment so the term of the loan remains the same or (b) maintaining the same monthly payment and increasing the term of the loan. Usually, the maximum term to which a 30-year loan may be extended is forty years. Once a forty-year term is reached, any increase in interest rate must increase the monthly payment. If the interest rate drops below the initial rate, the borrower can continue the existing payments (which will shorten the term) or decrease the monthly payments. However, in recent years, fewer lenders are offering this feature.

8. The borrower must be given advanced notice prior to a change in rate.

9. Some ARMs may be negative amortized loans. This means the payments may not cover the annual interest. The unpaid interest is added to the principal, making the loan larger. This can cause some problems in later years.

10. Some lenders offer a convertible feature that allows the borrower to convert an ARM loan to a fixed interest rate loan or a fixed rate loan to an ARM. The conversion is only offered during a certain "window period," usually from the beginning of the second year through the end of the fifth year. The borrower may be required to meet credit standards at the time of the conversion and is usually required to pay extra fees.

Other Alternative Types of Real Estate Loans

Other experimental types of loans include names such as FLIP (flexible payment mortgage), GPM (graduated payment mortgage), and SAM (shared appreciation mortgage), in addition to many other loans called *alphabet soup financing.* The details of these alternative loan types can be found in a textbook on real estate finance, such as *California Real Estate Finance,* 9th ed., by Robert J. Bond et al.[*]

Purpose of Adjustable Rate and Other Alternative Loans

Alternative real estate loans have been recommended by financial experts and real estate economists for many years. Here are some of the reasons.

Institutional lenders and secondary market investors have a constant problem with cycles of tight and loose money. This unsteady flow of funds is disruptive to their operations and the housing industry. When money is tight, it flows out of savings institutions because depositors can obtain higher yields elsewhere.

Advocates of alternative loans say this problem can be reduced through the use of ARMs. If money gets tight and interest rates rise, the savings institutions should be allowed to increase the rate they pay their depositors in order to prevent an outflow of savings. However, to pay higher interest on savings accounts, lenders must receive a higher interest rate on their existing loans. With an ARM, lenders can increase interest rates on their existing loans when they increase the interest they pay on a depositor's savings account.

Another problem facing lending institutions and secondary market investors deals with old, low fixed interest rate loans currently on the lender's books. If the current cost of money exceeds the interest rates on these older loans, the institutions are losing money on these loans. That means that the interest rate on new loans must be increased to compensate for the loss on these old loans. In effect, new borrowers are subsidizing the old borrowers. If all borrowers were on an adjustable rate, this subsidizing process would not be as severe. Those who are opposed to alternative loans argue that lenders are merely shifting the risk of rising interest rates to the borrower.

Adjustable rate mortgages are not new. They have been used for many years in Canada and in some European countries. In

---

[*] Robert J. Bond, Dennis J. McKenzie, John Fesler, and Rick Boone, *California Real Estate Finance,* 9th ed. (Cincinnati, OH: Cengage Learning, 2011).

California, the Cal-Vet loan program has been using adjustable rates since the program was started over eighty years ago.

Deeds of Trust

To give added insurance that a borrower will repay a loan, lenders require collateral or security for the loan. To give something as security for a loan without giving possession is called **hypothecation**. A real estate lender's most logical security is real property owned or about to be acquired by the borrower. To secure an interest in the borrower's real property, lenders in California use a deed of trust (also called a *trust deed*).

A **deed of trust** is a three-party instrument consisting of a borrower (**trustor**), a lender (**beneficiary**), and a neutral third party (**trustee**). Under a deed of trust (trust deed), the trustor deeds legal title (sometimes called *bare legal title* or *naked title*) to the trustee, who keeps the title as security until the promissory note is repaid. Once the debt is repaid, the beneficiary (lender) orders the trustee to reconvey the title back to the trustor (borrower). If the trustor should default on the loan, the beneficiary can order the trustee to hold a trustee's sale and sell the property to obtain the cash needed to pay the loan. Figure 7.2 illustrates how title is passed between a trustor and a trustee in a deed of trust and a deed of reconveyance.

In other states, frequently a mortgage is used to secure a real estate loan instead of a deed of trust. But in California, mortgages are rare—most lenders insist on deeds of trust instead. Why? Because in most cases, deeds of trust favor the lender over the borrower. If the borrower should default under a deed of trust, the lender can order the trustee to sell the property without a court proceeding, and it can be accomplished in approximately four months. Once

FIGURE 7.2

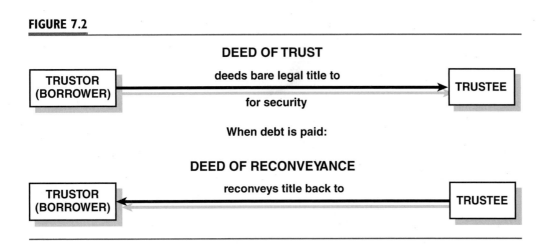

the sale takes place, the borrower loses all rights to redeem the property.

Foreclosure under a mortgage usually requires a court proceeding and can take up to one year. Why does it take so long? Under a mortgage, the title does not pass to a third party, such as a trustee under a deed of trust. So an expensive court action is needed to divest the borrower from the title. Then, after a court foreclosure, the borrower may have up to a one-year right of redemption. In short, California real estate lenders prefer to use deeds of trust rather than mortgages as a security instrument because foreclosure is quicker and cheaper with a deed of trust.

Special Clauses

In addition to repayment terms, many real estate financing instruments contain special clauses or loan conditions that the borrower and lender agree to honor. Two common clauses that appear in most promissory notes and deeds of trust are as follows:

1. **Acceleration clause.** An **acceleration clause** gives the lender the right to call all sums immediately due and payable upon the happening of certain events, such as nonpayment of monthly obligations, nonpayment of real property taxes, or willful destruction of the subject property.

2. **Alienation (due-on-sale) clause.** An **alienation (due-on-sale) clause** is a specific type of acceleration clause that gives the lender the right to call the loan due and payable if the borrower conveys legal title to a new owner. After a period of controversy, the due-on-sale issue has been settled. Per federal law, effective October 15, 1985, all-due-on sale clauses are enforceable, except for transfers between spouses and family trusts.

Other major clauses, although not as common, that occasionally appear in promissory notes and deeds of trust include the following:

1. **Subordination clause.** A **subordination clause** is where the holder of a senior (first) deed of trust agrees to become a junior lien (second) to pave the way for a new senior (first) deed of trust. This is most common when the holder of the first loan on vacant land agrees to allow a new construction loan to be put on record as a first deed of trust.

2. **Prepayment penalty clause.** A **prepayment penalty clause** that allows a lender to charge the borrower a penalty if the loan is paid before the scheduled due date. A typical prepayment penalty is 80 percent of six months' interest on the remaining balance of the loan.

However, penalties do vary with the lender. In today's real estate market, most loans have no prepayment penalty. A 2006 California law prohibits lenders from charging a prepayment penalty on owner-occupied home loans if the loan has been on the lender's books for more than three years. But if the lender is supervised by a federal agency, this California regulation does not apply. There is no prepayment penalty on FHA-insured, VA-guaranteed, or Cal-Vet home loans.

A financing instrument may contain several other special clauses depending on the operating policies of the lender. Borrowers should carefully read all documents to make certain they completely understand what all clauses mean. This will help to assure harmony between the lender and the borrower during the life of the loan.

Junior Deed of Trust

Any trust deed other than a first is called a **junior deed of trust** or a junior loan or lien. When a buyer does not have enough cash down payment to cover the gap between the sales price and the first deed of trust loan, a junior (or second) deed of trust loan is frequently carried back by the seller.

> *Example :* Sales price $500,000; buyer has a $50,000 cash down payment and is willing to secure a first deed of trust bank loan of $400,000. Therefore, $400,000 + 50,000 = $450,000. The buyer is short $50,000. To cover the gap, the seller agrees to carry back a $50,000 promissory note secured by a second deed of trust. This can be illustrated as follows:

$500,000	Sales price
−$400,000	First deed of trust
$100,000	Required to close the sale (excluding closing costs)
−$50,000	Cash down payment
$50,000	Size of second deed of trust

Homeowner equity loans are another common example of the use of junior (second) deeds of trust. Many banks and finance companies advertise their home equity loan programs, where the lender grants a loan based on the homeowner's increase in equity caused by appreciation of property values or earlier loan paydown. Home equity loans are usually secured by junior deeds of trust. Because junior trust deeds are less secure than first trust deeds, lenders usually demand a higher interest rate on home equity loans.

Taking Over a Seller's Existing Loan

The placement of a new real estate loan from an institutional lender requires the payment of loan fees, appraisal fees, credit report charges, and other loan closing costs.

In addition, the interest rate paid by a buyer is at the current prevailing market rate. If a buyer has enough cash down payment and if legally possible, it is usually cheaper to take over the seller's existing loan, rather than obtain a new loan. Many of the loan costs are avoided, and in some cases, the interest rate on the seller's loan is less than the prevailing interest rates on new real estate loans.

There are two ways a buyer can take over a seller's existing loan. A buyer can *assume* a seller's existing loan, or a buyer can purchase subject to a seller's existing loan. When a buyer assumes a seller's existing loan, the buyer agrees to take over the payments and to become personally liable for the debt. But when a buyer purchases subject to the existing loan, the buyer agrees to take over the payments, but not the primary liability for the debt; the seller remains personally liable. This distinction becomes important if a lender should foreclose and sue for a deficiency judgment.

A **deficiency judgment** is where a lender sues a borrower after a foreclosure when the proceeds from a foreclosure are not enough to cover the outstanding loan amount. An example: A real estate lender is owed $300,000, there is a default on the loan, and the lender sells the property in a foreclosure sale for $250,000. The amount owed was $300,000, and the proceeds from the foreclosure were $250,000; therefore, the deficiency is $50,000.

If the lender is allowed to sue for the $50,000 deficiency, the question arises, "Who shall be sued?" The answer is "Whoever is personally liable for the debt." If a buyer assumed a seller's existing loan, the action would be brought against the buyer, as he or she is personally liable. On the other hand, if a buyer purchased subject to a seller's existing loan, the seller is still primarily liable and the deficiency action would be brought against the seller. Deficiency judgments on residential dwellings are difficult to obtain in California because of special laws protecting purchase money, owner-occupied homeowners. But deficiency judgments are obtainable on VA-guaranteed home loans because these are federally backed loans, and federal law supersedes state antideficiency laws.

Installment Sales Contracts (Land Contracts)

Another real estate financing instrument is an installment sales contract, also called a contract of sale or agreement of sale or land contract. An **installment sales contract** is an agreement between the seller, called the *vendor,* and the buyer, called the *vendee,* where the buyer is given possession and use of the property. In exchange for possession and use, the buyer agrees to make regular payments to the seller. Legal title to the property remains with the seller until an agreed amount has been paid, at which time the seller formally deeds title to the buyer. In essence, under an installment sales contract, the seller becomes the lender. Outside lending institutions, such as banks and mortgage companies, are not needed in such a transaction.

The lack of immediate title poses some risks for the buyer. If the seller should die, become bankrupt, or become incompetent or encumber the title during the contract, the buyer could become involved in legal entanglements.

Recent court cases have greatly restricted the ease by which a seller can remove a buyer if he or she defaults on the payments. A long, expensive court action may be needed to remove a defaulted buyer from possession. In light of the disadvantage for the buyer and the seller, installment sales contracts are no longer popular in California. They are still used on a regular basis in other states.

7.2 FORECLOSURE PROCESS: TRUSTEE'S SALE

Borrowers default on repayment of loans for a variety of reasons, usually because of events beyond their control. Financial reversals such as loss of a business or job probably head the list, but other circumstances are closely related: death, disability, bankruptcy, dissolution of marriage, drop in property values, and poor budgeting. When a borrower defaults on a real estate loan, unless arrangements can be made with the lender to work out a satisfactory schedule for repayment, foreclosure takes place. However, most lenders try to avoid foreclosure whenever possible and use it only as a last resort. Lenders are in the business of lending money and do not want to become involved in owning and managing real estate.

A borrower can be in default for reasons other than nonpayment. There may be a violation of other terms listed on the trust deed, such as failure to maintain the property or failure to pay property taxes and fire insurance. Regardless of the violation, lenders in California must follow a prescribed procedure to take title from a delinquent debtor. Here is a summary of the process, which is also illustrated in Figure 7.3.

FIGURE 7.3

TRUSTEE'S SALE (FORECLOSURE)

| Borrower defaults | Trustee records notice of default | Starts reinstatement period; runs until 5 business days prior to sale | Trustee records and publishes notice of sale | Trustee's sale is held | Successful bidder receives trustee's deed |

Trustee's Sale

Virtually all trust deeds contain a power-of-sale clause, which empowers the trustee, in the event of default by the trustor, to sell the property at public auction. Although the provisions of the power-of-sale clause are a matter of contract and may vary from instrument to instrument, there are laws that specifically regulate foreclosure through a trustee's sale. The statutory requirements are as follows:

1. *Notice of default (NOD).* Once the beneficiary is reasonably certain that a trustor is unable to make good on the loan and any statutory grace period required by law (ninety days as of 2009), the beneficiary orders the trustee to record a notice of default in the county where the property is located. This begins a reinstatement period. The notice must contain a correct legal description of the property, the name of the trustor, the nature of the breach, and a statement to the effect that the party executing the notice of default has elected to sell the property to satisfy the obligation. Within ten days after filing the notice of default, a copy must be sent by registered or certified mail to the borrower, junior lienholders, and anyone whose "request for notice" appears on record. During this reinstatement period, which runs until five days before the date of sale, the trustor (borrower) can reinstate the loan by paying all delinquent installments. The trustor must also pay foreclosure costs and trustee's fees. This is referred to as the *right of reinstatement.*

2. *Notice of sale.* In addition to recording a notice of default, a trustee must also record a notice of sale. This notice of sale is filed if the borrower fails to reinstate the loan. The notice must contain a correct identification of the property, such as the street address or legal description. It must be published in a newspaper of general circulation in the county or jurisdiction in which the property is located. The publication must appear at least once a week for three consecutive calendar weeks. Moreover, the notice must

also be posted in a public place, such as a courthouse, and in some conspicuous place on the property, such as the front door. The sale must be held in a public place during business hours on a weekday (Monday through Friday).

3. *Final sale.* Any person, including the trustor and beneficiary, may bid on the property via public auction. All bids must be in cash or its equivalent. However, the lender foreclosing can submit the amount owed the lender as a bid in lieu of cash. A trustee's deed is issued to the highest bidder. Any surplus funds (that is, funds remaining after paying off the lender; foreclosure costs; and junior liens, if any) are given to the trustor.

No right of redemption exists after a trustee's sale. The purchaser acquires all rights held by the former owner, becoming the successor in interest, and is entitled to immediate possession, subject to those having superior rights over the trust deed that was foreclosed.

Rights of Holders of Junior Trust Deeds

When a trustee's sale is held on behalf of a first trust deed lender, junior trust deeds can be eliminated. Therefore, it is important to examine what rights a junior trust deed holder has in the foreclosure process.

Assume a homeowner has a first and a second trust deed loan against the property and is in default on the loans. If the first trust deed lender begins to foreclose, the second trust deed lender can step in and make the payments due on the first loan. This will stop the first lender from foreclosing. *The second trust deed lender then adds the payments made on the first trust deed loan to the balance the borrower owes on the second trust deed loan.* The holder of the second trust deed loan then demands repayment from the borrower. If the borrower fails to repay, the holder of the second trust deed forecloses under the trustee sale provisions of the second trust deed. The successful bidder at the trustee's sale becomes the owner of the property, subject to the first trust deed—that is, takes over the property and is required to make all future payments on the first trust deed loan. In short, a holder of a junior trust deed can stop the first lender from foreclosing on the first trust deed. This, in turn, keeps the second trust deed from being eliminated. The holder of the second trust deed gets title to the property as the lone bidder at the trustee's sale or cash from a third party who is the successful bidder at the trustee's sale on the second trust deed.

How does a holder of a second trust deed know when a borrower has defaulted on the first trust deed? The law requires senior trust deed holders to send a certified copy of any notice of default and sale to all holders of junior trust deeds. To be doubly sure, a holder of a junior trust deed may also wish to record an instrument called a *request for copy of notice of default*. This places on public record a notice to the senior trust deed holder that the junior trust deed holder wishes to be informed when a default is declared on the first loan.

Loan Modifications

Rather than facing foreclosure, borrowers may try to renegotiate their loan terms with their lender; this is known as a *loan modification*. Borrowers need to understand that the lender is not required to participate in a loan modification but may do so if the property is worth less than the loan amount and the lender believes it may see a larger loss if it forecloses on the property. To be successful, a borrower will need to present the following to the lender:

- A formal application, including a description of the hardship created by the mortgage
- Proof of income, such as two recent pay stubs or the most recent profit-and-loss statement for self-employed borrowers
- A form authorizing the Internal Revenue Service to release tax data to the servicer

It is also helpful if the borrower provides an estimate of what the property is worth, either an appraisal from a licensed appraiser or a broker price opinion from a reputable real estate agent.

7.3 TRUTH-IN-LENDING, EQUAL CREDIT OPPORTUNITY, AND THE REAL ESTATE SETTLEMENT PROCEDURES ACT

Many years ago Congress passed the **Truth-in-Lending Law**, which resulted in a provision called *Regulation Z*. The purpose of the law is to help borrowers understand how much it costs to borrow money. The law requires all lenders to show loan costs in the same way. This allows borrowers to compare one lender's cost against another lender's cost. The law requires lenders to quote the cost of borrowing, using what is called an **annual percentage rate (APR)**. The APR is not an interest rate, but rather a percentage rate that reflects the effective interest rate on the loan, including other prepaid financing charges such as loan fees, prepaid interest, and tax service fees.

Regulation Z requires a lender to give the borrower a disclosure statement showing a complete breakdown of all loan costs, in addition to other loan information. The law also says that certain loans are rescindable within three business days. This means borrowers have three days after they agree to a loan to cancel if they so wish. Generally, the rescindable right applies only to loans to refinance a borrower's home and to certain types of junior deeds of trust, including home improvement loans. First deeds of trust to purchase a home do not carry a three-day right to rescind, nor do loans carried back by a seller of real estate.

Real Estate Advertisements

Real estate advertisements must comply with Regulation Z. If one financial term (such as *interest rate* or *no money down*) is mentioned, all financing terms (*interest rate, monthly payments, length of loan,* and so on) must be stated in the ad. There are severe penalties for people who incorrectly advertise real estate loan terms.

Equal Credit Opportunity Act

The **Equal Credit Opportunity Act** prohibits lenders from discriminating on the basis of race, color, religion, national origin, age, sex, family size, handicap, or marital status or on the grounds of receipt of income from a public assistance program.

Some of the basic provisions of the act are as follows:

1. A lender cannot ask if the borrower is divorced or widowed. The lender can ask if the borrower is married, unmarried, or separated. For purposes of the law, *unmarried* means single, divorced, or widowed.

2. A lender cannot ask the borrower about receiving alimony or child support unless the borrower is first notified that the information need not be revealed; unless the borrower wishes to use such income to qualify for a loan, he or she need not disclose the source of income. However, the lender can ask about obligations to pay alimony or child support.

3. A lender cannot ask about birth control practices or childbearing intentions or capabilities.

4. A lender must notify the borrower within thirty days about what action has been taken on his or her loan application. In case of disapproval, if requested, the reason must be given.

5. If the borrower requests, the lender must consider information provided by the borrower indicating that a bad history of a joint account does not reflect on his or her credit.

In short, the Equal Credit Opportunity Act assures that all qualified persons shall have equal access to credit. This law has been especially helpful in assuring that women are not discriminated against because of their gender.

Real Estate Settlement Procedures Act

The **Real Estate Settlement Procedures Act (RESPA)** is a federal law requiring that certain forms be provided with regard to closing costs. The law applies whenever a person purchases an owner-occupied residence using funds obtained from institutional lenders that are regulated by a federal agency. Virtually all banks and thrift institutions, and most other lenders, fall directly or indirectly under RESPA's rules. The one major exception is real estate loans made by private parties.

RESPA rules require the lender to furnish the borrower with a special information booklet and a good faith estimate of closing costs three days from the time the prospective borrower files an application for a real estate loan. RESPA rules prohibit any kickbacks or unearned fees from being charged or listed as closing costs. The law states that only valid, earned closing costs shall be charged to the buyer or seller. Violators can be punished by up to one year in jail and/or a $10,000 fine. Most of the burden for implementing RESPA falls upon the real estate lender. However, escrow agents are also involved. RESPA requires the use of a Uniform Settlement Statement (HUD-1), which itemizes all final closing charges. Upon request, the escrow agent must let the borrower-buyer inspect the Uniform Settlement Statement one day before the close of escrow. In addition, the escrow officer must see that all parties receive a copy of the Uniform Settlement Statement after the close of escrow.

7.4 REAL PROPERTY LOAN LAW

Another consumer-oriented law is the Real Property Loan Law found in Sections 10240 48 of the California Business and Professions Code (Article 7). This segment of the law is commonly called the *Mortgage Loan Broker Law*. The purpose of this law is to protect borrowers who use the services of mortgage loan brokers. The law requires mortgage brokers to give a loan disclosure statement to all borrowers before they become obligated for the loan. The disclosure statement itemizes all closing costs, loan expenses, and commissions to be paid, thereby showing the borrower how much he or she will net from the loan.

Exceptions to the Mortgage Loan Broker Law

It is easier to state which lenders and what transactions are not covered by the law than to list those that are. As of July 2006, the following are exempt from the Real Property Loan Law:

1. Regulated institutional lenders, such as banks, thrift institutions, credit unions, and finance companies.
2. Purchase money transactions where a seller carries back the loan as part of the sale price; however, if a seller carries back the loan for more than seven transactions in one year, the Mortgage Loan Broker Law does apply.
3. Loans secured by first trust deeds when the principal amount is $30,000 or more.
4. Loans secured by junior trust deeds when the principal amount is $20,000 or more.

Maximum Commissions

Mortgage loan brokers are limited in the amount of commissions they can charge as a percentage, as shown in Table 7.1. As is evident in Table 7.1, the shorter the term of the loan, the less commission the broker can charge as a percentage of the face amount of the loan. On loans of $30,000 and over for first liens and $20,000 for junior liens, the broker can charge as much as the borrower agrees to pay. For loans covered by the law, however, competition frequently keeps rates below the maximum allowed.

TABLE 7.1   Maximum Commission as a Percentage.

	Less Than Two Years	Two Years but Less Than Three	Three Years and Over	Exempt Transactions
Type and Length of Loan First Trust Deeds	5%	5%	10%	Loans of $30,000 and over
Junior Trust Deeds	5%	10%	15%	Loans of $20,000 and over

SPECIAL INTEREST
TOPIC

Usury Law

Many states have passed laws establishing the maximum rate of interest that can be charged on various types of loans. Interest rates that exceed the maximum rate are considered usurious and, therefore, illegal. In some instances, if a lender is found guilty of usury, the borrower does not have to repay the interest due on the loan.

In California, the maximum rate is 10 percent or 5 percent above the Federal Reserve discount rate, whichever is greater, unless the lender is exempt from the law. California regulations exempt banks, thrift institutions, and several other recognized lenders from the usury law. Any real estate transaction handled by a licensed broker is also exempt from the usury law. However, private parties lending directly to private borrowers are not exempt. For example, real estate loans from institutional lenders can be at any rate agreed upon, while real estate loans from private lenders cannot. There is at least one exception: Sellers carrying back a purchase money deed of trust as part of their equity on a real estate sale can charge interest at any agreed-upon rate. However, this transaction should be cleared with an attorney to make sure the law has not changed.

The pros and cons of usury laws are currently being debated. Proponents believe that usury laws protect consumers against lenders, while opponents believe usury laws restrict the supply of loan funds and drive some borrowers to illegal loan sharks. From time to time, the federal government passes temporary laws that override state usury laws during periods of tight mortgage money.

Source: From R. J. Bond, D. J. McKenzie, J. Fesler, and Rick Boone, *California Real Estate Finance*, 9th ed. (Cincinnati, OH: Cengage, 2011).

Other Costs and Expenses

Under transactions covered by the Real Property Loan Law, brokers are also limited in the amount of costs and expenses, other than commissions, they can charge a borrower for arranging a loan. Such costs and expenses cannot exceed 5 percent of the amount of the loan. However, if 5 percent of the loan is less than $390, the broker can charge up to that amount, provided the charges do not exceed actual costs and expenses paid, incurred, or reasonably earned by the broker.

Regardless of the size of the loan, the borrower cannot be charged more than $700 for miscellaneous costs and expenses, excluding commission and title and recording fees, as of July 2006.

Balloon Payments

A balloon payment is prohibited if (1) the term of the loan is for six years or less and (2) the loan is secured by the dwelling place of the borrower. Again, this provision does not apply to loans carried by sellers.

Insurance

A borrower is not required to purchase credit life or disability insurance as a condition for obtaining a loan. However, a lender may insist, for self-protection, that fire and hazard insurance be obtained on the property until the loan has been repaid. If licensed to sell such insurance, the mortgage broker can act as the agent for the borrower, but the borrower is not obligated to purchase the insurance coverage through the mortgage loan broker.

Miscellaneous Provisions

Mortgage brokers are prohibited from charging a borrower for loan-servicing or collection fees. Late charges, if any, may not exceed $5 or 10 percent of the principal and interest part of an installment payment, whichever is greater. If an installment payment is made within ten days of its due date, however, no late charge can be assessed.

In case of early repayment of a loan, there can be no prepayment penalty against the borrower when the loan is over seven years old. During the first seven years, a borrower is allowed to pay up to 20 percent of the remaining principal balance of the loan during any twelve-month period without a penalty. The remaining balance may then be subjected to a maximum prepayment penalty of six months' unearned interest. Mortgage brokers must keep copies of all loan papers for at least four years.

CHAPTER SUMMARY

The financing of real estate usually involves a five-phase process consisting of the loan application, analysis, processing, closing, and servicing phases. In California, the major instruments of finance are promissory notes and deeds of trust (trust deeds). Promissory notes can be straight notes, which contain interest-only payments, or installment notes, which include payments of principal and interest. The most common promissory note is the fully amortized installment note. In addition to fixed interest rate loans, adjustable rate loans are also popular.

Real estate loans in California are secured by deeds of trust, also called trust deeds. A deed of trust is a three-party instrument consisting of a trustor (borrower), a trustee (title holder), and a beneficiary (lender). Upon repayment of a loan, the trustee reconveys title back to the trustor. If the trustor (borrower) should default on the loan, the trustee forecloses on the property under what is called a trustee's sale.

Many promissory notes and deeds of trust contain special clauses that outline the duties and responsibilities of the borrower. Acceleration and alienation (due-on-sale) are most common. Subordination Practical Application and prepayment penalty clauses also exist. Junior deeds of trust are used in any real estate transactions when the buyer does not have enough money to cover the gap between the sales price and the first loan. Installment sales contracts are no longer popular for the purchase and financing of real estate.

The Truth-in-Lending Act, the Equal Credit Opportunity Act, and the Real Estate Settlement Procedures Act (RESPA) are examples of federal laws designed to assure proper disclosure to and equal treatment of prospective real estate borrowers. The Real Property Loan Law is a California law that requires full disclosure when a borrower procures a loan through a mortgage loan broker. This law also regulates maximum commissions and closing costs that can be charged to a borrower. The Real Property Loan Law does not apply to first deed of trust loans of $30,000 or more or second deed of trust loans of $20,000 or more.

IMPORTANT TERMS AND CONCEPTS

acceleration clause

adjustable rate

alienation (due-on-sale) clause

annual percentage rate (APR)

balloon payment

beneficiary

deed of trust

deficiency judgment

Equal Credit Opportunity Act

installment note

installment sales contract

hypothecation

junior deed of trust

leverage

negative amortized loan

prepayment penalty clause

Real Estate Settlement Procedures Act (RESPA)

straight note

subordination clause

trustee

trustor

truth-in-lending law

PRACTICAL APPLICATION

1. A homeowner has a $200,000 interest-only ARM loan with a current interest rate of 6 percent with a 2 percent margin over the 11th District Cost-of-Funds Index with a cap rate of 11 percent. What are the current monthly loan payments? With an annual maximum increase of 2 percent per year, under worst-case circumstances, what are the maximum monthly loan payments for the second, third, and fourth years?

2. An owner is in financial trouble and is behind $2,000 in payments on a $175,000 studio condo loan. The lender files a notice of default and begins to foreclose. To date, foreclosure costs total $1,000, plus the $2,000 back payments. Explain what the owner must do to save the home.

3. Using the services of a mortgage loan broker, a homeowner borrows a $15,000 junior loan for a ten-year period to pay off consumer debts. Assuming the loan broker charges the maximum commission and fees allowed by law, how much will the homeowner net after paying these fees?

REVIEWING YOUR UNDERSTANDING

1. A fully amortized promissory note with equal payments to liquidate a debt would be a(n)
    a. straight note.
    b. principal plus interest note.
    c. conventional note.
    d. installment note.

2. Sales price $220,000; $30,000 cash down; seller carries $190,000 loan; seller continues to pay on an existing $50,000 bank loan against the property. The seller carry loan is a(n)
    a. first deed of trust.
    b. senior lien.
    c. wraparound mortgage, or all-inclusive deed of trust (AITD).
    d. institutional loan.

3. Under a deed of trust (trust deed), the lender is
   a. the beneficiary.
   b. the trustee.
   c. the trustor.
   d. the mortgagor.

4. A due-on-sale clause is correctly called a(n)
   a. subordination clause.
   b. alienation clause.
   c. escalation clause.
   d. prepayment clause.

5. Which real estate sale will make use of a junior lien?
   a. An all-cash sale.
   b. The buyer puts 20 percent down and obtains an 80 percent loan.
   c. The seller carries the first deed of trust.
   d. The buyer puts 10 percent down and obtains an 80 percent loan; the seller carries a 10 percent second deed of trust.

6. Under which financing instrument is the seller known as the vendor?
   a. An installment sales contract
   b. A contract of sale
   c. An agreement of sale
   d. All of the above

7. Once a trustee records a notice of default, how much time does the borrower have to make up the delinquencies and stop the foreclosure?
   a. Five days prior to sale
   b. Ninety days prior to sale
   c. Twenty-one days prior to sale
   d. One hundred and eighty days prior to sale

8. The law that requires a lender to quote the cost of borrowing as an annual percentage rate is the
   a. Real Estate Settlement Procedures Act (RESPA).
   b. Truth-in-Lending Act.
   c. Equal Credit Opportunity Act.
   d. Fair Credit Reporting Act.

9. Under the Real Property Loan Law, the maximum commission a mortgage broker can charge for a $19,000 junior trust deed loan payable in thirty-seven equal installments is
    a. $2,850.
    b. $1,900.
    c. $950.
    d. no maximum commission.

10. Regarding question 9, what is the maximum amount the borrower can be charged for actual fees and expenses, excluding commission, title, and recording fees?
    a. $700
    b. $950
    c. $390
    d. No maximum amount

11. A $200,000 note at 7 percent interest, payable at $1,166.67 per month, is what kind of note?
    a. Principal and interest included
    b. Fully amortized
    c. Accommodation
    d. Straight

12. In a normal sale using a grant deed and deed of trust, the buyer is the
    a. grantee and trustee.
    b. grantor and trustor.
    c. grantee and trustor.
    d. grantor and trustee.

13. A clause where the holder of the first loan agrees to become second in favor of a new construction loan is
    a. prepayment penalty.
    b. alienation.
    c. subordination.
    d. acceleration.

14. Under an adjustable rate mortgage (ARM), the distance between the actual rate paid by the borrower and the index is called the
    a. cap.
    b. margin.
    c. term.
    d. adjustment.

15. The maximum interest rate on an ARM loan is called the
    a. cap.
    b. margin.
    c. term.
    d. adjustment.

16. Giving something as security for a loan without giving up possession is called
    a. pledging.
    b. granting.
    c. hypothecating.
    d. vesting.

17. If a lender calls a loan due and payable because the borrower is willfully destroying the property, the lender is exercising which clause?
    a. Alienation
    b. Acceleration
    c. Subservient
    d. Subordination

18. Which law requires a lender to give a borrower a good faith estimate of closing costs and requires a HUD-1 closing statement?
    a. Regulation Z
    b. Equal Credit Opportunity Act
    c. Truth in Lending Law
    d. RESPA

19. A buyer purchases subject to a seller's existing loan. Later a foreclosure occurs and the lender sues for a deficiency judgment. Who has prime liability?
    a. Buyer
    b. Seller
    c. Lender
    d. Beneficiary

20. For nonexempt lenders, the maximum interest that can be charged under California usury law is
    a. 10 percent.
    b. 5 percent above the Federal Reserve discount rate.
    c. 10 percent or 5 percent above the Federal Reserve discount rate, whichever is greater.
    d. 10 percent or 5 percent above the Federal Reserve discount rate, whichever is lesser.

Appendix A

Wraparound Deed of Trust

A *wraparound mortgage or deed of trust*, also called an all-inclusive trust deed (AITD), is a financing device used to increase the lender's yield upon the sale of real property and to make it easier for the buyer to finance the purchase.

> *Example:* An owner has a $200,000 parcel of land with an existing loan of $100,000 at 7 percent interest, payable at $800 per month. The owner sells for $200,000; the buyer puts down $50,000 cash; and the seller carries a wraparound deed of trust for $150,000 at 10 percent payable at $1,100 per month. The buyer makes the $1,100 payments to the seller on the $150,000 wraparound loan. The seller then makes the $800 payments on the $100,000 underlying loan, keeping the $300 difference ($1,100 − $800 = $300).

The seller's yield is increased because the seller receives 10 percent on $150,000, but pays only 7 percent on $100,000.

The buyer does not assume the seller's existing loan, but rather makes payments only on the wraparound deed of trust (AITD). The seller is responsible for all existing liens. By having the seller carry a wraparound deed of trust, the buyer avoids the new loan fees charged by institutional lenders.

A wraparound deed of trust is a complicated financing device that should be used only if all parties understand its details. Also, adequate provisions should be inserted to protect the buyer's interest in case the seller fails to make the payments on the underlying loan(s) after receiving the buyer's payment on the wraparound deed of trust.

Many existing real estate loans may have enforceable due-on-sale clauses that prohibit the use of a wraparound deed of trust. A wraparound deed of trust can also be used to refinance a property. A lender makes a new wraparound loan, and the lender agrees to make payments on the underlying existing loan(s).

Appendix B

Leverage

Leverage can be described as using a small amount of your money (equity capital) and a large amount of someone else's money (borrowed capital) to buy real estate. Leverage can be advantageous if the property increases in value.

For example, assume you can purchase land for $100,000 and resell it later for $150,000. If you pay $100,000 all cash and sell the property for $150,000, you realize a $50,000 gain, or a 50 percent return on your investment.

All-Cash Transaction

$150,000   Resale price
−100,000   Purchase price
$50,000   Gain

$$\frac{\$50,000 \text{ Gain}}{\$100,000 \text{ Investment}} = 50\%$$

On the other hand, if you could obtain a $90,000 real estate loan, you would need to invest only $10,000 as a down payment. If you resell the land for $150,000 and pay off the $90,000 loan, you would have a $50,000 gain, or a 500 percent return on your investment.

Leverage Transaction

$100,000   Purchase price
−90,000   Loan
$10,000   Down payment (investment)

$150,000   Resale price
−90,000   Loan
$60,000

−$10,000   Down payment
$50,000   Gain

$$\frac{\$50,000}{\$10,000} \quad \text{Gain} = 500\%$$
     Investment

Of course, the percentage return is reduced by income taxes, closing costs, and interest on the loan, but they have been omitted to stress the impact of leverage. However, leverage is rosy only if property values increase. If property values decrease, look out! See the following section on pitfalls.Introduction to Real Estate Finance

PITFALLS

Leverage can work in reverse if the value of the property declines. Here is what happens if the land in the example has declined in value by 10% upon resale.

All-Cash Transaction

$100,000	Purchase price
−90,000	Resale price
(10,000)	Loss on resale

$$\frac{\$10,000 \text{ Loss}}{\$100,000 \text{ Invested}} = -10\% \text{ Loss on investment}$$

Leverage Transaction

$90,000	Resale price
−90,000	Loan
0	Gain

$$\frac{0 \text{ Gain}}{\$10,000 \text{ Invested}} = -100\% \text{ Loss on investment}$$

If you paid $100,000 all cash, your loss was 10 percent. But if you paid $100,000 by borrowing $90,000 and putting $10,000 as down payment and the property resold for only $90,000, you were just able to repay the lender, and you lost all of your $10,000 down payment! If the property were to decline in value more than 10 percent you would owe more than what the property is worth. If this becomes the case and the buyer "walks away" from the property and the lender forecloses, the buyer's credit rating is destroyed. In addition, any difference between the loan amount and the lower amount the lender receives from the resale of the property can, in some cases, result in an income tax liability for the former owner.

Example :

$90,000	Loan balance owed at the time of foreclosure
−70,000	Resale price lender receives for the property after foreclosure
$20,000	Difference is known as *debt forgiveness* and could be taxable to the former owner as income (see a tax expert for details)

Chapter 8

This chapter is divided into two parts. Part I covers the main types of real estate lenders found in California. Part 2 discusses government's role in real estate financing, stressing the main points of the Federal Housing Administration (FHA), Department of Veterans Affairs (VA), and California Department of Veterans Affairs (Cal-Vet) programs. At the conclusion of Part I of the chapter, you will be able to do the following:

1. Compute the multipliers and ratios used by many real estate lenders to qualify borrowers.

2. List three institutional and noninstitutional real estate lenders.

3. Describe how private mortgage insurance has changed real estate lending practices in California.

Part I: Real Estate Lenders

8.1 QUALIFYING FOR A REAL ESTATE LOAN

When qualifying a borrower, a lender tries to determine whether a borrower will make his or her loan payments in the future. To make this determination, a loan officer analyzes two major characteristics:

1. *Capacity to pay.* To determine capacity to pay, these questions must be asked: Does the borrower make enough money to make the payments? If so, is it a stable source of income? Does the borrower have enough cash to buy this property? What other assets does the borrower have? The answers to all of these questions affect the borrower's capacity to pay.

2. *Desire to pay.* Desire to pay is the other major factor a lender must analyze. A person may have the capacity to pay but lack the desire to do so. The desire to pay is just as important as the capacity to pay, but it is more difficult to measure. The desire to pay is generally reflected by the past credit history of a borrower. The Federal Fair Credit Report Act allows a person to obtain a free copy of a credit report once per year. Contact the credit agencies for details.

Credit (FICO) Score

Credit scoring is how most lenders evaluate a person's credit history. Credit scores are also called *FICO scores,* a term that comes from Fair, Isaac & Company, who designed a matrix of more than thirty items used to predict the likelihood that a loan will be repaid as agreed. Scores range from a low of 300 to a high of approximately 900. A score below 650 usually triggers a closer examination by a lender. Most lenders used to require a score of 720; however, lenders are frequently requiring scores of 740 and above for a borrower to get the best loan terms. Examples of major items that influence a credit score include the following:

1. The number of credit accounts and cards. Are the cards "maxed out" or at a zero balance? Too many credit accounts, even with zero balances, lower a score. Why? Because they may be "maxed out" after a loan is granted, overloading the borrower.
2. The number of credit inquiries. How recent were the inquiries? A lot of recent inquiries indicates a hunt for credit.
3. Any late payments, collections, judgments, credit write-offs, bankruptcy, or other similar items.

Three credit-reporting agencies—Equifax, Experian, and Trans-Union—issue a credit score. A lender tends to use the mid-score of all three scores. After a credit report has been issued, a borrower has the right to see a copy and his or her credit score.

In short, for a potential borrower, a good credit score is good news. A low score is not good news. For information about your credit score, access www.myfico.com, www.equifax.com, or another website you locate using a search engine. A fee may be charged.

Special note: As of July 2006 the credit-scoring system is undergoing revisions that may change the numbering system in the future.

Old Rule of Thumb Is Inadequate

The old lender's rule, "A home should not cost more than 2.5 times a buyer's (borrower's) gross income," is inadequate. The rule ignores the real issue—the buyer's ability to pay the monthly housing payment. This rule also ignores the issue of a buyer's personal debts. Isn't a buyer who is free of debt able to pay more for housing than a buyer heavily in debt? Most lenders today recognize that "2.5 times the gross income" rule is riddled with errors and pitfalls.

Use of Multipliers and Ratios

Most lenders qualify borrowers by using income multipliers or ratios. The ratios can vary from lender to lender; however, the traditional 4:1 multiplier has been used by conservative real estate lenders for many years.

A 4:1 multiplier simply means that the monthly income of the borrower should be approximately four times the monthly housing payment. Thus, if the monthly housing payment (principal +

interest + monthly taxes, private mortgage insurance [if any], and hazard insurance) will be $1,000, four times this amount ($1,000 × 4), or $4,000, should be the borrower's gross monthly income. When converted to a ratio, the 4:1 multiplier means that a borrower's monthly housing payment should not be much more than 25 percent of the borrower's gross monthly income. Gross income must include all stable income of the borrower and co-borrowers, such as a spouse's income, alimony payments, and public assistance payments as well as regular wages, commissions, and salaries.

Trend Toward More Liberal Ratios

Recently there has been a move toward the use of 3.5:1 multipliers. This means that the borrower's monthly housing payments should not exceed approximately 30 percent of the borrower's gross income. Lenders recognize that because of higher costs for homes in California, more of a borrower's income must be used to cover housing payments. Therefore, if a borrower's monthly housing payment (principal + interest + monthly taxes, private mortgage insurance [if any], and hazard insurance) will be $1,000, three and one-half times this amount, or $3,500, should be the borrower's gross monthly income. Contrast this $3,500 with the $4,000 required when a lender uses the 4:1 multiplier, and you can see that the lower the ratio, the less gross income is needed to qualify for a real estate loan.

What Counts as Income?

Generally, lenders would like the borrower to have at least a two-year work history, preferably with the same employer or in the same vocation. Acceptable income includes wages, commissions, alimony, child support, pensions, Social Security benefits, positive cash flow from rentals, and self-employment income. In most cases, the lender would want to see current pay stubs, and in the case of alimony and child support a history of consistent payments. Rental and self-employment income are usually verified by submitting the last two years of income tax filings. Under some circumstances, a lender may also count overtime, bonuses, and part-time work if the borrower can show a consistent pattern of receiving steady payment from these sources.

Debts

A lender must also consider a borrower's debts in order to determine the capacity to pay. A borrower's debts may be short term or long term.

Short-term debts may be ignored, and long-term debts are counted. The definition of long- versus short-term debts can vary depending on the lender. However, many lenders consider long-term debts to be obligations that exist for six to ten months or more.

When considering debts, conventional lenders traditionally have used the following guidelines: the monthly housing payment + long-term debts = total monthly expenses. Traditionally the total monthly expenses should not exceed 33 to 38 percent of the borrower's gross monthly income. However, in times of liberal financing, some lenders will boost this to 40+ percent.

Example : $1,000 monthly housing expense + $250 long-term monthly debts = $1,250 × 3 = $3,750, the gross monthly income required from the borrower.

Summary of Qualifying Guidelines

1. (Principal + interest + monthly taxes, PMI, and hazard insurance)

$$\frac{\text{Monthly housing payments}}{\text{Gross monthly income}} = \text{Percentage \%}$$

Ideally this rate should not exceed 25 to 30 percent, with 28 percent commonly used by many lenders.

2. (Monthly housing payments + long-term monthly debts)

$$\frac{\text{Total monthly expenses}}{\text{Gross monthly income}} = \text{Percentage \%}$$

This ratio should not exceed 33 to 38 percent, with 36 percent commonly used by many lenders.

Most real estate lenders require that borrowers qualify under both tests. Some borrowers can qualify on the first test but not on the second because they are too heavily in debt. These guidelines can vary from lender to lender; thus, consumers and real estate agents should contact local lenders to obtain specific guidelines. Market conditions, the secondary mortgage market, and government regulations may also affect lender policies; the previous examples should be used as a guide. (See the case study on qualifying for a home loan in the appendix of this chapter.)

8.2 INSTITUTIONAL LENDERS

An institutional lender is a financial depository that gathers deposits from the general public and then invests these funds. As indicated in Figure 8.1, California has three major types of institutional

FIGURE 8.1

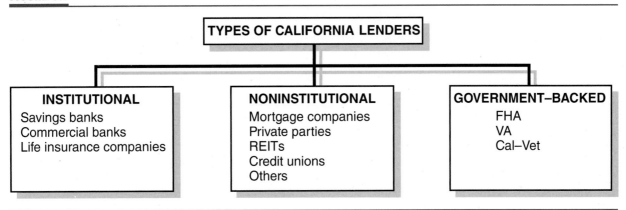

lenders: commercial banks, savings banks (formerly called savings and loan associations), and life insurance companies. All three of these institutions pour billions of dollars into California real estate loans. Before studying institutional lenders, it is helpful to review the characteristics of the California mortgage market and the concept of savings forming the pool for borrowing.

The California Mortgage Market

The characteristics of the California mortgage market can be summarized as follows:

1. *Usually high demand.* Because of its large economy, California traditionally has needed large amounts of mortgage funds. However, in periods of recession and economic slowdown, the demand for real estate loans declines.

2. *Population growth.* California is the most populous state. High population means high demand for housing to own or rent.

3. *Financial institutions.* California has many of the nation's largest commercial and savings banks.

4. *Mortgage loan correspondents.* California has many experienced mortgage companies that represent out-of-state life insurance companies and other lenders that, in boom times, are eager to invest in California real estate loans.

5. *Title and escrow companies.* Title insurance and escrow companies originated in California. Many of the nation's largest are in California, and they provide fast and efficient service for real estate lenders.

6. *Use of deeds of trust.* The deed of trust (trust deed) is used rather than mortgage instruments for securing real estate loans. Deeds of trust give lenders more flexibility than mortgages.

7. *Active secondary market.* Existing real estate loans are sold to out-of-state lenders. These include mutual savings banks, which are not located in California but which make the capital available through secondary purchases.

Savings Form the Pool for Borrowing

Profits and income can be taxed, spent, or saved. For most people, taxes are taken out first, and the remainder is used for consumer or business expenditures. If any funds remain after expenditures, they are saved or invested, which is a form of saving.

Sometimes people spend more than they earn and need to borrow to cover the excess spending. Where do the funds come from when people borrow? (Answer: from someone else's savings.) If all income were taxed or spent, there wouldn't be any savings left over to borrow, and it would be impossible to obtain a loan. Thus, all private funds for loans, including real estate loans, can be traced back to some form of savings. These savings can come from both domestic and foreign sources. With this background, turn your attention to the characteristics of institutional real estate lenders.

Commercial Banks

Commercial banks operate under a license or charter from the state or federal government. As far as real estate loans are concerned, there is little difference between a state and a national bank.

In recent years, commercial banks have been a powerful source for home loans, be they for purchase or refinance. Commercial banks also specialize in short-term construction financing, where the builder or developer has a "take-out" commitment from some other lender—most often, an insurance company or a savings bank—for the permanent mortgage loan. Large commercial banks play a major role in financing business and commercial properties, whereas some smaller banks deal exclusively with home loans.

Bankers may make conventional real estate loans for up to 95 percent or more of appraised value and for as long as 30–50 years on single-family dwellings. Many banks require private mortgage insurance on loans whose loan-to-value ratio is in excess of 80 percent. Bankers are sometimes authorized to grant FHA-insured and VA-guaranteed loans. Bankers are active seekers of home improvement and home equity loans.

Savings Banks (Formerly Called Savings and Loans)

A **savings bank** is a financial institution that accepts savings from the public and invests these savings mainly in real estate trust deeds and mortgages. The majority of savings bank loans are in residential properties, mostly single-family dwellings. A savings bank is also classified as either a state-chartered or a federally chartered institution. As far as real estate lending is concerned, there is little difference.

Under certain conditions, up to 95 percent or more loan-to-value ratio loans are obtainable at some savings banks if the loans are covered by private mortgage insurance. Most savings banks limit their loans to 30 years. Their prime real estate loan is on owner-occupied dwellings. But in a favorable market, savings banks also grant mobile home loans and apartment loans. Also common are combination loans that unite home construction and long-term take-out financing in one package.

The Savings and Loan Crisis

What happened? Why was there a massive savings and loan crisis in the 1980s? Some blame the economic stimulus provisions in the Economic Recovery Act of 1981. In the act, savings and loans were allowed to compete with commercial banks in more risky ventures; previously, they were restricted to single-family residential loans. Then in 1986, significant changes were made to the tax code that took away many of the tax advantages or shelters associated with investment real estate and the deductibility of interest. As a result, investment properties lost value and borrowers, unable to cover their mortgage payments, walked away from their properties.

Life Insurance Companies

Life insurance companies are another important source for real estate financing, particularly for large commercial and industrial properties such as shopping centers, office buildings, and warehouses. Life insurance companies also provide a significant amount of money for new housing subdivisions. In general, life insurance companies have broad lending powers.

Loan-to-value ratios are usually on the conservative side, generally in the 60 to 75 percent range for conventional financing, commonly with 30-year terms. Historically, insurance companies have preferred to grant large commercial and industrial real estate loans, but only if they are occupied by owners and tenants who have excellent credit and good company balance sheets.

Loan correspondents, such as mortgage companies, are widely used as agents of insurance companies. In this way, the insurance company is relieved of the burden of originating and processing loans as well as the responsibility of some administrative and service functions.

8.3 NONINSTITUTIONAL LENDERS

Institutional lenders such as commercial banks, savings banks, and life insurance companies accept deposits from the general public and are highly regulated by state and federal agencies.

Noninstitutional lenders do not accept deposits from the general public and are not as strictly regulated as institutional lenders. Major noninstitutional lenders include mortgage companies, private parties, real estate investment trusts, credit unions, and pension funds.

Mortgage Companies

Mortgage companies are a major type of noninstitutional real estate lender. When a mortgage company represents a life insurance company, a commercial bank, a savings bank, or another lender, it is called a *mortgage or loan correspondent*. It "corresponds" on behalf of its principal(s) in dealing with prospective borrowers. The mortgage correspondent is paid a fee in exchange for originating, processing, closing, and servicing loans. A loan correspondent serves a valuable function in the field of real estate financing for lenders whose headquarters or principal offices are located great distances from the properties on which they make loans.

Rules Regarding Mortgage Companies

Mortgage companies that do not use their own funds are subject in their lending activities to the same restrictions that govern their principal(s). Thus, if a California mortgage correspondent or banker represents an eastern life insurance company, the correspondent would have the same loan-to-value limitations placed on its loans as the insurance company.

Mortgage companies have special restrictions placed upon them. In California, they must be licensed and state approved. Even though they may not be lending money belonging to third parties, they are subject to the Real Property Loan Law when they make loans that are not specifically exempt under that law. They are also subject to some lending and other business regulations.

Mortgage Banker versus Mortgage Broker

A mortgage company could be a mortgage banker, a mortgage broker, or both. **Mortgage bankers** lend their own money and then either resell the loan to another lender or keep the loan for an investment. **Mortgage brokers** do not lend their own money; rather, they find a lender and a borrower and get a fee for bringing them together.

Major Player

Mortgage companies have become a dominant force in the California real estate market. In some areas, mortgage companies place more home loans than do institutional lenders. Many traditional real estate brokerage offices have added a mortgage brokerage division to give buyers a "one-stop shopping" option of buying and financing a purchase at the same office.

The Financial Crisis of 2008

One might have thought lenders would have learned their lesson in the early 1990s. But as real estate prices began soaring in 2002, fueled by low interest rates and increasing demand, lenders again began making risky loans. These loans were based on the "stated income" (without any documentation) of the borrower and provided straight or "interest-only" junior loans to achieve 100 percent financing without any type of mortgage insurance. As the market continued to heat up, lenders in increasing competition with each other began extending financing to borrowers with lower credit scores.

When the market began to slow down due to rising interest rates, borrowers unable to meet the interest rate adjustments on their adjustable rate loans began defaulting. This time, not only were commercial banks and savings banks caught off-guard, but also insurance companies, investment banks, and pension funds saw their investments in mortgage-backed securities lose value.

Far more extensive than the recession of the early 1990s, in 2008 Wall Street investment firms saw their portfolios filled with mortgage investments drop in value as much as 50 percent. As the economy entered 2010, a stabilization of the real estate market began, but with a continuance of borrower defaults and a flat real estate market, most economists predicted a slow economic recovery.

New Regulations for Mortgage Companies

As a result of the financial crisis of 2008, Congress enacted the Secure and Fair Enforcement for Mortgage Licensing (SAFE) Act on July 30, 2008 which requires the federal registration of all mortgage lenders, brokers, branches, and mortgage loan originators (MLOs) making loans secured by real estate. Implemented in California by SB 36, mortgage brokers are now required to obtain an MLO endorsement from the California Department of Real Estate to do loans in California.

The SAFE Act is designed to enhance consumer protection and reduce fraud through the setting of minimum standards for the licensing and registration of state-licensed mortgage loan originators. Additional educational requirements, licensing, and background checks will be required as these laws are implemented in 2010 for all real estate lenders, including mortgage brokers. Specifically, the licensing requirements include a twenty-hour prelicensure education course, which is to be completed through an Nationwide Mortgage Licensing System (NMLS) approved provider and contains the following:

- Three hours of federal law and regulations
- Three hours of ethics, including fraud, consumer protection, and fair lending issues
- Two hours of training related to lending standards for the nontraditional mortgage product marketplace

Upon completion of the prelicensure course, all applicants must pass a national and state-specific exam. Real estate licensees acting as mortgage brokers who fail to obtain this endorsement will face fines of $50 a day up to a maximum fine of $10,000.

Private Lenders

Private lenders are individuals who invest their savings in real estate loans. Private individuals can invest directly by granting loans to borrowers, or they can invest indirectly by turning to mortgage brokers who find borrowers for the private lender. Sellers frequently become private lenders when they carry back trust deeds in order to facilitate the sale of their property.

The prime motivation of private lenders is to earn a high yield, with some degree of safety. Some private lenders become investors by entering into partnership with young homebuyers in equity-share programs for the purchasing and financing of homes.

On seller carry loans on one to four residential units, a *seller financial disclosure statement* is required. This disclosure statement gives the buyer-borrower and the seller-lender an extensive breakdown of the major financial terms in the seller carry loan. Most real estate brokers have preprinted forms that satisfy this disclosure requirement.

Characteristics of Private Lenders

Private lenders generally share common characteristics, regardless of whether the loan is made directly by the individual or indirectly through a loan broker:

1. Most private lenders operate in the second trust deed market. Frequently, these loans are seller carry-back seconds that, thereafter, are sold to investors, usually at a discount, when the seller needs cash.

2. Most loans are on single-family homes and condos because this type of property is most familiar to the typical private investor and because the size of the loan is usually small.

3. The term of a private loan is usually short and often calls for a balloon payment. Three to six years are the most common maturities.

Real Estate Investment Trusts

The **real estate investment trust (REIT)** is a creature of the federal tax law. It was created in 1960 with the goal of encouraging small investors to pool their resources with others in order to raise venture capital for real estate transactions. It has been called the "mutual funds" of the real estate business. Just as mutual funds invest in a diversified portfolio of corporate stocks and bonds, REITs invest in a diversified portfolio of real estate and mortgage investments.

Credit Unions

A **credit union** is a mutual, voluntary-membership, cooperative organization of people who agree to save their money together to provide money for loans to each other. There are many credit unions throughout the United States, and their numbers are growing rapidly. For the most part, credit union lending in the field of real estate has been short term, but law changes now allow long-term real estate loans.

Syndicates, pension funds, trust funds, and various types of endowment funds are also noninstitutional real estate lenders. However, their lending practices are beyond the scope of this course.

To qualify as a trust, there are many tests that must be met, such as the requirement that at least 95 percent of the REIT's net income be distributed annually to the investors to qualify for favorable tax treatment. The legal ramifications of REITs are beyond the scope of this course; anyone interested in forming or participating in REITs should seek legal counsel.

Investing in Trust Deeds

TRUST DEEDS

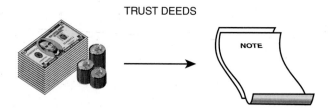

Some private investors prefer to purchase existing notes and trust deeds instead of granting a loan directly to a borrower. These investors search for a sale where the seller carries back the paper. They then attempt to purchase existing seller carry loans at a discount. Many times the seller is willing to sell the note for cash rather than wait several years for the buyer to pay off the loan.

The investor usually buys the note at a discount, which increases the investor's yield to a rate higher than the amount of interest on the face of the note. The size of the discount varies with the quality of the borrowers, the equity in the property, and current money market conditions. Some mortgage brokers earn commissions by bringing buyers and sellers of notes together.

Here are two legal terms regarding the selling of existing notes and trust deeds:

1. *Negotiable instrument* This is a promissory note that is a written promise or order to pay an amount of money at a definite time or on demand. Negotiable instruments are allowed to be freely sold.

2. *Holder in due course* This is a person who in good faith has purchased a note for value without any knowledge about defects or past due payments. A person who purchased a note as a holder in due course has some superior rights if the borrower on the note refuses to pay based on certain disputes with the former owner of the note.

8.4 PRIVATE MORTGAGE INSURANCE

What is **private mortgage insurance?** It is insurance that is used to guarantee lenders the payment of the upper portion of a conventional loan if a borrower defaults and a deficiency occurs at the foreclosure sale. Private mortgage insurance, formerly called *mortgage guaranty insurance,* is sold by private insurance companies, and in the lending business it is referred to as *PMI.*

The private mortgage system stimulates the housing market by allowing buyers with smaller down payments to qualify for a loan. Lenders who normally want buyer-borrowers to put at least 20 percent cash down will allow qualified buyer-borrowers to put less down if they purchase private mortgage insurance for a minimum of 24 months.

Coverage and Cost of Private Mortgage Insurance

Private mortgage insurance is available on one-to-four-unit dwellings. It generally covers the top 20 to 25 percent of the loan amount based on the value of the property. For example, if a condo sold for $380,000 and the loan was 90 percent, the loan would be $380,000 × 90% = $342,000. The private mortgage insurance coverage to the lender would be 20% × $342,000 loan = $68,400.

The initial insurance premium fee varies with PMI companies, but it is usually paid by the borrower. In addition, an annual premium that is divided by 12 is added to the borrower's monthly payment. There are also plans whereby you can pay one fee at the time of closing and no annual premium. Recent laws allow the borrower to cancel the PMI once the homeowner achieves 20 percent or more equity.

CHAPTER SUMMARY, PART I

Real estate lenders are concerned about a borrower's ability to repay a loan. To screen loan applicants, lenders use qualifying ratios coupled with an examination of the borrower's credit history and net worth.

Real estate lenders can be divided into three categories: (1) institutional lenders, (2) noninstitutional lenders, and (3) government-backed programs. Institutional real estate lenders are commercial banks, savings banks (savings and loan associations), and life insurance companies.

Noninstitutional real estate lenders include mortgage companies, private lenders, REITs, credit unions, and pension funds. The main government-backed programs include FHA, VA, and Cal-Vet.

Private mortgage insurance (PMI) is used to guarantee a lender the payment of the upper portion of a loan if a borrower should default and a foreclosure sale does not generate enough money to cover the loan. PMI allows lenders to grant higher loans, thereby requiring less down payment.

IMPORTANT TERMS AND CONCEPTS

commercial banks

credit union

institutional lenders

life insurance companies

mortgage bankers

mortgage brokers

mortgage companies

noninstitutional   private mortgage   real estate
lenders   insurance (PMI)   investment trust
private lenders   (REIT)
                                                     savings bank

PRACTICAL APPLICATION

1. A borrower earns $5,000 gross income per month and has $600 in long-term monthly debts. The lender's maximum qualifying ratios are 28 and 36 percent. Assuming good credit, what is the maximum monthly housing payment this borrower is qualified to pay?

2. Economists state that people can do only two things with their after-tax income and profits. What are these two things? Explain how the real estate market is affected by these two choices.

3. Stories have surfaced about borrowers being overcharged for their PMI coverage. A recent law requires PMI insurers to cancel the PMI coverage once a loan amount is reduced to 80 percent or less of the value of the home. Assume that a loan balance is $180,000 and re-presents 80 percent or less of the value of the condo. If the annual PMI charge is .0025 of the loan amount (.25 of 1 percent), how much will a borrower's loan payment be reduced by canceling the PMI?

REVIEWING YOUR UNDERSTANDING

1. A borrower's total monthly housing payments will be $1,000. The borrower's other long-term debts are $300 per month. The borrower's gross monthly income is $3,600. What are the borrower's qualifying ratios?
   a. 25 and 33.3 percent
   b. 27.8 and 36.1 percent
   c. 30 and 38.9 percent
   d. 31.2 and 37.3 percent

2. Which of the following is a noninstitutional lender?
   a. Commercial bank
   b. Life insurance company
   c. Pension fund
   d. Savings bank

3. Private mortgage insurance (PMI) usually covers what percent of the loan?

    a. 100 percent

    b. 80–90 percent

    c. 50–60 percent

    d. 20–25 percent

4. Which real estate lender frequently acts as a loan correspondent for other lenders?

    a. Pension funds

    b. Mortgage companies

    c. Real estate investment trusts

    d. Private lenders

5. The use of private mortgage insurance permits lenders to make up to what percent loans on owner-occupied homes?

    a. 80 percent or less

    b. More than 80 percent

    c. Any amount the lender wishes

    d. None of these

6. Which of the following statements is false?

    a. Commercial banks are considered institutional lenders.

    b. Savings form the pool for borrowing.

    c. Life insurance companies specialize in making individual homeowner loans.

    d. Private lenders, who grant hard-money loans to private individuals, are not exempt from usury laws.

7. A person who purchases a note for value at good faith without prior notice of a default or defect is a

    a. holder in due course.

    b. negotiable buyer.

    c. mortgage broker.

    d. loan correspondent.

8. A lender that makes hard-money loans by lending its own money is a
   a. seller, through seller carry loans.
   b. mortgage broker.
   c. mortgage banker.
   d. purchaser of existing trust deeds.

9. A lender that tends to use the lowest loan-to-value ratios is a
   a. savings bank.
   b. commercial bank.
   c. mortgage company.
   d. life insurance company.

10. In the financing of the sale of a home, which lender is required to complete a seller financial disclosure statement?
    a. Seller carry backs
    b. Credit union
    c. Savings banks
    d. Commercial banks

Part II: FHA, VA, and Cal-Vet Loans and the Secondary Mortgage Market

STUDENT LEARNING OUTCOMES, PART II

Part 2 of this chapter focuses on specific government programs designed to help people acquire their own home. Three programs presented in detail are the Federal Housing Administration (FHA), Department of Veterans Affairs (VA), and California Department of Veterans Affairs (Cal-Vet) programs. In addition, the purpose and function of the secondary mortgage market are discussed. At the conclusion of Part 2, you will be able to do the following:

1. Discuss the main characteristics of FHA-insured, VA-guaranteed, and Cal-Vet loans.
2. Define the secondary mortgage market, and discuss the role played by government agencies in this market.

8.5 GOVERNMENT ROLE IN REAL ESTATE FINANCING

The government has become heavily involved in helping consumers acquire decent housing. There are many government housing programs, but in this text, only FHA-insured, VA-guaranteed, Cal-Vet loan, and CalHFA programs are discussed.

Federal Housing Administration (FHA)

The Federal Housing Administration (FHA), a part of the Department of Housing and Urban Development (HUD), was established in 1934 to improve the construction and financing of housing. Since its creation, the FHA has had a major influence on real estate financing. Some of today's loan features that are taken for granted were initiated by the FHA.

The FHA is not a lender; *it does not make loans.* Approved lenders such as mortgage companies, insurance companies, and banks make the loans. However, the loans must be granted under FHA guidelines. Once the loan is granted, if the borrower defaults on the loan, the FHA insures the lender against foreclosure loss.

The FHA collects a fee for this insurance, which is called the *Mortgage Insurance Premium (MIP).* The MIP fees are paid up front in cash or financed as part of the loan.

This insurance should not be confused with credit life insurance. An FHA mortgage insurance policy does not insure the borrower's life. A mortgage insurance policy is used by the FHA to reimburse a lender if the borrower defaults on mortgage payments and the foreclosure results in a loss for the insured lender.

Advantages of FHA Loans

1. *Low down payment.* The main advantage of an FHA-insured loan is the low down payment. It used to be that FHA interest rates were set below the conventional rates. But deregulation now allows the FHA interest rate to float with the market. Therefore, sellers are no longer required to pay discount points to increase the lender's yield. Any loan fees or points charged by the lender are an item of negotiation and can be paid by the buyer or the seller.

2. *No prepayment penalty.* An FHA-insured loan does not allow a prepayment penalty.

3. *Under some circumstances, FHA-insured loans are assumable.* FHA-insured loans do not allow alienation clauses (due-on-sale clauses). This makes it possible to buy property and, with FHA approval, take over the seller's existing FHA-insured loan. At one time, all FHA-insured loans were assumable without requiring a credit and/or income check. But beginning with FHA-insured loans originating as of December 15, 1989, all assumptions must be approved by the FHA. In addition, non-owner-occupied assumptions are prohibited on FHA-insured loans as of the same date.

4. *All cash to the seller.* New FHA-insured loans cash out the seller. In a down real estate market, many sellers may need to carry a second, also known as a piggyback loan which is a combination of two loans that close at the same time to purchase a home to help

finance a conventional loan for a buyer. Under FHA terms, the high loan-to-value ratio gives the seller all cash.

5. *Minimum property standards.* FHA will not allow a lender to grant a loan unless the property meets FHA housing standards, which, in some cases, are more stringent than what some conventional lenders allow.

Disadvantages of FHA Loans

1. *Low loan amounts.* As a result of high home prices in many areas of California, the FHA program is often not practical because of the cap the FHA sets on its maximum loan amount allowed. (See "How to Calculate FHA-Insured Loan Amounts.")

2. *Red tape and processing time.* The FHA is a large federal agency; therefore, the problem of dealing with a bureaucracy becomes an issue. However, some FHA-insured lenders have preapproval rights that can speed up the FHA process.

3. *Repairs on existing property.* The FHA-appointed appraiser also checks for repairs that he or she believes are necessary. The FHA then requires that these repairs be made before the property is approved. Sellers may not wish to make these repairs and may refuse to sell to an FHA-insured buyer.

Federal Housing Administration Programs

Here are some general rules that apply to all FHA homeowner programs:

1. FHA will approve loans on owner-occupied 1 to 4-residential dwellings, units in planned unit developments (PUDs), condominiums, and mobile homes.

2. The maximum loan fee is 1 percent of the loan amount, and the buyer normally pays this fee.

3. The Mortgage Insurance Premium upfront fee (as of 2010) is 2 1/4 percent of the loan amount.

4. The maximum loan term is 30 years or three-quarters of the remaining economic life of the property, whichever is less.

5. The FHA requires that monthly payments include principal, interest, and 1/12 of the annual property taxes, hazard insurance premium, and Mortgage Insurance Premium.

6. There is no maximum purchase price. The buyer can pay more than the FHA appraisal. However, the loan is based on the FHA appraisal if it is lower than the sales price.

7. The interest rates on FHA-backed loans now float with the market instead of being fixed by the FHA.

8. FHA appraisals are good for six months on existing property and one year on new construction.

How to Calculate FHA-Insured Loan Amounts (As of February 2010)

FHA calculates the loan amount based on the home's sales price or the FHA-approved appraisal, whichever is less.

As of 2009, the maximum loan amount was set at 96.5 percent (or a 3.5 percent down payment). The FHA then sets a ceiling on the maximum loan allowed based on the median home prices in various geographic areas. The dollar amounts can change each year depending on the trend in home prices. Of California's 58 counties, the following 15 counties are considered especially high-cost areas and are allowed the largest FHA loan amounts in the continental United States: Alameda, Contra Costa, Los Angeles, Marin, Monterey, Orange, San Diego, San Francisco, San Joaquin, San Mateo, Santa Barbara, Santa Clara, Santa Cruz, Sonoma, and Ventura counties. In the remaining 43 California counties, the maximum FHA loan amounts are less. Dollar amounts are not quoted here, because they vary among California counties. For the maximum FHA-approved loan amount for your area, contact any local FHA-approved lender. You can also access HUD's website at www.hud.gov and get the latest quote for your county.

Required Cash Investment

The FHA requires a minimum 3.5 percent cash investment based on the sales price or appraisal, whichever is less. This 3.5 percent cash investment can come from an approved gift and need not be the FHA buyer's own personal money (larger down payments may be required for borrowers with low credit scores).

Therefore, with a 3.5 percent required cash investment, the buyer will be paying for some of the closing costs. If the buyer pays no more than the required 3.5 percent cash investment, the remaining closing costs, after applying the 3.5 percent rule, must be paid by the seller or some other party. The buyer can finance the required MIP by increasing the loan amount.

Under previous FHA rules, only the seller, not the buyer, must pay for the following closing costs: tax service fee, loan document fee, processing fee, flood certification fee, and termite costs, if any.

Currently, the payment of nonrecurring closing costs is negotiable between the seller and the buyer. See Chapter 10, "The Role of Escrow and Title Insurance Companies," for a complete discussion of the difference between recurring and nonrecurring closing costs. However, in 2010 the FHA limited seller's concessions to buyers to 3 percent of the sales price.

FHA Programs

The National Housing Act of 1934 created the Federal Housing Administration. The act has 11 subdivisions, or "Titles," with further subdivisions called "Sections." This chapter deals only with Section 203b because this is the most important section for the average homebuyer or real estate agent.

Section 203b

Under the **FHA 203b program:**

1. Anyone who is financially qualified is eligible.
2. Loans are available on properties from one to four units.
3. The maximum FHA loan amounts vary from region to region, with high-cost areas of California allowed larger loan amounts than lower-cost areas within the state.
4. Although a buyer's credit history is important, it does not need to be perfect.
5. The buyer must make a minimum cash investment of 3.5 percent, but this can come from an approved gift from family members and certain nonprofit groups.
6. The mortgage insurance premium (MIP) must be obtained and can be purchased up front or financed as part of the loan. The MIP added to the loan is allowed to exceed maximum FHA loan limits.
7. The FHA permits a borrower to carry more debt than most conventional lenders will allow.

> *Example:* A buyer wishes to purchase a small condo under the FHA 203b program. The buyer agrees to pay $230,000, and the FHA-approved appraisal comes in at $232,000. What is the maximum FHA loan amount? What is the minimum cash the buyer must invest?
>
> *Step 1:* The lesser of the price or appraisal is $230,000 × 96.5 % = $221,950, or the maximum loan for the area, whichever is less, plus any amount for the MIP.
>
> *Step 2:* The lesser of the price or appraisal is $230,000 × 3.5 % = $8,050 minimum cash investment required from the

buyer. If more cash is needed to pay for closing costs, the buyer can add more money or the seller or some other party can agree to pay the remaining costs. This will be determined on a case-by-case basis.

Department of Veterans Affairs (VA or G.I.) Loans

In 1944, Congress passed the G.I. Bill of Rights to provide benefits to veterans, including provisions for making real estate loans.

Like the FHA, the VA is not a lender. However, if no approved private lender is located in the area, the VA will make direct loans under certain conditions. One difference between the FHA and the VA is that the **Department of Veterans Affairs** guarantees a portion of the loan, while the Federal Housing Administration insures the loan.

The VA guaranteed amount is calculated as 25 percent of the current Federal Home Loan Mortgage Corporation (Freddie Mac) conforming loan amount. Each year, if the Freddie Mac conforming loan amount increases, the VA guarantee to an approved lender also increases. For example, as of January 2006, the maximum Freddie Mac conforming loan was $417,000; thus, 25% × 417,000 = $104,250 was the maximum VA lender guarantee.

Then, most VA-approved lenders simply reverse the process and will grant a no-money-down loan to qualified veterans that is four times the VA guarantee. For 2006 this would be the $104,250 guarantee × 25% = $417,000 maximum no-down-payment VA-guaranteed loan. The bottom line is that the maximum VA no-money-down loan amount is usually the same as the maximum Freddie Mac conforming loan amount.

In 2010, VA limits were increased based on property values in the county where the property is located. Since these limits change, you are encouraged to go to the Department of Veterans Affairs website at www.homeloans.va.gov to get the latest quote for your county.

Whether a loan is insured or guaranteed is important only if a foreclosure occurs. If a foreclosure does occur, the VA has two options:

1. It can pay the lender the loan balance and take over the property.
2. It can give the lender the property and pay it the amount of the deficiency, if any, up to the maximum amount of the VA guarantee.

However, if a foreclosure occurs under the FHA program, the lender is paid off and the property is taken over by the FHA.

Advantages and Disadvantages of VA (G.I.) Loans

Advantages of VA Loans

1. *No down payment.* The VA does not require a borrower to make any down payment on loans up to the current maximum loan amount if the borrower pays the VA-appraised value for the property. Caution: VA no-down loan amounts can change. Access the VA's website at www.homeloans.va.gov for the latest loan amounts.
2. *No mortgage insurance payment.*
3. *No prepayment penalty.*

Disadvantages of VA Loans

1. *Creditworthiness qualification for assumptions.* Effective March 1, 1988, VA loans are no longer automatically assumable. The VA requires a creditworthiness qualification before an existing loan can be taken over by a new buyer. A fee is charged for a VA loan assumption.
2. *Seller may need to pay discount points.* The VA point system is explained later.
3. *Red tape and processing time.* Processing time, inflexibility, and paperwork occasionally are problems in dealing with a large government agency.
4. *Loans can only be obtained by qualified veterans.*

Who is Eligible for VA Loans?

To be eligible, a veteran must have a discharge or release that is not dishonorable and must have served a minimum number of days depending on the time period in the service. The usual minimum is 181 days of active duty. National Guard and other military reserves who served at least six years are also eligible.

Those who served less than the required time but were released or discharged because of a service-connected disability are also eligible for VA loans. In addition, many other classifications of veterans are eligible for a VA-guaranteed loan depending on the circumstances. Also, a veteran can use his or her VA loan more than once.

General Information on VA Loans

1. *Type of property.* The VA will guarantee loans on properties of one to four units and on units in planned unit developments (PUDs), condominiums, and mobile homes.
2. *Interest rate.* Within VA guidelines, the interest rate is negotiable between the veteran and the lender.

3. *Loan fee.* The amount of the loan origination fee paid by the borrower is negotiable. Prior to a 1993 law change, the loan fee could be only 1 percent of the loan amount.

4. *Funding fee.* A separate fee on top of the loan fee is paid by the borrower for granting the loan. This fund fee usually varies from 2 to 3 percent of the loan amount. The funding fee can be financed by adding it to the loan amount.

5. *Term of loan.* The maximum term is 30 years.

6. *Down payment.* The VA does not require a down payment on loans up to current designed amounts. The veteran is frequently allowed to borrow the full amount of the purchase price. What happens if the VA appraisal is less than the purchase price? The loan amount cannot exceed the appraisal. The difference between the purchase price and the appraisal must be paid by the borrower in cash.

7. *Maximum loan.* There is no maximum loan amount on a VA loan. This does not mean you can obtain a no-down-payment VA loan in any amount. Since the VA guarantees only a portion of the loan, lenders limit the amount they will lend on VA loans. Many lenders will not lend more than four times the guarantee.

8. *Occupying the property.* The veteran must occupy the property. The VA does not have a program for veterans who do not intend to occupy the property.

9. *Monthly payments.* Included are principal, interest, and 1/12 the annual property taxes and hazard insurance premiums.

10. *Appraisal.* The VA appraisal is called the *certificate of reasonable value (CRV).* To the VA, *reasonable value* means current market value.

11. *Structural pest control report.* The VA requires that a report be obtained from a licensed structural pest control company. Any required work must be done, and the veteran must certify that the work has been done satisfactorily.

Calculating Discount Points for VA Loans

Under VA terms, a lender and the veteran negotiate the interest rate. If this negotiated rate is not sufficient to cope with today's cost of overhead and profit, a lender simply refuses to grant a loan under VA terms. This may cause the sale to fall through. Under these circumstances, a motivated seller might be willing to pay a discount fee to increase the lender's yield, thereby encouraging the lender to grant a VA loan and allow the sale to close.

Example: Assume the home sales price and appraisal both are $333,700 and the maximum VA-guaranteed loan available is $333,700. Also assume the negotiated VA interest rate the veteran qualifies for is 6 percent, but lenders can get 7 percent interest on government-backed real estate loans. To entice the lender to make the VA-backed loan at 6 percent, the seller agrees to pay the 1 percent difference. This fee is called a *mortgage discount,* or *points.*

As a rule of thumb, points are calculated as follows (based on current interest rates for 2010): each 1 percent of discount (1 point) is equal to one-sixth of 1 percent interest. For a lender to increase the yield on a loan by 1 percent, the lender must charge 6 percent, or 6 points, of the loan amount, which is deducted from the seller's net proceeds from the sale. Again, the seller is made aware of this before accepting the buyer's offer to purchase the home.

Thus, in the following example:

7% – 6% = 1% = 6/6 = 6 points or .06 of the loan amount

Therefore:

$333,700 loan amount × .06 = $20,022, which is the discount fee the seller must pay the lender up front from the seller's sale proceeds

The 1 percent difference in the previous example is used for simplicity's sake to explain VA discount points. In the real world, the interest rate spread between the VA and conventional rate may be only $1/8$ percent to $1/4$ percent, resulting in only 1 to 2 discount points to be paid by the seller.

In an active market where there are numerous buyers, sellers tend not to sell to VA buyers who require the payment of discount points. But in a slow market, a seller may be more than willing to pay discount points just to get rid of the property.

Cal-Vet Loans

The **Cal-Vet loans** program is administered by the State of California, Department of Veterans Affairs, Division of Farms and Home Purchases. The veteran (buyer) normally deals directly with this agency, although recent rules allow a mortgage loan broker to start the loan process on behalf of the buyer. No other lender is involved; the state makes the loan to the veteran directly. The money is obtained from the sale of State Veteran Bonds.

Who Is Eligible for Cal-Vet Loans?

To qualify, a veteran must meet these requirements:

1. Have had 90 days' active duty
2. Have been given an honorable discharge or, if still on active duty, a *Statement of Service* verifying his or her status
3. Be willing to buy a California home or farm

Both peacetime and wartime veterans are eligible for a Cal-Vet loan. But if loan funds are limited, a preference is given to wartime veterans. The highest priority is given to war veterans with a service-connected disability. Unremarried surviving spouses or registered domestic partners of an eligible veteran may also be qualified for a Cal-Vet loan. A Cal-Vet loan may be used more than once, as long as the previous Cal-Vet loan has been paid in full or awarded in a divorce to a nonveteran spouse.

General Information About Cal-Vet Loans

1. *Property.* Cal-Vet has generally the same property standards as FHA and VA. The property must be a single-family dwelling or a unit in a PUD, condominium, or mobile home. Certain farm loans are also approved. Cal-Vet requires both a structural pest control report and a roof inspection.
2. *Maximum loan.* The maximum Cal-Vet loan amounts can vary each year. There are separate maximums for single-family dwellings, farms, and mobile homes. To find the current maximum for each, go to the Cal-Vet website (www.cdva.ca.gov).
3. *Down payment and loan fees.* Cal-Vet loans guaranteed by the VA are called *Cal-Vet/VA loans* and are available for no money down up to the current maximum VA-guaranteed loan, which is usually four times the maximum VA guarantee (discussed earlier in the chapter). On straight Cal-Vet loans, without the VA guarantee, the down payment is usually 2 to 3 percent of the purchase price or appraised value, whichever is the lesser.
4. *Term of loan.* Most loans are approved for a term of thirty years.
5. *Interest rate.* The interest rate is variable. The rate is checked periodically to determine whether a change is necessary. The costs of the bonds and of running the program determine the interest rate.
6. *Secondary financing.* This is permitted under special circumstances. However, the provisions are too complex to be covered in this text.

7. *No prepayment penalty.* There is no penalty to pay off a Cal-Vet Loan early.

8. *Occupancy.* The veteran must occupy the property.

9. *Monthly payments.* Principal, interest, and 1/12 the annual property taxes, hazard insurance, disability, and life insurance premiums are included in monthly loan payments.

10. *Title to property.* When a property is being financed with a regular Cal-Vet loan, title is first conveyed to the Department of Veterans Affairs by the seller. The department then sells the property to the veteran under a land contract of sale. The department continues to hold title until the veteran has paid the loan in full.

Advantages and Disadvantages of Cal-Vet Loans

The main advantages of Cal-Vet loans are low interest rate, inexpensive life and hazard insurance, and low closing costs. In the past, the main disadvantage was the long time it took to process a Cal-Vet loan. But recent changes by the California Department of Veterans Affairs have attempted to address this issue. Cal-Vet now has several district offices throughout the state with trained personnel to provide the latest information and the help needed to prepare the required forms for faster loan processing. In addition, many mortgage brokers have completed Cal-Vet loan-processing seminars and are equipped to help a veteran process a loan. If a private mortgage loan broker is used, the seller and buyer must pay the broker's fee; it cannot be financed as part of a Cal-Vet loan. For more information, the website is www.cdva.ca.gov.

See Table 8.1 for a comparison of the government programs designed for obtaining loans.

8.6 THE CALIFORNIA HOUSING FINANCE AGENCY (CᴀʟHFA) PROGRAM

The **CalHFA** program is designed to help first-time homebuyers acquire a home in California's expensive housing market. This state agency sells mortgage revenue bonds to investors, and then uses the funds to buy loans from approved lenders who make loans under CalHFA guidelines. Thus, like FHA and VA, CalHFA does not make loans directly to borrowers. Instead, this state agency purchases the loans made by approved lenders. CalHFA prides itself on not using state funds and taxpayer dollars to operate its program. Full details regarding CalHFA can be found at their website (www.calhfa.ca.gov).

TABLE 8.1   Comparison of Government-Backed Loans (excluding CalHFA) as of July 2006.

	Federal Housing Administration (FHA)	Department of Veterans Affairs (VA)	Cal-Vet
Purpose of loan	1–4 units	1–4 units	Home or farm
Eligibility	Any U.S. resident	U.S. veteran	U.S. veteran
Maximum purchase price	None	None	None
Maximum loan	Varies by geographic area	None by the VA, but the VA restricts the guarantee	Varies each year
Down payment	3.5% minimum cash investment	None, but loan limited to the CRV	2% or 3% of sale price or appraisal, whichever is less
Maximum term	Usually 30 years	Usually 30 years	Usually 30 years
Interest rate	Market rate	Negotiated rate	Variable rate
Prepayment penalty	None	None	None

Two Main Programs

CalHFA offers a thirty-year, fixed-rate conventional loan program and what it calls an interest-only PLUS plan.

Thirty-Year, Fixed-Rate Conventional Loan Program

This program features a below-market fixed interest rate amortized for thirty years and a maximum loan-to-value ratio of 100 percent. In special circumstances, the loan can be as high as a 107 percent loan-to-value ratio. The loan origination fee cannot exceed 1.5 percent of the loan amount. Mortgage insurance is required, and CalHFA provides this coverage at a very low fee.

Property Eligibility: The property must meet all of the following requirements:

1. Sales price of the home cannot exceed CalHFA price limits. Said price limits vary by county. See the CalHFA website for your area.
2. It must be an owner-occupied, single-family, one-unit home, condo, or PUD.
3. Manufactured homes are allowed if they meet CalHFA construction standards.

   Borrower Eligibility: The borrower must meet the following requirements:

1. Be a U.S. citizen, permanent resident alien, or qualified alien.
2. Be a first-time homebuyer, unless the home is located in a federally designated *targeted area* that is deemed to need an infusion of investment.

3. Occupy the home as a principal or primary residence; non-owner-occupied loans are not allowed.

4. Have an income within CalHFA income limits established for each county where the home is located.

5. Meet CalHFA credit requirements.

There are certain special circumstances in which homes or borrowers may still qualify even if they cannot quite meet all the requirements listed above. See the CalHFA website for additional details.

Interest-Only PLUS Program

This CalHFA plan features a conventional loan with a below-market fixed interest rate, a thirty-five-year term, and interest-only payments for the first five years. Then the payments switch to an amortized loan for the remaining thirty years. The interest rate remains fixed for the entire thirty-five-year term. The loan-to-value ratio is 100 percent, rising to 107 percent under special circumstances. Mortgage insurance is required and is provided by CalHFA at very low rates. The property and borrower eligibility requirements are identical to the ones listed above under the thirty-year fixed-rate program.

For more information about this first-time homebuyer program, contact CalHFA at their website (www.calhfa.ca.gov).

8.7 SECONDARY MORTGAGE MARKET

The **secondary mortgage market** is a market where existing real estate loans are bought and sold—in other words, lenders sell their loans to other lenders and investors. The secondary mortgage market should not be confused with secondary financing. Secondary financing is a loan secured by a second or junior deed of trust, whereas a secondary market is the sale of an existing loan by one lender to another lender or investor. (See Figure 8.2.)

FIGURE 8.2

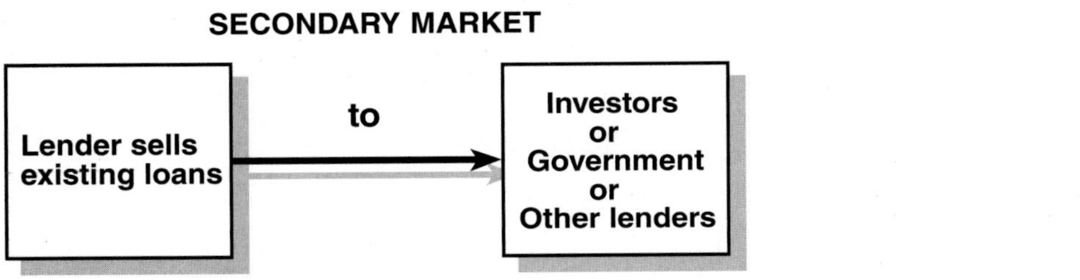

SECONDARY MARKET

Lender sells existing loans → to → Investors or Government or Other lenders

Purpose of the Secondary Mortgage Market

Flow of Money

Why do lenders need a secondary mortgage market? Why don't they just make a loan and keep it? That would be fine if every lender always had a perfect balance between the demand for loans and its supply of money. However, in the real world, this balance rarely exists. For example, a lender in California may have a greater demand for loans than it can meet. Another lender in Texas might have the opposite problem—surplus funds because of lack of demand in Texas. The solution to this problem is to have the Texas lender buy loans from the California lender. Both would be satisfying their needs. The Texas lender would be putting idle money to work, and the California lender would obtain additional funds to use to make new loans. Thus, one of the main purposes of the secondary market is to shift mortgage funds to areas where they are needed.

Generate New Loan Fees

A second reason why lenders resell their loans in the secondary market is to generate loan and collection fees. When a lender grants a loan, the lender generates a loan fee.

Some lenders prefer to sell a recently granted loan quickly to reinvest the proceeds into another new loan and generate a new loan fee (and so on). In addition, when a lender sells a loan, the purchaser of the loan may ask the original lender to continue to collect the loan payments and forward said payments to the purchaser. The original lender is paid a collection fee for this service.

Stabilize the Mortgage Market

The mortgage market is never static. Instead, it moves through cycles of tight and loose money. The market can be stabilized by providing funds to buy loans during tight money periods and providing loans to be purchased during loose money periods. Three main organizations are designed to help stabilize the mortgage market:

1. Federal National Mortgage Association
2. Federal Home Loan Mortgage Corporation
3. Government National Mortgage Association

Federal National Mortgage Association

The **Federal National Mortgage Association** (Fannie Mae) is usually called by its nickname. Established in 1938 by the U.S. Congress, its main job is to provide a secondary market for mortgages. Fannie Mae remained a part of the federal government until 1968, when it became a private corporation. Its main function today is still to maintain a secondary market.

To maintain a secondary market, Fannie Mae buys and sells mortgages. Where does it get the money to do this? It borrows money in the capital market by selling notes and bonds. Fannie Mae can usually obtain a more favorable rate than another corporate borrower because its obligations carry the indirect backing of the U.S. government.

What type of loans can Fannie Mae buy and sell? Fannie Mae can purchase government-backed and conventional loans on one- to four-unit dwellings, units in PUDs, and condominiums. Fannie Mae buys conventional loans only if the loans have been issued using Fannie Mae guidelines. Once purchased, the loans are either held as an investment or resold to other lenders and investors.

For more consumer information about Fannie Mae, access their website at www.fanniemaefoundation.org.

Federal Home Loan Mortgage Corporation

The **Federal Home Loan Mortgage Corporation (Freddie Mac)** was created in 1970 under the Emergency Home Finance Act. The main function of Freddie Mac was to provide a secondary mortgage market for the savings and loan associations. However, today it also deals with other institutional lenders.

Freddie Mac buys FHA, VA, and conventional loans. It purchases conventional loans on one- to four-unit buildings, units in PUDs, and condominiums. Freddie Mac and Fannie Mae usually have identical loan applications, maximum loan amounts, appraisal standards, and borrower loan qualification guidelines. Freddie Mac is a government-chartered stockholder-owned corporation, and information on it and its programs can be found at www.freddiemac.com.

The Secondary Mortgage Market Financial Crisis

Due to the large number of foreclosures following the depreciating real estate market in 2008, the federal government took conservatorship over both Fannie Mae and Freddie Mac. While some have suggested this might mean the demise of these two organizations, most financial experts agree that their role in the secondary market is too great and their presence is necessary.

Government National Mortgage Association

The **Government National Mortgage Association (Ginnie Mae)** is a wholly owned corporation of the U.S. government.

It was created in 1968, when Fannie Mae became a private corporation. At the time, Fannie Mae was relieved of two of its duties, which were given to Ginnie Mae. These were as follows:

1. The management and liquidation of certain mortgages previously acquired by the U.S. government
2. Special assistance functions, including the development of a mortgage-backed security program

By directly and indirectly providing low-interest-rate loans, Ginnie Mae encourages people to buy new homes. The increased demand for new homes results in more work and more jobs for the construction industry.

The real impact of Ginnie Mae is in its mortgage-backed security program. This program was established to attract additional money into the housing market. The mortgage-backed security was created to make investing in mortgages as simple as buying stocks and bonds. Under this mortgage program, an investor purchases a pool of mortgages and receives a certificate. There is no need to examine each mortgage. All the time-consuming paperwork is eliminated. Since Ginnie Mae is a federal corporation, its guarantee is backed by the "full faith and credit" of the U.S. government.

In short, the Ginnie Mae programs in the secondary mortgage market have added to the funds made available for real estate borrowers.

Special First-Time Homebuyer Programs

The Federal National Mortgage Association (Fannie Mae) has a first-time homebuyer program called the Community Home Buyer's Program. This program has lower down payment requirements and more generous qualifying ratios. To qualify, the borrower's income cannot exceed 115 to 120 percent of the median income in the area. See the Fannie Mae website noted above for more details.

Some local lenders, in an effort to place loans throughout the communities they serve, have their own first-time homebuyer programs.

Many of these lower-cost programs are for people who purchase in designated zip codes and U.S. census tracts.

Real Estate Loan Jargon

Real estate lenders speak a language of their own. Here are some key terms regarding real estate loans:

Conventional loans. Any non-government-backed loan

Conforming loans. Loans that meet the guidelines of Fannie Mae or Freddie Mac

Nonconforming loans. Loans that do not meet the guidelines of Fannie Mae or Freddie Mac

Jumbo loans. Loans that exceed the loan limits of Fannie Mae or Freddie Mac

Portfolio loans. Loans that will not be sold in the secondary mortgage market, but will be held by the lender as an investment

CHAPTER SUMMARY, PART II

Government has taken an active role in the field of real estate finance. On the federal level, the Federal Housing Administration (FHA) has several programs. The 203b program is the most popular. The Department of Veterans Affairs (VA) has a no-down-payment program for qualified veterans. The state of California's Cal-Vet loan program has been a huge success, with demand usually exceeding the supply of loans available. The low interest rate paid by the California veteran is the main attraction.

The secondary mortgage market consists of real estate lenders who sell existing mortgages to other real estate lenders. The main purpose of the secondary mortgage market is to help strike a balance between the demand for real estate loans and the supply of money available for them. The Federal National Mortgage Association (Fannie Mae), the Federal Home Loan Mortgage Corporation (Freddie Mac), and the Government National Mortgage Association (Ginnie Mae) participate in this secondary mortgage market.

IMPORTANT TERMS AND CONCEPTS

CalHFA

Department of Veterans Affairs (VA)

Cal-Vet loans

Federal Home Loan Mortgage Corporation (Freddie Mac)

Federal Housing Administration (FHA)

Federal National Mortgage Association (Fannie Mae)

FHA 203b program

Government National Mortgage Association (Ginnie Mae)

secondary mortgage market

PRACTICAL APPLICATION

1. A buyer agrees to purchase an older studio condo using the FHA 203b program. The price and FHA-approved appraisal are both $150,000, and the seller agrees to pay all closing costs above the buyer's minimum cash investment. Based only on this information, how much cash is the buyer required to invest to close escrow?

2. Referring to question 1, assume the buyer used the VA program and paid a 1 percent loan fee, plus a 1.5 percent funding fee and $500 in other closing costs. Based only on this information, how much cash does the buyer-veteran need to close escrow?

3. Referring to question 1, assume the buyer used the Cal-Vet program and paid the 2 percent down payment and $700 in closing costs, with the seller agreeing to pay all other remaining costs. Based only on this information, how much cash does the buyer-veteran need to close escrow?

REVIEWING YOUR UNDERSTANDING

1. Assuming the county qualifies, with no loan increase for MIP, and with an approved FHA price and appraisal of $250,000, what is the maximum FHA-insured amount?
   a. $250,000
   b. $247,250
   c. $241,250
   d. $238,625

2. Of the following government programs, which usually has the lowest interest rate?
   a. Cal-Vet
   b. VA
   c. FHA
   d. Fannie Mae

3. If the maximum VA-negotiated interest rate a veteran is able to pay is 7.5 percent, but a lender wants a rate of 8 percent, what is the difference in points between these two rates?

   a. .5 point

   b. 3 points

   c. 5 points

   d. 6 points

4. Which statement is true about a VA-guaranteed loan?

   a. The buyer must pay the discount points, if any.

   b. The down payment requirement is 3 percent of the first $25,000 and 5 percent of the remainder.

   c. The maximum loan amount for a home is $60,000.

   d. The veteran can use a VA loan more than once.

5. The least down payment for a home appraised at $300,000 would be from

   a. FHA.

   b. VA.

   c. Cal-Vet.

   d. Fannie Mae.

6. During a Cal-Vet loan, title to the real property usually rests with

   a. the institutional lender.

   b. the borrower.

   c. the Department of Veterans Affairs.

   d. the buyer.

7. A secondary mortgage market is where

   a. second loans are placed against real estate.

   b. existing real estate loans are bought and sold.

   c. an insurance company guarantees the loan payments.

   d. mortgage brokers arrange loans to borrowers.

8. Fannie Mae refers to

   a. the Government National Mortgage Association.

   b. the Federal National Mortgage Association.

   c. the Federal Home Loan Mortgage Corporation.

   d. the Department of Veterans Affairs.

9. A loan that meets Fannie Mae and Freddie Mac guidelines is known as a
   a. jumbo loan.
   b. portfolio loan.
   c. conventional loan.
   d. conforming loan.

10. When a seller carries back a junior loan, this is best described as
    a. secondary financing.
    b. the secondary mortgage market.
    c. an equity line of credit.
    d. investing in a second trust deed.

Appendix A

Case Study—Qualifying for a Home Loan

As a general rule of thumb, there are ideally two percentages to be aware of: 28 percent and 36 percent.

1. No more than 28 percent of your gross monthly income should be used for your total monthly house payment, consisting of principal, interest, taxes, insurance, and (if need be) association dues and private mortgage insurance.

$$\frac{\text{Total monthly house payment}}{\text{Gross monthly income}} = \text{No more than } 28\%$$

2. No more than 36 percent of your gross monthly income should be used for your total monthly credit obligations (monthly house payments plus all other monthly credit obligations such as car loans, credit cards, and so on that have six months or more to run).

$$\frac{\text{Total monthly credit obligation}}{\text{Gross monthly income}} = \text{No more than } 36\%$$

Mr. and Mrs. First-Time Buyer wish to purchase a small older $180,000 condo. Mr. Buyer has a yearly salary of $33,000, and Mrs. Buyer earns $34,000 per year. They have both been with their employers for more than four years. Their monthly bills are as follows: car payments, three years remaining at $375 per month; furniture payment, $125 per month for 13 months; and a student loan, $75 per month with four months remaining. If they buy the home, their annual property taxes will be $2,100, and homeowner's insurance and dues will cost $504 per year.

A local lender is willing to make a $162,000 (90 percent) loan at 8.5 percent for 30 years, payable at $1,245 per month, plus $38 per month for private mortgage insurance. Assuming the buyers have the required cash down payment and have a good credit history, do they have the income to qualify for this loan? Do they meet the 28 and 36 percent ratios?

After you have done your computations, check your answer by turning to the section titled "Answers to Reviewing Your Understanding Questions" toward the end of the book.

Chapter

9

STUDENT LEARNING OUTCOMES

An appraisal is an essential part of a real estate transaction. Many times the decision to buy, sell, or grant a loan on real estate hinges on a real estate appraiser's estimate of a property's value. At the conclusion of the chapter, you will be able to do the following:

1. Define appraisal, and list four elements and forces that influence value.

2. Distinguish between utility value and market value.

3. Define depreciation, outline the causes of depreciation, and describe how to calculate depreciation.

4. Discuss the three approaches or methods used to determine value, outline the steps in each approach, and define gross multipliers.

Real Estate Appraisal

9.1 APPRAISAL CONCEPTS

An **appraisal** is defined as an estimate or an opinion of value. Real estate appraisals are needed to do the following:

1. Set sales prices on property.
2. Estimate real estate loan values.
3. Determine values for real property taxes.
4. Help set premiums on fire insurance policies.

Other reasons include determining estate taxes and values for government acquisition. Real estate appraisal is not an exact science; therefore, the accuracy of an appraisal is related to the skill, experience, and judgment of the appraiser.

Real Estate Appraisal License Requirements

Any appraisal for a real estate transaction involving federal insurance or assistance must be done by a licensed or certified appraiser. This includes an appraisal for any lender whose deposits are insured or regulated by a federal agency. For these appraisals, the appraiser must have a special license or certificate issued by the California Office of Real Estate Appraisers. A real estate license alone does not qualify; the appraisal license or certification is completely different from a real estate license. The basic appraisal categories of license or certification are as of January 2007:

1. *Licensed:* Allowed to appraise noncomplex one- to four-unit residential properties up to $1 million. On nonresidential transactions, the dollar limit is only $250,000.
2. *Certified (Residential):* Allowed to appraise all one- to four-unit residential properties regardless of the value. On nonresidential transactions, the dollar limit is $250,000.

3. *Certified (General):* Allowed to appraise any real estate regardless of type or value.

All appraisers must take a minimum number of hours of real estate appraisal and related educational courses as follows:

Licensed: 150 hours

Certified-Residential: 200 hours

Certified-General: 300 hours

All of the educational hours listed above must include the fifteen-hour course on the Uniform Standards of Professional Appraisal Practice (USPAP). *Minimum on-the-job experience requirements are as follows:*

Licensed: 2,000 hours

Certified—Residential: 2,500 hours plus 2.5 years experience

Certified—General: 3,000 hours (at least 1,500 hours must be with nonresidential properties) plus 2.5 years experience

Effective January 1, 2008, any new certified—residential license applicant will need an associate's degree or higher from an accredited college or, in lieu of the degree, at least twenty-one semester units of specifically designated courses. Any new certified—general license applicant will need a bachelor's degree or higher from an accredited college or, in lieu of the degree, at least thirty semester units of specifically designated courses. No college degree is required for the licensed-level appraiser. See the Office of Real Estate Appraisers' (OREA) website at www.orea.ca.gov for additional details.

After meeting these requirements, a person must pass an examination, then an appraisal license or certification is issued for a two-year period. To renew the license, a designated number of hours of approved continuing education courses must be taken. For people who have the education but not the experience, upon passing the examination, a training license is issued for the least complicated appraisals. No training license exists at the higher certification level. For more information about a real estate appraiser's license, access the OREA's website at www.orea.ca.gov.

Professional Designations

In addition to a state-issued license or certificate, several professional real estate appraisal organizations in the United States issue highly prized professional designations. Two of the largest appraisal trade associations are the American Institute of Real Estate Appraisers, which issues the widely recognized Member of the Appraisal Institute (MAI) designation, and the Society of Real Estate Appraisers, which issues the designation SRPA.

Home Valuation Code of Conduct (HVCC)

Effective May 1, 2009, Fannie Mae and Freddie Mac will not purchase loans from lenders who do not subscribe to the Home Valuation Code of Conduct (HVCC). The HVCC is designed to prevent lenders, borrowers, and sellers from influencing an appraisal report in single-family residential transactions. Specifically, the HVCC does the following:

- Prohibits lenders and third parties from influencing appraisers in the preparation of their appraisal reports.
- Mandates standards for appraisal reports, and for hiring and compensating appraisers in the preparation of reports.
- Lenders must provide a copy of the appraisal report to the borrower within three days of the preparation of the report.
- Insures independence of appraisers from the influence of lenders and third parties.

Because of Fannie Mae and Freddie Mac's dominance in the secondary mortgage market, the Home Valuation Code of Conduct has standardized the appraisal process in residential lending.

Market Value

The purpose of an appraisal is to determine a value for a property. Although there are various types of value—sales value, loan value, tax value, and insurance value—two major categories of value are value in use (utility value) and market value.

Value in use (utility value) refers to the value of a particular property to a particular owner or user of real estate. The value of property to a particular owner may be emotional as well as economic; thus, value in use is also known as *subjective value*. For example, the value that you place in a property that has been in your family for over one hundred years might be different than what an outside buyer views as value.

On the other hand, **market value** is value in exchange as determined by supply and demand in the open real estate market. Market value is also referred to as *objective value*. Between utility and market value, without question, most appraisals are for the purpose of establishing market value. Market value can be briefly defined as "the highest price in terms of money for which a property would sell in the open market, with the seller not being obligated to sell, the buyer not being obligated to buy, and allowing a reasonable length of time to effect the sale." This also assumes that the buyer and the seller are fully knowledgeable persons. In short, when a buyer or seller asks the question, "What is the property worth?" he or she is asking for an estimate or opinion of the market value as of a certain date.

Market Value versus Price Paid

Price paid may or may not be the same as market value. A person may pay $500,000 for a home that has a market value of $480,000, or he or she may do just the opposite—pay a price of $480,000 for a home with a market value of $500,000. On the other hand, a person may pay $500,000 for a home that has a market value of $500,000. The key point is this: Price trends establish market value, but for any given single sale, the price actually paid may be equal to, higher than, or lower than market value.

Essential Elements of Value

For property to have value, four elements or characteristics must be present: (1) utility, (2) scarcity, (3) demand, and (4) transferability. *Utility* refers to usefulness—the more useful a property, the greater its potential value. *Scarcity* means lack of abundance. When utility exists, the scarcer an item, the greater its value. *Demand* refers to the desire to own real estate, coupled with the financial ability to buy. Assuming a scarce number of properties for sale, the greater the number of ready, willing, and able buyers (demand), the greater the likelihood that the property offered for sale will increase in value.

Transferability refers to the ability to transfer identifiable ownership. A beautiful home on the California coast may be a scarce commodity, with great utility and high demand. But if the property's title is clouded and uncertain, not many people will be willing to buy the home. The clearer the title, the more valuable the property. When a title is clouded, the property is less valuable.

Utility, scarcity, demand, and transferability are the essential elements that create value. If all are present in a favorable combination, a property's value may increase. If one or more elements are flawed or missing, a property's value may be declining, or in a worst-case scenario it becomes worthless. (See Figure 9.1.)

Four Forces that Influence Value

Once a property's value has been established, there are four forces that can change its value. These forces (shown in Figure 9.1) are as follows:

1. *Social forces,* such as changes in population, marriage trends, and family size, and changes in attitudes toward education, recreation, and lifestyles.
2. *Economic forces,* which include changes in income levels, employment opportunities, the cost of money and credit, taxes, and the availability of energy and natural resources.

FIGURE 9.1

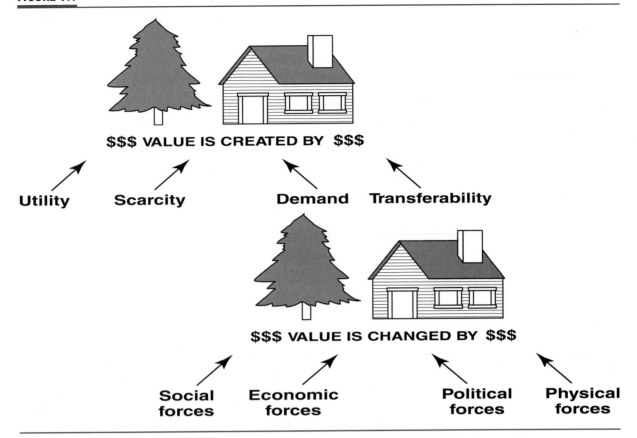

3. *Political forces,* such as changes in zoning, building codes, construction moratoriums, government housing programs, and pro-growth or no-growth government philosophies.

4. *Physical forces* that affect the physical aspects of the property, such as size and shape of the parcel, location, climate, and soil conditions.

These four forces continually bombard every parcel of real estate and cause values to shift positively or negatively. Which of these forces is the single most important? There is no simple answer! This is where the skill, experience, and judgment of an appraiser weigh in. However, an old saying states, "The three most important factors of value are location, location, location."

Basic Principles of Valuation

Appraisal theory and practice are based on several principles or assumptions:

1. *Principle of highest and best use.* The best use of land is that which produces the greatest net return to the land.

2. *Principle of change.* Real estate values are constantly changing as a result of social, economic, political, and physical forces within a region, city, and neighborhood.

3. *Principle of supply and demand.* The interaction of supply and demand causes real estate values to change. For example, assuming a fixed supply of homes for sale, an increase in demand should cause prices to increase.

4. *Principle of substitution.* The value of a property tends to be influenced by the price of acquiring an equally desirable substitute property. For example, the value of property A is somewhat determined by the value of comparable properties B, C, and D.

5. *Principle of conformity.* In a residential neighborhood, the maximum value is found where there is a high degree of conformity, such as homes of similar design, architecture, and upkeep.

6. *Principle of contribution.* In making improvements to a property, a property's value should increase by at least the amount spent on the improvement. For example, if you spend $50,000 remodeling a house, the house should increase in value by at least $50,000.

Several other principles are the principles of progression, regression, anticipation, competition, and surplus productivity. But these are beyond the scope of this book. For specific details, consult any appraisal textbook.

All the principles mentioned previously form the theoretical foundation upon which real estate appraisers rely to estimate value.

9.2 DEPRECIATION

Depreciation is defined as a loss in value from any cause.

Depreciation is usually measured as the difference between the new replacement cost of a building or improvement and its value as of the date of the appraisal. If an existing building (excluding land) is appraised at $450,000, but its replacement cost (if it were destroyed and needed to be rebuilt) is calculated to be $500,000, the $50,000 difference ($500,000 less $450,000) is the amount of the depreciation.

Causes of Depreciation

The causes or reasons for a loss in real estate value can be grouped into three categories.

1. **Physical deterioration** is a loss in value caused by (a) wear and tear from use; (b) deferred maintenance and lack of upkeep;

(c) damage by termites, dry rot, and so on; and (d) weather conditions. A run-down home in need of paint and repairs is an example of depreciation caused by physical deterioration.

2. **Functional obsolescence** is a loss in value caused by (a) an unpopular floor plan and layout; (b) a lack of updated, modern appliances and equipment; and (c) a poor or unpopular architectural design and style. A three-bedroom, one-bath home with a wall heater and single-car garage is an example of depreciation caused by functional obsolescence. Why? Because most buyers of three-bedroom homes prefer one and one-half or two bathrooms, a two-car garage, and a forced-air heating system. Therefore, all other things being equal, the three-bedroom, one-bath home usually sells at a lower price.

3. **Economic obsolescence** is a loss in value resulting from (a) zoning and other government actions; (b) misplaced improvements, such as a home built next to an all-night service station; and (c) a drop in demand for real estate, or overbuilding, creating an excessive supply of homes. An example of economic obsolescence would be a neighborhood street, recently declared a truck route, whose increased traffic brings noise and fumes into the area. This could cause home values to decline. In short, economic obsolescence is caused by factors outside the boundaries of the property—items beyond the control of the owners.

Curable versus Incurable Depreciation

Physical deterioration and functional obsolescence can be classified as curable or incurable. **Curable depreciation** means that if repairs and/or remodeling are undertaken, the expense incurred will be less than the value added to the property. If you spend $30,000 to repair your home and in the process this adds $30,000 or more in value, this is considered curable.

Incurable depreciation means the cost to repair or remodel exceeds the value added to the property. If you pay $30,000 to repair your home and in the process this adds less than $30,000 in value, this is considered incurable (in other words, it violates the principle of contribution). Physical deterioration and functional obsolescence can be classified as curable or incurable per the guidelines noted earlier. However, economic obsolescence is almost always considered incurable because the loss in value is caused by negative factors outside the property's boundaries. Therefore, it is assumed that these negative factors are beyond the control of any single property owner.

Accrued Depreciation versus Recapture for Depreciation

Accrued depreciation is the loss in value that has already occurred in a building. Recapture for depreciation (sometimes called *accrual for depreciation*) is an estimate for depreciation that will occur in the future. Accrued (past) depreciation is used in an appraisal technique called the *cost approach*. A recapture for depreciation is used in an appraisal technique called the *income approach*. These approaches to value are discussed in the next section of this chapter.

An Additional Word about Depreciation

Depreciation for appraisal purposes is different from depreciation for income tax purposes. The appraiser looks at depreciation as being an actual decline in value. For income tax purposes, an accountant uses book depreciation (also called *cost recovery*) as a basis for an income tax deduction. The two concepts are not the same. The accountant uses a theoretical figure allowed by the Internal Revenue Service, whereas an appraiser uses economic analysis to arrive at an actual decline in value.

Appreciation is an increase in value that can result from inflation or from the interaction of supply and demand forces. All real estate improvements suffer some form of depreciation, but simultaneously many properties are appreciating. The question then becomes this: Is the rate of appreciation exceeding the rate of depreciation? If so, overall value of the property increases. But if the rate of depreciation is exceeding appreciation, the overall value of the property decreases.

9.3 APPRAISAL METHODS

When an appraiser is hired, the appraiser's estimate of value is submitted as a report. Three common types of appraisal reports are as follows:

1. Restricted appraisal report
2. Summary appraisal report
3. Self-contained appraisal report

The restricted form is the least comprehensive report. It is used when a client is familiar with the area and therefore does not need appraisal details. It requires a prominent disclaimer that the appraisal is limited in scope. This is the least expensive type of report and formerly was referred to as a *letter form report*.

The summary report is most commonly used by real estate appraisers when appraising property for loan purposes. The short-form report consists of check sheets and spaces to be filled in by the appraiser. In recent years, there has been a tendency to standardize the short-form report using guidelines established by government-backed agencies that operate in the secondary mortgage market. This report was formerly referred to as a *short-form report*. (See Figure 9.2.)

The self-contained report is the most comprehensive and expensive appraisal report. It is a complete documentation of the entire appraisal process, including computation, maps, photographs, and detailed analysis. This report is used in court cases, in condemnation proceedings, and for expensive commercial and industrial properties. Because of its size, detail, and cost, a self-contained appraisal report is not commonly used in the home market. A self-contained report was formerly referred to as a *narrative report*.

Appraisal Process

As in many other professional occupations, real estate appraisers have developed a system for conducting their work. The appraisal of real estate can be viewed as a series of steps, with each step logically following the preceding, until a final estimate of value is reached. Figure 9.3 is a flowchart of the real estate appraisal process.

As shown in Figure 9.3, the appraiser starts with a definition of the problem. What is the reason for the appraisal? Why does the client need the appraisal? Then the needed data are gathered and classified. The data are run through three approaches or techniques of analysis called the cost, market (comparable sales), and income approaches. A separate value is arrived at under each approach, and these three values are correlated, or reconciled. From this reconciliation process, one final estimate of value is given to the client. Reconciliation is not the averaging of the results from the three approaches, but rather a weighted blend based on what is most appropriate for the property.

Although this appraisal process has its roots in scientific analysis, the appraisal of real estate is still somewhat judgmental. Therefore, the accuracy of the appraisal depends not only on the data gathered but also on the judgment, skill, and experience of the person doing the appraisal.

FIGURE 9.2

Uniform Residential Appraisal Report

File #

The purpose of this summary appraisal report is to provide the lender/client with an accurate, and adequately supported, opinion of the market value of the subject property.

SUBJECT

Property Address		City	State	Zip Code

Borrower   Owner of Public Record   County

Legal Description

Assessor's Parcel #   Tax Year   R.E. Taxes $

Neighborhood Name   Map Reference   Census Tract

Occupant ☐ Owner ☐ Tenant ☐ Vacant   Special Assessments $ ☐ PUD   HOA $ ☐ per year ☐ per month

Property Rights Appraised ☐ Fee Simple ☐ Leasehold ☐ Other (describe)

Assignment Type ☐ Purchase Transaction ☐ Refinance Transaction ☐ Other (describe)

Lender/Client   Address

Is the subject property currently offered for sale or has it been offered for sale in the twelve months prior to the effective date of this appraisal? ☐ Yes ☐ No

Report data source(s) used, offering price(s), and date(s).

CONTRACT

I ☐ did ☐ did not analyze the contract for sale for the subject purchase transaction. Explain the results of the analysis of the contract for sale or why the analysis was not performed.

Contract Price $ Date of Contract   Is the property seller the owner of public record? ☐ Yes ☐ No   Data Source(s)

Is there any financial assistance (loan charges, sale concessions, gift or downpayment assistance, etc.) to be paid by any party on behalf of the borrower? ☐ Yes ☐ No
If Yes, report the total dollar amount and describe the items to be paid.

NEIGHBORHOOD

Note: Race and the racial composition of the neighborhood are not appraisal factors.

Neighborhood Characteristics	One-Unit Housing Trends	One-Unit Housing	Present Land Use %
Location ☐ Urban ☐ Suburban ☐ Rural	Property Values ☐ Increasing ☐ Stable ☐ Declining	PRICE AGE	One-Unit %
Built-Up ☐ Over 75% ☐ 25–75% ☐ Under 25%	Demand/Supply ☐ Shortage ☐ In Balance ☐ Over Supply	$ (000) (yrs)	2-4 Unit %
Growth ☐ Rapid ☐ Stable ☐ Slow	Marketing Time ☐ Under 3 mths ☐ 3–6 mths ☐ Over 6 mths	Low	Multi-Family %
Neighborhood Boundaries		High	Commercial %
		Pred.	Other %

Neighborhood Description

Market Conditions (including support for the above conclusions)

SITE

Dimensions   Area   Shape   View

Specific Zoning Classification   Zoning Description

Zoning Compliance ☐ Legal ☐ Legal Nonconforming (Grandfathered Use) ☐ No Zoning ☐ Illegal (describe)

Is the highest and best use of the subject property as improved (or as proposed per plans and specifications) the present use? ☐ Yes ☐ No If No, describe

Utilities	Public	Other (describe)		Public	Other (describe)	Off-site Improvements—Type	Public	Private
Electricity	☐	☐	Water	☐	☐	Street	☐	☐
Gas	☐	☐	Sanitary Sewer	☐	☐	Alley	☐	☐

FEMA Special Flood Hazard Area ☐ Yes ☐ No FEMA Flood Zone   FEMA Map #   FEMA Map Date

Are the utilities and off-site improvements typical for the market area? ☐ Yes ☐ No If No, describe

Are there any adverse site conditions or external factors (easements, encroachments, environmental conditions, land uses, etc.)? ☐ Yes ☐ No If Yes, describe

IMPROVEMENTS

General Description	Foundation	Exterior Description	materials/condition	Interior	materials/condition
Units ☐ One ☐ One with Accessory Unit	☐ Concrete Slab ☐ Crawl Space	Foundation Walls		Floors	
# of Stories	☐ Full Basement ☐ Partial Basement	Exterior Walls		Walls	
Type ☐ Det. ☐ Att. ☐ S-Det./End Unit	Basement Area sq. ft.	Roof Surface		Trim/Finish	
☐ Existing ☐ Proposed ☐ Under Const.	Basement Finish %	Gutters & Downspouts		Bath Floor	
Design (Style)	☐ Outside Entry/Exit ☐ Sump Pump	Window Type		Bath Wainscot	
Year Built	Evidence of ☐ Infestation	Storm Sash/Insulated		Car Storage ☐ None	
Effective Age (Yrs)	☐ Dampness ☐ Settlement	Screens		☐ Driveway # of Cars	
Attic ☐ None	Heating ☐ FWA ☐ HWBB ☐ Radiant	Amenities ☐ Woodstove(s) #		Driveway Surface	
☐ Drop Stair ☐ Stairs	☐ Other Fuel	☐ Fireplace(s) # ☐ Fence		☐ Garage # of Cars	
☐ Floor ☐ Scuttle	Cooling ☐ Central Air Conditioning	☐ Patio/Deck ☐ Porch		☐ Carport # of Cars	
☐ Finished ☐ Heated	☐ Individual ☐ Other	☐ Pool ☐ Other		☐ Att. ☐ Det. ☐ Built-in	

Appliances ☐ Refrigerator ☐ Range/Oven ☐ Dishwasher ☐ Disposal ☐ Microwave ☐ Washer/Dryer ☐ Other (describe)

Finished area **above** grade contains: Rooms   Bedrooms   Bath(s)   Square Feet of Gross Living Area Above Grade

Additional features (special energy efficient items, etc.)

Describe the condition of the property (including needed repairs, deterioration, renovations, remodeling, etc.).

Are there any physical deficiencies or adverse conditions that affect the livability, soundness, or structural integrity of the property? ☐ Yes ☐ No If Yes, describe

Does the property generally conform to the neighborhood (functional utility, style, condition, use, construction, etc.)? ☐ Yes ☐ No If No, describe

Freddie Mac Form 70 March 2005   Page 1 of 6   Fannie Mae Form 1004 March 2005

FIGURE 9.2 *(continued)*

Uniform Residential Appraisal Report   File

There are	comparable properties currently offered for sale in the subject neighborhood ranging in price from $		to $	
There are	comparable sales in the subject neighborhood within the past twelve months ranging in sale price from $		to $	

FEATURE	SUBJECT	COMPARABLE SALE # 1		COMPARABLE SALE # 2		COMPARABLE SALE # 3	
Address							
Proximity to Subject							
Sale Price	$		$		$		$
Sale Price/Gross Liv. Area	$ sq. ft.	$ sq. ft.		$ sq. ft.		$ sq. ft.	
Data Source(s)							
Verification Source(s)							
VALUE ADJUSTMENTS	DESCRIPTION	DESCRIPTION	+(-) $ Adjustment	DESCRIPTION	+(-) $ Adjustment	DESCRIPTION	+(-) $ Adjustment
Sale or Financing Concessions							
Date of Sale/Time							
Location							
Leasehold/Fee Simple							
Site							
View							
Design (Style)							
Quality of Construction							
Actual Age							
Condition							
Above Grade	Total Bdrms. Baths	Total Bdrms. Baths		Total Bdrms. Baths		Total Bdrms. Baths	
Room Count							
Gross Living Area	sq. ft.	sq. ft.		sq. ft.		sq. ft.	
Basement & Finished Rooms Below Grade							
Functional Utility							
Heating/Cooling							
Energy Efficient Items							
Garage/Carport							
Porch/Patio/Deck							
Net Adjustment (Total)		☐ + ☐ -	$	☐ + ☐ -	$	☐ + ☐ -	$
Adjusted Sale Price of Comparables		Net Adj. % Gross Adj. %	$	Net Adj. % Gross Adj. %	$	Net Adj. % Gross Adj. %	$

I ☐ did ☐ did not research the sale or transfer history of the subject property and comparable sales. If not, explain

My research ☐ did ☐ did not reveal any prior sales or transfers of the subject property for the three years prior to the effective date of this appraisal.

Data source(s)

My research ☐ did ☐ did not reveal any prior sales or transfers of the comparable sales for the year prior to the date of sale of the comparable sale.

Data source(s)

Report the results of the research and analysis of the prior sale or transfer history of the subject property and comparable sales (report additional prior sales on page 3).

ITEM	SUBJECT	COMPARABLE SALE # 1	COMPARABLE SALE # 2	COMPARABLE SALE # 3
Date of Prior Sale/Transfer				
Price of Prior Sale/Transfer				
Data Source(s)				
Effective Date of Data Source(s)				

Analysis of prior sale or transfer history of the subject property and comparable sales

Summary of Sales Comparison Approach

Indicated Value by Sales Comparison Approach $

Indicated Value by: Sales Comparison Approach $ **Cost Approach (if developed) $**   **Income Approach (if developed) $**

This appraisal is made ☐ "as is", ☐ subject to completion per plans and specifications on the basis of a hypothetical condition that the improvements have been completed, ☐ subject to the following repairs or alterations on the basis of a hypothetical condition that the repairs or alterations have been completed, or ☐ subject to the following required inspection based on the extraordinary assumption that the condition or deficiency does not require alteration or repair:

Based on a complete visual inspection of the interior and exterior areas of the subject property, defined scope of work, statement of assumptions and limiting conditions, and appraiser's certification, my (our) opinion of the market value, as defined, of the real property that is the subject of this report is
$ **, as of**   **, which is the date of inspection and the effective date of this appraisal.**

Freddie Mac Form 70 March 2005	Page 2 of 6	Fannie Mae Form 1004 March 2005

(Left margin vertical labels: SALES COMPARISON APPROACH / RECONCILIATION)

FIGURE 9.2 (*continued*)

Uniform Residential Appraisal Report

File #

ADDITIONAL COMMENTS

COST APPROACH TO VALUE (not required by Fannie Mae)

Provide adequate information for the lender/client to replicate the below cost figures and calculations.

Support for the opinion of site value (summary of comparable land sales or other methods for estimating site value)

ESTIMATED ☐ REPRODUCTION OR ☐ REPLACEMENT COST NEW	OPINION OF SITE VALUE .... = $
Source of cost data	Dwelling Sq. Ft. @ $ .... =$
Quality rating from cost service Effective date of cost data	Sq. Ft. @ $ .... =$
Comments on Cost Approach (gross living area calculations, depreciation, etc.)	
	Garage/Carport Sq. Ft. @ $ .... =$
	Total Estimate of Cost-New .... = $
	Less Physical	Functional	External
	Depreciation =$( )
	Depreciated Cost of Improvements..=$
	"As-is" Value of Site Improvements...=$
Estimated Remaining Economic Life (HUD and VA only) Years	Indicated Value By Cost Approach ....=$

INCOME APPROACH TO VALUE (not required by Fannie Mae)

Estimated Monthly Market Rent $ X Gross Rent Multiplier   = $ Indicated Value by Income Approach

Summary of Income Approach (including support for market rent and GRM)

PROJECT INFORMATION FOR PUDs (if applicable)

Is the developer/builder in control of the Homeowners' Association (HOA)? ☐ Yes ☐ No   Unit type(s) ☐ Detached ☐ Attached

Provide the following information for PUDs ONLY if the developer/builder is in control of the HOA and the subject property is an attached dwelling unit.

Legal name of project

Total number of phases   Total number of units   Total number of units sold

Total number of units rented   Total number of units for sale   Data source(s)

Was the project created by the conversion of an existing building(s) into a PUD? ☐ Yes ☐ No If Yes, date of conversion

Does the project contain any multi-dwelling units? ☐ Yes ☐ No Data source(s)

Are the units, common elements, and recreation facilities complete? ☐ Yes ☐ No If No, describe the status of completion.

Are the common elements leased to or by the Homeowners' Association? ☐ Yes ☐ No If Yes, describe the rental terms and options.

Describe common elements and recreational facilities

FIGURE 9.2   *(continued)*

Uniform Residential Appraisal Report   File

This report form is designed to report an appraisal of a one-unit property or a one-unit property with an accessory unit; including a unit in a planned unit development (PUD). This report form is not designed to report an appraisal of a manufactured home or a unit in a condominium or cooperative project.

This appraisal report is subject to the following scope of work, intended use, intended user, definition of market value, statement of assumptions and limiting conditions, and certifications. Modifications, additions, or deletions to the intended use, intended user, definition of market value, or assumptions and limiting conditions are not permitted. The appraiser may expand the scope of work to include any additional research or analysis necessary based on the complexity of this appraisal assignment. Modifications or deletions to the certifications are also not permitted. However, additional certifications that do not constitute material alterations to this appraisal report, such as those required by law or those related to the appraiser's continuing education or membership in an appraisal organization, are permitted.

SCOPE OF WORK: The scope of work for this appraisal is defined by the complexity of this appraisal assignment and the reporting requirements of this appraisal report form, including the following definition of market value, statement of assumptions and limiting conditions, and certifications. The appraiser must, at a minimum: (1) perform a complete visual inspection of the interior and exterior areas of the subject property, (2) inspect the neighborhood, (3) inspect each of the comparable sales from at least the street, (4) research, verify, and analyze data from reliable public and/or private sources, and (5) report his or her analysis, opinions, and conclusions in this appraisal report.

INTENDED USE: The intended use of this appraisal report is for the lender/client to evaluate the property that is the subject of this appraisal for a mortgage finance transaction.

INTENDED USER: The intended user of this appraisal report is the lender/client.

DEFINITION OF MARKET VALUE: The most probable price which a property should bring in a competitive and open market under all conditions requisite to a fair sale, the buyer and seller, each acting prudently, knowledgeably and assuming the price is not affected by undue stimulus. Implicit in this definition is the consummation of a sale as of a specified date and the passing of title from seller to buyer under conditions whereby: (1) buyer and seller are typically motivated; (2) both parties are well informed or well advised, and each acting in what he or she considers his or her own best interest; (3) a reasonable time is allowed for exposure in the open market; (4) payment is made in terms of cash in U. S. dollars or in terms of financial arrangements comparable thereto; and (5) the price represents the normal consideration for the property sold unaffected by special or creative financing or sales concessions* granted by anyone associated with the sale.

*Adjustments to the comparables must be made for special or creative financing or sales concessions. No adjustments are necessary for those costs which are normally paid by sellers as a result of tradition or law in a market area; these costs are readily identifiable since the seller pays these costs in virtually all sales transactions. Special or creative financing adjustments can be made to the comparable property by comparisons to financing terms offered by a third party institutional lender that is not already involved in the property or transaction. Any adjustment should not be calculated on a mechanical dollar for dollar cost of the financing or concession but the dollar amount of any adjustment should approximate the market's reaction to the financing or concessions based on the appraiser's judgment.

STATEMENT OF ASSUMPTIONS AND LIMITING CONDITIONS: The appraiser's certification in this report is subject to the following assumptions and limiting conditions:

1. The appraiser will not be responsible for matters of a legal nature that affect either the property being appraised or the title to it, except for information that he or she became aware of during the research involved in performing this appraisal. The appraiser assumes that the title is good and marketable and will not render any opinions about the title.

2. The appraiser has provided a sketch in this appraisal report to show the approximate dimensions of the improvements. The sketch is included only to assist the reader in visualizing the property and understanding the appraiser's determination of its size.

3. The appraiser has examined the available flood maps that are provided by the Federal Emergency Management Agency (or other data sources) and has noted in this appraisal report whether any portion of the subject site is located in an identified Special Flood Hazard Area. Because the appraiser is not a surveyor, he or she makes no guarantees, express or implied, regarding this determination.

4. The appraiser will not give testimony or appear in court because he or she made an appraisal of the property in question, unless specific arrangements to do so have been made beforehand, or as otherwise required by law.

5. The appraiser has noted in this appraisal report any adverse conditions (such as needed repairs, deterioration, the presence of hazardous wastes, toxic substances, etc.) observed during the inspection of the subject property or that he or she became aware of during the research involved in performing this appraisal. Unless otherwise stated in this appraisal report, the appraiser has no knowledge of any hidden or unapparent physical deficiencies or adverse conditions of the property (such as, but not limited to, needed repairs, deterioration, the presence of hazardous wastes, toxic substances, adverse environmental conditions, etc.) that would make the property less valuable, and has assumed that there are no such conditions and makes no guarantees or warranties, express or implied. The appraiser will not be responsible for any such conditions that do exist or for any engineering or testing that might be required to discover whether such conditions exist. Because the appraiser is not an expert in the field of environmental hazards, this appraisal report must not be considered as an environmental assessment of the property.

6. The appraiser has based his or her appraisal report and valuation conclusion for an appraisal that is subject to satisfactory completion, repairs, or alterations on the assumption that the completion, repairs, or alterations of the subject property will be performed in a professional manner.

FIGURE 9.2   *(continued)*

Uniform Residential Appraisal Report   File

APPRAISER'S CERTIFICATION: The Appraiser certifies and agrees that:

1. I have, at a minimum, developed and reported this appraisal in accordance with the scope of work requirements stated in this appraisal report.

2. I performed a complete visual inspection of the interior and exterior areas of the subject property. I reported the condition of the improvements in factual, specific terms. I identified and reported the physical deficiencies that could affect the livability, soundness, or structural integrity of the property.

3. I performed this appraisal in accordance with the requirements of the Uniform Standards of Professional Appraisal Practice that were adopted and promulgated by the Appraisal Standards Board of The Appraisal Foundation and that were in place at the time this appraisal report was prepared.

4. I developed my opinion of the market value of the real property that is the subject of this report based on the sales comparison approach to value. I have adequate comparable market data to develop a reliable sales comparison approach for this appraisal assignment. I further certify that I considered the cost and income approaches to value but did not develop them, unless otherwise indicated in this report.

5. I researched, verified, analyzed, and reported on any current agreement for sale for the subject property, any offering for sale of the subject property in the twelve months prior to the effective date of this appraisal, and the prior sales of the subject property for a minimum of three years prior to the effective date of this appraisal, unless otherwise indicated in this report.

6. I researched, verified, analyzed, and reported on the prior sales of the comparable sales for a minimum of one year prior to the date of sale of the comparable sale, unless otherwise indicated in this report.

7. I selected and used comparable sales that are locationally, physically, and functionally the most similar to the subject property.

8. I have not used comparable sales that were the result of combining a land sale with the contract purchase price of a home that has been built or will be built on the land.

9. I have reported adjustments to the comparable sales that reflect the market's reaction to the differences between the subject property and the comparable sales.

10. I verified, from a disinterested source, all information in this report that was provided by parties who have a financial interest in the sale or financing of the subject property.

11. I have knowledge and experience in appraising this type of property in this market area.

12. I am aware of, and have access to, the necessary and appropriate public and private data sources, such as multiple listing services, tax assessment records, public land records and other such data sources for the area in which the property is located.

13. I obtained the information, estimates, and opinions furnished by other parties and expressed in this appraisal report from reliable sources that I believe to be true and correct.

14. I have taken into consideration the factors that have an impact on value with respect to the subject neighborhood, subject property, and the proximity of the subject property to adverse influences in the development of my opinion of market value. I have noted in this appraisal report any adverse conditions (such as, but not limited to, needed repairs, deterioration, the presence of hazardous wastes, toxic substances, adverse environmental conditions, etc.) observed during the inspection of the subject property or that I became aware of during the research involved in performing this appraisal. I have considered these adverse conditions in my analysis of the property value, and have reported on the effect of the conditions on the value and marketability of the subject property.

15. I have not knowingly withheld any significant information from this appraisal report and, to the best of my knowledge, all statements and information in this appraisal report are true and correct.

16. I stated in this appraisal report my own personal, unbiased, and professional analysis, opinions, and conclusions, which are subject only to the assumptions and limiting conditions in this appraisal report.

17. I have no present or prospective interest in the property that is the subject of this report, and I have no present or prospective personal interest or bias with respect to the participants in the transaction. I did not base, either partially or completely, my analysis and/or opinion of market value in this appraisal report on the race, color, religion, sex, age, marital status, handicap, familial status, or national origin of either the prospective owners or occupants of the subject property or of the present owners or occupants of the properties in the vicinity of the subject property or on any other basis prohibited by law.

18. My employment and/or compensation for performing this appraisal or any future or anticipated appraisals was not conditioned on any agreement or understanding, written or otherwise, that I would report (or present analysis supporting) a predetermined specific value, a predetermined minimum value, a range or direction in value, a value that favors the cause of any party, or the attainment of a specific result or occurrence of a specific subsequent event (such as approval of a pending mortgage loan application).

19. I personally prepared all conclusions and opinions about the real estate that were set forth in this appraisal report. If I relied on significant real property appraisal assistance from any individual or individuals in the performance of this appraisal or the preparation of this appraisal report, I have named such individual(s) and disclosed the specific tasks performed in this appraisal report. I certify that any individual so named is qualified to perform the tasks. I have not authorized anyone to make a change to any item in this appraisal report; therefore, any change made to this appraisal is unauthorized and I will take no responsibility for it.

20. I identified the lender/client in this appraisal report who is the individual, organization, or agent for the organization that ordered and will receive this appraisal report.

FIGURE 9.2   *(continued)*

Uniform Residential Appraisal Report   File

21. The lender/client may disclose or distribute this appraisal report to: the borrower; another lender at the request of the borrower; the mortgagee or its successors and assigns; mortgage insurers; government sponsored enterprises; other secondary market participants; data collection or reporting services; professional appraisal organizations; any department, agency, or instrumentality of the United States; and any state, the District of Columbia, or other jurisdictions; without having to obtain the appraiser's or supervisory appraiser's (if applicable) consent. Such consent must be obtained before this appraisal report may be disclosed or distributed to any other party (including, but not limited to, the public through advertising, public relations, news, sales, or other media).

22. I am aware that any disclosure or distribution of this appraisal report by me or the lender/client may be subject to certain laws and regulations. Further, I am also subject to the provisions of the Uniform Standards of Professional Appraisal Practice that pertain to disclosure or distribution by me.

23. The borrower, another lender at the request of the borrower, the mortgagee or its successors and assigns, mortgage insurers, government sponsored enterprises, and other secondary market participants may rely on this appraisal report as part of any mortgage finance transaction that involves any one or more of these parties.

24. If this appraisal report was transmitted as an "electronic record" containing my "electronic signature," as those terms are defined in applicable federal and/or state laws (excluding audio and video recordings), or a facsimile transmission of this appraisal report containing a copy or representation of my signature, the appraisal report shall be as effective, enforceable and valid as if a paper version of this appraisal report were delivered containing my original hand written signature.

25. Any intentional or negligent misrepresentation(s) contained in this appraisal report may result in civil liability and/or criminal penalties including, but not limited to, fine or imprisonment or both under the provisions of Title 18, United States Code, Section 1001, et seq., or similar state laws.

SUPERVISORY APPRAISER'S CERTIFICATION: The Supervisory Appraiser certifies and agrees that:

1. I directly supervised the appraiser for this appraisal assignment, have read the appraisal report, and agree with the appraiser's analysis, opinions, statements, conclusions, and the appraiser's certification.

2. I accept full responsibility for the contents of this appraisal report including, but not limited to, the appraiser's analysis, opinions, statements, conclusions, and the appraiser's certification.

3. The appraiser identified in this appraisal report is either a sub-contractor or an employee of the supervisory appraiser (or the appraisal firm), is qualified to perform this appraisal, and is acceptable to perform this appraisal under the applicable state law.

4. This appraisal report complies with the Uniform Standards of Professional Appraisal Practice that were adopted and promulgated by the Appraisal Standards Board of The Appraisal Foundation and that were in place at the time this appraisal report was prepared.

5. If this appraisal report was transmitted as an "electronic record" containing my "electronic signature," as those terms are defined in applicable federal and/or state laws (excluding audio and video recordings), or a facsimile transmission of this appraisal report containing a copy or representation of my signature, the appraisal report shall be as effective, enforceable and valid as if a paper version of this appraisal report were delivered containing my original hand written signature.

APPRAISER

Signature_____
Name _____
Company Name _____
Company Address_____
_____
Telephone Number _____
Email Address_____
Date of Signature and Report_____
Effective Date of Appraisal _____
State Certification #_____
or State License #_____
or Other (describe) _____ State # _____
State _____
Expiration Date of Certification or License _____

ADDRESS OF PROPERTY APPRAISED

_____
_____

APPRAISED VALUE OF SUBJECT PROPERTY $ _____
LENDER/CLIENT
Name _____
Company Name _____
Company Address_____
_____
Email Address_____

SUPERVISORY APPRAISER (ONLY IF REQUIRED)

Signature_____
Name_____
Company Name _____
Company Address_____
_____
Telephone Number _____
Email Address _____
Date of Signature _____
State Certification #_____
or State License #_____
State _____
Expiration Date of Certification or License _____

SUBJECT PROPERTY

☐ Did not inspect subject property
☐ Did inspect exterior of subject property from street
   Date of Inspection _____
☐ Did inspect interior and exterior of subject property
   Date of Inspection _____

COMPARABLE SALES

☐ Did not inspect exterior of comparable sales from street
☐ Did inspect exterior of comparable sales from street
   Date of Inspection _____

FIGURE 9.3

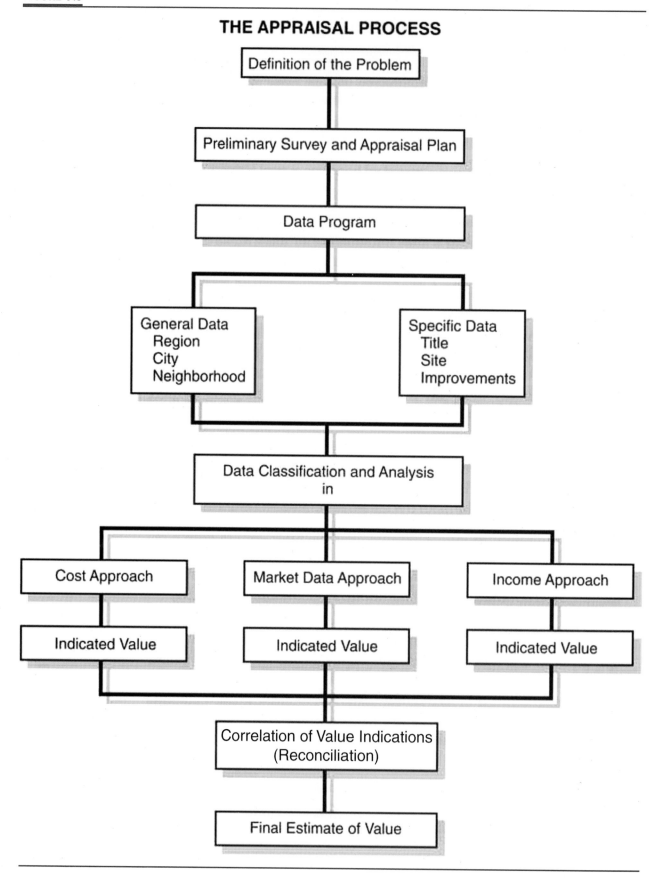

THE APPRAISAL PROCESS

Definition of the Problem

Preliminary Survey and Appraisal Plan

Data Program

General Data
  Region
  City
  Neighborhood

Specific Data
  Title
  Site
  Improvements

Data Classification and Analysis
in

Cost Approach

Market Data Approach

Income Approach

Indicated Value

Indicated Value

Indicated Value

Correlation of Value Indications
(Reconciliation)

Final Estimate of Value

Three Approaches to Value

Cost Approach to Value

The cost approach to value comprises four basic steps:

1. *Estimate the value of the land.* Compare recent lot sales prices.
2. *Estimate the current replacement costs of the improvements.* Building square footage × cost per square foot; also estimate price of fencing, cement work, and landscaping.
3. *Estimate and then subtract accrued depreciation to arrive at the present value of the improvement.* Current replacement cost to build new less depreciation = present value of the improvements.
4. *Add value of land to the present value of the improvements.* Land value + present value of improvements = estimate of value.

To estimate the value of the land, appraisers usually compare recent vacant lot sales, adjusting their estimates for the differences in location, topography, size, shape, and so on.

Estimating Replacement Cost

To estimate the current replacement cost of buildings, appraisers first measure the square footage (exterior length × width). The square footage of the house is measured separately from the garage, patios, and porches. Based on the construction quality of the building they are appraising, appraisers obtain estimates from local contractors regarding construction costs per square foot. In addition to local contractors, square foot costs and other construction information can be obtained by subscribing to cost-estimating publications. Once accurate costs per square foot are obtained, the appraiser multiplies this figure times the square footage of the building. Figures for fencing, cement work, and landscaping are then added to arrive at the current replacement cost of the improvement.

Estimating Depreciation

To estimate accrued depreciation, appraisers can use several techniques. The two most common methods of determining depreciation are the straight-line/age-life method and the cost-to-cure/observed condition method. The straight-line/age-life method assumes that depreciation occurs annually at an even rate over the estimated life of the improvement. For example, if a new building has an estimated life of 50 years, the straight-line/age-life method would assume a rate of depreciation of 2 percent per year ($100\% \div 50$ year life = 2%). Thus, if an appraiser were appraising a building with an effective age of ten years, the subtraction for depreciation would be 20 percent of the current replacement cost (10 years × 2% per year = 20%).

To estimate accrued depreciation using the cost-to-cure/observed condition method requires the appraiser to carefully observe physical, functional, and economic depreciation; then the appraiser estimates what it would cost to cure this depreciation. If some of the depreciation is incurable, the appraiser estimates the permanent loss in value. The sum of the cost to cure plus the permanent loss in value equals the estimated depreciation. Once the accrued depreciation has been estimated, this figure is subtracted from the current replacement cost to arrive at the present value of the improvements.

The final step in the cost approach is the easiest. The estimated value of the land is added to the estimated present value of the improvements to arrive at the estimated value of the total real property.

Advantages and Disadvantages of the Cost Approach

The **cost approach** is appropriate for appraising newly constructed buildings and unique special-purpose properties and public buildings such as schools and libraries. The cost approach usually sets the highest limits on value—the thought being that the most a person will pay for real property is what it would cost to replace the property.

On the negative side, the cost approach does not always measure the individual amenities of the property, such as location, or the outside influences, such as neighborhood surroundings. Also, it is difficult to accurately convert depreciation into dollar figures. Thus, on older properties, the likelihood of errors in estimating depreciation increases with the age of the building. Also, in a declining real estate market, the cost to build a property may be much higher than what buyers are currently willing to pay. Figure 9.4 is an example of an appraisal using the cost approach.

Income Approach

The **income approach** to value is based on the premise that a property is worth the present value of the future income to be produced by the property. In other words, what an investor should be willing to pay today for a property is directly related to what the investor expects to receive from the property in the future. Financial analysts have developed a technique called *capitalization,* which mathematically computes the present value of the future income produced by real estate.

The determination of value by the income approach can be viewed as a series of steps:

1. Estimate gross annual income.

2. Estimate vacancies and uncollectible rents, and subtract this from gross annual income to arrive at the effective gross income, also called the *gross operating income.*

3. Estimate annual expenses and subtract these from the effective gross income to arrive at the net operating income.

4. Select the proper capitalization rate.

5. Divide the capitalization rate into the net operating income to arrive at an estimate of value.

These steps can be summarized as follows:

	Gross annual income
Less	−Vacancy factor and uncollectible rents
Equals	Effective gross income
Less	−Annual expenses
Equals	Net operating income

$$\frac{\text{Net operating income}}{\text{Capitalization rate}} = \text{Estimate of property's value}$$

Explanation of the Income Approach

Gross annual income is the maximum amount of income a property can expect to make if fully occupied 100 percent of the time and assuming rents are at the going market rate. Appraisers recognize that 100 percent occupancy all the time is unrealistic. Vacancies and turnovers occur. Also, some tenants skip out on their rent. Therefore, appraisers subtract an estimate for vacancies and uncollectibles to arrive at the effective gross income.

After computing the effective gross income, the appraiser totals the annual operating expenses. Operating expenses are the costs of running and maintaining the property. Examples include the following:

Property taxes	Supplies
Insurance premiums	Utilities
Repairs	Accounting and legal advice
Maintenance	Advertising
Management fees	Reserves for replacement

Real estate loan payments and income tax depreciation deductions are not considered operating expenses because they are not costs incurred to run the building. Therefore, they are not deducted to arrive at net income.

Once annual operating expenses are calculated, they are subtracted from the effective gross income to arrive at the net operating

FIGURE 9.4

Example Using Cost Approach

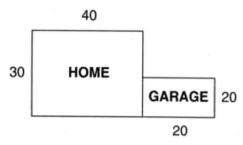

Cost New per Square Foot
Home = $150 per sq. ft.
Garage = $50 per sq. ft.

Depreciation Information
Estimated life new = 50 years

Present effective age = 10 years

Land Value
$150,000 based on recent comparable sales

Solution

```
  30  ft.
x 40  ft.        (Home)
1,200  sq. ft.
```

```
1,200  sq. ft.
x $150  per sq. ft.
$180,000  replacement value of home
```

```
  20  ft
x 20  ft.        (Garage)
 400  sq. ft.
```

```
 400  sq. ft.
x $50  per sq. ft.
$20,000  replacement value of garage
```

```
 $180,000  replacement value of home
 +20,000  replacement value of garage
 $200,000  before depreciation
```

Depreciation

$$\frac{100\%}{50 \text{ yrs.}} = 2\% \text{ depreciation per year} \times 10 \text{ years} = 20\%$$

(200,000 x 20% depreciation = $40,000 depreciation)

```
$200,000  before depreciation
 −40,000  depreciation
$160,000  present value of improvement
+150,000  land
$310,000  estimate of value
```

income. Net operating income is the income the property produces after the deduction of operating expenses, but before the payment of real estate loans.

The next step in the income approach is to select the appropriate capitalization rate. A **capitalization rate** can be defined as the rate necessary to attract an average investor to invest in the property being appraised. The capitalization rate reflects a return on the funds invested, as well as a return (recapture) of the investment. This is not unlike opening a savings account with $100. If at the end of the year you received $10 in interest, you would have a 10% return or 10% capitalization rate. The determination of the appropriate capitalization rate is the most difficult aspect of the income approach to value. The techniques for the selection of a capitalization rate are complex and beyond the scope of this book. For example, visualize the capitalization rate as being the rate that other like properties that are returning to their owners.

The final step in the income approach is to divide the capitalization rate into net operating income to arrive at an estimate of value.

$$\frac{\text{Net operating income}}{\text{Capitalization rate}} = \text{Estimate of value}$$

The income approach to value is appropriate for income-producing properties such as apartment buildings, commercial office buildings, and retail stores. Figure 9.5 is an example of an appraisal using the income approach.

Market Approach (Comparable Sales)

The **market approach** to value is based on the principle of substitution. The **principle of substitution** states that a buyer should not pay more for a home than the price it takes to acquire a comparable home. Therefore, the market approach is also known as the *comparison sales approach to value.*

To apply the market approach, an appraiser gathers data on current sales of properties that are similar to the property being appraised. Ideally, the comparable properties should be in the same neighborhood; be similar in size, style, and quality; and contain similar internal characteristics as the subject property. Comparables should be recent sales.

Each comparable used must also be what is called a *market sale.* A market sale is a sale in which a property is sold using normal financing techniques and the buyer and the seller were fully informed and knowledgeable about the real estate market. If either the buyer

FIGURE 9.5

Example Using Income Approach

The property is a clean, but modest, 15-unit apartment with fair market rents of $700 per unit. The estimated factor for vacancies and uncollectibles is 5%. Annual operating expenses include:

Property taxes	$9,450
Insurance	$1,000
Management and accounting	$10,000
Repairs and others	$12,000

The capitalization rate selected by the appraiser is 7%.

Solution

Gross annual income	$126,000	($700 x 15 units x 12 months)
Less vacancies and uncollectibles	−6,300	($126,000 x 5%)
Effective gross income	$119,700	
Less annual expenses	−32,450	($9,450 + 1,000 + 10,000 + 12,000)
Net operating income	$87,250	

$$\frac{\text{Net operating income}}{\text{Capitalization rate}} \qquad \frac{\$87,250}{7\%} = \$1,246,000 \text{ Estimate of value}$$
(rounded to nearest $1,000)

If the capitalization rate selected had been 6%, the value would be:

$$\frac{\$87,250}{6\%} = \$1,454,000 \text{ rounded to nearest } \$1,000$$

If the capitalization rate were 8%, the value would be:

$$\frac{\$87,250}{8\%} = \$1,091,000 \text{ rounded to nearest } \$1,000$$

Observe this rule: *The higher the capitalization rate, the lower the value.* Therefore, you can see that the selection of the appropriate capitalization rate is very critical! *The selection of an inappropriate capitalization rate can greatly distort value.*

or the seller was under any duress or strain, such as divorce, death in the family, or financial reversals, the appraiser would discard the sale as not being a good comparable sale. For the market approach to be valid, the sales used for comparison must reflect normal market conditions, not sales sold under abnormal circumstances.

Once the comparable properties are selected (three properties are usually the minimum; five are better), the appraiser makes adjustments for the differences between the comparable properties and the subject property being appraised. The appraiser takes sales prices of the comparable properties and adjusts these prices to reflect what the comparable properties would have sold for if they had the features or characteristics of the subject property. It is important to remember that you always adjust the feature values of the comparable properties, never the subject property. The results of this process produce an indicated market value range for the property being appraised. Figure 9.6 is an example of an appraisal using the market approach.

Value Range for Market Approach Example

If the comparables in the market approach example (Figure 9.6) were near the location of the subject home and had the same lot size and overall condition of the subject home, the comparables A, B, and C would have sold for somewhere between $319,900 and $320,500; these figures reflect the indicated market value range.

Value Conclusions for Market Approach Example

Subject home in Figure 9.6 should sell for somewhere between $319,900 and $320,500. Final estimate is $320,000, as Comparable B is most comparable in the opinion of the appraiser.

This is a highly simplified example of the market approach, but it does show the basic concept of how the market approach attempts to adjust known comparable sales to reflect what the comparables should have sold for if the comparables had the characteristics of the subject property. As consumers, people use an informal market approach when they shop for automobiles, furniture, clothes, and most other types of consumer purchases. When it comes to real estate, appraisers simply formalize the process by reducing the comparative facts to writing.

The market approach to value is not the main technique used when appraising income property, but it is an excellent approach to use when appraising homes, especially when the local home market is highly active with many comparable sales in the immediate neighborhood.

FIGURE 9.6

Example Using Market Approach

Assume that the subject property is an older two-bedroom home with a one-car garage. The square footage for the home is 1,100 square feet. The appraiser locates three similar homes that have recently sold in the neighborhood at fair market prices. All have identical square footage and number of rooms.

Comparables

Data	Comparable A	Comparable B	Comparable C
Price paid	$323,900	$321,500	$316,000
Location	better than subject property	equal to subject property	equal to subject property
Lot size	equal to subject property	larger than subject property	smaller than subject property
Overall condition	better than subject property	equal to subject property	worse than subject property

Dollar Adjustment Factors per the Opinion of the Appraiser

Location difference	$1,000
Lot size difference	$1,500
Overall condition difference	$3,000

Adjustments

Data	Comparable A	Comparable B	Comparable C
Price paid	$323,900	$321,500	$316,000
Location	−1,000	0	0
Lot size	0	−1,500	+1,500
Overall condition	−3,000	0	+3,000
Price comparables would have sold for if they were like the subject home	$319,900	$320,000	$320,500

Use of Gross Multipliers

Appraisers have designed a method for quickly obtaining a rough estimate of value using what are called *gross monthly rent multipliers* (GMRM), also known as *gross rent multipliers* (GRM), if annual rents, instead of monthly rents, are used. A **gross multiplier** is a ratio between sales price and rental rates. The GMRM is found by dividing the sales price of a home by its monthly rent.

Example:

$$\frac{\text{Sales price}}{\text{Monthly rental rate}} \qquad \frac{\$300,000}{\$2,000} = 150 \text{ Gross monthly rent multiplier}$$

The gross rent multiplier is found by dividing the sales price of a home by its annual rent.

$$\frac{\text{Sales price}}{\text{Annual rate}} \qquad \frac{\$300,000}{\$24,000} = 12.5 \text{ Gross rent multiplier}$$
$$(\$2,000/\text{mo.} \times 12)$$

An appraiser does this for many sales until a trend develops. When asked to conduct an appraisal on a home, the appraiser does a complete market approach (comparable sales) to arrive at an estimate of value. To recheck the results of the market approach, the appraiser may also do a cost approach and an income approach. For a home, a full-blown income approach is not needed, so the gross rent multiplier approach is often used instead.

The appraiser locates comparable homes, determines their gross multipliers, and selects the most appropriate multiplier. Next, the appraiser determines the fair market rent of the subject home. Then the gross multiplier is multiplied by the fair market rent to arrive at an estimate of value.

Example: After carefully selecting comparable sales, the appraiser determines that the gross monthly rent multiplier should be 200. The fair market rent of the home is $1,500. Therefore, gross monthly rent multiplier × monthly rent = estimate of value.

$$200 \times \$1,500 = \$300,000 \text{ Estimate of value}$$

Because smaller residential properties have a higher expense ratio, gross multipliers are more frequently used on 1–4 residential units, while larger properties are values with a capitalization rate.

Reconciliation and Final Estimate of Value

The process of bringing together the three indications of value derived through the market, cost, and income approaches is the final step in the appraisal process. This process is called **correlation (reconciliation)**. When reconciling, the appraiser gives full consideration to each approach; then, based on judgment and experience, the appraiser arrives at one final value or price.

Correlation or reconciliation is not the averaging of the three approaches! Averaging gives equal weight to each approach, which is wrong. For any given property, one of the approaches is better and should be given more weight.

The final value estimate is not given in odd dollars and cents. The final estimate of value usually is rounded to the nearest $100, $500, or $1,000, depending on the value of the property.

CHAPTER SUMMARY

Appraisers are required to be licensed or certified for all transactions involving federal insurance or regulation. An appraisal license or certificate is distinct and separate from a real estate license.

An appraisal is defined as an estimate or opinion of value. Although there are many types of value, the value sought most often is the market value.

For a property to have value, four elements are necessary: utility, scarcity, demand, and transferability. Once value has been established, social, economic, political, and physical forces cause value to change. Appraisal theory rests on certain principles, such as highest and best use, change, supply and demand, substitution, and conformity, in addition to several others.

Depreciation is defined as a loss in value from any cause. Depreciation of real estate is caused by physical deterioration, functional obsolescence, and economic obsolescence. Depreciation can be classified as curable or incurable or as accrued or accrual for depreciation.

The appraisal process can be viewed as a series of steps leading to a final estimate of value. The appraisal techniques include the cost approach, income approach, and market approach. In certain instances, the gross multiplier technique is also used to estimate value.

The selection of a single final estimate of value is called correlation or reconciliation. Final value conclusions are submitted in a written report, which may be a restricted, summary, or self-contained appraisal report.

IMPORTANT TERMS AND CONCEPTS

appraisal

appreciation

capitalization rate

correlation
(reconciliation)

cost approach

curable
depreciation

depreciation

economic
obsolescence

functional
obsolescence

gross multiplier

income approach

incurable
depreciation

market approach

market value

physical
deterioration

principle of
substitution

value in use (utility
value)

PRACTICAL APPLICATION

1. A steel building property consists of the following: the land value is $300,000, the main structure is 200 feet × 40 feet, and a storage building is 35 feet × 15 feet. A cement slab and other improvements have a present value of $27,000. The main structure has an effective age of twenty years with an estimated life of fifty years. The replacement cost of the main structure is $65 per square foot. The storage building has an effective age of fifteen years with an estimated life new of thirty years. The replacement cost of the storage building is $20 per square foot. Using the cost approach, what is the estimated value of the property? (Round answer to nearest $1,000.)

2. An 11,000-square-foot commercial property rents for $1 per square foot per month on a triple net lease to a highly rated tenant with ten years to go on the lease. The only cost to the landlord is 5% of gross rents for miscellaneous expenses not covered by the net lease. A comparable property sold for $1,500,000 and had a net operating income of $135,000. Based only on this information, what is the estimated value of the commercial property? (Round answer to nearest $1,000.)

3. You are doing a listing presentation for Ms. Seller's home, which does not have a spa. You found three comparable homes that sold recently in the subdivision: Comparable A sold for $357,000, is in better condition, and has a larger lot in addition to a spa. Comparable B sold for $340,000 and is in similar

condition to Ms. Seller's home, but it has a smaller lot and no spa. Comparable C sold for $325,000, is in worse condition than Ms. Seller's home, and has a smaller lot and no spa. The adjustments are as follows: for spa, $1,000; condition, $3,000; and lot size, $10,000. Based only on this information, what do you think should be the listing price of Ms. Seller's home? (Round answer to nearest $1,000.)

REVIEWING YOUR UNDERSTANDING

1. An appraisal is defined as
   a. the market price.
   b. an estimate of value.
   c. the loan value.
   d. the actual selling price.

2. For most homebuyers, the value they want to know is the
   a. market value.
   b. tax value.
   c. insurance value.
   d. resale value.

3. The best use of land is that which produces the greatest net return to the land. This is the
   a. principle of change.
   b. principle of substitution.
   c. principle of conformity.
   d. principle of highest and best use.

4. Loss in value in a home because of a poor floor plan is called
   a. physical determination.
   b. functional obsolescence.
   c. economic obsolescence.
   d. book depreciation.

5. The most comprehensive type of appraisal report is the
   a. restricted (letter) report.
   b. summary (short-form) report.
   c. self-contained (narrative) report.
   d. negotiated (based on estimated value) report.

6. For existing residential homes, the best appraisal approach is usually the
   a. market approach.
   b. income approach.
   c. cost approach.
   d. capitalization approach.

7. Given: land valued at $100,000. Cost new per square foot: home, $150; garage, $50. Estimated life: new, fifty years; present effective age, ten years. What is the estimated value of the property? (See Figure 9.7.)
   a. $240,000
   b. $260,000
   c. $292,000
   d. $308,000

FIGURE 9.7

8. Find the value by use of the income approach (round to nearest $100). Given: four-unit apartment rents for $700 per unit per month; vacancy factor is 5 percent; annual expenses are $11,000; and capitalization rate is 6 percent.
   a. $348,700
   b. $351,800
   c. $424,300
   d. $419,100

9. Gross monthly multiplier is 200, and fair market rent of condo is $1,275 per month. The estimate of value is
   a. $255,000.
   b. $240,500.
   c. $233,000.
   d. $275,500.

10. According to the California Office of Real Estate Appraisers, the most comprehensive appraisal skill level is a
    a. licensed appraiser.
    b. Certified—Residential.
    c. Certified—General.
    d. broker.

11. When evaluating a twenty-year-old home, the appraiser assigns it an age of only ten years because of the extremely good care taken by the owner. This is an example of
    a. effective age.
    b. chronological age.
    c. actual age.
    d. physical age.

12. The rule is the higher the capitalization rate, the
    a. higher the value.
    b. lower the value.
    c. lower the risk.
    d. higher the net income.

13. Which of the following is false?
    a. All things equal, the higher the demand, the higher the price.
    b. An example of physical deterioration is a worn-out roof.
    c. Depreciation for income tax purposes is different from depreciation for appraisal purposes.
    d. Price, value, and cost are the same concept.

14. A change in zoning is what type of force that influences values?
    a. Functional
    b. Physical
    c. Political
    d. Observed

15. The principle that states that the value of one home tends to be influenced by the price of acquiring equally desirable homes is called the principle of
    a. progression.
    b. supply and demand.
    c. substitution.
    d. conformity.

16. Which of the following best describes the cost approach to value?

    a. Land value + replacement cost = value
    b. Land value + replacement cost − depreciation = value
    c. Land value + net income ÷ capitalization rate = value
    d. Land value + adjusted value of comparables = value

17. Similar condos rent for $1,600 per month and sell for $352,000. The condo you want to buy could rent for $1,800. What is its estimate of value?

    a. $379,000
    b. $388,500
    c. $396,000
    d. $402,000

18. When considering the purchase of a home with fix-up potential, the most difficult depreciation to cure (correct) is

    a. physical.
    b. functional.
    c. economic.
    d. deferred.

19. For property to have value, there must be four elements. All of the following are elements of value, except for

    a. transferability.
    b. scarcity.
    c. utility.
    d. price.

20. One of the last steps in the appraisal process is known as correlation, also known as

    a. averaging the three values.
    b. reconciliation.
    c. establishing the median value.
    d. discounting the values to a single value.

STUDENT LEARNING OUTCOMES

Closing a real estate transaction is a highly technical process. Escrow and title insurance companies provide valuable services that help consumers and real estate agents smoothly and efficiently close a real estate transaction. At the conclusion of the chapter, you will be able to do the following:

1. Define escrow and list the legal requirements for a valid escrow.
2. Describe the basic services provided by title insurance companies.
3. Explain the difference between a CLTA standard and an ALTA extended-coverage policy of title insurance.
4. Explain various closing costs and indicate who normally pays for each closing cost.

The Role of Escrow and Title Insurance Companies

10.1 ESCROW

Definition of Escrow

In a real estate sale, an **escrow** is a process whereby a neutral third party acts as the closing agent for the buyer and the seller. (See Figure 10.1.) The escrow officer assumes the responsibility of handling all the paperwork and disbursement of funds to close out a real estate transaction. The Civil Code defines an escrow as follows:

A grant may be deposited by the grantor with a third person, to be delivered on the performance of a condition, and, on delivery by the depository, it will take effect. While in the possession of the third person, and subject to condition, it is called an escrow.

Escrows can be used for a variety of business transactions, such as sale or exchange of real estate, sale or encumbrance of personal property, sale or pledging of securities, sale of the assets of a business (bulk sale), sale of a promissory note secured by a deed of trust, and transfer of liquor licenses. By far, the most common

FIGURE 10.1

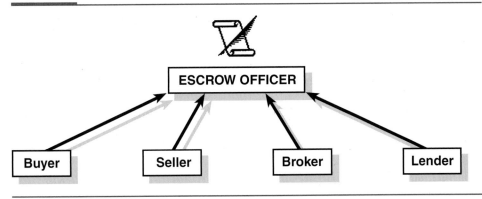

reason for the use of an escrow is to handle the sale and transfer of real estate. The clerical aspects of transferring title to real estate are detailed and complicated; therefore, buyers, sellers, lenders, and real estate agents prefer to use trained escrow officers.

Legal Requirements for a Valid Escrow

There are two essential requirements for a valid real estate escrow:

1. There must be a binding contract between the seller (grantor) and the buyer (grantee).
2. There must be the conditional delivery of transfer instruments and monies to a neutral third party.

The binding contract can be in any legal form, such as a deposit receipt, an agreement of sale, an exchange agreement, or mutual instructions from the buyer and the seller. The escrow instructions signed by the buyer and seller supplement the terms of the original purchase agreement, and the two contracts are interpreted together. If there is a conflict between the purchase contract and the escrow instructions, the usual rule is that the most recent contract prevails. In most cases, this is the signed escrow instructions. Prior to signing the escrow instructions, every signee should check to see that the instructions reflect the most current purchase agreement.

Confidentiality of Escrows

Escrow instructions are confidential. Only the principals and their agents in the transaction are entitled to see the escrow instructions, and then only insofar as the instructions pertain to mutual items in the transaction. For example, the buyer and the seller are entitled to see each other's escrow instructions regarding the sales price, down payment, and other terms of the sale. But how much the seller is netting from the sale is no business of the buyer. Likewise, the buyer's financing arrangement with an institutional lender is no business of the seller, who is cashing out of the transaction.

If the escrow holder receives conflicting instructions from the principals, the escrow officer simply refuses to proceed until the parties settle their differences. An escrow officer cannot give legal advice and may bring an action in court forcing the principals in the escrow to litigate their differences. This legal action is called an *interpleader action.*

Status of the Escrow Holder

An escrow is a limited agency. The only obligations to be fulfilled by the escrow holder are those set forth in the instructions connected with the transaction. Before a real estate sale is recorded, the escrow officer is the dual agent for the buyer and the seller. After the deed is recorded, the escrow officer becomes the individual agent for each party.

This distinction is important, especially if an unethical escrow officer should steal money from the escrow company. If the escrow officer embezzles the money before the seller is entitled to it, the buyer suffers the loss. But if the money is embezzled after the seller becomes entitled to it, the loss falls on the seller because the money is now considered to be the seller's.

Regulation of Escrow Holders

Title insurance companies, banks, trust companies, and attorneys can handle escrows without obtaining an escrow license. However, independent escrow companies must be incorporated and can handle escrows only after obtaining a special license from the Department of Corporations (DOC). Independent escrow companies are common in southern California, whereas title insurance companies handle most of the escrows in northern California.

Who Decides Which Escrow Company to Use?

The selection of an escrow company is negotiated between the buyer and seller. The real estate agent cannot dictate which escrow company to use. If a real estate agent has a financial interest in an escrow company, the law requires the agent to disclose this interest to the buyer and the seller before a final selection is made. Real estate brokers can legally handle escrows without obtaining a special escrow license if the broker is an agent for the buyer or the seller in the transaction.

Once an escrow company is selected, who pays the fee? The payment of the escrow fee is an item that is negotiable between buyer and seller. The decision as to who pays this fee varies throughout the state. In some geographic areas, the seller usually pays; in other areas, the buyer usually pays; in some areas, the fee is split between the buyer and the seller.

Services Provided by Escrow Holders

For a fee, the escrow holder carefully collects, prepares, and safeguards the instructions, documents, and monies required to close the transaction. Upon receipt of written instructions from all parties (that is, buyer, seller, lender, and real estate agent), the escrow instructions are compared to determine whether the parties are in mutual agreement. An escrow officer can do no more or no less than the instructions dictate.

When the parties are in agreement and all instruments and monies have been deposited, the escrow officer sees that title is transferred. The following are some of the services performed by an escrow company:

1. Prepares buyer's and seller's escrow instructions; prepares deed and other needed documents, such as promissory notes and deeds of trust as instructed from all parties

2. Requests the demand for payoff for the seller's loan from the lending institution or, in the case of an assumption, requests a beneficiary statement from the lending institution

3. Collects the structural pest control report and the notice of work completed, if any

4. Collects the required fire insurance policy

5. Balances the accounting details, including adjustments and prorations of the taxes, interest, insurance, and assessments and rents (if any)

6. Collects the balance of monies required to close the transaction

7. Verifies that the appropriate documents are recorded; after transfer has occurred, the escrow file is audited; the escrow officer then disburses the monies, issues itemized closing statements to all parties, and orders the title insurance policy

---

SPECIAL INTEREST TOPIC

North versus South

Escrow practices differ between southern and northern California. In southern California, independent escrow companies are common, and they handle a considerable number of the real estate transactions. Title insurance companies provide the title services, but escrow companies do the actual closing of the sale. Because of a severe real estate recession in the early 1990s, many southern California independent escrow companies have gone out of business, have merged with other escrow companies, or were purchased by title companies. Some lending institutions also provide escrow services in southern California. In northern California, most escrows are handled by title insurance companies that have extensive escrow departments with many branch offices.

One other point of difference has to do with the timing of the signing of escrow instructions. In southern California, it is common to have the buyer and seller sign escrow instructions shortly after they sign their purchase agreement. This may be 30 or 60 days before the actual close of escrow. In many northern California counties, escrow instructions are usually not signed until a day or two before the actual close of escrow.

Termination of Escrows

Escrows are usually terminated by completion of the sale and, in the case of a refinance, upon completion of the loan process. If the transaction is not completed, the escrow may be canceled by mutual agreement of all parties. The escrow company is entitled to receive partial payment of escrow fees for services rendered to date.

All the conditions required by escrow instructions must be performed within the time limit set forth in the escrow agreement. The escrow officer has no authority to enforce or accept the performance after the time limit provided in the instructions. When the time limit provided in the escrow has expired and neither party to the escrow has performed in accordance with the terms, upon receiving mutual written releases, the parties are entitled to the return of their respective papers, documents, and money from the escrow officer.

Escrows and RESPA

The **Real Estate Settlement Procedures Act (RESPA)** is a federal law that requires certain forms to be provided regarding closing costs. The law applies whenever a person purchases an owner-occupied residence using funds obtained from institutional lenders regulated by a federal agency. Virtually all banks and most other lenders fall directly or indirectly under RESPA's rules. The one major exception is real estate loans by private parties, which are usually exempt from RESPA.

RESPA rules require a lender to furnish the borrower with a special information booklet and a good faith estimate of closing costs when the prospective borrower files an application for a real estate loan. RESPA rules prohibit any kickbacks or unearned fees from being listed as closing costs. The law expressly states that only valid, earned closing costs shall be charged to the buyer or seller. Violators can be punished by up to one year in jail and/or a $10,000 fine.

Most of the burden for implementing RESPA falls upon the real estate lender. However, escrow agents are also involved. RESPA requires the use of a Uniform Settlement Statement (HUD-1), which must itemize all closing charges. Upon request, the escrow agent must let the borrower-buyer inspect the Uniform Settlement Statement one day before the close of escrow. In addition, the escrow officer must see that all parties receive a copy of the Uniform Settlement Statement after the close of escrow.

Escrows—Summarized

An escrow holder is a neutral third party who, for a fee, will handle the paperwork involved in transferring title and/or in placing a new loan on real property. Escrow companies are licensed by the state of California. However, banks, attorneys, and title insurance companies can act as escrow holders without obtaining a special license. A real estate broker can act as an escrow holder only if the broker is an agent for the buyer or the seller.

TECHNICAL REASONS FOR AN ESCROW

1. To provide a custodian for funds and documents who can make concurrent delivery
2. To provide a clearinghouse for payments
3. To provide an agency for computing prorations

ESSENTIALS OF A VALID ESCROW

1. Must have a binding contract between buyer and seller
2. Must have conditional delivery of transfer instruments to a third party

TERMINATION OF AN ESCROW

1. By full performance and closing
2. By mutual cancellation by the parties
3. By revocation by a party

10.2 TITLE INSURANCE COMPANIES

Title insurance companies are incorporated businesses that provide these basic services:

1. Search and gather public records relating to the legal title of real property.
2. Examine and interpret the title records that have been gathered.
3. Insure an owner or lender against financial loss resulting from certain unreported defects in the title.

Title Search

A *title search* can be conducted in one of two ways. The first is the *courthouse search*. Under this method, a title person goes to the county courthouse and searches through the public records, seeking information pertaining to a particular property under examination. The title searcher reproduces the information and presents the items to a title examiner for interpretation.

The second method is for a title company to maintain its own *title plant*. A title plant is really a condensed courthouse where records affecting real property are copied, usually microfilmed or computerized, and filed for future reference. When a title search is ordered, the title person has only to select the needed information from the title plant. This reduces the need for frequent trips to the county courthouse, thereby saving valuable time for the title company and the customer.

Title Examination

The actual examination and interpretation of a title is done by a highly skilled title examiner (not an attorney) whose task is to review each document and create what is known as a **chain of title**. A chain of title is an unbroken history of all the title transfers, beginning with the document originally transferring title from the government to private ownership and ending with the document vesting title in the current owner.

In addition to identifying the correct owner, the title examiner determines what and how various encumbrances (such as taxes, deeds of trust, easements, and so on) affect the ownership. When the examination is complete, the information is compiled into a *preliminary title report* that lists the name of the owner(s), the legal description of the property, the status of property taxes and special assessments, and the various encumbrances against the property. This preliminary title report is not the actual title policy, but it is the basis upon which a title company is willing to insure the owner's title.

Title Insurance

In the early days of California, title insurance did not exist. Land holdings were large, and population was sparse. Property frequently was transferred simply by the delivery of a symbol in the presence of a witness.

As population and migration increased, land holdings were divided and sold to incoming strangers. Boundaries became confused, and it was difficult to identify ownership. To combat this confusion, when California became a state in 1850, the legislature enacted recording statutes. These recording statutes created depositories (namely, the county recorder's office) to collect and file title documents for public use. Soon the recorder's offices became too complex for many laypeople to use. Specialists called **abstractors** began searching and compiling courthouse records. For a fee, these abstractors would publish their findings on a specific parcel of land.

To protect the public, the need arose for a system to guard against the errors, omissions, and incorrect judgments that abstractors might make. This need for additional assurance led to the concept of title insurance.

Today a title insurance policy insures the ownership of land and the priority of a lien (deed of trust, contract of sale, and so on) subject to the encumbrances revealed in the title examination. The owner and/or lender is assured that a thorough search has been made of all public records affecting a particular property. (See Figure 10.2.)

Types of Title Insurance Policies

Title insurance policies are divided into two basic groups, the standard policy and the extended-coverage policy. The **standard policy** is the most widely used and can be divided into three subtypes:

1. *Standard owner's policy,* which insures the owner for the amount of the purchase price
2. *Standard lender's policy,* which insures the lender for the amount of the loan
3. *Standard joint protection policy,* which co-insures the owner and lender under one policy

The standard policy is frequently referred to as a **CLTA policy.** CLTA stands for California Land Title Association, a state trade association for title insurance companies.

Included in the standard coverage policy is the assurance that title is free and clear of all encumbrances of public record, other

FIGURE 10.2

TITLE INSURANCE PROCESS

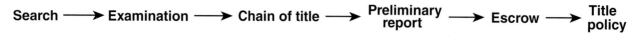

Search ⟶ Examination ⟶ Chain of title ⟶ Preliminary report ⟶ Escrow ⟶ Title policy

than the items revealed in the title examination and listed as exceptions in the title policy. Under the standard policy, the title company does not make a physical inspection of the property and therefore excludes from coverage unrecorded items that could affect the title. For example, unrecorded easements are excluded, as well as the rights of parties in possession other than the owner, such as tenants or squatters. Also excluded from standard policy coverage are violations of environmental laws, zoning and other government ordinances affecting the use of the property, nondeclared assessments, and some items regarding mining and water claims.

Extended-Coverage Policy

The **extended-coverage policy** was originally established for real estate lenders. This policy requires the title company to make a physical inspection of the property and insures against certain unrecorded title risks excluded under the standard policy. In some cases, the extended-coverage policy is requested and issued to homeowners, but not to other types of property owners. The extended-coverage policy is commonly referred to as an **ALTA policy**. ALTA stands for American Land Title Association, a national trade association for title insurance companies.

How Much Does Title Insurance Cost?

Title insurance premiums, like most other types of insurance premiums, are calculated based upon the dollar amount of insurance coverage. Owners' title policies are issued for the purchase price of the property, whereas lenders' title policies are issued for the loan amount. Therefore, owners of more expensive property pay higher title fees than owners of less expensive property. Title fees are established by title companies themselves, not by any government agency. Competition keeps rates between title companies comparable.

Unlike other forms of insurance (such as automobile, fire, and life insurance), which require annual premiums, a title insurance fee is paid only once. The title policy stays in force as long as the owner retains title to the property. A new title insurance policy is required by the lender; otherwise, the lender will not make the loan on the property.

Who Pays for the Title Insurance?

The payment of the owner's policy fee is a negotiable item between the buyer and the seller. However, in different geographic areas, the method of payment varies. In some areas, it is customary to split the title fee between the buyer and the seller. In some areas, the seller normally pays the title fee; in others, the buyer pays. The lender's policy title fee is almost always paid by the borrower-buyer.

SPECIAL INTEREST TOPIC		Evolution of Title Protection
	FIRST CAME	*Abstract of Title* A summary of title prepared by an early-day specialist, with no guarantee of accuracy
	THEN	*Certificate of Title* A certificate stating the name of the owner and a list of encumbrances, with no guarantee of accuracy
	THEN	*Guarantee of Title* A title search in which an abstract company guaranteed the accuracy of the search
	AND TODAY	*Title insurance* Creation of an insurance company that issues a title policy and insures the accuracy of results. If insured suffers an insured loss, a claim is filed similar in nature to any other type of insurance. Title insurance led to the use of the grant deed and elimination of the warranty deed in California. (See Chapter 2 for details regarding deeds.)

Who Decides Which Title Insurance Company to Use?

This is another negotiable item between the buyer and the seller. The usual custom is for the party paying the title fee to select the title company. As discussed above, real estate regulations prohibit a real estate agent from dictating which title insurance company to use. If the real estate agent should happen to have a financial interest in the title company selected, the agent must disclose this fact to the buyer and the seller.

Title Insurance Summarized

A title insurance policy ensures that a thorough examination has been made of all public records affecting the property in question and that the owner has acquired ownership free from title defects of public record, subject only to the encumbrances revealed in the title examination and the exceptions recited in the title insurance policy. It means that the owner has a marketable title that can be transferred to others.

STANDARD COVERAGE POLICY (CLTA)

1. Risks normally insured against the following:
    (a) Most matters disclosed by public records
    (b) Certain off-record risks, such as forgery or incompetence of parties
2. Risks not normally insured against the following:
    (a) Matters not disclosed by public records
    (b) Environmental laws, zoning, and other government ordinances regarding the use of the property
    (c) Certain mining and water claims
    (d) Defects known to the insured before the property was purchased and not revealed to the title company before the sale

EXTENDED-COVERAGE POLICY (ALTA)

1. Risks covered:
    (a) All those listed under the standard coverage policy
    (b) Unperfected mechanics' liens
    (c) Unrecorded physical easements
    (d) Facts a correct survey would show
    (e) Certain water claims
    (f) Rights of parties in possession, including tenants and owners under unrecorded instruments
2. Risks not normally covered:
    (a) Environmental laws, zoning, and other government ordinances affecting the use of the property
    (b) Defects known to the insured before the property was insured but not revealed to title company by the insured

For an additional charge, an insured can purchase special endorsements to cover items normally excluded under the CLTA or ALTA policies.

10.3 CLOSING COSTS

Closing costs refer to the expenses paid by the buyer and the seller upon the sale of property. Some people attempt to estimate closing costs by using simple rules of thumb, such as "3 percent of the sales price" or some other rough figure. However, rules of thumb are not accurate. The only sure way to determine actual closing costs is to list and price each individual item.

The payment of the closing costs is a negotiable topic between the buyer and seller. No law requires that certain closing costs are the responsibility of the buyer or the seller. The only exception deals with some government-backed loans where regulations prohibit the buyer from paying certain closing costs. However, by custom, certain closing costs are typically paid by the buyer, and other costs are usually paid by the seller.

Buyer's Closing Costs

A buyer's (borrower) closing costs can be divided into two categories: (1) nonrecurring closing costs, and (2) recurring closing costs.

Nonrecurring closing costs are one-time charges paid upon the close of escrow. Recurring closing costs are prepaid items that the buyer pays in advance to help offset expenses that will continue as long as the buyer owns the property.

Nonrecurring Closing Costs Usually Paid by the Buyer

1. *Loan origination fee.* A fee charged by a lender to cover the expenses of processing a loan. The fee is usually quoted as a percentage of the loan amount. For example, a 1% loan fee for a $300,000 loan would be 1% × $300,000 = $3,000 loan fee.

2. *Appraisal fee.* A fee charged by an appraiser for giving an estimate of property value. The fee for a simple appraisal varies throughout the state, with $350 or more being a typical charge for a single-family residence. Appraisal fees for income properties such as apartments and office buildings are considerably higher.

3. *Credit report fee.* Before a lender grants a loan, the borrower's credit is checked at a credit agency. The credit report usually costs from $40 to $60.

4. *Structural pest control inspection fee.* A fee charged by a licensed inspector who checks for termites, fungus, dry rot, pests, and other items that might cause structural damage. For a home in an urban area, the fee is usually $75-125.

5. *Tax service fee.* A fee paid to a tax service company that, for the life of the loan, each year reviews the tax collector's records. If a borrower fails to pay property taxes, the tax service company reports this fact to the lender, who then takes steps to protect the loan against a tax foreclosure sale. This fee usually runs from $50 to $80.

6. *Recording fees.* This covers the cost of recording the deed, the deed of trust, and other buyer-related documents. Most counties charge $10 to $15 to record a single-page document.

7. *Notary fees.* Signatures on documents to be recorded must be notarized. Notary public fees are set by law.

8. *Assumption fee.* A fee paid to a lender if the buyer "assumes" the loan, that is, agrees to take over and continue to pay the seller's existing loan.

9. *Title and escrow fees.* Buyer's responsibility in buyer-pays areas, areas where it is customary for the buyer to pay the title and escrow fees.

Recurring Closing Costs Usually Paid by the Buyer

1. *Hazard insurance.* A one-year premium for insurance against fire, storm, and other risks. The minimum coverage is the amount of the real estate loan, but buyers are advised to purchase greater amounts if they make a large down payment toward the purchase price. Many owners purchase comprehensive homeowner's packages.

2. *Tax proration.* In California, the property tax year runs from July 1 through June 30 of the following year. If the seller has prepaid the taxes, the buyer reimburses the seller for the prepaid portion. Prorations are discussed in detail in Chapter 6.

3. *Tax and insurance reserves.* This is also known as an *impound account* or *trust account.* If a buyer's (borrower's) monthly loan payment is to include taxes and insurance, as well as principal and interest, the lender sets up a reserve account. Depending on the time of the year (the date taxes and insurance are due relative to the date escrow closes), a lender will want the buyer to prepay one to six months of taxes and insurance premiums into this reserve account. Once an adequate reserve account is established, tax and insurance bills are forwarded to the lender for payment. At the end of the year, adjustments are made to assure that adequate amounts are in the trust fund for the next year.

4. *Interest due before the first loan payment.* Interest on real estate loans is typically paid in arrears. For example: Escrow closes September 15 with the first loan payment due November 1. The payment due November 1 covers the interest due for the month of October. How is the interest from September 15 to September 30 collected? It is collected in advance at the close of escrow and is called *prepaid interest.* If escrow closed on the first of the month, there would be no prepaid interest if the first payment was due on the first of the following month.

Seller's Closing Costs

The closing costs paid by a seller are one-time, nonrecurring expenses. After the close of escrow, the seller is divested of ownership and, therefore, has no recurring expenses attached to ownership such as property taxes and hazard insurance. Remember that the payment of a particular closing expense is negotiable between the buyer and seller. The following list is merely a guideline to closing costs usually paid by the seller as the result of custom and/or agreement.

Closing Costs Usually Paid by the Seller

1. *Transfer tax.* A tax charged when title is transferred. The county has a documentary transfer tax that is computed at $1.10 per $1,000 (or 55 cents per $500 or fraction thereof) of the sales price. For example, if a $500,000 home is sold for cash or all-new financing, the state documentary transfer tax would be as follows:

   $500,000 sales price ÷ 1,000 = 500 × $1.10 = $550 tax

   For a more detailed explanation of the documentary transfer tax, see Chapter 6. In addition to the documentary transfer tax, some cities in California have enacted a municipal transfer tax that must be collected and disbursed at the close of escrow.

2. *Prepayment penalty.* A charge by a lender when a borrower pays off a loan before the required due date. Many times when a property is sold, the buyer obtains financing to cover the sales price. In the process, the seller's existing mortgage is paid off to make way for the buyer's new mortgage. If the seller's mortgage has a prepayment clause, the seller pays this penalty as a closing cost. Most loans do not have prepayment penalties. But if they do, the actual prepayment penalties vary by lender. A typical prepayment penalty might be six months' interest on the outstanding loan balance at the time of payoff, after subtracting

20 percent of the original loan amount. (See Chapter 7 for details.)

3. *Structural pest control work.* Customarily the buyer pays for the structural pest control inspection fee, and the seller pays for corrective work. However, in some areas, the seller pays for both the inspection and the corrective work.

4. *Real estate brokerage commission.* The commission is normally quoted as a percentage of the sales price. A 6 percent commission with a sales price of $500,000 would be a $30,000 closing cost for the seller.

5. *Discount points.* On some government-backed loans, the seller may pay discount points to increase a lender's yield on a loan. One point is equal to 1 percent of the buyer's loan amount.

6. *Recording and notary fees.* Fees for recording seller-oriented documents, such as a deed of reconveyance to clear off an old loan.

7. *Title and escrow fees.* Seller's responsibility in seller-pays areas, where it is customary for the seller to pay the title and escrow fees.

8. *Natural hazard disclosure fees.* To provide seller-required disclosures for earthquake, flood, fire, and other hazards.

Summary of Closing Costs

BUYER USUALLY PAYS

1. Loan origination fee
2. Appraisal fee
3. Credit report
4. Structural pest control inspection fee
5. Tax service fee
6. Recording fees
7. Notary fees
8. Assumption fee, if any
9. Title and escrow fees in buyer-pays areas
10. Hazard insurance
11. Interest on loan before first payment

SELLER USUALLY PAYS

1. Transfer tax
2. Prepayment penalty
3. Structural pest control work and report fee

(continued)

4. Real estate brokerage commission
5. Discount points on government-backed loans
6. Recording and notary fees
7. Title and escrow fees in seller-pays areas
8. Natural hazard disclosure fees

USUALLY PRORATED BETWEEN THE BUYER AND SELLER

1. Property taxes
2. Interest if loan is assumed by buyer
3. Rents if the property is tenant-occupied income property

CHAPTER SUMMARY

Escrow is the use of a neutral third party to act as the closing agent in a real estate transaction. To be valid, an escrow requires a binding contract and a conditional delivery of transfer instruments. Escrow companies must comply with the Real Estate Settlement Procedures Act (RESPA).

Title insurance companies, institutional lenders, attorneys, and independently licensed companies can handle escrows. A real estate broker can handle an escrow if he or she is an agent for the buyer or the seller in the transaction.

Title insurance companies search and gather public title records, examine and interpret the records, and then issue policies of title insurance. The two major types of title insurance policies are the CLTA standard and the ALTA extended-coverage policies. Certain items are not included in title insurance coverage; therefore, consumers should be aware that these excluded items are their responsibility.

Closing costs can be classified as recurring and nonrecurring. Recurring closing costs are prepaid items that the buyer pays in advance to help offset expenses that will continue as long as the buyer owns the property. Nonrecurring closing costs are one-time charges paid upon the close of escrow.

The payment of escrow fees, title insurance, and closing costs is an item of negotiation between the buyer and the seller. However, by custom, certain closing costs are typically paid by the buyer, whereas other costs are usually paid by the seller. This custom varies throughout the state of California. Escrow and closing practices differ between northern and southern California.

IMPORTANT TERMS AND CONCEPTS

abstractors

ALTA policy

chain of title

closing costs

CLTA policy

escrow

extended-coverage
policy

Real Estate
Settlement
Procedures Act
(RESPA)

standard policy

PRACTICAL APPLICATION

1. Seller and buyer are in escrow for the sale of a home. In the area, it is customary for the seller to pay for the CLTA title policy. The deposit receipt states that the seller will pay for the title policy, but the escrow instructions signed by all parties state that all title and escrow fees will be split 50/50. Just prior to close of escrow, the buyer submits amended instructions for the escrow officer to charge the entire CLTA policy to the seller. The seller refuses to proceed with the escrow. As the buyer's real estate agent, what might you do to solve this problem?

2. Acme Title Company has a policy of giving real estate licensees who refer business to the company a dinner for two and tickets to a professional sporting event. Without your suggestion, the buyer and the seller asked that Acme Title Company be the title insurer. As the real estate agent in the transaction, what are the legal and ethical issues?

3. A $413,575 existing ARM loan at 7 percent will be assumed by the buyer. The seller has made the October 1 payment, and escrow will close on October 19 (use 18 days since buyer is responsible for the day escrow closes). Using a 360-day year, what are the escrow debit and credit charges to the buyer and seller for the interest proration?

REVIEWING YOUR UNDERSTANDING

1. For an escrow to be binding, there must be
   a. a conditional delivery of transfer instruments.
   b. a contract between the parties.
   c. a neutral third party.
   d. all of the above.

2. Which of the following must have an escrow license?
   a. Title insurance companies
   b. Independent escrow companies
   c. Real estate brokers if they handle escrows in which they are also the agent
   d. All of the above

3. A history of all title transfers of a particular parcel of land is called a(n)
   a. preliminary report.
   b. chain of title.
   c. abstract of title.
   d. guarantee of title.

4. A CLTA title policy is also known as a(n)
   a. extended-coverage policy.
   b. ALTA coverage policy.
   c. standard coverage policy.
   d. all-inclusive policy.

5. Which of the following is a nonrecurring closing cost?
   a. Title insurance fee
   b. Real property tax proration
   c. Interest on a new real estate loan
   d. Hazard insurance premium

6. A title insurance policy especially designed for lenders, which requires the title company to make a physical inspection of the property, is called a(n)
   a. CLTA standard policy.
   b. joint protection policy.
   c. all-inclusive policy.
   d. ALTA extended-coverage policy.

7. Annual real property taxes for a lot are $720 and are paid for the current fiscal year. Escrow closes April 1, and the taxes are to be prorated. Therefore:
   a. The seller will be charged (debited) $180.
   b. The seller will be credited $180.
   c. The buyer will be credited $180.
   d. The buyer will be debited $540.

8. The sales price for a small condo is $300,000, with the buyer obtaining a new loan. The seller agrees to pay off the existing $100,000 loan. The seller also agrees to pay the county documentary transfer tax, which is
   a. $55.
   b. $110.
   c. $220.
   d. $330.

9. Although the payment of closing costs is negotiable between the buyer and seller, the buyer usually pays for the
   a. loan origination fee.
   b. broker's commission.
   c. prepayment penalty.
   d. transfer tax.

10. The sales price for a rural lot is $80,000; the buyer pays all cash, and the seller pays off the old loan of $45,000. The seller also pays a 5 percent broker commission, documentary transfer tax, a $300 prepayment penalty, plus $500 in other closing costs. How much will the seller net from escrow?
    a. $35,000
    b. $30,112
    c. $49,888
    d. $45,000

11. All of the following are covered by title insurance policies, except
    a. forged deeds.
    b. liens of record.
    c. environmental violations.
    d. incompetent owners of record.

12. If the parties in an escrow are in conflict and cannot agree as to what to do, the escrow officer can bring a court action called a(n)
    a. abstractor.
    b. interpleader.
    c. judgment.
    d. writ.

13. The use of the HUD-1 closing statement is required by
    a. Regulation Z.
    b. Truth-in-lending.
    c. ECOA.
    d. RESPA.

14. The title records in the office of the title company are called a title
    a. survey.
    b. examination.
    c. plant.
    d. chain.

15. Which of the following is a recurring closing cost?
    a. Tax service
    b. Property taxes
    c. Credit report
    d. Recording fee

16. Which of the following is a nonrecurring closing cost?
    a. Notary fee
    b. Homeowner association dues
    c. Interest on existing loans
    d. Fire insurance

17. The sales price is $300,000; the buyer obtains a new 80 percent loan and pays a 1 percent loan fee, a $25 tax service fee, a $350 property tax proration, a $100 structural pest control inspection charge, $825 in hazard insurance, and one-half of the $900 escrow fee. Based on this information, how much total cash will the buyer need to close escrow?
    a. $1,450
    b. $3,750
    c. $64,150
    d. $64,950

18. The most extensive title assurance is
    a. certificate of title.
    b. abstract of title.
    c. guarantee of title.
    d. insurance of title.

19. Escrow officers cannot
    a. give legal advice.
    b. draft deeds for the parties in escrow.
    c. prepare documents for recording.
    d. do any of the above.

20. Property taxes for the year are $2,400, paid up to July 1 of the year. Escrow closes May 1; therefore, the escrow officer will prorate the prepaid property taxes as follows:
    a. $400 credit to seller
    b. $400 credit to buyer
    c. $2,000 debit to seller
    d. $2,000 debit to buyer

Chapter

11

STUDENT LEARNING OUTCOMES

The relationship between landlords and tenants can be calm and enjoyable, or it can be turbulent, with frustration and confusion on both sides. The California legislature is constantly passing laws related to landlords and tenants. Many problems between landlords and tenants are caused by a lack of understanding of the legal rights and duties of each party. At the conclusion of the chapter, you will be able to do the following:

1. Define a lease and list four types of leasehold estates.
2. Outline the requirements needed for a valid lease or rental agreement.
3. Explain the difference between a sublease and an assignment of a lease.
4. Discuss the duties and responsibilities that landlords and tenants owe to each other.
5. Describe how tenants can be lawfully evicted.
6. Explain the services provided by professional property managers.

Landlord and Tenant Relations

11.1 LEASES

A lease is a contract between an owner, called a **lessor** (or landlord), and a **lessee** (or tenant). A tenant is given the right to possess and use the landlord's property in exchange for rent. *California law requires that all leases for more than one year must be in writing to be valid.*

A lease or rental agreement for one year or less need not be in writing to be valid. However, a prudent person should reduce all rental and lease agreements to writing. In this chapter, the terms *lease* and *rental agreement* are used interchangeably.

Types of Leasehold Estates

In Chapter 2, a distinction was made between a *freehold estate and a less-than-freehold estate.* A freehold estate is an interest in real property as an owner; a less-than-freehold estate is an interest in real property as a tenant. Less-than-freehold estates are also known as *leasehold estates* or *chattel real.* There are four types of leasehold estates, as illustrated in Figure 11.1 and described in the following list.

1. **Estate for years** *(tenancy for a fixed term)*. A leasehold that continues for a fixed time span. The term *estate for years* is misleading because the fixed time span can be for a day, a week, a month, a year, or years. Therefore, a signed lease for five years and a signed lease for one month are both estates for years. To eliminate this confusion, the term *estate for years* is beginning to be called a *tenancy for a fixed term.*

2. **Estate from period to period** *(periodic tenancy)*. A leasehold that continues from period to period (day, week, month, or

FIGURE 11.1

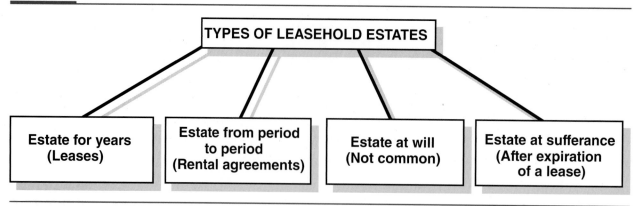

year) with no specified termination date. Each party agrees to renew or terminate at the end of each period. A month-to-month rental agreement is an example of an estate from period to period.

3. **Estate at will.** A leasehold that can be terminated without notice at any time by the lessor or the lessee. An estate at will has no definite termination date listed in the lease. The California legislature has passed laws stating that the lessor and the lessee must give advance notice prior to the termination of an estate at will. Today we would describe a tenancy where there is no agreement between a landlord and a tenant (someone moves into a property without permission and establishes residency) as an estate at will. An example of a tenancy at will would include a defaulting trustor (borrower) in possession following a nonjudicial foreclosure action. The lender (or successful bidder at the foreclosure sale), now the new owner of the property, would have to evict the former owner (trustor/borrower) who is still in possession. Since there is no agreement between the new and former owner, but the former owner is in possession and considered a tenant, this would be a tenancy at will.

4. **Estate at sufferance.** A leasehold where a lessee retains possession of the property after the expiration of a lease. For example, a lessee has a five-year lease that expired today. The lessor and the lessee have not decided on renewal terms. Under these circumstances, the lessee's estate for years is converted to an estate at sufferance until a decision is made about the future rights of the lessee. The landlord can enter into another lease agreement or ask the lessee to leave. After a period of time, an estate at sufferance may be considered a periodic (month-to-month) tenancy.

Requirements for a Valid Lease

For a lease to be valid, it must have the following characteristics:

1. Be in writing if the term is for more than one year. Any alterations must also be in writing.
2. Contain the names of the lessor and lessee.
3. Contain a sufficient description of the property. In some cases, a street address is sufficient for a simple residential lease. In other cases, it may be wise to include a complete legal description in addition to the common street address.
4. Show the amount of rent and the manner of payment. An example might be a rent of $60,000, payable $1,000 per month for five years.
5. State the duration or time period the lease is to run or, in the case of a periodic tenancy, the periods involved. *According to law, urban property cannot be leased for more than 99 years and rural agricultural land for more than 51 years.*
6. Be signed by the lessor. Technically a lessee does not need to sign the lease to make it valid. The lessee's possession of the property is considered to be acceptance of the agreement. However, to eliminate misunderstanding, a landlord should insist that the tenant sign the lease.
7. Have a lessor and a lessee who are legally able to contract.
8. Have any renewal or extension provisions in boldface type. A renewal or extension provision is a clause that automatically renews or extends the lease if the lessee remains in possession after expiration of the lease.

See Figure 11.2 for a sample residential rental agreement form.

Other Provisions

Although not legally required, a lease should also state who is responsible for utilities and maintenance. If there are special rules regarding noise, guests, parking, pets, and so on, they should be noted in the rental agreement. The intended use of the property should be specified, as well as the maximum number of tenant occupants per rental unit as allowed by law. A lease should also note the right, if any, the tenant may have to remove fixtures attached by him or her.

Security Deposits

On a residential rental, a security deposit cannot exceed more than two months' rent on unfurnished dwellings or three months' rent

FIGURE 11.2

CALIFORNIA
ASSOCIATION
OF REALTORS ®

RESIDENTIAL LEASE OR
MONTH-TO-MONTH RENTAL AGREEMENT
(C.A.R. Form LR, Revised 11/08)

Date _____, _____ ("Landlord") and
_____ ("Tenant") agree as follows:

1. PROPERTY:
    A. Landlord rents to Tenant and Tenant rents from Landlord, the real property and improvements described as: _____
    _____ ("Premises").
    B. The Premises are for the sole use as a personal residence by the following named person(s) **only:** _____
    _____.
    C. The following personal property, maintained pursuant to paragraph 11, is included: _____
    _____ or ☐ (if checked) the personal property on the attached addendum.

2. TERM: The term begins on (date) _____ ("Commencement Date"), **(Check A or B):**
    ☐ **A. Month-to-Month:** and continues as a month-to-month tenancy. Tenant may terminate the tenancy by giving written notice
         at least 30 days prior to the intended termination date. Landlord may terminate the tenancy by giving written notice as
         provided by law. Such notices may be given on any date.
    ☐ **B. Lease:** and shall terminate on (date) _____ at _____ ☐ AM/☐ PM.
         Tenant shall vacate the Premises upon termination of the Agreement, unless: **(i)** Landlord and Tenant have extended this
         agreement in writing or signed a new agreement; **(ii)** mandated by local rent control law; or **(iii)** Landlord accepts Rent from
         Tenant (other than past due Rent), in which case a month-to-month tenancy shall be created which either party may
         terminate as specified in paragraph 2A. Rent shall be at a rate agreed to by Landlord and Tenant, or as allowed by law. All
         other terms and conditions of this Agreement shall remain in full force and effect.

3. RENT: "Rent" shall mean all monetary obligations of Tenant to Landlord under the terms of the Agreement, except security deposit.
    A. Tenant agrees to pay $ _____ per month for the term of the Agreement.
    B. Rent is payable in advance on the **1st (or ☐ _____) day** of each calendar month, and is delinquent on the next day.
    C. If Commencement Date falls on any day other than the day Rent is payable under paragraph 3B, and Tenant has paid one full
         month's Rent in advance of Commencement Date, Rent for the second calendar month shall be prorated based on a 30-day
         period.
    D. **PAYMENT:** Rent shall be paid by ☐ personal check, ☐ money order, ☐ cashier's check, or ☐ other _____,
         to (name) _____ (phone) _____ at (address)
         _____, (or at any other location
         subsequently specified by Landlord in writing to Tenant) (and ☐ if checked, rent may be paid personally, between the hours of
         _____ and _____ on the following days _____). If any payment is
         returned for non-sufficient funds ("NSF") or because tenant stops payment, then, after that: (i) Landlord may, in writing, require
         Tenant to pay Rent in cash for three months and (ii) all future Rent shall be paid by ☐ money order, or ☐ cashier's check.

4. SECURITY DEPOSIT:
    A. Tenant agrees to pay $ _____ as a security deposit. Security deposit will be
         ☐ transferred to and held by the Owner of the Premises, or ☐ held in Owner's Broker's trust account.
    B. All or any portion of the security deposit may be used, as reasonably necessary, to: **(i)** cure Tenant's default in payment of Rent (which
         includes Late Charges, NSF fees or other sums due); **(ii)** repair damage, excluding ordinary wear and tear, caused by Tenant or by a
         guest or licensee of Tenant; **(iii)** clean Premises, if necessary, upon termination of the tenancy; and **(iv)** replace or return personal
         property or appurtenances. **SECURITY DEPOSIT SHALL NOT BE USED BY TENANT IN LIEU OF PAYMENT OF LAST
         MONTH'S RENT.** If all or any portion of the security deposit is used during the tenancy, Tenant agrees to reinstate the total security
         deposit within five days after written notice is delivered to Tenant. Within 21 days after Tenant vacates the Premises, Landlord shall:
         (1) furnish Tenant an itemized statement indicating the amount of any security deposit received and the basis for its
         disposition and supporting documentation as required by California Civil Code § 1950.5(g); and **(2)** return any remaining
         portion of the security deposit to Tenant.
    C. Security deposit will not be returned until all Tenants have vacated the Premises and all keys returned. Any security
         deposit returned by check shall be made out to all Tenants named on this Agreement, or as subsequently modified.
    D. No interest will be paid on security deposit unless required by local law.
    E. If the security deposit is held by Owner, Tenant agrees not to hold Broker responsible for its return. If the security deposit is held
         in Owner's Broker's trust account, **and** Broker's authority is terminated before expiration of this Agreement, **and** security deposit
         is released to someone other than Tenant, **then** Broker shall notify Tenant, in writing, where and to whom security deposit has
         been released. Once Tenant has been provided such notice, Tenant agrees not to hold Broker responsible for the security
         deposit.

5. MOVE-IN COSTS RECEIVED/DUE: Move-in funds made payable to _____
    shall be paid by ☐ personal check, ☐ money order, or ☐ cashier's check.

Category	Total Due	Payment Received	Balance Due	Date Due
Rent from _____ to _____ (date)				
*Security Deposit				
Other _____				
Other _____				
Total				

*The maximum amount Landlord may receive as security deposit, however designated, cannot exceed two months' Rent for
unfurnished premises, or three months' Rent for furnished premises.

LR REVISED 11/08 (PAGE 1 OF 6) Print Date

Tenant's Initials (_____)(_____)
Landlord's Initials (_____)(_____)

Reviewed by _____ Date _____

EQUAL HOUSING
OPPORTUNITY

RESIDENTIAL LEASE OR MONTH-TO-MONTH RENTAL AGREEMENT (LR PAGE 1 OF 6)

FIGURE 11.2 (*continued*)

Premises: _____ Date: _____

6. **LATE CHARGE; RETURNED CHECKS:**
   A. Tenant acknowledges either late payment of Rent or issuance of a returned check may cause Landlord to incur costs and expenses, the exact amounts of which are extremely difficult and impractical to determine. These costs may include, but are not limited to, processing, enforcement and accounting expenses, and late charges imposed on Landlord. If any installment of Rent due from Tenant is not received by Landlord within **5 (or ☐ _____) calendar days** after the date due, or if a check is returned, Tenant shall pay to Landlord, respectively, an additional sum of $ _____ or _____% of the Rent due as a Late Charge and $25.00 as a NSF fee for the first returned check and $35.00 as a NSF fee for each additional returned check, either or both of which shall be deemed additional Rent.
   B. Landlord and Tenant agree that these charges represent a fair and reasonable estimate of the costs Landlord may incur by reason of Tenant's late or NSF payment. Any Late Charge or NSF fee due shall be paid with the current installment of Rent. Landlord's acceptance of any Late Charge or NSF fee shall not constitute a waiver as to any default of Tenant. Landlord's right to collect a Late Charge or NSF fee shall not be deemed an extension of the date Rent is due under paragraph 3 or prevent Landlord from exercising any other rights and remedies under this Agreement and as provided by law.

7. **PARKING: (Check A or B)**
   ☐ **A.** Parking is permitted as follows: _____
   _____.
   The right to parking ☐ is ☐ is not included in the Rent charged pursuant to paragraph 3. If not included in the Rent, the parking rental fee shall be an additional $ _____ per month. Parking space(s) are to be used for parking properly licensed and operable motor vehicles, except for trailers, boats, campers, buses or trucks (other than pick-up trucks). Tenant shall park in assigned space(s) only. Parking space(s) are to be kept clean. Vehicles leaking oil, gas or other motor vehicle fluids shall not be parked on the Premises. Mechanical work or storage of inoperable vehicles is not permitted in parking space(s) or elsewhere on the Premises.
   OR ☐ **B.** Parking is not permitted on the Premises.

8. **STORAGE: (Check A or B)**
   ☐ **A.** Storage is permitted as follows: _____
   The right to storage space ☐ is, ☐ is not, included in the Rent charged pursuant to paragraph 3. If not included in the Rent, storage space fee shall be an additional $ _____ per month. Tenant shall store only personal property Tenant owns, and shall not store property claimed by another or in which another has any right, title or interest. Tenant shall not store any improperly packaged food or perishable goods, flammable materials, explosives, hazardous waste or other inherently dangerous material, or illegal substances.
   OR ☐ **B.** Storage is not permitted on the Premises.

9. **UTILITIES:** Tenant agrees to pay for all utilities and services, and the following charges: _____
   except _____, which shall be paid for by Landlord. If any utilities are not separately metered, Tenant shall pay Tenant's proportional share, as reasonably determined and directed by Landlord. If utilities are separately metered, Tenant shall place utilities in Tenant's name as of the Commencement Date. Landlord is only responsible for installing and maintaining one usable telephone jack and one telephone line to the Premises. Tenant shall pay any cost for conversion from existing utilities service provider.

10. **CONDITION OF PREMISES:** Tenant has examined Premises and, if any, all furniture, furnishings, appliances, landscaping and fixtures, including smoke detector(s).
    (Check all that apply:)
    ☐ **A.** Tenant acknowledges these items are clean and in operable condition, with the following exceptions: _____
    _____.
    ☐ **B.** Tenant's acknowledgment of the condition of these items is contained in an attached statement of condition (C.A.R. Form MIMO).
    ☐ **C.** Tenant will provide Landlord a list of items that are damaged or not in operable condition within **3 (or ☐ _____) days** after Commencement Date, not as a contingency of this Agreement but rather as an acknowledgment of the condition of the Premises.
    ☐ **D.** Other: _____.

11. **MAINTENANCE:**
    A. Tenant shall properly use, operate and safeguard Premises, including if applicable, any landscaping, furniture, furnishings and appliances, and all mechanical, electrical, gas and plumbing fixtures, and keep them and the Premises clean, sanitary and well ventilated. Tenant shall be responsible for checking and maintaining all smoke detectors and any additional phone lines beyond the one line and jack that Landlord shall provide and maintain. Tenant shall immediately notify Landlord, in writing, of any problem, malfunction or damage. Tenant shall be charged for all repairs or replacements caused by Tenant, pets, guests or licensees of Tenant, excluding ordinary wear and tear. Tenant shall be charged for all damage to Premises as a result of failure to report a problem in a timely manner. Tenant shall be charged for repair of drain blockages or stoppages, unless caused by defective plumbing parts or tree roots invading sewer lines.
    B. ☐ Landlord ☐ Tenant shall water the garden, landscaping, trees and shrubs, except: _____
    _____.
    C. ☐ Landlord ☐ Tenant shall maintain the garden, landscaping, trees and shrubs, except: _____
    _____.
    D. ☐ Landlord ☐ Tenant shall maintain _____.
    E. Tenant's failure to maintain any item for which Tenant is responsible shall give Landlord the right to hire someone to perform such maintenance and charge Tenant to cover the cost of such maintenance.
    F. The following items of personal property are included in the Premises without warranty and Landlord will not maintain, repair or replace them: _____.

Tenant's Initials (_____)(_____)
Landlord's Initials (_____)(_____)

Reviewed by _____ Date _____

EQUAL HOUSING OPPORTUNITY

LR REVISED 11/08 (PAGE 2 OF 6)

RESIDENTIAL LEASE OR MONTH-TO-MONTH RENTAL AGREEMENT (LR PAGE 2 OF 6)

FIGURE 11.2 *(continued)*

Premises: _____ Date: _____

12. **NEIGHBORHOOD CONDITIONS:** Tenant is advised to satisfy him or herself as to neighborhood or area conditions, including schools, proximity and adequacy of law enforcement, crime statistics, proximity of registered felons or offenders, fire protection, other governmental services, availability, adequacy and cost of any wired, wireless internet connections or other telecommunications or other technology services and installations, proximity to commercial, industrial or agricultural activities, existing and proposed transportation, construction and development that may affect noise, view, or traffic, airport noise, noise or odor from any source, wild and domestic animals, other nuisances, hazards, or circumstances, cemeteries, facilities and condition of common areas, conditions and influences of significance to certain cultures and/or religions, and personal needs, requirements and preferences of Tenant.

13. **PETS:** Unless otherwise provided in California Civil Code § 54.2, no animal or pet shall be kept on or about the Premises without Landlord's prior written consent, except: _____.

14. ☐ (If checked) **NO SMOKING:** No smoking is allowed on the Premises. If smoking does occur on the Premises, **(i)** Tenant is responsible for all damage caused by the smoking including, but not limited to, stains, burns, odors and removal of debris; **(ii)** Tenant is in breach of this Agreement; **(iii)** Tenant, Authorized Guests, and all others may be required to leave the Premises; and **(iv)** Tenant acknowledges that in order to remove odor caused by smoking, Landlord may need to replace carpet and drapes and paint entire premises regardless of when these items were last cleaned or replaced. Such actions and other necessary steps will impact the return of any security deposit.

15. **RULES/REGULATIONS:**
    A. Tenant agrees to comply with all Landlord rules and regulations that are at any time posted on the Premises or delivered to Tenant. Tenant shall not, and shall ensure that guests and licensees of Tenant shall not, disturb, annoy, endanger or interfere with other tenants of the building or neighbors, or use the Premises for any unlawful purposes, including, but not limited to, using, manufacturing, selling, storing or transporting illicit drugs or other contraband, or violate any law or ordinance, or commit a waste or nuisance on or about the Premises.
    B. **(If applicable, check one)**
       ☐ 1. Landlord shall provide Tenant with a copy of the rules and regulations within _____ days
          or _____.
       OR ☐ 2. Tenant has been provided with, and acknowledges receipt of, a copy of the rules and regulations.

16. ☐ (If checked) **CONDOMINIUM; PLANNED UNIT DEVELOPMENT:**
    A. The Premises is a unit in a condominium, planned unit development, common interest subdivision or other development governed by a homeowners' association ("HOA"). The name of the HOA is _____. Tenant agrees to comply with all HOA covenants, conditions and restrictions, bylaws, rules and regulations and decisions. Landlord shall provide Tenant copies of rules and regulations, if any. Tenant shall reimburse Landlord for any fines or charges imposed by HOA or other authorities, due to any violation by Tenant, or the guests or licensees of Tenant.
    B. **(Check one)**
       ☐ 1. Landlord shall provide Tenant with a copy of the HOA rules and regulations within _____ days
          or _____.
       OR ☐ 2. Tenant has been provided with, and acknowledges receipt of, a copy of the HOA rules and regulations.

17. **ALTERATIONS; REPAIRS:** Unless otherwise specified by law or paragraph 29C, without Landlord's prior written consent, **(i)** Tenant shall not make any repairs, alterations or improvements in or about the Premises including: painting, wallpapering, adding or changing locks, installing antenna or satellite dish(es), placing signs, displays or exhibits, or using screws, fastening devices, large nails or adhesive materials; **(ii)** Landlord shall not be responsible for the costs of alterations or repairs made by Tenant; **(iii)** Tenant shall not deduct from Rent the costs of any repairs, alterations or improvements; and **(iv)** any deduction made by Tenant shall be considered unpaid Rent.

18. **KEYS; LOCKS:**
    A. Tenant acknowledges receipt of (or Tenant will receive ☐ prior to the Commencement Date, or ☐ _____):
       ☐ _____ key(s) to Premises,   ☐ _____ remote control device(s) for garage door/gate opener(s),
       ☐ _____ key(s) to mailbox,   ☐ _____
       ☐ _____ key(s) to common area(s),   ☐ _____.
    B. Tenant acknowledges that locks to the Premises ☐ have, ☐ have not, been re-keyed.
    C. If Tenant re-keys existing locks or opening devices, Tenant shall immediately deliver copies of all keys to Landlord. Tenant shall pay all costs and charges related to loss of any keys or opening devices. Tenant may not remove locks, even if installed by Tenant.

19. **ENTRY:**
    A. Tenant shall make Premises available to Landlord or Landlord's representative for the purpose of entering to make necessary or agreed repairs, decorations, alterations, or improvements, or to supply necessary or agreed services, or to show Premises to prospective or actual purchasers, tenants, mortgagees, lenders, appraisers, or contractors.
    B. Landlord and Tenant agree that 24-hour written notice shall be reasonable and sufficient notice, except as follows. 48-hour written notice is required to conduct an inspection of the Premises prior to the Tenant moving out, unless the Tenant waives the right to such notice. Notice may be given orally to show the Premises to actual or prospective purchasers provided Tenant has been notified in writing within 120 days preceding the oral notice that the Premises are for sale and that oral notice may be given to show the Premises. No notice is required: **(i)** to enter in case of an emergency; **(ii)** if the Tenant is present and consents at the time of entry or **(iii)** if the Tenant has abandoned or surrendered the Premises. No written notice is required if Landlord and Tenant orally agree to an entry for agreed services or repairs if the date and time of entry are within one week of the oral agreement.
    C. ☐ (If checked) Tenant authorizes the use of a keysafe/lockbox to allow entry into the Premises and agrees to sign a keysafe/lockbox addendum (C.A.R. Form KLA).

20. **SIGNS:** Tenant authorizes Landlord to place FOR SALE/LEASE signs on the Premises.

21. **ASSIGNMENT; SUBLETTING:** Tenant shall not sublet all or any part of Premises, or assign or transfer this Agreement or any interest in it, without Landlord's prior written consent. Unless such consent is obtained, any assignment, transfer or subletting of Premises or this Agreement or tenancy, by voluntary act of Tenant, operation of law or otherwise, shall, at the option of Landlord,

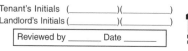

Tenant's Initials (_____)(_____)
Landlord's Initials (_____)(_____)

| Reviewed by _____ Date _____ |

EQUAL HOUSING
OPPORTUNITY

RESIDENTIAL LEASE OR MONTH-TO-MONTH RENTAL AGREEMENT (LR PAGE 3 OF 6)

FIGURE 11.2 *(continued)*

Premises: _____   Date: _____

terminate this Agreement. Any proposed assignee, transferee or sublessee shall submit to Landlord an application and credit information for Landlord's approval and, if approved, sign a separate written agreement with Landlord and Tenant. Landlord's consent to any one assignment, transfer or sublease, shall not be construed as consent to any subsequent assignment, transfer or sublease and does not release Tenant of Tenant's obligations under this Agreement.

22. **JOINT AND INDIVIDUAL OBLIGATIONS:** If there is more than one Tenant, each one shall be individually and completely responsible for the performance of all obligations of Tenant under this Agreement, jointly with every other Tenant, and individually, whether or not in possession.

23. ☐ **LEAD-BASED PAINT (If checked):** Premises was constructed prior to 1978. In accordance with federal law, Landlord gives and Tenant acknowledges receipt of the disclosures on the attached form (C.A.R. Form FLD) and a federally approved lead pamphlet.

24. ☐ **MILITARY ORDNANCE DISCLOSURE:** (If applicable and known to Landlord) Premises is located within one mile of an area once used for military training, and may contain potentially explosive munitions.

25. ☐ **PERIODIC PEST CONTROL:** Landlord has entered into a contract for periodic pest control treatment of the Premises and shall give Tenant a copy of the notice originally given to Landlord by the pest control company.

26. ☐ **METHAMPHETAMINE CONTAMINATION:** Prior to signing this Agreement, Landlord has given Tenant a notice that a health official has issued an order prohibiting occupancy of the property because of methamphetamine contamination. A copy of the notice and order are attached.

27. **MEGAN'S LAW DATABASE DISCLOSURE:** Notice: Pursuant to Section 290.46 of the Penal Code, information about specified registered sex offenders is made available to the public via an Internet Web site maintained by the Department of Justice at www.meganslaw.ca.gov. Depending on an offender's criminal history, this information will include either the address at which the offender resides or the community of residence and ZIP Code in which he or she resides. (Neither Landlord nor Brokers, if any, are required to check this website. If Tenant wants further information, Tenant should obtain information directly from this website.)

28. **POSSESSION:**
    A. Tenant is not in possession of the premises. If Landlord is unable to deliver possession of Premises on Commencement Date, such Date shall be extended to the date on which possession is made available to Tenant. If Landlord is unable to deliver possession within **5 (or ☐ _____) calendar days** after agreed Commencement Date, Tenant may terminate this Agreement by giving written notice to Landlord, and shall be refunded all Rent and security deposit paid. Possession is deemed terminated when Tenant has returned all keys to the Premises to Landlord.
    B. ☐ Tenant is already in possession of the Premises.

29. **TENANT'S OBLIGATIONS UPON VACATING PREMISES:**
    A. Upon termination of this Agreement, Tenant shall: **(i)** give Landlord all copies of all keys or opening devices to Premises, including any common areas; **(ii)** vacate and surrender Premises to Landlord, empty of all persons; **(iii)** vacate any/all parking and/or storage space; **(iv)** clean and deliver Premises, as specified in paragraph C below, to Landlord in the same condition as referenced in paragraph 10; **(v)** remove all debris; **(vi)** give written notice to Landlord of Tenant's forwarding address; and **(vii)** _____
    B. All alterations/improvements made by or caused to be made by Tenant, with or without Landlord's consent, become the property of Landlord upon termination. Landlord may charge Tenant for restoration of the Premises to the condition it was in prior to any alterations/improvements.
    C. **Right to Pre-Move-Out Inspection and Repairs: (i)** After giving or receiving notice of termination of a tenancy (C.A.R. Form NTT), or before the end of a lease, Tenant has the right to request that an inspection of the Premises take place prior to termination of the lease or rental (C.A.R. Form NRI). If Tenant requests such an inspection, Tenant shall be given an opportunity to remedy identified deficiencies prior to termination, consistent with the terms of this Agreement. **(ii)** Any repairs or alterations made to the Premises as a result of this inspection (collectively, "Repairs") shall be made at Tenant's expense. Repairs may be performed by Tenant or through others, who have adequate insurance and licenses and are approved by Landlord. The work shall comply with applicable law, including governmental permit, inspection and approval requirements. Repairs shall be performed in a good, skillful manner with materials of quality and appearance comparable to existing materials. It is understood that exact restoration of appearance or cosmetic items following all Repairs may not be possible. **(iii)** Tenant shall: **(a)** obtain receipts for Repairs performed by others; **(b)** prepare a written statement indicating the Repairs performed by Tenant and the date of such Repairs; and **(c)** provide copies of receipts and statements to Landlord prior to termination. Paragraph 29C does not apply when the tenancy is terminated pursuant to California Code of Civil Procedure § 1161(2), (3) or (4).

30. **BREACH OF CONTRACT; EARLY TERMINATION:** In addition to any obligations established by paragraph 29, in the event of termination by Tenant prior to completion of the original term of the Agreement, Tenant shall also be responsible for lost Rent, rental commissions, advertising expenses and painting costs necessary to ready Premises for re-rental. Landlord may withhold any such amounts from Tenant's security deposit.

31. **TEMPORARY RELOCATION:** Subject to local law, Tenant agrees, upon demand of Landlord, to temporarily vacate Premises for a reasonable period, to allow for fumigation (or other methods) to control wood destroying pests or organisms, or other repairs to Premises. Tenant agrees to comply with all instructions and requirements necessary to prepare Premises to accommodate pest control, fumigation or other work, including bagging or storage of food and medicine, and removal of perishables and valuables. Tenant shall only be entitled to a credit of Rent equal to the per diem Rent for the period of time Tenant is required to vacate Premises.

32. **DAMAGE TO PREMISES:** If, by no fault of Tenant, Premises are totally or partially damaged or destroyed by fire, earthquake, accident or other casualty that render Premises totally or partially uninhabitable, either Landlord or Tenant may terminate this Agreement by giving the other written notice. Rent shall be abated as of the date Premises become totally or partially uninhabitable. The abated amount shall be the current monthly Rent prorated on a 30-day period. If the Agreement is not terminated, Landlord shall promptly repair the damage, and Rent shall be reduced based on the extent to which the damage interferes with Tenant's reasonable use of Premises. If damage occurs as a result of an act of Tenant or Tenant's guests, only Landlord shall have the right of termination, and no reduction in Rent shall be made.

33. **INSURANCE:** Tenant's or guest's personal property and vehicles are not insured by Landlord, manager or, if applicable, HOA, against loss or damage due to fire, theft, vandalism, rain, water, criminal or negligent acts of others, or any other cause. **Tenant**

Tenant's Initials (_____)(_____)
Landlord's Initials (_____)(_____)

Reviewed by _____ Date _____

LR REVISED 11/08 (PAGE 4 OF 6)

RESIDENTIAL LEASE OR MONTH-TO-MONTH RENTAL AGREEMENT (LR PAGE 4 OF 6)

FIGURE 11.2 (*continued*)

Premises: _____ Date: _____

is advised to carry Tenant's own insurance (renter's insurance) to protect Tenant from any such loss or damage. Tenant shall comply with any requirement imposed on Tenant by Landlord's insurer to avoid: **(i)** an increase in Landlord's insurance premium (or Tenant shall pay for the increase in premium); or **(ii)** loss of insurance.

34. **WATERBEDS:** Tenant shall not use or have waterbeds on the Premises unless: **(i)** Tenant obtains a valid waterbed insurance policy; **(ii)** Tenant increases the security deposit in an amount equal to one-half of one month's Rent; and **(iii)** the bed conforms to the floor load capacity of Premises.

35. **WAIVER:** The waiver of any breach shall not be construed as a continuing waiver of the same or any subsequent breach.

36. **NOTICE:** Notices may be served at the following address, or at any other location subsequently designated:
Landlord: _____   Tenant: _____
_____   _____
_____   _____

37. **TENANT ESTOPPEL CERTIFICATE:** Tenant shall execute and return a tenant estoppel certificate delivered to Tenant by Landlord or Landlord's agent within 3 days after its receipt. Failure to comply with this requirement shall be deemed Tenant's acknowledgment that the tenant estoppel certificate is true and correct, and may be relied upon by a lender or purchaser.

38. **TENANT REPRESENTATIONS; CREDIT:** Tenant warrants that all statements in Tenant's rental application are accurate. Tenant authorizes Landlord and Broker(s) to obtain Tenant's credit report periodically during the tenancy in connection with the modification or enforcement of this Agreement. Landlord may cancel this Agreement: **(i)** before occupancy begins; **(ii)** upon disapproval of the credit report(s); or **(iii)** at any time, upon discovering that information in Tenant's application is false. A negative credit report reflecting on Tenant's record may be submitted to a credit reporting agency if Tenant fails to fulfill the terms of payment and other obligations under this Agreement.

39. **MEDIATION:**
    A. Consistent with paragraphs B and C below, Landlord and Tenant agree to mediate any dispute or claim arising between them out of this Agreement, or any resulting transaction, before resorting to court action. Mediation fees, if any, shall be divided equally among the parties involved. If, for any dispute or claim to which this paragraph applies, any party commences an action without first attempting to resolve the matter through mediation, or refuses to mediate after a request has been made, then that party shall not be entitled to recover attorney fees, even if they would otherwise be available to that party in any such action.
    B. The following matters are excluded from mediation: **(i)** an unlawful detainer action; **(ii)** the filing or enforcement of a mechanic's lien; and **(iii)** any matter within the jurisdiction of a probate, small claims or bankruptcy court. The filing of a court action to enable the recording of a notice of pending action, for order of attachment, receivership, injunction, or other provisional remedies, shall not constitute a waiver of the mediation provision.
    C. Landlord and Tenant agree to mediate disputes or claims involving Listing Agent, Leasing Agent or property manager ("Broker"), provided Broker shall have agreed to such mediation prior to, or within a reasonable time after, the dispute or claim is presented to such Broker. Any election by Broker to participate in mediation shall not result in Broker being deemed a party to this Agreement.

40. **ATTORNEY FEES:** In any action or proceeding arising out of this Agreement, the prevailing party between Landlord and Tenant shall be entitled to reasonable attorney fees and costs, except as provided in paragraph 39A.

41. **C.A.R. FORM:** C.A.R. Form means the specific form referenced or another comparable from agreed to by the parties.

42. **OTHER TERMS AND CONDITIONS;SUPPLEMENTS:** ☐ Interpreter/Translator Agreement (C.A.R. Form ITA);
    ☐ Keysafe/Lockbox Addendum (C.A.R. Form KLA); ☐ Lead-Based Paint and Lead-Based Paint Hazards Disclosure (C.A.R. Form FLD)
    _____
    _____
    The following ATTACHED supplements are incorporated in this Agreement: _____
    _____
    _____

43. **TIME OF ESSENCE; ENTIRE CONTRACT; CHANGES:** Time is of the essence. All understandings between the parties are incorporated in this Agreement. Its terms are intended by the parties as a final, complete and exclusive expression of their Agreement with respect to its subject matter, and may not be contradicted by evidence of any prior agreement or contemporaneous oral agreement. If any provision of this Agreement is held to be ineffective or invalid, the remaining provisions will nevertheless be given full force and effect. Neither this Agreement nor any provision in it may be extended, amended, modified, altered or changed except in writing. This Agreement is subject to California landlord-tenant law and shall incorporate all changes required by amendment or successors to such law. This Agreement and any supplement, addendum or modification, including any copy, may be signed in two or more counterparts, all of which shall constitute one and the same writing.

44. **AGENCY:**
    A. **CONFIRMATION:** The following agency relationship(s) are hereby confirmed for this transaction:
    Listing Agent: (Print firm name) _____ is the agent of
    (check one): ☐ the Landlord exclusively; or ☐ both the Landlord and Tenant.
    Leasing Agent: (Print firm name) _____ (if not same as Listing
    Agent) is the agent of (check one): ☐ the Tenant exclusively; or ☐ the Landlord exclusively; or ☐ both the Tenant and Landlord.
    B. **DISCLOSURE:** ☐ (If checked): The term of this lease exceeds one year. A disclosure regarding real estate agency relationships (C.A.R. Form AD) has been provided to Landlord and Tenant, who each acknowledge its receipt.

45. ☐ **TENANT COMPENSATION TO BROKER:** Upon execution of this Agreement, Tenant agrees to pay compensation to Broker as specified in a separate written agreement between Tenant and Broker.

Tenant's Initials (_____)(_____)
Landlord's Initials (_____)(_____)

LR REVISED 11/08 (PAGE 5 OF 6)

Reviewed by _____ Date _____

RESIDENTIAL LEASE OR MONTH-TO-MONTH RENTAL AGREEMENT (LR PAGE 5 OF 6)

FIGURE 11.2 *(continued)*

Premises: _____ Date: _____

46. ☐ **INTERPRETER/TRANSLATOR:** The terms of this Agreement have been interpreted for Tenant into the following language: _____. Landlord and Tenant acknowledge receipt of the attached interpretor/translator agreement (C.A.R. Form ITA).

47. **FOREIGN LANGUAGE NEGOTIATION:** If this Agreement has been negotiated by Landlord and Tenant primarily in Spanish, Chinese, Tagalog, Korean or Vietnamese, pursuant to the California Civil Code, Tenant shall be provided a translation of this Agreement in the language used for the negotiation.

48. **OWNER COMPENSATION TO BROKER:** Upon execution of this Agreement, Owner agrees to pay compensation to Broker as specified in a separate written agreement between Owner and Broker (C.A.R. Form LCA).

49. **RECEIPT**: If specified in paragraph 5, Landlord or Broker, acknowledges receipt of move-in funds.

> Landlord and Tenant acknowledge and agree Brokers: **(a)** do not guarantee the condition of the Premises; **(b)** cannot verify representations made by others; **(c)** cannot provide legal or tax advice; **(d)** will not provide other advice or information that exceeds the knowledge, education or experience required to obtain a real estate license. Furthermore, if Brokers are not also acting as Landlord in this Agreement, Brokers: **(e)** do not decide what rental rate a Tenant should pay or Landlord should accept; and **(f)** do not decide upon the length or other terms of tenancy. Landlord and Tenant agree that they will seek legal, tax, insurance and other desired assistance from appropriate professionals.

Tenant agrees to rent the Premises on the above terms and conditions.

Tenant _____ Date _____
Address _____ City _____ State _____ Zip _____
Telephone _____ Fax _____ E-mail_____
Tenant _____ Date _____
Address _____ City _____ State _____ Zip _____
Telephone _____ Fax _____ E-mail_____

☐ **GUARANTEE:** In consideration of the execution of this Agreement by and between Landlord and Tenant and for valuable consideration, receipt of which is hereby acknowledged, the undersigned ("Guarantor") does hereby: **(i)** guarantee unconditionally to Landlord and Landlord's agents, successors and assigns, the prompt payment of Rent or other sums that become due pursuant to this Agreement, including any and all court costs and attorney fees included in enforcing the Agreement; **(ii)** consent to any changes, modifications or alterations of any term in this Agreement agreed to by Landlord and Tenant; and **(iii)** waive any right to require Landlord and/or Landlord's agents to proceed against Tenant for any default occurring under this Agreement before seeking to enforce this Guarantee.

Guarantor (Print Name) _____
Guarantor _____ Date _____
Address _____ City _____ State _____ Zip _____
Telephone_____ Fax _____ E-mail_____

Landlord agrees to rent the Premises on the above terms and conditions.

Landlord _____ Landlord _____
Address _____
Telephone _____ Fax _____ E-mail_____

> **REAL ESTATE BROKERS:**
> **A.** Real estate brokers who are not also Landlord under this Agreement are not parties to the Agreement between Landlord and Tenant.
> **B.** Agency relationships are confirmed in paragraph 44.
> **C.** COOPERATING BROKER COMPENSATION: Listing Broker agrees to pay Cooperating Broker (Leasing Firm) and Cooperating Broker agrees to accept: **(i)** the amount specified in the MLS, provided Cooperating Broker is a Participant of the MLS in which the Property is offered for sale or a reciprocal MLS; or **(ii)** ☐ (if checked) the amount specified in a separate written agreement between Listing Broker and Cooperating Broker.

Real Estate Broker (Listing Firm) _____ DRE Lic. # _____
By (Agent) _____ DRE Lic. # _____ Date _____
Address _____ City _____ State _____ Zip _____
Telephone _____ Fax _____ E-mail_____

Real Estate Broker (Leasing Firm) _____ DRE Lic. # _____
By (Agent) _____ DRE Lic. # _____ Date _____
Address _____ City _____ State _____ Zip _____
Telephone _____ Fax _____ E-mail_____

Published and Distributed by:
REAL ESTATE BUSINESS SERVICES, INC.
a subsidiary of the California Association of REALTORS®
525 South Virgil Avenue, Los Angeles, California 90020

Reviewed by _____ Date _____   EQUAL HOUSING OPPORTUNITY

LR REVISED 11/08 (PAGE 6 OF 6)

RESIDENTIAL LEASE OR MONTH-TO-MONTH RENTAL AGREEMENT (LR PAGE 6 OF 6)

Source: Reprinted with permission of California Association of REALTORS®

on furnished units. The security deposit must be refunded within 21 days after the tenant vacates the property.

However, if properly worded, the security deposit can be used to offset back rent and damages caused by the tenant or to clean the premises left dirty by the tenant. If an offset is used, the landlord must provide the tenant with an itemized statement showing all charges within 21 days after the tenant vacates. *No security deposit can be labeled as nonrefundable.* The landlord is still allowed to collect the first month's rent in addition to the security deposit already noted.

Assignment Versus Sublease of the Lease

An assignment of a lease transfers the entire leasehold interest to another party, including the prime liability and responsibility to make payments to the lessor (landlord). Figure 11.3 illustrates an assignment of a lease.

Under an assignment, the original Lessee A is removed from the transaction and all rights and duties pass to Assignee B. Assignee B is now primarily liable for the lease.

A **sublease** transfers only a part of the term of the lessee to a sublessee. The original lessee is still liable to the lessor (landlord) for the terms and conditions of the lease. Figure 11.4 illustrates a sublease.

Sublessee B pays Lessee A, who pays the lessor. In essence, there are two contracts—the original lease between lessor and Lessee A and another contract between Lessee A and Sublessee B. Each contract stands alone. If Sublessee B does not pay Lessee A, Lessee A must still pay the lessor. In Figure 11.4, Lessee A is said to hold a **sandwich lease.** In other words, Lessee A is wedged between the lessor and the sublessee. A lessor can insert a clause in the lease, prohibiting any assignment or sublease without the prior written approval of the lessor.

FIGURE 11.3

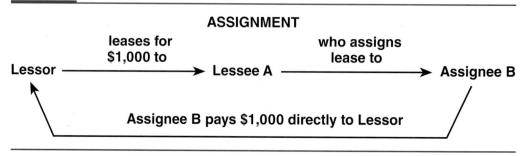

ASSIGNMENT

FIGURE 11.4

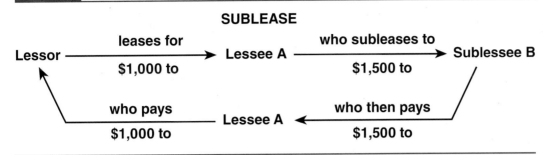

Lease with Option to Buy

Under a **lease with option to buy** (purchase), property is rented for a period of time, at the end of which the lessee is given the right to purchase per a set of agreed terms. The lessee (tenant/optionee) is not required to buy, but may if he or she wishes. If the lessee does exercise the option, the lessor/optionor must sell.

A lease with option to buy should not be confused with a concept known as *first right of refusal*. Under a first right of refusal, the lessor (landlord) is not required to sell. However, if the lessor does wish to sell, the lessee (tenant) is given the first chance to buy.

Major Types of Leases

1. **Gross lease.** The tenant pays a flat rental amount, and the landlord is responsible for taxes, maintenance, and insurance.
2. *Triple net lease.* The tenant pays rent; the tenant also pays the landlord's property taxes, hazard insurance, and maintenance (a helpful acronym is *TIM*).

   This type of lease is used when commercial property is leased on a long-term basis. It is also sometimes referred to as a **net lease.**
3. **Percentage lease.** Rent is based on a percentage of the tenant's gross sales—this type of lease often uses a combination flat rent plus a certain percentage of the tenant's gross sales. Usually, the higher the tenant's gross sales, the smaller the percentage; and the lower the tenant's sales volume, the higher the percentage.

Important Concepts

1. *Extension of a lease.* The continuation of an old lease is an *extension.* For example, an existing lease is about to expire, so the lessor and lessee agree to extend the lease for one year using the same terms and conditions.

2. *Renewal of a lease.* This occurs when the existing lessor and lessee renegotiate a new lease upon the expiration of the existing lease. The terms and conditions are frequently different from those of the old lease.

3. *Escalator clause.* This clause allows the landlord to increase the rent during the term of the lease if costs increase. It is frequently tied to the Consumer Price Index or Producer Price Index.

11.2 DUTIES AND RESPONSIBILITIES OF LANDLORDS AND TENANTS

Landlord's Duties and Rights

In exchange for rent, a landlord surrenders use and possession of the property to a tenant. Under this arrangement, a landlord owes the tenant certain duties and responsibilities, which include these:

1. If the property is residential, there is an *implied right of habitability.* The landlord, in essence, guarantees that the dwelling meets minimum housing and health codes.

2. Landlords have the right to inspect the property periodically, but they must give *advance notice.* Most lease agreements state that the landlord must give 24 or 48 hours' notice. In cases of emergency, to protect the property, a landlord is allowed to enter the premises without giving advance notice.

3. With residential property, a landlord is usually held liable for injuries resulting from unsafe conditions in common areas such as stairwells, hallways, and the surrounding grounds. If the defects or dangers are caused by tenant negligence, the liability for injuries may shift from the landlord to the tenant. On nonresidential structures, the liability for keeping the premises safe is frequently shifted from landlord to tenant via the use of triple net lease terms.

4. A landlord is not allowed to interfere with the tenant's use and quiet enjoyment of the property. If the tenant is abiding by the terms of the rental agreement, frequent and uncalled-for intrusions by a pesky landlord can be grounds for the tenant to cancel the rental agreement and possibly seek damages in court.

5. According to state and federal laws, a landlord cannot refuse to rent to a tenant based on (1) race, color, or national origin; (2) religion or creed; (3) sex, sexual orientation, or marital status and registered domestic partnership; and (4) physical handicap unless it can be proven that the building poses a danger to the handicapped person. Also, landlords cannot refuse to rent to

families with children; however, certain senior citizen housing projects are allowed to exclude children.

6. Under current law (as of January 2010), a landlord can terminate a month-to-month rental agreement by serving the tenant with a 60-day notice if the tenant has been in the property for over a year. If the tenant has occupied the property for less than a year, then the landlord can give the tenant a 30-day notice. The landlord does not need to give the tenant a reason, nor does the tenant need to be in violation of the terms of the rental agreement. However, if the tenant can prove that the landlord's actions are unfair based upon the antidiscriminatory laws noted above, the tenant can sue the landlord. Also, if a tenant has a signed lease for a specified duration (estate for years), a landlord cannot force the tenant (lessee) to leave unless the tenant violates the terms of the lease agreement. Note: if a landlord has entered into a Section 8 agreement with a local housing authority to provide housing for low- and moderate-income tenants, special rules apply that may be different from those noted above.

Tenant's Duties and Rights

A tenant owes a landlord certain duties and responsibilities. In turn, a tenant has certain rights. Tenant duties and rights are summarized as follows:

1. Tenants are expected to pay the rent when due and not to damage the property beyond normal wear and tear.

2. Tenants who have month-to-month rental agreements are required to give at least a 30-day notice (regardless of how long the tenant has occupied the property) before vacating the property. A landlord can sue for 30 days' rent if a tenant fails to give the landlord a 30-day notice before vacating.

3. Tenants can be held liable for injuries to guests or customers resulting from unsafe conditions caused by the tenant's negligence. Tenants should purchase their own renter's insurance policy to protect their valuables in case of fire, storm damage, and theft. Most renter's insurance policies also provide personal liability protection for the tenant.

4. Tenants have a duty not to interfere with the rights of other tenants.

5. A tenant has the right to use and enjoy the property. If the tenant is unreasonably bothered by the landlord or another person, the tenant has the right to abandon the property and pay no further rent. This process is called *constructive eviction*.

SPECIAL INTEREST TOPIC

Rent Controls

Rent control is a controversial topic, with emotions and misconceptions running rampant on both sides of the issue. From a purely economic point of view, rent controls make little sense. The issue has been studied repeatedly by liberal and conservative economists, and most agree that rent controls do not solve housing problems. Rents are high because demand for apartment housing is high and supply is inadequate. The solution is to decrease demand for rental units or increase supply.

Rent controls do neither. Rent controls artificially depress rent levels, which, in turn, stimulates demand instead of reducing demand. Rent controls reduce returns and yields on apartment investments, thereby discouraging the construction of new units or the conversion of large homes into apartments. In the long term, rent controls can actually cause landlords to defer needed maintenance, resulting in a property's deterioration. In short, rent controls tend to perpetuate the ill they are supposed to cure!

A danger accompanying long-term rent control is the departure of investors in rental property altogether. If investors are unable to make a reasonable return on any specific type of investment, they will abandon it as an investment vehicle. The result over time is likely to be an ever-decreasing number of available rental opportunities for tenants.

Never fully explored is the hostage-like situation that is established for tenants unwilling to move from their rent-controlled apartments. Artificially maintained low rents can create difficult decisions for tenants who may have to move to areas where market rents prevail even when such a move may be to their overall economic benefit.

Source: From *California Real Estate Finance*, 9th ed., by R. J. Bond, D. J. McKenzie, John Fesler, and Rick Boone (Cincinnati, OH: Cengage Learning, 2011).

6. In California, all residential rentals must meet minimum housing and health codes. The responsibility for meeting the codes rests with the landlord. If the property falls below standards because of damage or negligence caused by the tenant, the landlord can bring legal action against the tenant. On the other hand, if, through no fault of the tenant, the dwelling falls below housing codes, the tenant can demand that the landlord make the needed repairs. If the landlord refuses, the tenant can abandon the property and not

be liable for future rent. The tenant may elect to use a rental offset procedure outlined in the California Civil Code.

Rental Offset

If a residential landlord refuses to make needed repairs, Section 1942 of the Civil Code allows a tenant to spend up to one month's rent to make the repairs. The paid repair bill can then be used to offset the next month's rent. The basic rules are as follows:

1. The tenant must give the landlord written notice and adequate time to make the repairs.

2. If the landlord refuses, the tenant can spend up to one month's rent on the repairs, then deduct the cost of repairs from the following month's rent.

3. A tenant can use a rental offset only twice in any 12-month period and can use it only for needed repairs, not decorative changes. In most cases, a tenant cannot charge for his or her own labor, only for repair parts. However, if a tradesperson makes the repairs, both parts and labor can be used for the offset. If a tenant spends more than one month's rent, the excess cannot be applied against subsequent rental payments.

Current law prohibits a landlord from taking retaliatory action, such as serving an eviction notice or raising the rent, for a period of 180 days after the tenant's use of the rental offset.

Rental Payments to Neutral Escrow

In some instances, needed repairs may exceed one month's rent and a tenant may be reluctant to use the limited offset provisions noted earlier. Under these circumstances, a tenant may be able to make rental payments to a neutral escrow, with instructions to deliver the rents to the landlord after the property has been brought up to minimum housing standards. *Caution: This is a controversial legal concept and should not be exercised without the advice of an attorney.*

11.3 EVICTIONS AND OTHER WAYS TO TERMINATE RENTAL AGREEMENTS

Eviction occurs when a tenant is dispossessed by operation of law. The eviction process is a legal procedure in court. Landlords cannot resort to "self-help" actions such as changing the locks, shutting off utility services, seizing the tenant's property in lieu of rent, or threatening the tenants with bodily harm. If a landlord commits an illegal act, such as the ones noted previously, the tenant can sue the landlord under the aforementioned theory known as *constructive eviction*.

Unlawful Detainer Action

The process of legally removing a tenant from possession involves a series of steps.

1. Landlord serves the tenant with a three-day or 30-day notice, depending on the circumstances.
2. If the tenant fails to abide by the notice, the landlord files an unlawful detainer action in court.
3. If the landlord wins, the court awards the landlord a judgment. The landlord then asks for a writ of possession authorizing the sheriff to evict the tenant.
4. The sheriff sends the tenant an eviction notice; if the tenant fails to leave, the sheriff physically removes the tenant.

Three-Day Notice Versus 30 or 60-Day Notice

A tenant is served a three-day notice when the tenant has defaulted on rent or has violated other terms of the rental agreement.

A 30-day notice is served when the tenant has not violated the rental agreement, but the landlord wants the tenant to leave. If the tenant has a fixed-term lease (estate for years), a landlord cannot serve a notice unless the terms of the lease have been violated by the lessee. The exception is serving notice to the lessee that the lease will not be renewed upon expiration.

Serving Notice

The procedure for serving notice can be summarized as follows:

1. The notice must be personally delivered to the tenant(s).

   OR

2. If the tenant(s) is absent, a copy should be left with someone of suitable age (typically 18 years old or older), then a copy must be mailed to the tenant(s) at place of residence.

   OR

3. If no one is home, a copy may be affixed in a conspicuous place on the property, then a copy must be mailed to the tenant(s).

Slipping the notice under the door or putting it in the mailbox is not sufficient delivery. Also, it is a good idea to have the notice served by someone other than the landlord. If a sheriff, marshal, or constable serves the notice, it will have the maximum impression on the tenant(s).

Superior Court[*]

Landlords bring unlawful detainer actions in superior court. In superior court, these actions have a priority on the court's calendar, and an early hearing is usually granted. An attorney generally is needed for a superior court action, and this helps assure the landlord that legal procedures will be correctly followed. This is important if a landlord or tenant appeals to a higher court. Unlawful detainer actions can no longer be heard in small claims court.

Sheriff Evicts the Tenant

After a writ of possession has been granted to the landlord, the sheriff sends the tenant an eviction notice. After approximately five days, if the tenant has not left, the sheriff physically removes the tenant, but not the tenant's possessions. The tenant's possessions are impounded according to the lien laws.

Delays and Appeals

With an increasing awareness of tenants' rights, many tenant action groups have effectively designed delay and appeal processes that can extend an unlawful detainer action for many months. This dramatically increases the landlord's costs, in both attorney time and lost rents. From the landlord's point of view, the best protection is to make sure that a lawful, careful screening takes place before a tenant moves in. Once an unethical tenant moves in, it can become very expensive to have the tenant removed.

Termination of Lease

Few leases or rental agreements are ever terminated because of eviction. Most leases are terminated for the following reasons:

1. *Expiration of time.* The time period for the lease is up, and new terms are not negotiated.
2. *Mutual consent.* The lessor and lessee agree to terminate the lease with no additional liability on either side.

---

[*]A law change combined municipal and superior courts in most counties.

In addition, leases can be terminated because of destruction of the premises; government action, such as condemnation; or a breach of terms and conditions by the lessor or lessee.

Mobile (Manufactured) Home Park Tenants[*]

A mobile home park is usually a development where lots are rented to mobile home owners. The tenants own their mobile homes, but they are tenants of the land. In California, special laws for mobile home park tenants differ from the typical landlord–tenant laws. A mobile home tenant in a park *cannot be evicted unless one of the following applies:*

1. The tenant fails to comply with local and state laws.
2. The tenant annoys other tenants.
3. The tenant fails to abide by reasonable park rules.
4. The tenant fails to pay the rent and other agreed-upon charges.
5. The tenant has his or her rights condemned by government.
6. The use of the park changes.

The mobile home tenant who is in violation must be given at least a 60-day notice, rather than the 3-day or 30-day notice rules for regular tenants.

If the mobile home cannot be moved without a permit, the law requires that a tenant must be given a reasonable notice to vacate. The tenant cannot be required to move merely to make space for a person purchasing a mobile home from the park owner. In addition, many other special rules apply to tenants in mobile home parks.

11.4 PROPERTY MANAGEMENT

As an investment, real estate offers a hedge against inflation; offers income tax advantages; and, in some cases, provides an annual cash income. However, real estate needs managerial attention, which frequently discourages investors who do not wish to be bothered by tenants. An alternative might be to employ a professional property manager.

Field of Property Management

Property management is a specialty within the real estate business. Property managers represent owners by screening tenants, negotiating

---

[*]Mobile and manufactured homes are one and the same for this discussion.

rental agreements, hiring personnel to maintain the building and grounds, and hiring on-site residential managers. *California rules state that an apartment building or complex with 16 or more rental units must have an on-site residential manager* (a real estate license is not required for on-site residential managers but is for off-site property managers). In addition, property managers are responsible for rent collection and the keeping of accounting records for income tax purposes.

Property managers range from real estate brokers who handle a few properties for their clients to large corporate firms that manage hundreds or thousands of units, including commercial properties such as office buildings and shopping centers.

As mentioned above, an off-site property manager must be a licensed real estate broker, but on-site residential managers do not need a real estate license. Key employees of the property management company must be bonded. The Institute of Real Estate Management, affiliated with the National Association of REALTORS®, issues the nationally recognized designation **Certified Property Manager (CPM)**. The CPM designation is achieved after meeting rigorous educational and experience requirements.

Compensation

Property management firms are usually paid a percentage of the rents collected. The percentage is negotiable and varies from firm to firm. For a large structure with many rental units, the fee may be as low as 1 percent or 2 percent of gross rents collected. On small units such as rental homes and duplexes, the fee may be 10 percent or more. The fee for renting resort properties may be 25 percent or more of rents collected. Some property managers may charge a flat rate rather than a percentage of rents collected.

Property management fees do not include the cost of maintenance, only the management of the property. If maintenance or repairs are needed, the manager sees that the work is done, but the bill is paid by the property owner or is deducted from the rent proceeds.

When a property manager is hired, the manager and the owner sign a management contract. This contract designates the property manager as the owner's agent and lists all the duties and responsibilities of the parties. To be enforceable, the management contract must meet the legal requirements of California contract law.

CHAPTER SUMMARY

A lease is a contract between an owner, called the lessor, and a tenant, called the lessee. A lessee is given possession in exchange for rent. Leases for more than one year must be in writing to be valid.

Types of leasehold estates are estate for years, estate from period to period, estate at will, and estate at sufferance. Leases on urban property cannot exceed 99 years, whereas leases for agricultural land cannot exceed 51 years. Security deposits on residential properties cannot exceed two months' rent on unfurnished dwellings and three months' rent on furnished dwellings.

An assignment of a lease transfers the entire leasehold interest to another person, whereas a sublease transfers only a part of the leasehold interest to a sublessee.

Rental payments can be paid on a gross, net, or percentage basis. An escalator clause allows the landlord to raise the rent during the term of the lease.

A landlord's duties and rights include an implied condition of habitability, advance notice prior to inspection, 30 or 60-day advance notice when ordering the tenant to vacate, and an obligation not to discriminate when renting property.

A tenant's duties and rights include paying the rent when due, not damaging the property, and giving the landlord 30 days' notice when vacating. Under certain conditions, a tenant can use a rent offset for repairs if the property falls below minimum housing standards. Eviction occurs when a tenant is dispossessed by process of law. The tenant must be served with a 3-day, 30 or 60-day notice, depending on the circumstances.

The action of suing for eviction is called unlawful detainer action. If a writ of possession is granted, the sheriff evicts the tenant. Delays and appeals by a tenant can extend the eviction process by several months.

In addition to eviction, leases can be terminated by expiration of time, mutual consent, destruction of the premises, government action, and breach of terms and conditions.

Property management is a specialty within the real estate business. Property managers represent owners by finding tenants, caring for the property, and maintaining proper accounting records. Property managers are usually paid a fee based on the rents collected.

IMPORTANT TERMS AND CONCEPTS

certified property manager (CPM)

estate at sufferance

estate at will

estate for years

estate from period to period

gross lease

lease with option to buy

lessee

lessor

net lease

percentage lease

sandwich lease

sublease

PRACTICAL APPLICATION

1. An apartment is rented for $800 per month with a $1,000 security deposit. While moving out, the tenant informs the landlord that the water heater leaks. After inspecting the water heater, the landlord believes the leak was the result of the tenant banging the water heater while moving out. The cost of the repair is $100. How would you handle the security deposit issue if you were the landlord?

2. A tenant has a one-year lease that terminates December 1, 2011. The terms of the lease state that no pets are allowed. On October 1, 2011, a neighbor calls the landlord to complain that the tenant's dog barks too much. The landlord tells the tenant that the dog must go, but the tenant refuses to remove the dog. List the next legal steps the landlord must take to get rid of the dog.

3. As an owner of a five-unit apartment complex, you are thinking about hiring a professional property manager. The property manager quotes a fee of 8% of collected rents. Each apartment rents for $750 per month with a vacancy factor of 5%. You are in a combined federal and state tax bracket of 31%. What is the annual after-tax cost of hiring the property manager?

REVIEWING YOUR UNDERSTANDING

1. Ms. Alvarez leases her summer cabin to Mr. Greene for the months of June, July, and August of a designated year. Mr. Greene has an estate:
   a. for years.
   b. from period to period.
   c. at sufferance.
   d. of monthly rental.

2. Urban property cannot be leased for more than:
   a. 99 years.
   b. 51 years.
   c. 15 years.
   d. no time limit.

3. An assignment of a lease differs from a sublease in that an assignment:
   a. transfers liability to the new occupant.
   b. involves two lease contracts: (1) lessor to lessee and (2) lessee to sublessee.
   c. requires that the original lessee still be primarily liable to the lessor.
   d. none of the above.

4. Under which lease does the tenant pay rent, property taxes, maintenance, and hazard insurance?
   a. gross lease
   b. triple net lease
   c. flat lease
   d. escalator lease

5. A residential tenant can expect the landlord to make necessary repairs to keep the dwelling habitable. If the landlord does not, the tenant can make repairs and offset the rent up to
   a. $700 maximum.
   b. one month's rent.
   c. reasonable cost.
   d. $1,000 maximum.

6. It is illegal to screen and eliminate potential tenants based on
   a. marital status, sex, sexual orientation, and family status.
   b. race, color, and creed.
   c. religion and physical handicap.
   d. all of the above.

7. If a tenant has violated the terms of the rental agreement or lease, before the tenant can be evicted, the tenant must be served a:
   a. 1-day notice.
   b. 3-day notice.
   c. 30-day notice.
   d. 60-day notice.

8. If a small unfurnished apartment rents for $800 per month, the maximum security deposit the landlord can ask for is
   a. $100.
   b. $500.
   c. $800.
   d. $1,600.

9. The legal process by which a tenant is evicted is called a(n):
   a. eviction action.
   b. ejectment action.
   c. possessory action.
   d. unlawful detainer action.

10. The professional designation CPM stands for
    a. Certificate of Public Management.
    b. Certified Practical Manager.
    c. Certificate of Practical Management.
    d. Certified Property Manager.

11. At the end of the lease, the lessee can purchase the property under agreed terms and the lessor must sell. This is an example of
    a. a lease with option to buy.
    b. first right of refusal.
    c. a sublease.
    d. assignment of lease.

12. The law that states that certain leases must be in writing to be enforceable is the:
    a. Statute of Escribe.
    b. Statute of Limitations.
    c. Statute of Conveyance.
    d. Statute of Frauds.

13. A landlord wants to ask the month-to-month tenant who has occupied the property for six months to leave because the landlord plans to occupy the rental home. Under state law, the landlord must serve the tenant with a(n):
    a. 30-day notice.
    b. 3-day notice.
    c. eviction order.
    d. writ of possession.

14. A landlord who is uniform in application can refuse to rent based upon all of the following, except:
    a. poor credit.
    b. inadequate income.
    c. the existence of children.
    d. too many pets.

15. Assuming the tenant takes possession, in order to be valid, a rental agreement for six months must contain
    a. signatures of the lessor and lessee.
    b. written terms.
    c. a legal description of the property.
    d. none of the above.

16. The interest a tenant has in real estate is known as a:
    a. freehold estate.
    b. less-than-freehold estate.
    c. tenant right estate.
    d. fee simple absolute estate.

17. Regarding security deposits:
    a. the maximum for an unfurnished apartment is three months' rent.
    b. no security deposit can be labeled nonrefundable.
    c. the deposit must be less than the first month's rent.
    d. all unused deposits must be refunded in seven days.

18. Month-to-month tenants in a mobile home park can be requested to leave only for specified reasons and must be served with at least a:
    a. 90-day notice.
    b. 60-day notice.
    c. 30-day notice.
    d. 3-day notice.

19. Most unlawful detainer actions are heard in
    a. superior court.
    b. small claims court.
    c. appellate court.
    d. Supreme Court.

20. In an apartment complex, an on-site resident manager is required if there are
    a. 4 or more units.
    b. 8 or more units.
    c. 12 or more units.
    d. 16 or more units.

Chapter 12

This chapter highlights the principles of government land-use planning and stresses zoning and subdivision regulations. Condominiums, planned unit developments, and the selling of undivided interests are also discussed. The chapter concludes with an explanation of fair housing laws. At the conclusion of the chapter, you will be able to do the following:

1. Describe the main goals of a community general plan.
2. Explain the difference between government use of police power and eminent domain, and give two examples of each.
3. List the major characteristics of the Subdivision Map Act and the Subdivided Lands Act.
4. Describe a common interest development and discuss the differences between a condominium and a planned unit development.
5. List the major fair housing laws that prohibit discrimination in the selling or renting of real estate.

Land-Use Planning, Subdivisions, Fair Housing, and Other Public Controls

12.1 GOVERNMENT LAND-USE PLANNING

Government land-use controls are controversial. Some people believe land is a commodity to be bought and sold like any other product. They consider any type of land-use control an infringement on free enterprise. At the other extreme are those who believe land is a resource that belongs to all the people, the use of which should be completely controlled by government. Somewhere in the middle is the view that land is a commodity and a resource that should be privately owned, but used constructively to benefit society.

Private Deed Restrictions

Most attention regarding land-use control has focused on government regulations. However, for many years, covenants, conditions, and restrictions (CC&Rs) in deeds have been used by private individuals to regulate real estate usage.

California owners are allowed to limit the use of land by contract as long as the restrictions are not a violation of the law. Thus, land-use controls are not new, but in the last 70 years, the bulk of the controls have shifted from private imposition to government imposition. Private deed restrictions were discussed in more detail in Chapter 3.

Public Land-Use Controls

Industrialization and urban crowding have created a need for public controls to maintain order and promote social harmony. One way to maintain order is to control the use of land. The two main powers that allow government to control land use are police power and the power of eminent domain.

Police power refers to the constitutional right of government to regulate private activity to promote the general health, welfare, and safety of society. Police power has often been used in the United States to direct land use. Major real estate examples of police power include zoning ordinances, building and health codes, setback requirements, environmental regulations, and rent controls. Of the many police power enactments, zoning, subdivision, and environmental regulations emerge as the most influential methods for controlling land use.

Police power allows government to regulate private land use without the payment of compensation. The power of **eminent domain** is different in that it allows the government to acquire title to private land for public use in exchange for the payment of just compensation. Eminent domain is used for a variety of government land-use projects, such as highways, public housing, and urban renewal.

Redevelopment agencies also have the power of eminent domain under California's Redevelopment Law. A redevelopment agency may condemn land within a redevelopment district that has been determined as being blighted and resell it to a private developer in an effort to revitalize urban areas or improve an area's economic climate; see *Kelo v. City of New London,* 545 U.S. 469 (2005).

All levels of government can exercise the power of eminent domain regardless of how unwilling the property owner may be. The main issue in most eminent domain cases is the amount of compensation. The courts have ruled that the property's fair market value is the proper basis for determining compensation. In addition, most federal and some state agencies must pay for moving and other miscellaneous expenses incurred by those being displaced.

Planning

The dictionary defines *planning* as "thinking out acts and purposes beforehand." When applied to cities and counties, planning can be defined as anticipating and achieving community goals in light of social, economic, and physical needs. Planning requires that a community analyze its assets and liabilities, establish its goals, and attempt to achieve these goals using land-use control as a primary tool. California law requires that every incorporated city and county must have a planning commission. A **planning commission** is composed of citizens appointed by the members of the city council or board of supervisors. Planning commissioners advise the elected officials on land-use matters. The planning commission typically only makes recommendations; the final decision on planning rests with the city council or board of supervisors, depending on who has jurisdiction.

In addition to planning commissions, many cities and counties have planning departments. **Planning departments** are agencies within city and county government, staffed with professionally trained planners. Planning department employees provide technical services for planning commissions, elected officials, and citizens.

State law requires every city and county to develop a general plan, which outlines the goals and objectives for the community. The general plan also lists the steps needed to achieve these goals.

General Plan

The establishment of a community general plan requires three major steps: (1) resource analysis, (2) formulation of community goals, and (3) implementation of the plan.

Resource Analysis

The first step is to recognize the individual character of the community. What are its strong points? What are its weaknesses? To accomplish this, several substudies are required, including an economic base study, a population trend study, a survey of existing land use, a housing needs study, a city facilities study, and an analysis of the community's financial resources. Once a resource inventory has been taken, the next step is to formulate community goals in light of the resources.

Formulation of Community Goals

The formulation of community goals is the most difficult phase of urban planning because of the conflict between various special interest groups, each trying to secure and establish its own definition of the community goal. In spite of this problem, citizen input should be encouraged. A community plan must be based on the desires of community residents as a whole, not on the desires of staff planners alone.

Once the goals are established, a comprehensive plan to achieve the objectives must be formulated. The plan is frequently referred to as the general plan or the master plan, and it should encompass all social, economic, and physical aspects of the projected growth.

The plan should be long-range but provide for short-range flexibility as the need for modification arises. Under no circumstances must the general plan be viewed as an inflexible, permanent fixture that never requires modification. A community's attitude and resources can change, and the general plan must be modified to comply with these changes.

Implementation of the Plan

The final step in urban planning is to implement the general plan. The implementation phase requires local government to use police power, eminent domain, taxation, and control over government spending to enact the plan. As previously indicated, the three most powerful tools for implementing a community plan are zoning, subdivision, and environmental regulations.

Zoning

Zoning refers to the division of land into designated land-use districts. In its simplest form, zoning districts are divided into residential use, commercial use, industrial use, and rural use. Each use, in turn, can have several subclasses. For example, residential can be broken down into single-family, multifamily, and mobile home zones. Commercial zones are usually divided into retail, office, and wholesale space. Industrial zones are divided into light industry and heavy industry; rural zones, into agricultural, resource, and recreational use.

Zoning as a land-control tool was not common in the United States until the 1920s; prior to this time, there was some doubt about the constitutionality of zoning, although early zoning laws can be traced to colonial times. However, in 1926, the U.S. Supreme Court held that zoning was a reasonable exercise of government police power. Since this decision, every state has passed legislation allowing individual cities and counties to enact zoning ordinances.

Early zoning ordinances were aimed at safety and nuisance control. The idea was to use zoning to protect individual property values by prohibiting offensive use of surrounding land. The use of zoning has gradually been expanded, and now it is used to "promote the general welfare" of the entire community.

Inclusionary Zoning

Inclusionary zoning is an ordinance that requires a builder of new residential housing to set aside a designated number of units for low- and moderate-income people. If the developer refuses to provide the designated units, the building permit is denied.

In some cases, instead of providing inclusionary units, the builder is required to pay into a fund that the government uses to provide low- and moderate-income housing. To encourage participation in the program, the builder is allowed to construct more units per acre than normal.

The economic reality is that the prices of the regular units are frequently increased to offset the builder's losses on the inclusionary units. This shifts the burden of providing affordable housing from the government to the private market.

Controversy: Local Versus State and Federal Planning

Historically, planning has been a local matter. Each community developed its own plans within the confines of its own territorial limits. In the process, each community attempted to optimize its own social and economic well-being, frequently at the expense of surrounding areas. For example, the planning of a smelly industrial plant on the border of one city has a spillover effect on the neighboring community located downwind.

The growth of multicity metropolitan areas has led the state to mandate planning on a regional basis. Water and sewage systems, rapid transit, highway traffic patterns, airports, and pollution controls are examples of regional planning. However, from a political point of view, there is wide-scale resistance to the creation of another layer of government. Moreover, local government officials are reluctant to surrender some of their power to regional or state commissioners.

Opposition to federal and state controls also comes from individuals who believe that the power of land regulation should be limited to local government. They fear that planning on a state and federal level is insensitive to local needs. Who is correct? Like most land-use controls, the correct answer depends on one's value judgment. However, the current trend is toward more regional, state, and federal control over land use.

Examples of federal laws include the **National Environmental Policy Act,** which requires an environmental impact report on all projects using federal funding, and the **Clean Air Act,** which requires businesses (including real estate developers) to meet air quality standards. The federal government has declared that development cannot take place in "wetlands" for fear of damaging wildlife habitat. The definition of what constitutes *wetlands* has created numerous lawsuits.

Examples of state laws include the Coastline Conservation Act, creating controls on the 1,000-mile California coast; the California Environmental Quality Act, which requires an environmental impact report on major real estate projects; and the Subdivision Map Act and Subdivided Lands Act, which control the creation of subdivisions in the state.

12.2 SUBDIVISIONS

Another important use of police power is *subdivision regulation*. Poorly conceived subdivisions, with inadequate streets and facilities, can become a burden to taxpayers in later years, when expensive redevelopment is needed to correct earlier oversights. Proponents of subdivision controls believe that the origin of slums and urban blight can be traced to inadequate regulations. Opponents disagree, stating that today's slums are the result of government ordinances that prevent land from rising to its economic highest and best use.

Today subdivision regulations are used in all areas of California. Real estate developers are frequently required to provide water, sewer, paved streets, sidewalks, street lights, and school and park sites as a condition of being allowed to subdivide. The idea is to plan for the future at the inception and to require the purchaser of the subdivided lot, not the community as a whole, to pay the expense of added community facilities. Like all public controls, subdivision regulations are controversial because they require the surrender of some individual rights in an attempt to promote the general welfare.

Summary of Planning Terms

Planning commission. An appointed body of citizens charged with the responsibility of advising the elected board of supervisors or city council members in matters of land use.

Planning department. City or county staff employees who lend professional and technical assistance to elected officials and citizens.

Zone. An area defined on a map by a boundary line within which the land-use regulations are the same.

Rezoning. The process of changing land-use regulations on property from one zone to another.

Variance. A deviation from the zoning regulations for a particular parcel. *Conditional use permit.* A requirement imposed by government in connection with the approval of a permit or a division of property.

Development plans. Plans showing the details of the proposed development. Normally includes plot plan, architectural renderings, and statistical information relative to acreage, building area, units, and parking. In most cases, an environmental impact study will be required.

Standard subdivision. A division of property into lots that does not include common areas.

Minor subdivision or lot split. A division of residential property into two, three, or four parcels.

Major subdivision. A division of residential property into five or more parcels. *Architectural review.* Certain zoning areas where a special citizens' group approves or rejects the proposal based on its architectural compatibility with the surrounding area.

Appeal. The right to request review of a negative planning commission decision. The appellate process goes from the planning commission to the board of supervisors or city council to the courts.

Source: From *Essentials of Real Estate Economics,* 6th ed., by D. J. McKenzie and R. M. Betts (Cincinnati, OH: South-Western, 2011).

Subdivision Laws

There are two basic laws under which subdivisions are controlled in California—the Subdivision Map Act and the Subdivided Lands Act. The **Subdivision Map Act** covers the division of land into two or more lots for the purpose of sale, lease, or financing, whether now or in the future. The Subdivision Map Act is administered by local officials and is concerned with the physical aspects of the subdivision, such as design, streets, water, sewers, and so on. The Subdivision Map Act outlines the procedure for filing subdivision maps to legally create a subdivision. (See Figure 12.1.)

The **Subdivided Lands Act** defines a subdivision as the division of land into five or more lots for the purpose of sale, lease, or financing, whether now or in the future. The Subdivided Lands Act is administered by the California real estate commissioner and

FIGURE 12.1

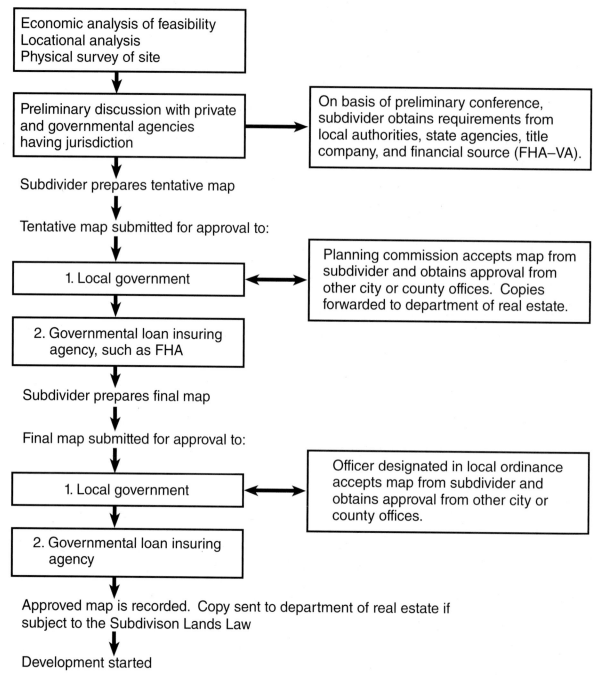

BASIC OUTLINE OF SUBDIVISION MAP PREPARATION AND APPROVAL

PRELIMINARY PLANNING

Economic analysis of feasibility
Locational analysis
Physical survey of site

Preliminary discussion with private and governmental agencies having jurisdiction

On basis of preliminary conference, subdivider obtains requirements from local authorities, state agencies, title company, and financial source (FHA–VA).

Subdivider prepares tentative map

Tentative map submitted for approval to:

1. Local government

Planning commission accepts map from subdivider and obtains approval from other city or county offices. Copies forwarded to department of real estate.

2. Governmental loan insuring agency, such as FHA

Subdivider prepares final map

Final map submitted for approval to:

1. Local government

Officer designated in local ordinance accepts map from subdivider and obtains approval from other city or county offices.

2. Governmental loan insuring agency

Approved map is recorded. Copy sent to department of real estate if subject to the Subdivison Lands Law

Development started

Source: From *Reference Book*, California Department of Real Estate.

is primarily concerned with the marketing aspects of the subdivision. The basic objective of the Subdivided Lands Act is to protect the purchasers of property in new subdivisions from fraud and misrepresentation when buying new subdivided land.

No new subdivision of five or more parcels located in California can be offered for sale until the real estate commissioner issues a public report. The final public report is not issued until the commissioner is satisfied that the developer has met all statutory requirements, with particular emphasis on the establishment of financial arrangements to assure completion of any promised facilities. *The issuance of a public report does not mean that in the eyes of the commissioner, the subdivision is a good investment.* It merely means that the subdivider has conformed to all laws and regulations.

Before each lot in a new subdivision can be sold, the subdivider must deliver a copy of the commissioner's final public report to the prospective buyer. The prospective buyer must then sign a statement acknowledging that he or she received and read the public report, and this signed copy must be kept on file by the subdivider for three years. Only after these steps have taken place can the subdivider sell each lot.

The public report is good for five years; however, the law requires the commissioner to issue an amended public report when a material change occurs regarding the subdivision. Examples of material changes include changes in contract forms, physical changes such as lot lines or street lines, and a sale of five or more lots to a single buyer.

Under certain circumstances, the commissioner can issue a preliminary **public report,** which allows the subdivider to take reservations for purchase pending the issuance of the final public report. A reservation is not binding upon the prospective buyer. The prospective buyer is allowed to back out and receive a full refund up until the final report is issued and a binding purchase agreement is signed.

The public report process applies only to the first sale of each lot in a new subdivision. A subsequent resale of a lot by the original purchaser does not require that the second buyer receive a public report.

Out-of-State and Foreign Land

Subdivided land projects located in other states and offered for sale in California do not need to obtain a formal public report from the

California Department of Real Estate (DRE). Instead, out-of-state subdividers must include specific disclaimers in all advertising and sales agreements. Foreign properties offered for sale in California have very few restrictions; a sale is basically a buyer-beware situation. All California buyers should seek legal advice before purchasing an out-of-state or out-of-country property.

Red Tape

The actual processing of a subdivision is frequently a costly and time-consuming process. The data needed to complete the required forms are highly technical and beyond the skills of average property owners. The services of title officers, surveyors or engineers, contractors, and attorneys often are required. The average subdivision takes many months to process and major development can take years. Delays are costly; in the end, these costs are borne by the consumer.

Land Project Right to Rescind Sale

A *land project* is defined as a speculative subdivision of 50 or more lots located in a sparsely populated area of the state. These types of subdivisions are frequently sold only after intensive promotion in urban areas, long distances away from the development.

A purchaser of a lot in the land project is allowed a limited time after the sale to "cool off" and rescind, or cancel, the purchase contract and receive a full refund with no further obligations. As of July 2007, the right to rescind extends for 14 days after the signing of the purchase agreement. But in the future, regulations might extend this period. (Also see the section "Time-Sharing Ownership" regarding the right to rescind sale.)

Interstate Land Sales Full-Disclosure Act

A federal law known as the Interstate Land Sales Full-Disclosure Act regulates land sales between two or more states. If a developer of 50 or more lots located in one state wishes to market the lots in another state(s), the developer must conform to this law.

Basically, the law requires the developer to obtain a public report issued by the Department of Housing and Urban Development (HUD) and to deliver a copy of the public report to each prospective buyer. This law is an attempt to reduce the number of fraudulent land sales that take place by mail or through out-of-state advertising.

Subdivision Laws Summarized

Subdivided Lands Act	Subdivision Map Act
Five or more lots or parcels	Two or more lots or parcels
No contiguity requirement	Land must be contiguous units
160-acre and larger parcels designated as such by government survey are exempt	No exemption for 160 acres and larger
Administered by California real estate commissioner	Administered by local officials
Requires a final public report	No public report required

Currently a debate is raging. On one hand, increased regulations are designed to protect the consumer and the environment; on the other hand, consumers must pay for these regulations via higher prices. Are the protections worth the price? This is a value judgment question that each person must answer.

12.3 COMMON INTEREST DEVELOPMENTS (CIDs)

An increase in population has caused an increase in urban land prices. As land becomes scarcer and prices begin to rise, there is a tendency to intensify development to obtain more living units per acre. **Common interest developments (CIDs)** in the form of condominiums, planned unit developments, stock cooperatives, and community apartments are examples of intensified owner-occupied developments that differ from the traditional single-family-home type of subdivision. All of these developments are considered subdivisions and are regulated by state law.

Condominiums

A **condominium** is a type of real estate ownership, not a type of structure. In a condominium, a person owns his or her own apartment-type living unit. In a legal sense, a condominium owner acquires a fee title interest in the airspace of the particular unit and an undivided interest (with other condominium owners) in the land in addition to all other common areas, such as hallways, elevators, carports, and recreational facilities. A condominium is sometimes called a *vertical subdivision*.

Each condominium owner has his or her own individual deed, real estate loan, and property tax assessment. A condominium interest is bought and sold like any other parcel of real estate.

All condominiums have homeowners' associations that elect a governing board. The governing board is responsible for the management of the complex and sees that the building and common areas are maintained. The owners' association also sets the dues for each owner's share of the maintenance.

Condominium developments are expected to continue to gain an increasing share of the housing market. In some areas, there has been a tendency to convert existing renter-occupied apartments into owner-occupied condominiums. This has caused controversy because condo conversion reduces the supply of rental units, thereby making it more difficult for renters to find affordable housing. On the other hand, a condo conversion increases the supply of owner-occupied housing, thereby making it easier for owners to find affordable housing. Therefore, it is expected that the condo conversion controversy will rage on for years.

Planned Unit Development (PUD)

A **planned unit development (PUD)** or planned development (PD) is often confused with a condominium. They are not the same. In a PUD, a person owns his or her own living unit and lot, in addition to an undivided interest in the common areas. A condominium owner owns his or her own living unit, but not his or her own lot. A PUD is often referred to as a *townhouse development,* but this is incorrect. A townhouse is a type of architecture and not a type of ownership. In a PUD, no one lives in the airspace above or below the owner, as is found in a condominium. PUDs are frequently located in the suburbs, whereas condominiums are usually located in urban areas. They are both found in resort areas such as Lake Tahoe and Palm Desert.

PUDs are similar in operation to condominiums. A homeowners' association levies dues for upkeep and maintenance of the common areas.

In addition, each property owner has CC&Rs in his or her deed that dictate the do's and don'ts of ownership.

Stock Cooperatives and Community Apartments

A **stock cooperative** is a corporation formed for the purpose of holding title to a building. Each shareholder of the entire corporation is given the right to occupy a living unit, but the entire building is owned by the corporation. A sale of a share in the corporation also passes the right of occupancy to a living unit within the stock cooperative.

A community apartment is created when a group of people jointly purchase an undivided interest in an entire apartment complex. Then each person is given the right to occupy a particular apartment unit. The undivided share can be sold, and the new purchaser acquires the right to live in the particular apartment.

Under a stock cooperative and a community apartment, each person does not receive an individual deed, real estate loan, or property tax assessment. All the shareholders and undivided interest owners must agree to pool their funds each month to make the mortgage payment, pay the property taxes, and pay for upkeep and maintenance.

Stock cooperatives and community apartments are not as popular as condominiums and PUDs. Most people prefer their own individual deed, real estate loan, and property tax assessment, which are present in condominiums and PUDs but not in stock cooperatives or community apartments.

Disclosure Requirements

When a unit in an existing common interest development is offered for sale, the seller must provide, as a *minimum*, to a prospective buyer prior to the close of escrow:

1. A copy of the existing conditions, covenants, and restrictions; the articles of incorporation; the owners' association by-laws; the governing documents; and a current financial statement on the owners' association
2. A written statement of any known pending special assessments, claims, or litigation against the seller or the owners' association
3. A current statement showing whether the seller has any unpaid assessments or dues owed to the owners' association

Recreational Developments Selling Undivided Interests

Recreational land developments can be found throughout California. The developer usually begins with a large parcel of land, subdivides the land, and then sells parcels to individual owners. In some cases, the parcels are fully developed; in other cases, vacant lots are sold.

An alternative to subdividing recreational land into individual parcels is keeping the original large parcel intact and **selling**

undivided interests or shares in the whole. An example is a developer who has 1,000 acres of land and is considering subdividing the land into 1,000 one-acre lots to be sold to 1,000 recreational users. An alternative might be to sell a 1/1000 undivided interest to 1,000 recreational users. With selling 1,000 undivided interests, each owner has the right to use all 1,000 acres instead of just one acre, as would be the case if a traditional subdivision were created.

The buyer of an undivided interest in a recreational land development has 7 days (from receipt of the Public Report or signing the contract) to rescind the purchase contract under the California Business and Professions Code for any reason and receive a full refund. The marketing of an undivided interest is controlled by the state subdivision laws and private deed restrictions, similar to condominiums and PUDs.

Time-Sharing Ownership

Another interesting concept is that of time-sharing ownership. Under time-sharing, a person buys an interest in a building—for example, a condominium in a resort area—where the right of occupancy is limited to a specified calendar time period. An example is 12 people who pool their funds and each person purchases a 1/12 interest in a Lake Tahoe condominium. Each person's 1/12 interest gives that person the right to occupy the condominium for a month. The month or the time period is designated in the deed or by a separate instrument. This is a way to own a vacation home for the exact time period you desire, for an expense that covers just the pro rata time of occupancy.

There are other derivations of time-sharing ownership, such as purchasing the right of occupancy for a designated time period each year. But the purchaser does not acquire an interest in the land. Many timeshare resorts have exchange privileges with other resorts, allowing a time-share owner to move from location to location.

The time-sharing owners need CC&Rs in deeds, as well as an owners' association to govern the use and maintenance of the unit. The buyer of a time-share has 7 days (from receipt of the Public Report or signing the contract) to rescind the purchase contract under the California Business and Professions Code for any reason and receive a full refund.

12.4 HOUSING AND CONSTRUCTION LAWS
State Laws and Regulations

State housing laws. State housing laws, or codes, establish minimum housing standards for the entire state. State housing and health and safety codes are enforced by local, not state, building inspectors. The state housing law is a uniform code that must be adopted by all cities and counties in California.

Local building codes. Until 1970, local codes were allowed to deviate from state housing laws. However, with the passage of the state uniform housing codes, local variances are permitted only if a study finds sufficient reason to deviate from the state uniform code.

Contractor's license law. State law requires every person who engages in the business of a contractor to be licensed. A property owner doing his or her own work for his or her own use must build according to codes, but is exempt from the contractor license law. On the other hand, if an owner wishes to build with the intention to offer the finished real estate project for sale, a licensed contractor must do the work.

Environmental impact regulations. A housing or real estate development usually requires an environmental review before a building permit is issued. The builder must prepare a negative impact report (NIR) if a project is minor, with no or limited environmental concern, or a costly, fully documented environmental impact report (EIR) if a project is major. The purpose of both reports is to address what impact the real estate construction will have on the social, economic, physical, and biological environment. Then the report must state what steps the builder will take to reduce the impact on the environment, including not building the project in the first place.

12.5 FAIR HOUSING
State Laws and Regulations

EQUAL HOUSING OPPORTUNITY

Over the years, several federal and state laws have been passed making it against public policy to discriminate in real estate based on race, color, religion, sex, sexual orientation, marital status or registered domestic partnership, national origin, ancestry, family status, or mental or physical handicap. The courts do not tolerate discrimination, and violators can expect to be fined and/or jailed.

Unruh Civil Rights Act. This state law makes it unlawful for people engaged in business in California, including real estate agents, to discriminate when providing business products and services. Examples of unlawful real estate agent conduct include steering and block busting. **Steering** is the unlawful directing of a prospective buyer or tenant to certain neighborhoods or the refusal to tell about the availability of housing in another neighborhood.

Block busting is attempting to create panic selling by telling existing property owners that minority groups have targeted their neighborhoods for purchase. Steering and block busting are illegal; the penalties include loss of a real estate license and severe criminal and civil charges, in addition to fines.

California Fair Housing Act (Rumford Act). This state law forbids discrimination in the sale, rental, lease, or financing of practically all types of housing. The staff of the Department of Fair Employment and Housing investigates complaints from people who believe they have been discriminated against in housing. If the staff thinks a violation has occurred, a hearing is held with the Commission of Fair Employment and Housing. If the commission rules that discrimination has occurred, it has the power to order the sale or rental of the property. In addition, the commission has the power to levy fines. A person who has suffered discrimination has a right to bypass the commission process and bring a direct lawsuit in court. The state of California believes that fair housing is so important that it requires all real estate agents to take a three-hour fair-housing course as a condition for keeping a real estate license.

Housing Financial Discrimination Act (Holden Act). This state law prohibits financial institutions from engaging in discriminatory loan practices. This law attempts to prohibit redlining. *Redlining* is a loan practice under which a lender refuses to grant a housing loan in certain geographic areas based on neighborhood trends, regardless of the merits of the borrower or of the individual home.

Commissioner's rules and regulations. The California real estate commissioner has issued numerous regulations regarding housing discrimination. These regulations detail the types of discriminatory conduct that, if practiced by a real estate licensee, are the basis for disciplinary action that can result in a suspension or fine or even in prosecution by the local district attorney.

Federal Laws

Civil Rights Act of 1968 and 1988 Amendments. This comprehensive law states that within constitutional limits, fair housing should prevail throughout the United States. This act left it up to the courts to determine the constitutionality of this law.

Jones v. Mayer Case. In this landmark case, the U.S. Supreme Court interpreted and applied an act of Congress passed in 1866 immediately after the Civil War. The constitutionality rested on the

Thirteenth Amendment, which prohibits slavery. Using the Act of 1866 and the Thirteenth Amendment, the U.S. Supreme Court held that the Civil Rights Act of 1866 bars all racial discrimination, private as well as public, in the sale or rental of property, and that the statute was a valid exercise of the power of Congress to enforce the Thirteenth Amendment.

1988 Amendments to the Civil Rights Act of 1968. The 1988 Amendments broaden the definition of *handicap* to include anyone with a disability that impairs "major life activities." Thus, property owners cannot discriminate because of AIDS, cancer, and alcoholism. People with mental disorders, including past drug users, are also protected. Per the 1988 Amendments, current drug abusers or anyone who can be proved to be a current threat to the health, safety, or property of others is not considered a protected class. To be safe, any refusal to sell or rent for any reason other than inadequate income or credit should first be reviewed by the property owner's attorney. The 1988 Amendments also make it a federal violation to discriminate against families with children unless the development is an approved senior citizen project.

Senior Citizen Housing

Due to public policy concerns for the availability of affordable housing for seniors, federal law provides an exception to antidiscrimination laws based on age, allowing certain apartment complexes, CIDs. and detached dwelling communities to designate themselves as senior communities.

There are two classifications for senior communities. The first is where every dwelling is occupied solely by persons age 62 or older. The second classification is where 80 percent or more of the dwellings must have at least one person age 55 or older and the community adheres to a policy that demonstrates intent to house persons who are 55 or older. The remaining 20 percent of the dwellings may be occupied solely by those under age 55. The purpose of the 20 percent classification is for surviving spouses. Let's say Ed, age 56 and Lavonne, age 52, move into a senior community. A year later, Ed dies, leaving his widow in the dwelling. If not for the 20 percent category, Lavonne would have to vacate since she is not 55 or older. Instead, she now moves over to the 20 percent category, and upon reaching age 55 would return to the 80 percent category.

While occupancy is restricted by age, ownership is not. For example, a 53-year-old couple could purchase a home in a 55-year-or-older community but would not be able to move in until one of them turns age 55. They could rent the residence to a qualifying tenant during the meantime. Agents representing buyers and sellers in senior communities must be very careful to fully disclose the community's requirements. Senior community management companies and homeowners' associations are diligent about disclosing to agents the requirements of occupancy. An agent is wise to attach any correspondence received from the community's management to their disclosure (see Chapter 5) for the buyer.

Many Other Laws

In addition to the laws listed previously, numerous other laws and regulations directly or indirectly attempt to prohibit discrimination in housing. All real estate owners, agents, managers, and lenders must give the public an equal opportunity to acquire real estate.

CHAPTER SUMMARY

Two powers that allow government to control land use are police power and the power of eminent domain. Major police power tools include zoning, building and health codes, and subdivision regulations.

Cities and counties in California must have a planning commission. In addition, most cities and counties also have planning departments. The planning commission and elected officials must adopt a general plan that outlines the goals and objectives for the community. The three most powerful tools for implementing the general plan are zoning, subdivision regulations, and environmental regulations. The two major subdivision laws are the Subdivision Map Act and the Subdivided Lands Act. The Subdivision Map Act is administered by local officials and is mostly concerned with the physical aspects of a subdivision. The Subdivided Lands Act is administered by the California real estate commissioner and is primarily concerned with the marketing aspects of a subdivision. The key element of the Subdivided Lands Act is the required public report, which must be delivered to each prospective buyer of a lot in a new California subdivision.

Common interest developments in the form of condominiums, PUDs stock cooperatives, and community apartments are examples of intensified owner-occupied developments, which differ from the traditional single-family-dwelling type of subdivision.

Over the years, laws have been passed making it against public policy to discriminate in the selling, leasing, or renting of housing. The Unruh Civil Rights Act and the California Fair Housing Act (Rumford Act) are two California antidiscrimination laws. The Civil Rights Act of 1968 and 1988 Amendments is a federal law that prohibits discrimination in housing.

IMPORTANT TERMS AND CONCEPTS

California Fair Housing Act (Rumford Act)

Civil Rights Act of 1968 and 1988 Amendments

Clean Air Act

common interest developments

condominium

eminent domain

inclusionary zoning

National Environmental Policy Act

planned unit development (PUD)

planning commission

planning departments

police power

public report

selling undivided interests

steering

stock cooperative

Subdivided Lands Act

Subdivision Map Act

Unruh Civil Rights Act

zoning

PRACTICAL APPLICATION

1. You are the real estate agent for an owner of vacant land currently zoned residential. You and the owner believe that growth trends have changed and that the highest and best use of the land would be for commercial development. You apply to the planning commission for a rezone to commercial use. The planning commission turns down your proposal. The owner wishes to appeal the planning commission decision. What is the appeal process?

2. Explain how a condominium differs from a PUD and a stock cooperative. Why are they all called *common interest developments*?

3. You just listed a $750,000 home for sale. Twenty days later, the seller calls to tell you that the neighbors are concerned that the home might be sold to a minority person and that the seller does not want the home shown to potential minority buyers. How should you respond?

REVIEWING YOUR UNDERSTANDING

1. Which of the following is an example of government use of police power?
   a. rent controls
   b. building codes
   c. zoning ordinances
   d. all of the above

2. The Subdivision Map Act is administered by
   a. the California real estate commissioner.
   b. local officials.
   c. the California Department of Urban Planning.
   d. the Department of Housing and Urban Development (HUD).

3. Before a developer can sell a lot in a new California subdivision containing five or more lots, the prospective buyer must receive a copy of the:
   a. preliminary title report.
   b. builder's warranties.
   c. public report.
   d. zoning ordinances.

4. A developer from Nevada wishes to sell 300 Las Vegas lots to California residents and open sales offices in Los Angeles and San Francisco. The developer need not conform to the:
   a. Subdivision Map Act.
   b. California Department of Real Estate sales agreement disclosures requirements.
   c. California Department of Real Estate advertising disclosures requirements.
   d. Interstate Land Sales Full-Disclosure Act.

5. The right of the consumer, within a specified time, to rescind a land purchase contract and receive a full refund applies to new:
   a. urban subdivisions of 50 lots or more.
   b. suburban subdivisions of 50 lots or more.
   c. farmland of 50 acres or more.
   d. land projects of 50 lots or more.

6. A development where a person individually owns his or her living unit but has an undivided interest with the other owners in the land and common areas is a:
   a. planned unit development.
   b. townhouse.
   c. condominium.
   d. stock cooperative.

7. The selling of a 1/2500 share in a northern California recreational ranch is an example of a(n):
   a. undivided interest.
   b. condominium.
   c. PUD.
   d. time-sharing ownership.

8. A person cannot refuse to sell a home based on a buyer's:
   a. physical handicap.
   b. marital status.
   c. sex.
   d. all of the above.

9. The law that prevents agents from discriminating when providing real estate services is the:
   a. Fair Housing Act.
   b. Rumford Act.
   c. Unruh Civil Rights Act.
   d. Housing Financial Discrimination Act.

10. The law that makes it illegal for real estate lenders to redline a neighborhood is the:
   a. California Fair Housing Act.
   b. Rumford Act.
   c. Unruh Civil Rights Act.
   d. Housing Financial Discrimination Act.

11. Which of the following is the best example of a common interest development?
   a. condominium
   b. single-family home
   c. tenant-occupied apartment building
   d. mobile home park

12. Recorded CC&Rs and an homeowners' association are mandatory for a:
   a. condominium.
   b. single-family home.
   c. tenant-occupied apartment building.
   d. mobile home park.

13. A deviation from the established zone requirements is called:
   a. a lot split.
   b. a negative impact report.
   c. rezoning.
   d. a variance.

14. If private deed restrictions allow some use that is prohibited by zoning, the rule is that
   a. zoning prevails.
   b. private deed restrictions prevail.
   c. rezoning is allowed.
   d. spot zoning is required.

15. A simple lot split is governed by the:
   a. Subdivided Lands Act.
   b. Subdivision Lot Division Act.
   c. Subdivision Map Act.
   d. Subdivision Land Project Act.

16. The Civil Rights Act of 1968 and 1988 Amendments does not protect against discrimination in housing if a person is
   a. a current controlled-substance abuser.
   b. an alcoholic.
   c. an AIDS victim.
   d. confined to a wheelchair.

17. The illegal act of directing potential buyers and tenants to certain neighborhoods is called
   a. block busting.
   b. directing.
   c. locating.
   d. steering.

18. If the real estate commissioner issues a Preliminary Public Report for a subdivision, a developer is allowed to
    a. sell the lots.
    b. reserve the lots.
    c. finance the lots.
    d. escrow the lots.

19. The power of eminent domain requires government agencies to
    a. regulate but not buy the private property.
    b. pay just compensation for the private property.
    c. include the private property in the general plan.
    d. take public property.

20. Prior to issuing a building permit involving a minor project with little if any environmental damage, the local government may require a(n):
    a. environmental impact report.
    b. public subdivision report.
    c. property tax report.
    d. negative impact report.

Chapter

13

Government levies taxes to generate revenue to help pay for government expenditures. This chapter presents the principles of real property and income taxation, two forms of taxation that have a direct impact on real estate ownership. At the conclusion of the chapter, you will be able to do the following:

1. Describe the real property assessment procedure as required by Proposition 13.

2. List the rules regarding the date and manner of payment of real property taxes, and describe the tax sale procedure in the event of nonpayment of property taxes.

3. Explain homeowners', veterans', and senior citizens' property tax exemptions.

4. List the income tax advantages of real estate ownership, including the changes resulting from recent revisions in tax laws.

Introduction to Taxation

13.1 REAL PROPERTY TAXES

In California, property taxes used to be levied by cities and counties on an ad valorem basis. **Ad valorem** is a Latin phrase that means "according to value." Under the concept of ad valorem, owners of higher valued property pay more in property taxes than owners of lower valued property. With the passage of Proposition 13, property taxes in California are now levied using a system based upon date of acquisition, which is not a pure ad valorem system.

Assessment Procedure

On June 6, 1978, the voters of California passed Proposition 13, the Jarvis-Gann initiative. **Proposition 13** limits real property taxes to 1 percent of the full cash value of the real property, plus an amount for local assessments and bonds.

No Change in Ownership Since March 1, 1975

Under the terms of Proposition 13, if there has been no change in ownership since March 1, 1975, the 1975 value shall be the initial full cash value. To this figure the assessor is allowed to add an inflation factor of 2 percent per year, *compounded* to arrive at full cash value for the present tax year. For example, assume that a person has owned his or her home since March 1, 1975. The 1975 value was $60,000. The 1976 full cash value would be $60,000 plus 2% (or $61,200), 1977 would be $61,200 plus 2% (or $62,424), and so on, until the present tax year is reached. In this example, for the year 2011, the value for tax purposes will be $113,073. Therefore, the maximum real property tax for the 2007–2008 tax year will be 1% of $113,073, or only $1,130.73, plus any amount needed to pay for voter-approved bonds, less any exemptions such as the California homeowner's exemption. Again, this applies only if there is no change in ownership since March 1, 1975.

In this example, the value for tax purposes bears no relationship to the actual current market value of the property. A home worth $60,000 in 1975 may be worth $500,000 or more currently. But the property would be taxed at a value of $113,073—a bargain for the property owner.

Change in Ownership Since March 1, 1975

When there is a change in ownership (such as a sale, a gift, or an inheritance), *the new owner's full cash value for tax purposes shall be the sales price or value of the property as of the date of transfer.* A supplemental tax bill is then mailed to the new owner.

Using the previous example, if a property worth $60,000 in 1975 is sold in January 2011 for $500,000, the new owner's full cash value for that tax year will be $500,000. Therefore, the maximum real property tax for the 2011–2012 tax year will be 1% of $500,000, or $5,000, plus any amount needed to pay for voter-approved bonds, less any exemptions such as the California homeowner's exemption.

As you can see, whenever there is a change in ownership, the full cash value for tax purposes is adjusted to the current market value of the property. In many cases, this can result in a dramatic increase in real property taxes from what the former owner was paying.

Supplemental Property Tax Bill

When a real estate transfer occurs that triggers a new property tax assessment, a supplemental tax bill is sent to the new owner. For example, assume that a transfer occurs in the middle of a tax year. The new owner will be required to pay the remaining portion of the former owner's property tax bill, plus an increase (or decrease, in some cases) in the form of a supplemental bill that reflects the increase in assessment due to the title transfer. This prevents a new owner from getting a windfall tax break based on the former owner's lower Proposition 13 assessment.

Is This Discrimination?

Opponents of Proposition 13 have long contended that this law discriminates against recent buyers. Opponents point out that similar properties side by side could have dramatically different property tax bills depending on when each owner purchased the property. Is this a form of discrimination based on unequal taxation? In a U.S. Supreme Court case, it was held that Proposition 13 is constitutional and not a form of illegal discrimination.

Other Adjustments

On new construction since March 1, 1975, full cash value for tax purposes is the real estate value at the time of completion plus the inflation factor of 2 percent per year to the present tax year. If you add improvements to your existing home, such as a swimming pool or a new bathroom, does this affect your tax bill? Yes. Does it mean that the entire home is brought up to current market value for tax purposes? No. What happens is that your home keeps its present full cash value as shown on the tax records before your new improvements. Then the new improvements are valued separately as of the date of completion. Each of these figures is adjusted by the 2 percent yearly figure, and the sum of these two figures equals full cash value for tax purposes.

Transfer Exclusions

Transfers between spouses and registered domestic partners—such as changing title from joint tenancy to community property or a deed from one spouse or partner to another—or deeding property to a living trust are not considered transfers for property tax purposes. A transfer of a principal residence worth $1 million or less from a parent(s) to children also is not considered a transfer for property tax purposes. Other transfer exclusions include replacing a property due to government eminent domain or replacing a property due to a disaster. This means that the county assessor *will not* reappraise the property and increase the property tax.

During the real estate crash of the early to mid-1990s, when property values dropped, the tax assessor did not automatically increase tax values by the 2 percent factor allowed under Proposition 13. In some cases, property tax values were lowered and property taxes owed declined.

Special Treatment for Senior Citizens

Another law, Proposition 60, allows homeowners 55 years of age and over to transfer their base-year property tax value to another home of equal or less value in the *same county* and keep the low assessment they had on their former home. Example: A couple purchased a home in 1985 for $100,000. For property tax purposes, the assessed value is now $121,900 but the home is worth $500,000. If the couple sells for $500,000 and buys a home in the same county for $490,000, they can take their $121,900 assessment to the new home, rather than be assessed for the $490,000 purchase price. This results in the following property tax savings: $121,900 × 1% = $1,219 property tax, versus $490,000 × 1% = $4,900 property tax.

Proposition 90 allows the same concept to be applied if a home is purchased in *another county*, but only if that county's Board of Supervisors chooses to apply Proposition 90.

Real Property Tax Dates

Real property taxes cover a fiscal year that begins July 1 and runs through June 30 of the following year. For example, the fiscal tax year for 2010–2011 would begin July 1, 2010, and end June 30, 2011.

The real property tax becomes a lien on the January 1 preceding the fiscal tax year. Using the previous example, on January 1, 2010, a lien is placed on all taxable real estate for the 2010–2011 tax year, which begins July 1, 2010. (See Figure 13.1.)

The real property tax can be paid in two equal installments. The first installment is due November 1 and is delinquent if not paid by 5 p.m. on December 10. If December 10 falls on a weekend or holiday, the tax is due by 5 p.m. the next business day. The second installment is due on February 1 and is delinquent if not paid by 5 p.m. on April 10. Again, if April 10 falls on a weekend or holiday, the tax is due by 5 p.m. the next business day.

FIGURE 13.1

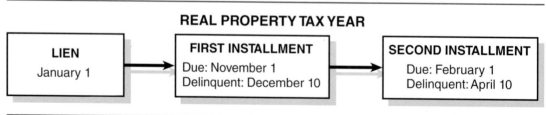

REAL PROPERTY TAX YEAR

LIEN	FIRST INSTALLMENT	SECOND INSTALLMENT
January 1	Due: November 1 Delinquent: December 10	Due: February 1 Delinquent: April 10

If a taxpayer wishes, both installments can be paid when the first installment is due. A 10 percent penalty is added to each installment that is not paid on time. If both installments become delinquent, a small additional charge is added to the 10 percent penalty. As a memory tool, some people use the acronym NDFA, which stands for "November, December, February, and April"—or "No Darn Fooling Around" with property taxes!

Memory Tool "NDFA"
November 1
December 10
February 1
April 10

Tax Sale

If an owner fails to pay real property taxes when due, on June 30 the tax collector publishes a notice of "intent to sell" the property to the state of California because of unpaid taxes. This sale is not a real sale, but rather what is known as a *book sale*. The property owner still owns the real estate, but the owner's name is entered into a delinquent account book, which begins a five-year redemption period. During this five-year period, an owner can redeem the property by paying back taxes, interests, and other penalties and costs. Delinquent taxes can be paid in five annual installments as long as the current taxes are paid on time. For example, assume that a taxpayer owes three years' worth of back property taxes. If the owner pays the current year's taxes, the tax collector will allow the owner to make partial payments on the back taxes, rather than demand full payment of all back taxes.

If after five years the property taxes are still unpaid, the delinquent property is deeded to the state, and the former owner loses title. But as long as the state holds title, the former owner still has the right of redemption.

However, the state also has the right to sell tax-deeded property to other public agencies or to private parties. Once the state sells the property, the former owner loses the right of redemption.

Public Auction

The sale of tax-deeded property is conducted by the county tax collector, who must first obtain the permission of the local board of supervisors and the state controller.

The actual sale is a public auction that begins with a minimum bid that varies with each parcel being sold. All tax sales are for cash, as the state or county will not finance the sale. The successful bidder receives a *tax deed*. Under current title insurance practices, the holder of tax-deeded property can acquire title insurance after a period of one year.

Real Property Tax Exemptions

Because of special laws, certain owners of real estate are partially or totally exempt from the payment of property taxes. For example, government-owned real estate such as public buildings, parks, and school sites are exempt from property taxation. Some churches and other religious properties are not charged property taxes. In addition, there are special exemptions for homeowners, veterans, and senior citizens.

California Homeowner's Exemption

Under current law (January 2007), an owner-occupied residential dwelling is entitled to a $7,000 deduction from full assessed value. For example, if an owner-occupied home is assigned a $350,000 full cash value by the assessor, a $7,000 homeowner's exemption is subtracted from this figure to obtain a $343,000 taxable value.

$350,000	Full cash value
− 7,000	Less homeowner's exemption
$343,000	Taxable value

Then, according to Proposition 13, the actual tax will be $3,430 ($343,000 × 1%), plus any amount needed to pay for voter-approved bonds. In short, the California Homeowner's Exemption is worth $70 ($7,000 × 1%).

To claim the homeowner's exemption, a person must have been the owner and in residence on or before January 1 and must file for the exemption with the assessor's office by February 15. Once filed, the exemption remains in effect until title is transferred or the exemption is terminated by actions of the owner. If a homeowner should miss the February 15 deadline, he or she can still file by December 1, but will receive only 80 percent ($5,600) of the $7,000 exemption.

Veteran's Exemption

A California resident who has served in the military during time of war is entitled to a $4,000 exemption on the full value of the property. However, a person may not have a homeowner's exemption and a veteran's exemption on the same property. Therefore, a veteran who owns one home is wise to take the homeowner's exemption of $7,000 instead of the veteran's exemption of $4,000. If a veteran owns other real estate in addition to a personal residence, the veteran's exemption can be applied against the other property. But current rules prohibit a veteran whose net worth exceeds a designated sum from using the veteran's exemption. The designated net worth is subject to change, so a veteran should contact a veteran's official or tax consultant before applying for the veteran's exemption.

Upon the death of an eligible veteran, the exemption rights are extended to the unmarried surviving spouse, registered domestic partner, or a pensioned father or mother. *Special rules exist for veterans who are disabled* because of injuries incurred in military service. In some cases, the disabled veteran may not be required to pay any property tax. The California Department of Veterans Affairs should be contacted regarding the special rules for disabled California veterans.

Exemptions for Senior Citizens

In recent years, several laws have been enacted to help senior citizens, many of whom live on fixed incomes. Under some laws, a senior citizen is defined as a person 55 years of age or older; under other laws, the age limit is moved up to 62 years or older.

In California, there are special laws that allow a partial or total refund of property taxes for certain senior citizens. In addition, the California legislature has passed laws allowing certain senior citizens to defer the payment of property taxes due on their home. In such a case the state pays the property taxes due the county and city. Then the state places a lien against the senior citizen's home, which accrues interest. The postponed taxes and interest run for an indefinite period. The state can recover on the lien only when the senior citizen dies, sells, or no longer occupies the home.

The rules that determine the eligibility of senior citizens for special tax treatment are constantly changing; therefore, senior citizens should contact the local tax assessor or senior citizen's action council for the latest information.

Other Exemptions

Property tax exemptions of one sort or another also exist for a variety of other owners of real estate. Owners who use the land for timber, growing crops, young orchard trees, grapevines less than three years old, as well as churches and nonprofit organizations all qualify in some way for property tax exemptions. In addition, property tax incentives are used to keep agricultural land from being converted to urban use.

Special Assessments

Special assessments are different from real property taxes. Real property taxes help pay for the general operation of local government, whereas **special assessments** are levied to pay for a specific improvement, such as streets and sewers. Special assessment liens usually are on a parity with property tax liens and often are collected at the same time.

A frequently used special assessment law is the Street Improvement Act of 1911. This law is used by cities and counties for street improvements. According to this law, local government or a specially formed district hires a contractor to install or improve streets. Each owner along the street is liable for a pro rata share of the cost. The owner can pay in full within 30 days after completion, or the local government can sell bonds to raise the revenue to pay the contractor. If the project goes to bond, the property owners can pay their pro-rated share in installments over a period of time. Failure to pay a special assessment can result in a loss in the property owner's title, similar in nature to a tax sale.

Another program is the Mello-Roos Community Facilities Act of 1982. This law is used to finance public services in newly developed areas. Examples of services include waste treatment plants, parks, schools, fire stations, and so on. Under this program, the owners in the assessment district pay for the facilities in their neighborhood, rather than owners in other neighborhoods paying for the facilities. The Mello-Roos Act can result in very high taxes, well above the normal property tax, and must be made known to any new buyer before a purchase takes place.

Taxing Personal Property

As a general rule, only tangible personal property used in business is subject to taxes. Intangible property (such as shares of stock, or loans due) as well as household furnishings and personal effects are not taxed.

Personal property taxes are divided into secured and unsecured categories, depending on whether the owner of the personal property also owns the real estate where the personal property is located. Many rules apply to personal property, but they are beyond the scope of this book. Local tax assessors have numerous pamphlets available that explain the personal property tax procedures. All businesspeople are encouraged to obtain and read these pamphlets.

13.2 INCOME TAXES

Income taxes are levied by the federal government and by the state of California. The income tax is a progressive tax. *Progressive* means that the federal and state rates increase as the income levels being taxed increase.

**Persons and Agencies Involved
in Property Taxes**

COURTHOUSE

County board of supervisors. Establishes county budgets and sets county property tax rates up to the maximum allowed by law.

City council members. Establish city budgets and set city property tax rates up to the maximum allowed by law.

City or county auditor. Maintains the tax rolls.

City or county assessor. Appraises property for tax purposes.

City or county tax collector. Is responsible for actually collecting the taxes.

Local board of equalization. Is composed of the members of the board of supervisors; hears appeals from citizens who believe they have been taxed unfairly. In some areas, this function is handled by an assessment appeals board, which consists of citizens appointed by the board of supervisors.

State board of equalization. Audits and offers guidance to local taxing agencies.

The buying and selling of real estate have significant income tax consequences. In some cases, the income tax aspects may be as important as the price of the property. Income tax aspects of a real estate transaction should be considered before the sale, not after. Once a sale takes place, it is too late to go back and restructure the sale to take advantage of any tax laws that were overlooked.

Special note: Registered domestic partners cannot file joint income tax forms for state and federal taxes. Therefore, the income tax privileges extended to married couples do not apply to registered domestic partners in California.

Income tax laws are complicated and constantly changing. Before entering into a complicated real estate transaction, a person should seek the advice of an income tax specialist, such as an attorney or accountant.

Major Income Tax Advantages for Homeowners

Income tax laws favor homeowners over renters by granting various income tax incentives for becoming a homeowner.

1. Interest paid on real estate loans is deductible against personal income to reduce tax liability, subject to the interest limitation noted on the next pages.

2. Property taxes paid are also deductible against personal income.

3. The old 24-month trade-up and 55-year-old rules have been abolished. The law now states that there will be no tax on gain up to $250,000 for singles and $500,000 for married couples who file joint returns. There are no age limits and no restrictions even if a person previously used the 55-year-old exemption. Unmarried co-owners get up to a $250,000 exclusion for each person if each meets the ownership and occupancy rules. Registered domestic partners come under this unmarried co-owner rule. To qualify, the home must have been the principal residence for at least a total of two years during the five years prior to the sale. Only one spouse must be the owner during this time. But both spouses must have lived there for the two-year period to get the maximum exemption of $500,000 with a joint filing.

4. The full exclusion can be used only once every two years. When the home is sold for a gain before the two-year holding period is achieved, the gain is fully taxable unless the sale is due to a job change, a major illness, or unforeseen circumstances. Then a pro rata formula is used to separate tax exempt from taxable gain.

> *Example:* Owned and lived in a home only 18 months; then due to a job change, sold it for a gain. The formula is as follows:
>
> $$\frac{18 \text{ months}}{24 \text{ months}} = 75\%$$
>
> For single exclusion $250,000 \times 75\% = \$187,500$ maximum
>
> For married $500,000 \times 75\% = \$375,000$ maximum exclusion

1997 Tax Law: Homeowner Problems

1. Homeowners with gains of more than $250,000 for singles and $500,000 for married couples filing jointly will be taxed at capital gain rates for the excess over these dollar amounts. No deferral techniques are available.

2. Loss on the sale of a personal home will not be tax deductible.

Major Income Advantages for Investment Property Owners

1. Interest on real estate loans and property taxes paid is deductible against the rental income earned by the property.

2. Repairs, maintenance, management, insurance, and other operating expenses are also deductible. *Note: Repairs, maintenance, and other operating expenses are not deductible for homeowners on their own residences, only on investment real estate.*

3. Depreciation deduction allowances, technically called *cost recovery*, can be used to shelter income. The **depreciation deduction** consists of a yearly allowance (the length depending on if it is residential or nonresidential) for wear, tear, and obsolescence, which permits the property owner to recover the original cost over the useful life of the property. Land is not depreciable, only the improvements such as buildings, fences, and so on. Depreciation cannot be taken on owner-occupied residential homes; it can be taken only on income real estate. Depreciation deductions reduce the taxable income, thereby giving the property owner more after-tax cash flow. However, tax law changes place restrictions on how real estate losses can be used to shelter income other than rents.

4. Under certain circumstances, an investment property owner can enter into a tax-deferred exchange. If properly structured, an investor can exchange one like property for another (typically defined as real for real, in business or investment use, for equal or greater value) without paying immediate income taxes on the former property. The tax liability is not eliminated, but rather postponed until the investor disposes of the new property in a taxable transaction—usually a sale. Some people incorrectly call this a "tax-free" exchange; technically it is only a tax-deferred exchange. To structure an Internal Revenue Code, Section 1031, tax-deferred exchange, an investor must not receive what is referred to as *boot*. **Boot** is defined as unlike property received in an exchange. The receipt of boot creates a tax liability on the boot. Examples of boot include cash, notes, personal property, mortgage relief, and so on. There are many technical rules regarding a tax-deferred exchange, and no one should proceed without the advice of tax counsel.

REAL ESTATE ASPECTS OF THE TAX REFORM ACT OF 1986, TAX REVENUE ACT OF 1987, TAXPAYER RELIEF ACT OF 1997, AND OTHER RECENT REVISIONS

Summary of Rules for Homeowners

1. Mortgage interest deductions are allowed for acquisition debt (purchase money loan) up to a maximum loan of $1 million on all combined mortgages on a first and second residence. If you borrow more than $1 million, the interest paid on the excess over $1 million is not deductible. No interest deduction is allowed for three or more personal-use homes.

2. For the refinance of an existing home, the remaining loan balance on acquisitions loan(s) plus $100,000 will be the maximum refinance loan allowed if the homeowner wishes to deduct all the interest as a qualified home loan. However, if a refinance loan exceeds the home's value, a portion of the interest paid is not deductible.

3. The $250,000 for singles and $500,000 for joint-filing married couples exemptions noted on previous pages are still valid.

4. Installment sale treatment is still allowed for homeowners.

Summary of Rules for Income Property Owners

1. Depreciation (cost recovery) on buildings and improvements is 27 ½ years for residential rental properties and 39 years for nonresidential properties. The straight-line method must be used.

2. Rental property mortgage interest is fully deductible against rental income, with no dollar loan limits such as the $1 million cap placed on homeowners. However, any tax loss created by interest and depreciation deductions falls under the passive tax loss rules listed herein.

3. Real estate rentals are considered "passive" investments and produce either passive income or passive loss, depending on the property's cash flow. The general rule is that a passive real estate loss can only be used to offset other passive income, *not* active or portfolio income such as salaries, commissions, profits, interest, and dividends. Prior to tax law changes, real estate losses could be used to offset active or portfolio income.

4. There is a special $25,000 exception to the passive loss rules if a person meets the following test:

   a. Is an individual owner of 10 percent or more interest in rental real estate

   b. Is actively involved in the management (owner can use property managers, but he or she must make the key decisions)

   c. Has a modified adjusted gross income of $100,000 or less

   If the owner of rental real estate meets this test, he or she can use up to $25,000 in passive losses from real estate to offset active or portfolio income, such as salaries and interest, after first offsetting passive income.

5. If the rental property owner's modified adjusted gross income exceeds $100,000, the $25,000 amount is reduced $1 for every $2 above the $100,000. Any unused passive losses from rental real estate can be carried forward to reduce future passive income and gain upon sale of the property. The passive loss rules do not eliminate the investor's right to use real estate losses. However, the law's changes will, in some cases, delay the right to use the loss until a later date, such as the date of resale.

6. The right for a real estate investor to do a 1031 tax-deferred exchange remains the same; recent tax law changes have not eliminated this technique.

7. Installment sales treatment for real estate investors is still allowed. Installment sale treatment for real estate dealers has been abolished.

There are many other tax law changes, but these are the items that have a major impact on real estate. The preceding is listed for information purposes and should not be considered tax advice. For tax advice, a person should seek competent tax advisors.

5. An installment sale is another way to reduce tax liability upon the sale of real estate. This method of selling allows the seller to carry back paper and spread the gain from the sale over a period of years. Rather than paying the entire tax in the year of sale, the seller pays income taxes only on that portion of the gain received in the form of payments in any one year. Once again, advice of tax counsel should be sought to make sure the sale qualifies for installment reporting.

State Income Tax

In some ways, California income tax law is patterned after the federal laws. However, some notable differences should be discussed with a tax expert. For example, the tax brackets for individuals and corporations are different for state income tax as opposed to federal income taxes. There are special rules regarding new residents and their need to file a California income tax statement. All of these state tax laws, in addition to many others, are administered by the California Franchise Tax Board.

For most real estate transactions, the impact of federal income taxes is more important than the impact of state income taxes. But careful tax planning should attempt to minimize both federal and state income taxes.

Special Withholding Rules for Foreign and Out-of-State Sellers

Under the Foreign Investment in Real Property Tax Act (FIRPTA), the federal government requires that 10 percent of the sales price of property owned by a foreigner must be withheld for a possible income tax liability. California Revenue and Taxation Code Sections 18805 and 26131 require a $3\frac{1}{3}$ percent withholding for state income taxes if the seller is a foreigner or a resident of another state. A recent law change also allows the state to withhold $3\frac{1}{3}$ percent from California residents who sell certain types of investment property. Both of these laws put the burden for compliance on the buyer, not the seller. Both of these laws have exceptions and exemptions that can be complicated and tricky. If a person is purchasing California property from a foreigner or a U.S. citizen who lives in another state, the buyer might wish to check with a tax expert before the sale takes place to make sure the income tax laws are being correctly applied.

13.3 OTHER TAXES

Documentary Transfer Tax

Upon the transfer of real estate, a documentary transfer tax of $0.55 per $500 of consideration, or fraction thereof (at a rate of $1.10 per $1,000), is levied. If the property being transferred is in an unincorporated area, all of the tax goes to the county where the property is located. If the property is located in an incorporated city, the city and county divide the tax proceeds.

The tax is levied on the full price of the property if there is an all-cash sale or if the buyer obtains a new loan that cashes the seller out. If the buyer assumes the seller's existing loan, the transfer tax is levied only on the equity being transferred. (See Chapter 6 for detailed examples of the documentary transfer tax.)

Estate and Inheritance Tax

In some cases, the federal government taxes the estates of deceased persons. The state of California has eliminated inheritance taxes. There are several ways to reduce or, in some cases, avoid the payment of estate taxes. The methods are technical and complicated, and the services of an attorney should be used. For further information, see Internal Revenue Publication 559.

Gift Taxes

The federal government, but not the state of California, has tax laws that apply to gifts of real and personal property. A gift is a voluntary transfer of property from the owner, called the *donor*, to the receiver, called the *donee*.

The federal law allows a tax-free gift (as of January 2006) of $13,000 of value per donee per year. This $13,000 is scheduled to increase slowly over time. The use of gift tax exclusions during the life of the donor can often be used to save estate taxes upon death. Gift tax laws are complicated, and professional tax advice should be sought when planning an estate to minimize taxes by use of gifts.

Miscellaneous Taxes

Sales and use taxes occasionally arise in certain broker transactions—for example, in the sale of a business opportunity or a mobile home. In circumstances where sales tax is involved, the real estate agent is responsible for seeing that escrow instructions are correctly drafted to account for the tax liability.

Unemployment insurance fees, worker's compensation fees, and Social Security taxes may need to be collected when a real estate salesperson is hired by a broker and acts as an employee instead of as an independent contractor.

CHAPTER SUMMARY

Property taxes in California are levied on a modified ad valorem basis and usually change when a property is transferred to a new owner. Two classifications of property taxes are real property taxes and personal property taxes. With passage of the Jarvis-Gann Initiative (Proposition 13), the maximum real property tax allowed is 1 percent of full cash value, plus 2 percent annual inflationary factor, plus an additional sum to pay for voter-approved bonds that affect the property.

If there has been no change in ownership since March 1, 1975, the tax year 1975–1976 is the base year for computing full cash value. A change in ownership after March 1, 1975, causes the full cash value for tax purposes to be increased to the sales price or value as of the date of transfer. There are special rules for the handling of remodeling and additions that cause the taxable value to rise.

Real property taxes are paid over a fiscal year beginning July 1 and ending June 30. The first installment is due November 1 and is delinquent if not paid by December 10. The second installment is due February 1 and is delinquent if not paid by April 10. Real property taxes become a lien on the January 1 preceding the fiscal tax year. If the required taxes are not paid, the owner's title will eventually revert to the state of California for delinquent taxes.

Real property tax exemptions include $7,000 on appraised value for homeowners, $4,000 for qualified veterans, and special exemptions for senior citizens. There are several other property tax exemptions for certain classes of property, such as timber and growing crops.

Income taxes are levied by both federal and state government. Income taxes are progressive—that is, the tax rate increases as the income level increases. The buying and selling of real estate have significant income tax consequences. Sometimes the income tax aspects are more important than the price. Income tax laws are complicated and constantly changing. Before entering into a real estate transaction, a person should seek the advice of a qualified tax expert.

Other taxes that can have an impact on real estate are estate taxes, gift taxes, transfer taxes, and use and sales taxes.

IMPORTANT TERMS AND CONCEPTS

ad valorem

boot

depreciation
deduction

proposition 13

special assessments

PRACTICAL APPLICATION

1. Counting local bonds, the typical property tax in your community runs .0125 of the sales price, and homeowner's insurance runs .005 of the sales price. As a real estate agent, you are showing potential buyers a $225,000 condo that requires an 80 percent loan at 8 percent amortized for 30 years. Based on this information, what will be the initial monthly housing payment of PITI (principal, interest, 1/12 taxes, and 1/12 insurance)? *Hint:* You need to use a financial calculator or the amortization table in Chapter 6.

2. Married homeowners who have owned and lived in their main home for eight years sell their $750,000 home and have a $300,000 gain. They file joint returns and their federal capital gain tax bracket is 20 percent. Based on this information, how much do they owe in federal taxes due to the sale of their home?

3. A homeowner refinances and takes out a 125 percent equity loan. How much of the interest on this loan is deductible for federal income taxes?

REVIEWING YOUR UNDERSTANDING

1. Under Proposition 13, the maximum real property tax cannot exceed what percent of full cash value after adjustments for inflation, voter-approved bonds, and exemptions?
   a. 1%
   b. 2%
   c. 5%
   d. 10%

2. Real property taxes become a lien on
   a. February 1.
   b. January 1.
   c. December 1.
   d. November 1.

3. Real property reverts to the state if property taxes are delinquent for
   a. one year.
   b. three years.
   c. five years.
   d. seven years.

4. If full cash value of a small condo is $290,000, what is the taxable value after subtracting for a homeowner's exemption?
   a. $281,000
   b. $297,000
   c. $290,000
   d. $283,000

5. The second installment of real property taxes is due
   a. November 1.
   b. December 10.
   c. February 1.
   d. April 10.

6. Which of the following is incorrect?
   a. To obtain the full homeowner's exemption, a person must file by February 15.
   b. The California veteran's exemption is $4,000.
   c. Property taxes are collected by the assessor.
   d. Special assessments are liens on real property.

7. A qualified single homeowner can exclude the taxable gains from the sale of a home up to
   a. $100,000.
   b. $150,000.
   c. $250,000.
   d. $500,000.

8. A qualified married couple who files joint returns can exclude gain on their home up to
   a. $100,000.
   b. $150,000.
   c. $250,000.
   d. $500,000.

9. Income real estate is entitled to use
   a. tax-deferred exchanges.
   b. installment sale provisions.
   c. depreciation deductions on improvements.
   d. all of the above.

10. The passive loss rules apply to
    a. principal residences.
    b. vacant land.
    c. rental real estate.
    d. personal automobiles.

11. In a Section 1031 tax-deferred exchange, the receipt of unlike property is called
    a. basis.
    b. boot.
    c. basics.
    d. bases.

12. Examples of laws that create special assessments above and beyond basic property taxes are the Street Improvement Act of 1911 and:
    a. Proposition 13.
    b. Proposition 60.
    c. the Assessment Act of 1974.
    d. the Mello-Roos Community Facilities Act of 1982.

13. The home sales price is $550,000, and the buyer is to assume an existing loan of $490,000; the documentary transfer tax is
    a. $605.
    b. $539.
    c. $110.
    d. $66.

14. The homeowner's property tax exemption is worth how much in actual annual tax savings?
    a. $7,000
    b. $700
    c. $70
    d. $7

15. When a seller carries paper to spread out the taxable gain over a series of years, this is called
    a. installment reporting.
    b. a 1031 exchange.
    c. a capital gain.
    d. tax elimination.

16. Which of the following cannot legally take a depreciation tax deduction on his or her property?
    a. An apartment building owner
    b. A retail store owner
    c. A farm building owner
    d. A homeowner, for that portion of the home not used as a business

17. Under certain guidelines, which proposition allows home-owners 55 years or older to transfer their property tax basis to another home in the same county?
    a. Proposition 13
    b. Proposition 60
    c. Proposition 90
    d. Proposition 1034

18. For a homeowner, which of the following expenses are deductible for income tax purposes?
    a. Condo association dues
    b. Fire insurance
    c. Property taxes
    d. All of the above

19. The government person who maintains the property tax rolls
    is the:
    a. assessor.
    b. collector.
    c. councilperson.
    d. none of the above.

20. A *book sale* refers to a sale:
    a. where income taxes are deferred.
    b. for accounting purposes for delinquent property taxes.
    c. where tax-delinquent property is deeded to a buyer.
    d. to remove paid liens.

Chapter

14

STUDENT LEARNING OUTCOMES

This chapter explores the characteristics of a house, including construction details, roof styles, and architectural designs. Mobile homes, condominiums, and vacation or second homes are also discussed. At the conclusion of the chapter, you will be able to do the following:

1. Identify major construction terms associated with home building.
2. Differentiate among various architectural styles.
3. List the advantages and disadvantages of buying versus renting a home.
4. Discuss the advantages and disadvantages of owning a mobile (manufactured) home, condominium, and vacation home.

Single-Family Homes and Mobile Homes

14.1 HOME CONSTRUCTION STYLES

There are many varieties of home construction styles, but the three most common types are one-story, split-level, and two-story homes.

The one-story home is the simplest to build and the easiest to maintain, but it occupies more land per square foot of living space than the other styles.

The split-level home is popular in California because of the better utilization of land of varying topography as well as the pleasing cosmetic effect. However, it is usually more expensive to build.

The two-story home has a lower cost per square foot because a single foundation and roof support two floors of living area. But the principal disadvantage is the stairs that must be climbed to reach the second floor. Also, the difficulty of reaching exterior portions for repair and maintenance presents some problems.

Roof Styles

The major roof styles are illustrated below.

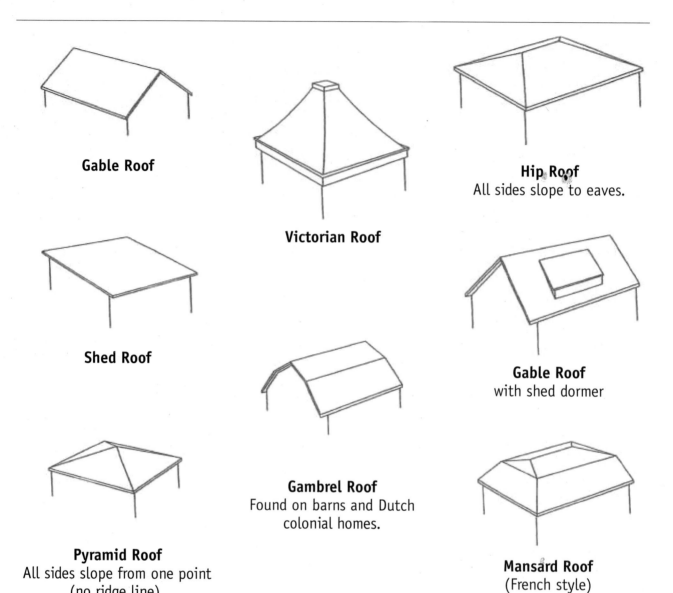

Gable Roof

Victorian Roof

Hip Roof
All sides slope to eaves.

Shed Roof

Gambrel Roof
Found on barns and Dutch
colonial homes.

Gable Roof
with shed dormer

Pyramid Roof
All sides slope from one point
(no ridge line).

Mansard Roof
(French style)

Source: *Real Estate California License Preparation Book* (Cincinnati, OH: South-Western, 2005).

Architectural Styles

The architectural styles of homes are illustrated and described here.

New England Colonial
A box-shaped two-story house with a center entrance, wood siding, and shutters.

Georgian Colonial
A brick two-story house with a center entrance and a hip roof.

Southern Colonial
A two-story house with pillars and shutters.

Dutch Colonial
A two-story house with a gambrel roof.

California Bungalow
A small one-story house with a low-pitched roof.

California Ranch
A one-story house with a low-pitched roof and a sprawling floor plan.

Spanish
A house with a tile roof and arches.

Cape Cod
A house with a second story above the eaves, a high-pitched roof, wood siding, and a large chimney.

French Provincial
A formal house with a high-pitched slate hip roof, a stone or brick exterior, and shutters.

Victorian
A house with
ornate gables.

English Elizabethan
A house with a high-
pitched slate roof,
rough half-timbers,
and a plaster exterior.

Monterey
A two-story
house with a
front balcony.

French Norman
A house with a tower
as the main entrance
and a steep roof.

English Tudor
A house with a high-pitched
slate roof, a cathedral-
like entrance, and a
masonry exterior.

Mediterranean or Italian
A house with a tile roof,
a stucco exterior, and
rounded decorative work
above the windows.

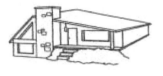

Contemporary
A house of
modern design.

Source: *Real Estate California License Preparation Book* (Cincinnati, OH: South-Western, 2005).

CONSTRUCTION DETAILS

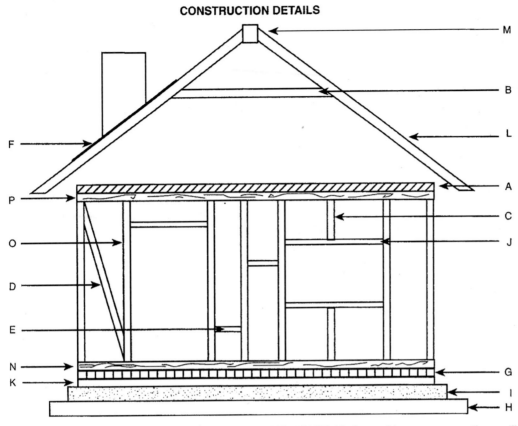

A CEILING JOIST. Horizontal beams supporting ceiling
B COLLAR BEAM. A beam that connects opposite rafters above the floor
C CRIPPLES. Short vertical piece 2 × 4 above or below an opening
D DIAGONAL BRACE. A brace across corner of structure to prevent swaying
E FIRE STOP. Short board or wall between studs to prevent fire spreading
F FLASHING. Metal sheet usually around chimney to prevent water seepage
G FLOOR JOIST. Horizontal beams supporting floor
H FOOTING. Base or bottom of a foundation wall
I FOUNDATION. The supporting portion of structure resting on footing
J LINTEL. A horizontal board over a door or window, also called header
K MUDSILL. Perimeter board anchored directly to foundation
L RAFTERS. Boards designed to support roof loads
M RIDGE BOARD. Highest board in the house supporting upper ends
N SOLE PLATE. Usually 2 × 4 on which wall and studs rest
O STUDS. Vertical boards 2 × 4 supporting the walls every 16″ (on center)
P TOP PLATE. A horizontal board fastened to upper end of studs

Other Construction Terms
  Board Foot = used to measure lumber, contains 144 cubic inches
  R–VALUE = ranking of insulation materials
  EER = Energy Efficiency Rating

14.2 MOBILE (MANUFACTURED) HOMES

Because building codes, zoning laws, and other practices, as well as inflation, make it difficult to build low-cost conventional houses, many families have turned to mobile homes as a solution.

The name *mobile* was changed to *manufactured* over 20 years ago, but most people still call them mobile homes. A mobile or manufactured home is defined by the California Health and Safety Code as "a vehicle designed and equipped to contain not more than two dwelling units, to be used without permanent foundation." Mobile homes in the past were confused with trailers. The major difference is that trailers usually provide temporary housing only, whereas a mobile home is a permanent living unit. The word *mobile* may be confusing; actually, studies show that once in place, mobile homes are seldom moved. They are usually located in mobile home parks, although in many rural areas, they can be found on individual lots. The Mobile Home Parks Act defines a **mobile home park** as "any area or tract of land where one or more mobile home lots are rented or leased." The rental operation of a mobile home park is within the jurisdiction of the State Department of Housing and Community Development. If a mobile home park has five or more lots for sale or lease, it is considered a subdivision and consequently subject to subdivision laws. Under certain circumstances, mobile homes purchased after July 1, 1980, can be taxed as real property if they are attached to a permanent foundation.

Types of Mobile Homes

The four basic types of mobile homes are illustrated here.

Single, 8-foot, and 10-foot-wide units

Single, 12-foot-wide units

Multiple-wide, double-wide, or triple-wide units

Quads—four units together

Legal Requirements Related to Mobile Homes

In order to list or sell a mobile home, a real estate licensee must comply with special aspects of the real estate law.

1. *New mobile homes cannot be sold by real estate licensees,* but only through mobile home dealers licensed by the Department of Housing and Community Development.
2. *A real estate licensee can sell used mobile homes* provided the mobile homes have already been registered with the state and are on a lot or in a mobile home park.
3. The mobile home must be capable of being transported over a road. The hitch must be attached to the unit or stored underneath, and the axles must still be attached to the frame.
4. The licensee is responsible to see that there is proper completion and delivery of the title to the buyer.
5. Notification of transfer of ownership must be made within 10 days of the sale date.
6. All fees must be paid to the state within 10 days of the sale date.
7. No concealment of a material fact or any other fraudulent act may be committed.
8. Mobile homeowners must pay an In Lieu Tax similar to regular property taxes paid by homeowners.
9. If the mobile home was manufactured after June 15, 1976, it must have a Department of Housing and Urban Development (HUD) tag, guaranteeing its proper construction.

Violations of Business and Professions Code

Under this code, real estate licensees may have their licenses suspended or revoked if they are found guilty of any of the following:

1. Failed to provide for the delivery of proper certificate of ownership of a mobile home
2. Knowingly participated in the purchase or sale of a stolen mobile home
3. Submitted a check, draft, or money order to the state for payment of mobile home fees and the draft is dishonored upon presentation to the bank

Financing Mobile Homes

Because mobile homes are considered to be personal property, the method of encumbering the ownership is through a security agreement instead of a deed of trust.

Mobile homes can be financed through FHA, VA, and Cal-Vet loans (see Chapter 8). In addition, conventional loans are available from banks and other real estate lenders. Most mobile home loans are amortized over a 15-year period. Interest rates on mobile home loans are usually higher than on conventional home loans.

Termination of Tenancy in a Mobile Home Park

The Civil Code provides for the termination of tenancy by the landlord of a mobile home park tenant when any of these occur:

1. Failure of the tenant to comply with local ordinances and state laws and regulations related to mobile homes
2. Conduct of the tenant upon park premises that constitutes a substantial annoyance to other tenants
3. Failure of the tenant to comply with reasonable rules and regulations of the mobile home park
4. Nonpayment of rent, utility charges, or incidental service charges
5. Failure to maintain the mobile home in a reasonable state of repair acceptable to park management

In recent years, there has been considerable legislation, as well as many disputes and lawsuits, regarding rents and other occupancy issues at mobile home parks. The complete rights and duties of landlords and tenants in a mobile home park are too extensive to cover in this textbook. Interested parties should research The Mobilehome Residency Law, Civil Code 798, and The Mobilehome Parks Act, Sections 18200, et. seq., of the California Health and Safety Code.

Advantages of Mobile Home Ownership

1. The price of traditional homes has risen so rapidly that many families, young adults, and senior citizens are purchasing mobile homes because of their lower prices as compared to conventional homes.
2. Mobile home parks are relatively quiet places to live.
3. Residents feel secure because there is usually only one entrance or exit to the mobile home and most residents know the other owners who live in the mobile home park.
4. Mobile homes are transportable.
5. The quality and amenities of mobile homes have improved over the years.
6. Better financing terms are now available for mobile home purchasers.
7. There is minimal yard maintenance or none at all.

Disadvantages of Mobile Home Ownership

1. Mobile homes can depreciate rapidly.
2. Mobile homes usually have a lower resale value than conventional houses.
3. The terms of loans offered by lenders are usually not as favorable as those for conventional homes.
4. When a mobile home is located in a mobile home park, the owner may be required to buy extras, such as steps with handrails or skirting to conceal wheels.
5. Cities and counties may have restrictions regarding the placement of mobile homes; therefore, sites may be difficult to obtain.

Converting a Mobile Home to Real Property

For a mobile home to become real property, the following four conditions must be met:

1. The mobile homeowner must obtain a building permit.
2. The mobile home must be placed on a permanent foundation.
3. The mobile homeowner must obtain a certificate of occupancy.
4. A document stating that the mobile home is attached to a permanent foundation must be recorded.

Once these conditions are met, a mobile home is considered real property, and all the laws of real estate apply.

Modular Homes

Although there are slight technical differences between a modular and a pre-paneled home, for our purposes a modular home will be considered a factory-built home, without wheels, that is intended from the beginning to be placed on a permanent foundation. **Modular homes** are not considered vehicles, as are mobile homes, and they immediately become real estate upon placement. Once placed, all the rules of real property apply to modular homes. They are allowed in areas zoned for single-family dwellings and compete in the marketplace with on-site constructed homes (sometimes called *stick-built homes*). Advocates of modular homes stress the consistent quality guaranteed in a factory setting, plus the lower cost per square foot, and the homes arrive at the building site 90 percent finished, which saves on-site construction time.

There are communities where lots are sold primarily for the placement of modular homes. Most of these are subdivisions with private deed restrictions and a homeowners' association for the common areas. Modular homes are entitled to all the financing packages that are granted to on-site constructed homes.

As with mobile homes, a real estate licensee is not allowed to sell a new modular unit from the factory or off a sales lot. But once a modular home is set in place, a real estate licensee is allowed to handle the sale of the property. If a real estate agent wishes to sell new mobile or modular homes, said agent must conform to retailer rules that come under the California State Board of Equalization and obtain additional special licenses that apply to mobile and modular homes.

14.3 CONDOMINIUMS

A **condominium** is a system of individual fee ownership of a unit in a multifamily structure combined with joint ownership of common areas of the structure and the land.

Advantages of Condominium Ownership

1. Owners can sell their units as they would a regular home.
2. Insurance companies offer special packages for condominium owners.
3. It combines the benefits of owning a house with the advantages of apartment living.
4. Owners receive the same income tax benefits as homeowners.

5. Owners build equity with each payment, as they do in a regular home.

6. There is little or no yard work to perform.

7. Common areas that are part of ownership can include game rooms, swimming pools, tennis courts, and putting greens.

8. The law offers some protection to owners, in that they cannot be made to leave because of certain infractions of by-laws and regulations of the governing owners' association.

Disadvantages of Condominium Ownership

1. Each owner is responsible for all building maintenance problems in his or her unit.

2. Owners may be required to pay their share of the association fees to cover maintenance costs in common areas even if they disagree with the expenditure.

3. Sometimes the developer controls parking and recreation areas, for which he or she may charge extra fees.

4. Owners may find themselves living rather compactly in close proximity to neighbors. Noises emanating from swimming pool and game areas may be distracting.

Basic Items to Check When Buying a Condominium

1. If the building is new, check on the reputation of the builder. If it is an existing building, check with agents, neighbors, home-owners' associations, and government agencies to see if there have been complaints regarding the quality of construction.

2. Read all legal documents carefully, including any conditions, covenants, and restrictions, as well as governing documents of the homeowners' association (consult an attorney if necessary).

3. Make sure you know the amount and coverage of any home-owners' association fees. What are they now? When were they raised last? Are there any pending lawsuits against the home-owners' association?

4. Ask yourself these specific questions:
   a. Is exterior and/or interior maintenance included in the established fees?
   b. Are there any restrictions on the sale or lease of individual units? How many units are tenant occupied, as opposed to owner occupied?

   c. Are there any warranties on equipment? If so, for how long?

   d. Does the developer and/or the association have reserve funds in case of an emergency?

   e. Are owners required to pay maintenance costs for unsold units?

   f. Is there enough insurance to protect against fire, liability, theft, and other risks?

5. What experience has the real estate agent had regarding the sale and financing of condominiums?

14.4 VACATION HOMES

Many people own a vacation or second home. Second homes typically include a cabin in the mountains, a cottage by the lake, a house near the beach, a chalet near a ski slope, or a home in a desert resort area.

Where You Buy Is Important

You should ask yourself these questions before you make your final decision regarding ownership of a second home:

1. Can I tolerate close neighbors, or do I want complete privacy?
2. Do I want a place close to everyday conveniences or one that is "out of sight and sound"?
3. Depending on the area chosen, can I afford it? If not, can I interest someone in a joint venture?
4. What is the resale potential? Will the home be difficult to resell if I need to get my money out?

A Second Home as an Investment

Five major factors determine investment potential. They are risk, liquidity, management, tax aspects, and appreciation potential. **Risk** is the possibility that you will lose all or part of your initial investment. The risk involved in a second home as an investment depends on the market conditions at the time of purchase and resale. Second-home investments are usually considered a greater risk than a principal residence, and this is reflected in the higher interest rates a lender may charge for a second-home loan compared to the interest rate on a loan to buy a principal residence.

    Liquidity refers to the ability to convert your investment to cash quickly. Real estate is not as liquid as other investments, such as stocks and bonds. However, if the second home is priced right, it can usually be sold in a reasonable amount of time.

Before you buy a second home, check out the resale history of the area.

Management refers to the cost and time involved in overseeing the investment. Real estate requires a considerable amount of management. On nearby real estate investments, you may choose to manage the property yourself. But when the second home is a considerable distance away, you need to pay for local management to oversee, maintain, and check up on the property.

Tax aspects refer to the income tax laws and their impact on the investment. Owners of second homes are allowed to deduct the interest on loans and payment of property taxes. If the second home is rented out for a portion of time, a complex set of income tax rules applies. If a second home is sold for a gain, homeowners are not allowed to use the $250,000 for singles and $500,000 for married couples income tax exclusions. A vacation or second home is no longer the tax haven it once was—see your tax advisor before you buy. Today most vacation homes are purchased to enjoy; they are not purchased as tax shelters.

Appreciation refers to an increase in value when demand exceeds supply. California real estate, as a whole over a length of time, has tended to increase significantly in value. But at any given time, prices can decline because of a current decline in demand. The vacation or second home market is usually more volatile than the regular home market.

14.5 SHOULD YOU RENT OR BUY?

Keep in mind that the advantages of renting closely parallel the disadvantages of buying, and the disadvantages of renting closely relate to the advantages of buying.

Advantages of Renting and Disadvantages of Buying

1. Only a comparatively small outlay of money is required to rent, usually the first and last months' rents and a security deposit. When you purchase a home, the lender may require a down payment of 5 to 20 percent of the price. If you put less money down on a home, you are usually charged a higher interest rate and loan fees, because of the risk involved to the lender.

2. There is less risk in renting because your initial outlay is limited. You do not stand to lose much even if you decide to move earlier than you had planned. In purchasing, whenever you invest

money, there is a greater risk that you might lose some or all of it if property values decline.

3. In the short run, when renting, your costs are fixed. You know how much your rent will be each month, so you can usually budget accordingly. In buying, the mortgage payment may or may not remain stable depending on whether the loan has a fixed or adjustable rate. When you own your property, taxes and maintenance costs increase over time.

4. In renting, if the neighborhood should decline, you can move without suffering a personal loss because of a decline in real estate values. Renting provides greater mobility than owning.

5. When you rent, you can take the money that otherwise would be used to buy a home and deposit it in a savings account or buy stocks and bonds, giving you greater liquidity. When you purchase real estate, your money is usually tied up and may be difficult to pull out to meet a financial emergency.

6. When you rent, you do not have the same responsibility for maintenance as you do when you own your own property. You can take a vacation trip without worrying about the maintenance and upkeep of the property. When you own, the responsibility for maintenance is yours.

Advantages of Buying and Disadvantages of Renting

1. Buying a home can be an investment for the future. Well-located properties usually increase in value over the long run. During recessions, there may be a short-term drop in prices, but over the long term, the average California home has experienced appreciation. When you rent, you have only rent receipts to show for your expenditure at the end of each month.

2. As a homeowner, you can deduct your property taxes and interest payments from personal income before paying federal or state income taxes.

3. Pride of ownership and security make people feel comfortable and permanent in their homes. Many homeowners cement that security by becoming involved in community affairs, working around the yard, and making minor repairs. On the other hand, it is difficult to establish permanence in a rented home. At the whim of the landlord, you may be asked to leave or to pay higher rent in order to stay.

4. A home is usually larger than an apartment unit, allowing plenty of room for activities. Few apartment units provide the same

freedom of movement as a home. In addition, you can build on to your home if you need more space.

5. There are fewer restrictions placed on homeowners. They can have pets if they wish. They can even play the stereo after 10 P.M. if they wish!

6. Homeowners are frequently viewed as more secure credit risks than renters.

These items are just a few of the advantages and disadvantages of owning versus renting.

CHAPTER SUMMARY

This chapter discussed the characteristics of one-story, two-story, and split-level homes. Various architectural designs, roof styles, and construction details were illustrated. The principles of mobile home, condominium, and vacation home ownership were discussed. The chapter ended with an explanation of the pros and cons of buying versus renting real estate.

IMPORTANT TERMS AND CONCEPTS

appreciation	management	risk
condominium	mobile home park	tax aspects
liquidity	modular homes	

PRACTICAL APPLICATION

1. Using the construction illustration in the book, starting from the ground and moving to the sole plate of a standard home, give the construction name for each item in the correct sequence.

2. List the four conditions required in California to convert a mobile home to real property.

3. As a real estate agent, you are attempting to convince a renter that buying a home makes more economic sense than renting. List five advantages of owning a home.

REVIEWING YOUR UNDERSTANDING

1. The ownership of a mobile home is transferred by means of a:
   a. deed.
   b. certificate of ownership.
   c. bill of sale.
   d. sales agreement.

2. All fees relating to licensing or transferring of title to mobile homes must be paid to the:
   a. Department of Housing and Community Development.
   b. Department of Motor Vehicles.
   c. Department of Real Estate.
   d. Division of Mobile Homes.

3. All things being equal, the least cost per square foot should be found in a:
   a. one-story home.
   b. split-level home.
   c. ranch-style home.
   d. two-story home.

4. When you rent rather than own, you have the ability to move to another location quickly. This is called
   a. liquidity.
   b. convenience.
   c. mobility.
   d. permanence.

5. Of the numerous roof styles, which of the following fits the description "All sides slope to eaves"?
   a. Gambrel
   b. Hip
   c. Mansard
   d. Gable

6. What style of house fits the description "A two-story house with a front balcony"?
   a. Contemporary
   b. California bungalow
   c. Monterey
   d. Dutch colonial

7. A real estate licensee can sell used mobile homes if the mobile home:
   a. is registered with the state.
   b. has at least 800 square feet.
   c. qualifies for conventional financing.
   d. is preapproved by the Department of Real Estate.

8. The proper payment for the transfer fee for the sale of a mobile home must be made within
   a. 5 days.
   b. 10 days.
   c. 15 days.
   d. 20 days.

9. For a mobile home to be considered real estate, it must be
   a. in a mobile home park.
   b. on a permanent foundation.
   c. approved by the FHA.
   d. preapproved by the Department of Real Estate.

10. Once a mobile home is converted to real property, title to the mobile home is transferred using a:
    a. deed.
    b. bill of sale.
    c. pink slip.
    d. certificate of ownership.

11. In terms of complication, the most difficult tenant to evict is one located in a(n):
    a. apartment building.
    b. mobile home park.
    c. duplex.
    d. home.

12. The highest point in a standard frame house is the:
    a. collar beam.
    b. rafters.
    c. ridge board.
    d. header.

13. In the construction of a home, the horizontal board above a window is called a:
    a. brace.
    b. sole plate.
    c. header.
    d. stud.

14. A piece of lumber 1 inch thick and 12 inches by 12 inches in size contains
    a. 1 board foot.
    b. 2 board feet.
    c. 3 board feet.
    d. 4 board feet.

15. The foundation of a standard built home sits on the:
    a. mudsill.
    b. collar beam.
    c. footing.
    d. stud.

16. The ultimate responsibility for the management of an entire condominium building after all the individual units have been sold rests with the:
    a. original developer.
    b. lender.
    c. owners' association.
    d. government.

17. Second homes:
    a. always make good investments.
    b. provide extraordinary tax write-offs.
    c. are easier to finance than a first home.
    d. are usually purchased to enjoy, not as investments.

18. An advantage of owning versus renting includes
    a. mobility.
    b. control.
    c. liquidity.
    d. less risk.

19. For income tax purposes, an owner of a second home who does not rent out the property is allowed to
    a. sell and, within 24 months, trade up into another second home and defer the gain on the sale.
    b. deduct property taxes and loan interest.
    c. deduct the cost of repairs and maintenance.
    d. sell and use the $250,000 and/or $500,000 tax exclusion rule.

20. The advantage of owning versus renting a home includes
    a. more liquidity.
    b. more mobility.
    c. less initial investment.
    d. income tax deductions.

Chapter

15

A career in real estate can be an exciting opportunity for certain people. The various types of job opportunities within the real estate industry may offer greater potential for movement and advancement than other areas of employment. The real estate business is a people-oriented industry. Real estate professionals help or assist customers and clients to achieve their housing financial and investment goals. Thus, a career in real estate can lead to a wide range of employment activities from the entry-level position of sales agent to the sophisticated role of the real estate counselor. However, there are pitfalls to consider! Not everyone can succeed in real estate. It is not to be viewed as a get-rich-quick industry. Success takes dedication and hard work. At the conclusion of Part I of this chapter, you will be able to do the following:

1. Describe the major career choices in the real estate industry.
2. List the requirements to become a licensed real estate salesperson or broker.
3. Examine personal questions to consider before becoming a real estate agent.
4. Explain special issues for real estate licensees who wish to sell business opportunities.

At the conclusion of Part II of this chapter, you will be able to do the following:

Describe the major aspects of the state real estate license examination.

At the end of Part II, you will have the opportunity to take a self-administered 150-question review examination of the entire course. Answers to these questions are provided to enhance your learning experience.

Part 1: A Career in Real Estate and the Department of Real Estate License Examination Requirements

15.1 STRUCTURE OF THE REAL ESTATE INDUSTRY

Although this chapter focuses on the rules for obtaining a real estate license, anyone interested in a career in real estate should recognize the diversity of the industry. In addition to acting as an agent for the buying and selling of properties, a person wanting a career in real estate could pursue many other activities. Real estate–oriented people are needed in the areas of construction, financing, escrow, appraising, property management, land development, and other related specialties. Each of these areas offers opportunities for well-trained people. Some of these specialties require a real estate license, whereas others require a different license or no license at all.

Real Estate Agents

The potential as a real estate sales agent is unlimited. A variety of opportunities exist as a result of the growth in the U.S. population and the continued expansion of the nation's economy. As a consequence, real estate agents are needed to assist people who wish to buy, sell, or develop real estate.

A real estate salesperson's license qualifies him or her to work for a real estate broker as a real estate agent. Although a new licensee may be considered an expert in the eyes of the public and the law, most new agents soon realize that additional training and education are necessary in order to live up to the public's expectations.

As a salesperson becomes more experienced, he or she may wish to become a real estate broker. Brokers are allowed to own and operate their own business. A real estate salesperson cannot solely own and operate a real estate firm; he or she must be affiliated with a broker.

Sometimes a real estate brokerage company handles all kinds of properties, or it may specialize in just residential, commercial, industrial, farm, or vacant land sales. Some real estate brokers may wish to become consultants and work on a fee-per-hour basis rather than be paid a sales commission.

Although the field of real estate is complex, anyone interested in a career has boundless opportunities for personal satisfaction as well as the potential to make above-average income. A person who plans on entering the field of real estate must remember that experience, education, integrity, and resourcefulness are the characteristics that the public expects to see in real estate agents.

However, success will not be easy. Real estate is a competitive business, and the failure and turnover rates for new licensees are very high. The reasons for failure are discussed in detail later in this chapter.

Real Estate Trade Associations

People who choose real estate as a career quickly become aware of real estate trade associations. The largest is the National Association of REALTORS® (NAR), which is identified by the symbol ®. The National Association of REALTORS® owns the nationally recognized designation REALTOR®. Only members of the National Association of REALTORS® can use the term REALTOR®. In California, the unauthorized use of the term REALTOR® constitutes a violation of California Department of Real Estate (DRE) regulations.

The **National Association of REALTORS®** is broken down into state associations, each of which provides services to their state members. The California Association of REALTORS® (CAR) is the state-affiliated group that provides services for California members. The major objectives of the **California Association of REALTORS® (CAR)**, as set forth in its constitution, are as follows:

1. To unite its members
2. To promote high standards
3. To safeguard the land-buying public
4. To foster legislation for the benefit and protection of real estate
5. To cooperate in the economic growth and development of the state

The California Association of REALTORS® is, in turn, divided into numerous local groups called the Association of REALTORS® or Boards of REALTORS®. Local associations are usually broken down by cities or counties.

The main thrust of REALTOR® trade groups is to provide information and education for their members and to pursue political agendas that are favorable to the ownership of real estate. This is achieved using publications, seminars, state-national-international conventions, videos, cassettes, online information, and various training sessions. Another advantage of association membership is the substantial savings on insurance and other health benefits through group rates.

Another national real estate organization is the National Association of Real Estate Brokers. This trade association was formed in 1947 and consists of predominantly African-American real estate brokers whose members are called REALTISTS®. The organization has several state chapters and local boards throughout the United States.

A REALTIST® must be a member of a local board as well as a member of the national organization. Both nationally and locally, REALTISTS® are working for better housing for the communities they serve. In many cases, individuals are both REALTORS® and REALTISTS® by virtue of voluntary dual membership.

Professional Designations and Code of Ethics

If an agent wishes to specialize in a particular aspect of real estate, trade associations provide advanced training leading to certified designations. Once earned, the professional designations enjoy a national recognition and usually lead to higher income for the designee.

Virtually all trade associations have a code of ethics for their members. If trade association members violate the code of ethics, it is grounds for dismissal from the group and the loss of the benefits of membership.

Other Real Estate Employment

In addition to sales jobs, real estate–trained salaried positions may be available as a loan officer, an appraiser, an escrow officer, or a title officer. These salaried jobs are with financial institutions, appraisal companies, escrow companies, title companies, and some government agencies. Real estate developers and contractors frequently hire salaried personnel who need a real estate background.

Additional opportunities for real estate students may exist in local, state, and federal governments. These include a variety of occupational levels, such as right-of-way agents, appraisers, leasing negotiators, planners, and HUD housing program staff.

15.2 LICENSE REQUIREMENTS AND COMPETITION

Real Estate Salespersons

The current requirements (October 1, 2007) to become a real estate salesperson are as follows:

1. Must be at least 18 years of age and a legal U.S. resident.
2. Conviction of a crime that is a felony or that involves moral turpitude may result in the denial of a license.
3. Effective October 1, 2007, the former 18-month conditional real estate sales license is abolished. All sales license applicants must complete college-level courses in real estate principles and real estate practice, plus one other DRE-approved statutory course, such as real estate finance, real estate appraisal, legal aspects of real estate, real estate economics, and so on, before being allowed to take the real estate sales license examination. These courses can be taken at an accredited college or at a private vocational school approved by the DRE.
4. Must be able to pass the state examination consisting of 150 multiple-choice questions to be answered within a three-and-one-quarter-hour time period. A passing score is 105 or more correct answers, representing 70 percent and up.

   The salesperson's examination is given as needed at designated locations in California, usually Oakland, Los Angeles, San Diego, Sacramento, and Fresno. The examination is difficult; a failure rate of 50 percent or more is common.
5. Upon completion of the examination, one must submit the required license fee on an approved application form along with a set of classifiable fingerprints.

Real Estate Brokers

Current requirements to become a real estate broker are as follows:

1. Must be at least 18 years of age and a legal U.S. resident.
2. Conviction of a crime that is a felony or that involves moral turpitude may result in the denial of a license.
3. Must complete at least eight approved real estate courses. The following five must be taken:
   a. Real Estate Practice
   b. Legal Aspects of Real Estate
   c. Real Estate Finance

    d. Real Estate Appraisal

    e. Real Estate Economics or Accounting

    Any three of the following courses must also be taken, for a total of eight courses: real estate principles, business law, property management, real estate office administration, escrow, mortgage loan brokering, real estate computer applications, common interest development, or another approved advanced real estate course. The courses must be taken through an accredited college or at a private vocational school approved by the real estate commissioner.

4. Must complete the experience requirements that consist of two years' full-time experience as a real estate salesperson or its equivalent. *Equivalent* is experience in an allied field such as title, escrow, or finance. Equivalence can, in some cases, include education in lieu of experience, such as an accredited college degree.

5. Must pass the state examination consisting of 200 multiple-choice questions to be answered within five hours with a score of 150 or more correct answers, representing a score of 75 percent or better.

    The test for the broker's license is more difficult than the salesperson's examination, and the failure rate is frequently high, averaging approximately 50 percent.

6. Must complete the license application and pay the proper fee.

7. The broker's examination is given monthly (or more often depending on demand) at the locations mentioned earlier for the sales examination.

Real estate licensees are allowed to sell business opportunities as well as real estate. See Section 15.4 of this chapter for details regarding business opportunities.

State Examination

For a detailed explanation of the state real estate examination and official DRE instructions, see Part II of this chapter. Also, a complete 150-question examination, including answers, in a format similar to the sales examination, is presented for your review in Part II.

Continuing Education Requirements

Real Estate Sales License

Effective July 1, 2007, during a new real estate sales licensee's first four years, he or she must take the following five separate three-hour DRE-approved courses for a total of 15 hours.

1. Ethics
2. Agency
3. Fair Housing
4. Trust Fund Handling
5. Risk Management

Once a real estate sales licensee completes his or her first renewal, any subsequent sales license renewal will require forty-five hours of DRE-approved continuing education. The following courses ethics, agency, fair housing, trust fund handling, and risk management must be taken. However, after the first renewal of a sales license an eight-hour combined survey course covering update issues on ethics, agency, fair housing, trust fund handling, and risk management can be taken. The remaining hours beyond the combined survey course can be DRE-approved continuing education courses of the sales licensee's choosing as long as said courses do not exceed the current DRE allotment of consumer service courses. See the DRE website at www.dre.ca.gov for the current allotment.

Real Estate Broker's License

Effective July 1, 2007, during a new real estate broker licensee's first four years, he or she must take 45 hours of DRE-approved continuing education, which must include these five separate three-hour DRE-approved courses for a total of 15 of the required 45 hours.

1. Ethics
2. Agency
3. Fair Housing
4. Trust Fund Handling
5. Risk Management

The remaining 30 hours for a total of 45 hours can be DRE-approved continuing education courses of the broker's choosing so long as said courses do not exceed the current DRE allotment of consumer service courses. See the DRE website at www.dre.ca.gov for the current allotment.

If a new broker licensee's first renewal date is before July 1, 2007, then only ethics, agency, fair housing, and trust fund handling are required. Risk management is not required for renewals prior to July 1, 2007. However, the broker will still need to accumulate 45 hours of DRE-approved continuing education.

Once a real estate broker licensee completes his or her first renewal, any subsequent broker license renewal will require forty-five hours of DRE-approved continuing education. The following courses ethics, agency, fair housing, trust fund handling, and risk management must be taken. However, after the first renewal of a broker's license an eight-hour combined survey course covering update issues on ethics, agency, fair housing, trust fund handling, and risk management can be taken. The remaining hours beyond the Combined Survey course can be DRE-approved continuing education courses of the licensee's choosing so long as said courses do not exceed the current DRE allotment of consumer service courses. See the DRE website at www.dre.ca.gov for the current allotment.

The California DRE: A Summary

The DRE is a public agency that has responsibility over certain real estate activities in California. Here are some key points.

1. The California **Real Estate Commissioner** is appointed by the governor and serves as the chief executive of the DRE.

2. The commissioner administers the Real Estate Law and issues regulations that have the force of law and become a part of the California Administrative Procedures Code.

3. The commissioner and members of the department screen applicants for licenses and investigate complaints against licensees. After a proper hearing, if a licensee has violated a law or regulation, the commissioner can restrict, suspend, or revoke a real estate license.

   Restricted license: allows licensee to continue to work, but under limited conditions

   Suspended license: a temporary loss of license

   Revoked license: a loss of license

   Once a real estate broker's license is suspended or revoked, any salesperson working under said broker's license must cease working for that broker. Any commissions earned by the salesperson prior to the date of the broker's suspension or revocation are allowed to be paid to the salesperson.

4. A real estate license is required when a person performs a real estate act for another for compensation. The compensation may be in the form of a commission, a fee, a salary, or anything of value. The following exceptions do not need a real estate license:

   a. Principal handling his or her own affairs.

   b. Attorney in fact acting under a power of attorney.

   c. Appraiser (needs special license not issued by the DRE, but rather issued by the Office of Real Estate Appraisers).

d. Attorney at law (lawyer) while performing duties as an attorney. If the attorney charges a fee as a broker, a real estate license is required.

e. Trustee selling under a deed of trust.

f. Residential on-site property manager. A full-service off-site property manager must have a real estate license.

5. As of January 2009, the fine for an unlicensed person who receives an illegal commission is $20,000 for an individual and $60,000 for a corporation. The fine for paying a commission to an unlicensed person is $100.

6. Fictitious business names: A licensed broker, corporation, or partnership may operate under a fictitious name (DBA, or *Doing Business As*) if the name is approved by the commissioner.

7. A corporate real estate license requires an officer to be licensed as a broker. A partnership real estate license requires one partner to be licensed as a broker. A real estate salesperson and a broker can form a real estate brokerage partnership.

8. Prepaid rental-listing license: A special license that allows a licensee to collect a fee for supplying a prospective tenant with a list of available rentals. This does not allow the licensee to negotiate rental contracts or perform any other real estate activity. Real estate brokers can collect a prepaid fee without a special license if done at their regular place of business.

Real Estate Licensees in California

Statistics provided by the DRE indicate that the total number of real estate licensees fluctuates with the real estate market. When the market is good, the number of real estate licensees increases. When the real estate market drops, so does the number of licensees, but this drop lags behind the drop in the market. As of February 2010, there were approximately 497,000 real estate licensees in California. Approximately 30 percent were brokers and 70 percent salespersons.

The greatest number of licensees is involved with the buying and selling of homes as opposed to other real estate activities. One can enter the real estate market as a salesperson with only a small amount of initial capital, and the opportunity does exist to earn a good income. Compensation, on the other hand, is largely based on earnings from commissions. As a consequence, anyone contemplating a real estate sales career should be aware that he or she is in direct competition with a large number of licensees whose numbers tend to expand with the real estate market.

How About a Part-Time Real Estate Job?

Several potential licensees hope to work part-time until their sales volume supports full-time employment. Brokers do hire part-time salespeople with the expectation that they will eventually become full-time agents. Brokers agree that they commit a great amount of time and resources to train part-time salespeople. In return, they want new salespeople to commit to becoming full-time agents in the future. The part-time agent is usually not as successful as fully committed salespeople.

Working Hours and Fringe Benefits

The person who decides to enter real estate on a full-time basis initially faces the prospect of long hours, including evenings and weekends. Evenings and weekends are the only hours some prospective buyers and sellers have free to discuss real estate needs.

In addition, the fringe benefits that often come with other jobs may not exist. For example, paid vacations, insurance benefits, or retirement funds are not common in the real estate business. If a real estate salesperson wants these items, he or she usually must pay for them out of his or her own earnings. If fringe benefits are of overriding concern, a prospective salesperson should explore these areas of question prior to joining a particular firm.

Realistic Picture

Real estate sales and related activities can offer unlimited opportunities for motivated individuals. Perseverance and hard work, coupled with good training and additional educational coursework, can help a person become financially independent and provide a valuable service for the public. Real estate is not a get-rich-quick business; it takes work and a willingness to be helpful and understanding.

15.3 PERSONAL PREPARATION TO ENTER THE REAL ESTATE INDUSTRY

Some people enter real estate sales with unrealistic expectations for earnings that do not materialize, and this results in a negative employment experience. If possible, a prospective licensee should meet with a real estate instructor or career counselor and an experienced real estate broker and discuss what it takes to succeed in the local real estate market. Some community colleges offer an internship program, where students work in a local real estate office while taking real estate courses.

Personal Checklist

1. If at all possible, an interest inventory test, such as the Strong Inventory Test, should be taken. These tests indicate a person's interests and what vocations are suited to these interests. These tests are available at most local community colleges. Call the college's registrar, student services office, or assessment center for information.

2. If the local college has a career center, check with a counselor to verify which real estate courses are required. A call to a DRE-approved private vocational school can provide the same information. Many are listed in the telephone book or online. Be sure to discuss (or research online) the cost for textbooks, registration fees, matriculation requirements, and class hours, as well as the total scope of real estate course offerings.

3. Once the arrangements for a course of study have been established, it is a good idea to check the local real estate employment market. The executive officers of local real estate associations and boards can give indications of the sales activities in the local area. These indicators might include a list of the number of real estate salespeople, listings and sales activities, and average dollar volume of business. The real estate sections of many local newspapers also publish these statistics.

4. Select an area where you might like to work, and survey the real estate offices within this territory. Visit several offices and take a look around. Although a brief look does not indicate the success of a real estate company, it does give some important first impressions.

5. Check local newspaper real estate advertisements to determine which real estate offices are working which neighborhoods.

6. Try to narrow the real estate office choices to one to five offices, and attempt to identify the personnel within these offices. If possible, make an appointment with an employed salesperson to discuss the activities within each office. This can provide valuable facts concerning management, number of employees, rapport, and so on. Many times, the decision to attempt to join a firm is made at this time.

7. Once the selection process is narrowed, an appointment should be made for an interview with the owner-broker or the personnel manager.

To assure a more informative interview, list specific questions to ask. The list should include questions regarding the existing number of salespeople, support personnel, training programs, commission splits, advertising and listing policies, employee-independent contractor arrangements, commission ratios once certain sales quotas have been reached, personal costs for office expenses (telephone), and fringe benefits (if any).

This suggested list of questions does not intend to imply that the applicant is to interview management! However, not asking enough questions can lead to regret later. A well-conducted interview usually brings out information that is useful for both the applicant and the real estate company.

Questions to Ask Yourself Before You Enter the Real Estate Business

1. Why am I leaving my current employment? Are my reasons valid and logical, or are they emotional?

2. How many sales per month will I need in order to generate enough commission dollars to equal my present salary? (This projection should include money set aside for income taxes and insurance.)

3. What arrangements will be made for annual vacations and holidays?

4. What about the fringe benefits—health, life, and dental packages? How will these be paid for?

5. Will I need to work on weekends and during evening hours? If so, will this be continuous? If not, how long will it last? How will this affect my lifestyle? My family?

6. Do I have the stamina and energy it takes to be in sales?

7. Are my personality traits such that I will be continually charged and challenged? Will I be able to take the peaks and valleys of real estate sales?

8. Am I financially prepared to begin a career in real estate sales? Do I have the money to carry myself and my family for a period of time before sales start to materialize? In addition, the prospective salesperson should recognize that there are continuing out-of-pocket expenses such as the following:

   a. Local board, state, and national professional fees.

   b. The cost to drive and maintain a suitable automobile for use in escorting clients to and from properties. (This includes repair costs, additional gasoline mileage, and comprehensive insurance coverage.)

   c. Incidental daily costs that arise in connection with food services for clients, such as coffee, luncheons, and dinners.

   d. Monthly office costs—telephone, listing materials, and keys for properties.

   e. Those pertaining to personal appearance, which requires a businesslike wardrobe, personal grooming, and the uniform wardrobe required by certain franchise offices.

9. How will my family or my other relationships cope with the change? Do they support my decision?

This list of questions is not intended to be a negative overview of real estate sales, but rather a serious review of what must be considered for a successful and professional entrance into the real estate field.

Ending Note

The real estate business provides an opportunity for a personally challenging and financially rewarding career, but it is not "easy for the taking." With dedication and hard work, you can become a successful real estate salesperson, earn a substantial income, and create opportunities for personal investments.

15.4 SELLING BUSINESS OPPORTUNITIES

A real estate license allows an agent to sell business opportunities. A business opportunity is defined as the sale or lease of a business, including stock, trade fixtures, trade name, and goodwill. This involves the sale of personal property, and all the rules of personal property apply.

The essential elements of the sale of a business opportunity include the following:

1. A bill of sale is the written instrument that passes title to personal property.

2. The financial statements needed when a business is sold are as follows:

   a. *Balance Sheet:* Shows the financial position of the business as of a given date

      Assets. Things of value owned by the business

      Liabilities. Unpaid debts and expenses of the business

      Net Worth. Owners' equity, the difference between the assets and liabilities

   b. *Profit and Loss Statement:* Shows the profit and loss of the business during a specific time period.

Gross Income   (Revenue from sales)

$\underline{- \text{Expenses}}$ (cost of goods and expenses)

Net income   (profit)

3. Bulk Sales Rules apply when a business is sold that involves inventory. A *bulk transfer* is defined as the transfer of a major portion of inventory other than a sale to customers. The transferee (buyer) must give public notice 12 business days before the transfer takes place. The notice requires recording a Notice of Intent to Sell Bulk and publishing it in a newspaper of general circulation. The purpose of this notice is to let creditors of the seller file a claim if trade credit is still owed on the inventory.

   If the buyer and seller do not comply with the bulk sale law, the sale is valid between them, but is void against the creditors who can then attach the inventory.

4. Other terms and definitions include the following:

   a. *Goodwill:* Expectation of continued public patronage.

   b. *Turnover:* Number of times the inventory is sold per year.

   c. *Sales and Use Tax:* A tax on the sale of personal property.

   d. *Alcoholic Beverage Control Act (ABC):* Rules involving the sale of a liquor license. One of these rules states that the person must be of good moral character. If a new license is issued by the state, the initial fees are relatively modest. But once a license is issued, because the number of liquor licenses is limited by population, a free market develops and the price for a liquor license can skyrocket.

CHAPTER SUMMARY, PART I

Real estate offers many avenues for employment. In addition to sales, opportunities exist in the fields of real estate appraisal, finance, escrow, title insurance, construction, and development. Real estate trade associations, such as the National Association of REALTORS®, the National Association of Real Estate Brokers, and the California Association of REALTORS®, provide valuable services to their members and the public.

Real estate licensees are regulated by the California Department of Real Estate (DRE). The DRE is headed by the real estate commissioner, who is appointed by the governor.

The basic requirements to become a real estate salesperson are being 18 years of age or older, being a legal U.S. resident, completing approved courses in real estate principles, real estate practice, and one other DRE broker-level course, passing the 150-question state examination with a score of 70 percent or better, completing an application along with a set of classifiable fingerprints, and paying all fees. A real estate salesperson must work for a broker.

The basic requirements to become a real estate broker are being 18 years of age or older, being a legal U.S. resident, completing eight approved real estate courses, having two years' experience as a real estate salesperson or its equivalent, passing a 200-question state examination with a score of 75 percent or better, completing an application, and paying all fees. A real estate broker's license is good for four years. A real estate broker is allowed to operate his or her own real estate office and to hire real estate salespeople.

To renew a real estate sales or broker's license, a person must complete 45 hours of DRE-approved continuing education classes. Within the first 45-hour renewal period, a licensee must take four separate three-hour courses in ethics, agency, fair housing, and trust fund handling.

Prior to entering the real estate business, a person should conduct a serious self-appraisal. The real estate business offers many opportunities for self-motivated people, but it is not a get-rich-quick business.

IMPORTANT TERMS AND CONCEPTS

business opportunities

California Association of REALTORS® (CAR)

National Association of REALTORS® (NAR)

real estate commissioner

REALTIST®

REALTOR®

PRACTICAL APPLICATION

1. As a new California real estate salesperson licensee, what are the educational requirements during the first four years of your license?

2. After being a California real estate salesperson for five years, you acquire your California real estate broker license. What are the continuing education requirements during the first four years of your broker license?

3. What is meant by the term *bulk sale*?

REVIEWING YOUR UNDERSTANDING

1. The term REALTOR® can only be used by a member of the:
   a. National Association of Real Estate Brokers.
   b. National Association of REALTORS®.
   c. National Association of Real Estate Councils.
   d. all of the above.

2. REALTISTS® are members of the:
   a. National Association of Real Estate Brokers.
   b. National Association of REALTORS®.
   c. National Association of Real Estate Councils.
   d. all of the above.

3. Real estate appraisers are licensed by the:
   a. Department of Property Valuation.
   b. Office of Real Estate Appraisers.
   c. Department of Real Estate.
   d. Office of Valuations and Standards.

4. A real estate salesperson is usually employed on a commission basis and receives payment directly from the:
   a. buyer.
   b. seller.
   c. broker.
   d. lender.

5. Which of the following best describes the real estate business?
   a. easy money
   b. competitive business
   c. noncompetitive business
   d. generous employer-paid benefits

6. In addition to real property, a real estate licensee is allowed to act as an agent for the sale of
   a. automobiles.
   b. new unregistered mobile homes.
   c. travel trailers.
   d. business opportunities.

7. Before being allowed to sit for the state real estate sales examination, an applicant must take a course in Real Estate Principles, Real Estate Practice, and
    a. take 45 hours of approved continuing education.
    b. be 21 years old.
    c. one other broker-level course.
    d. be a registered voter.

8. All of the following continuing education courses are required to renew a salesperson's license except:
    a. ethics
    b. agency
    c. real estate practice
    d. trust fund handling

9. To sit for the real estate broker's examination, an applicant must first do all the following, except
    a. take 45 hours of approved continuing education.
    b. take eight approved college-level broker courses.
    c. have two years' real estate sales experience or its equivalent.
    d. pay the required examination fee.

10. After the first renewal of the salesperson's license, subsequent renewal of the license every four years requires
    a. 45 hours of approved continuing education.
    b. a re-examination.
    c. two approved college-level broker courses.
    d. two years of full-time real estate experience or its equivalent.

11. The California Real Estate Commissioner is
    a. elected by the voters.
    b. appointed by the California Association of REALTORS®.
    c. appointed by the governor.
    d. elected by the California legislature.

12. After a proper hearing, if a licensee has violated a law or regulation, the real estate commissioner can restrict, suspend, or revoke a real estate license. If a licensee is allowed to continue to work under limited outlined conditions, the real estate license is called a:

    a. restricted license.

    b. suspended license.

    c. revoked license.

    d. temporary license.

13. The maximum fine for an unlicensed individual who receives an illegal commission is

    a. $200.

    b. $2,000.

    c. $20,000.

    d. $200,000.

14. In a typical real estate sale, which of the following does not need a real estate license to handle his or her portion of the transaction?

    a. Listing salesperson

    b. Selling agent

    c. Original broker

    d. Buyer's attorney

15. The real estate business is:

    a. very easy.

    b. competitive.

    c. mostly salary based.

    d. none of the above.

16. A business opportunity is defined as the sale of all of the following, except

    a. operating business.

    b. inventory.

    c. goodwill.

    d. real estate.

17. The financial statement that shows the position of a business on a given day is called a:
    a. profit and loss statement.
    b. balance sheet.
    c. net worth sheet.
    d. cash flow statement.

18. The financial statement that shows the operations of a business over a period of time, usually one year, is called a:
    a. profit and loss statement.
    b. balance sheet.
    c. net worth sheet.
    d. cash flow statement.

19. Under bulk sales rules, the buyer must give public notice at least:
    a. 5 days before transfer takes place.
    b. 7 days before transfer takes place.
    c. 10 days before transfer takes place.
    d. 12 days before transfer takes place.

20. The expectation of continued patronage is called
    a. blue sky.
    b. intangible goods.
    c. goodwill.
    d. site value.

Part II

15.5 THE REAL ESTATE LICENSE EXAMINATION IN DETAIL

The requirements to become a real estate salesperson or broker were discussed in Part I of this chapter. The discussion below outlines in more detail the state examination and the steps required to obtain a license once the examination has been passed.

The state real estate examination was created using guidelines originally outlined by a research project conducted by the University of California. The examination has been updated several times using generally accepted scientific studies. All questions are based on the knowledge necessary to competently perform the tasks of a real estate broker and salesperson. The real estate salesperson examination and the real estate broker examination are weighted by topics chosen to reflect the differences in the level and amount of knowledge required by each job. As the real estate business changes, and the separate roles of a salesperson and a broker change, the Department of Real Estate attempts to alter the examination to reflect these changes. **The examination weightings as of April 2010 follow. The weightings may be subject to change in the future.**

SPECIAL INTEREST TOPIC

AREA 1—PROPERTY OWNERSHIP AND LAND USE CONTROLS AND REGULATIONS

Approximately 18 percent of the Sales Exam and 15 percent of the Broker Exam

Classes of property

Property characteristics

Encumbrances

Types of ownership

Description of property

Government rights in land Public controls

Environmental hazards and regulations Private controls

Water rights

Special categories of land

AREA 2—LAWS OF AGENCY

Approximately 12 percent of the Sales Exam and 12 percent of the Broker Exam

Law, definition, and nature of agency relationships; types of agencies and agents

Creation of agency and agency agreements

Responsibilities of agent to seller and buyer as principal

Disclosure of acting as a principal or other interest

Termination of agency

Commissions and fees

AREA 3—VALUATION AND MARKET ANALYSIS

Approximately 12 percent of the Sales Exam and 11 percent of the Broker Exam

Value

Methods of estimating value

AREA 4—FINANCING

Approximately 13 percent of the Sales Exam and 13 percent of the Broker Exam

General concepts

Types of loans

Sources of financing

How to deal with lenders

Government programs

Mortgages, deeds of trust, and notes

Financing credit laws

Loan brokerage

AREA 5—TRANSFER OF PROPERTY

Approximately 9 percent of the Sales Exam and 10 percent of the Broker Exam

Title insurance

Deeds

Escrow

Reports

Tax aspects

Special process

AREA 6—PRACTICE OF REAL ESTATE AND MANDATED DISCLOSURES

Approximately 24 percent of the Sales Exam and 27 percent of the Broker Exam

Trust account management

Fair housing laws

Truth in advertising

Recordkeeping requirements

Agent supervision

Permitted activities of unlicensed sales assistants

DRE jurisdiction and disciplinary actions

Licensing, and continuing education requirements and procedures

California Real Estate Recovery Fund

General ethics

Technology

Property management and landlord and tenant rights

Commercial, industrial, and income properties

Specialty areas

Transfer disclosure statements

Material facts affecting property value

Need for inspection and obtaining and verifying information

AREA 7—CONTRACTS

Approximately 12 percent of the Sales Exam and 12 percent of the Broker Exam

General

Listing agreements

Buyer broker agreements

Offers and purchase contracts

Counteroffers and multiple counteroffers

Leases

Agreements

Promissory notes and securities

BASIC RULES AND PROCEDURES

Conduct that constitutes subversion and is grounds for denial, suspension, revocation, or restriction of a license includes, but is not limited to, the following:

1. Removing or reproducing examination material without authorization

2. Paying a test taker to reconstruct the examination

3. Using improperly obtained test questions to prepare for the examination

4. Selling, distributing, or buying state examination material

5. Cheating during the examination

6. Possessing unauthorized equipment or information during the examination

7. Impersonating an examinee or having an impersonator take the examination

EXAMINATION BOOKLET	ANSWER SHEET
22. When examinees and licensees refer to the Reference Book, as published by the Department of Real Estate, they should use: (a) the first edition (b) any edition available (c) the 1960 edition (d) the latest edition published	A B C D 22 ○ ○ ○ ○ A B C D 23 ○ ○ ○ ○ A B C D 24 ○ ○ ○ ○ A B C D 25 ○ ○ ○ ○

All examinations are multiple-choice tests. Each question gives four possible answers, only one of which is correct. You may think more than one answer has some element of correctness, but only one answer is the most complete and best answer. No question is intended to be tricky; therefore, you should interpret words according to their common meaning.

The only materials allowed are the DRE-provided examination, an answer sheet, and a special pencil. used at the Los Angeles, Sacramento, and San Diego locations. The Fresno and Oakland locations offer the examination in an electronic format. At the Los Angeles, Sacramento, and San Diego locations, an examinee is allowed to use a silent battery-operated calculator only if it does not have a printout capability or an alphabetic keyboard. The DRE supplies a single piece of scratch paper, which you must turn in with your answer sheet and examination.

HOW TO APPLY FOR THE SALESPERSON EXAMINATION

1. Complete an original Salesperson Examination Application (RE 400A) or a combination Examination and License Application (RE 435). No changes of any kind can be made to an application once it has been received by the DRE. Do not submit more than one application.

2. Attach the current examination fee. This fee varies from time to time. The DRE accepts checks, money orders, and (in most cases) credit cards. For the current fee and payment procedure, visit the DRE website at www.dre.ca.gov or call the DRE at (916) 227-0900.

3. Send official transcripts or photocopies of approved certificates of completion.

4. Applicants with limitations requiring special accommodations must submit a physician's letter with the application to verify the nature of the limitation. The DRE's ability to honor special requests is limited by scheduling constraints and cannot be guaranteed.

5. Send the application, official transcripts, and appropriate fee to the most current DRE address in Sacramento. The wait time for a response depends on the DRE's workload. If you do not receive an official notice within four weeks, contact the DRE for a follow-up. Your official Examination Schedule Notice (RE 401A) will list the date, time, and official location based on your selection on the application form.

RESCHEDULING PROCEDURES

If you change your mind and do not wish to take the examination as scheduled, you can apply for another examination date or location. You do this by completing and returning the Examination Schedule Notice (RE 401A). A fee is charged for any rescheduled examination.

NOTIFICATION OF EXAMINATION RESULTS

Examination results are usually mailed out within five days of your taking the examination, unless the DRE is under an abnormal workload. You can visit the DRE website at www.dre.ca.gov or use a touchtone phone and call the Examination Section at (916) 227-0900 to obtain your results within three working days. The passing score is 70 percent or better. You are not given your test score when you pass. You are given your test score when you fail.

REEXAMINATION IF YOU FAIL

You may not apply for reexamination until after you receive notification that you failed the prior test. There is no limit on the number of re-examinations you can take during a two-year period following the filing of your original examination application. If you wish to be reexamined after this two-year period, you must file a new application. All reexaminations require the payment of a fee.

ONCE YOU PASS THE EXAMINATION

When you pass, you are sent a Salesperson License Application (RE 202), if you have not already completed RE 435. Within one year of the examination date, you must complete this form and send it to the DRE along with the appropriate license fee. A complete fingerprint set on the Live Scan is required. Out-of-state applicants must complete different forms.

(See the DRE website for details.) The application must also include proof of legal residence (e.g., a birth certificate or resident alien card). This must be submitted with a State Public Benefits Statement (RE 205) before a license will be issued. In addition, a license may be denied if an applicant has violated California law regarding the payment of child support. If you fail to apply for your license within one year of passing the examination, your test score is no longer valid and you need to retake and pass the examination again before being eligible to apply for a real estate salesperson license.

HOW TO APPLY FOR THE BROKER EXAMINATION

1. Complete an original Broker Examination Application (RE 400B) or a combination Examination and License Application (RE 436). No changes of any kind can be made to an application once it has been received by the DRE. Do not submit more than one application.

2. Attach the current examination fee. This fee varies from time to time. The DRE accepts checks, money orders, and (in most cases) credit cards. For the current fee and payment procedure, visit the DRE website at www.dre.ca.gov or call the DRE at (916) 227-0900.

3. Submit an official transcript or approved certificate of completion showing successful completion of all of the eight required statutory college-level real estate courses. Photocopies of transcripts are not acceptable.

4. Submit a completed Employment Verification form(s) (RE 226) to verify the required two years of licensed real estate salesperson experience or a copy of a diploma or transcript to verify a

four-year college degree earned through a regionally accredited college, or an Equivalent Experience Verification form(s) (RE 227) to verify nonlicensed real estate–related experience.

5. Applicants with limitations requiring special accommodations must submit a physician's letter with the application to verify the nature of the limitation. The DRE's ability to honor special requests is limited by scheduling constraints and cannot be guaranteed.

6. Send the application, official transcripts, and appropriate fee to the most current DRE address in Sacramento. The wait time for a response depends on the DRE's workload. If you do not receive an official notice within four weeks, contact the DRE for a follow-up. Your official Examination Schedule Notice (RE 401B) will list the date, time, and official location based on your selection on the application form.

RESCHEDULING PROCEDURES

If you change your mind and do not wish to take the examination as scheduled, you can apply for another examination date or location. You do this by completing and returning the Examination Schedule Notice (RE 401B). A fee is charged for any rescheduled examination.

NOTIFICATION OF EXAMINATION RESULTS

Examination results are usually mailed to you within five days of your taking the examination, unless the DRE is under an abnormal workload. You can visit the DRE website at www.dre.ca.gov or use a touchtone phone and call the Examination Section at (916) 227-0900 to obtain your results within three working days. The passing score is 75 percent or better. You are not given your test score when you pass. You are given your test score when you fail.

REEXAMINATION IF YOU FAIL

You may not apply for reexamination until after you receive notification that you failed the prior test. There is no limit on the number of re-examinations you can take during a two-year period following the filing of your original examination application. If you wish to be reexamined after this two-year period, you must file a new application. All reexaminations require the payment of a fee.

ONCE YOU PASS THE EXAMINATION

When you pass, you are sent a Broker License Application (RE 200) if you have not completed RE 436. Within one year of the examination date, you must complete this form and send it to the DRE along with the appropriate license fee and a complete fingerprint set on Live Scan.

Out-of-state applicants must complete different forms. (See the DRE website for details.) The application must also include proof of legal residence (e.g., birth certificate or resident alien card). This must be submitted with a State Public Benefits Statement (RE 205) before a license will be issued. In addition, a license may be denied if an applicant has violated California law regarding the payment of child support. If you fail to apply for your license within one year of passing the examination, your test score is no longer valid and you need to retake and pass the examination again before being eligible to apply for a real estate broker's license.

15.6 COMPREHENSIVE REAL ESTATE PRINCIPLES PRACTICE EXAMINATION WITH ANSWERS

An old education adage says the best way to learn is to "read, recite, and review." To help with your review, a 150-question practice examination is presented. Real estate principles cover such a vast amount of material that every single topic cannot be tested.

But the questions that follow are a representative sample of the types of questions that frequently appear in examinations. The questions have been created to match the weighting breakdown found in the state examination. Answers appear at the end of the examination.

Test-Taking Tips

1. Take three passes through the examination. The first time through, answer only the questions you know for sure, skipping everything else. This will give you a sense of success and allow you to get a feel for the examination. The second time through, answer those questions you think you know, skipping those that are completely unfamiliar to you. The third time through, guess. **Remember to go back and answer all the questions**.

2. Reading pitfalls: Make sure you read all the answer choices. Sometimes an answer may appear correct, but another reading reveals the actual correct answer. Watch out for questions that say "except for," "which is not," and so on. The wording is confusing and you may select the wrong answer if you are not careful.

3. Here are some guessing suggestions:
   a. Choose the longest answer.
   b. Do not choose "all of the above" unless you can identify two answers as being right.
   c. Two answers will be close, and two answers will be obviously wrong. Eliminate the obviously wrong two answers, and select the most logical of the remaining two.

4. Math phobia: If math is not your strong point, leave the math until last. If you have done well on the rest of the examination, missing every math question will not usually cause you to fail. If you cannot do a math question, just guess at the correct answer.

5. Take the entire exam in one sitting in quiet surroundings. Upon completion, check your answers and look up the textbook discussion regarding the questions you missed.

DO NOT WRITE ON THE EXAMINATION. RUN SEVERAL PHOTOCOPIES OF THE ANSWER SHEET ON THE NEXT PAGES. THIS TYPE OF ANSWER SHEET IS OFTEN USED BY THE DEPARTMENT OF REAL ESTATE FOR THE STATE EXAMINATION. THIS PROCEDURE WILL ALLOW YOU TO RETAKE THE EXAMINATION SEVERAL TIMES FOR PRACTICE.

NCS Trans-Optic 08-15193:321

SIDE 1

1. WRITE YOUR IDENTIFICATION NUMBER IN THE SPACES PROVIDED BELOW.

2. BELOW EACH DIGIT OF YOUR IDENTIFICATION NUMBER BLACKEN THE CIRCLE THAT CORRESPONDS TO THE DIGIT IN THAT COLUMN.

IDENTIFICATION NUMBER

DEPT. OF REAL ESTATE - ANSWER SHEET

RE FORM-420 (12/81)

PRINT CLEARLY

1. EXAMINEE NAME (LAST, FIRST, & MIDDLE)

2. EXAMINEE SIGNATURE ▶

3. TITLE ☐ BROKER ☐ SALESPERSON

4. SESSION ☐ AM ☐ PM

5. EXAMINATION DATE

6. BIRTHDATE

7. EXAMINATION LOCATION ☐ LA ☐ SAC ☐ SF ☐ SD ☐ SA ☐ FR ☐ _____

8. EXAMINATION CODE NUMBER

9. BOOK NUMBER

PROPER MARK ● IMPROPER MARKS ⊙ ◔ ⊘ ⊗

IMPORTANT: ERASE CLEANLY ANY ANSWER YOU WISH TO CHANGE.
SEE IMPORTANT MARKING INSTRUCTIONS ON SIDE 2.

ENTER FIRST 3 LETTERS OF LAST NAME

(A B C D answer bubbles for questions 1–100, arranged in five columns: 1–20, 21–40, 41–60, 61–80, 81–100)

SIDE 2

DEPT. OF REAL ESTATE—ANSWER SHEET

IMPORTANT DIRECTIONS FOR MARKING ANSWERS

PRACTICE

	A	B	C	D
1	○	○	○	○
2	○	○	○	○
3	○	○	○	○
4	○	○	○	○
5	○	○	○	○

- Use only the black lead pencil provided.
- Do NOT use ink or ballpoint pens.
- Make heavy black marks that fill the circle completely.
- Erase cleanly any answer you wish to change.
- Make no stray marks on the answer sheet.
- NOTE: IMPROPER MARKS MAY SIGNIFICANTLY DELAY THE RELEASE OF YOUR RESULTS.

EXAMPLES

RIGHT
1 ● ○ ○ ○

WRONG
2 ⊘ ○ ○ ○

WRONG
3 ○ ○ ⊗ ○

WRONG
4 ○ ○ ○ ◎

WRONG
5 ○ ○ ○ ◉

DO NOT WRITE IN THIS SPACE

	A B C D		A B C D		A B C D		A B C D		A B C D
101	○○○○	121	○○○○	141	○○○○	161	○○○○	181	○○○○
102	○○○○	122	○○○○	142	○○○○	162	○○○○	182	○○○○
103	○○○○	123	○○○○	143	○○○○	163	○○○○	183	○○○○
104	○○○○	124	○○○○	144	○○○○	164	○○○○	184	○○○○
105	○○○○	125	○○○○	145	○○○○	165	○○○○	185	○○○○
106	○○○○	126	○○○○	146	○○○○	166	○○○○	186	○○○○
107	○○○○	127	○○○○	147	○○○○	167	○○○○	187	○○○○
108	○○○○	128	○○○○	148	○○○○	168	○○○○	188	○○○○
109	○○○○	129	○○○○	149	○○○○	169	○○○○	189	○○○○
110	○○○○	130	○○○○	150	○○○○	170	○○○○	190	○○○○
111	○○○○	131	○○○○	151	○○○○	171	○○○○	191	○○○○
112	○○○○	132	○○○○	152	○○○○	172	○○○○	192	○○○○
113	○○○○	133	○○○○	153	○○○○	173	○○○○	193	○○○○
114	○○○○	134	○○○○	154	○○○○	174	○○○○	194	○○○○
115	○○○○	135	○○○○	155	○○○○	175	○○○○	195	○○○○
116	○○○○	136	○○○○	156	○○○○	176	○○○○	196	○○○○
117	○○○○	137	○○○○	157	○○○○	177	○○○○	197	○○○○
118	○○○○	138	○○○○	158	○○○○	178	○○○○	198	○○○○
119	○○○○	139	○○○○	159	○○○○	179	○○○○	199	○○○○
120	○○○○	140	○○○○	160	○○○○	180	○○○○	200	○○○○

DO NOT WRITE IN THIS SPACE

NCS Trans-Optic 08-15193:321

DEPT. OF REAL ESTATE - ANSWER SHEET

RE FORM-420 (12/81)　　　　PRINT CLEARLY

SIDE 1

1. WRITE YOUR IDENTIFICATION NUMBER IN THE SPACES PROVIDED BELOW.
2. BELOW EACH DIGIT OF YOUR IDENTIFICATION NUMBER BLACKEN THE CIRCLE THAT CORRESPONDS TO THE DIGIT IN THAT COLUMN.

IDENTIFICATION NUMBER

1. EXAMINEE NAME (LAST, FIRST, & MIDDLE)

2. EXAMINEE SIGNATURE

3. TITLE ☐ BROKER ☐ SALESPERSON
4. SESSION ☐ AM ☐ PM
5. EXAMINATION DATE
6. BIRTHDATE
7. EXAMINATION LOCATION ☐ LA ☐ SAC ☐ SF ☐ SD ☐ SA ☐ FR ☐ ____
8. EXAMINATION CODE NUMBER
9. BOOK NUMBER

PROPER MARK ●   IMPROPER MARKS ⊙◑◌⊗

IMPORTANT: ERASE CLEANLY ANY ANSWER YOU WISH TO CHANGE. SEE IMPORTANT MARKING INSTRUCTIONS ON SIDE 2.

ENTER FIRST 3 LETTERS OF LAST NAME

(Answer grid, questions 1–100, each with A B C D bubbles)

SIDE 2

DEPT. OF REAL ESTATE—ANSWER SHEET

IMPORTANT DIRECTIONS FOR MARKING ANSWERS

PRACTICE

	A B C D
1	○○○○
2	○○○○
3	○○○○
4	○○○○
5	○○○○

- Use only the black lead pencil provided.
- Do NOT use ink or ballpoint pens.
- Make heavy black marks that fill the circle completely.
- Erase cleanly any answer you wish to change.
- Make no stray marks on the answer sheet.
- NOTE: IMPROPER MARKS MAY SIGNIFICANTLY DELAY THE RELEASE OF YOUR RESULTS.

EXAMPLES

RIGHT
1 ●○○○

WRONG
2 ⊘○○

WRONG
3 ○○⊗○

WRONG
4 ○○○◉

WRONG
5 ○○○◉

DO NOT WRITE IN THIS SPACE

DO NOT WRITE IN THIS SPACE

	A B C D		A B C D		A B C D		A B C D		A B C D
101	○○○○	121	○○○○	141	○○○○	161	○○○○	181	○○○○
102	○○○○	122	○○○○	142	○○○○	162	○○○○	182	○○○○
103	○○○○	123	○○○○	143	○○○○	163	○○○○	183	○○○○
104	○○○○	124	○○○○	144	○○○○	164	○○○○	184	○○○○
105	○○○○	125	○○○○	145	○○○○	165	○○○○	185	○○○○
106	○○○○	126	○○○○	146	○○○○	166	○○○○	186	○○○○
107	○○○○	127	○○○○	147	○○○○	167	○○○○	187	○○○○
108	○○○○	128	○○○○	148	○○○○	168	○○○○	188	○○○○
109	○○○○	129	○○○○	149	○○○○	169	○○○○	189	○○○○
110	○○○○	130	○○○○	150	○○○○	170	○○○○	190	○○○○
111	○○○○	131	○○○○	151	○○○○	171	○○○○	191	○○○○
112	○○○○	132	○○○○	152	○○○○	172	○○○○	192	○○○○
113	○○○○	133	○○○○	153	○○○○	173	○○○○	193	○○○○
114	○○○○	134	○○○○	154	○○○○	174	○○○○	194	○○○○
115	○○○○	135	○○○○	155	○○○○	175	○○○○	195	○○○○
116	○○○○	136	○○○○	156	○○○○	176	○○○○	196	○○○○
117	○○○○	137	○○○○	157	○○○○	177	○○○○	197	○○○○
118	○○○○	138	○○○○	158	○○○○	178	○○○○	198	○○○○
119	○○○○	139	○○○○	159	○○○○	179	○○○○	199	○○○○
120	○○○○	140	○○○○	160	○○○○	180	○○○○	200	○○○○

DO NOT WRITE IN THIS SPACE

PRACTICE EXAMINATION

1. A "loss in value from any cause" is a definition of
   a. economic obsolescence.
   b. depreciation.
   c. leverage.
   d. goodwill.

2. A couple recently married and each person had children from a previous marriage. They wish to take title to property so they can pass their share to their own children by will. The best form of title would be
   a. joint tenancy.
   b. severalty.
   c. community property.
   d. tenancy in whole.

3. A valid deed passes title when it is
   a. signed.
   b. recorded.
   c. delivered and accepted.
   d. acknowledged.

4. In July, Easton bought Rothchild's home through the listing broker, McGrew. After a hard rain in November, the roof developed a severe leak. Easton sued Rothchild and McGrew for the cost of a new roof. Testimony in court revealed that Rothchild mentioned the need for a new roof to Broker McGrew. McGrew did not tell Easton about the need for a new roof. What would most likely occur?
   a. Easton would collect from Rothchild; Rothchild would then seek recourse from McGrew.
   b. Easton would recover from Rothchild, but McGrew would not be liable to Rothchild.
   c. McGrew would be liable to Easton, but Rothchild would not be liable.
   d. Easton would not recover from Rothchild or McGrew based on the principle of caveat emptor.

5. The main purpose of the Truth-in-Lending Act is to
   a. prevent usury.
   b. require disclosure of credit terms.
   c. reduce the cost of credit.
   d. regulate annual percentage rates.

6. The difference between judgment liens and mechanics' liens is that
   a. mechanics' liens are general liens.
   b. mechanics' liens can take priority before they are recorded.
   c. mechanics' liens are voluntary liens.
   d. judgment liens are involuntary liens.

7. Broker Santos is in the process of listing a home. The agency disclosure must be given
   a. within five days.
   b. prior to close of escrow.
   c. prior to the seller signing the listing agreement.
   d. immediately after the seller signs the listing agreement.

8. On October 1, 2008, Garcia agreed to purchase Chan's home. Both parties agreed that escrow would close on December 1, 2008, and that property taxes would be prorated as of date of possession. On November 1, 2008, Chan paid the property taxes for the year 2008–2009. According to the escrow closing statement, which of the following is true?
   a. Garcia paid Chan for 8 months' taxes.
   b. Garcia paid Chan for 1 month's taxes.
   c. Chan paid Garcia for 8 months' taxes.
   d. Chan paid Garcia for 1 month's taxes.

9. A quitclaim deed conveys only the present rights of the:
   a. grantor.
   b. servient tenant.
   c. grantee.
   d. trustee.

10. To have a valid recorded homestead, certain elements are essential. Which of the following is not essential?
   a. a description of the property
   b. a statement of residence
   c. to be a married person
   d. to be recorded

11. A licensed loan broker arranged for a loan and has the borrower sign the required statement. The broker then discovers a lien that the borrower did not disclose. If the loan cannot be arranged due to the lien, the borrower is liable for
   a. cost and expenses incurred to date.
   b. no cost and expenses.
   c. all cost and expenses and half the commission.
   d. none of the above.

12. A person purchased a property for $200,000, which was equal to $4.75 per square foot. The rectangular lot was 300 feet deep. The cost per front foot was
   a. $1,425.
   b. $950.
   c. $827.
   d. $793.

13. Which of the following is not essential to form an agency?
   a. a fiduciary relationship
   b. agreement of the parties
   c. consideration
   d. competent parties

14. An owner sells a lot for cash and receives $67,100 from escrow. The only expenses were a 6 percent commission and $517 in other expenses. The property sold for
   a. $71,643.
   b. $71,933.
   c. $72,591.
   d. $73,137.

15. A real estate agent must disclose all material facts to a seller principal. Which of the following is considered a material fact?
    a. the buyer's racial background
    b. the agent's knowledge of a pending better offer
    c. the lender's requirement that a buyer pay a loan fee
    d. that the buyer has a medical problem

16. In appraising improved property, the least important factor is
    a. sales price.
    b. highest and best use.
    c. prices of comparables.
    d. assessed value.

17. Common interest developments in the form of community apartments and condominium projects fall within the California Subdivision Act and
    a. are illegal.
    b. are regulated by state law.
    c. are rarely approved.
    d. have fewer units per acre.

18. Studs are attached to rest upon the:
    a. mud sill.
    b. subfloor.
    c. header.
    d. sole plate.

19. A person borrowed 80 percent of the value of a studio condo. The loan interest rate was 7 percent. The first-year interest was $10,500. The value of the condo was
    a. $173,500.
    b. $182,900.
    c. $187,500.
    d. none of the above.

20. Adams, Brown, and Chow are owners of commercial land as joint tenants. Adams dies and is survived by Brown and Chow. Which is correct?
   a. Brown and Chow receive title by succession.
   b. The joint tenancy is terminated.
   c. Adams's interest terminates.
   d. Brown and Chow are now tenants in common.

21. To completely fence the NW quarter of the SE quarter of Section 3 would take how much fencing?
   a. 2 miles
   b. 1 mile
   c. ½ mile
   d. ¼ mile

22. When the landlord and the tenant mutually agree to cancel a lease, their action is called a(n):
   a. mutually agreed upon termination.
   b. rescission.
   c. release.
   d. abandonment.

23. An amortized loan has equal monthly installments consisting of
   a. interest alone.
   b. principal alone.
   c. principal and interest.
   d. principal, interest, taxes, and insurance.

24. Which of the following is an operating expense to be subtracted from gross income when appraising a property using the income approach?
   a. interest payments
   b. principal payments
   c. property taxes
   d. all of the above

25. The word *emblements* refers to
    a. attachments to a contract.
    b. growing crops.
    c. machinery.
    d. fixtures on a building.

26. A salesperson working for a broker had been wrongfully selling information to a loan company. When the broker, who had been using reasonable supervision, discovered this, the salesperson was fired. Based upon the information given,
    a. the broker is probably not liable if he or she had no knowledge of the wrongdoing.
    b. both the salesperson and the broker are liable.
    c. there is no liability.
    d. a salesperson is licensed to sell loan information in his or her name only.

27. Which of the following is worded incorrectly?
    a. Federal National Mortgage Association (Fannie Mae)
    b. Government National Mortgage Association (Ginnie Mae)
    c. Federal Housing Association (FHA)
    d. Department of Veterans Affairs (DVA)

28. Williams entered into a nine-month oral lease on July 1 to start on September 1 at a rate of $1,000 per month. On August 15, Williams backed out of the lease. The lease is
    a. unenforceable.
    b. enforceable.
    c. void.
    d. restricted by the Statute of Frauds.

29. Title insurance does not protect a buyer against
    a. forgery in the chain of title.
    b. lack of capacity of the grantor.
    c. recorded easements.
    d. zoning restrictions.

30. If state housing codes conflict with local codes, usually:
    a. state codes prevail.
    b. local codes prevail.
    c. the stricter of the two prevails.
    d. the more lenient of the two prevails.

31. A broker received deposits from principals and incorrectly placed the funds in a safe for several days before putting the funds in the broker's trust fund account at the bank. The broker is guilty of
    a. conversion.
    b. commingling.
    c. misrepresentation.
    d. fraud.

32. A husband dies intestate. His separate property is distributed to his wife and two children as follows:
    a. all to the wife
    b. half to the wife and half to the children
    c. all to the children
    d. one third to the wife, the rest to the children

33. Under the Subdivided Lands Act, the Real Estate Commissioner is primarily concerned with
    a. physical design and layout.
    b. health facilities.
    c. financing and marketing arrangements.
    d. none of the above.

34. Jones leases a home from Santos under a three-month written lease. Upon expiration of the lease, Jones retains possession. Santos has not decided on the next step. Jones has an estate at
    a. will.
    b. sufferance.
    c. years.
    d. tenancy.

35. An investor has an apartment building with no vacancies in which each unit rents for $600. The investor raises the rent 15 percent and suffers a 15 percent vacancy factor. Rental income:

    a. increases.

    b. decreases.

    c. remains the same.

    d. the question cannot be answered with the information given.

36. A real estate agent is asked to hold the buyer's deposit uncashed until acceptance of the offer by the seller. Upon the seller's acceptance, the agent must put the deposit in escrow or in a trust fund or give the deposit to the seller within how many business days?

    a. 5

    b. 3

    c. 2

    d. 1

37. The maximum amount of personal funds a broker may have in a trust fund account to cover charges and not be guilty of commingling is

    a. $50.

    b. $200.

    c. $500.

    d. $1,000.

38. Property is being sold where the buyer is going to take over the seller's existing loan. To avoid legal conflict before closing, the real estate agent should check to be sure the loan does not include a(n):

    a. release clause.

    b. prepayment penalty.

    c. alienation clause.

    d. subordination clause.

39. The stated policy of the Real Estate Commissioner is to create an equal opportunity industry. This means agents should
    a. maintain an attitude free from bias.
    b. realize that race, creed, and color are not material facts.
    c. do unto others as you would have them do unto you.
    d. all of the above.

40. A subdivider sold five lots to one buyer and optioned five other lots to another buyer. The subdivider must
    a. notify the Department of Real Estate of a material change.
    b. close the option sales within three business days.
    c. record the sales within five business days.
    d. not sell five lots to a single purchaser.

41. Under the Federal Truth-in-Lending Law (Regulation Z), certain borrowers have ___ days to rescind the loan.
    a. 30
    b. 10
    c. 5
    d. 3

42. A seller employed a broker under an open listing. The seller indicated to the broker that the roof leaked. While showing the home to a buyer, the broker stated that the roof was in good condition. After the sale, the buyer discovered that the roof leaked. The broker is guilty of
    a. false promise.
    b. the Statute of Frauds.
    c. misrepresentation.
    d. all of the above.

43. Under Division 6 of the Uniform Commercial Code (Bulk Sale), a public notice must be given 12 days before transfer by the:
    a. seller.
    b. buyer.
    c. creditors.
    d. all of the above.

44. The value of the subject property as set by the price of comparable properties is based on the principle of
    a. change.
    b. regression.
    c. substitution.
    d. highest and best use.

45. A California real estate broker sold a ranch in Montana to a California resident. A Montana broker assisted in the sale. To show appreciation, the California broker gave part of the commission to the Montana broker. This action was
    a. unlawful because the California broker was not licensed in Montana.
    b. unlawful because the Montana broker was not licensed in California.
    c. lawful.
    d. none of the above.

46. Income tax benefits for homeowners include deductions for
    a. interest on home loans.
    b. depreciation on buildings.
    c. expenses and repairs.
    d. all of the above.

47. All REALTORS® in California are bound by which Code of Ethics?
    a. National Mortgage Brokers Association
    b. National Association of Real Estate Brokers
    c. National Association of REALTORS®
    d. All of the above

48. In issuing a policy of title insurance, the title company is least likely to make an on-site inspection if the policy is a(n):
    a. CLTA standard owner's policy.
    b. ALTA extended policy.
    c. construction loan policy.
    d. lender's policy.

49. A real estate broker must retain copies of all listings and deposit receipts for how many years?
    a. 1
    b. 3
    c. 4
    d. 5

50. The first half of real property taxes are due and payable on November 1. They become delinquent after December 10, at which time, if not paid, a penalty is added to the amount. The penalty is
    a. 10 percent.
    b. 8 percent.
    c. 6 percent.
    d. 3 percent.

51. A Notice of Non-responsibility is usually posted and recorded by an owner when a:
    a. bulk sale takes place.
    b. tenant approves repairs without consent from the landlord.
    c. transfer of title takes place.
    d. mechanic's lien is filed.

52. Covenants and conditions are frequently placed in deeds. If a covenant or condition is breached, the enforcement is
    a. more severe for a condition.
    b. more severe for a covenant.
    c. equal for both a condition and a covenant.
    d. under current law neither can be enforced.

53. Which of the following is not a fiduciary relationship?
    a. broker to seller
    b. trustor to beneficiary
    c. attorney to client
    d. attorney-in-fact to principal

54. An appraiser determines that the market rent for a parcel of land is $700 per month and that interest (capitalization) rates should be 11 percent. The approximate value is
    a. $54,545.
    b. $69,280.
    c. $76,360.
    d. $105,000.

55. An owner plans to divide a parcel of land into nine parcels, with the intention of selling three parcels per year for each of the next three years. The owner:
    a. must satisfy the Subdivision Map Act.
    b. must report to the Real Estate Commissioner, but need not conform to the Subdivision Map Act
    c. must comply with the Subdivision Map Act and the Subdivided Lands Act.
    d. need not comply with any special law, as fewer than five lots are being sold in any one year.

56. Which of the following is a less-than-freehold estate?
    a. fee simple defeasible
    b. fee simple absolute
    c. leasehold estate
    d. life estate

57. A lease that lies between the primary lease and the sublessee is a:
    a. sandwich lease.
    b. percentage lease.
    c. ground lease.
    d. wedge lease.

58. An easement acquired by prescription can be lost by nonuse for a period of
    a. 5 years.
    b. 3 years.
    c. 2 years.
    d. 1 year.

59. A corporation built a large tract of homes and hired a handyperson to take care of the maintenance. The handyperson was given extra compensation for showing the homes on weekends to prospective buyers.
    a. The corporation is not in violation of real estate regulations.
    b. The handyperson could be fined for showing homes without a license.
    c. As an employee, the handyperson does not need a license to show homes.
    d. All corporate employees and officers selling the homes must be licensed.

60. After a trustee's sale, any money remaining after paying lienholders and costs is remitted to the:
    a. trustor.
    b. trustee.
    c. beneficiary.
    d. mortgagor.

61. The person who acquires title to real property under the terms of a will is known as the:
    a. devisee.
    b. administrator.
    c. testator.
    d. executrix.

62. A "commercial acre" is
    a. 43,560 sq. ft.
    b. a normal acre, less deductions for streets and setbacks.
    c. an acre zoned for commercial use.
    d. 42,513 sq. ft.

63. As required by law and regulations, a real estate broker must have a:
    a. trust fund account.
    b. trust fund logbook.
    c. credit card for business use only.
    d. both (a) and (b) are correct.

64. Shay gives a quitclaim deed to Wilson for a parcel of real estate. Wilson does not record the deed. Which of the following is true?
    a. Deed is invalid as between Shay and Wilson.
    b. Deed is invalid as between Shay and Wilson, but valid to subsequent recorded interest.
    c. Deed is valid as between Shay and Wilson, but invalid as to subsequent recorded interest without notice.
    d. Deed is valid as between Shay and Wilson and valid as to subsequent recorded interest without notice.

65. When public records are used to establish a chain of title, a written summary of the results is known as a(n):
    a. guarantee of title.
    b. abstract of title.
    c. opinion of title.
    d. affidavit of title.

66. After a mortgage is executed and recorded, title:
    a. remains with the mortgagor.
    b. transfers to the mortgagee.
    c. is given to the trustee.
    d. remains with the trustor.

67. A real estate contract by a married couple under the age of 18 is
    a. void.
    b. voidable.
    c. unenforceable.
    d. valid.

68. An exclusive agency listing differs from an exclusive right-to-sell listing in that
    a. only the exclusive right-to-sell listing must have a definite termination date.
    b. the broker is entitled to a commission if the owner sells the property under the exclusive agency listing.
    c. only the exclusive right-to-sell listing must be in writing to be enforceable.
    d. under the exclusive right-to-sell listing, the broker is entitled to a commission no matter who sells the property during the term of the listing.

69. A buyer in a land project can rescind the purchase for any reason and obtain a refund within
    a. 3 days.
    b. 5 days.
    c. 10 days.
    d. 14 days.

70. Which of the following represents the four essentials of value?
    a. scarcity, cost, demand, utility
    b. utility, transferability, cost, demand
    c. transferability, utility, demand, scarcity
    d. demand, cost, utility, price

71. All of the following are contracts, except
    a. escrow instructions.
    b. a listing agreement.
    c. a deed.
    d. a deposit receipt.

72. The cost approach to value has limited use when appraising
    a. a new building.
    b. tract homes.
    c. museum buildings.
    d. special-purpose properties.

73. When an agent violates antidiscrimination regulations, the Real Estate Commissioner can
    a. sue for damages.
    b. file a criminal action.
    c. revoke a license.
    d. all of the above.

74. Zowski holds a life estate measured by his own life. He leased the property to Anderson for five years, but died two months later. The lease is
    a. still valid.
    b. no longer valid.
    c. invalid from the inception.
    d. binding on the heirs of Zowski.

75. An owner sold a lot for $70,400, realizing a 20 percent profit over what was originally paid for the lot. The profit is
    a. $11,733.
    b. $14,080.
    c. $13,714.
    d. $12,509.

76. Which of the following is not essential to a general contract?
    a. that it be in writing
    b. mutual consent
    c. capable parties
    d. lawful object

77. An example of a lender who frequently uses loan correspondents and funds large commercial loans is a:
    a. savings bank.
    b. commercial bank.
    c. credit union.
    d. life insurance company.

78. RESPA (Real Estate Settlement Procedures Act) requires that certain lenders and/or closers must deliver a Uniform Settlement Statement to the borrower and seller within
    a. 10 days after the loan commitment.
    b. 3 days prior to closing.
    c. 5 days after closing.
    d. on or before the date of closing.

79. A deeds a title to B with the condition that B never sell alcoholic beverages on the property. B has a:
    a. less-than-freehold estate.
    b. fee simple absolute.
    c. fee simple defeasible.
    d. periodic tenancy.

80. An abstract of judgment can be recorded
    a. in any county.
    b. only in the county where the judgment is to be placed.
    c. only in the county where the debtor has real property.
    d. only in the county where the creditor resides.

81. The amount of real estate sales commission is
    a. regulated by the real estate commissioner.
    b. subject to negotiation.
    c. fixed by trade groups.
    d. governed by state law.

82. A roof that is pitched with two sloping sides is called a:
    a. hip.
    b. gable.
    c. mansard.
    d. gambrel.

83. A contract that is executory:
    a. has not been performed.
    b. has been signed.
    c. is completed.
    d. has been notarized.

84. How much money would have to be invested at a 7 percent
    return to give an investor $200 per month?
    a. $34,286
    b. $48,000
    c. $43,705
    d. $39,325

85. A person who believes he or she has been discriminated
    against in seeking housing can file a complaint with
    a. the Federal Trade Commission.
    b. the Rumford Commission.
    c. the Unruh Commission.
    d. the Fair Employment and Housing Commission.

86. If a borrower fails to make a loan payment, which financing
    instrument would be to the borrower's advantage?
    a. deed of trust
    b. mortgage
    c. contract of sale
    d. lease

87. After a loan has been granted, rapid unanticipated inflation would most benefit a:
    a. borrower with an ARM loan.
    b. fixed-interest rate beneficiary.
    c. trustor with a fixed interest rate.
    d. trustee.

88. The most difficult depreciation to correct is
    a. physical.
    b. economic.
    c. functional.
    d. accrued.

89. Properties A and B each have a value of $200,000. Property A was appraised using a capitalization rate of 6 percent, whereas Property B was appraised using a capitalization rate of 7 percent.
    a. Property B has more income than Property A.
    b. Property B has less income than Property A.
    c. Property A and Property B have the same income.
    d. None of the above.

90. Which of the following is not appurtenant or incidental to the land?
    a. stock in a mutual water company
    b. an easement
    c. reasonable airspace
    d. a picked crop

91. Recording of an instrument gives
    a. actual notice.
    b. constructive notice.
    c. preliminary notice.
    d. recorded notice.

92. A rate of interest that exceeds the legal rate is the:
    a. nominal rate.
    b. going rate.
    c. stated rate.
    d. none of the above.

93. The Federal National Mortgage Association (Fannie Mae) was primarily created to
    a. insure low-income housing loans.
    b. increase the amount of money available to finance housing.
    c. insure bank depositors for up to $250,000 per account.
    d. lengthen the term for real estate loans.

94. Broker Sanchez and Broker Roberts both have an open listing on a home. Broker Sanchez showed the home to a buyer who decided not to make an offer. A month later, Broker Roberts showed the same home to the same buyer, who then decided to buy. The seller owes a commission to
    a. Broker Sanchez only.
    b. Broker Sanchez and Broker Roberts.
    c. Broker Roberts only.
    d. Broker Sanchez, who needs to split it with Broker Roberts.

95. Both the buyer and the seller initial the liquidated damages clause in a deposit receipt. Later the buyer backs out. The seller is entitled to
    a. actual damages.
    b. no damages.
    c. punitive damages.
    d. liquidated damages.

96. A person borrowed $2,500 on a straight note. In eight months, $150 in interest was paid. The interest rate is
    a. 8.4 percent.
    b. 9 percent.
    c. 10.1 percent.
    d. 10.6 percent.

97. If a dispute arises during escrow and the buyer and seller cannot agree, the escrow holder may legally:
    a. file an interpleader action.
    b. return all funds to the respective parties.
    c. cancel the escrow.
    d. do all of the above.

98. The SW quarter of the NW quarter of the SE quarter of the SE quarter of the NW quarter of a section contains
    a. 1¼ acres.
    b. 2½ acres.
    c. 5 acres.
    d. none of the above.

99. Which of the following requires a real estate agent to do a physical inspection of a home and then report the results of said inspection?
    a. Disclosure Regarding Real Estate Agency Relationship
    b. Real Estate Transfer Disclosure Statement
    c. Natural Hazard Disclosure Statement
    d. Independent Real Estate Inspection Report

100. An owner hired a broker to act as property manager and collect rent from tenants. Rents are due on the first of the month. On June 1, the broker collected rents from all but one of the tenants. The next day, the owner died. On June 2, the broker asked the remaining tenant for the rent. The tenant refused to give the rent money to the broker. The tenant:
    a. must give the rent to the broker.
    b. should not give the rent to anyone but the heirs or the court.
    c. is in default by not giving the rent to the broker.
    d. need not pay the rent.

101. Which of the following employment situations is primarily concerned with the results, not the direction, of work?
    a. employer–employee
    b. jobber
    c. independent contractor
    d. agent

102. If there is no notice of completion, a subcontractor must file a mechanic's lien in
    a. 10 days.
    b. 30 days.
    c. 60 days.
    d. 90 days.

103. Which of the following is not issued by the Department of Real Estate?
    a. Real estate broker license
    b. Prepaid rental listing license
    c. Real estate sales license
    d. Escrow license

104. The fine for an unlicensed individual who receives a real estate commission is
    a. $20,000.
    b. $2,000.
    c. $200.
    d. none of the above.

105. When a buyer purchases a condominium, the buyer must be given which of the following regarding CC&Rs, the amount of homeowner dues, and financial and pending lawsuits (if any) about the homeowners' association?
    a. Common Interest Development General Information
    b. Real Estate Transfer Disclosure Statement
    c. Natural Hazard Disclosure Statement
    d. Seller Financing Disclosure Statement

106. An out-of-state developer wishes to sell lots to Californians. All of the following apply, except that
    a. sales agreements must carry a disclaimer approved by the California Real Estate Commissioner.
    b. advertising must carry a disclaimer approved by the California Real Estate Commissioner.
    c. the Subdivision Map Act will be enforced.
    d. all of the above apply.

107. The $500,000 exemption on the profits from the sale of a qualified principal residence apply for homeowners who are
    a. 50 years or older.
    b. married and file joint tax returns.
    c. native Californians only.
    d. earning an income of $125,000 or less.

108. Equity in real property is the:
    a. cash flow value.
    b. total of all mortgages.
    c. difference between the mortgage balance and value.
    d. appraised value.

109. The maximum time that urban real estate can be leased is
    a. 99 years.
    b. 51 years.
    c. 30 years.
    d. 15 years.

110. Which of the following is not required to obtain title to unimproved land by adverse possession?
    a. minimum of five years
    b. open and notorious use
    c. Color of title or claim of right
    d. that the acquiring party live on the property

111. Certain unities are required to maintain a joint tenancy relationship. They are
    a. grantee, unity, possession, and claim.
    b. time, title, interest, and unity.
    c. interest, time, title, and possession.
    d. ownership, time, title, and interest.

112. The Health and Safety Code specifies minimum standards for water and sewer facilities in a new subdivision. Approval and control for local water and sewer rest with the:
    a. local officials.
    b. Real Estate Commissioner.
    c. state officials.
    d. Planning Commissioner.

113. Most real estate syndicates in California use which form of ownership?
    a. Corporation
    b. Limited partnership
    c. Real estate investment trust
    d. Joint venture

114. The words *procuring cause* would have the most important meaning under which circumstance?
     a. a lawsuit by the buyer
     b. a dispute between brokers over a commission
     c. a disagreement between buyer and seller
     d. a dispute over loan proceeds

115. Which of the following would violate the advertising provisions of the Truth-in-Lending Law? Ads that state
     a. no money down.
     b. $100,000 all-cash sale.
     c. $200,000 price, easy terms.
     d. qualification for FHA financing.

116. In the event that a seller backs out of a valid purchase contract, all of the following are true, except
     a. the buyer could sue for damages.
     b. the buyer could sue for specific performance.
     c. the broker could sue for damages.
     d. the broker could sue for specific performance.

117. A federal law regarding the sale of subdivided lots is the:
     a. Subdivision Map Act.
     b. Interstate Land Sales Full Disclosure Act.
     c. Land Project Act.
     d. Subdivided Lands Act.

118. The instrument used to transfer title to personal property is the:
     a. deed.
     b. bill of lading.
     c. lease.
     d. bill of sale.

119. An example of functional obsolescence is a:
     a. one-car garage.
     b. cracked foundation.
     c. truck route in front of a home.
     d. detrimental change in zoning.

120. When the Real Estate Commissioner receives a valid complaint against a licensee, the commissioner institutes action against the licensee under the:
    a. Business and Professions Code.
    b. Administrative Procedures Code.
    c. Real Estate Code.
    d. Rules and Regulations Code.

121. When a business opportunity is sold, a price is often paid for continued patronage. This continued patronage is called
    a. goodwill.
    b. blue sky.
    c. turnover.
    d. future sales.

122. A cloud on the title could be created by
    a. a recorded homestead.
    b. a deed of trust paid, but never reconveyed.
    c. an easement for utility poles.
    d. recorded covenants and conditions.

123. A written agency between a real estate broker and a principal would not be
    a. executed.
    b. implied.
    c. expressed.
    d. a contract.

124. Which act of California law prohibits real estate agents from discriminating while conducting business?
    a. Unruh Civil Rights Act
    b. Housing Financial Discrimination Act
    c. Holden Act
    d. Civil Rights Act of 1968 and 1988 Amendments

125. When a real estate broker acts exclusively for the buyer or seller, but not for both, it is called a(n):
    a. dual agency.
    b. exclusive agency.
    c. divided agency.
    d. single agency.

126. The most important factor in estimating the value of residential homes is
    a. square footage.
    b. demand by ready, willing, and able buyers.
    c. floor plan.
    d. rent.

127. Which of the following is correct regarding net listings?
    a. They are not allowed in California.
    b. The broker has the exclusive right to sell the property.
    c. The broker is required to disclose the full commission prior to close of sale.
    d. The seller's net cannot exceed the difference between the sales price and the appraised value.

128. Once an abstract of judgment is recorded, it remains in force for
    a. 1 year.
    b. 3 years.
    c. 5 years.
    d. 10 years.

129. The *secondary mortgage market* refers to
    a. the resale of existing loans.
    b. the granting of second loans.
    c. mortgage brokers who arrange loans.
    d. none of the above.

130. Real estate loans that are pegged to some index and in which the interest rate may change during the term of the loan are called
    a. conventional loans.
    b. FHA loans.
    c. ARM loans.
    d. seller carry loans.

131. The unauthorized use of the term REALTOR® is
    a. a criminal offense.
    b. a violation of California Real Estate Law.
    c. not a problem if the person is a licensed broker.
    d. not punishable in California.

132. If a tenant is late on the rent, an owner should serve a(n):
    a. 30-day notice.
    b. 3-day notice.
    c. unlawful detainer warrant.
    d. eviction notice.

133. Once a real estate broker's license has been revoked or suspended, his or her sales associates can
    a. be paid commissions earned prior to the suspension.
    b. collect rents as property managers.
    c. continue to work on existing listings.
    d. take new listings with a post date on the contract.

134. A woman died and left an estate. Thirty-seven percent went to her husband; 18 percent each went to each of the two sons and one daughter. The rest went to a college foundation. The college foundation received $37,000. The daughter's share was
    a. $74,000.
    b. $84,000.
    c. $96,000.
    d. $124,000.

135. Adams sells Blackacre to Baker. Baker places the deed to Blackacre in his safety deposit box without recording same. Baker lets Adams retain possession of Blackacre. Some time later, Adams sells Blackacre to Collins. Collins records her deed and takes possession of Blackacre from Adams. When Baker gains knowledge of the transfer from Adams to Collins, he could do which of the following?
    a. Record his prior deed and charge Collins rent.
    b. Take possession away from Collins and let Collins collect the money she paid to Adams.
    c. Sue Collins.
    d. Do nothing regarding Collins if she had no prior knowledge of the transfer to Baker.

136. Personal property attached to a building in such a way that it becomes part of the building is known as a(n):
    a. appurtenance.
    b. fixture.
    c. attachment.
    d. dedication.

137. The situation by which property reverts to the state for lack of heirs is called
    a. escheat.
    b. eminent domain.
    c. condemnation.
    d. intestate succession.

138. When work is done per the Street Improvement Act of 1911, property owners are allowed to pay their pro rata share within how many days before it goes to bond?
    a. 30
    b. 60
    c. 90
    d. 180

139. The real property tax year runs from
    a. January 1 to December 31.
    b. March 1 to February 28.
    c. July 1 to June 30.
    d. December 10 to December 9.

140. Which of the following is correct regarding an "as is" home sale?
    a. Caveat emptor is the only rule.
    b. The real estate agent is not required to physically inspect the home.
    c. All material facts about the home must still be disclosed.
    d. "As is" home sales are not allowed in California.

141. In qualifying married buyers for a loan, the least important is
    a. regular income.
    b. spouse's income.
    c. monthly debts.
    d. overtime pay.

142. Rates for title insurance are established by
    a. title insurance companies.
    b. the Department of Real Estate.
    c. the Department of Insurance.
    d. the corporation commissioner.

143. A duly licensed real estate salesperson may lawfully receive a commission from the:
    a. seller.
    b. escrow holder.
    c. broker.
    d. all of the above.

144. A real estate broker would not be disciplined by the real estate commissioner for
    a. making a secret profit.
    b. making a false promise.
    c. making a misrepresentation.
    d. acting as a dual agent with the full knowledge and approval of all parties.

145. A Real Estate Purchase Contract is frequently referred to as a(n):
    a. deposit receipt.
    b. listing agreement.
    c. option.
    d. lease.

146. The important case of the U.S. Supreme Court that prohibits discrimination in housing is
    a. *Wellenkamp v. Wilson.*
    b. *Jones v. Mayer.*
    c. *Unruh v. Smith.*
    d. *Rumford v. Brown.*

147. The maximum mortgage broker commission allowed on a
     $5,000 second trust deed loan due in seven years is
     a. $250.
     b. $500.
     c. $750.
     d. $1,000.

148. The maximum amount allowed from the Real Estate
     Recovery Fund for all parties in a single-judgment case
     against a broker is
     a. $100,000.
     b. $125,000.
     c. $150,000.
     d. $250,000.

149. A corporation is prohibited from holding title as
     a. joint tenants.
     b. tenancy in partnership.
     c. tenants in common.
     d. severalty.

150. In a 1031 real estate exchange, taxable unlike property is
     called
     a. like for like.
     b. basis.
     c. foreign property.
     d. boot.

ANSWERS TO PRACTICE EXAMINATION

As you grade your practice examination, keep track of each
question missed. A passing score is 105 questions correct
(70 percent).

   After you compute your score, go back and reread each question
missed; then look up the explanation in the textbook. Wait a day or
two, review the glossary in the textbook, and take the examination
again.

   1. (b) Chapter 9
   2. (c) Chapter 2
   3. (c) Chapter 2

4. (a) Chapter 4
5. (b) Chapter 7
6. (b) Chapter 3
7. (c) Chapter 4
8. (a) Chapter 6
9. (a) Chapter 2
10. (c) Chapter 3
11. (c) Chapter 7
12. (a) $200,000/$4.75 = 42,105.26$ sq. ft./$300 =$ ft. 140.35 front ft., then $200,000/140.35 = $1,425$
13. (a) Chapter 5 (fiduciary is a result of agency, but not needed to form an agency)
14. (b) $67,100 + 517 = (94$ percent of total$)$67,617/0.94 = $71,933$
15. (b) Chapter 5
16. (d) Chapter 9
17. (b) Chapter 12 (Subdivision Map Act 2 or more units)
18. (d) Chapter 14
19. (c) $10,500/0.07 = 150,000/0.80 = $181,500$ value
20. (c) Chapter 2
21. (b) Chapter 2
22. (a) Chapter 11
23. (c) Chapter 7
24. (c) Chapter 9
25. (b) Chapter 1
26. (b) Chapter 4
27. (c) Chapter 8
28. (b) Chapter 11
29. (d) Chapter 10
30. (c) Chapter 12
31. (b) Chapter 4
32. (d) Chapter 2
33. (c) Chapter 12
34. (b) Chapter 11
35. (b) Chapter 9 (15 percent rent increase will not cover 15 percent vacancy)
36. (b) Chapter 4
37. (b) Chapter 4

38. (c) Chapter 7
39. (d) Chapter 12
40. (a) Chapter 12
41. (d) Chapter 7
42. (c) Chapter 4
43. (b) Chapter 15
44. (c) Chapter 9
45. (c) Chapter 4
46. (a) Chapter 13
47. (c) Chapter 15
48. (a) Chapter 10
49. (b) Chapter 5
50. (a) Chapter 13
51. (b) Chapter 3
52. (a) Chapter 3
53. (b) Chapter 7
54. (c) $\$700 \times 12$ mo. $= \$8,400/0.11 = \$76,364$
55. (c) Chapter 12
56. (c) Chapter 11
57. (a) Chapter 11
58. (a) Chapter 3
59. (b) Chapter 15
60. (a) Chapter 7
61. (a) Chapter 2
62. (b) Chapter 2
63. (b) Chapter 4
64. (c) Chapter 2
65. (b) Chapter 11
66. (a) Chapter 7
67. (d) Chapter 5
68. (d) Chapter 5
69. (d) Chapter 12
70. (c) Chapter 9
71. (c) Chapter 5
72. (b) Chapter 9
73. (c) Chapter 15
74. (b) Chapter 3

75. (a) $70,400/1.20 = $58,667, then $70,400 less $58,667 = $11,733

76. (a) Chapter 5 (only contracts under the Statute of Frauds need be in writing, not a general contract)

77. (d) Chapter 8

78. (d) Chapter 10

79. (c) Chapter 2

80. (a) Chapter 3

81. (b) Chapter 5

82. (b) Chapter 14

83. (a) Chapter 5

84. (a) $200 mo. × 12 mo. = $2,400/0.07 = $34,286

85. (d) Chapter 12

86. (b) Chapter 7

87. (c) Chapter 7

88. (b) Chapter 9

89. (a) Chapter 6

90. (d) Chapter 1

91. (b) Chapter 2

92. (d) Chapter 7 (usury)

93. (b) Chapter 8

94. (c) Chapter 5

95. (d) Chapter 5

96. (b) $150/8 = $18.75 mo. × 12 mo. = $225 int. yr./$2,500 loan = 9%

97. (a) Chapter 10

98. (d) Chapter 2

99. (b) Chapter 5

100. (b) Chapter 4

101. (c) Chapter 4

102. (d) Chapter 3

103. (d) Chapter 15

104. (a) Chapter 15

105. (a) Chapter 5

106. (c) Chapter 12

107. (b) Chapter 13

108. (c) Glossary

109. (a) Chapter 11

110. (d) Chapter 2
111. (c) Chapter 2
112. (a) Chapter 12
113. (b) Chapter 2
114. (b) Glossary
115. (a) Chapter 7
116. (d) Chapter 5
117. (b) Chapter 12
118. (d) Chapter 15
119. (a) Chapter 9
120. (b) Chapter 15
121. (a) Chapter 15
122. (b) Chapter 7
123. (b) Chapter 5
124. (a) Chapter 12
125. (d) Chapter 4
126. (b) Chapter 9
127. (c) Chapter 5
128. (d) Chapter 3
129. (a) Chapter 8
130. (c) Chapter 7
131. (b) Chapter 15
132. (b) Chapter 11
133. (a) Chapter 15
134. (a) $18\% \times 3 = 54\%$ children's share, then $54\% + 37\% = 91\%$ husband and children combined, then $100\% - 91\% = 9\%$ college share, then daughter has twice as much as college, $\$37,000 \times 2 = \$74,000$
135. (d) Chapter 2
136. (b) Chapter 1
137. (a) Chapter 2
138. (a) Chapter 13
139. (c) Chapter 13
140. (c) Chapter 4
141. (d) Chapter 8
142. (a) Chapter 10
143. (c) Chapter 4
144. (d) Chapter 4

145. (a) Chapter 5
146. (b) Chapter 12
147. (c) Chapter 7
148. (d) Chapter 4
149. (a) Chapter 2
150. (d) Chapter 13

Answers to Chapter Practical Application Questions

CHAPTER I

1. Requiring an application fee and a set of approved plans infringes on the right to use and the right to enjoy by placing a cost on the homeowner. On the other hand, requiring that the new addition meets housing codes ensures that the existing and subsequent owner(s) will have a safer home. As mentioned in the textbook, the bundle of rights is not absolute or unlimited; these rights are subject to the actions of government, which, in turn, is accountable to the people via the election process.

2. In the absence of an agreement to the contrary, all items of personal property can usually be removed by the seller. If the facts of the case show that the prefab storage shed merely rested on the ground, it is probably personal property. If it was bolted down on a cement slab or attached to a foundation, it probably is real property and should stay with the land. If the issue is too close to call, the courts tend to favor the buyer. This entire issue could have been avoided if the parties had mentioned the outcome of the shed in the purchase contract.

3. Trade fixtures are added by tenants as items needed to run a business, while regular fixtures are added by tenants for personal use. The presumption is that business tenants are automatically allowed to remove trade fixtures when they leave. Personal fixtures carry no automatic removal presumption. Whether regular fixtures can or cannot be removed depends on individual circumstances. In both cases, any legal removal carries with it the responsibility to repair all damages the removal may cause. Once again, any conflict can be avoided by discussing the issue in the rental contract.

CHAPTER 2: PART I

1. 165 acres, which looks like the shaded area below.

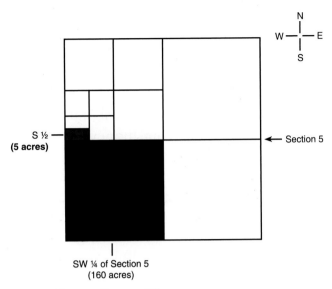

2. The basic rule is that the first additional bid over the initial accepted bid must be 10% of the first $10,000 and 5% of any excess.

    Therefore: $200,000 initial bid
    $$\frac{-\ 10,000 \times 10\% \qquad = \$1,000}{\$190,000 \times 5\% \qquad = \$9,500}$$
    $$\overline{\qquad\qquad\qquad\qquad \$10,500}$$

    $200,000 initial bid + $10,500 = $210,500 required for the first additional bid over the initial bid. Any bids after this may be in any amounts at the pleasure of the probate judge.

3. Williams is probably right because a grant deed carries after-acquired title, which means that after the grantor deeds the property, if he or she should later acquire an additional interest in the property, that interest automatically passes to the grantee.

CHAPTER 2: PART 2

1. Upon Washington's death, the lease with Santos is canceled since a life tenant cannot lease beyond the life of the designated person in a life estate. Possession will go to the heirs of Adams.

2. Nguyen and Battino are tenants in common as they do not have the unities of time, title, or interest. The percentage of interest in the properties is as follows: Nguyen now has his original 50% + Harris's 25%, for a total of 75% interest in the 20 acres.

Battino has a 25% interest in the 20 acres. When Harris sold one half to Battino, Harris was still a joint tenant with Nguyen on the remaining one half, and the right of survivorship applies. This illustrates how confusing things can get when joint tenants sell off portions of their interest in real estate.

3. The community property issues for the court to look at are as follows: The family home is obviously community property, but the five-unit apartment is going to be a legal issue. When Sara's parents left her the apartments, the inheritance was her separate property. The placing of the rental money in a separate account in her name alone showed intent to keep it separate property. But Sara's using the rental income to pay for the children's college tuition may be perceived as using the funds for a community property responsibility and a form of commingling. Sara's attorney will try to prove the money was a mere gift and not a pledging of the rental proceeds for a community purpose. Bill's attorney may take the opposite argument, which could create a nasty situation. The moral to the story is that if you are married and wish to maintain separate property, it is best to operate under the guidance of a competent attorney.

CHAPTER 3

1. An easement by prescription is an attempt to obtain the right to travel over the land of another, while adverse possession is an attempt to take title to the land of another. Both require hostile, open, and notorious use for at least five years under a claim of right or color of title. But adverse possession also requires the payment of the property taxes for at least five years, while easement by prescription does not.

2. a. Preliminary Notice should be served within 20 days from the first furnishing of labor or materials on your home site.

    b. A Notice of Completion should be filed by you within 10 days after the completion of the home.

    c. After filing your Notice of Completion, the general contractor has 60 days to file a lien, while the subcontractors have 30 days.

    d. If your Notice of Completion is filed incorrectly and, therefore, is invalid, all workers have 90 days to file a lien.

    e. If a mechanics' lien is filed, it will automatically terminate if court action is not instituted within 90 days.

3. $250,000   condo value
     − 125,000   to holder of first loan
      − 35,000   to holder of home equity second loan
      − 75,000   to owner of home per head of household exemption
     $ 15,000   remainder to be applied toward the judgment creditor's $25,000
                 debt

CHAPTER 4

1.   Vista Realty is probably a dual agent for Alvarez and Patel because both salespeople work for the same real estate office. Or maybe Patel is completely unrepresented. If Salesperson Ames and Salesperson Jones worked for different real estate companies, Vista Realty could represent just the seller and the other real estate company could represent just the buyer.

2.   Both Acme Properties and Lake Realty are probably guilty of misrepresentation. The incorrect square footage and wrong lot size were probably honest mistakes and not outright fraud, but a misrepresentation is a misrepresentation. Acme Properties will have a difficult time declaring they are innocent because they relied on the information supplied by Lake Realty. The salesperson from Acme Properties should have said, "Here are the measurements provided by Lake Realty, the listing agent. I have not verified the numbers, and you should not make any decisions until you have an appraiser or another qualified person check their accuracy."

3.   The heirs are right. The seller's death prior to accepting the offer automatically canceled the listing contract with Excellent Realty. Excellent Realty's contention that a commission was earned prior to the seller's death due to the $360,000 offer is incorrect. $360,000 is less than the listed price of $375,000, and it would take the seller's formal acceptance of the $360,000 offer to waive the required $375,000 listing price.

CHAPTER 5

1.   Sally has a bilateral (promise for a promise; e.g., rent for occupancy), expressed (written), executed (signed and moved in), valid real estate contract (lease). Although she is only 17, by virtue of her military service, she is an emancipated minor and legally able to contract.

2.   The legal issues to consider: Sunrise Realty was given the exclusive authorization and right to sell the listing for 180 days. Vargas canceled the listing in 90 days without a legal release from Sunrise

Realty. The sale took place through Ambrosini Properties during the 180-day time period that Vargas had given to Sunrise Realty. In a similar situation, a California court ruled that a seller could not unilaterally cancel the listing, that the permission of the listing agent was required, and that the seller must pay a second full commission to the original listing company.

3. A Real Estate Transfer Disclosure Statement is required on all one-to-four residential units, even rental units, even if the property is being sold "as is" and even if the buyer does not care about the condition of the house. The parties cannot agree to "waive" the Real Estate Transfer Disclosure Statement on residential one-to-four-unit sales. The seller is legally liable to disclose all known defects, and the agent is responsible for conducting a physical inspection and disclosing the results of said inspection. Agents are not normally liable for hidden defects neither disclosed by sellers nor revealed to the agent or buyer. However, the agent should submit in writing a suggestion to the buyer to seek out and use professional contractors and inspectors prior to purchasing the property "as is" to determine the extent of the physical damage. Frequently, the purchase contract, signed by the buyer, seller, and real estate agent, has this provision preprinted. But to be extra safe, an additional separate notice to this effect would not hurt.

CHAPTER 6

1. $244.75 divided by $1.10 = $222.50 × $1,000 = $222,500 originally paid by the seller. Then $400,000 less $222,500 = $177,500 profit divided by $222,500 paid = 79.78% approximate gross profit.

2. The N ½ and the NW ¼ of the SW ¼ of Section 9 = 360 acres × $5,000 per acre = $1,800,000 sale price × 10% commission = $180,000 total commission × 50% = Broker B's share of $90,000 × 60% = $54,000, your share as the salesperson.

3. 2,000 square feet × $125 per square foot = $250,000, and 500 square feet × $30 per square foot = $15,000. Thus, $250,000 home + $15,000 garage + $60,000 land and other improvements = $325,000. Then $325,000 × $1.20 = $390,000 resale price to make a 20% profit. Proof: $390,000 resale price divided by 1.20 = $325,000 cost.

CHAPTER 7

1. $200,000 interest-only loan × 6% = $12,000 divided by 12 months = $1,000 current monthly payment. Second year

equals $200,000 × 8% = $16,000 divided by 12 months = $1,333.33 monthly payment. Third year equals $200,000 × 10% = $20,000 divided by 12 months = $1,666.67 monthly payment. Fourth year 11% cap rate is reached; therefore, $200,000 × 11% = $22,000 divided by 12 months = $1,833.33 monthly payment.

2. The homeowner has until five days prior to the date of the foreclosure sale to make up back payments and all foreclosure costs to save the home. Using the figures given, that would be $2,000 back payments + $1,000 foreclosure costs, for a total of $3,000. If the homeowner waits until the five days prior or the date of sale, the lender can then demand the entire loan balance of $175,000 + $2,000 back payments + $1,000 in foreclosure costs. Some owners who find themselves in this predicament use the services of an attorney to file bankruptcy in an attempt to buy some time against the foreclosure.

3. $15,000 junior lien for ten years has a maximum commission rate of 15%, plus a maximum of 5% of the loan amount for additional costs and expenses, not to exceed $700. Therefore, $15,000 × 15% = $2,250 commission; $15,000 × 5% = $750 other costs, with a maximum allowed of only $700. Thus, $15,000 less $2,250 commission less $700 additional costs and expenses = $12,050 net to the homeowner. But the homeowner will be required to repay $15,000 plus interest on the $15,000, driving the effective rate of interest considerably higher than the interest rate stated on the note.

CHAPTER 8: PART I

1. $5,000 gross monthly income × 28% = $1,400 qualified maximum housing payments not counting debts. $5,000 × 36% = $1,800 less $600 long-term monthly debts = $1,200 qualified, counting monthly debts. Therefore, $1,200—the lesser of the two—applies. This illustrates how too much long-term debt reduces a person's ability to qualify for a larger loan, which, in turn, reduces his or her ability to qualify for a more expensive home.

2. People can spend or save (invest) their after-tax income and profits. When people decide to spend excessively, this reduces the supply of savings available for loans. This, in turn, can drive up interest rates and make it more difficult for people to qualify for real estate loans, slowing down the real estate market. On the other hand, when people choose to raise their level of savings, all things being equal, this increases the supply of funds available for loans,

and interest rates remain affordable. Affordable interest rates tend to stimulate the real estate market. Of course, if taken to extremes, if everybody only saved and did not spend, the economy would crash; then nobody would borrow to buy anything at any interest rate!

3. $180,000 loan balance × .0025 = $450 annual PMI cost divided by 12 months = $37.50 reduction in the monthly loan payment if the PMI coverage is canceled.

CHAPTER 8: PART 2

1.   Minimum cash required is 3%; therefore, $150,000 price × 3% = $4,500 cash required to close escrow if the seller pays all other closing costs.

2.   Due to no down payment on this VA-guaranteed loan, the sales price and the loan amount are the same. Therefore, $150,000 loan × 2.5% (1% loan fee + 1.5% funding fee) = $3,750 + $500 other closing costs = $4,250 cash to close escrow.

3. $150,000 Cal-Vet price × 2% down payment = $3,000 + $700 other costs = $3,700 cash required to close escrow.

CHAPTER 9

1.   200-foot × 40-foot main structure = 8,000 square feet × $65 per square foot = $520,000 replacement cost new; 20-year effective life × 2% (100% divided by 50 years) = 40% depreciation factor; $520,000 × 40% = $208,000 depreciation. Therefore:

$520,000	replacement cost new
−208,000	depreciation
$312,000	present value of main structure

35-foot × 15-foot storage building = 525 square feet × $20 per square foot = $10,500 replacement cost new; 15-year effective life × 3.33% (100% divided by 30 years) = 50% depreciation factor; $10,500 × 50% = $5,250 depreciation. Therefore:

$ 10,500	replacement cost new
− 5,250	depreciation
$ 5,250	present value of storage building

$312,000	present value of main structure
+ 5,250	present value of storage building
+ 27,000	present value of cement slab and other improvements
+300,000	land value
$644,250	or $644,000 estimated value of special use property

2. 11,000 square feet $\times$ \$1 $\times$ 12 months = \$132,000 gross rents

$132,000   gross rents
−   6,600   expenses ($132,000 × 5%)
$125,400   net operating income

$$\frac{\$135,000 \text{ net income of comparable property}}{\$1,500,000 \text{ comparable property}} = \begin{array}{c} 9\%\text{comparable} \\ \text{cap rate} \end{array}$$

$$\frac{\$125,400 \text{ net operating income}}{.09 \text{ capitalization rate}} = \begin{array}{c} \$1,393,333 \text{ or } \$1,393,000 \\ \text{estimated value} \end{array}$$

3.

	Comparable A	Comparable B	Comparable C
Price paid	$357,000	$340,000	$ 325,000
Spa	− 1,000	0	0
Condition	− 3,000	0	+ 3,000
Lot size	− 10,000	+ 10,000	+ 10,000
	$343,000	$350,000	$ 338,000

$350,000 is the best listing price estimate based on Comparable B having the least number of adjustments.

CHAPTER 10

1. The issue here is to save the transaction. The buyer's agent might mention that the buyer signed escrow instructions to split the title fee 50/50, even though the original deposit receipt said the seller would pay. The latest contract usually applies unless the buyer made an honest mistake and misread the instructions. The agent might mention that if the transaction falls through, the buyer could lose his or her deposit. Also, the issue of a court action interpleader might be pursued by the escrow holder. The bottom line is that if the transaction falls apart, the buyer will not get the home, the seller will not get the full sale proceeds, and the agent will not get a full commission. If the issue is a total stumbling block, ultimately the agent might agree to pay the buyer's 50 percent portion just to close the transaction. This may not be "fair," but it might be what is needed to solve the problem.

2. There are many issues here: California has an anti-rebate law that prohibits title companies from paying real estate licensees for the placement of title insurance. The fine can be up to \$10,000 and/or one year in jail for both the title representative and the real estate agent. Federal RESPA rules prohibit kickbacks and unearned fees paid to real estate agents. Real estate commissioner regulations prohibit "secret profit" by real estate agents. The

issue is whether unsolicited dinner and sporting event tickets come under the anti- rebate, RESPA, and secret profit rules. It would take an attorney to check out each law! It is probably best to pass on the whole thing and tell the title company, "NO THANKS!"

3. $413,575 × 7% = $28,950.25 divided by 360 days = $80.42 per day × 18 days = $1,447.51 pro ration, which will be a debit for the seller and a credit for the buyer because interest is paid in arrears on real estate loans.

CHAPTER 11

1. The landlord could proceed as follows: Within 21 days, refund the security deposit, less damages beyond normal wear and tear. If the $100 damage to the water heater is beyond normal, the landlord should withhold the $100 from the security deposit. The problem is proving that the leak was caused by damage, not normal wear and tear. From a practical point of view, many landlords will not hold the $100 from the security deposit for fear the tenant will make an issue, causing legal hassles, which could end up costing a landlord much more than $100.

2. The landlord should serve a three-day (not a 30-day) notice to remove the dog or quit possession. If the tenant complies, the issue is settled. If the tenant does not remove the dog or move out, the next step for the landlord is to proceed with a formal unlawful detainer action. From a pure cost point of view, some- times it is cheaper to pay the tenant to move, rather than bear the cost of an unlawful detainer action.

3. 5 units × $750 per month × 12 months = $45,000 gross scheduled income per year; then:

$45,000	
−2,250	vacancy factor ($45,000 × 5%)
$42,750	collected rents
× .08	property management rate
$ 3,420	property management fee paid
× .31	combined tax bracket
$ 1,060.20	tax savings when management fee is deducted

Therefore:

$3,420.00	property management fee paid
−1,060.20	tax savings
$2,359.80	after-tax cost of property management

CHAPTER 12

1. The appeal process is as follows: The planning commission decision can be appealed to the city council or to the board of supervisors depending on who has jurisdiction. If a person does not like the decision of the city council or board of supervisors, he or she can appeal to the courts. The decision of the highest court is final.

2. An owner of a condominium owns exclusively his or her airspace within the condo unit and has an undivided interest with the other owners in the building and land. A PUD owner owns his or her individual unit, inside and out, and owns the land immediately under the PUD. He or she has an equal undivided interest with the other PUD owners in the common areas. Under a stock cooperative, a corporation owns the property and each shareholder in the corporation is given the right to occupy a living unit. They are all called common interest developments because they feature some joint form of ownership in common with other co-owners.

3. The agent should respond by stating that any form of discrimination is illegal and carries a stiff fine and/or jail term for agents and owners. Also, good business ethics and a sense of fair play mean that all financially qualified people should have an equal right to own a home. Finally, if the owner insists upon discriminating, the agent should immediately cancel the listing.

CHAPTER 13

1. $225,000 × 80% = $180,000 loan at 8% for 30 years = $1,320.78 monthly payment using a financial calculator or 7.34 × 180 = $1,321.20 approximate monthly payment using the amortization table in Chapter 6. $225,000 price × .017 (.012 property taxes plus .005 insurance) = $3,825 divided by 12 months = $318.75 per month for property taxes and insurance. Therefore, $1,320.78 + $318.75 = $1,639.53 by financial calculator or $1,321.20 + $318.75 = $1,639.95 using the amortization table in Chapter 6.

2. No federal capital gains tax is owed as the first $500,000 of gain is excluded for married homeowners who file joint returns and live in their main home for more than two years.

3. The federal tax code allows homeowners to deduct interest on the home equity loan up to the market value of the home. The interest paid on 25% of a 125% loan that exceeds the market

value of the home will not be deductible if said funds are used to pay personal debts or expenditures. Homeowners should check with a tax specialist before entering into an equity loan to determine the current IRS rulings.

CHAPTER 14

1. Using the illustration in the book, starting with the ground and building up, a standard home has the footings, then the foundation, then the mudsill, then the floor joist, and finally the sole plate.
2. The four conditions are as follows: (1) must obtain a building permit, (2) must be placed on a permanent foundation, (3) must obtain a certificate of occupancy, and (4) must record a document stating that the mobile home is attached to a permanent foundation.
3. Advantages of owning your home include appreciation potential, tax advantages, privacy and control, pride of ownership, and better access to credit.

CHAPTER 15

1. As a new California real estate salesperson licensee, the educational requirements during the first four years of your license are as follows: If not previously completed, during the first 18 months of your license, you must complete two college or private vocational school (approved by DRE) college-level real estate courses consisting of real estate practice and finance or appraisal or legal aspects or economics or accounting or business law or property management or escrows or office administration or mortgage loan brokering or real estate computer applications or other advanced real estate courses approved by the DRE. Then within the first four years, you must complete four 3-hour DRE-approved courses in ethics, agency, fair housing, and trust fund handling. After July 1, 2007, you must also take a 3-hour course in risk management.
2. As a California real estate broker licensee, the continuing educational requirements during the first four years of your license are as follows: You must complete 45 hours of DRE-approved continuing education, including one 6-hour survey course updating ethics, agency, fair housing, and trust fund handling. After July 1,

2007 the survey course must be 8 hours and include risk management.

3. A bulk sale occurs when a business that has inventory is sold. When the bulk sale rules are not followed, a buyer of a business may find that he or she paid twice for the same inventory: once to the seller who did not own the inventory outright and again to the creditor who has a claim on the inventory. All purchasers of businesses should seek the advice and guidance of an attorney to be sure that all bulk sale rules are followed.

Answers to Chapter Reviewing Your Understanding Questions

Chapter 1

1. (c), 2. (b), 3. (d), 4. (c), 5. (a), 6. (d), 7. (b), 8. (d), 9. (d), 10. (d), 11. (c), 12. (a), 13. (b), 14. (d), 15. (b), 16. (c), 17. (b), 18. (a), 19. (d), 20. (a)

Chapter 2: Part 1

1. (d), 2. (d), 3. (b), 4. (d), 5. (d), 6. (a), 7. (b), 8. (c), 9. (c), 10. (a), 11. (a), 12. (c), 13. (a), 14. (d), 15. (c), 16. (b), 17. (b), 18. (c), 19. (a), 20. (d)
(Hint: Question 3: Read legal description backward and divide to solve for acres. Thus, Section 5 has 640 acres, so the SW 1/4 of that totals 160 acres, and the NE 1/4 of that totals 40 acres. The word "and" or a comma means "the sum of." Next, go back to Section 5's 640 acres, then jump to the NW 1/4 of that, which is 160 acres, and then you can see that the E 1/2 of that is 80 acres. Now go back again to Section 5's 640 acres, then the SW 1/4 of that has 160 acres, and the NW 1/4 of that has 40 acres. Thus, 40 + 80 + 40 = 160 acres.)

Chapter 2: Part 2

1. (a), 2. (d), 3. (c), 4. (c), 5. (b), 6. (c), 7. (c), 8. (c), 9. (b), 10. (b), 11. (b), 12. (a), 13. (b), 14. (d), 15. (c), 16. (c), 17. (c), 18. (a), 19. (d), 20. (b)

Chapter 3

1. (c), 2. (b), 3. (d), 4. (b), 5. (a), 6. (c), 7. (d), 8. (b), 9. (a), 10. (b), 11. (c), 12. (a), 13. (c), 14. (d), 15. (b), 16. (a), 17. (b), 18. (c), 19. (d), 20. (d)

Chapter 4

1. (b), 2. (d), 3. (b), 4. (b), 5. (d), 6. (a), 7. (d), 8. (c), 9. (b), 10. (d), 11. (b), 12. (a), 13. (c), 14. (b), 15. (c), 16. (b), 17. (a), 18. (c), 19. (b), 20. (d), 21. (a), 22. (c), 23. (c), 24. (c), 25. (b)

Chapter 5

1. (d), 2. (d), 3. (c), 4. (b), 5. (d), 6. (a), 7. (b), 8. (d), 9. (c), 10. (c), 11. (a), 12. (c), 13. (c), 14. (a), 15. (d), 16. (d), 17. (a), 18. (b), 19. (c), 20. (c), 21. (c), 22. (d), 23. (a), 24. (d), 25. (b)

Chapter 6

1. (d) $600 × 4 units × 12 months = $28,800 for the year

   $28,800
   − 1,440   5% vacancy ($28,800 × 5%)
   − 8,000   operating expenses
   $19,360   net income; then $19,360 ÷ .06 cap rate = $322,667

2. (b) $63,000 ÷ 1.20 = $52,500 paid; then,

   $63,000   sales price − $52,500 = $10,500 gross profit, then
   $10,500   gross profit
   − 3,780   selling cost ($63,000 × .06)
   $ 6,720   net profit

3. (d) $150 per month × 12 months = $1,800 year ÷ .06 interest = $30,000

4. (b) $170,000 price − $140,000 loan = $30,000 equity, then $30,000 ÷ 1,000 = 30 × $1.10 = $33

5. (d) $720 ÷ 12 months = $60 per month, then April 1st to July 1st = 3 months, then 3 months × $60 = $180 prepaid by seller, debit to buyer

6. (b) $600,000 − $400,000 = $200,000 gross profit, then $200,000 profit ÷ $400,000 cost = 50% gross profit

7. (c) $18,000 ÷ .06 = $300,000

8. (a) Table 6.6: 15 year @ 9% = $10.15 factor per $1,000, then $10.15 × 42 = $426.30 payment

9. (b) 4 acres × 43,560 sq. ft. per acre = 174,240 sq. ft., then 174,240 ÷ 8 lots = 21,780 sq. ft. per lot ÷ 400 ft. = 54.45 ft. wide per lot

10. (d) $66,000 × .10 = $6,600 interest for 1 year ÷ 12 months = $550 interest first month, then first-month payment principal + interest $840; − $550 interest = $290 principal

11. (a) 1,920 sq. ft. × $100 = $192,000 home
    425 sq. ft. × $ 30 = $ 12,750 garage
    8,000 sq. ft. × $ 15 = $120,000 lot
    $324,750 total

12. (c) Table 6.6: $3,861.98 pmt. ÷ 425 = $9.09, then down 10% column find 9.09 at 25 years

13. (d) $60,000 net income ÷ .08 cap rate = $750,000 price

14. (c) $179,500 × .07 = $12,565 × .40 B's share = $5,026

15. (d) $225,000 × .90 = $202,500 loan × .07 interest = $14,175 interest per year, then $14,175 ÷ 12 months = $1,181.25 interest-only payment.

16. (a) $206.25 ÷ 1.10 = 187.50 × $1,000 = $187,500

17. (b) 43,560 sq. ft. per acre ÷ 5 = 8,712 sq. ft. × $13 = $113,256 price × .09 = $10,193.04, then $10,193.04 × .50 = $5,096.52, round to $5,097

18. (b) With Table 6.5: 20 days @ 9% = 5.000, then $150,000 ÷ $1,000 = 150, then 5.000 × 150 = $750 interest for 20 days owed lender

    Without Table 6.5: $150,000 ×.09 = $13,500 interest for 1 year ÷ 360 days = $37.50 per day × 20 days = $750

19. (c) Table 6.6: $127,000 × .80 = $101,600 ÷ 1,000 = 101.6 @ 9% for 30 years = 8.05 factor, then 8.05 × 101.6 = $817.88 pmt. 1st loan

    2nd loan $127,000 × .10 = $12,750 ÷ 1,000 @ 10% for 20 years = 9.66 factor, then 9.66 × 12.7 = $122.68 pmt. 2nd loan, then $817.88 + $122.68 = $940.56, approx. $941

20. (d) $2,500,000 × .09 = $225,000 per year ÷ 12 months = $18,750

Chapter 7

1. (d), 2. (c), 3. (a), 4. (b), 5. (d), 6. (d), 7. (a), 8. (b), 9. (a), 10. (a), 11. (d), 12. (c), 13. (c), 14. (b), 15. (a), 16. (c), 17. (b), 18. (d), 19. (b), 20. (c)

Chapter 8: Part 1

1. (b), 2. (c), 3. (d), 4. (b), 5. (b), 6. (c), 7. (a), 8. (c), 9. (d), 10. (a)

Chapter 8: Part 2

1. (c), 2. (a), 3. (b), 4. (d), 5. (b), 6. (c), 7. (b), 8. (b), 9. (d), 10. (a)

Appendix Case Study

$1,245	Principal and interest
+ 175	Property taxes (2,100 ÷ 12)
+ 42	Property insurance and dues (504 ÷ 12)
+ 38	Private mortgage insurance (PMI)
$1,500	Total monthly housing payment

$33,000 + 34,000 = $67,000 per year ÷ 12 months
= $5,583 per month

$1,500 ÷ $5,583 = 26.9%

$1,500	Total monthly housing payment
+ 375	Car payment
+ 125	Furniture payment
$2,000	Total monthly credit obligations

$2,000 ÷ $5,583 = 35.8%

Yes, they qualify for the loan.

Chapter 9

1. (b), 2. (a), 3. (d), 4. (b), 5. (c), 6. (a), 7. (d), 8. (a), 9. (a), 10. (c), 11. (a), 12. (b), 13. (d), 14. (c), 15. (c), 16. (b), 17. (c), 18. (c), 19. (d), 20. (b)

Chapter 10

1. (d), 2. (b), 3. (b), 4. (c), 5. (a), 6. (d), 7. (b), 8. (d), 9. (a), 10. (b), 11. (c), 12. (b), 13. (d), 14. (c), 15. (b), 16. (a), 17. (c), 18. (d), 19. (a), 20. (a)

Chapter 11

1. (a), 2. (a), 3. (a), 4. (b), 5. (b), 6. (d), 7. (b), 8. (d), 9. (d), 10. (d), 11. (a), 12. (d), 13. (a), 14. (c), 15. (d), 16. (b), 17. (b), 18. (b), 19. (a), 20. (d)

Chapter 12

1. (d), 2. (b), 3. (c), 4. (a), 5. (d), 6. (c), 7. (a), 8. (d), 9. (c), 10. (d), 11. (a), 12. (a), 13. (d), 14. (a), 15. (c), 16. (a), 17. (d), 18. (b), 19. (b), 20. (d)

Chapter 13

1. (a), 2. (b), 3. (c), 4. (d), 5. (c), 6. (c), 7. (c), 8. (d), 9. (d), 10. (c), 11. (b), 12. (d), 13. (d), 14. (c), 15. (a), 16. (d), 17. (b), 18. (c), 19. (d), 20. (b)

Chapter 14

1. (b), 2. (a), 3. (d), 4. (c), 5. (b), 6. (c), 7. (a), 8. (b), 9. (b), 10. (a), 11. (b), 12. (c), 13. (c), 14. (a), 15. (c), 16. (c), 17. (d), 18. (b), 19. (b), 20. (d)

Chapter 15

1. (b), 2. (a), 3. (b), 4. (c), 5. (b), 6. (d), 7. (d), 8. (d), 9. (a), 10. (a), 11. (c), 12. (a), 13. (c), 14. (d), 15. (b), 16. (d), 17. (b), 18. (a), 19. (d), 20. (c)

Glossary

A

ALTA Owner's Policy A residential owner's extended coverage policy that provides buyers or owners the same protection the ALTA policy gives to lenders. Also called an ALTA-R policy.

ALTA Title Policy An American Land Title Association–approved title policy. A type of title insurance policy that expands the risks normally insured against under the standard type of policy to include unrecorded mechanics' liens; unrecorded physical easements; facts a physical survey would show; water and mineral rights; and rights of parties in possession, such as tenants and buyers under unrecorded instruments.

Absolute Fee-Simple Title Title that is absolute and unqualified. It is the best title one can have.

Abstract of Judgment A condensation of the essential provisions of a court judgment.

Abstract of Title A summary or digest of the conveyances, transfers, and any other facts relied on as evidence of title, together with any other elements of record that may impair the title.

Abstraction A method of valuing land. The indicated value of the improvement is deducted from the sales price.

Acceleration Clause A clause in a trust deed or mortgage giving the lender the right to call all sums owed to the lender to be immediately due and payable upon the happening of a certain event.

Acceptance When the seller or agent's principal agrees to the terms of the agreement of sale and approves the negotiation on the part of the agent and acknowledges receipt of the deposit in subscribing to the agreement of sale.

Access Right The right of an owner to have ingress and egress to and from his or her property. Also called right of way.

Accretion An addition to land from natural causes as, for example, from gradual action of the ocean or river waters.

Accrued Depreciation The difference between the cost of replacement new as of the date of the appraisal and the present appraised value.

Accrued Items of Expense Those incurred expenses that are not yet payable. The seller's accrued expenses are credited to the purchaser in a closing statement.

Acknowledgment A formal declaration before a duly authorized officer by a person who has executed an instrument that such execution is his or her act and deed.

Acquisition The act or process by which a person procures property.

Acre A measure of land equaling 160 square rods, or 4,840 square yards, or 43,560 square feet, or a tract about 208.71 feet square.

Ad Valorem A Latin phrase meaning "according to value." Usually used in connection with real estate taxation.

Administrator/Administratrix A person appointed by the probate court to administer the estate of a person deceased.

Adjustable Rate Loan A mortgage where the interest rate may go up or down, thereby the monthly payment may decrease or increase over the life of the loan.

Advance Commitment The institutional investor's prior agreement to provide long-term financing upon completion of construction.

Advance Fee A fee paid in advance of any services rendered. The practice of obtaining a fee in advance for the advertising of property or businesses for sale. Said fees can be incorrectly obtained, thereby becoming a violation of real estate laws and regulations.

Adverse Possession The open and notorious possession and occupancy under an evident claim or right, in denial or opposition to the title of another claimant.

Affiant A person who makes an affidavit.

Affidavit A statement or declaration reduced to writing, sworn to or affirmed before some officer who has authority to administer an oath or affirmation.

Agency The relationship between principal and agent that arises out of a contract, either expressed or implied, written or oral, wherein the agent is employed by the principal to do certain acts dealing with a third party.

Agent One who represents another from whom he or she has derived authority.

Agreement of Sale A written agreement or contract between seller and purchaser in which they reach a meeting of minds on the terms and conditions of the sale. Often called a deposit receipt.

Air Rights The rights in real property to use the airspace above the surface of the land.

Alienation The transferring of property to another; the transfer of property and possession of lands or other things from one person to another.

Alienation Clause A clause that gives the lender the right to call a loan upon sale of real estate. Also called a due-on-sale clause.

Alluvion (Alluvium) Soil deposited by accretion; increase of earth on a shore or bank of a river.

Amenities Satisfaction of enjoyable living to be derived from a home; conditions of agreeable living or a beneficial influence arising from location or improvements.

AMO Accredited Management Organization.

Amortization The liquidation of a financial obligation on an installment basis; also, recovery, over a period, of cost or value.

Amortized Loan A loan that is completely paid off, interest and principal, by a series of regular payments that are equal or nearly equal. Also called a level payments loan.

Annual Percentage Rate (APR) Not an interest rate, but rather percentage rate that reflects the effective interest rate on the loan, including other prepaid financing charges such as loan fees, prepaid interest, and tax service fees.

Annuity A series of assured equal or nearly equal payments to be made over a period of time or a lump-sum payment to be made in the future. The series of installment payments due to the landlord under a lease. The series of installment payments due to a lender. Real estate finance is most concerned with the first definition.

Anticipation, Principle of Affirms that value is created by anticipated benefits to be derived in the future.

Appraisal An estimate and opinion of value; a conclusion resulting from the analysis of facts.

Appraiser One qualified by education, training, and experience and tested by the state who is hired to estimate the value of real and personal property based on experience, judgment, facts, and use of formal appraisal processes.

Appreciation An increase in value that can result from inflation or from the interaction of supply and demand forces.

Appropriation of A legal term including the act or acts involved in the taking and reducing to personal possession of water occurring in a stream or another body of water and of applying such water to beneficial uses or purposes.

Appurtenance Something annexed to another thing that may be transferred incident to it. That which belongs to another thing, such as a barn, a dwelling, a garage, or an orchard, is incident to the land to which it is attached.

Architectural Style Generally, the appearance and character of a building's design and construction.

Assessed Valuation A valuation placed upon property by a public officer or board as a basis for taxation.

Assessed Value Value placed upon property as a basis for taxation.

Assessment The valuation of property for the purpose of levying a tax or the amount of the tax levied.

Assessor The official who has the responsibility of determining assessed values for property taxes.

Assignment A transfer or making over to another of the whole of any property, real or personal, in possession or in action, or of any estate or right therein.

Assignment of Lease The original lessee is removed from the transaction and the rights and duties pass to a new assignee, who is now primarily liable for the lease.

Assignor One who assigns or transfers property.

Assigns; Assignees Those to whom property is transferred.

Assumption Agreement An undertaking or adoption of a debt or an obligation resting primarily upon another person.

Assumption Fee A lender's charge for changing over and processing new records for a new owner who is assuming an existing loan.

Assumption of Mortgage The taking of title to property by a grantee, wherein he or she assumes liability for payment of an existing note secured by a mortgage or deed of trust against the property; becoming a co-guarantor for the payment of a mortgage or deed of trust note.

Attachment Seizure of property by court order, usually done to have the property available in the event a judgment is obtained in a pending suit.

Attest To affirm to be true or genuine; an official act establishing authenticity.

Attorney in Fact One who is authorized to perform certain acts for another under a power of attorney; power of attorney may be limited to a specific act or acts or be general.

Avulsion The sudden tearing away or removal of land by action of water flowing over or through it.

Axial Growth City growth that occurs along main transportation routes. Usually takes the form of star-shaped extensions outward from the center.

B

Backfill The replacement of excavated earth into a hole or against a structure.

Balloon Payment Where the final installment payment on a note is more than twice as great as the preceding installment payments, paying the note in full.

Baseboard A board placed against the wall around a room next to the floor.

Baseline and Meridian Imaginary lines used by surveyors to find and describe the location of private or public lands.

Batten Narrow strips of wood or metal used to cover joints interiorly or exteriorly; also used for decorative effect.

Beam A structural member transversely supporting a load.

Bearing Wall or Partition A wall or partition supporting any vertical load in addition to its own weight.

Bench Marks A location indicated on a durable marker by surveyors.

Beneficiary (1) One entitled to the benefit of a trust; (2) one who receives profit from an estate, the title of which is vested in a trustee; or (3) the lender on the security of a note and deed of trust.

Bequeath To give or hand down by will; to leave by will.

Bequest That which is given by the terms of a will.

Betterment An improvement upon property that increases the property value and is considered a capital asset, as distinguished from repairs or replacements where the original character or cost is unchanged.

Bilateral Contract Contract in which a promise from one person is made in exchange for a promise from another person.

Bill of Sale A written instrument given to pass title of personal property from the vendor to the vendee.

Binder An agreement to consider a down payment for the purchase of real estate as evidence of good faith on the part of the purchaser. Also, a notation of coverage on an insurance policy that is issued by an agent and given to the insured prior to the issuing of the policy.

Blacktop Asphalt paving used in streets and driveways.

Blanket Mortgage A single mortgage that covers more than one piece of real estate.

Board Foot A unit of measurement of lumber that is one foot wide, one foot long, and one inch thick; 144 cubic inches.

Bona Fide In good faith; without fraud.

Boot Unlike property received in an exchange that creates an income tax liability; for example, cash, notes, and personal property.

Bracing Framing lumber nailed at an angle to provide rigidity.

Breach The breaking of a law or failure of duty by either omission or commission.

Breezeway A covered porch or passage that is open on two sides and that connects the house and the garage or two parts of the house.

Bridging Small wood or metal pieces used to brace floor joists.

Broker A person employed by another for a fee to carry on any of the activities listed in the license law definition of a broker.

B.T.U. (British thermal unit) The quantity of heat required to raise the temperature of one pound of water by one degree Fahrenheit.

Building Code A systematic regulation of construction of buildings within a municipality established by ordinance or law.

Building Line A line set by law a certain distance from a street line in front of which an owner cannot build on his or her lot (a setback line).

Building, Market Value of The sum of money that the presence of a structure adds to or subtracts from the value of the land it occupies. Land valued on the basis of highest and best use.

Built-in Cabinets or similar features built as part of a house.

Bundle of Rights Rights the law designates that accompany ownership.

Buyer's Agent Real estate broker appointed by a buyer to be the buyer's agent to find property for the buyer.

C

California Association of Realtors (CAR) State-affiliated group that provides services for California members.

California Housing Finance Agency Program (CalHFA) Program designed to help first-time homebuyers acquire a home in California's expensive housing market.

California Land Title Association (CLTA) Trade association for title insurance companies that issues standard policies of title insurance.

Cal-Vet Loan Loan made directly to a veteran by the state of California. The money is obtained from the sale of State Veteran Bonds.

California Fair Housing Act (Rumford Act) State law that forbids discrimination in the sale, rental, lease, or financing of practically all types of housing.

Capital Assets Assets of a permanent nature used in the production of an income, such as land, buildings, machinery, and equipment. Under income tax law, they are usually distinguishable from "inventory," which comprises assets held for sale to customers in ordinary course of the taxpayers' trade or business.

Capital Gain Income from the sale of an asset rather than from the general business activity. Capital gains are generally taxed at a lower rate than ordinary income.

Capitalization In appraising, determining value of property by considering net income and percentage of reasonable return on the investment. Thus, the value of an income property is determined by dividing annual net income by the capitalization rate.

Capitalization Rate The rate of interest that is considered a reasonable return on the investment and used in the process of determining value based on net income. It may also be described as the yield rate that is necessary to attract the money of the average investor to a particular kind of investment. This amortization factor can be determined in various ways; for example, by the straight-line depreciation method. (To explore this subject in greater depth, refer to current real estate appraisal texts.)

Casement Window Frames of wood or metal that swing outward.

Cash Flow The net income generated by a property before depreciation and other noncash expenses.

Caveat Emptor Let the buyer beware. The buyer must examine the goods or property and buy at his or her own risk.

CBD Central business district.

CC&Rs Covenants, conditions, and restrictions.

Center of Influence One who, by nature of his or her relationships, is in a position to sway others.

Central Business District (CBC) An area in a city's downtown core noted for its commercial, office, and other business-related activities.

Certificate of Reasonable Value (CRV) The Department of Veterans Affairs appraisal commitment of property value.

Certificate of Taxes Due A written statement or guarantee of the condition of the taxes on a certain property made by the county treasurer of the county in which the property is located. Any loss resulting to any person from an error in a tax certificate is paid by the county the treasurer represents.

Chain A unit of measurement used by surveyors. A chain consists of 100 links equal to 66 feet.

Chain of Title A history of conveyances and encumbrances affecting the title from the time the original patent was granted or as far back as records are available.

Change, Principle of Holds that it is the future, not the past, that is of prime importance in estimating value.

Characteristics Distinguishing features of a (residential) property.

Chattel Mortgage A claim on personal property (instead of real property) used to secure or guarantee a promissory note. (See Security Agreement and Security Interest.)

Chattel Real An estate related to real estate, such as a lease on real property.

Chattels Goods or every species of property, movable or immovable, that are not real property.

Circuit Breaker An electrical device that automatically interrupts an electric circuit when an overload occurs. Used instead of a fuse to protect each circuit; can be reset.

Civil Rights Act of 1968 and 1988 Amendments Laws stating that within constitutional limits, fair housing should prevail throughout the United States.

Clapboard Boards, usually thicker at one edge, used for siding.

Clean Air Act Requires businesses (including real estate developers) to meet air quality standards.

Closing Costs Expenses paid by the buyer and the seller upon the sale of the property.

Closing Statement An accounting of funds made to the buyer and seller separately. Required by law to be made at the completion of every real estate transaction.

Cloud on the Title Any conditions revealed by a title search that affect the title to property; these are usually relatively unimportant items, but cannot be removed without a quitclaim deed or court action.

Code of Ethics (See Ethics.)

Collar Beam A beam that connects the pairs of opposite roof rafters above the attic floor.

Collateral The property subject to the security interest. (See Security Interest.)

Collateral Security A separate obligation attached to a contract to guarantee its performance; the transfer of property or of other contracts or valuables to ensure the performance of a principal agreement.

Collusion An agreement between two or more persons to defraud another's rights by the forms of law or to obtain an object forbidden by law.

Color of Title That which appears to be good title but which is not title in fact.

Commercial Acre A term applied to the remainder of an acre of newly subdivided land after the area devoted to streets, sidewalks and curbs, and so on has been deducted from the acre.

Commercial Banks Operate under license or charter from the state of federal government.

Commercial Paper Bills of exchange used in commercial trade.

Commingling A broker has mixed the funds of his or her principal with the broker's own money.

Commission An agent's compensation for performing agency duties; in real estate practice, a percentage of the selling price of property, percentage of rentals, and so on.

Commitment A pledge or a promise or firm agreement.

Common Interest Developments Projects with individual ownership of buildings and common ownership of land; for example, condominiums and planned unit developments.

Common Law The body of law that grew from customs and practices developed and used in England "since the memory of man runneth not to the contrary."

Community A part of a metropolitan area that has a number of neighborhoods that have a tendency toward common interests and problems.

Community Property Property accumulated through joint efforts of a married couple or registered domestic partners.

Compaction Whenever extra soil is added to a lot to fill in low places or to raise the level of the lot, the added soil is often too loose and soft to sustain the weight of the buildings. Therefore, it is necessary to compact the added soil so it can carry the weight of buildings without the danger of their tilting, settling, or cracking.

Comparable Sales Sales that have similar characteristics as the subject property and are used for analysis in the appraisal process.

Competent Legally qualified.

Competition, Principle of Holds that profits tend to breed competition and that excess profits tend to breed ruinous competition.

Component One of the features making up the whole property.

Compound Interest Interest paid on original principal and on the accrued and unpaid interest that has accumulated.

Conclusion The final estimate of value realized from facts, data, experience, and judgment.

Condemnation The act of taking private property for public use by a political subdivision; declaration that a structure is unfit for use.

Condition A qualification of an estate granted that can be imposed only in conveyances. They are classified as conditions precedent and conditions subsequent.

Condition Precedent A condition that requires a certain action or the happening of a specified event before the estate granted can take effect; for example, most installment real estate sales contracts, which state that before the buyer can demand transfer of title, all payments shall be made at the time specified.

Condition Subsequent When there is a condition subsequent in a deed, the title vests immediately in the grantee. But upon breach of the condition, the grantor has the power to terminate the estate; for example, a condition in the deed prohibiting the grantee from using the premises as a liquor store.

Conditional Commitment A commitment of a definite loan amount for some future unknown purchaser of satisfactory credit standing.

Conditional Sales Contract A contract for the sale of property stating that delivery is to be made to the buyer but title is to remain vested in the seller until the conditions of the contract have been fulfilled. (See Security Interest.)

Condominium A system of individual fee ownership of units in a multifamily structure combined with joint ownership of common areas of the structure and the land. (Sometimes referred to as a vertical subdivision.)

Conduit Usually, a metal pipe in which electrical wiring is installed.

Confession of Judgment An entry of judgment upon the debtor's voluntary admission or confession.

Confirmation of Sale A court approval of the sale of property by an executor, an administrator, a guardian, or a conservator.

Confiscation The seizing of property without compensation.

Conformity, Principle of Holds that the maximum of value is realized when a reasonable degree of homogeneity of improvements is present.

Conservation The process of utilizing resources in such a manner that minimizes their depletion.

Consideration Anything of value given to induce one entering into a contract; it may be money, personal services, or even love and affection.

Constant The percentage that, when applied directly to the face value of a debt, develops the annual amount of money necessary to pay a specified net rate of interest on the reducing balance and to liquidate the debt in a specified time period. For example, a 6% loan with a 20-year amortization has a constant of approximately 8½%. Thus, a $10,000 loan amortized over 20 years requires an annual payment of approximately $850.

Construction Loans Loans made for the construction of homes or commercial buildings. Usually, funds are disbursed to the contractor-builder during construction and after periodic inspections. Disbursements are based on an agreement between borrower and lender.

Constructive Eviction Breach of a covenant of warranty or quiet enjoyment; for example the inability of a lessee to obtain possession because of a paramount defect in title or a condition making occupancy hazardous.

Constructive Notice Notice given by the public records.

Consumer Goods Used or bought for use primarily for personal, family, or household purposes.

Contour The surface configuration of land.

Contract An agreement, either written or oral, to do or not to do certain things.

Contribution, Principle of Holds that maximum real property values are achieved when the improvements on the site produce the highest (net) return, commensurate with the investment.

Conventional Mortgage A mortgage securing a loan made by investors without governmental underwriting; that is, not FHA insured or VA guaranteed.

Conversion Change from one character or use to another.

Conveyance As a verb, refers to the process of transferring title to property from one person to another. As a noun, refers to the document used to effect the transfer of title (usually some kind of deed).

Cooperative Ownership A form of apartment ownership. Ownership of shares in a cooperative venture that entitles the owner to use, rent, or sell a specific apartment unit. The corporation usually reserves the right to approve certain actions, such as a sale or an improvement.

Corner Influence Table A statistical table used to estimate the added value of a corner lot.

Corporation A group or body of persons established and treated by law as an individual or unit with rights and liabilities or both, distinct and apart from those of the persons composing it. A corporation is a creature of law having certain powers and duties of a natural person. Being created by law, it can continue for any length of time the law prescribes.

Corporeal Rights Possessory rights in real property.

Correction Lines A system of compensating for inaccuracies in the government rectangular survey system due to the curvature of the earth. Every fourth township line, 24-mile intervals, is used as a correction line on which the intervals between the north and south range lines are remeasured and corrected to a full six miles.

Correlate the Findings To interpret the data and value estimates to bring them together to a final conclusion of appraised value.

Correlation The result of bringing the indicated values developed by the three appraisal approaches into mutual relationship with each other.

Cost A historical record of past expenditures or an amount given in exchange for other things.

Cost Approach One of three methods in the appraisal process. An analysis in which a value estimate of a property is derived by estimating the replacement cost of the improvements, deducting therefrom the estimated accrued depreciation, then adding the market value of the land.

Counterflashing Flashing used on chimneys at roofline to cover shingle flashing and to prevent moisture entry.

Counteroffer Automatically does away with the buyer's original offer; in effect, is merely an offer made by the seller to the buyer.

Covenant Agreements written into deeds and other instruments promising performance or nonperformance of certain acts or stipulating certain uses or nonuses of the property.

CPM Certified property manager; a designation of the Institute of Real Estate Management.

Crawl Space An exterior or interior opening permitting access underneath a building, as required by building codes.

CRB Certified residential broker.

Credit Unions Mutual, voluntary-membership, cooperative organization of people who agree to save their money together to provide money for loans to each other.

Cubage The number or product resulting from the multiplication of the width of a thing by its height and by its depth and length.

Curable Depreciation Items of physical deterioration and functional obsolescence that are customarily repaired or replaced by a prudent property owner.

Curtail Schedule A listing of the amounts by which the principal sum of an obligation is to be reduced by partial payments and of the dates when each payment will become payable.

Curtesy The right that a husband has in his wife's estate at her death.

D

Damages The indemnity recoverable by a person who has sustained an injury, in his or her person, property, or relative rights, through the act or default of another.

Data Plant An appraiser's file of information on real estate.

Debenture Bonds issued without security.

Debtor The party who "owns" the property that is subject to the security interest—previously known as the mortgagor or the pledgor.

Deciduous Trees Trees that lose their leaves in the autumn and winter.

Deck Usually, an open porch on the roof of a ground or lower floor, porch, or wing.

Decree of Foreclosure Decree by a court in the completion of foreclosure of a mortgage, contract, or lien.

Dedication An appropriation of land by its owner for some public use accepted for such use by authorized public officials on behalf of the public.

Deed Written instrument that, when properly executed and delivered, conveys title.

Deed Restriction A limitation in the deed to a property that dictates certain uses that may or may not be made of the property.

Default Failure to fulfill a duty or promise or to discharge an obligation; omission or failure to perform any act.

Defeasance Clause The clause in a mortgage that gives the mortgagor the right to redeem his or her property upon the payment of obligations to the mortgagee.

Defeasible Fee Sometimes called a base fee or qualified fee; a fee-simple absolute interest in land that is capable of being defeated or terminated upon the happening of a specified event.

Deferred Maintenance Existing but unfulfilled requirements for repairs and rehabilitation.

Deficiency Judgment A judgment given when the security pledge for a loan does not satisfy the debt upon its default.

Depreciation Loss of value in real property brought about by age, physical deterioration, or functional or economic obsolescence. Broadly, a loss in value from any cause.

Depth Table A statistical table used to estimate the value of the added depth of a lot.

Desist and Refrain Order An order directing a person to desist and refrain from committing an act in violation of the real estate law.

Deterioration Impairment of condition. One of the causes of depreciation and reflecting the loss in value brought about by wear and tear, disintegration, use in service, and the action of the elements.

Devisee One who receives a bequest made by will.

Devisor One who bequeaths by will.

Directional Growth The location or direction toward which the residential sections of a city are destined or determined to grow.

Discount An amount deducted in advance from the principal before the borrower is given the use of the principal. (See Point[s].)

Disintermediation The relatively sudden withdrawal of substantial sums of money that savers have deposited with savings banks, commercial banks, and mutual savings banks. This term also includes life insurance policy purchasers borrowing against the value of their policies. The essence of this phenomenon is that within a short period of time, financial intermediaries lose billions of dollars as owners of funds held by those institutional lenders exercise their prerogative of withdrawing their money from these financial institutions.

Disposable Income The after-tax income a household receives to spend on personal consumption.

Dispossess To deprive one of the use of real estate.

Documentary Transfer Tax A state-enabling act that allows a county to adopt a documentary transfer tax to apply on all transfers of real property located in the county. Notice of payment is entered on the face of the deed or on a separate paper filed with the deed.

Dominant Tenement Term used in connection with right-of-way rights and is the property that benefits from the use of the easement.

Donee A person to whom a gift is made.

Donor A person who makes a gift.

Dower The right that a wife has in her husband's estate at his death.

Dual Agency Where a broker represents the buyer and the seller in a real estate transaction.

Duress Unlawful constraint exercised upon a person whereby the person is forced to do some act unwillingly.

E

Earnest Money The down payment made by a purchaser of real estate as evidence of good faith.

Easement Created by grant or agreement for a specific purpose, an easement is the right, privilege, or interest one party has in the land of another; for example, right of way.

Easement in Gross An easement that does not have a dominant tenement.

Eaves The lower part of a roof projecting over the wall.

Ecology The relationship between organisms and their environment.

Economic Life The period over which a property will yield a return on the investment, over and above the economic or ground rent due to land.

Economic Obsolescence A loss in value caused by factors away from the subject property but adversely affecting the value of the subject property.

Economic Rent The reasonable rental expectancy if the property were available for renting at the time of its valuation.

Effective Age of Improvement The number of years of age that is indicated by the condition of the structure.

Effective Interest Rate The percentage of interest that is actually being paid by a borrower for the use of money.

Emblements Growing vegetable crops.

Eminent Domain The right of the government to acquire property for necessary public or quasi-public use by condemnation; the owner must be fairly compensated. The right of the government to do this and the right of the private citizen to get paid is spelled out in the Fifth Amendment to the U.S. Constitution.

Encroachment Trespass The building of a structure or construction of any improvements partly or wholly on the property of another.

Encumbrance Anything that affects or limits the fee-simple title to property, such as mortgages, easements, or restrictions of any kind. Liens are special encumbrances that make the property security for the payment of a debt or an obligation, such as mortgages and taxes.

Endorsement The act of signing one's name on the back of a check or note, with or without further qualification.

Equal Credit Opportunity Act Federal law that prohibits lenders, when granting a loan, from discriminating based on a borrower's sex, race, color, religion, age, marital status, or handicap, in addition to other items.

Equity The interest or value an owner has in real estate over and above the liens against it; branch of remedial justice by and through which relief is afforded to suitors in courts of equity.

Equity of Redemption The right to redeem property during the foreclosure period, such as a mortgagor's right to redeem.

Equity Sharing Where an owner-occupant and a nonowner investor pool their money to buy a home. A contract sets out the arrangements between the occupying owner and the nonoccupying investor.

Erosion The wearing away of land by the action of water, wind, rain, or glacial ice.

Escalation The right reserved by the lender to increase the amount of the payments and/or interest upon the happening of a certain event.

Escalator Clause A clause in a contract providing for the upward or downward adjustment of certain items to cover specified contingencies.

Escheat The reverting of property to the state when heirs capable of inheriting are lacking.

Escrow The deposit of instruments and funds with instructions to a third neutral party to carry out the provisions of an agreement or a contract; when everything is deposited to enable carrying out the instructions, it is called a complete or perfect escrow.

Estate As applied to the real estate practice, signifies the quantity of interest, share, right, or equity of which riches or fortune may consist in real property. The degree, quantity, nature, and extent of interest that a person has in real property.

Estate of Inheritance An estate that descends to heirs. All freehold estates are estates of inheritance, except estates for life.

Estate for Life A freehold estate; not an estate of inheritance, but one that is held by the life tenant for his or her own life or the life or lives of one or more other persons.

Estate from Period to Period An interest in land where there is no definite termination date but the rental period is fixed at a certain sum per week, month, or year. Also called a periodic tenancy.

Estate at Sufferance An estate arising when the tenant wrongfully holds over after the expiration of his or her term. The landlord has the choice of evicting the tenant as a trespasser or accepting such tenant for a similar term under the conditions of the tenant's previous holding. Also called a tenancy at sufferance.

Estate of Will The occupation of lands and tenements by a tenant for an indefinite period, terminable by one or both parties without notice. Estates of will are not recognized in California.

Estate for Years An interest in lands by virtue of a contract for the possession of them for a definite and limited period of time. A lease may be said to be an estate for years.

Estimated Remaining Life The period of time (years) it takes for improvements to become valueless.

Estoppel A doctrine that bars one from asserting rights that are inconsistent with a previous position or representation.

Ethics The branch of moral science, idealism, justness, and fairness dealing with the duties that a member of a profession or craft owes to the public, to clients or patrons, and to other professional members. Various real estate trade associations have codes of ethics that govern their members.

Eviction Dispossession by process of law. The act of depriving a person of the possession of lands in pursuance of the judgment of a court.

Exchange Officially called an Internal Revenue Code 1031 exchange that allows an owner to trade one property for another and to defer the income tax.

Exclusive Agency Listing A written instrument giving one agent the right to sell property for a specified time but reserving the right of the owner to sell the property without the payment of a commission.

Exclusive Right-to-Sell Listing A written agreement between the owner and agent giving the agent the right to collect a commission if the property is sold by anyone during the term of the agreement.

Execute To complete, to make, to perform, to do, to follow out; to execute a deed; to make a deed, including especially signing, sealing, and delivering; to execute a contract is to perform the contract, to follow out to the end, to complete.

Executor/Executrix A person named in a will to carry out its provisions as to the disposition of the estate of a deceased person.

Expansible House A home designed for further expansion and additions in the future.

Expansion Joint A bituminous fiber strip used to separate units of concrete to prevent cracking caused by expansion as a result of temperature changes.

Expenses Certain items that appear on a closing statement in connection with a real estate sale.

Expressed Contract Contract wherein the parties have agreed to perform an act or acts verbally or under a written agreement.

Extended Coverage Originally established for real estate lenders, this policy requires the title company to make a physical inspection of the property and insures against certain unrecorded title risks excluded under the standard policy.

F

Facade Front of a building.

Fair Market Value The amount of money that would be paid for a property offered on the open market for a reasonable period of time with the buyer and the seller knowing all the uses to which the property could be put and with neither party being under pressure to buy or sell.

Fair Housing (See Open Housing Law.)

False Promise False statement about what the promise is going to do in the future.

Farmers Home Administration An agency of the Department of Agriculture. Its primary responsibility is to provide financial assistance for farmers and others living in rural areas where financing is not available on reasonable terms from private sources.

Federal Deposit Insurance Corporation (FDIC) An agency of the federal government that insures deposits at commercial banks and savings banks.

Federal Housing Administration (FHA) An agency of the federal government that insures mortgage loans.

Federal National Mortgage Association (FNMA) "Fanny Mae" A private corporation whose primary function is to buy and sell existing mortgages in the secondary market.

Fee An estate of inheritance in real property.

Fee Simple In modern estates, the terms fee and fee simple are substantially synonymous. The term "fee" is of Old English derivation. Fee-simple absolute is an estate in real property by which the owner has the greatest power over the title that it is possible to have, being an absolute estate. In modern use, it expressly establishes the title of real property in the owner, without limitation or end. The owner can dispose of it by sale, trade, or will.

FHA 203b Program The most important section for the average home buyer or real estate agent. Under this program anyone who is financially qualified is eligible. Their credit history is important but need not be perfect. The buyer must have a minimum cash investment but it can come from an approved gift from family members and certain non-profits. The borrower is allowed to carry more debt than most conventional lenders allow. The Mortgage Insurance Premium (MIP) must be obtained and can be either purchased up front or financed as part of the loan. The MIP added to the loan is allowed to exceed maximum FHA loan limits. Loans are available up to four units. The maximum FHA loan amounts vary from region to region.

Fidelity Bond A security posted for the discharge of an obligation of personal services.

Fiduciary A person in a position of trust and confidence, as between principal and broker; the broker as fiduciary owes certain loyalty that cannot be breached under the rules of agency.

Filtering Down The process of making housing available to successively lower-income groups.

Financial Intermediary Financial institutions such as commercial banks, savings banks, mutual savings banks, and life insurance companies that receive relatively small sums of money from the public and invest them in the form of large sums. A considerable portion of these funds are loaned on real estate.

Financing Statement An instrument filed to give public notice of the security interest and thereby protect the interest of the secured parties in the collateral. (See Security Interest and Secured Party.)

Finish Floor Finish floor strips are applied over wood joists, deadening felt, and diagonal subflooring before finish floor is installed; finish floor is the final covering on the floor: wood, linoleum, cork, tile, or carpet.

Fire Stop A solid, tight closure of a concealed space that is placed to prevent the spread of fire and smoke through such a space.

Fiscal Controls Federal tax revenue and expenditure policies used to control the level of economic activity.

Fixity of Location The physical characteristic of real estate that subjects it to the influence of its surroundings.

Fixtures Appurtenances attached to the land or improvements, which usually cannot be removed without agreement, as they become real property; for example, plumbing fixtures or store fixtures built into the property.

Flashing Sheet metal or other material used to protect a building from seepage of water.

Footing The base or bottom of a foundation wall, pier, or column.

Foreclosure Procedure whereby property pledged as security for a debt is sold to pay the debt in the event of default in payments or terms.

Forfeiture Loss of money or anything of value resulting from failure to perform.

Foundation The supporting portion of a structure below the first-floor construction or below grade, including the footings.

Franchise A specified privilege awarded by a government or business firm that awards an exclusive dealership.

Fraud The intentional and successful employment of any cunning, deception, collusion, or artifice used to circumvent, cheat, or deceive another person, whereby that person acts upon it to the loss of his or her property and legal injury.

Freehold An estate of indeterminable duration, such as fee simple or life estate.

Frontage Land bordering a street.

Front Foot Property measurement for sale or valuation purposes; the property measures by the front foot on its street line each front foot extending the depth of the lot.

Front Money The minimum amount of money necessary to initiate a real estate venture.

Frostline The depth of frost penetration in the soil. Varies in different parts of the country. Footings should be placed below this depth to prevent movement.

Full Performance All parties to the contract accomplish what they set out to do in the contract.

Functional Obsolescence A loss of value caused by adverse factors from within the structure that affect the utility of the structure.

Furring Strips of wood or metal applied to a wall or another surface to even it, to form airspace, or to give the wall an appearance of greater thickness.

Future Benefits The anticipated benefits the present owner will receive from property in the future.

G

Gable Roof A pitched roof with sloping sides.

Gambrel Roof A curb roof, having a steep lower slope with a flatter upper slope above.

General Lien A lien on all property of a debtor.

Gift Deed A deed for which the consideration is love and affection and where there is not material consideration.

Girder A large beam used to support beams, joists, and partitions.

Government National Mortgage Association (Ginnie Mae) Wholly owned corporation of the U.S. government, created in 1968 when Fannie Mae became a private corporation.

Grade Ground level at the foundation.

Graduated Lease A lease that provides for a varying rental rate, often based on future determination; sometimes rent is based on the result of periodical appraisals; used largely in long-term leases.

Grant A technical term used in deeds of conveyance of lands to signify an intent to transfer title.

Grant Deed A deed in which "grant" is used as the word of conveyance. The grantor implicitly warrants that he or she has not already conveyed to any other person and that the estate conveyed is free from encumbrances done, made, or suffered by the grantor or any person claiming under him or her, including taxes, assessments, and other liens.

Grantee The purchaser; a person to whom a grant is made.

Grantor Seller of property; one who signs a deed.

GRI Graduate, Realtors Institute.

Grid A chart used in rating borrower risk, property, and the neighborhood.

Gross Domestic Product (GDP) The total value of all goods and services produced in an economy during a given period of time using resources located in the country.

Gross Income Total income from property before any expenses are deducted.

Gross Lease Lease where the tenant pays a flat rental amount and the landlord is responsible for property taxes, hazard insurance, and maintenance.

Gross Rate A method of collecting interest by adding total interest to the principal of the loan at the outset of the term.

Gross Rent Multiplier A figure that, when multiplied by the gross income of a property, produces an estimate of value of the property.

Ground Lease An agreement for use of the land only; sometimes secured by improvements placed on the land by the user.

Ground Rent Earnings of improved property credited to earnings of the ground itself after allowance is made for earnings of improvements; often termed economic rent.

H

Habendum Clause The "to have and to hold" clause in a deed.

Header A beam placed perpendicular to joists and to which joists are nailed in framing for a chimney, a stairway, or another opening.

Highest and Best Use An appraisal phrase meaning that use which, at the time of an appraisal, is most likely to produce the greatest net return to the land and/or buildings over a given period of time; that use which will produce the greatest amount of amenities or profit. This is the starting point for appraisal.

Hip Roof A pitched roof with sloping sides and ends.

Holder in Due Course One who has taken a note, check, or bill of exchange in due course (1) before it was overdue, (2) in good faith and for value, and (3) without knowledge that it was previously dishonored and without notice of any defect at the time it was negotiated to him or her.

Holdover Tenant A tenant who remains in possession of leased property after the expiration of the lease term.

Holographic Will Document written, dated, and signed in its entirety in the handwriting of the maker. It requires no witnesses.

Homestead Law Designed to protect a homeowner's equity in a personal residence from forced sale by certain types of creditors.

Hundred Percent Location A city retail business location that is considered the best available for attracting business.

Hypothecate To give a thing as security without the necessity of giving up possession of it.

I

Implied Contract Contract wherein the parties have not formally agreed verbally or through a written agreement to perform an act.

Impounds A trust type of account established by lenders for the accumulation of funds to meet taxes, FHA mortgage insurance premiums, and/or future insurance policy premiums required to protect their security. Impounds are usually collected with the note payment.

Inclusionary Zoning An ordinance that requires a builder of new housing to set aside a designated number of units for low- and moderate-income people.

Income Approach One of the three methods in the appraisal process; an analysis in which the estimated gross income from the subject residence is used as a basis for estimating value along with gross rent multipliers derived.

Incompetent One who is mentally incompetent, incapable; any person who, though not insane, is, by reason of old age, disease, weakness of mind, or any other cause, unable, unassisted, to properly manage and take care of him or herself or property and, by reason thereof, is likely to be deceived or imposed upon by artful or designing persons.

Incorporeal Rights Nonpossessory rights in real estate.

Increment An increase. Most frequently used to refer to the increase of value of land that accompanies population growth and increasing wealth in the community. The term unearned increment is used in this connection since values are supposed to have increased without effort on the part of the owner.

Incurable Depreciation When the cost of the repair or remodel exceeds the value added to the property.

Independent Contractor An individual who is hired to accomplish results and little or no supervision is required.

Indirect Lighting Reflected from the ceiling or another object external to the fixture.

Injunction A writ or an order issued under the seal of a court to restrain one or more parties to a suit or proceeding from doing an act that is deemed to be inequitable or unjust in regard to the rights of some other party or parties in the suit or proceeding.

Input Data, information, and so on that is fed into a computer or another system.

Installment Contract Purchase of real estate wherein the purchase price is paid in installments over a long period of time; title is retained by seller, and upon default, the payments are forfeited. Also known as a land contract.

Installment Note A note that provides that payments of a certain sum or amount be paid on the dates specified in the instrument.

Installment Reporting A method of reporting capital gains by installments for successive tax years to minimize the impact of the totality of the capital gains tax in the year of the sale.

Institutional Lender A financial depository that gathers deposits from the general public and then invests these funds.

Instrument A written legal document created to effect the rights of the parties.

Interest The charge, in dollars, for the use of money for a period of time. In a sense, the "rent" paid for the use of money.

Interest Rate The percentage of a sum of money charged for its use.

Intestate A person who dies having made no will or a will that is defective in form, in which case the estate descends to the heirs at law or next of kin.

Involuntary Lien A lien imposed against property without consent of an owner; for example, taxes, special assessments, and federal income tax liens.

Irrevocable Incapable of being recalled or revoked; unchangeable.

Irrigation Districts Quasi-political districts created under special laws to provide for water services to property owners in the district; an operation governed to a great extent by law.

J

Jalousie A slatted blind or shutter like a Venetian blind, but used on the exterior to protect against rain as well as to control sunlight.

Jamb The side post or lining of a doorway, a window, or another opening.

Joint The space between the adjacent surfaces of two components joined and held together by nails, glue, cement, or mortar.

Joint Note A note signed by two or more persons who have equal liability for payment.

Joint Tenancy Joint ownership by two or more persons with right of survivorship; all joint tenants own equal interest and have equal rights in the property.

Joint Venture Two or more individuals or firms joining together on a single project as partners.

Joist One of a series of parallel beams to which the boards of a floor and ceiling laths are nailed; supported, in turn, by larger beams, girders, or bearing walls.

Judgment The final determination of a court of competent jurisdiction of a matter presented to it; money judgments provide for the payment of claims presented to the court or are awarded as damages.

Judgment Lien A legal claim on all property of a judgment debtor that enables the judgment creditor to have the property sold for payment of the amount of the judgment.

Junior Mortgage A mortgage second in lien to a previous mortgage.

Jurisdiction The authority by which judicial officers take cognizance of and decide causes; the power to hear and determine a cause; the right and power a judicial officer has to enter upon the inquiry.

L

Laches Delay or negligence in asserting one's legal rights.

Land Contract A contract ordinarily used in connection with the sale of property in cases where the seller does not wish to convey title until all or a certain part of the purchase price is paid by the buyer; often used when property is sold on a small down payment. (See Installment Contract and Installment Reporting.)

Land and Improvement Loan A loan obtained by the builder-developer for the purchase of land and to cover expenses for subdividing.

Landlord One who rents property to another.

Later Date Order The commitment for an owner's title insurance policy issued by a title insurance company that covers the seller's title as of the date of the contract. When the sale closes, the purchaser orders the title company to record the deed to purchaser and show that the examination covers this later date so as to establish the purchaser as owner of the property.

Lateral Support The support that the soil of an adjoining owner gives to a neighbor's land.

Lath A building material of wood, metal, gypsum, or insulating board fastened to the frame of a building to act as a plaster base.

Lease A contract between owner and tenant setting forth conditions upon which the tenant can occupy and use the property and the term of the occupancy.

Lease with Option to Buy Under this type of contract the property is rented for a period of time, at the end which the lessee is given the right to purchase per a set of agreed terms.

Leasehold Estate A tenant's right to occupy real estate during the term of the lease. This is a personal property interest.

Legal Description A description recognized by law; a description by which property can be definitely located by reference to government surveys or approved recorded maps; for example, Lot, Block, and Tract; U.S. Government Survey; and Metes and Bounds.

Less-Than-Freehold Estate An interest held by tenants who rent or lease property.

Lessee One who contracts to rent property under a lease contract.

Lessor An owner who enters into a lease with a tenant.

Level-Payment Mortgage A loan on real estate that is paid off by making a series of equal (or nearly equal) regular payments. Part of the payment is usually interest on the loan, and part of it reduces the amount of the unpaid balance of the loan. Also sometimes called an amortized mortgage.

Leverage The use of borrowed funds to obtain an asset.

Lien A form of encumbrance that usually makes property security for the payment of a debt or discharge of an obligation; for example, judgments, taxes, mortgages, and deeds of trust.

Life Estate An estate or interest in real property that is held for the duration of the life of some certain person.

Life Insurance Companies Can be a source for real estate financing, particularly for large commercial and industrial properties such as shopping centers, office buildings, and warehouses. Life insurance companies also provide a significant amount of money for new housing subdivisions.

Limited Partnership A partnership composed of some partners whose contribution and liability are limited.

Lintel A horizontal board that supports the load over an opening such as a door or window.

Liquidated Damages A sum agreed upon by the parties to be full damages if a certain event occurs.

Liquidity The ability to convert your investment to cash quickly.

Lis Pendens Suit pending, usually recorded so as to give constructive notice of pending litigation.

Listing An employment contract between principal and agent authorizing the agent to perform services for the principal involving the latter's property; listing contracts are entered into for the purpose of securing persons to buy, lease, or rent property. Employment of an agent by a prospective purchaser or lessee to locate property for purchase or lease may be considered a listing.

Living Trust Created during a person's lifetime to avoid probate proceedings.

Loan Administration Mortgage bankers not only originate loans, but also "service" them from origination to maturity of the loan. Also called loan servicing.

Loan Application A source of information on which the lender decides whether to make the loan; defines the terms of the loan contract; gives the name of the borrower, place of employment, salary, bank accounts, and credit references; and describes the real estate that is to be mortgaged. It also stipulates the amount of the loan being applied for and repayment terms.

Loan Closing When all conditions have been met, the loan officer authorizes the recording of the trust deed or mortgage. The disbursal procedure of funds is similar to the closing of a real estate sales escrow. The borrower can expect to receive less than the amount of the loan (as title, recording, service, and other fees may be withheld), or he or she can expect to deposit the cost of these items into the loan escrow. This process is sometimes called funding the loan.

Loan Commitment Lender's contractual commitment to a loan based on the appraisal and underwriting.

Loan Qualification Ratios One of the methods a lender uses to qualify a borrower.

Louver An opening with a series of horizontal slats set at an angle to permit ventilation without admitting rain or sunlight.

M

MAI Member of the Appraisal Institute. Designates a person who is a member of the American Institute of Real Estate Appraisers.

Margin of Security The difference between the amount of the mortgage loan(s) and the appraised value of the property.

Marginal Land Land that barely pays the cost of working or using.

Market Data Approach One of the three methods in the appraisal process. A means of comparing similar types of residential properties that have recently sold to the subject property.

Market Price The price paid regardless of pressures, motives, or intelligence.

Market Value The price at which a willing seller would sell and a willing buyer would buy, neither being under abnormal pressure. As defined by the courts, the highest price estimated in terms of money that a property will bring if exposed for sale in the open market, allowing a reasonable time to find a purchaser with knowledge of the property's use and capabilities for use.

Marketable Title Merchantable title; title free and clear of objectionable liens or encumbrances.

Material Fact One the agent should realize will likely affect the judgment of the principal in giving consent to the agent to enter into the particular transaction on the specified terms.

Mechanic's Lien A lien created by statute that exists against real property in favor of persons who have performed work or furnished materials for the improvement of the real estate.

Metes and Bounds A term used in describing the boundary lines of land, setting forth all the boundary lines together with their terminal points and angles.

Minor Any person under 18 years of age.

Misplaced Improvements Improvements on land that do not conform to the most profitable use of the site.

Mobile Home Defined by California health and safety code as "a vehicle designed and equipped to contain no more than two dwelling units, to be used without a permanent foundation."

Modular A building composed of modules constructed on an assembly line in a factory. Usually, the modules are self-contained.

Moldings Usually, patterned strips used to provide ornamental variation of outline or contour, such as cornices, bases, and window and door jambs.

Monetary Controls Federal Reserve tools for regulating the availability of money and credit to influence the level of economic activity.

Monument A fixed object and point established by surveyors to establish land locations.

Moratorium The temporary suspension, usually by statute, of the enforcement of liability for debt.

Mortgage An instrument recognized by law by which property is hypothecated to secure the payment of a debt or an obligation; the procedure for foreclosure in the event default is established by statute.

Mortgage Bankers Lend their own money and then either resell the loan to another lender or keep the loan for an investment.

Mortgage Brokers Do not lend their own money. Instead, they find a lender and a borrower and get a fee for bringing them together.

Mortgage Companies Place more home loans than do institutional lenders.

Mortgage Contracts with Warrants Warrants make the mortgage more attractive to the lender by providing the greater security that goes with a mortgage and a greater return through the right to buy stock in the borrower's company or a portion of the income property itself.

Mortgage Insurance Insurance against financial loss available to mortgage lenders to protect against loss resulting from default by borrowers.

Mortgagee One to whom a mortgagor gives a mortgage to secure a loan or performance of an obligation; a lender. (See Secured Party.)

Mortgagor One who gives a mortgage on his or her property to secure a loan or assure performance of an obligation; a borrower. (See Debtor.)

Multiple Listing A listing, usually an exclusive right to sell, taken by a member of an organization composed of real estate brokers with the provision that all members will have the opportunity to find an interested client; a cooperative listing.

Mutual Water Company A water company organized by or for water users in a given district with the goal of securing an ample water supply at a reasonable rate; stock is issued to users.

N

NAR National Association of REALTORS®.

NAREB National Association of Real Estate Brokers.

Narrative Appraisal An extensive written report of all factual materials, techniques, and appraisal methods used by an appraiser to determine value.

National Environmental Policy Act requiring an environmental impact report on all projects using federal funding.

Negative Amortized Note The loan payment does not cover even the monthly interest. Each month this shortage is added to the principal owed, resulting in an increased loan balance, which in turn, incurs additional interest.

Negotiable Capable of being negotiated; assignable or transferable in the ordinary course of business.

Net Lease Sometimes referred as a triple net lease. The tenant pays rent along with the landlord's property taxes, hazard insurance, and maintenance.

Net Listing A listing with the provision that the agent retains as compensation all sums received over and above a net price to the owner.

Nominal Interest Rates The percentage of interest stated in loan documents.

Non-Institutional Lenders Do not accept deposits from the general public and are not as strictly regulated as institutional lenders.

Notary Public An appointed officer with authority to take the acknowledgment of persons executing documents, to sign the certificate, and to affix a seal.

Note A signed written instrument acknowledging a debt and promising payment.

Notice Actual knowledge acquired by being present at the occurrence.

Notice of Completion Document that an owner of real property files at the County Recorder's office once construction work on the property is completed.

Notice of Nonresponsibility A notice provided by law designed to relieve a property owner from responsibility for the cost of work done by a tenant on the property or materials furnished therefore notice must be verified, recorded, and posted.

Notice to Quit A notice to a tenant to vacate rented property.

O

Offset Statement Statement by owner of property or owner of lien against property, setting forth the present status of liens against said property.

Open-End Mortgage A mortgage containing a clause that permits the mortgagor to borrow additional money after the loan has been reduced without rewriting the mortgage.

Open Housing LAW Passed by Congress in 1968 and 1988 to prohibit discrimination in the sale of real estate because of race, color, religion, sex, or handicap of buyers.

Open Listing An authorization given by a property owner to a real estate agent wherein said agent is given the nonexclusive right to secure a purchaser; open listings may be given to any number of agents without liability to compensate any except the one who first secures a buyer ready, willing, and able to meet the terms of the listing or who first secures acceptance by the seller of a satisfactory offer.

Opinion of Title An attorney's evaluation of the condition of the title to a parcel of land after examination of the abstract of title to the land.

Option A right given for a consideration to purchase or lease a property upon specified terms within a specified time.

Oral Contract A verbal agreement; one that is not reduced to writing.

Orientation Placing a house on its lot with regard to its exposure to the rays of the sun, prevailing winds, privacy from the street, and protection from outside noises.

Overhang The part of the roof extending beyond the walls to shade buildings and to cover walks.

Overimprovement An improvement that is not the highest and best use for the site on which it is placed by reason of excess size or cost.

Ownership in Severalty When a person acquires real property and holds title solely in his or her own name.

P

Participation In addition to base interest on mortgage loans on income properties, a small percentage of gross income is required, sometimes predicated on the fulfillment of certain conditions, such as minimum occupancy or a percentage of net income after expenses, debt service, and taxes.

Partition Action Court proceedings by which co-owners seek to sever their joint ownership.

Partnership A decision of the California Supreme Court has defined a partnership in the following terms: "A partnership as between partners themselves may be defined to be a contract of two or more persons to unite their property, labor or skill, or some of them, in prosecution of some joint or lawful business, and to share the profits in certain proportions."

Party Wall A wall erected on the line between two adjoining properties, which are under different ownership, for the use of both properties.

Par Value Market value, nominal value.

Patent Conveyance of title to government land.

Penalty An extra payment or charge required of the borrower for deviating from the terms of the original loan agreement. Usually levied for being late in making regular payment or for paying off the loan before it is due.

Penny The term, as applied to nails, serves as a measure of nail length and is abbreviated by the letter d.

Percentage Lease Lease on the property, the rental for which is determined by the amount of business done by the lessee; usually, a percentage of gross receipts from the business with provision for a minimum rental.

Perimeter Heating Baseboard heating, or any system in which the heat registers are located along the outside walls of a room, especially under the windows.

Personal Property Any property that is not real property.

Physical Deterioration Impairment of condition. Loss in value brought about by wear and tear, disintegration, use, and actions of the elements.

Pier A column of masonry, usually rectangular in horizontal cross section, used to support other structural members.

Pitch The incline or rise of a roof.

Planned Unit Development (PUD) A land-use design that provides intensive utilization of the land through a combination of private and common areas with prearranged sharing of responsibilities for the common areas.

Planning Commission An appointed body of citizens charged with the responsibility of advising the elected board of supervisors or city council members in matters of land use.

Planning Departments Agencies within city and county government, staffed with professionally trained planners. The planning department employees provide technical services for planning commissions, elected officials, and citizens.

Plate A horizontal board placed on a wall or supported on posts or studs to carry the trusses of a roof or rafters directly; a shoe, or base member as of a partition or other frame; a small flat board placed on or in a wall to support girders, rafters, and so on.

Pledge The depositing of personal property by a debtor with a creditor as security for a debt or engagement.

Pledgee One who is given a pledge or a security. (See Secured Party.)

Pledgor One who offers a pledge or gives security. (See Debtor.)

Plottage Increment The appreciation in unit value created by joining smaller ownerships into one large single ownership.

Plywood Laminated wood made up in panels; several thicknesses of wood glued together with grain at different angles for strength.

Points Under certain loans, discounts, or points, paid to lenders are, in effect, prepaid interest and are used by lenders to adjust the effective interest rate so it is equal to or nearly equal to the prevailing market rate (the rate charged on conventional loans).

Police Power The right of the state to enact laws and enforce them for the order, safety, health, morals, and general welfare of the public.

Prefabricated House A house manufactured and sometimes partly assembled before delivery to the building site.

Prepaid Items of Expense Prorations of prepaid items of expense that are credited to the seller in the closing statement.

Prepayment Provision made for loan payments to be larger than those specified in the note.

Prepayment Penalty Penalty for the payment of a mortgage or trust deed note before it actually becomes due if the note does not provide for prepayment.

Present Value The lump-sum value today of an annuity. A $100 bill to be paid to someone in one year is worth less than if it were a $100 bill to be paid to someone today—for several reasons, one of which is that the money has time value. How much the $100 bill to be paid in one year is worth today will depend on the interest rate that seems proper for the particular circumstances. For example, if 6% is the appropriate rate, the $100 to be paid one year from now would be worth $94.34 today.

Presumption A rule of law that courts and judges shall draw a particular inference from a particular fact or from particular evidence unless and until the truth of such inference is disproved.

Prima Facie Presumptive on its face.

Principal The employer of an agent or the amount of money borrowed or the amount of a loan.

Principal Note The promissory note that is secured by the mortgage or trust deed.

Private Grant An owner voluntarily conveys his or her ownership rights to another.

Private Lenders Individuals who invest their savings in real estate loans either by directly granting loans to borrowers or by turning to mortgage brokers who find borrowers for the private lender.

Private Mortgage Insurance (PMI) Insurance used to guarantee lenders the payment of the upper portion of a conventional loan if a borrower defaults and a deficiency occurs at the foreclosure sale.

Privity Mutual relationship to the same rights of property; contractual relationship.

Probate An action that takes place in superior court, and the estate property may be sold during the probate period for the benefit of the heirs or to cover court costs.

Procuring Cause That cause originating from a series of events that, without break in continuity, results in the prime object of an agent's employment producing a final buyer.

Progression, Principle of The worth of a lesser-valued residence tends to be enhanced by association with many higher-valued residences in the same area.

Promissory Note Following a loan commitment from the lender, the borrower signs a note, promising to repay the loan under stipulated terms. The promissory note establishes personal liability for its repayment.

Property The rights of ownership. The right to use, possess, enjoy, and dispose of a thing in every legal way and to exclude everyone else from interfering with these rights. Property is generally classified into two groups: personal property and real property.

Proposition 13 Limits real property taxes to one percent of the full cash value of the real property, plus an amount for local assessments and bonds.

Proration Adjustments of interest, taxes, and insurance on a pro rata basis as of the closing date. Fire insurance is normally paid for three years in advance. When a property is sold during this time, the seller wants a refund on that portion of the advance payment that has not been used at the time the title to the property is transferred. For example, when the property is sold two years later, the original buyer wants to receive one-third of the advance premium that was paid.

Proration of Taxes To divide or prorate taxes equally or proportionately to time of use.

Proximate Cause That cause of an event which, in a natural and continuous sequence unbroken by any new cause, produced that event and without which the event would not have happened. Also, the procuring cause.

Public Grant A governmental agency deeds property to an individual or an institution.

Public Report Report issued by the real estate commissioner which merely states that the sub-divider has conformed to all laws and regulations.

Purchase and Installment Saleback Involves purchase of the property upon completion of construction and immediate saleback on a long-term installment contract.

Purchase of Land, Leaseback, and Leasehold Mortgages An arrangement whereby land is purchased by the lender and leased back to the developer with a mortgage negotiated on the resulting leasehold of the income property constructed. The lender receives an annual ground rent, plus a percentage of income from the property.

Purchase and Leaseback Involves the purchase of property subject to an existing mortgage and immediate leaseback.

Purchase Money Mortgage or Trust Deed A trust deed or mortgage given as part or all of the purchase consideration for property. In some states, the purchase money mortgage or trust deed loan can be made by a seller who extends credit to the buyer of property or by a third-party lender (typically a financial institution) that makes a loan to the buyer of real property for a portion of the purchase price to be paid for the property. (In many states, there are legal limitations upon mortgagees and trust deed beneficiaries collecting deficiency judgments against the purchase money borrower after the collateral hypothecated under such security instruments has been sold through the foreclosure process. Generally, no deficiency judgment is allowed if the collateral property under the mortgage or trust deed is residential property of four units or less with the debtor occupying the property as a place of residence.)

Q

Quantity Survey A highly technical process in arriving at a cost estimate of new construction, sometimes referred to in the building trade as the price take-off method. It involves a detailed estimate of the quantities of raw material (lumber, plaster, brick, cement) used, as well as the current price of the material and installation costs. These factors are added together to arrive at the cost of a structure. It is usually used by contractors and experienced estimators.

Quiet Title A court action brought to establish title; to remove a cloud on the title.

Quitclaim Deed A deed to relinquish any interest in property the grantor may have.

R

Radiant Heating A method of heating, usually consisting of coils or pipes placed in the floor, wall, or ceiling.

Rafter One of a series of boards of a roof designed to support roof loads. The rafters of a flat roof are sometimes called roof joists.

Range A strip of land six miles wide determined by a government survey, running in a north-to-south direction.

Ratification The adoption or approval of an act performed on behalf of a person without previous authorization.

Real Estate Association or Board An organization whose members consist primarily of real estate brokers and salespersons.

Real Estate Settlement Procedures Act A federal disclosure law effective June 20, 1975, requiring new procedures and forms for settlements (closing costs) involving federally related loans.

Real Estate Trust A special arrangement under federal and state law whereby investors pool funds for investments in real estate and mortgages and yet escape corporation taxes.

Realtist A real estate broker holding active membership in a real estate board affiliated with the National Association of Real Estate Brokers.

Realtor A real estate broker holding active membership in a real estate board affiliated with the National Association of Realtors.

Recapture The rate of interest necessary to provide for the return of an investment. Not to be confused with interest rate, which is a rate of interest on an investment.

Reconciliation (See Correlation.)

Recording The process of placing a document on file with a designated public official for everyone to see. This public official is usually a county officer known as the county recorder. The recorder designates the fact that a document has been given to him or her by stamping it and indicating the time of day and the date when it was officially placed on file. Documents filed with the recorder are considered to be placed on open notice to the general public of that county. Claims against property usually are given a priority on the basis of the time and the date they are recorded, with the most preferred claim status going to the earliest one recorded, the next claim going to the next earliest one recorded, and so on. This type of notice is called constructive notice or legal notice.

Recovery Fund Fund established by the state of California whereby the public can recover money when there are certain uncollectable court judgments obtained against a real estate licensee on the basis of fraud, misrepresentation, deceit, or conversion of trust funds in a transaction.

Redemption Buying back one's property after a judicial sale.

Refinancing The paying off of an existing obligation and assuming a new obligation in its place.

Reformation An action to correct a mistake in a deed or another document.

Registered Domestic Partnership Established when persons meeting the criteria specified by Family Code section 297 file a Declaration of Domestic Partnership with the Secretary of State of California.

Rehabilitation The restoration of a property to satisfactory condition without drastically changing the plan, form, or style of architecture.

Release Clause This is a stipulation that upon the payment of a specific sum of money to the holder of a trust deed or mortgage, the lien of the instrument as to a specific described lot or area shall be removed from the blanket lien on the whole area involved.

Release Deed An instrument executed by the mortgagee or the trustee reconveying to the mortgagor the real estate that secured the mortgage loan after the debt has been paid in full. Upon recording, it cancels the mortgage lien created when the mortgage or trust deed was recorded.

Remainder An estate that takes effect after the termination of the prior estate, such as a life estate.

Remainder Depreciation The possible loss in value of an improvement that will occur in the future.

Rental Offset Section 1942 of the Civil Code allows a tenant to spend up to one month's rent to make repairs. The repair bill can then be used to offset the next month's rent as long as some basic rules are followed.

Replacement Cost The cost to replace a structure with another having utility equivalent to that being appraised, but constructed with modern materials and according to current standards, design, and layout.

Reproduction Cost The cost of replacing the subject improvement with one that is the exact replica, having the same quality of workmanship, design, and layout.

Rescission of Contract The abrogation or annulling of contract; the revocation or repealing of contract by mutual consent by parties to the contract or for cause by either party to the contract.

Reservation A right retained by a grantor in conveying property.

RESPA Real Estate Settlement Procedures Act.

Restriction Relating to real property, the owner of real property is restricted or prohibited from doing certain things relating to the property or from using the property for certain purposes. Property restrictions fall into two general classifications—public and private. Zoning ordinances are examples of the former type. Restrictions can be created by private owners, typically by appropriate clauses in deeds or in agreements, or in the general plans of entire subdivisions. Usually, they assume the form of a covenant or promise to do or not to do a certain thing. They cover a multitude of matters, including use for residential or business purposes; for example, houses in tract must cost more than $100,000.

Reversion The right to future possession or enjoyment by the person or heirs creating the preceding estate.

Reversionary Interest The interest a person has in lands or other property upon the termination of the preceding estate.

Ridge The horizontal line at the junction of the top edges of two sloping roof surfaces. The rafters at both slopes are nailed at the ridge.

Ridge Board The board placed on edge at the ridge of the roof to support the upper ends of the rafters; also called roof tree, ridge piece, ridge plate, or ridgepole.

Right of Survivorship The right to acquire the interest of a deceased joint owner; a distinguishing feature of a joint tenancy.

Right of Way A privilege operating as an easement upon land, whereby the owner does by grant or by agreement give to another the right to pass over the land, construct a roadway, or use as a roadway; the right to a specific part of the land; the right to construct through and over the land telephone, telegraph, or electric power lines; or the right to place underground water mains, gas mains, or sewer mains.

Riparian Rights The right of a landowner to the water on, under, or adjacent to his or her land.

Riser The upright board at the back of each step of a stairway. In heating, a riser is a duct slanted upward to carry hot air from the furnace to the room above.

Risk Analysis A study made, usually by a lender, of the various factors that might affect the repayment of a loan.

Risk Rating A process used by a lender to decide on the soundness of making a loan and to reduce all the various factors affecting the repayment of the loan to a qualified rating of some kind.

S

Sale-Leaseback A situation where the owner of a piece of property wishes to sell the property and retain occupancy by leasing it from the buyer.

Sales Contract A contract by which buyer and seller agree to terms of a sale.

Sandwich Lease A leasehold interest that lies between the primary lease and the operating lease.

Sash Wood or metal frames containing one or more window panes.

Satisfaction The discharge of mortgage or trust deed lien from the records upon payment of the evidenced debt.

Satisfaction Piece An instrument for recording and acknowledging payment of an indebtedness secured by a mortgage.

Savings Bank (Savings and Loan) Financial institution that accepts savings from the public and invests these savings mainly in real estate trust deeds and mortgages.

Seal An impression made to attest the execution of an instrument; for example, a notary public's seal.

Secondary Financing A loan secured by a second mortgage or trust deed on real property. These can be third, fourth, fifth, sixth, and so on, ad infinitum.

Secondary Mortgage Market A market where existing real estate loans are bought and sold.

Secret Profit If the real estate agent derives any profit other than the agreed commission without disclosing the nature of the profits to the principal.

Section Section of land is established by government survey and contains 640 acres.

Secured Party The party having the security interest. Thus, the mortgagee, the conditional seller, the pledgee, and so on are all referred to as the secured party.

Security Agreement An agreement between the secured party and the debtor that creates the security interest.

Security Interest Designating the interest of the creditor in the property of the debtor in all types of credit transactions. It replaces such terms as the following: chattel mortgage, pledge, trust receipt, chattel trust, equipment trust, conditional sale, and inventory lien.

Seizin Possession of real estate by one entitled thereto.

Self-Contained Appraisal Report (See Narrative Report.)

Seller's Agent The seller appoints a real estate broker to find a buyer for the seller's property.

Separate Property Property owned by a husband or wife or registered domestic partners that is not community property; property acquired by either spouse or registered domestic partners prior to marriage or registered domestic partnership or by gift or device after marriage or registered domestic partnership.

Septic Tank An underground tank in which sewage from a house is reduced to liquid by bacterial action and drained off.

Servicing Supervising and administering a loan after it has been made. This involves such things as collecting payments, keeping accounting records, computing interest and principal, foreclosing on defaulted loans, and so on.

Servient Tenement Property that is subject to an easement or upon which the easement is imposed.

Severalty Ownership Owned by one person only; sole ownership.

Shake A hand-split shingle, usually edge grained.

Sheathing A structural covering, usually boards, plywood, or wallboards, placed over exterior studding or rafters of a house.

Sheriff's Deed A deed given by court order in connection with sale of property to satisfy a judgment.

Shopping Center, Regional A large shopping center with 250,000 to 1,000,000 square feet of store area, serving 200,000 people or more.

Sill The lowest part of the frame of a house, resting on the foundation and supporting the uprights of the frame; the board or metal forming the lower side of an opening, as a door sill or windowsill.

Single Agency Where a broker represents either the buyer or the seller, not both, in a real estate transaction.

Sinking Fund A fund set aside from the income of property that, with accrued interest, will eventually pay for replacement of the improvements.

Six-Month Rule A homeowner with a valid formal declaration of homestead has six-months in which to invest his or her equity money into the purchase of another home, thereby continuing to protect the equity against creditors up to the exemption amount.

Soil Pipe A pipe carrying waste out off a house to the main sewer line.

Sole or Sole Plate A member, usually a two-by-four, on which wall and partition studs rest.

Span The distance between structural supports such as walls, columns, piers, beams, girders, and trusses.

Special Agency An agent has limited or well-defined powers, perhaps confined to a single transaction.

Special Assessment A legal charge against real estate by a public authority to pay the cost of public improvements such as streetlights, sidewalks, and street improvements.

Specific Liens Liens that attach to only a certain, specific parcel of land or piece of property.

Specific Performance An action to compel performance of an agreement; for example, the sale of land.

Standard Depth Generally, the most typical lot depth in a neighborhood.

Standard Policy The assurance that title is free and clear of all encumbrances of public record, other than the items revealed in the title examination and listed exceptions in the title policy.

Standby Commitment The mortgage banker frequently protects a builder by a "standby" agreement, under which the banker agrees to make mortgage loans at an agreed price for many months in the future. The builder deposits a "standby fee" with the mortgage banker for this service. Frequently, the mortgage banker secures a "standby" from a long-term investor for the same period of time, who pays a fee for this privilege.

Statute of Frauds State law that provides that certain contracts must be in writing in order to be enforceable; for example, a real property lease for more than one year and an agent's authorization to sell real estate.

Statute of Limitations States that you must begin the lawsuit within a legally prescribed time period.

Statutory Will A preprinted form approved by the state in which a person merely fills in the blanks, usually without formal legal assistance. This statutory will requires at least two witnesses.

Steering The unlawful directing of a perspective buyer or tenant to certain neighborhoods or the refusal to tell about the availability of housing in another neighborhood.

Stock Cooperative Corporation formed for the purpose of holding title to a building.

Straight-Line Depreciation A definite sum set aside annually from income to pay the cost of replacing improvements, without reference to interest it earns.

String, Stringer A timber or another support for cross members. In stairs, the support on which the stair treads rest.

Straight Note Commonly referred to as an "interest-only" note. Under the straight note, the borrower agrees to pay the interest, usually monthly, and to pay the entire principal in a lump sum on the due date.

Studs or Studding Vertical supporting timbers in walls and partitions.

Subdivided Lands Act Defines a subdivision as the division of land into five or more lots for the purpose of sale, lease or financing, whether now or in the future.

Subdivision Map Act Covers the division of land into two or more lots for the purpose of sale, lease or financing, whether now or in the future.

Subject to Mortgage When a grantee takes a title to real property subject to mortgage, he or she is not responsible to the holder of the promissory note for the payment of any portion of the amount due. The most the grantee can lose in the event of a foreclosure is equity in the property. (See Assumption of Mortgage.) In neither case is the original maker of the note released from his or her responsibility.

Sublease A lease given by a lessee.

Subordinate To make subject to or junior to.

Subordination Clause A clause in a junior or a second lien permitting retention of priority for prior liens. A subordination clause is also used in a first deed of trust, permitting it to be subordinated to subsequent liens as, for example, the liens of construction loans.

Subpoena A process to cause a witness to appear and give testimony.

Subrogation The substitution of another person in place of the creditor, to whose rights the former succeeds in relation to the debt. The doctrine is often used when one person agrees to stand surety for the performance of a contract by another person.

Substitution, Principle of Affirms that the maximum value of a property tends to be set by the cost of acquiring an equally desirable and valuable substitute property, assuming no costly delay is encountered in making the substitution.

Succession The handing down of property to another person.

Sum of the Years Digits An accelerated depreciation method.

Summary Appraisal Report A uniform short-form appraisal frequently used for loan purposes.

Supply and Demand, Principle of Affirms that price or value varies directly, but not necessarily proportionally, with demand and inversely, but not necessarily proportionally, with supply.

Surety One who guarantees the performance of another; a guarantor.

Surplus Productivity, Principle of Affirms the net income that remains after the proper costs of labor, organization, and capital have been paid, which is imputable to the land and tends to fix the value thereof.

Survey The process by which a parcel of land is measured and its area is ascertained.

Syndicate A partnership organized for participation in a real estate venture. Partners may be limited or unlimited in their liability.

T

Take-Out Loan The loan arranged by the owner or builder-developer for a buyer. The construction loan made for construction of the improvements is usually paid from the proceeds of this loan.

Tax Sale Sale of property after a period of nonpayment of taxes.

Tenancy in Common Ownership by two or more persons who hold undivided interest, without right of survivorship; interests need not be equal.

Tenancy in Partnership Exists when two or more persons, as partners, pool their interests, assets, and efforts in a business venture, with each to share in the profits or the losses.

Tentative Map The Subdivision Map Act requires subdividers to submit initially a tentative map of their tract to the local planning commission for study. The approval or disapproval of the planning commission is noted on the map. Thereafter a final map of the tract embodying any changes requested by the planning commission is required to be filed with the planning commission.

Tenure in Land The mode or manner by which an estate in lands is held.

Termite Shield A shield, usually of noncorrodible metal, placed on top of the foundation wall or around pipes to prevent passage of termites.

Termites Antlike insects that feed on wood.

Testator One who leaves a will in force upon death.

Threshold A strip of wood or metal beveled on each edge and used above the finished floor under outside doors.

Title Insurance Insurance written by a title company to protect property owner against loss if title is imperfect.

Title Report A report that discloses the condition of the title, made by a title company preliminary to issuance of title insurance.

Title Theory Mortgage arrangement whereby title to mortgaged real property vests in the lender.

Topography Nature of the surface of land; topography may be level, rolling, or mountainous.

Tort A wrongful act; wrong, injury; violation of a legal right.

Township A territorial subdivision six miles long and six miles wide containing 36 sections, each one mile square.

Trade Fixtures Articles of personal property annexed to real property, but which are necessary to the carrying on of a trade and are removable by the owner.

Trade-In An increasingly popular method of guaranteeing an owner a minimum amount of cash upon sale of present property to permit the purchase of another. If the property is not sold within a specified time at the listed price, the broker agrees to arrange financing to purchase the property at an agreed-upon discount.

Treads Horizontal boards of a stairway.

Treaty of Guadalupe Hidalgo Ended the war with Mexico and whereby California became a territory of the United States.

Trim The finish materials in a building, such as moldings, applied around openings (window trim, door trim) or at the floor and ceiling (baseboard, cornice, picture molding).

Trust Account An account separate and apart and physically segregated from broker's own funds in which a broker deposits funds collected for clients.

Trust Deed Just as with a mortgage, this is a legal document by which a borrower pledges certain real property or collateral as guarantee for the repayment of a loan. However, it differs from a mortgage in a number of important respects. For example, instead of having two parties to the transaction, there are three. There is the borrower, who gives the trust deed and who is called the trustor. There is the third neutral party (just as there is with an escrow), who receives the trust deed and who is called the trustee. And, finally, there is the lender, who is called the beneficiary because the lender benefits from the pledge arrangement. In the event of a default, the trustee can sell the property and transfer the money obtained at the sale to the lender as payment of the debt.

Trustee One who holds property in trust for another to secure the performance of an obligation.

Trust Funds Money or other items of value that an agent receives on behalf of a principal in the course of a real estate transaction that requires a license.

Trustor One who deeds property to a trustee to be held as security until the trustor has performed any obligations to a lender under terms of a deed of trust.

Truth-in-Lending Law Law with the purpose of helping borrowers understand how much it costs to borrow money.

U

Underimprovement An improvement that, because of its deficiency in size or cost, is not the highest and best use of the site.

Underwriting The technical analysis by a lender to determine the borrower's ability to repay a contemplated loan.

Undue Influence Taking any fraudulent or unfair advantage of another's weakness of mind or distress or necessity.

Unearned Increment An increase in value of real estate resulting from no effort on the part of the owner; often caused by an increase in population.

Unenforceable Contract A contract that appears to be valid, but it cannot be sued upon.

Uniform Commercial Code Establishes a unified and comprehensive scheme for the regulation of security transactions in personal property, superseding the existing statutes on chattel mortgages, conditional sales, trust receipts, assignment of accounts receivable, and others in this field.

Unilateral Contract Created by only one party extending a promise without a reciprocal promise by another party.

Unit-in-Place Method The cost of erecting a building by estimating the cost of each component part; that is, foundations, floors, walls, windows, ceilings, and roofs (including labor and overhead).

Unlawful Detainer Action Process of legally removing a tenant from possession which involves a series of steps.

Unruh Civil Rights Act State law that makes it unlawful for people engaging in business in California, including real estate agents, to discriminate when providing business products and services.

Usury On a loan, claiming a rate of interest greater than that permitted by law.

Utilities Refers to services rendered by public utility companies, such as water, gas, electricity, and telephone.

Utility The ability to give satisfaction and/or excite desire for possession.

V

VA Loans Department of Veteran's Affairs guarantees a portion of a loan.

Valid Having force or binding force; legally sufficient and authorized by law.

Valley The internal angle formed by the junction of two sloping sides of a roof.

Valuation Estimated worth or price; estimation: the act of valuing by appraisal.

Vendee A purchaser; buyer.

Vendor A seller; one who disposes of a thing in consideration of money.

Veneer Thin sheets of wood.

Vent A pipe installed to provide a flow of air to or from a drainage system or to provide a circulation of air within such system to protect trap seals from siphonage and back pressure.

Verification Sworn statement before a duly qualified officer to the correctness of contents of an instrument.

Vested Bestowed upon someone; secured by someone, such as a title to property.

Void To have no force or effect; that which is unenforceable.

Voidable That which is capable of being adjudged void, but is not void unless action is taken to make it so.

Voluntary Lien Any lien placed on property with consent of or as a result of the voluntary act of the owner.

W

Wainscoting Wood lining of an interior wall; lower section of a wall when finished differently from the upper part.

Waive To relinquish or abandon; to forego a right to enforce or require anything.

Warranty Deed A deed used to convey real property that contains warranties of title and quiet possession, and the grantor thus agrees to defend the premises against the lawful claims of third persons. It is commonly used in many states, but in others, the grant deed has supplanted it because of the modern practice of securing title insurance policies that have reduced the importance of express and implied warranty in deeds.

Waste The destruction of, or material alteration of, or injury to premises by a tenant for life or years.

Water Table The distance from surface of ground to a depth at which natural groundwater is found.

Will An instrument that leaves real estate of a decedent to an heir(s); for example, witnessed will, holographic will, and statutory will.

Witnessed Will A formal typewritten document signed by the individual who is making it, wherein he or she declares in the presence of at least two witnesses that it is his or her own will.

Writ of Execution An order from the court allowing the judgment holder to attach or seize real or personal property belonging to the judgment debtor.

Y

Yield The interest earned by an investor on his or her investment (or bank, on the money it has lent). Also called return.

Yield Rate The yield expressed as a percentage of the total investment. Also called rate of return.

Z

Zone The area set off by the proper authorities for specific use, subject to certain restrictions or restraints.

Zoning The act of city or county authorities specifying type of use to which property may be put in specific areas.

Index